SAGE was founded in 1965 by Sara Miller McCune to support the dissemination of usable knowledge by publishing innovative and high-quality research and teaching content. Today, we publish over 900 journals, including those of more than 400 learned societies, more than 800 new books per year, and a growing range of library products including archives, data, case studies, reports, and video. SAGE remains majority-owned by our founder, and after Sara's lifetime will become owned by a charitable trust that secures our continued independence.

Los Angeles | London | New Delhi | Singapore | Washington DC | Melbourne

Economic Challenges for the Contemporary World

Thank you for choosing a SAGE product!
If you have any comment, observation or feedback,
I would like to personally hear from you.
Please write to me at **contactceo@sagepub.in**

Vivek Mehra, Managing Director and CEO, SAGE India.

Bulk Sales

SAGE India offers special discounts
for purchase of books in bulk.
We also make available special imprints
and excerpts from our books on demand.

For orders and enquiries, write to us at

Marketing Department
SAGE Publications India Pvt Ltd
B1/I-1, Mohan Cooperative Industrial Area
Mathura Road, Post Bag 7
New Delhi 110044, India

E-mail us at **marketing@sagepub.in**

Get to know more about SAGE

Be invited to SAGE events, get on our mailing list.
Write today to **marketing@sagepub.in**

This book is also available as an e-book.

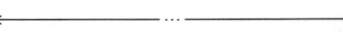

Economic Challenges for the Contemporary World

Essays in Honour of
PRABHAT
PATNAIK

EDITED BY
Mausumi Das
Sabyasachi Kar
Nandan Nawn

Los Angeles | London | New Delhi
Singapore | Washington DC | Melbourne

Copyright © Mausumi Das, Sabyasachi Kar and Nandan Nawn, 2016

All rights reserved. No part of this book may be reproduced or utilised in any form or by any means, electronic or mechanical, including photocopying, recording or by any information storage or retrieval system, without permission in writing from the publisher.

First published in 2016 by

SAGE Publications India Pvt Ltd
B1/I-1 Mohan Cooperative Industrial Area
Mathura Road, New Delhi 110 044, India
www.sagepub.in

SAGE Publications Inc
2455 Teller Road
Thousand Oaks, California 91320, USA

SAGE Publications Ltd
1 Oliver's Yard, 55 City Road
London EC1Y 1SP, United Kingdom

SAGE Publications Asia-Pacific Pte Ltd
3 Church Street
#10-04 Samsung Hub
Singapore 049483

Published by Vivek Mehra for SAGE Publications India Pvt Ltd, typeset in Minion 10/12.5 pts by Zaza Eunice, Hosur, Tamil Nadu and printed at Chaman Enterprises, New Delhi.

Library of Congress Cataloging-in-Publication Data

Names: Das, Mausumi, editor. | Kar, Sabyasachi, editor. | Nawn, Nandan, editor. | Patnaik, Prabhat, honoree.
Title: Economic challenges for the contemporary world : essays in honour of Prabhat Patnaik / edited by Mausumi Das, Sabyasachi Kar and Nandan Nawn.
Description: New Delhi ; Thousand Oaks : SAGE, 2016.
Identifiers: LCCN 2015049015| ISBN 9789351508786 (hardback : alk. paper) | ISBN 9789351508779 (epub) | ISBN 9789351508793 (ebook)
Subjects: LCSH: Economic development. | Economics.
Classification: LCC HD82 .E27 2016 | DDC 330—dc23
LC record available at http://lccn.loc.gov/2015049015

ISBN: 978-93-515-0878-6 (HB)

The SAGE Team: Supriya Das, Isha Sachdeva and Rajinder Kaur

Contents

List of Tables	ix
List of Figures	xi
Foreword by Kaushik Basu	xv
Acknowledgements	xvii

CHAPTER 1
Introduction 1
Mausumi Das, Sabyasachi Kar and Nandan Nawn

SECTION 1
Sustaining the Growth Process 21

CHAPTER 2
Financial Development and Growth under Capitalism 23
C.P. Chandrasekhar

CHAPTER 3
Global Economic Challenges: Alone We Lag, Together We Grow 33
Pranab Mukhopadhyay

CHAPTER 4
Sustainability, Surplus and Survival: Explorations through Agricultural Energetics 52
Nandan Nawn

SECTION 2
Dealing with Globalisation: Trade, Capital, Technology 73

CHAPTER 5
Secular Movements in the International Terms of Trade of Primary Commodities
vis-à-vis Manufactured Goods: Towards an Explanation 75
Shouvik Chakraborty

CHAPTER 6
Global Rebalancing: Limitations of the East-Asia-centric Approach and the Role of Europe 88
Sabyasachi Kar

CHAPTER 7
Effect of Fiscal Policy on Level of Activity under Capital Flows 114
Surajit Das

CHAPTER 8
Foreign Direct Investment, Intellectual Property Rights and Technology Transfer 131
Biswajit Dhar and Reji Joseph

SECTION 3
Mitigating Immiserisation: Poverty, Inequality, Joblessness 143

CHAPTER 9
Aspiration, Inequality and Growth 145
Mausumi Das

CHAPTER 10
A Proposition on Convergence to Equality in a Growth Model with Bliss 162
Subrata Guha

CHAPTER 11
Education, Equity and Development 178
Sudhanshu Bhushan

CHAPTER 12
Employment Growth and Informalisation of Workers in the Organised Manufacturing Sector 191
Shuji Uchikawa

SECTION 4
Envisioning the Institutional Changes 211

CHAPTER 13
Monetary Equilibrium and Inertial Expectations 213
Jyotirmoy Bhattacharya

CHAPTER 14
Stock Markets, Finance and Development: A View from History 229
Vineet Kohli

CHAPTER 15
Corporate Retailing in the Advanced Countries: Some Salient Features 240
Pradip Kumar Biswas

SECTION 5
Reimagining the Political Hegemony **255**

CHAPTER 16
Empire or Imperialism? 257
Prasenjit Bose

CHAPTER 17
Output and Price (In)Stability under Neoliberalism: A Kaleckian Approach 267
Rohit

CHAPTER 18
Agricultural Investment in India in Recent Decades: A Political Economic Note of Its Causes and Consequences 286
Debarshi Das

CHAPTER 19
Political Economy of Contemporary Indian Agricultural and Rural Dynamics 300
Praveen Jha

About the Editors and Contributors 317
Index 321

List of Tables

4.1	Energy Analysis of Different Types of Land Use in France, 1870s	60
4.2	Energy Values for Labour under Alternative Framework of Accounting without Hired-in or Hired-out (in calorie)	64
4.3	Energy Value of Active and Inactive Days of Labourer with Hired-in and Hired-out (in calorie)	65
5.1	Regression Results of the Share of Profits in Gross Output of the Manufacturing Sector on the Terms of Trade (1970–2005)	86
5.2	Regression Results of the Share of Profits in Gross Output of the Manufacturing Sector on the Terms of Trade (1974–2005)	86
7.1	Top 20 Countries in Terms of FDI Inflow/Outflow during 2003–2007	119
7.2	Top 20 Countries vis-à-vis Net Inflow/Outflow of Portfolio Capital during 2003–2007	120
7.3	Correlation between Capital Flows and Interest Rates	121
7.4	Relation of Trade Deficit with Exchange Rate during 1977–1978 to 2007–2008 in India	122
7A.1	Interest Rate and Exchange Rate Fluctuation of 48 Countries during 2003–2007	130
11.1	Regression Statistics Dependent Variable in Average Monthly per Capita Expenditure	182
11.2	Average Years of Schooling and Education Gini by Caste and Religion: India and Bihar	184
11.3	Regression Statistics Dependent Variable Expenditure Inequality Measured in Terms of Standard Deviation	185
11.4	Regression Statistics Dependent Variable Expenditure Inequality Measured in Terms of Gini Coefficient	185
11.5	Income Inequality to Social Expenditure as a Ratio to Total Expenditure (2007–2008)	186
11A.1	Construction of Educational Level from Educational Attainment of Individuals	189
12.1	Growth Rates of GVA and Capital–Labour Ratio in the Organised Manufacturing Sector	192
12.2	Growth Rates of Man-days Worked by Directly Employed Workers and Contract Workers	205
12.3	Annual Wages per Worker in the Organised and Annual Emoluments per Hired Worker in 2010–2011	207
14.1	Ratio of Market Capitalisation to GNP	234
14.2	Ratio of Market Capitalisation to Value of Structures and Equipment	235
14.3	Ratio of Financial Assets to National Assets	235

15.1	Firm Entry and Exit Rates for the US Retail Sector (Mean by Market Type, 1976–2000)	243
15.2	Supermarket Convenience Store Acquisitions	244
15.3	Sale of Clothing by Type of Outlet (in percentages)	245
15.4	Supermarket Practices Concerning Relations with Suppliers	247
15.5	Change in Real Farm-gate Prices (1990–2002)	250
15.6	Change in Agriculture Output and Consumer Prices in EU-15 in Percentage (1990–2002)	251
15.7	Farm-gate and Retail Price Spreads Ratio in EU Member States (2001)	251
15.8	Percentage Change in Farm-gate and Retail Price Spreads Ratio in EU Member States (1990–1991 to 2000–2001)	251
17.1	Comparative Analysis of Growth in the US: 1955.4–2006.4	282
18.1	Net Private Investment as a Percentage of Agricultural Income	289
18.2	Public and Private Investment in First Three Five-year Plans (Crores of Rupees at 1960–1961 Prices)	289
18.3	Percentage Growth of Inputs Use, Irrigated Area in Different Periods	289
18.4	Annual Percentage Change in Capital Formation in Indian Agriculture, at 1980–1981 Prices	290
18.5	Annual Growth Rate of Yield of Food Grains	292
18.6	Annual Growth Rate of Employment in the Organised Sector	293
19.1	Distribution of Number of Holdings and Area Operated in India as per Agricultural Census 2010–2011	302
19.2	Cropping Pattern in India (Area in million ha)	303
19.3	Trends in Cropping Pattern in India (Percentage Share—Crop Wise)	304
19.4	Growth Rates of Production of Cereals, Pulses and Total Food Grains since the 1950s	305
19.5	Growth Rates of Yield of Cereals and Pulses and Total Food Grains in India since the 1950s	306
19.6	Agriculture Labour Households with/without Access to Cultivable Land (Percentage of Total Agricultural Labour Households)	307
19.7	Share of Expenditure on Rural Economy in Total Budgetary Expenditure since the 1990s (in percentage)	312

List of Figures

3.1	Illustration of the Interaction between Different Sectors/Variables in the CAM Model	36
3.2	Growth in per Capita Income 2000–2030 (Baseline)	37
3.3	Employment Rates 2000–2030 (Baseline)	38
3.4	Growth in per Capita Income 2000–2030 (Scenario 1)	40
3.5	Employment Rates (per cent) 2000–2030 (Scenario 1)	41
3.6	Growth in per Capita Income 2000–2030 (Scenario 2)	42
3.7	Employment Rates (per cent) (Scenario 2)	42
3.8	US Public Debt and Net Export of Assets (as a Percentage of GDP) (Scenario 2)	43
3.9	Growth Rate in per Capita Income 2000–2030 (Scenario 3)	44
3.10	Employment Rates 2000–2030 (Scenario 3)	45
3.11	Current Account Balance as a Percentage of GDP (Scenario 3)	45
3.12	Public Debt (as a Percentage of GDP) in Europe (2000–2030) (Scenario 3)	46
3.13	Growth in per Capita Income 2000–2030 in BRICS and USA (Comparing Scenario 4 and Baseline)	47
3.14	Growth in per Capita Income 2000–2030 in Europe (Comparing Scenario 4 and Baseline)	47
3.15	Comparing Employment Rates in Europe (Scenario 4 and Baseline)	48
3.16	Comparing Employment Rates in Other Countries (Scenario 4 and Baseline)	48
3.17	Public Debt (as a Percentage of GDP) (Scenario 4 and Baseline)	49
4.1	Surplus per Hectare, under Three Approaches, against GCA (in ha)	66
4.2	EROI under Three Approaches, against GCA (in ha)	66
4.3	Surplus per Hectare, against EROI, Scale P	67
4.4	Surplus per Hectare, against EROI, Scale PM	67
4.5	Surplus per Hectare, against EROI, Scale HM	67
5.1	Time Path of the Rate of Profit	81
5.2	Share of Developed Countries among the Major Exporters of Manufactured Goods (1970–2011)	84
5.3	Share of G7 Countries among the Major Manufacture Exporters: Developed Countries (1980–2011)	85
5.4	Ratio of Wages to Gross Output in the Manufacturing Sector of the G7 Countries (1970–2005)	85
5.5	Ratio of Profits to Gross Output in the Manufacturing Sector of the G7 Countries (1970–2005)	85

6.1	GDP Growth: World Economy and Individual Blocs	95
6.2	Current Account Balance as a Ratio to GDP	96
6.3	Net External Assets as a Ratio to GDP	97
6.4	External Sector Balances of the US and Major East-Asian Economies	98
6.5	Current Account Balance as a Ratio to GDP	100
6.6	Net External Assets as a Ratio to GDP	101
6.7	Current Account Balance of the US	102
6.8	Major Gainers (Current Account Balance) from a Reduction of East-Asian Current Account Surplus	102
6.9	Trade Balance of Some Major Deficit and Surplus Countries/Blocs	103
6.10	Trade Balance of the US	104
6.11	Net Invisibles of Some Major Deficit and Surplus Countries/Blocs	105
6.12	Net Invisibles of the US	106
6.13	Current Account Balance (in million dollars, 2005 Prices)	107
6.14	Current Account Balance as a Ratio to GDP	108
6.15	Net External Assets as a Ratio to GDP	109
6.16	Current Account Balance of the US	110
8.1	Share of Residents in Total Patents Granted in China (per cent)	140
9.1	Income Dynamics of the Rich: Perpetual Growth	152
9.2	Income Dynamics of the Rich: Convergence to a Steady State	152
9.3	Income Dynamics of the Poor: Poverty Trap Scenario	155
9.4	Income Dynamics of the Poor: Escape from Poverty Trap	156
9.5	Income Dynamics of the Poor: Low Aspiration	157
9.6	Income Dynamics of the Poor: High Aspiration	158
10.1	Phase Diagram for the System (10.5)–(10.6)	168
11.1	Gross Attendance Rates by Social and Religious Groups (2007–2008)	181
11.2	Inequality in Level Participation	181
11.3	Education Gini Coefficient across States over the Years	183
11.4	Predicted Value of Overall Education Gini by Average Years of Schooling in Urban and Rural	184
12.1	Production and Exports of Cotton Yarn	198
12.2	Production of Crude Steel (million tonnes)	199
12.3	Distribution of Motor Vehicle Census Sector Factories Operating in 2007–2008	201
12.4	Trends in Number of Workers and per Capita Wages in the Organised Manufacturing Sector	206
17.1	(Im)Possibility of a Viable Range	271
17.2	Questioning the Viability of the Capitalist Core	273
17.3	Periphery Ensures the Viability of the Capitalist Core	275
17.4	Transitional Dynamics from the Golden Age to Neoliberalism	280

18.1	Public Investment in Agricultural Sector, Agricultural Investment and Total Investment	291
19.1	Share of Agriculture in Total GDP (at Constant 2004–2005 Prices, in percentage)	301
19.2	Share of Public Sector GCF in Agriculture and Allied Sector in the Total GCF (in Percentage and Figures are Based on 2004–2005 Prices)	306
19.3	Share of Combined Budgetary Expenditure towards Rural Economy (RE) out of Total Combined Budgetary Expenditure and GDP since 1950–1951 (in percentage)	310

Foreword

This unusual collection of essays, utilising diverse methodologies and addressing numerous, varied challenges faced by the world economy today, has one common feature. All the chapters are authored by PhD students of Prabhat Patnaik. This is a richly deserved tribute to a remarkable intellectual. Prabhat Patnaik is a brilliant thinker, India's pre-eminent heterodox, Marxist economist, one of the finest orators anywhere and an individually generous person. The diversity of the volume, in terms of the kinds of methodology used, conclusions reached and intellectual orientations of the authors, reflects well Prabhat's own openness and instinctive generosity with friends and students.

I had the pleasure of working with Prabhat over several years as 'series editors' for two Oxford University Press series—Themes in Economics and Readings in Economics. Themes in Economics was started by Sukhamoy Chakravarty, who invited Prabhat and me to join him as series editors. The aim was to bring out books that commissioned various authors to write papers and would be edited by the volume editor, lightly supervised by the three of us. Those were wonderful days of long discussions about what topics to cover, whom to invite as volume editors, all transacted over endless cups of coffee and conversation about philosophy, politics and economics. After Sukhamoy's premature death in 1990—he was 56 at that time—Prabhat and I decided to carry on the editorial work, and both series continued for several more years. It was an excellent experience, trying to draw the best talents from around the country and to put together some of the most interesting ideas in economics for policymakers and students to read and do research on.

Prabhat was several years my senior at St. Stephen's College, and we had had no overlap. While I was familiar with his phenomenally prodigious writings, it was during this editorial work that I got to know him well. It was wonderful to see how open he was to different schools of thoughts and methodologies, even though he himself had his own beliefs. We both felt that students ought to have the option about which ideas to accept and which ones to reject, and though we had our disagreements about which ones are best kept and which ones best rejected, we worked extremely well in choosing which ones should be read.

One can see the diversity of intellectual schools in this book as well, which includes chapters on mainstream mathematical economics covering general equilibrium theory and neoclassical growth theory, analysis of financial and stock markets, political economy, and heterodox and descriptive essays.

Although the book is meant for the global economy and is on economics in general, it is particularly relevant for contemporary India. After decades of running a relatively closed economy, starting in 1991, India reformed and opened up. Among other changes, the Indian rupee was allowed to float with minimal interventions from the Reserve Bank of India—often described as a managed float—many quantity restrictions on imports were removed and import duties were sharply lowered, and restrictions on foreign direct investments coming into India were reduced.

It is not surprising that India would soon be feeling the ebbs and flows of the global economy. India, in my view, did very well by the reforms, growing at around 7 per cent per annum from 1994, which would have been unthinkable even four or five years prior to that; but India was also exposed to global highs and downturns in ways it was not used to. The 1997 East Asian crisis hit India hard, as did the global financial crisis of 2008. Being, still, a relatively new globalised economy, India has a lot to learn on how to navigate global fluctuations and flows and get more out of being a globalised economy.

This collection of papers, apart from celebrating Prabhat Patnaik's outstanding career as an economist and teacher, also tries to chip away at the large task ahead for India, as the nation's economy grows and integrates into the world.

Mausumi Das, Sabyasachi Kar and Nandan Nawn deserve congratulations for organising and editing this excellent compendium.

Kaushik Basu
Senior Vice President and Chief Economist, The World Bank
Professor of Economics and the C. Marks Professor of International Studies, Cornell University

Acknowledgements

We would like to express our sincere gratitude to all the authors of this volume for their cooperation. Our special thanks to C.P. Chandrasekhar for his comments and suggestions on the introductory chapter and to Praveen Jha for his help at a crucial point in publishing this volume.

We are grateful to Kaushik Basu for making time from his busy schedule and writing the Foreword to this volume.

We would like to thank N. Unni Nair, former Commissioning Editor at SAGE, for his interest, effort and most importantly patience in supporting this long-drawn project. We would also like to thank Isha Sachdeva, Production Editor, for efficiently leading the production team working on this book, and Neena Ganjoo and Pranab Jyoti Sarma for their excellent copy-editing.

Editors

1
Introduction

Mausumi Das, Sabyasachi Kar and Nandan Nawn

Prabhat Patnaik is a highly respected name in the academic and professional fraternity, both in India and abroad. His reputation as an economist belonging to the Marxist and Heterodox traditions is formidable. He has enthralled successive generations of students at the Centre for Economic Studies and Planning (hereafter, the Centre) at the Jawaharlal Nehru University (JNU), New Delhi, not only by his personal academic brilliance, but also by his exceptional ability to motivate, to inspire and to encourage students to constantly challenge the conventional wisdom and seek new answers. This volume is a tribute to that spirit of intellectual engagement.

Edited volumes that pay a tribute to a scholar usually consist of contributions from peers and colleagues who have been intellectually influenced by him/her. In this regard, this volume is unique. Here, the contributors were all doctoral students of Prabhat Patnaik at the Centre at various points of time. Prabhat's own work spans a vast area, in terms of both issues and analytical frameworks. It, therefore, does not come as a surprise to find the amazing width and breadth of topics that have been explored by the contributors to this volume—ranging from political economy to modern monetary economics, from international economics to growth theory, and from agriculture and industry to finance and environment.

All these works are not necessarily confined within the bounds of heterodox economics. Nor is there a common methodological thread that binds them together. Nevertheless, there is a common line of thinking that runs through all of them, and this entails a critical way of looking at the functioning of the contemporary capitalist system. Prabhat's own work has consistently underscored the weaknesses of the capitalist system, particularly its impact on the process of development. The works of his students reflect this line of thinking and emphasise the economic challenges that are thrown up by the problems and weaknesses of this system. In a broad sense, this critical approach towards the contemporary capitalist system is indeed the intellectual legacy of Prabhat Patnaik. This is evident in all the essays included here and is reflected in the title of the volume.

The idea of this volume dates back to October 2010, around the time when the students and teachers of the Centre had arranged a common 'farewell' for Anjan Mukherji, Utsa Patnaik and Prabhat Patnaik, the last three of the sextet that had started the Centre and who took formal retirement from the JNU within a period of barely four months, in July, August and October of 2010, respectively. Admittedly, there were many possible ways to pay a tribute to this scholar: conferences, seminars, lectures and, of course, books. A certain way to resolve this issue was to choose an option that would create new and lasting knowledge and at the same time reach the maximum number of people. Accumulation of knowledge, embodied in a *Festschrift*, was considered to be the best candidate to serve this purpose. Since this *Festschrift* would be for Prabhat Patnaik, there would never be a shortage of willing contributors: his students, colleagues, comrades, readers and even followers are just too many. This problem of plenty led us to limit ourselves to a very exclusive club—Prabhat's doctoral students.

It was, however, not easy to locate his students. The thesis section of the JNU library had to be searched manually, as bibliographic information in the catalogue did not include the name of supervisors. In any case, this effort was without much success, as record keeping is not one of the priorities in the educational institutions in India. Even the data entered in the register at the Centre was incomplete. Bereft of any other option, the editors then approached Prabhat Patnaik himself for a complete list of his doctoral students. All those who have been awarded a degree by 2012 and were working on contemporary economic problems were contacted. Subsequently, the 'Festschrift project' started with those from whom we had received a positive response.

We are certain that there will be more endeavours similar to this one. This volume is unique though to the extent that it was conceived, contributed and delivered exclusively by Prabhat's students. After all, for a teacher, can anybody be more worthy as an associate than her or his own students?

Academic and Professional Life of Prabhat Patnaik

Prabhat Patnaik was born on 19 September 1945 to Prananath and Manjari Patnaik in Jatani in the Khordha (aka Jatni and Khurdha Road, respectively) district of Odisha, India.

His brilliant student life benefitted from numerous scholarships—a Government of India Merit Scholarship in 1957 during his early schooling and later in Daly College, Indore, and another one for pursuing BA (honours) programme in Economics in St. Stephens College, Delhi University. From there, he joined the Delhi School of Economics for MA in Economics programme. His teachers at the Delhi School of Economics included Amartya Sen, Sukhamoy Chakravarty and K.N. Raj.

In 1966, on a Rhodes scholarship, he joined Balliol College, Oxford University, in its BPhil programme. A year later he moved to the Faculty of Social Studies, Nuffield College, where he would submit his DPhil thesis in 1973, titled 'Private corporate industrial investment in India, 1947–1967: factors affecting its size, cyclical fluctuation and sectoral distribution'.

After the completion of the Rhodes scholarship in 1969, he joined the Faculty of Economics and Politics, University of Cambridge, and was elected a Fellow of Clare College, Cambridge. In 1974, he came back to India and joined—as an Associate Professor—the then newly formed Centre for Economic Studies and Planning at the JNU, New Delhi, to complete the initial sextet that had laid its foundation stones—others being Anjan Mukherji, Utsa Patnaik, Amit Bhaduri, Sunanda Sen and (late) Krishna Bharadwaj, the founder Chairperson. He became a Professor in 1983 and has remained associated with the Centre till date. He was the Sukhamoy Chakravarty Chair in Planning and Development when he took formal 'retirement' in September 2010. Subsequently, he was an Adjunct Faculty at the Centre, and since January 2013, he has been a Professor Emeritus.

He received the V.K.R.V. Rao Prize in Social Science Research instituted by the Institute for Social and Economic Change, Bangalore, in 1986. In July 2012, the School of African and Oriental Studies, University of London, bestowed the Honorary Doctorate Degree of Science and Economics (DSc Econ) on him.

He had been Vice-Chairman of the Kerala State Planning Board from June 2006 to July 2011. In 2008, he was appointed by the President of the United Nations General Assembly to be a part of the four-member high-power task force to recommend reforms of the global financial system, led by Joseph Stiglitz.

Since the last number of its ninth volume in December 1981, he has been the Editor of *Social Scientist*, a journal known for its radical content, from theoretical and applied to contemporary and historical.

Works of Prabhat Patnaik

The works of Prabhat Patnaik are vast and varied. For a remarkable political economist who had started expressing his thoughts in the written form while he was just 21 and continues till this day with an enormous frequency, he has put together a stupendous body of work. Besides regular contributions in most accessible public domains like newspapers (*People's Democracy* and the *Telegraph*, Kolkata, for example) and web sites of the Economic Research Foundation, New Delhi (http://www.macroscan.org/), and the International Development Economics Associates (http://www.networkideas.org), his publications in journals exceed 100, along with seven books and a considerable number of chapters in edited volumes.

Clearly, it is impossible for anyone to even make an attempt to pen an exhaustive summary of his intellectual achievements, more so, given the variety of areas on which he has written. Rather than providing an exhaustive account of his works, in this section we attempt to familiarise the readers with some of the dominant strands of thoughts and chain of arguments that seem to have persisted in Patnaik's writings over the years. The central focus in the large corpus of his work during the last half a century since the first publication (1966) has been the nature and causes of underdevelopment and pathways to development in India in general, with particular concerns for social injustice and deep-rooted poverty. In disciplinary terms, his works can be located at the cusp of macroeconomics and political economy. Sifting through the huge volume of journal articles, book chapters, invited lectures and books, one can discern three dominant themes that underlie much of his work:

1. Growth in the Indian economy—its nature and consequences
2. Capitalism—its internal contradictions and external supports
3. Socialism—its desirability and feasibility in today's world

Each of these three themes is discussed below with the appropriate references.

Growth in the Indian Economy

The first theme—the nature and consequences of growth in the Indian economy—has spanned over Patnaik's whole academic life. There are two important issues that have largely defined this strand of his works. The first is the role of demand in the growth process of a developing economy like India, while the second is the impact of globalisation—particularly financial globalisation—on such an economy. On the role of demand, his early writings focus on the constraints imposed by the agricultural sector on manufacturing, thereby limiting the scope of expansion of the latter. A slightly different argument, which appears in the more recent writings of Patnaik, highlights the changing composition of demand from wage goods to luxury consumption goods, which may generate self-sustaining demand for the non-agricultural sector while the agricultural sector stagnates. Patnaik's analysis of the impact of globalisation of the Indian economy—expanded later to include other emerging economies like China—shows that these processes lead to increasing unemployment, poverty and inequality in these countries.

Patnaik has been one of the few economists who consistently drew attention to the role of demand constraints in determining growth rates, especially in less-developed economies like India. Early contributions analysed the factors behind the rise and fall of industrial growth rates in India over the 1950s and 1960s, showing that the stimulus for the spurt in the post-independence economy came from two sources, the import substitution policies based on protection and high public investments, leading to very significant industrial growth rates during this period (Patnaik, 1979). However, since there was no egalitarian shift in the pattern of asset and income distribution, which would have boosted domestic demand and expanded the markets for mass consumer goods, this resulted in a top-heavy industrialisation. As a result, once the opportunities provided by import substitution were exhausted, the growth petered out by the early 1970s. Elsewhere, it was argued that it was the lack of a growth in domestic demand from agriculture that led to adverse economic consequences during the late 1980s (Patnaik, 1987). According to Patnaik, in an economy like India, the stimulus for industrialisation has to come from agriculture rather than from the external sector. He shows that a systematic squeeze on the agricultural sector during the 1970s and the early 1980s—in terms of both low growth and adverse movement of terms of trade—led to a low demand for food and an increasing demand for luxury imports. This trend resulted in unsold foodstocks, high unemployment, as well as an external deficit during the late 1980s. Together with a fiscal crisis, these challenges led to an increasing tendency towards privatisation and demand for a freer play of the markets during the end of the 1980s.

By the early 1990s, of course, the Indian economy changed course and adopted market-friendly reforms, which, among other things, implied a movement towards increased globalisation. As is well-known, Patnaik was, and continues to be, extremely critical of these policies. Writing during the early years of the post-reform period, he claimed that the international economic system—particularly the mobility of international capital—would undermine the autonomy of national policymaking, making it very difficult for developing countries to sustain economic growth with free markets (Patnaik, 1994). In particular, the fear of capital flights would stop governments from any policy to stimulate demand and hence the growth of the economy. Taking this argument forward, Patnaik (2000b) argued that in the post-reform period, the Indian economy turned into a chronic demand-constrained economy. It was no longer constrained by foodgrain production or foreign exchange reserves and manifested unutilised capacities in many sectors. This change was due to a shift in income distribution against agricultural workers, a decline in the role of the state in stimulating demand in the economy and a rise in net imports, all of which were themselves a result of policies trying to attract international capital flows. The research work gave empirical evidence to validate the above claims and argued that all of these led to fall in growth rates during the end of the 1990s.

On the impact of financial globalisation on the growth of the Indian economy, another work highlights the fact that the capital flowing into India following the economic liberalisation was not 'capital for production' but 'capital as finance' (Patnaik, 1997a). While the long-term flows (capital in production or direct foreign investment) into the economy have been meagre, it has received a large amount of speculative flows (capital as finance) in the form of foreign currency deposits and portfolio investment. However, these have not generated higher economic growth. Patnaik argued that the government attempted to counter this tendency of falling growth rates by increasing the fiscal deficit, but even this strategy showed diminishing returns, significantly because revenue expenditures increased at the cost of capital expenditures. The article concluded that liberalisation and globalisation had caused economic stagnation, decline in domestic food availability and increases in rural poverty.

Despite the increase in volatility in growth rates in the post-reform period, it is irrefutable that average growth rates did go up during this period. In fact, by the early years of the new century, growth rates seemed to have gone up even further. It is in his efforts to explain this trend that Patnaik started to emphasise the critical role played by increases in the demand for 'luxury consumption'. Thus, Patnaik (2007d) questions why a rising share of economic surplus in output has not created any serious realisation problem in a demand-constrained economy like India, and hence any consequent tendency towards stagnation. He reasoned out that this was not because of exogenous countervailing factors like state expenditure or an export surplus of goods and services. Rather, the article attributed this phenomenon to the fact that the rising share of economic surplus in output has been accompanied by greater consumption by the surplus earners themselves and also by greater investment that has been stimulated by such consumption, leading to an increase in the rate of economic growth. He developed a theoretical model of this phenomenon, showing that such growth leads to slow growth of employment due to a rapid increase in labour productivity, leading to rising unemployment. Patnaik went on to generalise this idea of an inequalising growth process to describe the nature of growth not only in India but also in other emerging economies like China. Contributions to this argument discuss how a shift in the income distribution from wages to surplus has led to a shift in demand in these countries towards products that require the use of technology with higher labour productivity (Patnaik, 2009c). This has led to a high rate of growth of labour productivity preventing them from using up of their labour reserves, and this makes the distribution even more unequal. Furthermore, he also theorised the possible impact such growth processes would have on poverty in countries with petty producers and reserves of unemployed labour (Patnaik, 2011). He argued that such a growth process involves dispossessing these petty producers without creating adequate employment growth in the formal sectors. As a result, there is an ever-increasing reserve of unemployed or underemployed labourers and higher incidence of poverty. Patnaik concluded that in order to address their social needs, the growth strategy for countries like India and China must be one that can rapidly use up their labour reserves through a peasant agriculture-led growth strategy.

Capitalism

The inherent contradictions of capitalism, and its resilience as an economic system despite these contradictions is another recurrent theme that appears in many of Patnaik's works. Marx himself, as well as the traditional Marxist theory, viewed capitalism as a transitory system—ridden with various internal contradictions that make the system inherently unstable and vulnerable to crises. Such crisis could manifest itself either in the form of overproduction, resulting in a falling rate of profit and/or growing unemployment, or in the form of spiralling inflation, culminating in a complete collapse of the modern monetary system whereby money ceases to have any positive value. Yet, advanced capitalism has exhibited exceptional resilience and stability and has remained a viable economic system, notwithstanding occasional crises. This has impelled Patnaik, a Marxist economist himself, to analyse the possible causes for this stability that defies the Marxist prediction of its inevitable eclipse. Patnaik's writings on the theme of capitalism can be classified into three distinct theses: (a) a theoretical critique of the mainstream representation of the capitalist system; (b) an alternative explanation for the observed stability of capitalism and (c) an analysis of the changing character of present-day capitalism with the advent of international finance capital (IFC).

A Critique of the Mainstream View

To the staunch believers of the capitalist system, its stability itself is a proof of its inherent efficiency—a validation of the smooth functioning of the 'invisible hand'. Others, including the Keynesians, recognise the underlying deficiencies of the system and attribute its stability to appropriate state interventions. Patnaik contests both these positions.

According to Patnaik, the theoretical underpinning of the laissez-faire market economy, namely the Walrasian/Arrow–Debreu framework, may fail to ensure the existence of an equilibrium with full employment once the role of expectations in influencing the current actions of agents is taken into account. In particular, the adjustment mechanism implied in the Walrasian system in terms of flexibility of the nominal wage rate and the price level may no longer work. For example, in the face of excess supply in the commodity market, if a downward adjustment in the nominal price level is accompanied by the expectation of a further fall in the prices, then aggregate demand will not pick up to mop up the excess supply. In such a scenario, the price level will keep spiralling down without the economy settling down to a full-employment equilibrium. Patnaik further argues that as opposed to the assumption of atomistic, price-taking agents in the Walrasian/Arrow–Debreu framework, the actual capitalist world is characterised by conglomerate agents who are price makers. In the absence of price-taking behaviour on part of the agents, the basic tenets of the laissez-faire economy fail to operate. Moreover, price-making behaviour on the part of the workers (through trade unions) as well as capitalists (in the form of mark-up pricing) would entail a distributive conflict over the share of the output, resulting in accelerating inflation (Patnaik, 1997c).

The conceptual inadequacy of the wage–price flexibility mechanism was recognised by Keynes, who used the rigidity of the nominal wage rate as an anchor that pins down the capitalist system to a well-defined equilibrium. But such an equilibrium would be characterised by involuntary unemployment. Thus, the Keynesian framework proposes demand creation through state intervention as a mechanism to stabilise the capitalist economy to the level of full employment. However, Patnaik rejects the claim that prudent state intervention is the reason behind the observed stability in the capitalist system on two counts. First, the state itself is influenced by interests of the economically dominant classes (namely the rentiers and the bourgeoisie), which may undermine its ability to lower unemployment and protect workers' interest. Second, even when the state acts as a neutral authority, it may have limited capacity to simultaneously control inflation or unemployment through the fiscal and monetary policies, as such policies may generate speculative behaviour riding on the agents' expectations (Patnaik, 1997c).

Patnaik (2008c) examines another foundation of advanced capitalism—the institution of fiat money, which acts as the medium of exchange as well as a store of value in any modern capitalist economy. The core question that Patnaik seeks to address here is the following: What breathes value into the intrinsically worthless bits of paper called 'money'? Note that the answer to this question is of fundamental importance for the stability of the modern capitalist system. If value of money tends to zero, then commodity prices would approach infinity, resulting in a complete collapse of the monetary system. Once again Patnaik argues that the mainstream Walrasian/monetarist view that attributes the value of money to its demand and supply (like any other commodity) is logically untenable. To the extent that money also acts as a store of value, expectations about future prices would directly influence the demand for money. And to the extent that expectations about future prices interact with the current price level, there may not actually exist any finite price level (and hence a finite value of money) at which the demand for money equals its supply. Indeed, money will have a positive value if and only if people have inelastic price expectations. This is tantamount to saying that money will have positive value if and only if people believe that money will have positive value in future. Patnaik argues that this assumption of inelastic price expectation contradicts the basic Walrasian premise that all prices are flexible, which by definition rules out any anchorage that can fix the value of money vis-à-vis a particular commodity. Indeed, such an anchorage is provided in Keynes in terms of the rigidity of the nominal wage, which immediately fixes the value of money vis-à-vis labour. However, according to Patnaik, even the Keynesian theory is incomplete since such exogenous determination of the value of money entails the possibility of deficiency of aggregate demand resulting in involuntary unemployment, which once again undermines the viability of the capitalist system.

Stability of Capitalism: An Alternative Explanation

Patnaik argues that the observed stability of capitalism in the advanced countries stems from the unequal interdependence between the capitalist core and the pre-capitalist or semi-capitalist periphery, the latter being characterised by the presence of a large unorganised reserve army of labour. Existence of such a periphery allows the capitalist core to simultaneously uphold the interests of its organised labour force as well as organised capital. Price stability at the core is attained by compressing the real wage of the unorganised workers in the periphery. At the same time, the periphery constitutes a ready market for the goods produced in the advanced capitalist countries, thereby allowing the latter economies to maintain full employment at the expense of the former (Patnaik, 1972, 1989, 1997a, 2010c).

According to Patnaik, this institutionalised global mechanism of unequal interdependence is a form of imperialism. In Patnaik's writings, the issue of endurance of capitalism is intertwined with the issue of imperialism. Indeed, the stability of capitalism has been attributed to the evolving nature of imperialism. At its initial phase, advance of capitalism in the western world depended heavily on its exploits in the colonies, while in its later phase, survival of capitalism has hinged crucially on the exploitation of the market as well as surplus labour in the less-developed economies.

While Patnaik attributes the apparent success of the core capitalist countries to this imperialist mechanism, which operates by subjugation of the labour force and exploitation of the markets in the less developed periphery in the interest of the capitalist core, he argues that this mechanism is different from the erstwhile colonial form of imperialism as it does not require explicit use of coercion to keep the system going. In fact, it mediates by the actions and choices of the capitalist and other dominant social groups in the backward economy who have a distinct preference for goods imported from the advanced countries over home-produced goods. This process contributes to the spontaneous reproduction of unequal interdependence, thereby enhancing its durability (Patnaik, 1997c).

In a similar vein, Patnaik argues that the stability of the capitalist monetary system is also attributable to this imperialist mechanism of unequal interdependence. In order to answer the question as to why money has a stable and positive value in a capitalist economy, Patnaik reverts back to the issue of external stimuli in the form of existence of a pre-capitalist market. Existence of such a pre-capitalist market absorbs the overproduction in the advanced capitalist economy without jeopardising its monetary foundation. Sticky wages continue to provide an anchor to the value of money at the capitalist core, while the concomitant demand constraint is overcome by reaching out to markets beyond the capitalist core (Patnaik, 2008c).

Changing Character of Capitalism

Writing at the beginning of this present millennium, Patnaik (2003) identified the rise of IFC as the most significant internal change that has occurred within capitalism. In particular, it was argued that this development reflects extraordinary predatoriness of capitalism, which not only halts but also reverses the progress along the road to the freedom by restricting, if not eliminating, the capacity of the nation-state to intervene (Patnaik, 2007b). The newness of predatory capitalism is articulated in Patnaik (1996, 1999c, 2000a, 2002, 2005, 2007b) and elsewhere, most recent being Patnaik (2010b). This movement of finance looking for opportunities all over the globe is not the same as what Kautsky had called 'internationally united finance capital'. Neither it is the same imperialism as Lenin construed it (this was discussed in detail in Patnaik, 1986), for this new entity is neither specifically nation-based, nor nation-state aided or is linked to some specific national capitalist strategy. Indeed, according to Patnaik, this new age of global finance leads to a stronger age of imperialism that brings about a transformation in the nature of the capitalist state such that it acts exclusively towards promotion of financial and corporate interests (Patnaik, 2007b).

The nature of economic growth in this new age of global finance is argued to have a dichotomous effect vis-à-vis the two global segments: (1) advanced capitalist countries and (2) third world. The growth in advanced capitalist countries is accompanied by persistence of poverty in the third world. Globalised finance capital makes the demand constraint more acute by thwarting any state-led demand management, which, in turn, fuels a process of de-industrialisation in the relatively backward economies due to lower 'staying power' of the domestic producers there. The Washington-based institutions of World Bank and International Monetary Fund defend the interests of IFC by ensuring price stability in the metropolitan centres through forced deflation and devaluation in the primary commodity-producing third-world countries (Patnaik, 1996). However, this prediction is contradicted by the apparent economic success of East Asian countries of Thailand, Indonesia, Malaysia and the Philippines despite their strong integration to imperialism. Patnaik (1999c) argues that the high growth of the East Asian 'tigers' could be explained by the restraint put on the financial interests to the extent of making it subordinate to the productive economy. This factor, which is analogous to the dirigisme pursued by newly industrialising third-world economies or the policies followed by 'miracle' economies of Germany and Japan in the post-war period, is however relatively unnoticed in the literature.

Towards a Socialist Project

The two strands of Patnaik's works discussed above underscore the realism that capitalism is inherently unequal and unstable and hence unable to fulfil the objectives of freedom, democracy and individual subjectivity. Even if there is state intervention in the form of Keynesian demand management, it can only block these inherent tendencies temporarily, and reversing them permanently is simply not possible. Based on this perspective, Patnaik has written on a large number of issues, all of which are related to a critique of the new face of capitalism and a justification for socialism. These contributions include an analysis of this new form of capitalism, including its implication for development, the necessity for reinterpreting Marxism in this new context, critiquing alternative approaches like reformism and finally a renewed agenda for socialism.

IFC and the New Face of Capitalism

According to Patnaik, capitalism may make concessions during times of crisis for ensuring its survival, providing a false impression on its ability in fulfilling its promise. However, subsequently, contradictions emerge and these lead to a return of those tendencies, indeed, in a stronger form. For instance, following the 'golden age of capitalism', centralisation of capital has taken the new form of IFC. Patnaik argues that IFC is a major cause of crisis and stagnation in the world of capitalism, contributing to this outcome in three major ways (Patnaik, 1999a). First, it creates competition between capitalist countries for a larger share of financial flows and hence gives rise to deflationary tendencies, as this competition forces countries to lower their fiscal deficits. Second, this competitive deflation affects even the United States (US), the leading capitalist country in the post-war period. Third, it limits the possibilities of demand management that could actually minimise any deflationary crisis. This stagnation and crisis in advanced capitalist countries result in further centralisation of capital.

According to Patnaik, this new form of capitalism has an inherent antipathy for an 'activist state'. Thus, demand management, or any other form of state activism, including national policymaking, becomes very difficult or simply impossible (Patnaik, 1997b, 2006). Extending this argument, Patnaik analysed the nature of the state in this era of neoliberalism, including the nature of the bureaucracy, other state personnel and the 'organic intellectuals' (Patnaik, 2007c). Here, he argues that whether the state remains as a bourgeois or a dirigiste one, it differs in a fundamental way from the past as the interests of the state personnel are now grossly similar to that of the world of finance and corporations. Such enmeshing makes the state personnel incapable of bringing any change in the living conditions of the poor, or for that matter even carrying out normal government functions.

Patnaik argues that this phase marks a change in the set of feasible interventions available to the nation-state (Patnaik, 1995). While elaborating on how the undermining of the traditional forms of intervention results in the virtual stagnation and high levels of unemployment in the capitalist world, he emphasised that such limitations in no way eliminate the scope for intervention altogether. Thus, the nation-states now need to recognise the new constraints posed by the fluidity of financial capital while planning any intervention.

IFC and the Struggle for Autonomous Trajectory of Development

In the third world, neoliberal policies pursued by the state under pressure from IFC result in jobless growth, rise in inequality and agrarian distress (Patnaik, 2006). Stagnation and accentuated unemployment result in social strife, including the emergence of all kinds of divisive forces. The third world is also affected politically in terms of a loss of its sovereignty as the ascendancy of IFC favours the scuttling of democracy (Patnaik, 1999a). Elaborating on this idea, Patnaik argued that the focus on retaining 'investors' confidence' as persuaded by IFC negates democracy by taking economic policymaking outside the purview of the elected governments (Patnaik, 2001). Describing these as the 'rolling back' of democracy, he argues that the 'global financial community' that includes 'financial oligarchy proper' and ideologues of IFC promote and perpetuate the hegemony of IFC, say, by exercising 'peer pressure' through publicising the apparent costs that the country could face for 'capital flights' (Patnaik, 2009b).

The collaborative character of the bourgeois state in the era of IFC, in contrast to European historical experience, ensures serving the interests of imperialism towards re-colonisation, rather than pursuing and sustaining an autonomous trajectory of development (Patnaik, 2000a). This, in turn, undermines the productive employment of capital, preventing improvement in the living standard of working people. Patnaik argues that the real reason behind the production success of East Asian economies was the subservience of finance by the industry—as was the case during the Indian dirigisme—and this has now undergone a reversal due to the rise of IFC (Patnaik, 1997b).

Patnaik argues that defending democracy is central to the pursuit of development. Contrary to the ultra-leftist position that puts struggle for a change in the form of government as distinct and secondary to struggle for a change in the class nature of the state, or the broad Marxist position that extends primacy over the form of the government, struggles over the form of government and the class nature of the state are intricately enmeshed together (Patnaik, 2000a). The importance of strengthening democratic structures arises also from the fact that the willingness of the state to transform itself to become neocolonial takes place through jettisoning of these very structures. Thus, defending these structures becomes directly anti-imperialist task, which is a part of socialist agenda (Patnaik, 1999a).

Reimagining Marxism for the New Era

Patnaik argued that all the theoretical positions that believe in resolving the contradictions within the capitalist system are 'partial', if not 'unscientific', in a fundamental sense (Patnaik, 2008b). The scientific basis of the Marxist position follows from its recognition of the self-driven nature of the capitalist system. This position assumes away the possibilities of any successful and permanent social engineering of capitalism. In order to arrive at this position, Marxism has borrowed specific scientific discoveries from other traditions but has also assimilated those within its own tradition. Such openness of Marxism in engaging with all theoretical tendencies irrespective of their ideological mooring has featured in many of Patnaik's writings (2007a, 2008b, 2009b).

Rejection of such openness turns Marxism into a closed and completed system that can be applied only in specific contexts. This rigid interpretation of Marxism is shared by both the old socialist view and 'a good deal of left thinking to this day' (Patnaik, 2007a), and according to Patnaik, it contributes to a theoretical enfeebling of Marxism (Patnaik, 2008b). Instead, he argues that the need of the hour is a sustained attempt to understand the present through a 'reconstruction of Marxism'. As in any theoretical effort, validity of such attempts is to be judged by whether it enables an understanding of the present rather than through its closeness or deviation from the 'text'. Indeed, a healthy debate on such alternative reconstructions using concepts offered by Marx, Marxists and others can provide the 'necessary oxygen' that a revolutionary party needs for its survival. Such 'openness' could prevent development of 'hardening' of group interests within the Party as happened in the Soviet Union (Patnaik, 2009b).

Patnaik points out that in contrast to the inter-war years when socialism was attractive to millions for the hope of emancipation of mankind that it offered, the post-war period had witnessed a reversal in this trend (Patnaik, 1997b). He argues that this is due to the inability of socialism to restructure itself. During the same phase, on the other hand, capitalism restructured itself to appear even humane and capable of diffusing into the third world. Instead of a parallel transformation, socialism witnessed an absence of inner-party democracy, continuation of the dictatorship of the party in the name of the proletariat and, most importantly, the de-politicisation of the working class. As an example of the lack of such restructuring, Patnaik pointed out that socialism did not make any attempt to provide alternative conceptualisations of use-value or lifestyles, as a result of which living standards, and hence aspirations, were defined by those prevailing in advanced capitalist countries. He showed why failing to prevent such inculcation of bourgeois values among the entire population was self-defeating for socialism (Patnaik, 1999a). Due to this lack of willingness to restructure itself, the demise of socialism was imminent.

Reformism or Socialism?

The necessity of transcending the capitalist system along with its institutions, to socialism, appears as another central thread in Patnaik's various writings (2006, 2009a, 2009b). Emphasising the self-driven property of the capitalist system, he argued that any approach that rejects socialism in favour of reformism ignores this very feature of capitalism (Patnaik, 2008a). A system must be 'malleable' enough for the state intervention to 'reform' it. However with capitalism, any sustained state intervention against its inherent tendencies makes the system lose its coherence and it starts becoming dysfunctional. This fear of dysfunctionality in turn puts limits on state intervention. Thus, irrespective of the nature or form of the reforms that may take place, they cannot achieve what capitalism promises, that is, there can never be a permanent 'welfare capitalism' or 'humane capitalism' or a 'half-way house' in between (Patnaik, 2009b). It is only socialism that envisions a break away from these constraints through a dual transformation, first, in the system of ownership and, second, in the nature of the state. In this context, Patnaik ponders why the discontentment with capitalism as espoused by various movements against gender discrimination, ecological degradation or even by the 'radical' opponents of capitalism does not visualise any transcendence of the capitalist system (Patnaik, 2010a). In seeking an alternative, they mostly limit themselves in calling for various kinds of reforms rather than socialism. He concludes that this is based on an implicit belief in the idea of capitalism being a durable mode of production endowed with near-permanence, which has been rejected, quite ironically, even by the leading lights of political economy.

Towards a Socialist Project: Retrospect and Prospect

Sometime towards the end of the previous millennium, Patnaik foresaw conditions promising a new stage of advance for the socialist project (Patnaik, 1997b). The most important of these conditions was the emergence of IFC, which signified the ascendancy of western metropolitan, in particular, the Anglo-Saxon powers. This era was also distinct from earlier ones in that the imperial powers worked with a common cause rather than with a sense of rivalry. This absence of inter-imperialist rivalry ensured non-discriminatory treatment to IFC, without which its unity could have been jeopardised. It also facilitated the unfettered movement of IFC across the globe (Patnaik, 1999a). These forces also found a far more willing bourgeoisie in the third world who made a common cause with imperialism (Patnaik, 1997b).

In order to advance socialism in the face of these conditions, Patnaik provided an alternative framework (Patnaik, 1999a). This framework involved disciplining capital flows and not just avoiding capital account convertibility. It also involved imposing trade controls to avoid the re-institutionalisation of a colonial economy. This framework focussed on maintaining the autonomy of the nation-state, mobilisation of workers and peasants and putting in place structures to enable them to exercise their political power. In terms of specific policy measures, he argued for land reform for developing productive forces in agriculture as well as larger levels of public investment in agriculture financed by direct taxation of the richer classes. Together with these, policy needed to ensure universal literacy, universal availability of minimum health facilities, generation of employment and complete eradication of poverty. On a deeper social level, defence of the secular character of the polity, defence of democratic institutions and their deepening through the decentralisation of resources and decision making, etc., were essential aspects of this framework for socialism. In order to achieve these goals, Patnaik called for the reorganisation of the entire mode of organisational functioning of socialist forces in a country like India, inculcating democratic participation within them. Extending these arguments, he evaluated the possibilities of socialist forces acquiring political power in some third-world country (Patnaik, 1999a). Furthermore, he explored how such countries should act in order to survive given the lessons from the historical experience of socialism.

Patnaik argued why it is important for socialists to fight for a 'democratic national agenda' and against 'bourgeois internationalism' (Patnaik, 1999b). According to him, the latter implies a unity among the advanced capitalist countries for a common purpose, namely denying space to third–world nationalism in terms of self-reliance and the resultant capitulation to the diktats of global order dominated by these powers. Extending this line of thought, he further argued that in the transition from bourgeois internationalism to a new internationalism based on the unity of working people, an interim anti-imperialist 'national agenda' based on the class support of workers and peasants is necessary (Patnaik, 1999c). This has to include not only those in the third world who are the most affected by the hegemony of IFC, but also the workers in the first world who are also affected by it.

A Brief Review of the Chapters

The contemporary economic world poses several challenges that have engaged attention of the profession. Some of these challenges are of relatively recent origin and stem from the emergence of a new global economic order, newer institutions and new socio-economic and political alliances. Addressing these issues requires new ways of approaching the problems. Some issues, on the other hand, are age-old, but may have acquired newer dimensions in the current economic milieu. These include the problems of persistence of poverty, inequality, unemployment, etc. The present volume addresses a select set of issues, both old and new, analyses their causes and consequences and, in some cases, offers solutions.

Each chapter in this volume can be identified in terms of a particular present-day economic problem that it seeks to address. Depending on the nature of the problem addressed, the chapters in this volume have been classified under five broad sections:

A. Sustaining the growth process
B. Dealing with globalisation: trade, capital, technology
C. Mitigating immiserisation: poverty, inequality, joblessness
D. Envisioning the institutional changes
E. Reimagining the political hegemony

Section A deals with the challenges of sustaining a steady growth process in the current economic environment. While the incidence of a positive trend growth rate in the world economy is indeed associated with emergence of modern capitalism during the industrial revolution, maintaining this steady trend over long run has remained a challenge even for the developed capitalist economies. The challenge is more pronounced in the developing economies, which have recently embarked on trajectories of high growth. This not only requires creating the right stimuli and a suitable environment, but for any growth process to be sustainable, it must also entail a mechanism of generating steady agricultural surplus to support the growth of non-agricultural sectors. In this context, this section examines whether factors such as financial expansion and deepening (Chapter 2) or global cooperation (Chapter 3) can be instrumental in sustaining growth within and across regions. It also examines the nature of land policies towards augmenting agricultural surplus necessary for sustaining growth (Chapter 4).

Section B confronts challenges that are associated with the process of globalisation. The world today is becoming increasingly globalised with augmented volumes of trade flows, capital flows and technology flows across international borders. However, the benefits of globalisation may not be equitably distributed across countries, especially between the developed North and the less-developed South. The essays in this section focus on various aspects of such imbalances that arise in the course of globalisation. These imbalances may manifest themselves in a secular decline in the terms of trade against the primary product exporting Southern countries (Chapter 5), or a growing current account deficit and a concomitant increase in the net foreign liabilities of the US economy (Chapter 6), or large and volatile inflows of speculative capital that undermine macroeconomic policies in the developing countries (Chapter 7). Globalisation may also promote technology transfer from the advanced to the developing countries (Chapter 8).

The essays belonging to Section C are concerned with locating the causes of perpetuating and intensifying economic misery, and finding ways to alleviate it. Immiserisation impinges on the economic behaviour of the poor in several ways. It discourages savings and investments, deters schooling and human capital formation and, in general, may lead to inefficient decision making, resulting in perpetuation of misery, hunger and malnourishment in the long run. Such sub-optimal behaviour may be more pronounced in an unequal society, where the neighbourhoods and demonstration effects further confound the choices of the poor. Essays in this section explore pathways by which initial inequality may beget more inequality and impoverishment either by affecting the aspiration levels of the poor (Chapter 9), or through institutions of private inheritance and bequests (Chapter 10), or due to the elite dominance of public institutions (Chapter 11). They also explore conditions under which growth can be jobless or job-creating, highlighting an important economic phenomenon affecting immiserisation (Chapter 12).

The essays in Section D deal with the evolving nature of economic institutions and its consequences. The contemporary world economy looks different from the past not only because economic activities have changed significantly over time but also because the institutional framework underlying these activities has undergone drastic changes in recent years. The changing nature of institutions is perhaps most pronounced in the context of the monetary and financial institutions. With the advent of credit cards and other money substitutes, exogenous money (strictly regulated by the central bank) has given way to a more fluid concept of endogenous money. Regulated banking institutions have given way to more hands-off stock markets. The essays in this section examine the role of monetary policy (Chapter 13) and financial markets (Chapter 14) in the context of the changing nature of these institutions. Another sector that has seen significant institutional changes is retail trade. The third essay in this section (Chapter 15) critically examines such changes associated with the corporatisation of the retail industry.

The final section of the volume (Section E) contemplates various challenges that emerge out of the changing power structure and concurrent political hegemony in the contemporary capitalist world. With the emergence of financial globalisation, the economic boundaries of nation-states have become less distinct. At the same time, the presence of the state within its own national boundary itself has become weaker. The essays in this section examine the implications of these changes on the role of the state within the nation-states (Chapter 16) as well as on the stability of the capitalist system (Chapter 17). Weakening of the state leads to political realignment of the dominant class within the domestic economy, which, in turn, affects public policies. The last two essays in this section (Chapters 18 and 19) analyse the consequences of such political realignment for the agrarian sector.

It is worth mentioning here that the essays in this volume do not follow a uniform analytical structure or a single methodological technique. In analysing the theory, some authors use mainstream tools, while others develop alternative theoretical constructs to critically examine the contemporary world. Likewise, in analysing the empirics, some essays use rigorous econometric techniques, while others take recourse to historical experience and case studies to explain the current economic predicament. What ties these seemingly disparate set of essays together is the fact that each of them seeks to address a certain economic challenge—a challenge that confronts us in today's world as we look for betterment of economic conditions in India and elsewhere. A brief overview of each of these chapters follows.

Sustaining the Growth Process

In the introductory chapter of this section, C.P. Chandrasekhar explores various stimuli—exogenous and endogenous—for their ability to generate and sustain capitalist growth. Such stimuli could include continued existence of a pre-capitalist periphery, a sustained stream of innovations or a demand-induced state expenditure with varying time frames and intensities, notwithstanding the limitations associated with each. The highlight of the chapter is to explore whether finance could play a similar role, by generating an 'autonomous' demand, and explain the episodes of growth under capitalism, as portrayed in the recent literature. It argues that there can be periods when financial expansion and deepening lead to private debt, which serves as an exogenous stimulus to growth, but the resulting boom could be unsustainable and self-destructive. Even if it is prolonged and recurring, it can have contrary effects, which can lead to contraction rather than growth. Moreover, it is neither as strong nor as persistent as public expenditure or a pre-capitalist periphery in inducing growth.

In Chapter 3, Pranab Mukhopadhyay argues in favour of coordinated economic policies between the developed countries of the West and the emerging economies of the South, in order to revive the world economy. While the West faces the challenge of growing unemployment, the South wants to grow faster in order to reduce poverty and improve the well-being of a large section of its impoverished population. The chapter uses alternative simulation exercises based on a global macro-econometric model to show that individual country or regional efforts would be inadequate to achieve these goals, which underscores the need for coordinated fiscal expansion and structural change. The chapter concludes that if in a coordinated effort, the West were to undertake demand priming and the emerging economies structurally expand their intra-regional trade, only then the global recovery would be hastened.

Positing sustainability of farming in terms of sustenance of labour power and maintenance of agro-ecosystem health, Nandan Nawn in Chapter 4 characterises farming households by their surplus generating status and 'energy efficiency'. This chapter also analyses this issue in terms of a non-negative surplus with energy as a standard of measure, and employs the method of energy (balance) analysis. It begins by testing the appropriateness of alternative frameworks, including the 'metabolic' one, towards accounting for human labour in energy terms. Using a theoretical construct as well as an empirical illustration, it questions the supposed negative relationship between energy efficiency and area under cultivation. The chapter argues that, provided the value of labour-power is accounted for, the relationship will in fact be a positive one. This, in turn, contests the economic basis of land redistribution policies. On a concluding note, the chapter suggests an integration of the metabolic framework of human labour into the energy balance analysis for emergence of an 'ecological Marxism'.

Dealing with Globalisation: Trade, Capital, Technology

In Chapter 5, Shouvik Chakraborty contributes to the literature on the Prebisch–Singer hypothesis, which seeks to explain the secular deterioration in the terms of trade of primary commodities vis-à-vis manufactured goods in terms of long-term factors like elasticity of demand and technological progress. Chakraborty questions the adequacy of the Prebisch–Singer hypothesis in explaining the secular decline in the terms of trade in an economy characterised by mark-up pricing of manufactured goods. It postulates that the secular increase in the wage share in the gross output and/or the increase in the ratio of the profits to the gross output in the manufacturing sector are the factors primarily responsible for the secular deterioration in terms of trade. The chapter then empirically tests this conjecture for the G7 countries over the period of 1974 to 2005 and shows that an increase in the share of profits in the gross output of the manufacturing sector leads to a corresponding decline in the terms of trade of primary commodities vis-à-vis manufactured goods.

In Chapter 6, Sabyasachi Kar looks at the possibility of global imbalances returning to haunt the global economy, which took the shape of large current account deficits of the US and corresponding surpluses in some Asian and European countries. The chapter analyses the feasibility and limitations of an East Asia-centric approach to rebalancing such imbalances. It argues that in the past, most policy discussions on rebalancing have focused exclusively on the role of the East Asian economies in general, and that of China in particular. Using a global macro-econometric model, the study shows that even in the extreme case where these economies are forced to bring down their current account surpluses to zero, the net external liability position of the US economy would keep increasing, reaching historically high levels in the long run. Alternative scenarios show that Europe needs to play an important role in this process. The essay concludes that in order to be successful, global rebalancing has to involve a genuine partnership between the US, Asia and Europe.

In Chapter 7, Surajit Das deals with the effectiveness of fiscal policy in a world where capital flows are determined by possibilities of capital gains rather than interest rate differentials. The chapter gives empirical evidence to establish that capital flows are not determined by interest differentials and argues for an alternative to the Mundell–Fleming framework that reflects this reality. It then constructs a comparative static model for an open economy with capital flows, where the equilibrium level of aggregate output and employment is determined by interactions between the commodity market and the foreign exchange market. The implication is that expansionary fiscal policies have to be coupled with some control over foreign capital flows in order to achieve desired policy objectives.

In Chapter 8, Biswajit Dhar and Reji Joseph deal with technology flows from the advanced to the developing countries and the factors influencing such flows. They focus on two important enablers of such flows–foreign direct investment (FDI) and intellectual property rights (IPRs). Proponents of unfettered globalisation have viewed FDI as one of the most important channels of acquiring knowledge-based assets. This chapter cites available evidence to contest this position, showing that FDI has its own independent motives to move into its host countries, which are essentially driven by the possibilities of enhancing their profits. Moreover, the evidence of technology spillovers occurring from the presence of the foreign firms is found to be few and far between. Moving on to IPRs, the essay argues that technology transfer expands with stronger patents only when other components of an innovation system are at a developed stage in the host country.

Mitigating Immiserisation: Poverty, Inequality and Joblessness

In Chapter 9, Mausumi Das explores the link between households' aspiration, inequality and development. The exiting literature attributes long-run poverty to the lack of aspiration on the part of the poorer households. This chapter, on the other hand, argues that aspiration is a double-edged sword and its role on the perpetuation of poverty could be ambiguous. It shows that it matters whether the aspiration level relates to the current consumption or to the future one. Poorer households aspiring to catch up with the current living standards of the rich may end up dissaving, propelling the households to a long-run poverty trap. A growing economy, where the benefits of growth are unevenly distributed to begin with, leads to a widening of the aspirational gap. This further encourages poorer people to overspend on current consumption, which, in turn, accentuates the initial inequality and hampers growth.

Subrata Guha in Chapter 10 examines the long-run distribution of wealth in the context of an infinite horizon neoclassical growth model where dynastic households optimally decide about their consumption and saving paths in a competitive environment. This chapter motivates the issue by referring to the role of private property and private inheritance of wealth in generating inequality of opportunities across agents born with similar capabilities. The existing results in this literature (with iso-elastic utility) suggest that the initial differences in wealth across households will persist even in the long run. This chapter, on the other hand, shows that if consumer preferences are such that there exists the possibility of satiation at a finite rate of consumption or a 'bliss point', then it is possible to have an equilibrium growth path in the Ramsey–Cass–Koopmans neoclassical growth model along which dynastic wealth per unit of effective labour converges asymptotically to a common value.

Sudhanshu Bhushan in Chapter 11 explores the link between education and development, with particular emphasis on equity and distributive justice. The chapter captures the trends in access to higher education during the post-independent era, using multiple indicators like gross attendance rate and participation rate of various social and religious groups. It shows that between 1993–1994 and 2007–2008, there has been a decline in the educational inequality amongst various social groups across all the 14 major states in India. The essay also empirically establishes a positive relationship between years of schooling and households' consumption expenditure, which indicates that providing access to higher education could be an important policy instrument towards mitigating poverty. However, no significant relationship between the share of social expenditure by the government and household's consumption inequality could be found, which has led to the conclusion that without breaking the hierarchical social structure, scope of using increased public investment to reduce inequality is rather limited.

Shuji Uchikawa, in Chapter 12, explores the relationship between employment growth, gross value added and wages in Indian-organised manufacturing sector from 1973–1974 to 2010–2011. In particular, it explains both the 'jobless growth' prior to the second half of the 2000s and the rise in employment afterwards. Using published Annual Survey of Industries (ASI) data, it examines the long-term changes in the production structure of four industries: textiles, basic metals, motor vehicles and apparel. This chapter argues that while the capital–labour ratio increased in all the four industries during the pre-reform period, the reasons were diverse and different. Stringent labour laws (in case of textiles industry), control of price, distribution and import of technologies (in case of basic metal), concentration of production of in-house and lack of competition (in case of motor vehicles) and restriction of size as well as access to the domestic market (in case of apparel industries) induced these industries to substitute capital by labour, resulting in jobless growth. However, post 2000, deregulation of various industrial laws led to the large-scale entry of firms and consequent investment boom, which increased overall employment. The essay further points to the recent labour shortage in some of these industries despite informalisation of the labour force, and advocates a few possible solutions to overcome this constraint.

Envisioning the Institutional Changes

In Chapter 13, Jyotirmoy Bhattacharya extends the earlier works of Jean-Michel Grandmont and Prabhat Patnaik emphasizing the importance of inelasticity of expectations for the existence of competitive equilibrium in a simple monetary model of exchange. It takes Grandmont's work forward in two directions. First, in contrast to Grandmont's assumption of a given distribution of outside money, the chapter shows that the requirement for expectations to be inertial would be equally applicable in a world where money is endogenous but where at each point of time there exist pre-existing nominal payment commitments. The second extension allows for monetary policy in the form of a nominal interest rate that is determined by the central bank. The sufficient condition for the existence of equilibrium now places a joint restriction on the expectations function and the interest rate rule. The chapter compares this restriction to the conditions that need to be imposed on new-Keynesian models under rational expectations in order to ensure determinacy of equilibrium.

In Chapter 14, Vineet Kohli critically examines the revisionist account of the role of stock markets in the early phases of development, as propounded by Raghuram R. Rajan and Luigi Zingales. This chapter challenges Rajan and Zingales's claim that historically strong stock markets and liberal policies on trade and financial flows played complementary roles in the process of development of the now advanced economies—including those of continental Europe and Japan. The essay presents historical case studies on Germany, Japan and the US to show that active government interventions in financial sector were critical in shaping the size and role of stock markets in these economies, and various non-market means (for example, promotion of cooperative banks) were often used to improve access to finance to the excluded groups. Using historical data, this essay also refutes the view that stock market-based systems, as opposed to bank-based systems, foster more competition and provide more liquidity.

In Chapter 15, Pradip Kumar Biswas discusses the effects of the emergence of the corporate retailing industry, specifically in the context of advanced countries. Analysing two and a half decades of experience of the US and the European Union (EU) in terms of several characteristics, including growth, wage, employment, short- and long-run prices, etc., this chapter shows the debilitating effects of this sector on the overall economy. Moreover, it documents the influence of large retailers on the design of the public policy that was favourable to them. It also shows that there was absence of due penalty on violation of law notwithstanding the more powerful regulatory mechanisms. The essay concludes by suggesting necessary institutional developments that developing countries like India must undertake, if they do open up to corporate retail and want to avoid the experience of the US or EU in this context.

Reimagining the Political Hegemony

In Chapter 16, Prasenjit Bose has contributed to the recent Marxist political economy literature that debunks the concept of imperialism and moves to the idea of 'Empire' by conceptualising a 'new phase' of imperialism. It motivates itself from the historical debate between Kautsky's idea of an internationally united finance capital and Lenin's contrasting assertion of contradictions, conflicts and convulsions among the imperialist nations preventing such a possibility. In particular, this chapter argues why and how only an adequate analysis of the political economy of globalisation and that of the economic roles played by the state are necessary towards explaining the process of capital accumulation, financialisation of contemporary capitalism and the resulting concentration of power with the global financial oligarchy. In particular, it analyses the imperialist appropriation of the actual primitive accumulation in the third world through the circuits of global finance. It affirms the validity and relevance of the consequent local and national struggles against these forms of appropriation.

In Chapter 17, Rohit revisits the literature on twin instability of output and prices in an isolated mature capitalist economy, emphasised by Prabhat Patnaik. While Patnaik argued that the observed stability of the capitalist system is explained by the existence of a non-capitalist periphery and/or an active welfare state, this chapter claims that the present neoliberal stage of capitalism is characterised by the absence of such welfare states together with the rising strength of the rentier class. It argues that while suppressing of workers' demand by a credible threat to move the work base to the periphery has continued to curb the price instability, the absence of active welfare states has reintroduced the problem of output instability. Moreover, the growing conflict between the working class and the rentier class has generated a new kind of instability—political instability—which again makes the capitalist system vulnerable to crisis.

In Chapter 18, Debarshi Das revisits the 'Mode of Production Debate' that sought to characterise the relations of production in agrarian India and its evolution. In this context, this chapter examines the validity of the presumption that the pre-capitalist agrarian structure would give way to capitalist farming, propelled by the reinvestment of accumulated surplus in production. It shows that capital formation in Indian agriculture has declined in the last three decades, hindering the process of capitalist transition, and argues that the factors responsible for it are located more in the realm of contractionary macroeconomic policies than in the semi-feudal production relations. This chapter identifies the decline in public investment in agriculture as the primary cause for low accumulation, with additional factors like dispersion of land holdings, lack of gainful opportunities outside agriculture and rising population pressure contributing to the slowing down of agricultural growth. In light of this, it argues that political movements involving the peasantry must shift focus from its traditional demand for land redistribution towards countering the detrimental macroeconomic policies of the state that operates at the behest of the corporate capital.

In the concluding chapter of this volume, Praveen Jha explores the nature and causes of India's agrarian crisis in the recent years, using multiple variables like average size of operated holding, shifts in cropping pattern, annual average rate of growth of foodgrains, etc. Analysing the trends and patterns of public investment and priorities accorded in different budgets towards the rural economy over the years, this chapter identifies poor performance of public investment in particular, and neglect with respect to public policies in general, as the causal factors behind such crisis in the post-liberalisation era. This chapter argues that such shifts in priorities in government policy reflect an increasing alienation between the politically powerful rural elite, whose interests over the years have become more aligned with the interests of the urban elite, and the overwhelming majority of the poor peasantry, who are most adversely affected by the transition since the early 1990s.

References

Patnaik, P. (1966). Expansion in spite of excess capacity : a possible explanation. *Economic and Political Weekly*, 1(11), 459–461.

———. (1972). A note on external markets and capitalist development. *Economic Journal*, 82(328), 1316–1323.

———. (1979). Industrial development in India since independence. *Social Scientist*, 7(11), 3–19.

———. (1986). Introduction. In Prabhat Patnaik (Ed.), *Lenin and imperialism: An appraisal of theories and contemporary reality*. New Delhi: Orient Longman. Reprinted in Patnaik, P. (1995). *Whatever happened to imperialism and other essays*. New Delhi: Tulika Books, New Delhi.

———. (1987). Recent growth experience of the Indian economy—some comments. *Economic and Political Weekly*, 22(19–21), AN49–AN51+AN54–AN56.

———. (1989). Some aspects of the world capitalist economy in the 1980s. *Economic and Political Weekly*, 24(35/36) (Sep. 2–9, 1989), 2011–2014.

———. (1994). International capital and national economic policy—a critique of India's economic reforms. *Economic and Political Weekly*, 29(12), 683–689.

Patnaik, P. (1995). Nation-state in the era of globalisation. VII Zakir Hussain Memorial Lecture, 23 February, Zakir Hussain College, New Delhi. Also published in *Economic and Political Weekly, 30*(33), 2049–2053.

———. (1996). Globalization of capital and the theory of imperialism. *Social Scientist, 24*(11), 5–17. Reprinted in Patnaik, P. (2003). *The retreat to unfreedom*. New Delhi: Tulika Books.

———. (1997a). The context and consequences of economic liberalization in India. *The Journal of International Trade & Economic Development: An International and Comparative Review, 6*(2), 165–178.

———. (1997b). The past and the future of the socialist project. Ved Gupta Memorial Lecture, University of Delhi, published in *Social Scientist, 25*(3/4), 3–18. Reprinted in Patnaik, *The retreat to unfreedom*.

———. (1997c). *Accumulation and stability under capitalism*. Oxford: Clarendon Press.

———. (1999a). Thoughts on the current conjuncture from a socialist perspective. *Social Scientist, 27*(9/10), 30–41. Reprinted in Patnaik, *The retreat to unfreedom*.

———. (1999b). On the pitfalls of 'Bourgeoisie Internationalism'. In R.M. Chilcote (Ed.), *The political economy of imperialism* (pp. 169–179). New Delhi: Springer. Reprinted in Patnaik, *The retreat to unfreedom*.

———. (1999c). Capitalism in Asia at the end of the millennium. *Monthly Review, 51*(3), 53–70. Reprinted in Patnaik, *The retreat to unfreedom*.

———. (2000a). Democracy as a site for class-struggle, Prabhat Kar Memorial Lecture, Centre for Marxian Studies, Jadavpur University, published in *Economic and Political Weekly, 35*(12), 1005–1011. Reprinted in Patnaik, *The retreat to unfreedom*.

———. (2000b). The performance of the Indian economy in the 1990s. *South Asia: Journal of South Asian Studies, 23*(supplement 1), 193–205.

———. (2001). Imperialism and the diffusion of development, Ansari memorial Lecture, March 15, Jamia Milia Islamia University, Delhi, published in *Social Scientist, 29*(3/4), 3–18. Reprinted in Patnaik, *The retreat to unfreedom*.

———. (2002). Globalization and the emerging global politics, Rajendra Joshi Memorial Lecture, Rajasthan University, Jaipur, published in *Social Scientist, 30*(11/12), 3–16. Reprinted in Patnaik, *The retreat to unfreedom*.

———. (2003). 'Introduction' in *The retreat to unfreedom*. New Delhi: Tulika Publications.

———. (2005). The economics of the new phase of imperialism. Paper presented at the International Conference, 'Acts of Resistance from the South against Globalization', Ankara, Turkey. Reprinted in Patnaik, P. (2012). *Re-envisioning socialism*. New Delhi: Tulika Books.

———. (2006). On the necessity of Marxism. *The Marxist, XXII*(2–3). Reprinted in Patnaik, *Re-envisioning socialism*.

———. (2007a). Re-envisioning socialism. *Economic and Political Weekly, 42*(44), 41–43, 45–48. Reprinted in Patnaik, *Re-envisioning socialism*.

———. (2007b). The ideological hegemony of finance capital, Inaugural speech delivered at an All-India Congress of the Janavadi Lekhak Sangh, published in Patnaik, *Re-envisioning socialism*.

———. (2007c). The state under neo-liberalism. *Social Scientist, 35*(1/2), 4–15. Reprinted in Patnaik, *Re-envisioning socialism*.

———. (2007d). A model of growth of the contemporary Indian economy. *Economic and Political Weekly, 42*(22), 2077–2081.

———. (2008a). Capitalism, freedom and democracy. *Social Scientist, 36*(7/8), 16–28. Reprinted in Patnaik, *Re-envisioning socialism*.

———. (2008b). The terrain of Marxist theory. *Social Scientist, 36*(11/12), 2–32. Reprinted in Patnaik, *Re-envisioning socialism*.

———. (2008c). *The value of money*. New Delhi: Tulika Books.

———. (2009a). Socialism and the peasantry. *Social Scientist, 37*(11/12), 22–33. Reprinted in Patnaik, *Re-envisioning socialism*.

———. (2009b). Concerning Bourgeois democracy and socialism. *Re-envisioning socialism*. New Delhi: Tulika Books.

———. (2009c). A perspective on the growth process in India and China. Paper no. 05/2009. The IDEAS Working Paper Series.

———. (2010a). Socialism or reformism? *Social Scientist, 38*(5/6), 3–21. Reprinted in Patnaik, *Re-envisioning socialism*.

Patnaik, P. (2010b). *Notes on contemporary imperialism.* Retrieved from http://www.networkideas.org/featart/dec2010/Notes.pdf on 5 January 2016.

———. (2010c). A Marxist perspective on the world economy. *Social Scientist, 38*(7/8), 3–14.

———. (2011). Growth and poverty in the Indian economy. *Social Scientist, 39*(9/10), 19–34.

Further Readings

Patnaik, P. (2000). Entry in P. Arestis & M. Sawyer, (Eds), *A biographical dictionary of dissenting economists* (pp. 487–494), second edition. Cheltenham, UK and Northampton, US: Edward Elgar.

———. (2009). Interview. *Frontiers for socialism in the 21st century: Conversations on a global journey.* Cooperative and Policy Alternatives Center (COPAC), Johannesburg, 91–105.

SOAS. (2012). *Recording of honorary doctorate awarded to Prabhat Patnaik.* SOAS Graduation Ceremony (2012). Retrieved from https://www.youtube.com/watch?v=zXKiFbdJzVc on 20 June 2015.

SECTION 1
Sustaining the Growth Process

2

Financial Development and Growth under Capitalism

C.P. Chandrasekhar*

Introduction

Ever since the push to financial deregulation resulted in the proliferation of finance in the Anglo-Saxon world, an argument has gained ground that financial development and deepening are good for growth. There are two means adopted to back that claim. The first is to 'uncover' an empirical relationship between indices, such as the ratio of financial assets to gross domestic product (GDP) or the share of financial assets issued by financial intermediaries in total financial assets and the rate of GDP growth (King & Levine, 1993). However, such relationships are neither consistently observed nor robust (Arestis & Demetriades, 2012). The second is to build a conceptual edifice that suggests that the direction of causality in that relationship is from finance to growth. Underlying that edifice is the argument that financial structures—markets, institutions and instruments—emerge and evolve to mitigate information and transaction costs and are, therefore, by definition 'efficiency' inducing and growth promoting (Levine, 1997).

The focus in that literature is on the supply-side functions that the financial system performs in mobilising resources, directing them to activities that expand supply, allocating resources to activities that deliver the highest yields, and ensuring that the resources provided are put to the best use. This is ostensibly done by facilitating the hedging, pooling and trading of liquidity and idiosyncratic risk, ensuring cost-efficient monitoring of managers and exerting corporate control, besides facilitating exchange, mobilising savings and allocating them. In attributing this 'real' and 'productive' role to finance, the literature assumes away the fact that financial markets that trade information with public good characteristics are more prone to failure than the market for goods. When let free to function, they often deliver results contrary to what the functional finance school predicts (Stiglitz, 1994).

Exogenous Stimuli and Capitalist Growth

But this is not our concern here. Rather what is of significance for what follows is the more recent references to the financial sector's role as an instrument to generate 'autonomous' demand that can

---

* I am grateful for comments from Surajit Das, Jayati Ghosh and Rohit on an earlier draft of this chapter.

induce investment and spur growth. Exogenous stimuli that induce investment have been established as critical for capitalist growth. Kalecki (1962: 134) had clearly laid out that "the 'Harrodian' rate of growth is ephemeral in the sense that any deviation from the path determined by it renders the system stationary—i.e., subject to cyclical fluctuations but no trend". In the event, "the system cannot break the *impasse* of fluctuations around a static position unless economic growth is generated by the impact of semi-exogenous factors such as the effect of innovations upon investment" (Kalecki, 1962: emphasis as in original). The formulation emerged from a system based on an investment function in which investment decisions today that materialised in capital formation with a lag were endogenously induced by the level of investment and the rate of change of investment. That relationship is adequate to express the business cycle theory as presented by Kalecki himself, as developed based on the acceleration principle and as formulated by Harrod. This system tends to be subject to cyclical fluctuations around a static position, and a trend, if any is observed, is ephemeral and insignificant. Any trend growth requires exogenous or semi-exogenous stimuli that have "an impact on investment similar to" (Kalecki 1962: 147) a continuous increase in profits or output.

Endogenous stimuli cannot generate trend growth because atomistic decision makers in capitalist economies must make 'guesstimates' of potential demand when deciding on investment, based on implicit or explicit assumptions of what other capitalists would do, thereby shaping the future trajectory of demand and supply. Such expectations of demand must be partly based on current or recent experience. That is, capitalists do not decide on investments based on the likely future outcomes of their own actions, or the fact that their investments, through purchases from other capitalists and payments of wages to workers employed by them, would spur demand, including demand for their own output. In such circumstances, if endogenous factors were the only stimuli for investment, individual capitalists will find their capacities fully utilised only by accident or in special circumstances. If unutilised capacities rise, investment could fall and growth could slow down. That slowdown of growth would be cumulative and a positive trend, if any had prevailed, would prove ephemeral (Patnaik, 1972).

There is, however, a strand of reasoning that suggests that the institutional structure of capitalism, involving intense competition among atomistic capitalists, would spur investment and unleash a process that keeps multiplying demand. Often the notion of 'animal spirits' emphasised by Keynesians (Robinson, 1956) is invoked to render this pressure independent of current circumstances or profit expectations. But this pressure or passion to accumulate cannot be independent of the expectations of capitalists as a group, and if the state of demand dampens expectations and confidence, investment will fall. This cannot, therefore, substitute for exogenous stimuli.

Patnaik (2013: 12) elaborates what constitutes an exogenous stimulus as follows:

> Once we reject Say's Law and recognize that capitalism is prone to deficiency in aggregate demand, we have to accept that sustained growth in this system requires exogenous stimuli. By exogenous stimuli I mean a set of factors which raise aggregate demand but are not themselves dependent upon the fact that growth has been occurring in the system; that is, they operate irrespective of whether or not growth has been occurring in the system. Moreover, they raise aggregate demand by a magnitude that increases with the size of the economy, for instance with the size of the capital stock. They are in other words different from 'erratic shocks' on the one hand, and 'endogenous stimuli', such as the multiplier-accelerator mechanism, on the other: the latter can perpetuate or accelerate growth *only if it has been occurring anyway* (emphasis as in original).

The difference between exogenous stimuli and the endogenous stimuli referred to earlier is that while the latter can explain the persistence of growth once it has been triggered, "they cannot explain why the system does not remain stuck at a stationary state; and they cannot also explain why, if growth perchance falters for some reason, it should revive again" (Patnaik, 2013: 12). These differences also imply a complex interaction between exogenous and endogenous stimuli.

Identifying Exogenous Stimuli

Defining the required exogenous stimulus as a factor that raises aggregate demand without itself being dependent on growth in the system helps identify the elements that drive capitalist growth in different periods. The ones normally referred to in the literature are external markets, state expenditure and innovation. Exports are an obvious and important 'external' inducement to investment, but their role in explaining capitalist growth is controversial. One way in which exports can drive investment and growth within a given tariff area is when exports to other countries or markets exceed imports from them. But such surpluses are difficult to sustain and not all countries can have surpluses vis-à-vis the rest of the world. Success itself—by raising wages, generating supply bottlenecks in areas like infrastructure, strengthening the domestic currency and leading to loss of trade preferences—results in a loss of competitiveness. Historically, individual countries have benefitted from net exports for periods of time, losing that advantage to new competitors. Growth can occur, but this cannot be a permanent inducement to invest in an individual nation. Nor does it resolve the problem for capitalism as a system.

Luxemburg (1964) had argued that a pre-capitalist periphery, the destruction of which provides markets and, thereby, an external source of demand for the capitalist sector, was a prerequisite for accumulation under capitalism. This view has been questioned (Kalecki, 1971) on the grounds that it confused between total exports and net exports. What mattered, it was argued, for a bounded capitalist sector was net exports, since a part of the additional demand generated by exports would be neutralised by the inflow of imports that satisfied some fraction of domestic demand, dampening the aggregate demand stimulus because of 'leakages' to the international system.

There is, however, a point to what Luxemburg was emphasising. The aggregate demand effects of positive net exports are obvious. But even when exports do not exceed imports, the presence of a pre-capitalist sector is an 'inducement' to invest, and increases in exports by triggering investment in individual sectors benefiting from growth in external demand can spur growth through its multiplier effects on consumption and investment. These 'multiplier' effects of the investment induced by exports could for a number of reasons make exports a stimulus to growth even when trade is balanced. The opening up of external markets can cause a net increase in investment or consumption, partly because the process of opening up would itself require investment such as in transport facilities, partly because the expansion of export industries and contraction of import-competing industries need not be identically equal and partly because the opening up may provide access to new commodities that stimulate additional capitalist consumption and may not displace domestic production (Patnaik, 1972).

It should be obvious that conceptually this stimulus to investment and growth under capitalism cannot be everlasting. In fact, Rose Luxemburg argued that the complete destruction of the available pre-capitalist periphery would—in time—undermine accumulation in capitalism, leading to its own stagnation. This presumes that the pre-capitalist periphery mainly serves as a market for capitalism, and that it is the only exogenous stimulus driving investment and growth under capitalism, necessitating its inevitable exhaustion. While that is obviously not true, it does point to the fact that any single exogenous stimulus cannot be a persistent driver of growth. External export markets can induce investment and drive growth in different regions and periods to different degrees, but cannot be a consistent and continuing driver of capitalist accumulation.

A second important source of stimulus to capitalist accumulation is state expenditure. Through the direct demand it gives rise to as a result of purchases made, and the indirect demand resulting from the employment and incomes it generates, state expenditure is an obvious inducement for private investment. Not itself being induced by current and/or past incomes or profits and capable of being financed with debt that is serviced through taxes imposed on the output increases it results in, such expenditure is in large part autonomous. In the event, state expenditure, by acting like an internal external market, serves as an exogenous stimulus for capitalist growth. In practice, for much of the recent history of capitalism in the developed and underdeveloped countries, this has been the leading driver of growth. However, there could, under different circumstances, be a host of reasons why state investment is constrained for extended periods of time, making it a stimulus that is difficult to consistently sustain in many contexts. For example, inflation resulting from demand induced by state expenditure running up against supply bottlenecks (say, in agriculture) that are not easily relaxed may necessitate a reduction in such expenditure and a dampening of the stimulus involved.

A third potential exogenous stimulus is innovation. Kalecki (1962: 147) himself emphasised the role of a continuous stream of innovations which "need not be identified with changes in technology. We can broaden the concept to include such a phenomenon as the opening up of new sources of raw materials, which induces additional investment in the productive and transportation facilities required." In fact, the emergence of new industries too can have a positive impact on growth and even account for the recovery from a crisis. According to Kalecki (1932: 54), "the overcoming of the crisis in the USA in 1921 was unquestionably accelerated by developing the production of inexpensive cars, radio sets, electrical household equipment, rayon, etc." This is because

> [...] as in business fluctuations in general, a major role is played here by the time taken to construct industrial plants. While factories that are to produce new articles are under construction, such articles have not yet appeared in the market, whereas investments have already caused an overall increase in employment and an expansion of the domestic market. Hence, for the moment, 'old' branches of industry gain from the construction of factories for new articles.

It is necessary to underline here the reference to a 'continuous' stream of inventions or innovations as a requirement for sustained growth. Only then would their impact be the same as a 'continuous increase in profits' or a 'continuous increase in output'. "Each new invention, like each increment of profits (or output), makes certain projects *ceteris paribus* more attractive. Thus a stream of inventions causes investment over and above the level which would otherwise obtain" (Kalecki, 1962: 147).

This, however, makes innovation a different kind of exogenous stimulus as compared with public expenditure, since the government can, for long periods, maintain a certain fiscal deficit relative to GDP, or a continuous stimulus, if it chooses to. But there is no guarantee that capitalist evolution will be characterised by a continuous stream of innovations of equal or even substantial significance. In fact, Schumpeter (1961: 223), who gave an important role for innovations or 'new combinations' in taking capitalism out of its circular flow, saw them as not being "evenly distributed through time" but as appearing, "if at all, discontinuously in groups or swarms", leading to cycles of different durations.

Moreover, invention and innovation are not completely exogenous. With the growing integration of science and production, invention depends on research and development (R&D) spending, which in turn would depend on firm growth and profitability. Moreover, inventions can remain in existence for long without being commercialised and exploited. The degree to which that happens, leading to innovation, also depends on economic circumstances. Finally, gross investment is the carrier of innovation or the application of invention in production. So, the greater the inducement to invest, the higher the level of investment and, therefore, faster will be the pace of innovation. Other prior stimuli that are more persistent can be more important than innovation as long-term drivers of growth.

This requirement for a persistent or continuous stimulus also makes the pre-capitalist periphery more significant than innovations. So long as they exist and can be broken into and their production systems dismantled to yield new markets and sources of raw materials, they are a source of inducement for capitalist investment. And whatever investment occurs on that account unleashes many rounds of the multiplier. Actual exports to the periphery may not be as important as the very existence of such potential markets.

Temporary Exogenous Stimuli

The fact that there can be significant differences in the strength and persistence of exogenous stimuli allows us to identify other potentially significant, but temporary, exogenous stimuli under capitalism. Consider the imposition of all-round protection in a hitherto open economy in which demand was being substantially met with imports from abroad. Inasmuch as protection imposes quantitative limits on the availability of, or renders prohibitively expensive some of these products, it delivers a captive market that induces investment in the creation of capacity in the domestic tariff area. Thus, state action provides a sudden exogenous inducement for investment with concomitant effects on growth. However, this market and the growth it entails are often seen as a 'once-for-all' or windfall opportunity, since once the demand it creates is met, there must be other factors that keep the market growing. This is not because the investment induced would only be in that amount of capacity required to satisfy the unmet demand generated by protection. Rather the investment induced thereby would have its multiplier effects on income, mediated by rounds of consumption and investment. The market created by protection is a 'once-for-all'—not just a 'one-period'—phenomenon only in the sense that once these rounds of demand generation have exhausted themselves, growth would have to again rely on other external stimuli. State action in this instance (as opposed to state expenditure) does serve as an exogenous stimulus to capitalist growth, but not in a sustainable fashion.

This argument is on occasion implicitly, even if not self-consciously, stretched to suggest that institutional change in the pre- or proto-capitalist segments of the economy can trigger demand growth and stimulate investment. The example being referred to here is land reform in predominantly agrarian societies, characterised by semi-feudal land relations. A combination of land monopoly, absentee landlordism, interlinked land, labour and credit markets and tenancy have two consequences here. The first is that investment is far short of that which is potentially possible (Patnaik, 1986). Those who own the land refrain from investing in agriculture, preferring to obtain their returns from activities other than productivity-enhancing cultivation practices. On the other hand, those who possess the land and are the actual cultivators have neither the means nor the incentive to invest, since they retain little of the surplus, being the victims of rack-renting and usurious money lending. The second fall out of this environment is that low productivity combines with a highly unequal distribution of income, so that the consumption, especially manufactured goods consumption, of a large proportion of the population is limited. There is no mass domestic market that can encourage and drive economic diversification and growth.

In this environment, if the state decides to undertake radical land reform, involving distributing land and ensuring ownership of the actual cultivator, the effect could be similar to giving an exogenous push to the system. On the one hand, the breakdown of land monopoly and the redistribution of ownership could provide the material basis and the incentives for productivity enhancing investment that generates new demands and induces further rounds of investment. On the other hand, the enhanced incomes would be more equally distributed and can result in an increase in consumption and expansion of the market for mass consumption goods, which too would have its multiplier effects. The intensity of this exogenous stimulus could be substantial and prolonged, but it too cannot be persistent in the senses that state expenditure or a continuous stream of innovations can be.

Finance as an Exogenous Stimulus

Given this perspective on alternative forms of exogenous stimuli with varying time frames and intensities, can the role that finance plays in stimulating demand in the neoliberal era be treated as a form of exogenous stimulus that explains episodes of growth under capitalism? If so, what can we say regarding its relative strength and permanence relative to the other kinds of such stimuli identified earlier?

The reason why financial expansion and deepening can at all be considered as being akin to an exogenous stimulus is that it allows, in certain circumstances, the level of consumption and investment to be untethered from current income and its rate of change. There can be periods of easy money when individuals and firms can access credit in excess of what may be 'warranted' by their levels of current income at relatively low rates of interest. This matters because, to recall, the term exogenous is used here in the sense that the demand that provides the stimulus in question is independent of the actual level of present or past income.

Domestic demand comes from two sources: investment and consumption. If investment expands autonomously, as happens, for example, when governments decide to invest heavily in infrastructure, such investment directly and indirectly (through its multiplier effects) expands demand and induces further rounds of investment and growth. This is the 'internal', exogenous stimulus discussed earlier. As compared to this, private investment is most often seen as induced and not autonomous, needing some external stimulus to occur. However, if governments adopt a strategy of implicitly or explicitly guaranteeing a minimal, acceptable return in particular sectors, and back this guarantee with easy access to adequate credit, debt-financed private investment can also function as a source of autonomous demand.

The more difficult case to understand is the one where growth is not only based largely on domestic demand, but much of that demand takes the form of consumption expenditure. Increased consumption, since it is tethered to increases in income, is not normally seen as a stimulus to investment and growth, but an outcome of the latter. However, there is one way in which consumption can be 'autonomous' in the sense that it is not tethered to current income. That would be true if a significant share of incremental consumption is financed with credit. In recent times, credit has played an important role in financing personal investment (in housing) and consumption in developed and developing economies alike. Pre-crisis growth in the US, which was accompanied by rising inequality and a large trade deficit, was sustained by debt-financed household expenditure. This trend is also seen in developing countries after financial liberalisation. To the extent that this tendency operates, 'autonomous' consumption can spur demand and growth.

Consider, for example, the boom that preceded the 2008 financial crisis in the US. A typical description of that process from a critical perspective (Wolff, 2008) goes as follows:

> In the 1970s, employers found a way to stop the long-term slow rise in real wages of their employees. [...] Thus, [...] another capitalist crisis loomed as a bad recession hit hard. But that crisis was kept short because US

capitalism found a way to postpone it: massive debt. Since employers succeeded in keeping wages from rising, the only way to sell the ever-expanding output was to lend workers the money to buy more. Corporations invested their soaring profits in buying new securities backed by workers' mortgages, auto loans, and credit-card loans. [...] Postponing the solution to crisis of the 1970s only prepared the way for the bigger one [...]. Booming consumer lending in the 1980s, 1990s, and since 2000, especially in the deregulated financial world of Reagan and Bush America, provoked wild profit-driven excesses [...]. It also loaded millions of Americans with unsustainable debts. By 2006, the most stressed borrowers—'sub-prime'—could no longer pay what they owed.

There are three aspects of this description that need to be noted. First, debt is a means to increasing the consumption of those whose incomes are stagnant, staving off recessions and even driving growth. This, however, is problematic, since households, unlike governments, cannot keep borrowing on the grounds that they can generate tax revenues partly because of and partly independent of the growth that their debt-financed expenditure stimulates. Debt helps smoothen consumption and therefore partly dissociate levels of consumption from the fluctuating incomes, but there are limits to household debt imposed from the side of lenders, which should be determined by the magnitude and stability of expected household incomes. That makes it difficult for this kind of debt to serve as an exogenous driver of growth.

However, this is where the second aspect of the description comes in. Debt can be a persisting and even an increasingly strong stimulus driving capitalist growth for a relatively prolonged period of time because of financial innovations that help transfer credit risk. Securitisation, which allows different credit assets to be bundled, makes debt a tradable asset, and permits risk to be transferred away from those creating the credit assets in the first place. This allows mortgage companies and the banks that finance them to create far more credit assets than they would do if they had to carry all the credit risk. To keep this process going, there needs to be adequate, reasonably cheap liquidity in the system, ensured in practice by a loose monetary policy on the part of central banks. Monetary policy rather than fiscal policy underlies this stimulus.

But there are other constraints to this process, since increasing the volume of credit assets requires expanding the universe of borrowers. This requires bringing into the credit net those who would earlier have been considered high risk or even unworthy of credit—the so-called sub-prime borrowers. Why then would any other financial institution or investor want to buy into and carry that risk even if for a premium? Financial expansion and innovation play a role here as well. Financial liberalisation and the securitisation that accompanies it, helps pool, slice and combine risk from different markets (housing, automobiles, etc.), different geographies and different income groups into a single asset. Since it is unlikely that there would be simultaneous default in these diverse markets, the risk of the security crafted from this combination of credit assets is considered low. Moreover, the securities themselves could be bundled up and sliced in ways in which risks and returns are differentially distributed across the segments, allowing investors to choose the slice that suits their risk aversion and appetite for returns. The process of expanding the universe of borrowers and increasing the volume of credit assets could be sustained for long, introducing an element of longevity to this form of stimulus.

The third aspect of note in this description is that this can go on only until at some point of time the share of sub-prime borrowers and assets in total debt exposure crosses some threshold (varying with historical circumstances). The process becomes unsustainable because the volume of simultaneous default crosses some level where the solvency of intermediary institutions is in question. In sum, in the final analysis this stimulus cannot be sustained and the crisis that ensues would be much more severe than the growth slowdown associated with the weakening of other kinds of exogenous stimuli, because the downturn is aggravated by a process of deleveraging, as levels of debt are sought to be brought down in ways that intensify the recession. But in the interim, for a reasonably long period, the demand infused into the system by debt-financed private expenditure that is autonomous of income, induces investment and drives growth.

There is, however, one other feature that needs to be noted. After a lag, this downturn can be halted and the credit-based stimulus revived. The way in which this is done is that when the bust occurs, the state takes over the losses incurred by the financial sector by buying up and writing off the non-performing or just plain worthless assets on the books of the financial system and by recapitalising banks so that the process of debt expansion can restart. This has been a common occurrence. The savings and loan crisis of the 1980s in the US was 'resolved' by the use of taxpayers' money to the tune of an estimated $200 billion. Quite a few billion dollars were spent by governments in South Korea and Indonesia (among other countries) to deal with the losses that resulted from the financial crisis in 1997, and to take over the short-term foreign debt of private financial institutions and convert it into long-term, state-guaranteed loans at relatively high interest rates. And trillions of dollars have been injected into the system by governments and central banks in the developed industrial world to address the crisis of 2008.

Thus, when the crisis occurs, there is indeed a sharp downturn. But besides responding with fiscal expenditures to stall the downturn, governments and central banks increasingly intervene to save the financial system through fiscal transfers to them in various forms. Banks and financial institutions, though diminished in number and restructured, soon return to profit. Since this is at the expense of ordinary citizens, the debt cycle does not register a recovery immediately, because of the burden of debt on the balance sheets of households and corporates. But the possibility of such a recovery exists, and in time, circumstances permitting, the system rides on another bubble.

It bears noting, however, that while monetary policy in the form of monetary easing appears to underlie the stimulus when it occurs, the ability of the system to rely repeatedly on such a boom and the periodicity and length of such booms depends on the fiscal flexibility that the concerned government has. The onus of resolving the crisis facilitated by monetary easing falls on the *fisc*. In the case of the 2008 boom, while the size of the intervention required was substantial, in many countries, such as those in the European periphery, governments were unable to mobilise the resources to finance the transfers. They chose or were forced instead to resort to austerity that, consequent to steep expenditure cuts, only worsened both the recession and the fiscal deficit, since revenues are adversely affected by low growth. So there are contexts when fiscal policy cannot help resolve a crisis and create the basis for another bubble-driven boom.

Adverse Effects of Finance on Growth

It needs to be noted here that the rise to dominance of finance capital also has some adverse effects on growth. In particular, as underlined by Patnaik (2013), for a number of reasons finance capital is opposed to debt-financed spending by the state. To start with, deficit financing is seen to increase the liquidity overhang in the system and therefore as being potentially inflationary. Inflation, which erodes the real value of financial assets, is anathema to finance. Second, government spending is 'autonomous' in character and the use of debt to finance such autonomous spending amounts to introducing into financial markets an arbitrary player whose activities can render interest rate differentials that determine financial profits more unpredictable. Finally, the use of deficit spending to support autonomous expenditures by the state amounts to an implicit legitimisation of an interventionist state and a delegitimisation of the market.

Any State action that operates independently of finance capital, that seeks to work directly instead of working through the promotion of corporate-financial interests, undermines the social legitimacy of capitalism, and especially of these corporate-financial interests, for it raises the question: if the State is required to fix the system, then why do we need the system at all, why not simply have State ownership as such? (Patnaik, 2013: 19)

It has also been argued that two consequences of 'finance-dominated capitalism are "a fall in animal spirits of the firm sector with respect to real investment in capital stock" and "redistribution of income at the expense of the labour income share", both of which can have depressing effects on growth, (Hein, 2011: 27). The overall effect of finance on demand and growth can be positive, only if debt financed private spending neutralises these adverse effects.

In sum, there can be periods when financial expansion and deepening lead to private debt, serving as an exogenous or autonomous stimulus to growth. But the boom that ensues is unsustainable and self-destructive. Only in certain contexts can it be prolonged and recur with lags more than once. Even when it does it can have contrary effects, which lead to contraction rather than growth. Thus, this form of 'exogenous' stimulus too is neither as strong nor as persistent as public expenditure or a pre-capitalist periphery.

What remains then is that while capitalist growth occurs as a result of exogenous stimuli, it does so in fits and starts. Episodes of growth (on which cycles are embedded) are discontinuous and of varying durations. This is because the exogenous stimuli themselves vary in terms of intensity and duration, need not operate simultaneously, are never enduring and recur, if at all, at unpredictable intervals. In intervening periods, the system is characterised by recession and unemployment. Relative, and for some even absolute, deprivation is the only perpetual.

References

Arestis, P., & Demetriades, P. (2012). Financial development and economic growth: Assessing the evidence. *The Economic Journal, 107*(442), 783–799.
Hein, E. (2011). *Finance-dominated capitalism, re-distribution, household debt and financial fragility in a Kaleckian distribution and growth model*. MPRA Paper No. 34115. Retrieved from http://mpra.ub.uni-muenchen.de/34115/ on 15 August 2013.
Kalecki, M. (1932). New industries and the overcoming of a crisis. In J. Osiatynski (Ed.), *Collected works of Michal Kalecki: Vol. 1. Capitalism: Business cycles and full employment*. Oxford: Oxford University Press.
———. (1962). Observations on the theory of growth. *The Economic Journal, 72*(285), 134–153.
———. (1971). The problem of effective demand with Tugan-Baranovsky and Rosa Luxemburg. In J. Osiatynski (Ed.), *Selected essays on the dynamics of the capitalist economy*. Cambridge: Cambridge University Press.
King, R.G., & Levine, R. (1993). Finance and growth: Schumpeter may be right. *The Quarterly Journal of Economics, 108*(3), 717–737.
Levine, R. (1997). Financial development and economic growth: views and agenda. *Journal of Economic Literature, 35*(2), 688–726.
Luxemburg, R. (1964). *Accumulation of capital*. New York: Monthly Review Press.
Patnaik, P. (1972). A note on external markets and capitalist development, *The Economic Journal, 82*(328), 1316–1323.
———. (2013). Finance and growth under capitalism. In B. Dasgupta (Ed.), *Non-mainstream dimensions of global political economy* (pp. 12–22). Oxford: Routledge.
Patnaik, U. (1986). *The agrarian question and the development of capitalism in India*. Delhi: Oxford University Press.
Robinson, J. (1956). *The accumulation of capital*. London: Macmillan and Co.
Schumpeter, J.A. (1961). *The theory of economic development: An inquiry into profits, capital, credit, interest, and the business cycle*. Oxford: Oxford University Press.

Stiglitz, J.E. (1994). The role of the state in financial markets. *Proceedings of the World Bank Annual Conference on Development Economics 1993*. (Supplement to the World Bank Economic Review and World Bank Research Observer), 19–61.

Wolff, R.D. (2008). *Capitalist crisis, Marx's shadow. MR Zine*, 26 September. Retrieved from http://mrzine.monthlyreview.org/2008/wolff260908.html on 11 August 2013.

3

Global Economic Challenges: Alone We Lag, Together We Grow

Pranab Mukhopadhyay*

Introduction: The European Dilemma

Europe's sluggish economic recovery has confirmed fears that a solution to the European economic crisis may be long drawn out. The protracted negotiations over Greece's bailout package has not only caused rumbles in EU's financial circles but made the Greeks for the first time give a majority vote to a left-wing party in the EU. Europe is economically divided between the richer North and the poorer South. The choices before it are: should the richer nations of Europe agree on high inflation and fiscal transfers to the poorer countries or allow the poorer neighbours to face falling wages and high unemployment (Irwin, 2015). The EU's political stability is being tested as the economic crisis threatens the Maastricht treaty. Would the EU survive or will it have to be renegotiated?

Backdrop of the Crisis

The recent history of the global economic turmoil is traced to the sub-prime crisis of 2007 in the US. Consequently, as one may recollect, it led to the US Treasury Bond rating being cut from AAA to AA+ by Standard and Poor (S&P) in August 2011. This was the first time since 1917 that US T-Bills had lost their highest rating (Jackson, 2011). In late September 2010, the National Bureau of Economic Research's official business cycle-dating committee announced that business activity had reached a trough in June 2009 and marked the end of the recession that began in December 2007. The trough was also expected to be the marker for recovery. In May 2015, it was still not clear that the US economy was on its way to recovery (Yellen, 2015).

The European crisis on the other hand emerged in Greece in 2008 and soon showed up as a wider malaise across Europe. By December 2011, S&P downgraded nine of the 27 EU country ratings, leaving

---

* We acknowledge financial support from the SOAS–AUGUR project. Francis Cripps provided extensive research advice and was a generous host during the writing of this paper. We would like to thank Terry Mckinley for research support and advice and Naret Khurasee for support with the programming. Discussions with Saumen Chattopadhyay, Atulan Guha, Sabyasachi Kar and Parthapratim Pal were helpful during various workshops. Comments from the editors on an earlier draft are acknowledged. The usual disclaimer applies.

only Germany and Finland in the Euro single-currency area with an AAA rating (Elliot & Inman, 2012). For the last seven years Europe has been at its wits end to find an acceptable politically mediated economic solution. And it is not clear at all whether they are anywhere near such a solution now. The EU's management team has suggested a conventional austerity package of structural change with reduced government expenditure for the crisis-ridden countries. Many of the indebted countries have been uneasy with the austerity package proposed by EU's management team. Given that Greece had pitched battles on the streets over the last seven years, it was probably only a matter of time that it would elect a party that was anti-bailout (Spillius, 2012). In the January 2015 elections, Greece became the first country to elect a radical left party in the Euro zone, with Alexis Tsipras taking over as Prime Minister. Spain followed soon with a divided Parliament and the two leading parties saw their share of votes fall below 50% for the first time in December 2015 elections (Badcock, 2015).

Similarly, in France, Mr Sarkozy lost the elections in 2012 to Mr Hollande, who based his campaign on a promise of reversing and re-negotiating the austerity package proposed by the EU (Traynor, 2012). In the Netherlands, the Prime Minister Mark Rutte had to resign in 2012 since his party's coalition partners withdrew support over proposals for budget cuts (Kreijger & Escritt, 2012).

The European Central Bank (ECB), headed by Frenchman Mario Draghi, responded in March 2015 with a quantitative easing package of a €1.1 trillion that would buy €50 billion of sovereign debt as well as other bank assets (Inman, 2014). The questions that are being asked are: Whether a monetary easing (as initiated by the ECB) will be adequate to pull Europe out of a crisis or does it need more? Would a fiscal intervention be needed to help generate demand and accelerate recovery, as is being attempted in US (Krugman, 2015)? Can Europe do it by itself or does it need to coordinate its efforts with others—for example the US and the Brazil, Russia, India, China and South Africa (BRICS) group?

Given Europe's strong global linkages, the emergent solution will have great repercussions not only within Europe but also on the world economy. The interest in EU's economic future is therefore a natural one in the emerging economies, especially the BRICS countries.

Developing Country Concerns

While Europe and the US have been busy sorting out their economic problems, China has officially become the largest economy [in purchasing power parity (PPP) terms] as of 2014, India is the third largest economy and Brazil and South Africa are not far away at 7th and 29th, respectively (Stiglitz, 2015). However, the EU as an economic zone is a little bigger than China with strong global trade links, but as group of nations has fallen behind BRICS.

Developing and emerging economies have begun to be more effective in regional trade blocs and in enlarging their trade without the mediation of the US or Europe. This approach has provided them with a cushion to respond to the economic crisis centred in the developed countries, upon whom in the past they have otherwise been dependent for export markets. Now, with the establishment of the Asian Infrastructure Investment Bank by China with about 57 members (significantly excluding the US) marks a break from the established global financial hierarchy dominated by US and its European allies.

What role can emerging economies play in easing the economic crisis? For example, would an independent expansionary policy initiated by India reflate the world economy? Unlikely. Its domestic economy is not large enough (India generated about 6.5 per cent of the world GDP in 2013, PPP) and its integration with the world economy is too limited (less than 2 per cent of the world trade) to make a difference. Therefore, if India wants to be part of the action, it will need to be a partner in a coordinated global policy action or at least an influential regional arrangement to make a difference to sustained world economic growth.

A natural place to start then is with the BRICS, which accounted for a quarter of the world gross domestic product (GDP) and a little less than a fifth of the world trade in 2014. Therefore, as a group it potentially could have reasonable influence in the world economy.

In this chapter, we pose the following questions:

(a) Would unilateral efforts by developing or developed nations help economic recovery?
(b) Would a globally coordinated fiscal policy be a reliable alternative strategy?

In order to address these questions, we use a global macro model called CAM (described later). We use the current policy discussion in the professional circles and popular media to present scenarios that we feel best reflect the options and dilemmas for the policymakers. In order to keep the discussion tractable, we have kept the policy choices simple without detracting from the major issues.

Data

We use a comparable multi-country (207 country) time-series dataset from 1970 to 2013 compiled for the Global Macroeconomic Modelling Project by Alphametrics (Cripps & Khurasee, 2008). It includes national income accounts (published by the UN Statistics Division), trade statistics (from the COMTRADE database) and the International Financial Statistics and Government Financial Statistics (from the International Monetary Fund). Other data sources are the OECD, Eurostat, the International Labour Organization and the World Bank. The main variables tracked are national income and population, employment, government accounts; private income, expenditure, capital and wealth, monetary policy and assets and liabilities of the banking system, exchange rates, reserves and external assets (foreign direct investment and portfolio investments) and liabilities, inflation and capacity utilisation; balance of payments current account; trade in goods and services by commodity group and production and use of primary energy.

In order to make meaningful inter-country and overtime comparisons, the database provides values that are calibrated to a real value at constant prices in terms of 2005 PPP measures. The 'real exchange rate' for each bloc is defined as the ratio of the domestic expenditure deflator to the world deflator (Cripps, Izurieta & Singh, 2011).

The Model

Many of the problems that we discuss here may seem to be isolated and a single nation's problem but are really global in nature as domestic macroeconomic policies have an impact on others in an interconnected world. Therefore, the only way to analyse the macro economy today is to use a global model. For this chapter, we use the CAM-AUGUR model of the world economy (Cripps, Izurieta & McKinley, 2007), which is post-Keynesian in nature and based on the CEPR model originally developed by Cripps and Godley (1976).

The CAM model is based on a demand-determined framework, does not assume full employment and uses actual data from 1970 to 2013 to simulate the period 2014–2030. It treats the world as an integrated and closed economic system. Total world exports are equated to total world imports, implying that the world as a whole has a zero current surplus/deficit. The global total of external assets is also equated to the total of external liabilities. At the same time, the model is flexible enough to accommodate different

Figure 3.1
Illustration of the Interaction between Different Sectors/Variables in the CAM Model

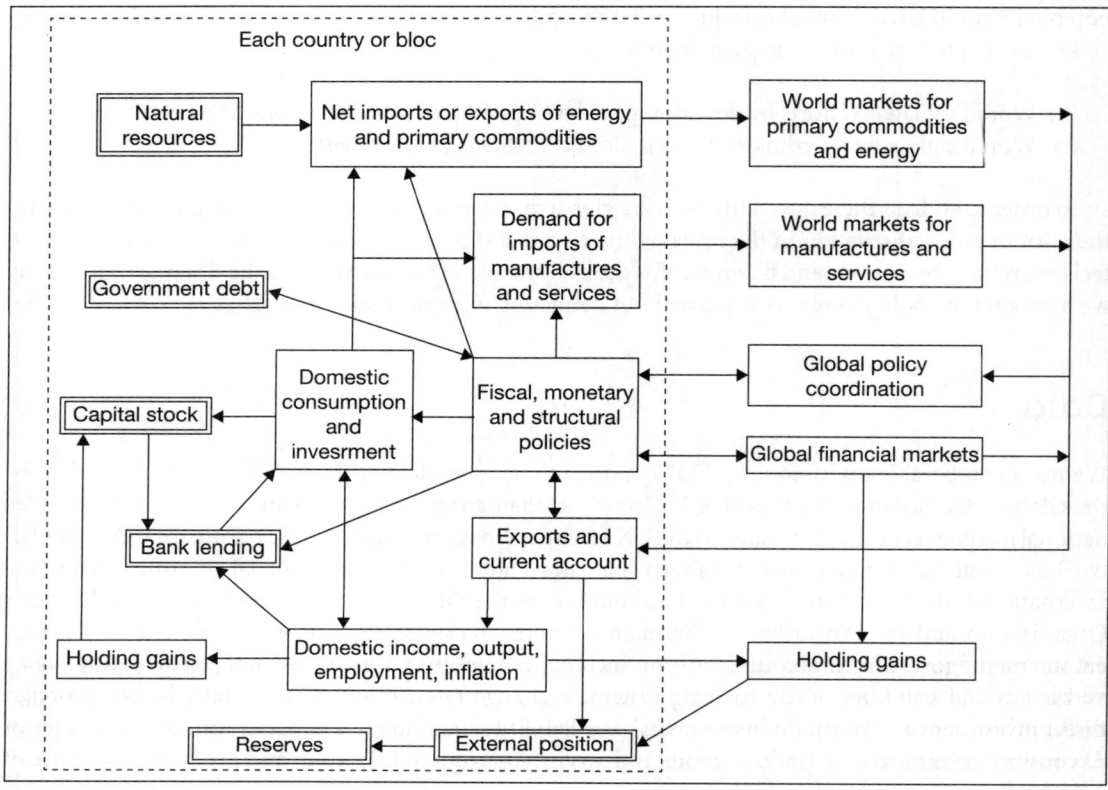

Source: Cripps and Khurasee (2008).

behavioural patterns of countries and blocs due to location, level of economic development, etc. At the base level, the model has a common set of identities and behavioural equations that is used for all blocs of countries. The main interactions are described in the flow diagram (see Figure 3.1).[1]

The CAM model (version 6.1) allows a flexible aggregation of countries to blocs to make the viewing of data and results more manageable. The model covers commonly used macroeconomic variables like investment, savings, prices, output, employment as well as international migration. In addition, private and government sectors' demand and income, international trade in manufactured goods, primary commodities, services and energy are covered. It also covers capital flows, international factor payments and transfers and exchange rates.

Our objective in this chapter is to forecast a medium-term outcome for different scenarios using the CAM (for baseline and projections) global macro-model. We make predictions for the period 2016–2030 for the commonly discussed macro variables, including growth, employment, prices, deficits and debt.

However, before we start on the scenarios, we will present the baseline scenario and predictions in a business-as-usual situation for per capita income growth and employment for the group of countries

---

[1] The behavioural equations are far too many to reproduce here for reasons of space but the interested reader may wish to see Cripps (2014).

Figure 3.2
Growth in per Capita Income 2000–2030 (Baseline)

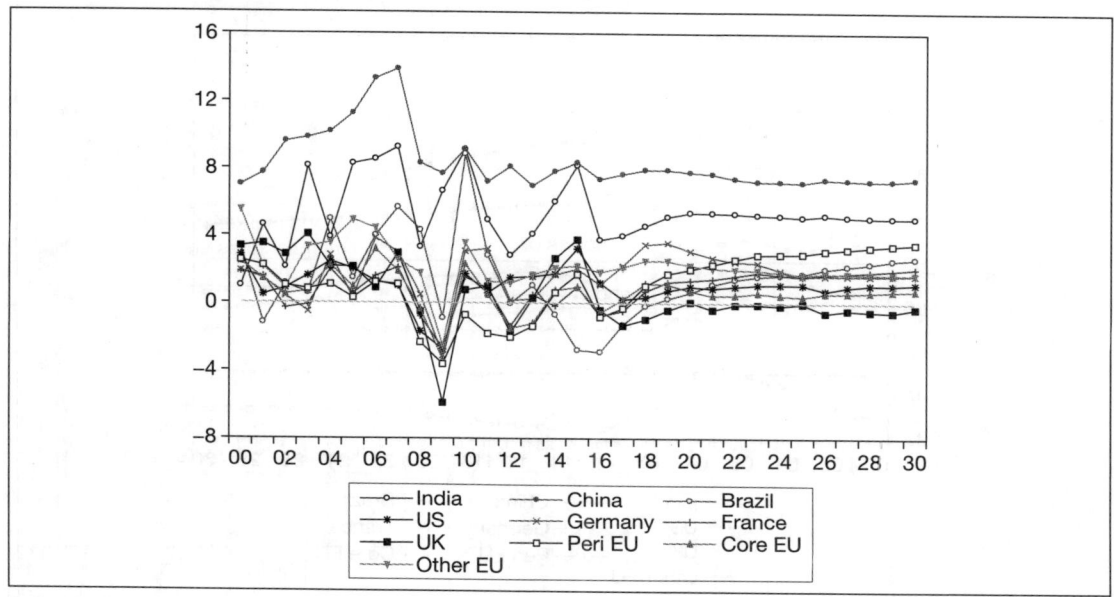

that we are interested in. China sees a decline in per capita income growth but stabilizes at a long-term average rate of about 8 per cent. It maintains the highest rate of growth followed by India and EU periphery countries. Among the group of countries considered, UK sees negative rates of growth and the core EU countries average about 1 per cent rate of growth (Figure 3.2).

As far as employment predictions are concerned, China is likely to see a drop in its employment rate, while Brazil is seen to stabilise its employment in this period (Figure 3.3). EU's periphery is expected to see a marginal increase but will have one of the lowest employment rates. France and other EU countries are expected to hover around 50 per cent, while Germany will decline from its current 57 per cent to about 54 per cent over the period. India is expected to maintain a steady level of about 54 per cent.

In the next section, we use the above model to describe our scenarios and present the outcomes.

Scenarios

In order to address the two questions posed in this chapter, we look at four scenarios explained as follows:

1. Scenario 1: BRICS goes it alone: This scenario assumes that India, Brazil and South Africa unilaterally decide to increase trade links with China, who as a BRICS partner agrees to provide a larger preferential market share to them. However, for its own economic management and to address concerns of critics about its large current account surplus, China also decides to maintain a current account balance. This essentially implies that it agrees to buy a lot more from the rest of the world. Such a strategy would placate its trade partners who have run large trade deficits with China, but also may increase export opportunities for smaller countries and neighbours, especially its BRICS partners.

Figure 3.3
Employment Rates 2000–2030 (Baseline)

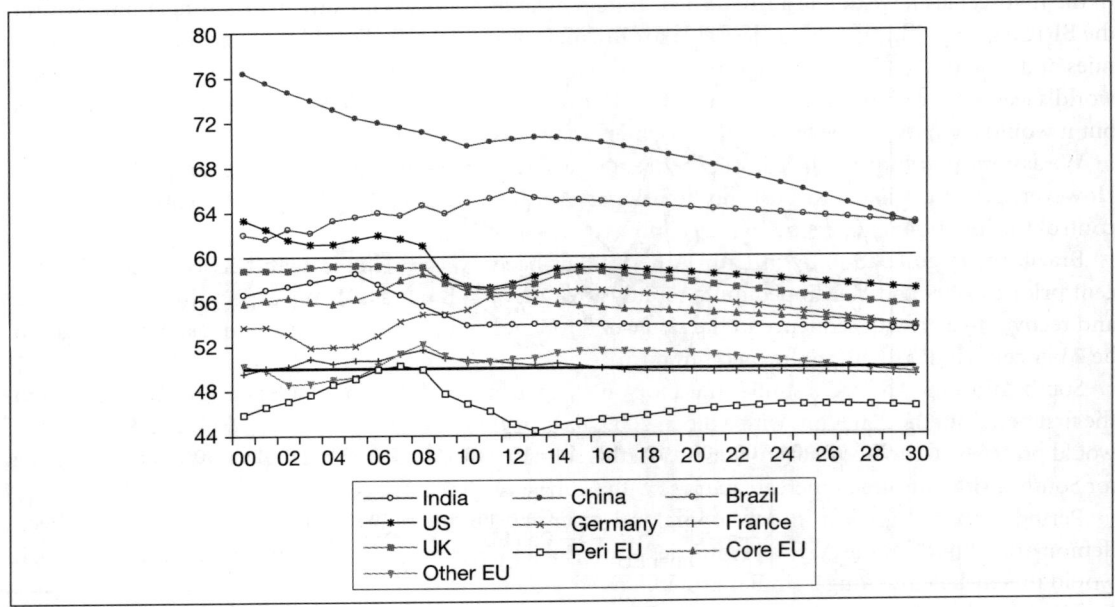

As we will see below, our findings suggest that this does not revive the US or the EU, let alone the world economy.

2. Scenario 2: US reflation: US decides to reflate its economy at a faster pace by allowing increased government expenditure. The demand for a fiscal stimulus has been voiced widely and some of this has helped US recover fractionally from the 2007 housing crisis and avoid some of the problems that the EU is facing (Ball, de Long & Summers, 2014).

   As we discuss later, while this reflationary strategy will help the US, but its global impact, especially in the EU, is not substantive.

3. Scenario 3: EU fiscal stimulus: In order to make the analysis tractable, CAM 6.1 has created three blocs in Europe—the core Eurozone (Austria, Belgium, Finland, Luxemburg and the Netherlands), EU periphery (Cyrpus, Spain, Greece, Ireland, Italy, Malta, Portugal and San Marino) and Other Europe (rest of Europe, which includes Czech Republic, Denmark, Estonia, Greenland, Croatia, etc.). Kept separately for analytical purposes are France, Germany and the UK. In 2014, Germany and the UK had an unemployment rate of little over 4 per cent, in France and Other Europe it was over 8 per cent and in the core EU countries it was about 6 per cent. However, in the EU periphery, it was over 16 per cent. Since neither the BRICS strategy nor the US fiscal expansion solves EU's crisis, the EU has to initiate its own recovery programme. A fiscal stimulus with the aim of increasing employment (avoiding austerity) would be in line with suggestions from many policymakers (Eatwell, McKinley & Petit, 2014). The EU could decide on an employment expansion scheme that targets the unemployment rate (number of unemployed as a ratio to the working-age population).

4. Scenario 4: Europe's task as well as that of the US and the BRICS countries becomes easier if country groups like G20 negotiated a coordinated policy where there is an expansion of the BRICS countries, along with US and EU. This would facilitate the world economy to regain normalcy quicker and with less pain.

BRICS Initiative with China's Balancing Act: Scenario 1

In the first scenario, we define a BRICS-led strategy. The partners would anticipate stronger links within the BRICS group. This would be desirable for Brazil, India and South Africa. These are emergent economies and would like to achieve high rates of growth. China, on the other hand, has already become the world's leading economy and world exporter. Its aspiration would therefore be different from the others but it would align its strategy with other partners in the BRICS group.

We assume that India is targeting a 9 per cent rate of GDP growth in the medium term (in PPP terms). However, growth is likely to push up inflationary pressures and real exchange rate would be used to control the inflationary pressure in the economy.

Brazil, the largest economy in Latin America, has been experiencing growth between 5 and 7.5 per cent prior to 2009 and has dipped quite rapidly after 2010 (WB undated). We expect that Brazil will try and recover to a growth sequence in the range of 5 to 7 per cent. In this scenario, we assume its target to be 7 per cent GDP growth in the medium term.

South Africa too has had a similar trajectory as Brazil being in the vicinity of 5 per cent GDP growth in the first decade of the 2000s but with a dip in 2009. Its growth recovery has been very slow. South Africa too would probably like to boost its growth rate. In this scenario, we do not assume a specific target growth rate for South Africa but similar increase in trade with China and favourable access to its domestic market.

Periods of rapid growth in developing and emerging countries are certainly possible, as has been demonstrated both in the ASEAN countries (until the mid-1990s), as well as in China. India and Brazil would merely be emulating a similar growth target.

The growth in India could be supported by expansionary government spending. Such expenditures could be in the area of infrastructure or energy supply. India's expansion of such programmes as the Employment Guarantee Schemes, Education Guarantee and Health for All is likely to lead to increased government expenditures in the social sectors. In this scenario, we expect that India's public expenditure would crowd-in private investment since we do not anticipate liquidity problems or supply bottlenecks (Bhaduri, 2009; Patnaik, 2007; Rakshit, 2005). Domestic expansion of aggregate demand could lead to temporary inflationary pressures, as has been experienced in India in the recent past. Typically, high and prolonged inflation is politically unacceptable. Since the government is sensitive to this issue, it could use the real exchange rate to manage the impact of inflation.

Growth in domestic expenditures could cause a ballooning of the current account deficit, which would be a deterrent to economic sustainability. In anticipation of this, India could make a concerted effort to reduce fossil fuel imports and substitute them with coal, even though it is more polluting. This option would at least allow it to reduce its import bill. In parallel, there could be an increased effort to export. The twin effort of curbing imports and expanding exports is likely to keep the current account under control.

China itself has had its own set of problems. Its growth rate has been fluctuating and declining and government intervention has been needed in recent years to revive growth (Cha & Fan, 2008; Economist, 2012). China has also been accused of being responsible for the crisis that the EU and US are facing. Since China has maintained large trade surpluses with both the EU and the US, it has been accused of not importing enough from its largest trade partners (Angang, 2003). In order to combat this criticism, China could relax its import strategy and move from a trade surplus situation to one of trade balance. This balance could be achieved by increasing imports of manufactured goods. This policy would be welcomed by its trading partners of the West. The instrument for balancing the current account could be a revaluation of China's real exchange rate. This has been an instrument that has been used quite effectively by China in the past for managing its external account. This scenario anticipates, in fact, the 12th Plan Strategy of China, which proposes to increase domestic consumption and reduce exports (APCO, 2010: 4).

Figure 3.4
Growth in per Capita Income 2000–2030 (Scenario 1)

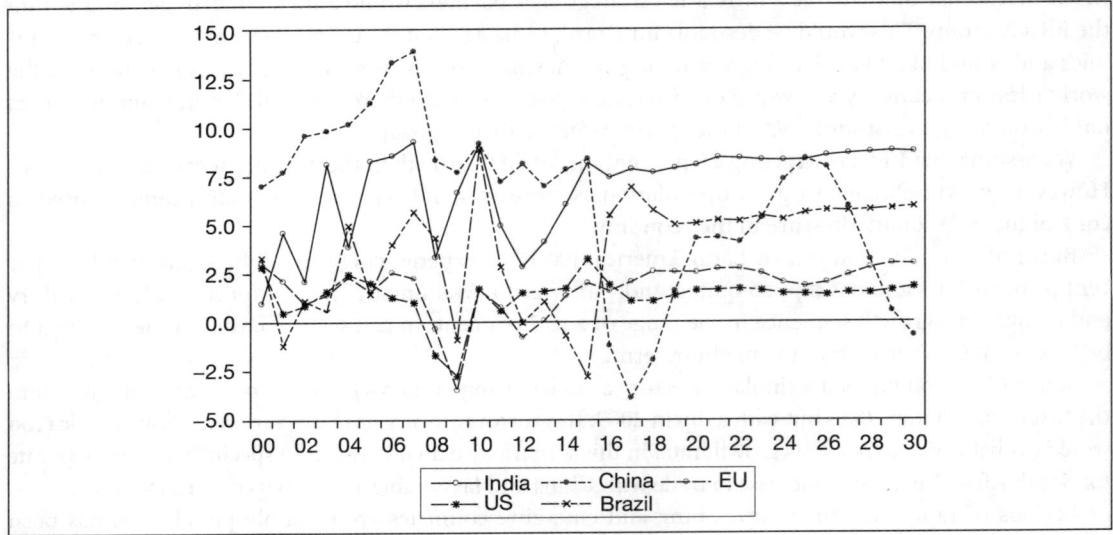

We next examine the possibility of a combined strategy: (a) India, Brazil and South Africa undertake expansion in trade and (b) China becomes more accommodative and chooses a strategy of greater internal absorption. In keeping with the emerging political dynamic at the global level, an optimist would anticipate that China would allow its BRICS partners preferential access to its domestic markets. This would boost India's export prospects without significantly affecting the access of either China or other countries to the large Chinese market.

India's trade with Latin America has been steadily improving. By 2013, Indo-Latin American trade had crossed the $42 billion mark, thereby registering more than a ten-fold rise over the decade. On the policy front, India and Mercosur have signed a preferential trade treaty effective from 2009 (Heine & Viswanathan, 2011). Within Latin America, Brazil dominates the trade with India. This situation is also reflected in the increased political coordination on the international arena that has emerged among India, Brazil and South Africa (the initiative that is nicknamed IBSA). Latin America, in turn, has benefitted from increased FDI flows from India.

It is, therefore, plausible that bilateral trade relations and the share of trade among countries such as India, Brazil and China could improve. As we see from the results below, there would be an improvement in the well-being in these countries (see Figures 3.4 and 3.5). But the fortunes of Europe and US would remain unaffected.

However, while this effort might improve India's economic fortunes, it would leave the rest of the world unaffected. In Europe and the US, for example, employment rates would remain low (see Figures 3.4 and 3.5). Hence, we pose a second scenario.

US Reflation: Scenario 2

The outcomes above bring us to consider options for the US economy, which has roughly recorded a decline in its employment rate by 5 per cent from its 2007 level to below 60 per cent in 2010. There is good reason to believe therefore, at least on economic grounds, that the US could be persuaded to adopt a more pro-employment fiscal expansion strategy. It is already reeling under severe pressure to stop the

Figure 3.5
Employment Rates (per cent) 2000–2030 (Scenario 1)

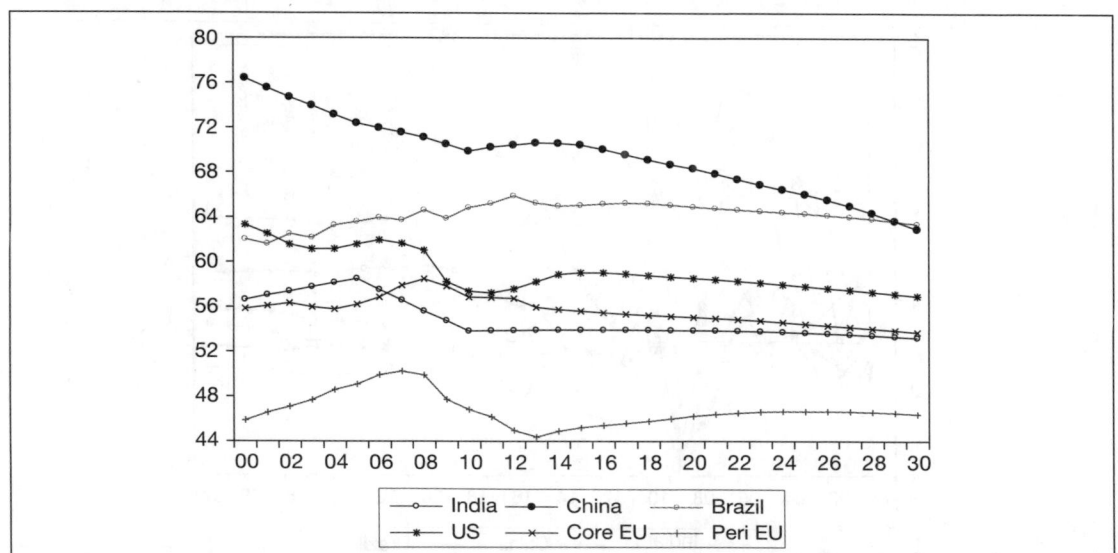

outsourcing of jobs by US companies, and the outcome of the forthcoming elections could be strongly influenced by the policies proposed for employment by the Republicans and Democrats. A fiscal expansion financed by additional borrowing (as proposed in this scenario) could lead to an increase in the employment in the US to 75 per cent. China and Latin America would experience a positive impact from such a policy, but the EU and India would not experience much effect (see Figures 3.6 and 3.7).

However, the public debt, as a percentage of GDP, in the US would rise (Figure 3.8). There would be an initial increase of this ratio to above 80 per cent, but it would then decline and stabilise at about 78 per cent. There would also be a decline in the net export of assets (see Figure 3.7). Employment would rise to reach the target of 75 per cent. But there would be no resultant inflationary pressures generated by this strategy.

What would happen, however, if the EU undertook expansionary fiscal policy alone? This is the basis of our next scenario.

European Reflation: Scenario 3

The focus of this scenario is to increase employment in Europe. If we look at the employment rate as the percentage of people currently employed as a percentage of the total working population, then Europe presents a varied picture. In 2014, the EU periphery had employment rate as low as about 45 per cent, while it was at about 58 per cent in the UK, followed closely by Germany. France was at about 50 per cent. As we have discussed before, this is not only an economic problem, but it has strong political repercussions—in countries like France, EU periphery and the rest of Europe (at about 51 per cent).

We assume that the EU targets a floor rate of unemployment at 6 per cent across all of Europe (unemployment here is defined as the number of people currently unemployed as a ratio of the labour force). This is expected to be achieved by using fiscal expansion to trigger both private investment and per capita income growth. Policymakers allow government expenditure and private investment to rise adequately to maintain at least 3 per cent rate of growth in per capita incomes.

Figure 3.6
Growth in per Capita Income 2000–2030 (Scenario 2)

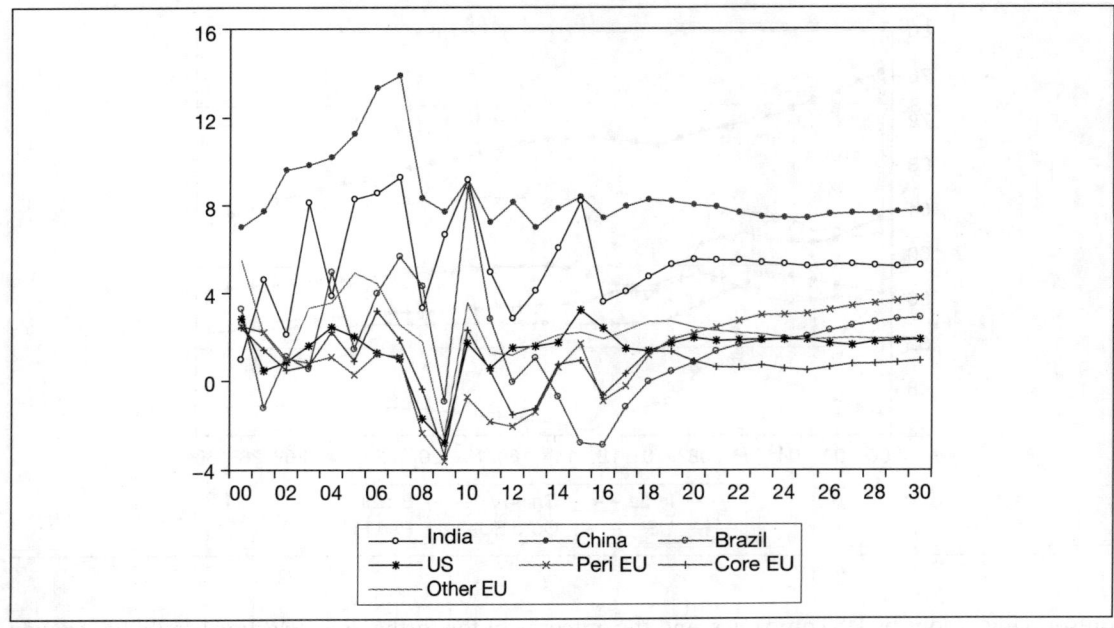

Figure 3.7
Employment Rates (per cent) (Scenario 2)

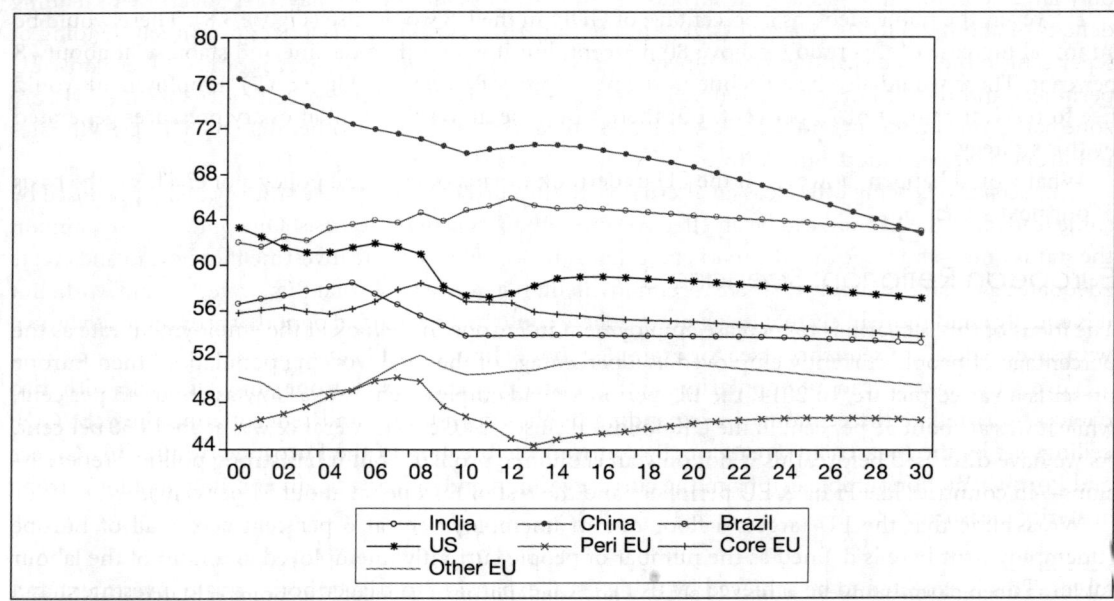

Figure 3.8
US Public Debt and Net Export of Assets (as a Percentage of GDP) (Scenario 2)

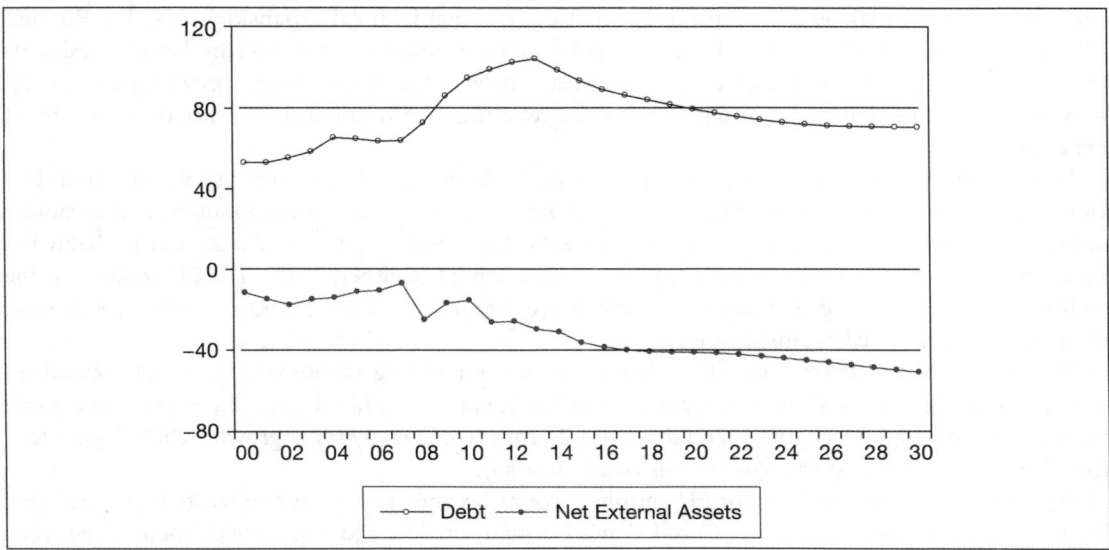

Government expenditure is expected to be financed by issue of sovereign bonds. While these policies are contrary to theories of sound finance (Buchanan & Wagner, 2000), they are very much part of the Keynesian legacy (Lerner, 1943), it would mean that EU blocs may have to re-negotiate the Maastricht treaty and allow member countries to have differential levels of debt and fiscal deficits. Germany is the only large economy that has a fiscal surplus in 2014. The UK and France have net government lending deficits of about 2.3 to 2.4 per cent GDP, but the Eurozone periphery has a net government lending of 5 per cent in the same year. Per capita income growth is also varied in these economies—Germany, EU periphery and rest of Europe showed a growth rate of about 2 per cent, while France and the EU core zone had about 1 per cent and the UK was about 3.6 per cent. Therefore, other than the UK, growth rates in Europe have been moderate or low.

This scenario is being offered as an alternative to the current conservative strategy being proposed by some leaders of the EU and can be an effective antidote to its economic crisis. One option is to maintain the status quo—and hope that the market mechanisms will allow private investment to flow in and create adequate aggregate demand and increase employment. It is conceivable that this strategy could work. But it is equally if not more likely that it will not. So there could be an extended period of economic downturn with severe social consequences (see for example Elliot & Inman, 2012).

Given the widespread unpopularity of the austerity measures, Europe might be left with two choices—(a) reflate the economy by expanding public expenditures and renegotiating the debt/GDP ceilings set by the Maastricht Treaty or (b) confront the breakup of the Eurozone by allowing Greece and Portugal an honourable exit from the currency union and obliging Spain and Italy to adopt strong austerity measures.[2]

---

[2] With an unemployment rate of almost 24 per cent and youth unemployment of 51 per cent in March 2012, Spain's economic managers would have difficulty in justifying austerity measures and might face unforeseen political fallout if they are unable to tackle the problem of unemployment quickly (Eurostat, 2012).

These are difficult choices. The exclusion of Greece and Portugal from the EU might permanently damage the dream of a unified Europe. It is not an option that would be politically desirable. The EU management team may be less averse to the first option, that is, fiscal expansion, now that Premier Merkel has less support because of the change of guard in France and the Netherlands. President-elect Hollande has already indicated his disagreement with the austerity strategy (Traynor, 2012). It is not impossible that the EU might reconsider reflating its economies by relying on government expenditure.

It is easy to assume that public expenditure could be financed by borrowing, but the question then would arise about who would buy these extra bonds since the markets are jittery about the manageability of the European debt, especially the debt of Greece, Portugal, Spain and Italy. The answer probably lies in instituting a federally backed issue of public bonds (Ewing & Geitner, 2012). The EU could treat the additional debt as federal debt (namely the debt above the 60 per cent level) and guarantee this portion of the debt through a federal institution.

This strategy is expected to lead to three levels of growth rates being established. The core EU countries would probably grow at a slower pace (about 1 per cent), France would achieve a 2 per cent growth rate while eurozone periphery countries and the rest of Europe would enjoy faster growth (about 3 per cent) from lower starting per capita income levels (see Figure 3.9).

Employment rates do look up for EU periphery countries and are expected to reach 49 per cent and France is likely to cross 51 per cent. Core EU and Germany are likely to end up with about 55 per cent employment rate in 2030 (see Figure 3.10).

As a result of these policies, the current account would head South in Europe (see Figure 3.11). The UK is expected to see the most rapid decline in its current account balance followed by France. Germany and rest of Europe are expected to maintain a positive balance on the current account.

Figure 3.9
Growth Rate in per Capita Income 2000–2030 (Scenario 3)

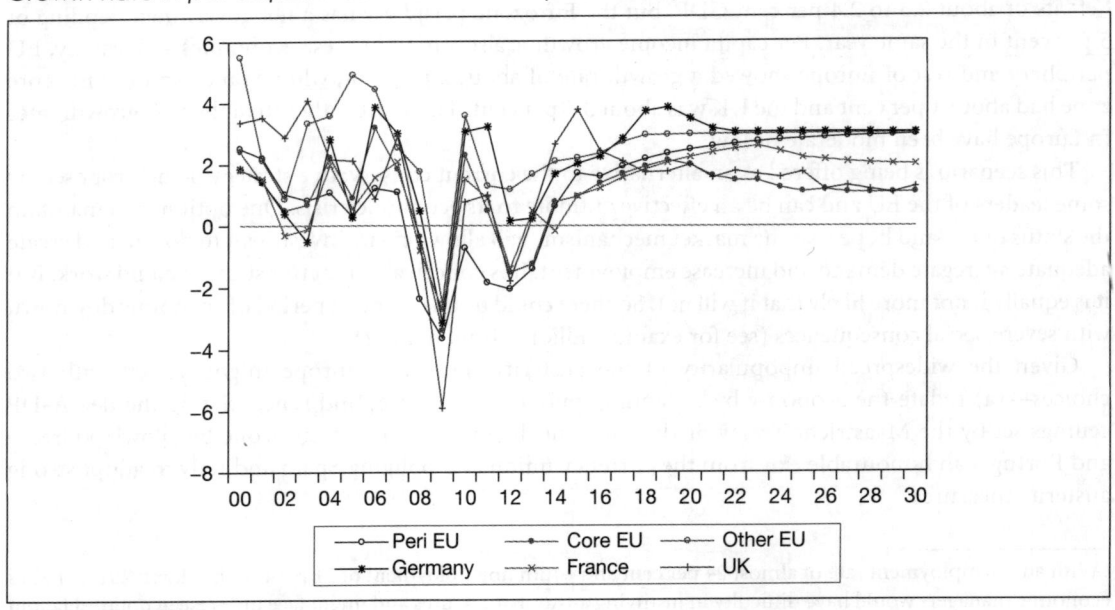

Figure 3.10
Employment Rates 2000–2030 (Scenario 3)

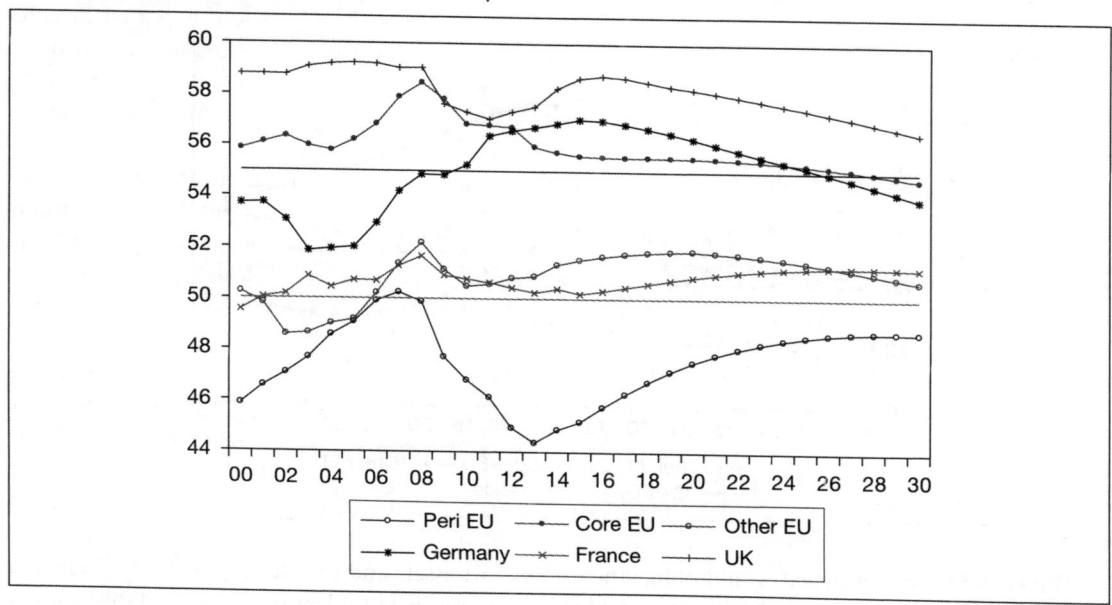

Figure 3.11
Current Account Balance as a Percentage of GDP (Scenario 3)

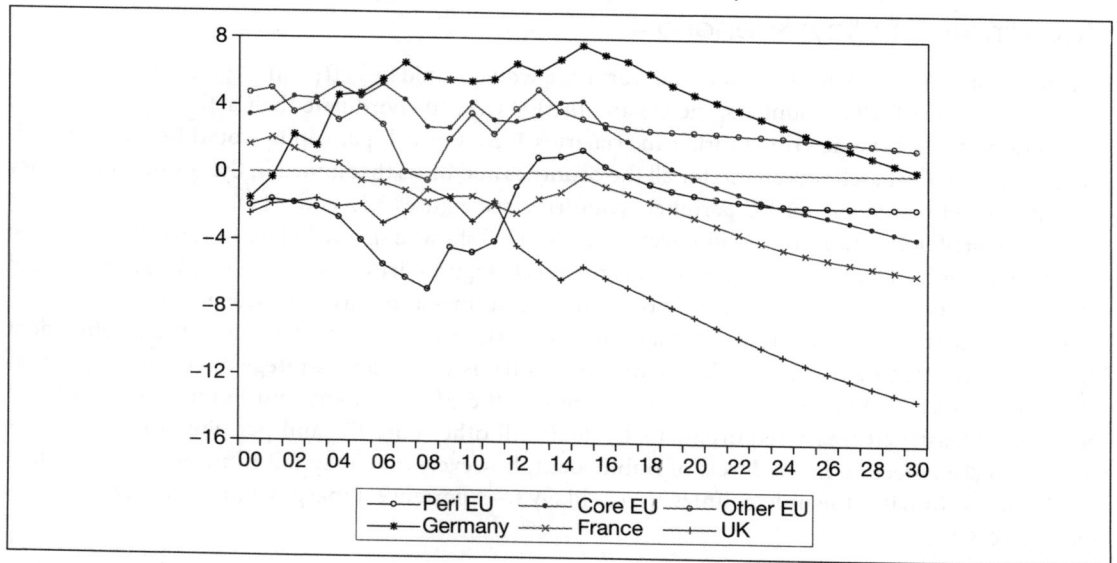

Figure 3.12
Public Debt (as a Percentage of GDP) in Europe (2000–2030) (Scenario 3)

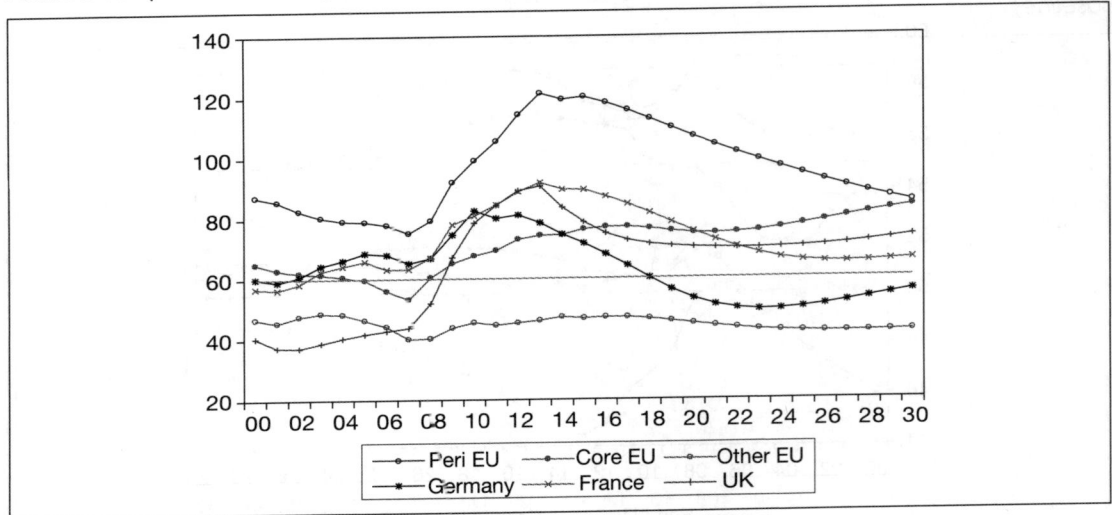

The current account deficit would oblige them to export assets and thus lead to a steady decline in their capital assets held abroad. Again, this might not pose a serious problem since much of this transfer would be taking place within Europe.

Many countries (except Germany and rest of Europe) would have a problem in meeting the Maastricht ceiling on the debt/GDP ratio of 60 per cent (see Figure 3.12). The periphery of the EU would initially have a high debt ratio but then taper down to about 80 per cent. This is where the critical issues of revising the debt ceiling would come in if employment is to be revived and fiscal expansion is the pathway taken.

Coordinated Policy: Scenario 4

The question we pose finally is whether the world as a whole would be better off if there was coordinated action—that is the BRICS countries, the US and the EU were to coordinate their action rather than act in isolation (as we have described earlier in scenarios 1–3). Growth per capita would be higher in this scenario than in the baseline scenario for all the countries and blocs that joined in the coordinated policy initiative except marginally for EU periphery countries (see Figures 3.13 and 3.14).

Employment too in all countries in Europe, Asia and US shows a marked increase under this scenario except China and India where there is no adverse effect (Figures 3.15 and 3.16). In any case, India and China do not undertake any targeted employment programmes as discussed in scenario 1.

An important gain in the process is that most countries would be able to reduce their public debt levels while attempting to manage their employment by using a global strategy of coordinated reflation (scenario 4). In Europe, for example, the rest of the EU, Germany and France will be able to meet their Maastricht treaty requirements by 2030. All other core EU and peripheral EU countries would also see a decline in the levels of public debt; however, they may fail to meet the Maastricht requirements. Brazil is the only country that is likely to experience a marginal increase in debt levels (see Figure 3.17).

Figure 3.13
Growth in per Capita Income 2000–2030 in BRICS and USA (Comparing Scenario 4 and Baseline)

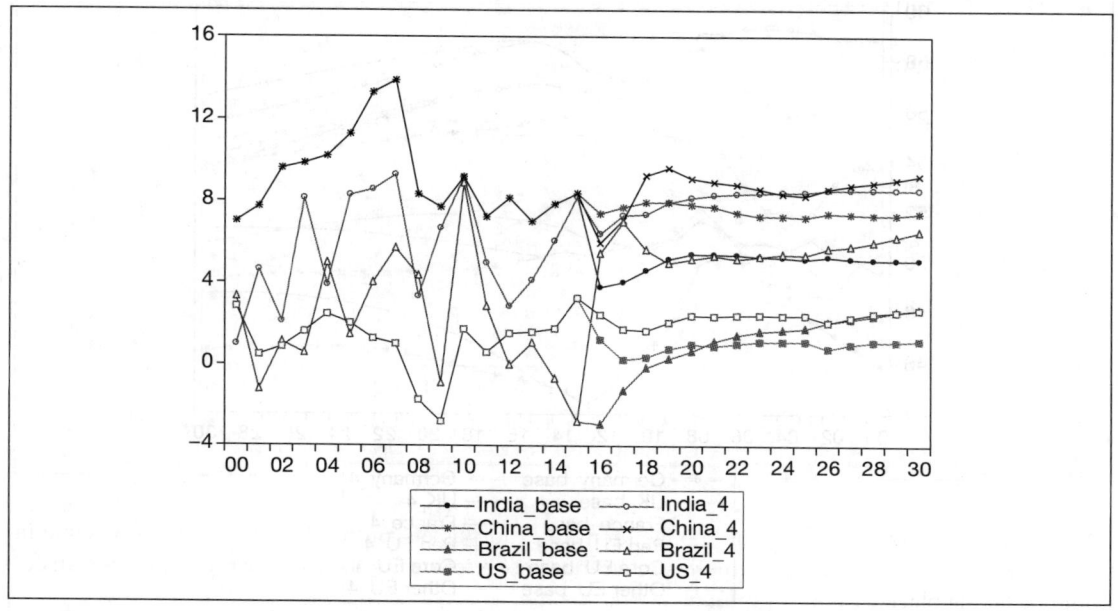

Figure 3.14
Growth in per Capita Income 2000–2030 in Europe (Comparing Scenario 4 and Baseline)

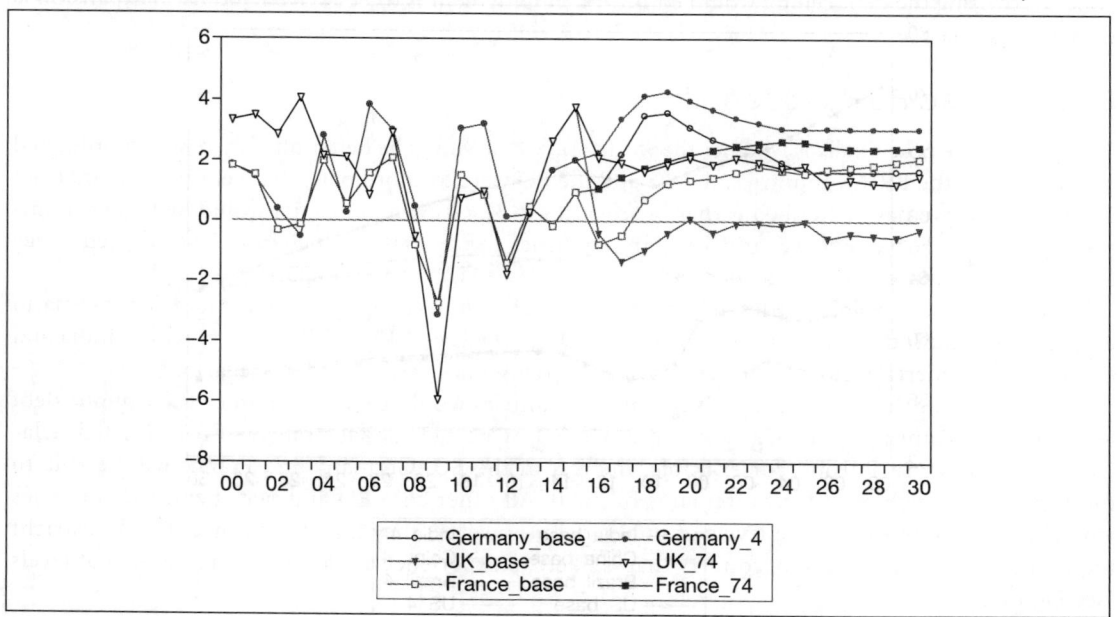

Figure 3.15
Comparing Employment Rates in Europe (Scenario 4 and Baseline)

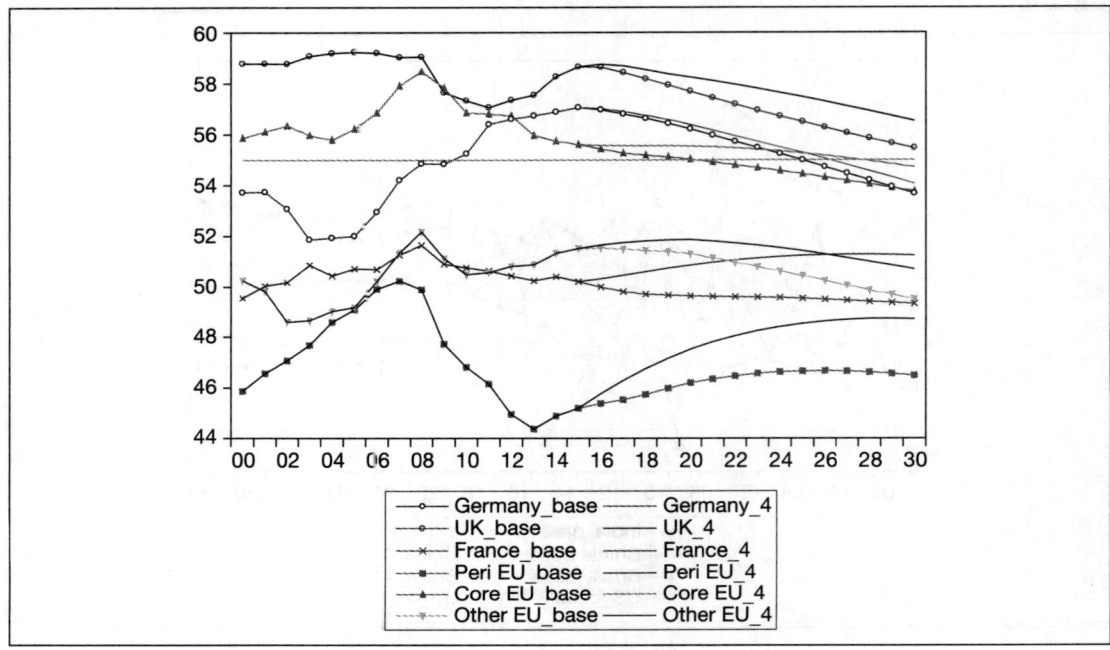

Figure 3.16
Comparing Employment Rates in Other Countries (Scenario 4 and Baseline)

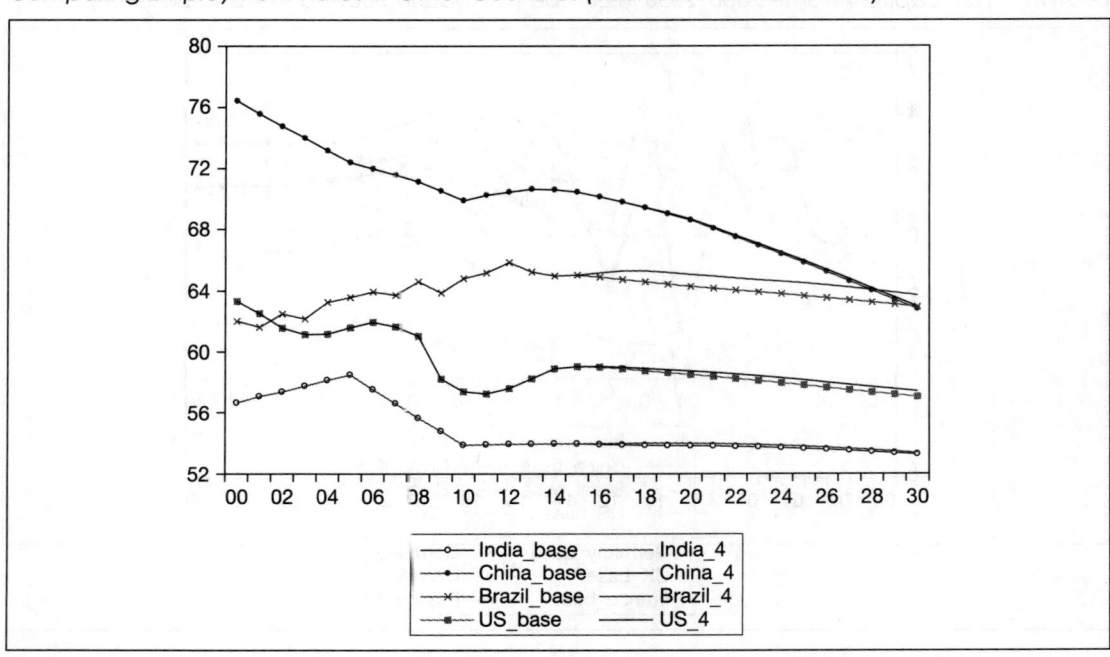

Figure 3.17
Public Debt (as a Percentage of GDP) (Scenario 4 and Baseline)

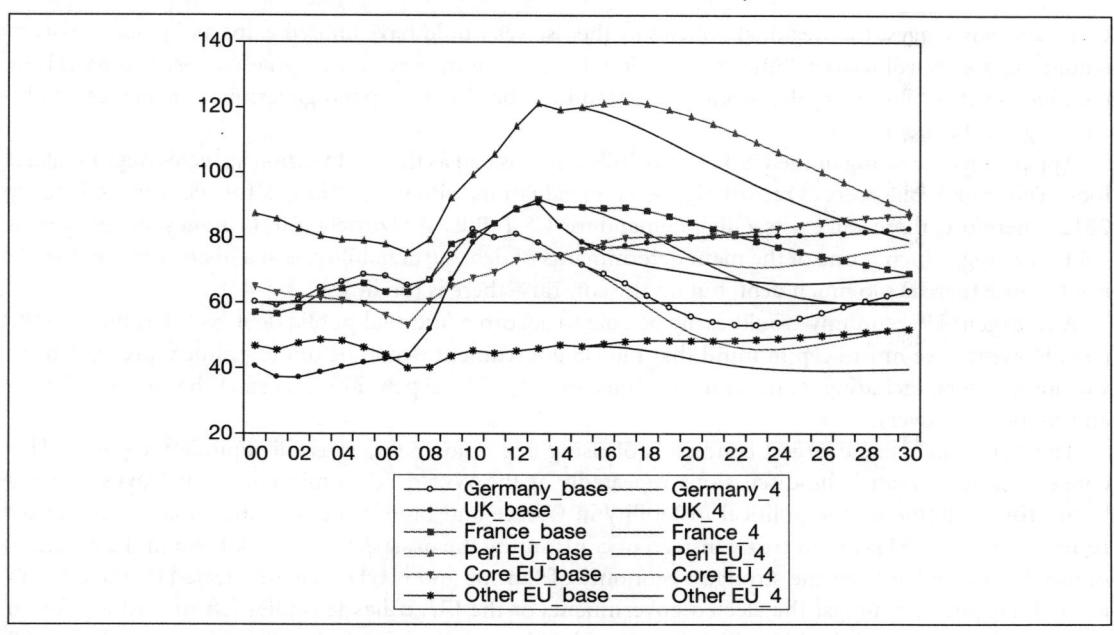

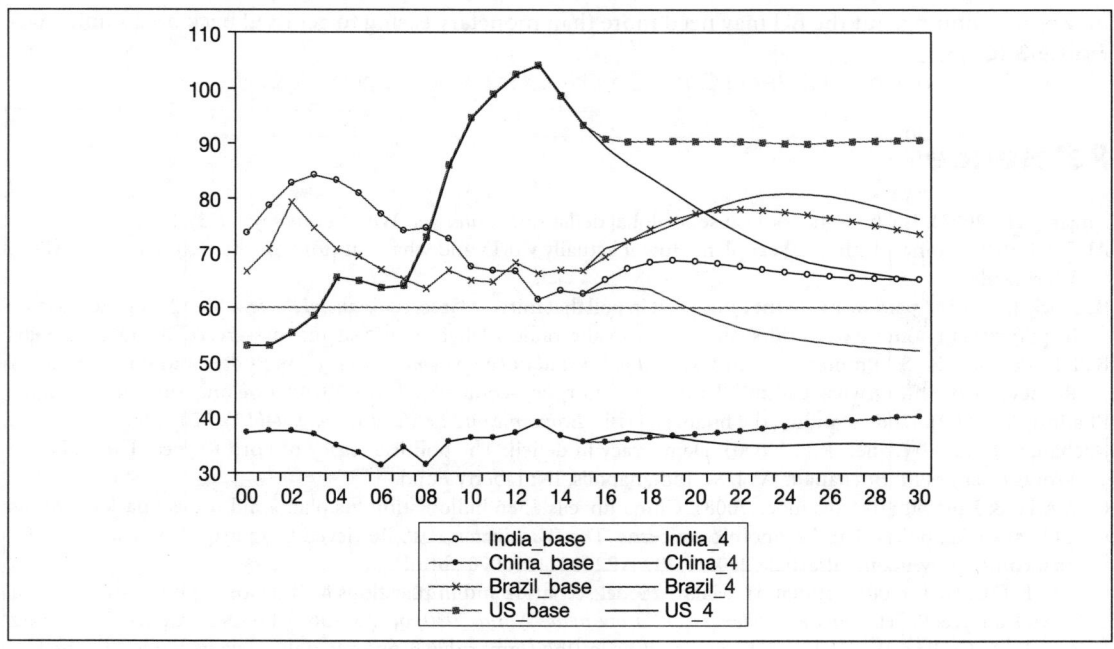

Discussion

Our scenarios suggest that regional policies by themselves would have limited gains and global recovery would require coordinated action. The question that faces us in view of the scenarios posed above is how credible are they? For example, would the US and EU be able to expand government expenditures by running fiscal deficits?

Apparently, the rating of the US Treasury Bills is not as bad as the credit rating agencies might make it look. Ten-year T-bills were at record high levels of valuation, with yield as low as 1.97 per cent in January 2012. Therefore, there still exists a high demand for US T-Bills. As Izurieta (2011) argues, the burden of debt servicing, which is one of the main determinants of debt sustainability, is at a historic low in the US not because there is too much debt, but on the contrary, there is too little.

A resurgent US economy would easily be able to absorb additional public debt, as it has done in the past. However, we must keep in mind that the US government would be under political pressure from various quarters, including financial institutions, to cut public expenditures, even at the cost of delaying an economic recovery.

The Eurozone's single largest concern is of rising unemployment, especially among the youth. This concern has dominated the discussions repeatedly at the World Economic Forum at Davos and has been brought home by the political instability in Greece and France. EU members may be better off re-negotiating the Maastricht treaty instead of confronting the prospect of a breakdown in the currency union. Germany has been the strongest economy of Europe and is relatively unaffected by the crisis in the EU. However, amongst the elected governments of the EU, it has few allies left in pushing for an austerity programme in the EU, which has earned widespread unpopularity. The initiatives of the ECB may be a beginning, but the EU may need more than monetary easing to get itself back on a stable macroeconomic track.

References

Angang, H. (2003). Is China the root cause of global deflation? *China and World Economy, 11*(3), 3–7.
APCO. (2010). China's 12th five-year plan: How it actually works and what's in store for the next five years. APCO Worldwide.
Badcock, J. (2015). Spain swings to the radical left in poll that mirrors Greece. *Financial Review*. May 26. Retrieved from http://www.afr.com/news/world/spain-swings-to-the-radical-left-in-poll-that-mirrors-greece-20150526-gh9q63
Ball, L., de Long, B., & Summers, L. (2014). *Fiscal policy and full employment*. Centre on Budget and Policy Analysis. Retrieved from http://www.pathtofullemployment.org/wp-content/uploads/2014/04/delong_summers_ball.pdf
Bhaduri, A. (2009). Understanding the financial crisis. *Economic and Political Weekly, 44*(13), 123–126.
Buchanan, J.M., & Wagner, R.E. (2000). Democracy in deficit: The political legacy of Lord Keynes. The Collected Works of James M. Buchanan. (Vol. 8). Indianapolis, IN: Liberty Fund.
Cha, A.E., & Fan, M. (10 November 2008). China unveils $586 billion stimulus plan amid unrest, package would address social, political and economic concerns. *The Washington Post*. Retrieved from http://www.washingtonpost.com/wp-dyn/content/article/2008/11/09/AR2008110900701.html
Cripps, F. (2014). Technical appendix: Macro-model scenarios and implications for European policy. In J. Eatwell, T. McKinley, & P. Petit (Eds.), *Challenges for Europe in the World, 2030* (pp. 351–368). London: Ashgate Publishing.
Cripps, F., & Godley, W. (1976). A formal analysis of the Cambridge economic policy group model. *Economica, 43*(172), 335–348.
Cripps, F., Izurieta, A., & McKinley, T. (2007). *Developing a global model for trade, finance and income distribution*. Technical paper 1. Brasilia: International Poverty Centre, UNDP. Retrieved from http://www.ipc-undp.org/pub/IPCTechnicalPaper1.pdf

Cripps, F., Izurieta, A., & Singh, A. (2011). Global imbalances, under-consumption and over-borrowing: The state of the world economy and future policies. *Development and Change, 42*(1), 228–261.

Cripps, F., & Khurasee, N. (2008). *CAM model of the world economy version 3.0, user guide*. Working Paper. Saraburi, Thailand. Retrieved from http://www.augurproject.eu/IMG/pdf/CAM_3-0_User_Guide_1-5.pdf

Eatwell, J., McKinley, T., & Petit, P. (2014). *Challenges for Europe in the world, 2030*. England: Ashgate Publishing.

Economist. (2 June 2012). The slowing economy stimulus or not ? *The Economist*. Retrieved from http://www.economist.com/node/21556308

Elliot, L., & Inman, P. (14 January 2012). Eurozone in new crisis as ratings agency downgrades nine countries. *The Guardian*. Retrieved from http://www.guardian.co.uk/business/2012/jan/13/eurozone-crisis-france-credit-rating-aaa

Eurostat. (2012). *Unemployment statistics*. European Commission. Retrieved from http://epp.eurostat.ec.europa.eu/statistics_explained/index.php/Unemployment_statistics

Ewing, J., & Geitner, P. (27 May 2012). As Euro bond wins supporters, details remain vague. *The New York Times*. Retrieved from http://www.nytimes.com/2012/05/28/business/global/in-euro-zone-a-debate-over-bonds.html?pagewanted=all

Heine, J., & Viswanathan, R. (2011). The other BRIC in Latin America: India. *Quarterly Americas* (Spring). Retrieved from http://americasquarterly.org/node/2422

Inman, P. (3 May 2014). European central bank fires starting gun on €1 tn stimulus. *The Guardian*. Internet edition. Retrieved from http://www.theguardian.com/business/2015/mar/05/european-central-bank-fires-starting-gun-on-1tn-stimulus

Irwin, N. (17 February 2015). A possible day of reckoning, again, for Greece and Europe. *The New York Times*. Retrieved from http://www.nytimes.com/2015/02/18/upshot/is-this-the-day-of-reckoning-for-greece-and-europe.html?ref=topics

Izurieta, A. (2011). Instability in the US: It is not debt but the lack of it. *Economic and Political Weekly, XLVI*(34), 34–38.

Jackson, H.C. (5 August 2011). S&P downgrades U.S. credit rating from AAA for the first time since 1917. *The Washington Post*. Retrieved from http://www.washingtontimes.com/news/2011/aug/5/sp-downgrades-us-credit-rating-aaa/?page=all

Kreijger, G., & Escritt, T. (23 April 2012). Dutch prime minister resigns in budget cuts row. *Reuters*. Retrieved from http://www.reuters.com/article/2012/04/23/us-dutch-politics-idUSBRE83M0PB20120423

Krugman, P. (17 April 2015). That old-time economics. *The New York Times*. Retrieved from http://www.nytimes.com/2015/04/17/opinion/paul-krugman-that-old-time-economics.html?ref=topics&_r=0

Lerner, A.P. (1943). Functional finance and the federal debt. *Social Research, 10*(1), 38–51.

Patnaik, P. (2007). A model of growth of the contemporary Indian economy. *Economic and Political Weekly, 42*(22), 2077–2081.

Rakshit, M. (2005). Some analytics and empirics of fiscal restructuring in India. *Economic and Political Weekly, 40*(31), 3440–3449.

Stiglitz, J.E. (2 January 2015). The politics of economic stupidity. *Live Mint*. Retrieved from http://www.livemint.com/Opinion/D6HPa2acTI77Si9eYF40BL/

Traynor, I. (7 May 2012). French and Greek elections renew fears for Euro's future. *The Guardian*. Retrieved from http://www.guardian.co.uk/business/2012/may/07/french-greek-elections-euro-future

WB. Undated. *Data*. The World Bank. Retrieved from http://data.worldbank.org/indicator/NY.GDP.MKTP.KD.ZG

Yellen, J. (2015). *The outlook for the economy*. Board of Governors of the Federal Reserve System. Retrieved from http://www.federalreserve.gov/newsevents/speech/yellen20150522a.htm

4
Sustainability, Surplus and Survival: Explorations through Agricultural Energetics

Nandan Nawn*

> *The Method I take to do this, is not yet very usual; for instead of using only comparative and superlative Words, and intellectual Arguments, I have taken the course [...] to express my self in Terms of Number, Weight, or Measure; to use only Arguments of Sense, and to consider only such Causes, as have visible Foundations in Nature; leaving those that depend upon the mutable Minds, Opinions, Appetites, and Passions of particular Men, to the Consideration of others.*
>
> —Sir William Petty (1662)

Introduction

The term 'sustain' variously means 'maintain', 'nourish' and 'suffer'. Despite the multiple meanings of the verb, the adjective or the noun is most commonly used in connection with matters related to ecology or environment. In agriculture, for example, as qualifiers to a particular practice, we notice the use of terms like 'organic', 'biological', 'ecological', 'low-input', 'regenerative', 'alternative', etc., as synonyms to 'sustainable'. In general, sustainability and its related terms are applied in diverse situations and contexts over multiple scales of time and space; more often than not it is just a feel-good buzzword with little substance: "[a]s a destination, sustainability is like truth and justice—concepts not readily captured in concise definitions" (Schaller, 1993: 91–92). Such ambiguities imply that "no one can ever

---

* Prabhat Patnaik's continuous encouragement (if not prodding) to his students for developing their own framework(s), eye for detail and meticulousness in every aspect of their work(s), and patient yet deft handling to mould somewhat incoherent thoughts of his students into a presentable work, had both intrinsic and instrumental values. He is responsible in more than one way in turning this author into an academic worker.

The main arguments of this chapter were presented with the title 'Is Small Really Beautiful? Hidden Agenda in the Era of Methodological Pluralism' as Seminar 4 in Seminar Series 2015 of the Centre for Economic Studies and Planning, JNU, on 17 February, 2015. The author wishes to thank the participants of the seminar, in particular Surajit Mazumdar, for his comments. Comments by Kanchan Chopra and the reviewer on the draft version have been greatly beneficial to the author as well.

know precisely and finally which farming practices may be the most sustainable in every location and circumstance" (Schaller, 1993: 91–92).

It remains, however, an incontrovertible fact that for sustainability (continuation) of economic activities outside of the agricultural sector, it is necessary for the latter not only to generate an adequate surplus but also to sustain (maintain) itself; such a possibility occurs quite obviously when the farm labour sustains (nourishes) itself. However, it can occur, even when the 'untrammelled owner' of the surplus sustains (suffers) exploitation, by the capitalist, landlord, household-head or even the self; generation of a positive surplus—albeit notionally—in such situations cannot continue beyond a limited period of time for the depleted 'cap-ability' of the labourer(s). Such a state can hardly be regarded as sustainable and it has adverse consequences for the sustainability of the economic system. Likewise, exploitation of the ecosystem, including soil and water, at a rate greater than that of their regeneration compromises the very basis of farming itself, making it unsustainable as well, as in the case of the labourer: "labour is not the only source of material wealth, of use values produced by labour. As William Petty puts it, labour is its father and the earth its mother. [...] Capitalist production, therefore, develops technology, and the combining together of various processes into a social whole, only by sapping the original sources of all wealth—the soil and the labourer" (Marx, 1867/1954: 50, 475).

Nevertheless, such connections are rare in the recent literature, be it on food, poverty or even political economy of agriculture. To illustrate, a typical contribution within the fold of 'sustainability of agriculture' includes biodiversity, resource efficiency, resilience, soil nutrient management, etc., but not labour (see, for example, *The Earthscan Reader in Sustainable Agriculture*). Conversely, it is livelihood, displacement, market for off-farm employment, etc., that are covered in the writings with a focus on agricultural labour (see, for example, Tripp, 2006), but not the agro-ecological environment within which the farming is practiced. Certainly, these discourses have been neglectful about the labour, which is responsible for the exchanges between human society and its environment, the part of nature that serves as a source of materials, energy and also as a sink for absorbing the waste: "Work is the process of contact between society and nature. By work, energy is transferred from nature to society; and it is on this energy that society lives and develops (if it develops at all)" (Bukharin, 1921/1969: 89–90).[1] It follows that, for enhancing the human well-being, sustaining (maintaining) the labour power is a necessary condition, as is sustaining the ecosystem health.[2]

It appears that in general the 'red' and the 'green' are hardly making any eye contact, either for being too close to each other, or, worse, for being too distant from each other. Else, it is difficult to explain the near-complete loss of interest in carrying forward the rich heritage of James Anderson, Josse Buel, James F.W. Johnston, Henry Carey, Justus von Liebig or even Karl H. Marx,[3] especially in a region like South Asia, where a sustained labour-power and maintenance of agro-ecosystem health assisted by a round-the-year sunshine could have contributed significantly in improving the overall well-being, and not just for those with farming as the primary source of livelihood. Contemporaneously, this assumes importance especially in India facing a multi-dimensional 'agrarian crises'.

This requires sustainability of agricultural practices to be defined in terms of the human well-being, which is not independent of preserving the integrity of the ecological system within which such practices are carried out. This chapter adopts such an eco-social approach.

---

[1] "[W]e know that the only means through which humanity is in a position to increase in any situation the quantity of energy is the use of his labour-power" (Podolinsky, 1883/2008: 181). Also see Marx (1867/1954: 173–174).
[2] In Aristotelian terms, the 'material cause' is the resources that are drawn out of the ecosystem, the 'formal cause' is the particular agricultural practice, the 'efficient cause' is the labour-power, including health and skills of the labourer, and the 'final cause' is the human well-being (see Falcon, 2015).
[3] See Anderson (1776, 1777), Buel (1847), Johnston (1851), Carey (1858), Liebig (1859) and Marx (1867/1954), respectively.

Admittedly, there have been a few efforts towards defining sustainable farming in relation to the human well-being: for instance, National Policy for Farmers (DAC, 2007: 1–2) of the Government of India recognised the need for "an appropriate policy [...] to be evolved to ensure that farming activity becomes more viable and the economic condition of farmers is improved on a sustainable basis" and also "to focus more on the economic well-being of the farmers, rather than just on production".[4] Here, well-being of the farmers has been accorded a particular importance which cannot be independent of the well-being of the other members of the farming household.

This approach warrants characterisation of such (sustaining) farming households that are generating a surplus while fulfilling the minimum requirement for ensuring their own well-being. Such an exercise is different from identifying those farms which are more 'efficient' as "even if output per unit area is higher on small holdings, given their tiny total area, is total output sufficient to meet the family's consumption requirement?" (Patnaik, 1981: 50). Indeed, no notion of 'sustainability' or 'viability' of the farms can be oblivious to the attainment of well-being of the members of the farming households.[5] Specifically, we may ask whether the farming households are being able to generate a surplus, when they are enjoying at least the necessary and appropriate food-calorie with respect to their age, sex and activity as per the norms. Adoption of food-calorie norms as an index of well-being and/or productive capacity of the labourers is well established in the academic literature as well as policy formulation, say, in the construction of poverty lines in India.[6]

For this purpose, rather than computing the surplus (output–input) in terms of its monetary equivalent, we shall be using energy as the standard. In particular, we define sustainability of agriculture in terms of whether the farm household is able to yield an energy surplus, when its members and animals in its possession are obtaining an appropriate calorie intake or 'energy income' (Hermann, 1875), following the norms recommended by the Indian Council of Medical Research (ICMR, 1990).[7]

The method employed here is that of energy (balance) analysis (EBA), situated at the boundary of ecology and economics.[8] In it, embodied energy is taken as a standard, like corn or embodied labour which had been used in the early years of economics towards the measurement of surplus. Like all the standards in the past two and half centuries of economic thought, this one too measures inputs and outputs in real terms, and is independent of prices, so that the problems related to imputation can be avoided altogether. After all, in agriculture, for most of the inputs and outputs, markets either do not exist or are heavily distorted. Ecological unsustainabilities in the form of depletion of water table or degradation of soil will prompt higher energy use in irrigation and fertiliser, respectively, which can be captured easily following this route, irrespective of the existence of the concerned 'markets', leave alone the imperfections within them. Further, the impending crisis facing the present mode of energy use

---

[4] Also see Schaller (1993: 96).
[5] See Patnaik (1981: 46).
[6] Arguably, in the conceptualisation of poverty line, it is "food calorie plus" for inclusion of non-food needs. However, for many, food expenditure accounts for a major share. Various reports, such as Nutritional Intake in India by the National Sample Survey Organisation (NSSO, 2007), show that for the three lowest (monthly per-capita consumer expenditure (MPCE) classes, an overwhelming proportion of expenditure is attributed to food, including cereals, in both rural and urban areas. It is the consumption of cereals which is responsible for most of the calorie intake, or, to put it alternatively, 'energy income'.
[7] Here, all the remaining inputs and outputs are valued in terms of their energy coefficients obtained from the literature; this follows Nawn (2012, 2014). Martinez-Alier (2011: 147) has offered a 'basic sustainability principle of an agricultural society' following a similar energetic route (see section 'Metabolic Framework of Human Labour').
[8] The common root (*oikos*) between the disciplines was to result in adoption of economic concepts in ecology. It was carried forward through parallel contributions from ecologists and economists in developing 'bio-economics'. 'Metabolic rate', 'energy budget', 'assimilative efficiency', 'production', 'growth efficiency', 'gross production', 'net production', 'gross primary productivity', 'net primary productivity', 'distribution' became important terms in ecology, with meanings very similar to that in economics (see Worster, 1994).

which is exhausting the non-renewable low entropy ones at a much faster rate than at which they could be produced justifies adoption of this standard.

A few qualifications are in order before we proceed further: first, given that every input other than (human and animal) labour and output is measured based on well-established energy coefficients, a negative surplus implies that the (assumed) calorie intake norms for the labour are not being fulfilled, implying under-consumption on the part of the latter; second, actual consumption against (human and animal) labour in energy terms will be much larger than the norms, for their inclusion of only the food consumption and hence the 'economic surplus' will be much less than the (energy) surplus in the way defined here;[9] third, generation of a positive surplus while fulfilling such norms is only a necessary, but not a sufficient condition for the generation of actual surplus, as our measurements do not take into account the consequences of expropriation of a portion of the surplus due to property relations, say, rent. Thus, the actual number of farming households with a negative (economic) surplus will be much larger than those identified following the energy route. However, even with these limitations, the framework (of agricultural energetics) and the method (of EBA) employed here offer ample insights into the state of agriculture. In particular, it will shed some new light on the characterisation of farming households that are 'efficient'.

The Energy Surplus

Ever since the Physiocrats, pioneers of a 'curious sociological phenomenon' called 'school of thought' in the history of economics (Meek, 1962: 27; Roll, 1938: 130), questions that had engaged the 'most speculative minds' began with "what does [the][...] surplus consist of and what determines its size" (Bharadwaj, 1978: 14). As it is well known, for this group of French economists, "[t]he produce of the land divides into two parts. The one comprehends the subsistence and the profits of the husbandman, which are the rewards of his labour, [...]; the other which remains is that independent and disposable part" (Anne-Robert-Jacques Turgot, 1774–1776, *Reflections on the Formation and Distribution of Wealth* as quoted in Stokes [1992: 24]).

Obviously the matter of interest was the disposable part, variously known as '*produit net*', 'net real income', 'disposable income' or 'surplus' (Meek, 1951: 27). Satisfaction of the other condition, that is, adequate compensation to the owners of physically exhausted inputs was implicitly assumed in various theoretical formulations as well as calculations, within the classical political economy; its violation was inconceivable.

The subsequent question that appeared in the classical economic thought was with respect to the quantification of surplus for spatio-temporal comparisons (Bharadwaj, 1978: 20), that is, valuation of surplus. Physiocrats did not have to face a value problem, however, for their focus: "In agriculture it [surplus] shows itself directly in the surplus of use-values produced over use-values consumed by the labourer, and can therefore be grasped without an analysis of value in general, without a clear understanding of the nature of value" (Marx, 1863/1963: 46). Thus, it could be concluded that "within the limits of agricultural labour, the Physiocrats have a correct grasp of surplus-value", even while it was "explained [...] in a feudal way, as derived from nature and not from society; from man's relation to the soil, not from his social relations. Value itself is resolved into mere use-value, and therefore into material substance" (Marx, 1863/1963: 52, 57).[10] It follows that, as long as it is the use-value, addressing the 'value problem' can be avoided.

---

[9] This is independent of the inclusion of 'aspirational' consumption.
[10] Also see Burkett (2003: 146).

Quantification of surplus involved adoption of a standard of measure, and it became a necessity when surplus became heterogeneous in content, especially after it was shown that the labour in manufacturing was also productive and thus capable of generating a 'value'. Further, recognition of net profit as a distinct and normal category of income had put the prevailing 'physical cost' theory into a difficulty.

Subsequent to Smith's 'Adding-up Theory' a la Sraffa or the simple 'Cost of Production Theory' (Dobb, 1973: 46), Ricardo in the first two editions of *Principles* (1817, 1819) contended that the 'stable' and 'invariant' standard—for assessment and spatio-temporal comparisons—to be the embodied labour, with distinct Aristotelian roots (see Aristotle, 350 BCE: 10), and inheritance of labour theory from Petty, Cantillon, and Smith; it was a 'simple' labour theory of value (Bharadwaj, 1989: 43). His subsequent attempts were to use different proportions of means of production to labour in different commodities; as long as the social product (net of rent) and wage were expressed in homogenous commodities (of corn, say) or homogenous magnitudes (of labour, say), there was no difficulty. Only when changes in wage resulted in variations in relative prices, problem of simultaneity appeared which Ricardo could not transcend.

It was then Marx's turn "to restate the problem of transforming labour values into prices of production" (Bharadwaj, 1989: 45): "What Lucretius says is self-evident; '*nil posse creari de nihilo*', out of nothing, nothing can be created. Creation of value is transformation of labour-power into labour. Labour-power itself is energy transferred to a human organism by means of nourishing matter" (Marx, 1867/1954: 207fn). Elsewhere, Marx had cited *Leviathan*: "The value or worth of a man, is as of all other things his price—that is to say, so much as would be given for the use of his power" (Marx, 1867/1954: 167fn); value of labour as that of all other commodities, in his other works, had followed from this: "After what has been said, it will be seen that the *value of labouring power* is determined by the *value of the necessaries* required to produce, develop, maintain, and perpetuate the labouring power" (Marx, 1865/1969).[11]

Quantitative assessment of value of labour-power as well as the value that such labour-power creates could be carried out following the energetic route, using the method of EBA employed by ecological economists.[12] The framework of the latter in fact is similar to the neo-Ricardians in more than one way, apart from viewing production as a circular process and linking it to the surplus.[13] Like Sraffa's framework involving 'dated labour' for conceiving cost (and price) of a commodity, the method of EBA is also based on a cost of production theory, where all the costs are carried back to the primary input, the only 'scarce' factor of production, the solar energy required to produce them, with labour, manufactured capital and natural capital as 'intermediate' inputs.[14] So far as the corresponding 'energy theory of value' is concerned, it is possible to limit the "question of value to that of finding some common measure of use value conceived apart from historically specific social relations of production" (Burkett, 2003: 151); thus, energy use-value is used here only as the standard of measure and not as a standard commodity.[15]

Accordingly, the 'energy surplus' or the "energy available to man in excess of that expended to make more energy available" (Cottrell 1955/2009) could be calculated. Some pioneering work in this direction was carried out by Sergei Podolinsky, Eduard Sacher, Patrick Geddes, Henry Adams and Wilhelm Ostwald, among others.[16]

---

[11] Emphasis as in original has been retained throughout, unless otherwise stated.
[12] For instance, value of labour-power can be calculated in calorie terms, by measuring the energy value of the 'means of subsistence' that is the "natural wants, such as food, clothing, fuel, and housing" (Marx, 1867/1954: 167). See Dobb (1973: 151) also: "[T]he 'nourishing matter' needed to replace the energy used-up in work was the material input into human labour".
[13] See England (1986) and Mayumi (2001).
[14] See Slesser (1978), Costanza (1980), Cleveland (1987) and Farber et al. (2002), among others.
[15] Like 'classicalist approaches to value', there exist variations on 'energy theory of value' as well; see Nawn (2015: 138).
[16] See Martinez-Alier (1987).

In sum, quantification of surplus in energy terms using energy use-value is an extension of the classical political economy framework, yet employing 'modern' tools. However, such an exercise, as is the EBA, is replete with methodical debates, in particular over the quantification of human labour, which is addressed in the following section.

Accounting for Human Labour Using Energy Values

The International Federation of Institutes of Advanced Study (IFIAS) in its first workshop established the conventions and methodology of what was then known as 'energy accounting': it was defined as "the determination of the energy sequestered in the process of making a good or service within the framework of an agreed set of conventions" (Nilsson, 1974: 222; de-emphasised). The second workshop (1975) prepared a summary of recommendations that included the nomenclature, method of analysis and the definition of terms (see IFIAS, 1978). It involves quantification of different types of 'embodied' energy, and thus conceptually it is identical to the method of direct and indirect labour embodied. However, these agreed set of conventions could not resolve a number of methodological debates,[17] most importantly, involving the treatment of human labour.[18]

The debate on human labour involves multiple elements, with the most obvious one hinging on the energy values per unit of labour (in hour or day). Jones (1989) had identified four such elements: (a) human metabolic energy expended, (b) 'lifestyle support' energy requirement, (c) marginal energy requirement of employment, and (d) a zero energy cost.[19]

In the industrialised agricultural systems, with almost all the activities being carried out in the mechanical form, the assumed energy values against human labour ranged from zero to a widely varying positive numbers: 6–7 MJ/day for Leach (1976) against food energy needed to maintain human activity during the working hours; 18.24 MJ/day for an eight-hour working day for Pimentel et al. (1973); 84 GJ/year against the 'energy for life support' for Slesser (1973)—just to illustrate the diversity in some of the 'classic' works. In the non-industrialised agricultural systems with labour inputs mostly in the manual form, the differences remain. For example, towards an energetic assessment of agricultural systems in India, Mitchell (1979: 84) had considered 10.04 and 7.95 MJ/day, respectively, for adult men and women for 'maintenance' of human labour, with additional increments for work, while it was 1.96 and 1.57 MJ/hour as 'energy coefficients' for adult men and women, respectively, by various studies in the Indian Council of Agricultural Research-sponsored All India Coordinated Research Project 'Energy Requirements in Agricultural Sector' (1971–2002; see De, 2005: 350). Clearly, the assumed energy value of labour is dependent upon the 'standard of living assumed' (Huettner, 1976: 102), and certainly it has important consequences for the corresponding economic analysis. Indeed, the debate on accounting for human labour is beyond the 'energy coefficients', as we will see soon.[20]

Consider cultivation in two contiguous plots which are identical in all respects (including output), except that in one the harvesting is carried out by a machine while it is through human labour in the

---

[17] See Nawn (2015: 137) for a summary of this debate.
[18] David Pimentel in the preface of his (edited) influential *Handbook of Energy Utilization in Agriculture* (1980) had defended the decision to exclude the energy value of 'manpower' by pointing towards the difficulties in doing so.
[19] For alternative lists see, Pimentel (1980: preface), Edwards (1976: fn1) and Giampietro, Bukkens and Pimentel (1993: 231).
[20] The other difficulty in accounting for labour is related to the measurement of energy against the control functions of human labour (Jones 1989), and this limitation is applicable to the method of EBA per se. It could be considerable in 'modern' societies where the human work involves managerial skill, technical knowledge and professional competence (Punti, 1988: 80), apart from designing. Also see Giampietro and Pimentel (1990).

other.[21] In the calculation of energy return on investment (EROI),[22] the numerator remains the same by construction, while the denominator differs. Here, alternative assumptions over the energy value against human labour will yield different results. For instance, zero energy cost will show the second plot to be much more efficient. Alternatively, the energy value of food necessary to obtain the energy for work may not enable a right comparison with its substitute, the oil fed machinery, as food can only be compared with "the cost of the 'oil' for the 'human machine', but not the consumption of energy necessary to build up this 'machine'" (Punti, 1988: 81).

Further, in contrast to the machinery, for which intensity increases together with the labour used and the material consumed directly as well as for repair/maintenance apart from the accelerated depreciation, for the living inputs, with the rising intensity of work only the recommended dietary allowance (RDA) increases.[23] While it is possible to account for an augmented health expenditure corresponding to the larger 'maintenance costs', conceptually it is difficult to consider anything analogous to the depreciation of the machine, leave alone the empirical difficulties.

In the literature on animal energetics, an alternative has been suggested in terms of considering the days of 'work' and 'rest' separately, as in a machine. The total calorie ingested during the average lifetime, say, for a pair of bullocks who were not engaged in 'any work', may provide the daily average against the 'maintenance'. Subsequently, corresponding to every type of intense work, an increment is added.[24] However, the corresponding measurement for the human labourers is usually carried out through a 'bomb caloriemeter', with individual days as the basis, and not the average of lifetime.

In this respect, Marx had provided a forward-looking alternative of maintaining the labour-power through its reproduction rather than the backward-looking one of depreciation (see section 'Metabolic Framework of Human Labour'). Both conceptually and methodically, this 'metabolic approach' is identical to the 'depreciation fund method' for fixed assets in business accounting. Before we delve into this approach, it will be useful to appreciate the significance, if not the centrality, of conceptualisation and quantification of the value of labour-power in the debate involving emergence of an 'ecological Marxism'. This can be best illustrated through a brief review of work of Sergei (or Serhii) Andreevich Podolinsky (1850–1891) that "has become a focal point in the debate over the potential for a Marxist ecological economics" (Burkett & Foster 2008: 116).[25]

The 'Podolinsky Business'

Podolinsky has been variously characterised as "an important socialist ecological thinker, […] socialist political economist" (Foster & Burkett, 2004: 33, 36), "a medical doctor, […] a Ukrainian narodnik activist, […] a Ukrainian nationalist", and "a Ukrainian federalist narodnik [but] [p]olitically […] not a Marxist" (Martinez-Alier, 1987: 5; 2006: 276); he has also been regarded as one of the founders of the trans-discipline of ecological economics for his pioneering contribution in conceptualising "energy return to energy input [or EROI and applying it] in different types of land-use" (Martinez-Alier, 2011: 152–153). Podolinsky had communicated with Marx in 1880 with his writings apparently aimed at

---

[21] This follows the illustration from Punti (1988).
[22] It is identical to energy returned on energy invested and is represented as the ratio of the amount of usable energy obtained from a particular energy resource to the amount of energy expended to obtain that same energy resource. For a review of various uses of EROI in economic analysis, see Murphy and Hall (2010).
[23] See, for example, ICMR (1990).
[24] See Rao (1984).
[25] See Burkett and Foster (2008: 120–124), Foster and Burkett (2004: 35–36) and Martinez-Alier (1987: 53–63; 2011: 152) for brief biographical sketches of Podolinsky.

establishing an energetic basis of the labour theory of value.[26] Upon Marx's request, Engels had assessed Podolinsky's work,[27] and it was argued that even though "Podolinsky wrote from the ecological point of view on the 'conditions of human life on earth' [which] [...] *could* have been easily connected with Marxism through an adequate definition of productive forces or productive powers" (Martinez-Alier, 1987: 5), it "was *not* done by Marx" (Martinez-Alier, 1987). Further, it was alleged that such 'reaction' on Engels' part and "Marx's silence from mid-1880 to the end of his life in early 1883, were a missed chance for a Marxian approach to agricultural and economic history based on the study of energy metabolism, and this omission affected the Marxian tradition long after" (Martinez-Alier, 2011: 152).[28]

This 'Podolinsky myth' was variously challenged.[29] Nevertheless, the proponents continued with the claim (see Martinez-Alier, 2011: 147, 153). In this debate[30] on the various strands of 'Podolinsky business',[31] accounting for living labour in energy terms assumes a central place for the same in Podolinsky's works. On the one hand, it was claimed that Podolinsky had "used the same methodology as modern energy accounting" (Martinez-Alierand Naredo, 1982: 213) notwithstanding the diversity within it, while on the other, it was argued that this "[e]nergy accounting [...] gave a scientific basis to the labour theory of value, a point that neither Marx nor Engels appreciated" (Martinez-Alier, 1987: 49).

Having identified "an accumulation of solar energy on the earth's surface" (Podolinsky 1883/2008: 166) as the "best means of employing human labour in order to draw upon a greater fraction of natural forces for the satisfaction of human needs" (Podolinsky 1883/2008: 163), identifying and influencing such 'activity of humans' (Podolinsky 1881/2004: 64) was found to be the most useful tool by Podolinsky for the purpose. Accordingly, labour was defined: 'such a use of the mechanical and intellectual energy accumulated in the organism, which has as a consequence an increase of the general energy budget of the earth's surface' (Podolinsky, 1883/2008: 172). Definition of 'surplus of energy' (Column 8 in Table 4.1) followed from it.

For this purpose, 'human (or animal) work' was measured as the "the energy input as the equivalent to work done, and not as the food energy intake" (Martinez-Alier, 1987: 49), which arguably was one of the most important aspects of Podolinsky's work. Accordingly, this student of Hermann (Martinez-Alier, 1987: 57) had used the results of the experiment by Gustave Adolphe Hirn towards measurements of human muscular labour, for defining the size of his celebrated 'economic coefficient' of the "human machine, that is, the percentage yield of the heat transformed during labour" (Podolinsky, 1883/2008: 176). It was stated to be 20 per cent, or one fifth, that is, "the human possesses the ability to transform 1/5 of the total energy added by nutrition into muscular labour" (Podolinsky, 1883/2008: 176), which was argued to be better than the "most advanced steam engines" (Podolinsky, 1883/2008). As we have seen above, comparing machines with human labour is not that simple as Podolinsky thought.

At the societal level, the coefficient was taken as 1/10 to reflect "the whole quantity of energy that is claimed by humanity for the satisfaction of its material and intellectual needs" (Podolinsky, 1883/2008: 177). This had apparently led him towards stating the "general theoretical principle" (Martinez-Alier & Naredo, 1982: 214) for sustaining the humanity. It was argued further that following Podolinsky's work, "one could determine the necessary minimum conditions of human survival on earth through an

---

[26] Podolinsky's letter to Marx dated 30 March and 4 April 1880, respectively, as cited in Martinez-Alier (1987: 62).
[27] See Engels (1882/1968a; 1882/1968b).
[28] See Foster and Burkett (2004: 48–54), who contested these allegations.
[29] See Foster and Burkett (2004) and Burkett and Foster (2006; 2008).
[30] See various works of Martinez-Alier, John Bellamy Foster and Paul Burkett in this regard.
[31] This phrase was used in Engels (1882/1968a).

Table 4.1
Energy Analysis of Different Types of Land Use in France, 1870s

Type of Land Use	Area (in mn ha)	Output (item)	Average Yield per Hectare (in kg/ha)	Unit Energy Value (in kcal/kg)	Labour Input (in hr)	Unit Energy Value (in kcal/hr)	Per Hectare Annual Accumulation of Energy (in kcal/ha)	Per Hectare 'Energy Surplus' in Comparison to Natural Pastures (in kcal/ha)	Per Hectare Hourly 'Net Energy Accumulation' per Unit Calorie Applied
	(1)	(2)	(3)	(4)	(5)	(6)	(7)=(3)×(4)	(8)	(9)=(8)/(6)
Forest	9	Dry wood	900	2,550	Nil	–	2,295,000	NA	NA
Natural pastures	4.2	Hay	2,500	2,550	Nil	–	6,375,000	NA	NA
Sown pastures	1.5	Hay (net of seed)	3,100	2,550	50 (horse) +80 (human)	37,450	7,905,000	1,530,000	40.85
Wheat cultivation	6	Wheat (net of seed)	8,000	3,750	100 (horse) +200 (human)	77,500	8,100,000	1,725,000	22.26
		Straw	2,000	2,550					

Source: Adapted from Podolinsky (1883/2008: 171–172).

Notes: 1. Column (8) was derived from column (7) by subtracting the figure against 'natural pastures'.
 2. Column (9) was interpreted as the 'net energy accumulation' against 'each calorie of labour applied' (Podolinksy, 1883/2008: 172) or 'energy return to the energy input from human (and animal) work' (Martinez-alier & Naredo, 1982: 212).
 3. Figures of energy accumulation "corresponds to the biologists' 'net production' [but without] the energy expended by plants in respiration" (Martinez-alier, 1987: 49; also see Foster and Burkett, 2004: 40).
 4. It can be derived from column(s) (5) and (6) that per hour 'Labour Input' to be 65 kcal or calorie. It is the 'energy at work' and not the nourishment required to perform such work. Thus, column (9) shows per unit of calorie applied and not per unit of food-calorie required for such application.

analysis of energy flows and energy efficiencies" (Martinez-Alier, 1987: 51). One wonders how, on the basis of a rate, a conclusion could be reached that involves absolute values! Indeed, the notion of 'energy surplus' that Podolinsky had conceptualised and measured does not follow from the classical political economy framework. Certainly, calculation of the rate of energy accumulation with respect to the expended energy, type of energy inputs, energy mix, etc., is an useful exercise per se, but that has hardly anything to do with exploring the principle that can lay the 'conditions for human survival'.

$$\text{Let us define per hectare energy surplus} = \text{Output/ha} - \text{Input/ha} \tag{4.1}$$

$$\text{EROI} = \text{Output/Input} = (\text{Output/ha})/(\text{Input/ha}) \tag{4.2}$$

and change in per hectare energy surplus in switching from natural pastures (j) to sown ones (i)

$$\begin{aligned} &= \text{Surplus}_i/\text{ha} - \text{Surplus}_j/\text{ha} \\ &= \Delta\text{Output/ha} - \Delta\text{Input/ha} \end{aligned} \tag{4.3}$$

For Podolinsky, per hectare 'energy surplus' (column 8 of Table 4.1) = ΔOutput/ha, and is different from Equation 4.1.

Similarly, per hectare hourly net accumulation per unit of calorie applied (column 9 of Table 4.1) = (ΔOutput/ha)/(ΔInput/ha) = ΔOutput/ΔInput is not the same as EROI in Equation 4.2.

$$\text{Equation 4.1 can be restated as (Surplus/ha)/(I/ha)} = \text{EROI} - 1 \tag{4.4}$$

This implies that an identical EROI can be associated with different levels of per hectare surplus (see Figures 4.3–4.5). To reiterate, it is only a non-negative surplus and not the rates like EROI or 'economic coefficient' that can ensure the sustainability of a farming household, and hence that of the economic system.

Engels' overall conclusion on Podolinsky was rather subtle: "[he] has strayed away from his very valuable discovery into mistaken paths because he was trying to find in natural science a new proof of the truth of socialism, and has therefore confused physics and economics" (Engels, 1882/1968a). However, one must record the pioneering contribution of Podolinsky: his "real discovery is that human labour has the power of detaining solar energy on the earth's surface and permitting its activity longer than would be the case without it" even if "[a]ll the economic conclusions he draws from this are wrong" (Engels, 1882/1968a).[32]

To appreciate the significance of Podolinsky's legacy, consider a numerical illustration from more than a century later in Payne (1985: 7): in dryland rice cultivation, 130 person-days were assumed as per-hectare labour input, and 1,000 kg (or 15 GJ) of 'net edible yield rice' as output. The '*average* energy cost of labour input per working day' was taken as 3 MJ (717 cal), implying per hectare per year 'human work input' as 390 MJ or 0.39 GJ.[33] No other material input was taken into consideration, leave alone the energy required for the labour during the non-active days of the year, presumably holding the assumption of full employment. The conclusion was that "to provide the 17 GJ per year needed for a family of five [5 persons × 2,200 kcal per day × 365 days = 16.798 GJ ≈ 17 GJ], 1.2 ha of land would be needed,

---

[32] For the record, it may be added here that Podolinsky had made several other computational errors, like ignoring the energy value of various inputs, including manure, guano or even coal (only seeds were included), in the accounting despite knowing about these. See Engels (1882/1968a), Burkett and Foster (2006; 2008) and Foster and Burkett (2004) on this matter.

[33] Oft-cited works like Dasgupta (1993: 278) and Dasgupta and Mäler (1995: 2391) had used the same illustration and assumed "average energy input in cultivation per working day" as the same 3 MJ (Payne, 1985), without even caring to mention that it includes only the labour at 'work'.

and a work input of 0.5 GJ per year [1.2×0.39 MJ]: a ratio of energy output to input of 34:1 [17:0.5]" (Payne, 1985). Such a fantastically (and impossibly) high EROI results from an atomistic understanding of treating human labourers as a machine, much like Podolinsky (see section 'An Empirical Illustration').

Metabolic Framework of Human Labour

The initial version of "basic sustainability principle" (Martinez-Alier, 2011: 147) had advocated inclusion of the total energy expenditure of workers (food and non-food) against human energy inputs, equivalent to the 'social reproduction' of workers, that includes not only the "physical energy to keep them in working order, but a variable historical element, which can be many times higher than the food and fuel energy physiologically needed" (Martinez-Alier, 1987: 28–30); this follows the metabolic framework for the accounting of living labour with roots which are more than a century old, and which was quite different from the route followed by Podolinsky.

The metabolic approach considers the amount of energy (from food) required to sustain the labourer and her dependants. This is conceptually similar to the consideration of energy required for the production of replacement animals in meat or milk production (Giampietro & Pimentel, 1990: 263). However, unlike the animals, whose number may be adjusted to the planned production requirements, human's "level of living" need to be met whether in "work" or not (Norum, 1983: 6) for obvious reasons.

The framework that Hermann had employed in *Elements of Human Physiology* (1875)[34] had established this principle; it involved a 'minimum exchange' of matter (and hence energy) differentiated with respect to age, sex and nature of activity so as to maintain the human body "at its usual standard of weight" (Hermann, 1875: 199, 205–206) through a balance between 'energy income' obtained from food and 'energy expenditure' involved.[35] This principle involving the 'minimum exchange of matter' for maintaining a particular weight has been employed in the measurement of Recommended Dietary Allowances (RDA) or the human energy income, and used by the World Health Organization, Food and Agriculture Organization of the United Nations and the Indian Council of Medical Research (ICMR).

> The energy allowances recommended are designed to provide enough to promote satisfactory growth in infants and children and to maintain constant body weight and good health in adults. […] In the case of energy, the input must equal to the output in order to be in energy balance which corresponds to a steady state. (ICMR, 1990: 11)

This approach took a social form in Marx's work, where it was the labour-power that was to be maintained or sustained. For him, labour is 'a process' where the labourer sets "in motion arms and legs, head and hands, the natural forces of his body, in order to appropriate Nature's productions in a form adapted to his own wants" (1867/1954: 173). Labour-power, in this framework, is the 'capacity for labour' represented by "the aggregate of those mental and physical capabilities existing in a human being, which he exercises whenever he produces a use-value of any description" (Marx, 1867/1954: 164).

Given that "the past labour […] is embodied in the labour-power, and the living labour that it can call into action", it was important for Marx to delineate the difference between the two, that is, "the daily cost of maintaining" the labourer, or, the corresponding energy income "transferred to a human organism by means of nourishing matter" (Marx, 1867/1954: 207fn), and, the "daily expenditure in work", or, the

---

[34] Even in its 140th year, notwithstanding the absence of copyright, this book is still sold by all the international bookselling sites like Amazon, Barnes and Noble, and even eBay!

[35] Using the calorimeter that allowed measurement of all kinds of 'energy expenditure' (Hermann, 1875: 220–221) and process of combustion of the 'alimentary substances of food' that could be perfected so as to mimic the process within the body (Hermann, 1875: 216) and Hirn's experiment (the one used by his student Podolinsky; referred earlier) Hermann had arrived at this conclusion.

energy expenditure by her (Marx, 1867/1954: 188); after all it is the "difference of the two values" that the "capitalist had in view" (Marx, 1867/1954).

The cost of "maintenance" is the cost of "reproduction" of the labourer herself (Marx, 1867/1954: 167). Alternatively, the *"value of labouring power* [...] is determined by the quantity of labour necessary to produce it" (Marx, 1865), which has three components. First is a "certain mass of necessaries" for the maintenance (besides growth) of the labourer in question, as labour-power gets depreciated with wear and tear, just like a machine, and thus requires rest to recuperate itself, just like the soil. Even while a "definite quantity of human muscle, nerve, brain, &c., is wasted" during work, it is essential for the labour-power to become a reality (Marx, 1867/1954: 167). This necessitates maintaining the labourer in her "normal state as a labouring individual" (Marx, 1867/1954: 168); this is synonymous with the requirement of stable weight for Hermann. This 'maintenance' is certainly different from what happens in a machine, unlike what Podolinsky had thought; for instance, 'means of subsistence' is also required during the period of rest.

A second set of 'necessities' is required for the replacement of the labourer in question so as to maintain the labour-power "at the very least, [with an] [...] equal amount of fresh labour-power", on a continuous basis as "wear and tear and death" results in the withdrawal of labour-power from the market at which it was brought (Marx, 1867/1954: 168); for this it is required to "bring up a certain quota of children [...] and to perpetuate the race of labourers" (Marx, 1865). For Hermann, the 'objective' of reproduction was "to maintain the number of individuals of the species approximately constant" (1875: 531). The final set of elements was required for developing the labour-power like skill, training, which was assumed to be small by Marx (1865).

Notwithstanding the variations in the climatic and other physical conditions of the country of the labourer, and modes of satisfaction of such 'natural' and 'necessary' wants that includes "food, clothing, fuel, and housing", "in a given country, at a given period, [...] is practically known" argued Marx (1867/1954: 168). Of course, there can be "difference between the labour-power of men and women, of children and adults" (1867/1954: 486) as the necessary (and varying) 'minimum exchange of matter' a la Hermann (1875: 206).

For absence of any accepted norm towards consumption of materials other than food for human-beings, we consider only a subset of the 'necessary and unavoidable' in terms of the nourishing matter which is undoubtedly lower than the entire 'means of subsistence'. Against raising 'a certain quota of children' we consider 'maintenance' of all the members of the household. But even with this limited version of metabolic framework, we shall be able to compare it with that of Podolinsky for showcasing the differences and implications including offering new insights into the debate involving 'small (farm) is beautiful'.

An Empirical Illustration

In this illustration, only the living labour—the main divergence among the accounting approaches—will be treated differentially. All the basic taxonomies of EBA in terms of scope (say, of ignoring sun's energy), system boundary (say, of considering the activities within the farm-gate), limitations (say, of ignoring energy quality issues), etc., will be retained; likewise, identical energy values against every input and identical annual rate of depreciation (8 per cent) of machines will be assumed.[36] In particular, the difference vis-à-vis treatment of living labour is in three respects—(a) basis (per hour/day), (b) scope

---

[36] See Table A2 in Nawn (2014) for the energy coefficients; for more details, see Nawn (2014: 12–16). Embodied energy of the standard machines of each type (say, thresher, submersible pumps, etc.) as prevalent in the state was computed based on standard energy value of the components, fabrication expenditure, etc.

Table 4.2
Energy Values for Labour under Alternative Framework of Accounting without Hired-in or Hired-out (in calorie)

Accounting Framework	For Active Hours or Days			For Inactive Hours or Days			Total	
	Men	Women	Children	Men	Women	Children	Per Day^	Per Season#
Podolinsky	468/hr	375/hr	234/hr	Nil	Nil	Nil	2,808	140,400
Podolinsky plus Maintenance	2,822/day	2,280/day	2,447/day	2,376/day	1,920/day	2,061/day	2,280	248,400
Hermann-Marx	2,822/day	2,280/day	2,447/day	2,376/day	1,920/day	2,061/day	2,280	780,840

Source: De (2005) for energy values for Podolinsky and ICMR (1990) for the other two.

Notes: 1. The household was assumed to consist of an adult farming woman aged 35 years, a 'dependent' adult man aged 40 years and a woman aged 17 years. The term 'dependent' concerns only to the production/availability of crop. See Table A1 in Nawn (2014) for specific energy values against all age-sex-actvity combinations.
2. Calorie values in Podolinsky was taken as identical for all men, and so was for all women or children, while it was age-specific under the other two.
^6 hours of activity is considered as an 'active' day.
#A season of 120 days with 50 active days and 70 inactive days was assumed. First two rows were derived as 50 days × corresponding energy value for a working day. For the third row it was sum of (a) 50 days × energy value of labour for active days, (b) 70 days × energy value of labour for inactive days and (c) 120 days × energy value of 'dependents' for inactive days.

(only active hours/days or with inactive ones) and (c) extent (only labourer or along with the other household members).

We shall be considering the following three progressively stricter scales for measuring the energy-value against human labour (see Tables 4.2 and 4.3 for a numerical illustration involving a hypothetical household):[37]

- Scale P (or Podolinsky): It takes account of only the energy for the working period of the labourers.
- Scale PM (or Podolinsky plus Maintenance of the Labourer): It considers as an input the energy for maintenance of the labourers over and above scale P.
- Scale HM (or Hermann–Marx): It considers as an input the energy for maintenance of the members of the household in question over and above scale PM.[38]

An analysis of farm-level primary data collected by a government agency,[39] of 590 farm households located across five agro-climatic zones for (*Aman*) paddy cultivation in the state of West Bengal during monsoon (*kharif*) season of 2004–2005, an agriculturally normal year, was undertaken.

---

[37] In Nawn (2014), we have designated these scales as definitions. They are identical in all respects, except the nomenclature.
[38] This corresponds to 'the reproduction of labour-power' in a loose sense. Identical treatment was extended to the animals as well. Thus, just not the animals kept for meeting the power requirements, but all animals in the possession of the household were considered in this scale.
[39] See Nawn (2013) for the details of this underutilised dataset.

Table 4.3
Energy Value of Active and Inactive Days of Labourer with Hired-in and Hired-out (in calorie)

Accounting Framework	Household Labour				Hired Labour			
	Active Days	Energy Value/Day	Inactive Days	Energy Value/Day	Active Days	Energy Value/Day	Inactive Days[2]	Energy Value/Day
Without hired in or hired out of household labour								
Podolinsky	50	2,808	70	n.a				
Podolinsky plus Maintenance	50	2,280	70	1,920				
Hermann-Marx	50	2,280	70	1,920				
With hired in labour of 30 days, in replacement of household labour								
Podolinsky	20	2,808	100	n.a	30	2,822	60	n.a
Podolinsky plus Maintenance	20	2,280	100	1,920	30	2,822	60	2,376
Hermann-Marx	20	2,280	100	1,920	30	2,822	60	2,376
With hired in labour of 30 days, in replacement of household labour, and hired out labour of 40 days in addition to own-farm work								
Podolinsky	20	2,808	60	n.a	30	2,822	60	n.a
Podolinsky plus Maintenance	20	2,280	60	1,920	30	2,822	60	2,376
Hermann-Marx	20	2,280	60	1,920	30	2,822	60	2,376

Notes: 1. An adult man of 45 hours was hired-in, it was assumed, for the specific energy-value.
2. Figures in this column are based on actual data pertaining to West Bengal, India in 2004–2005; thus it will vary spatio-temporally.
3. In the 2004–2005 West Bengal dataset, the members of the households with crop cultivation as the occupation, adult female and male labourers, on average, were engaged with 44 and 32 days of work respectively during the Kharif season with an average length of 120 days. Thus, on average, of the duration of the season, the number of active days was one-third. It follows that for every active day, there were two inactive days, within the season. In other words, in the calculation only the nourishment towards 'own maintenance' of hired-in labour was taken into consideration, but not the reproduction of the associated labour-power.

The empirical illustration in Figure 4.1 shows a positive per-hectare surplus against gross cultivated area (GCA) for the scale(s) P and PM belonging to every size-class.[40] This impression is countered by the negative surplus against HM. We maintain that it is only the scale HM that incorporates the energy value against labour correctly following the metabolic framework; and it also shows the extent of unsustainability of farming households, as defined in this chapter. Even with the consideration of only the energy value of food, leaving aside all the remaining elements of 'means of subsistence', such a negative surplus was arrived at. To reiterate, the actual number of households with a negative actual surplus will be far more for the limitations of our method as stated earlier in this chapter. While it may be possible for some of them to yield a monetary surplus, but in real terms, they yield only a negative surplus.

Second, EROI of scale HM was lower than that of scale PM, which was lower than that of scale P, independent of the GCA; EROI falls under scale P against GCA, remains almost static under scale PM and rises under scale HM (Figure 4.2). These show, among other things, that possibilities of the so-called

---

[40] These size-classes were arrived at by dividing all households into 14 cohorts nearly equal in size, based on the GCA.

Figure 4.1
Surplus per Hectare, under Three Approaches, against GCA (in ha)

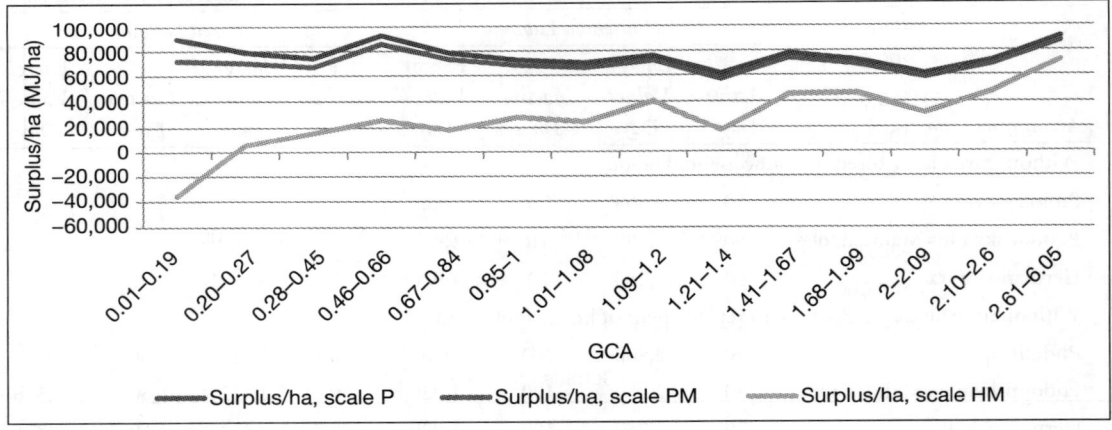

Figure 4.2
EROI under Three Approaches, against GCA (in ha)

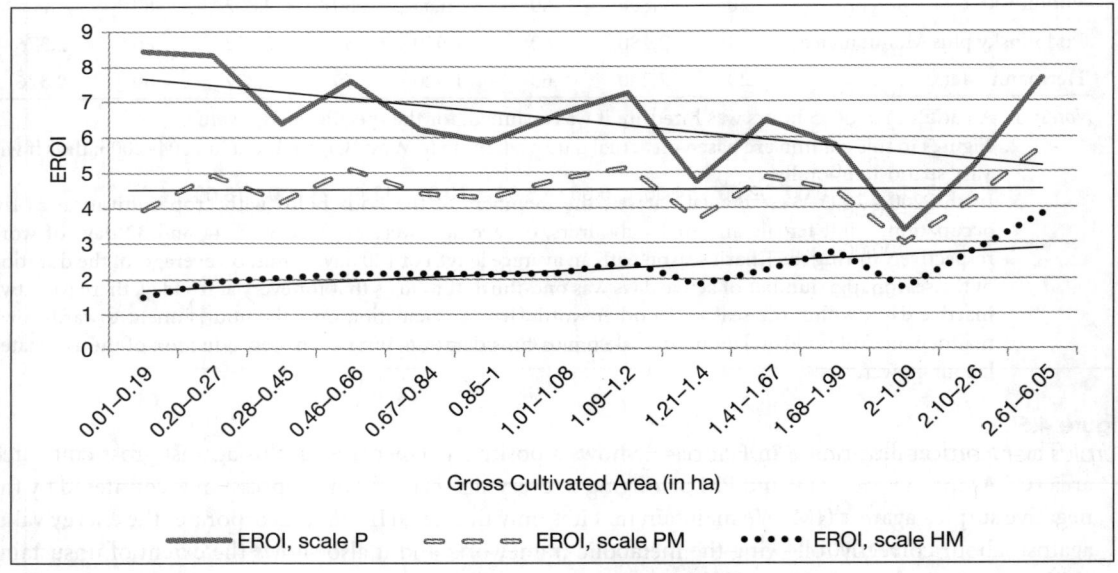

higher energy efficiency of small farms arise only under certain specific (and unrealistic) assumptions against human labour. In scale P, farming was considered merely as an 'activity' for the concerned labourer; in scale PM, it was regarded as 'livelihood', for inclusion of energy required for the non-active days but only for the labourer. On the other hand, scale HM considers many other 'supporting' activities that are carried out outside the farm boundary; such 'non-activities' are necessary for the sustenance of the labour-power—this inclusion underscores the social character of the scale HM. To put it differently, it is only under scale HM that the value of labour-power was attributed, and the result is an increasing EROI or energy efficiency with a rise in the area under cultivation.

Finally, Figures 4.3–4.5 illustrate the theoretical relationship stated earlier between per hectare surplus and EROI. It graphically shows that an identical per hectare surplus (and not surplus, as it depends on

Figure 4.3
Surplus per Hectare, against EROI, Scale P

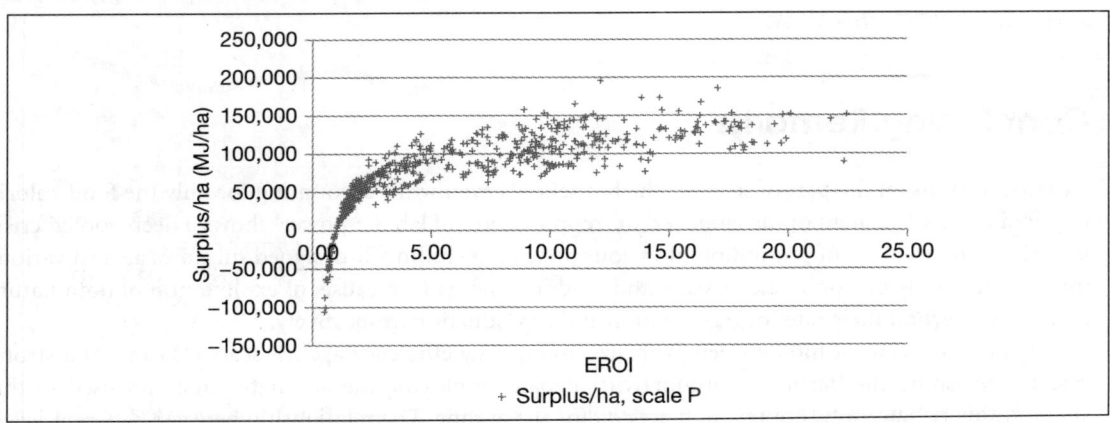

Figure 4.4
Surplus per Hectare, against EROI, Scale PM

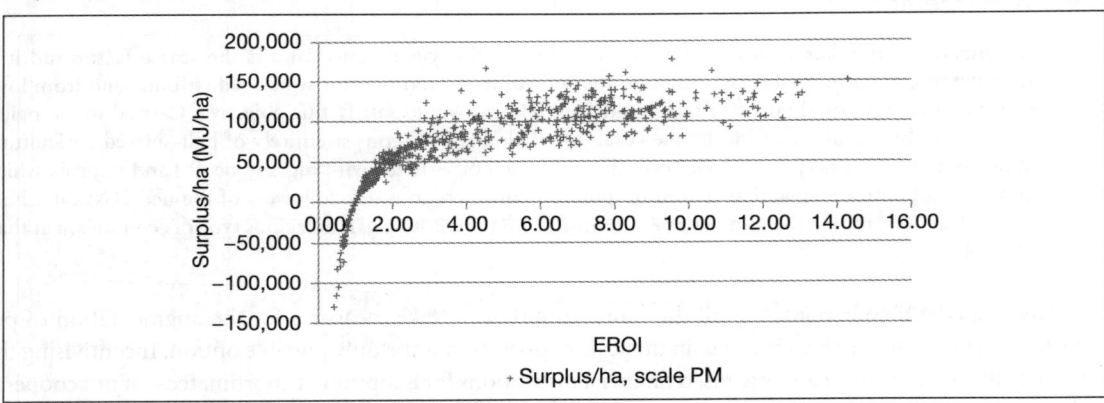

Figure 4.5
Surplus per Hectare, against EROI, Scale HM

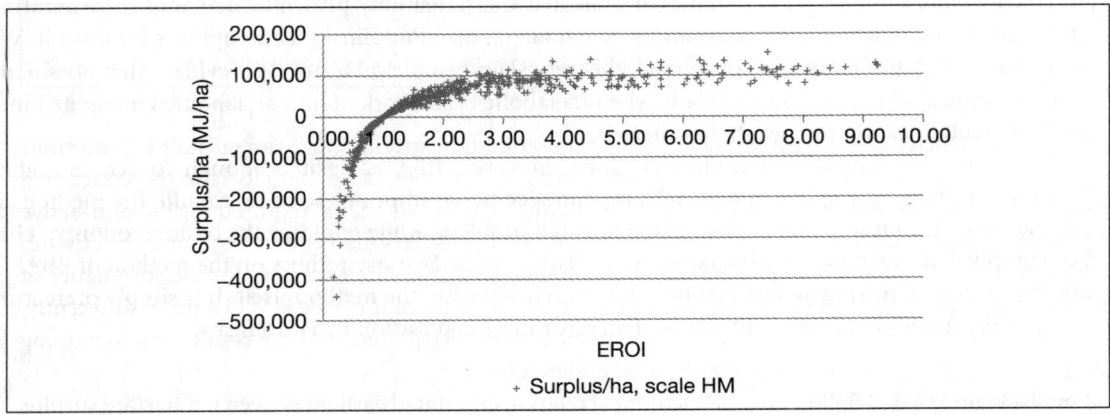

the GCA) can be obtained with a variety of EROI—alternatively, given an EROI the per hectare surplus can be increased by decreasing per hectare input, or a more intensive operation, the possibility of which arises only with a higher GCA.

Concluding Remarks

Negative surplus on the part of some of the households even while accounting for only the food-calorie required for 'replacement of the labourer' or 'reproduction of labour-power' shows a deep-rooted crisis in agriculture. Decades of promotion of various policies, including ill-designed subsidies against various inputs, could only postpone the crisis, without addressing its root cause, of exploitation of both nature and labour beyond their rates of regeneration and reproduction, respectively.

The positive relationship between farm size and energy efficiency against scale HM makes a strong case for revisiting the 'farm size productivity' debate employing the alternative method used in this chapter; this remains a future research agenda for the author. The relationship between different levels of EROI with identical per hectare surplus, among other things, reiterates the importance of economics of scale for augmentation of per hectare (and hence absolute) surplus, contesting the alleged economic basis of land re-distribution.

> The smallest family labour-based holdings have the highest yields; since land is the scarce factor and it is desirable to maximize output per unit area and total output, land reforms which redistribute land from low-yield hired labour-based farms to high-yield family farms would satisfy this objective. Carried to its logical conclusion, this implies that ideally the rural population should consist entirely of half-starved agricultural labour households since, as we have seen, these are the house-holds with highest yield! Land reforms which should be a political demand advanced on political considerations, the followers of the neo-classical school seek instead to garb it in the raiment of economism, and the most vulgar, fallacious type of economism at that. (Patnaik, 1982: 22)

Given the land constraint, it is all the more important to take measures for the augmentation of per hectare surplus, for which an increase in the scale of operation is the only possible option. Incentivising the farmers through credits from organised financial institutions for adoption of coordinated—if not cooperative—farming practices will certainly make both economic and ecological sense. While the ownership of land through land distribution or other reasons may provide a legal security or social prestige, it however cannot ensure economic well-being or livelihood security. Small may be beautiful, but not always.

To conclude, this chapter has shown that the 'basic sustainability principle' demands incorporation of the metabolic framework for accounting of human labour; Podolinsky's attempt was far from it. We have shown such limitations in conceptual, theoretical and empirical terms. It is evident that possibility of an 'ecological Marxism' can arise only when metabolic framework of human labour is integrated into the EBA; fault lines will remain sharp otherwise.

There is no reason why it cannot be done, however. EBA is flexible enough to accommodate 'heterodoxy', leaving ample scope for relaxing the specific assumptions so as to 'mould' the method, as per the context, contours and content of the research problem, while retaining the basic taxonomy; it has been amply demonstrated in this chapter. Criticism by some Marxist authors on the method of EBA[41] is arguably a case of mixing an application 'of' the method 'with' the method itself. It is simply premature to reject the method of EBA on the basis of an error in its application by Podolinsky.

---

[41] See Burkett and Foster (2008).

References

Anderson, J. (1776/1800). *Essays relating to agriculture and rural affairs* (5th edition, Vol. 3). London: Robinson and Cumming.

———. (1777). *An enquiry into the nature of the corn laws: With a view to the new corn bill proposed for Scotland.* Edinburgh: Mundell.

Aristotle. (350 BCE/2005). *Politics*, book one (trans. Benjamin Jowett). Retrieved from Digireads.com.

Bharadwaj, K. (1978). *Classical political economy and rise to dominance of supply and demand theories* (Romesh Chunder Dutt lectures on political economy). Kolkata: Centre for Studies in Social Sciences and Orient Longman.

———. (1989). *Themes in value and distribution.* Delhi: Oxford University Press.

Buel, J. (1847). *The farmer's instructor: Consisting of essays, practical directions, and hints for the management of the farm and the garden.* New York: Harper and Collins.

Bukharin, N. (1921/1969). *Historical materialism: A system of sociology* (translated from third Russian edition) (paperbacks for the study of Communism and Marxism). Ann Arbor, MI: University of Michigan Press.

Burkett, P. (2003). The value problem in ecological economics: Lessons from the Physiocrats and Marx. *Organization Environment, 16*(2), 137–167.

Burkett, P., & Foster, J.B. (2006). Metabolism, energy, and entropy in Marx's critique of political economy: Beyond the Podolinsky myth. *Theory and Society, 35*(1), 109–156.

———. (2008). The Podolinsky myth: An obituary introduction to 'human labour and unity of force' by Sergei Podolinsky. *Historical Materialism, 16*(1), 115–161.

Carey, H.C. (1858–1859). *The principles of social science* (Vol. 3). Philadelphia, PA: J.B. Lippincott & Co; London: Trubner & Co; and Paris: Guillamin & Co.

Cleveland, C.J. (1987). Biophysical economics. *Ecological Modelling, 38*(1–2), 47–73.

Costanza, R. (1980). Embodied energy and economic valuation. *Science, 210*(4475), 1219–1224.

Cottrell, F. (1955/2009). *Energy and society: The relationship between energy, social change, and economic development* (revised edition). New York: AuthorHouse, McGraw-Hill.

Dasgupta, P. (1993). *An inquiry into well-being and destitution.* Oxford: Clarendon Press.

Dasgupta, P., & Mäler, K.G. (1995). Poverty, institutions and the environmental resource-base. In J. Behrman & T.N. Srinivasan (Eds.), *Handbook of Development Economics* (Vol. 3A; pp. 2371–2463). Amsterdam: Elsevier Science.

De, D. (2005). *Energy use in crop production systems in India.* Bhopal: Central Institute of Agricultural Engineering.

Department of Agriculture and Cooperation (DAC). (2007). *National policy for farmers.* New Delhi: DAC, Ministry of Agriculture, Government of India.

Dobb, M. (1973). *Theories of value and distribution since Adam Smith: Ideology and economic theory.* London: Cambridge University Press.

Edwards, G.W. (1976). Energy budgeting: Joules or Dollars. *Australian Journal of Agricultural Economics, 20*(3), 179–191.

Engels, F. (1882/1968a). Engels to Marx in Ventnor; Marx-Engels Correspondence 1882. London: International Publishers. Retrieved from http://www.marxists.org/archive/marx/works/1882/letters/82_12_19.htm on 12 January 2016.

———. (1882/1968b). Engels to Marx in Ventnor; Marx-Engels Correspondence 1882. London: International Publishers. Retrieved from http://www.marxists.org/archive/marx/works/1882/letters/82_12_22.htm on 12 January 2016.

England, R. (1986). Production, distribution, and environmental quality: Mr. Sraffa reinterpreted as an ecologist. *Kyklos, 39*(2), 230–244.

Falcon, A. (2015). Aristotle on causality. In E.N. Zalta (Ed.), *The Stanford encyclopedia of philosophy.* Retrieved from http://plato.stanford.edu/archives/spr2015/entries/aristotle-causality on 13 January 2016.

Farber, S.C., Costanza, R., & Wilson, M.A. (2002). Economic and ecological concepts for valuing ecosystem services. *Ecological Economics, 41*(3), 375–392.

Foster, J.B., & Burkett, P. (2004). Ecological economics and classical Marxism: The "Podolinsky business" reconsidered. *Organization and Environment, 17*(1), 32–60.

Giampietro, M., Bukkens, S.G.F., & Pimentel, D. (1993). Labor productivity: A biophysical definition and assessment. *Human Ecology, 21*(3), 229–260.

Giampietro, M., & Pimentel, D. (1990). Assessment of energetics of human labor. *Agriculture, Ecosystems and Environment, 32*(3–4), 257–272.

Hermann, L. (1875). *Elements of human physiology* (translated from the 5th edition by Arthus Gamgee). London: Smith, Elder and Co.

Huettner, D.A. (1976). Net energy analysis: An economic assessment. *Science, New Series, 192*(4235), 101–104.

ICMR. (1990). *Nutrient requirements and recommended dietary allowances for Indians: A report of the expert group of ICMR*. Hyderabad: National Institute of Nutrition, Indian Council of Medical Research.

IFIAS. (1978). Energy analysis and economics: IFIAS workshop report. *Resources and Energy, 1,* 151–204.

Johnston, J. F. W. (1851). *Notes on North America: Agricultural, economical and social* (2 Vol.). Edinburgh & London: Charles C Little & James Brown; William Blackwood & Sons.

Jones, M.R. (1989). Analysis of the use of energy in agriculture: Approaches and problems. *Agricultural Systems, 29*(4), 339–355.

Leach, G. (1976). *Energy and food production*. Surrey, UK: IPC Science and Technology Press.

Liebig, J von. (1859). 'Letter X' in *Letters on modern agriculture: With addenda by a practical agriculturist embracing valuable suggestions* (adapted to the wants of American farmers). New York: J. Wiley.

Martinez-Alier, J. (2011). The EROI of agriculture and its use by the Via Campesina. *The Journal of Peasant Studies, 38*(1), 145–160.

Martinez-Alier, J. & Naredo, J.M. (1982). A Marxist precursor of energy economics: Podolinsky. *Journal of Peasant Studies, 9*(2), 207–224.

Martinez-Alier, J., & Schlüpmann, K. (1987). *Ecological economics: Energy, environment and society*. Oxford: Basil Blackwell.

Marx, K.H. (1867/1954). *Capital*. Three Vols.; Vol. 1 (translated by Samuel Moore and Edward Aveling, edited by Frederick Engels). Moscow: Progress Publishers.

Marx, K.H. (1863/1963). *Theories of surplus value*, 3 parts; part 1 (translated in English by Emile Burns, edited by S. Ryazanskaya). Moscow: Progress Publishers.

———. (1865/1969). *Value, price and profit: Speech by Marx to the first international working men's association*. New York: International Co. Inc. Retrieved from http://www.marxists.org/archive/marx/works/1865/value-price-profit/ on 11 January 2016.

Mayumi, K. (2001). Embodied energy analysis, Sraffa's analysis, Georgescu-Roegen's flow-fund model and viability of solar technology. In *The origins of ecological economics: The bioeconomics of Georgescu-Roegen*. London & New York: Routledge.

Meek, R.L. (1951). Physiocracy and classicism in Britain. *Economic Journal, 61*(241), 26–47.

———. (1962). *The economics of physiocracy: Essays and translations*. London: Ruskin House and George Allen & Unwin.

Mitchell, R. (1979). *The analysis of Indian agro-ecosystems*. New Delhi: Interprint.

Murphy, D.J., & Hall, C.A.S. (2010). Year in review—EROI or energy return on (energy) invested. *Annals of the New York Academy of Sciences, 1185*, 102–118.

National Sample Survey Organisation (NSSO). (2007). *Nutritional intake in India: 2004–2005*. New Delhi: NSSO, Ministry of Statistics and Programme Implementation, Government of India.

Nawn, N. (2012). *A comparative study of modern chemical-based agriculture and organic farms in terms of sustainability*. PhD thesis. New Delhi: Jawaharlal Nehru University, Mimeo.

———. (2013). Using cost of cultivation survey data: Changing challenges for researchers. *Economic and Political Weekly, 58*(26–27), 139–147.

———. (2014). Sustaining the farming household for sustaining the farming. *Journal of Agrarian Change*. Retrieved from http://onlinelibrary.wiley.com/doi/10.1111/joac.12085/pdf on 21 January 2016. Also published as Nawn, N. (2016). Sustaining the farming household for sustaining the farming. *Journal of Agrarian Change, 16*(1), January, 94–122.

———. (2015). Energetics of Irrigation under surplus rainfall conditions. In A. Shah, M. Panda, N. Ghosh, & P. Mukhopadhyay (Eds.), *Nature, economy, and society: Understanding the linkages* (pp. 133–161). Delhi: Indian Society for Ecological Economics and Springer.

Nilsson, S. (1974). Energy analysis: A more sensitive instrument for determining costs of goods and services. *Ambio, 3*(6), 222–224.

Norum, L. (1983). Problem formulation and quantification in energy analysis. *Energy in Agriculture, 2*, 1–10.
Patnaik, U. (1981). Neo-populism and Marxism: The Chayanovian view of the agrarian question and its fundamental fallacy: Part one. *Social Scientist, 9*(12), 26–35.
———. (1982). Neo-populism and Marxism: The Chayanovian view of the agrarian question and its fundamental fallacy: Part two. *Social Scientist, 10*(1), 11–35. (Originally published together as (1979) Neo-populism and Marxism: The Chayanovian view of the agrarian question and its fundamental fallacy. *The Journal of Peasant Studies, 6*(4), 375–420.)
Payne, P.R. (1985). The nature of malnutrition. In M. Biswas & P. Pinstrup-Andersen (Eds.), *Nutrition and development* (pp. 1–19). Oxford, New York, Tokyo: United Nations University and Oxford University Press.
Petty, W. (1662). 'Preface' to *Political Arithmetick*. In Charles Henry Hull (Ed.). 1899, *The economic writings of Sir William Petty* (2 vols), vol. 1, p. 244. Cambridge: Cambridge University Press.
Pimentel, D. (Ed.) (1980). *Handbook of energy utilization in agriculture*. Boca Raton, FL: CRC Press.
Pimentel, D., Hurd, L.E., Bellotti, A.C., Forster, M.J., Oka, I.N., Sholes, O.D., & Whitman, R.J. (1973). Food production and the energy crisis. *Nature, 182*(4111), 443–449.
Podolinsky, S. (1881/2004). Socialism and the unity of physical forces (originally *La Plebe, 14*(3), 13–16 and *14*(4), 5–15; English translation by A.D. Salvo and M. Hudson). *Organization and Environment, 17*(1), 61–75.
———. (1883/2008). *Human labour and unity of force* (translated in English by P. Thomas, editing and annotation by Paul Burkett and John Bellamy Foster). *Historical Materialism, 16*(1), 163–183.
Pretty, J.N. (Ed.). (2005). *The Earthscan reader in sustainable agriculture*. London and Sterling: Earthscan.
Punti, A. (1988). Energy accounting: Some new proposals. *Human Ecology, 16*(1), 79–86.
Rao, A.R. (1984). Bioenergetics of bullock power. *Energy, 9*(6), 541–543.
Roll, E. (1938). *History of economic thought* (5th impression). London: Faber and Faber.
Schaller, N. (1993). The concept of agricultural sustainability. *Agriculture, Ecosystems and Environment, 46*(1–4), 89–97.
Slesser, M. 1973. Energy subsidy as a criterion in food policy planning. *Journal of the Science of Food and Agriculture, 24*(10), 1193–1207.
———. (1978). *Energy analysis: Its utility and limits* (Research Memorandum No. RM-78-46). Laxenburg, Austria: International Institute for Applied Systems Analysis.
Stokes, K.M. (1992). *Man and the biosphere: Toward a coevolutionary political economy*. Armonk, NY: M.E. Sharpe.
Tripp, R. (2006). *Self-sufficient agriculture: Labour and knowledge in small-scale farming*. London and Sterling: Earthscan.
Worster, D. (1994). *Nature's economy: A history of ecological ideas* (2nd edition). New York: Cambridge University Press.

SECTION 2
Dealing with Globalisation: Trade, Capital, Technology

5

Secular Movements in the International Terms of Trade of Primary Commodities vis-à-vis Manufactured Goods: Towards an Explanation

Shouvik Chakraborty*

Introduction

> *No questions in political economy are of greater practical importance than those which relate to the terms of international exchange, or, in other words, to the causes which determine whether the produce of a given quantity of the labour of one country shall exchange for and be equivalent to the produce of an equal, or of a greater, or of a lesser quantity of labour of another country.*
>
> —Robert Torrens (1852: 32)

The issues related to the terms of international exchange assume immense significance in the sphere of economic discussions and in particular the discussions on political economy. Nearly all classical economists were convinced that the prices of primary produce had a tendency to rise over time relative to the prices of manufactures since production in the primary-producing sector was governed by the law of diminishing returns, whereas the manufacturing sector was subject to increasing returns and cost-reducing technical progress. For instance, the outstanding classical economist David Ricardo (1871/2004) had argued that the process of accumulation of capital would lead to a rise in terms of trade for primary commodities that are subject to diminishing returns; a rise that, with fixed subsistence real wages, causes the rate of profit to decline.

With the passage of time, a sharp contrast in the international distribution of wealth became apparent between the 'industrialised' and the 'primary-producing' countries; the widely held belief that the benefits of technological progress in the developed countries would trickle down to the underdeveloped

---

* The author is grateful to Prabhat Patnaik, Deepankar Basu, the referees and editors of this volume for their valuable inputs and comments on an earlier draft of this chapter. The author is also thankful to Robert Pollin for his support during the course of this research.

nations turned out to be a chimera. Even the view of the classical economists that the terms of trade of primary commodities vis-à-vis manufactures will show a secular upward trend did not seem to have any empirical validity. A report published by the United Nations (New York, 1949a) entitled *Relative prices of exports and imports of underdeveloped countries* provided statistics on the terms of trade.[1] It was constructed by dividing an import price index of Britain by a corresponding index of the export prices. The general trend during the whole period from 1876 to 1938 was markedly downward—average prices of primary commodities relative to manufactured goods had been declining over a period of more than half a century. This meant that, in 1938, a given quantity of primary exports would receive on average only 60 per cent of the quantity of manufactured goods which it could buy in the 1870s.

It is important here to mention the independent works of two great economists—Raul Prebisch and Hans Singer. Assuming that the developing countries are the major exporters of primary commodities while the developed countries primarily export manufactured goods, the research of Prebisch–Singer hypothesised a secular deterioration in the terms of the trade of the 'primary-producing' developing region (i.e., the periphery or the south) vis-à-vis the 'industrialised' developed region (i.e., the centre or the north). Both these authors provided the theoretical underpinnings behind the 'deterioration hypothesis', which later came to be popularly known as the Prebisch–Singer hypothesis in the economic literature.

The explanation put forward by Prebisch (United Nations 1949b, 1950, 1959) and Singer (1950) is mainly in terms of an unequal distribution of the fruits of technological progress. According to this hypothesis, the benefits of technological progress in the two sectors, that is, the manufactured goods sector and the primary commodity sector, percolate down very differently. In the former case, these benefits are distributed to the producers in the form of higher income. However, in the latter case, they get reflected in the form of lower prices. Singer (1950: 478) argued that technological progress in the manufacturing industries leads to a rise in incomes, whereas technological progress in the production of food and raw materials in the developing countries leads to a fall in their prices. Furthermore, the rise in the real income of the manufacturing sector through technological progress has different effects on the demand for primary commodities (that is, food and raw materials) and manufactured goods. This is due to the low income elasticity of demand for the primary commodities, through the operation of Engel's law, accompanied by the low price elasticity of demand for primary commodities compared to manufactured goods. In the case of food, the demand is not very sensitive to the rise in the real income and also there is a low price elasticity of demand. This is because food is a basic need–any income set free due to lower food prices will be devoted to the consumption of other goods rather than an increase in food consumption. In the case of raw materials, the technological improvement of the developed countries is devoted to economies in the use of primary commodities, that is, a reduction in the amount of raw materials used per unit of manufactured output and the development of synthetic substitutes for primary commodities. Hence, the demand for primary commodities is bound to expand less than the demand for manufactured goods with a rise in the real income of the manufacturing sector. Therefore, Singer (1950: 479) argued, "This lack of an automatic multiplication in demand, coupled with the low price elasticity of demand for both raw materials and food, results in large price falls, not only cyclical but also structural."

Prebisch (United Nations 1949b, 1950) independently discussed that the international division of labour was a major factor responsible for this secular decline. He argued that with the technological advancement in industrialised countries, the demand for raw materials would decline over time resulting in a displacement of labour from the primary-producing sector. Given the world political system of limited migration to industrialised nations and the obstacles hindering late industrialisation of the developing nations, the relative surplus labour displaced from primary activities tends to concentrate in the developing countries.

---

[1] While using the phrase 'terms of trade' in this chapter, I mainly refer to net barter terms of trade (NBTT) of primary commodities vis-à-vis manufactured goods.

This generates a huge labour surplus in the primary-commodity-producing sector, which tends to keep the real wages at their subsistence levels in the developing countries (Prebisch, 1964). Hence, technological progress and increased productivity results in lower prices rather than higher factor incomes in the primary commodity sector of the developing countries. On the other hand, in the industrialised countries, labour is organised into strong trade unions, and producers in strong monopolistic firms and producer organisations. This essentially means that the benefits of technological progress and increased productivity get largely absorbed in higher factor incomes rather than lower prices for consumers. Thus, Prebisch suggested that technological progress, resulting in an increase in the labour productivity, and its differential impact on the primary-commodity-producing sector and the manufactured goods sector was a major cause for the terms of trade deterioration.[2] The next section will argue that in an economy characterised by mark-up pricing of manufactured goods, the above-mentioned factors pointed out by Prebisch-Singer are inadequate to explain the secular decline in the terms of trade.

A Critique of Prebisch–Singer's Explanations on the Terms of Trade Deterioration

Prebisch and Singer and, in following their footsteps, many other economists (Sarkar, 1991) have argued that an increase in labour productivity results in a decline in the terms of trade. However, these arguments do not suffice as a proper explanation of the secular decline in the terms of trade when the pricing behaviour of the manufacturing sector is assumed to be based on prime cost plus profit mark–ups.[3]

Suppose p_a and p_i denote the prices in the primary commodity sector and the manufacturing sector, respectively. Then, the terms of trade is denoted by τ (that is equal to p_a/p_i). Let us also assume that α denotes the amount of primary commodity input required per unit of manufactured sector's output and λ_i denotes the labour input per unit of manufacturing output. We further assume that ω_i and μ_i denote the (fixed) product wage rate[4] and the profit mark-up in the industrial goods sector.

In a world of mark-up pricing, the industrial commodity price can be defined as

$$p_i = (\alpha \cdot p_a + \omega_i \cdot p_i \cdot \lambda_i)(1 + \mu_i) \qquad (5.1)$$

Rearranging the terms and dividing both sides by the industrial prices (p_i), we get

$$\tau = (1/\alpha) \cdot [1/(1+\mu_i) - \omega_i \cdot \lambda_i]. \qquad (5.2)$$

In this mathematical illustration, the capitalists in the manufacturing sector follow a prime cost plus pricing behaviour, that is, the prices are determined on a profit mark-up basis over the unit cost of production that includes the cost of raw materials and labour per unit of output. Now, we assume that labour productivity in the agricultural sector goes up. Further, we assume that money wages do not change in this sector. With a reduction in the labour coefficient at given money wages, the unit cost of labour falls, and *ceteris paribus* (with other conditions remaining the same) reduces the prices of the primary

---

[2] For a detailed discussion on the factors responsible for the secular fall in the terms of trade of primary commodities as formulated by Prebisch and Singer see Prebisch (1950, 1959, 1962, 1964), Singer (1950, 1975a,b, 1982/1984, 1987) and Singer and Meier (1958).
[3] This idea was originally developed in Patnaik (1997; 2002).
[4] Here, the assumption of a fixed product wage rate is a simplifying one. Even if the product wage rate is assumed alternatively to be fixed in terms of the primary commodity commanded, then also the argument would have remained the same. A similar assumption was also made by Patnaik (2002).

commodities. Since primary commodities constitute an essential input in the form of raw materials in the production of the manufactured goods, it would reduce the unit costs of production, and also reduce the cost of living of the workers in the manufacturing sector. A reduction in the cost of living index would lead to a fall in the money wages in the manufacturing sector, and hence, reduce the unit labour costs.[5] This, along with a fall in the unit raw material cost, would lead to a reduction in the unit prime cost of the manufacturing sector. Assuming that mark-up in the manufacturing sector is given, a reduction in the unit prime cost of production results in a proportionate fall in the price of manufactured goods and leaves the terms of trade unaffected. Mathematically, this implies that if any increase in labour productivity in the primary commodity sector lowers the prices of these commodities, then from Equation 5.2 it can be observed that, *ceteris paribus*, it equivalently leads to a reduction in the prices of the manufactured goods, leaving the terms of trade unaffected.[6] Hence, any increase in productivity in the primary commodity sector, even if 'passed on' in the form of lower prices, leaves the terms of trade unaffected.[7] Moreover, if such an increase in labour productivity does not lower the prices of primary commodities, then also the terms of trade remains unaltered (since left hand side of Equation 5.2 remains unchanged). Therefore, one can conclude, whether the labour productivity growth is 'passed on' in the form of lower prices in the primary commodity sector or not, the terms of trade are left unchanged.

Similarly, increases in the product wage rate of the industrial sectors in proportion to the increases in the labour productivity of the manufacturing sector leaves the prices of the manufacturing sector unaffected and thereby leaves the terms of trade unaffected. This implies that a reduction in λ_i (due to an increase in labour productivity by means of technological progress) is matched by a corresponding rise in ω_i. Therefore, from Equation 5.1, one can see that the industrial prices (p_i) remain unaffected; from Equation 5.2, it becomes evident that the terms of trade also remains unaltered.

The Impact of Demand–Supply Imbalance on the Terms of Trade

Bernstein (1960) was of the view that with technological progress in the manufacturing sector, the industrial production units of the developed countries would require less and less of primary commodities per unit of that output causing a secular fall in the raw material content of the industrial output. This would lead to a chronic surplus of the primary commodities causing a secular fall in the relative prices of these commodities. This argument also gets support in the writings of Prebisch (1950), Singer (1950) and Sundrum (1983), who feel that many of the commodities exported by the developing countries were subject to synthetic substitution and, hence, to a decline in demand.

This argument has deep implications, some beyond the issue of reduction in the terms of trade, and hence, merits a detailed discussion. An important implication is that the dependence of the industrialised countries on the developing countries as a source of raw materials for their industrial production has declined over the years. One may further extend the argument to put forward the hypothesis that, with technological progress, the requirement of raw materials for the production of manufactured goods in the industrial countries may not exist at all in the near future. However, these arguments are fallacious. For instance, Harry Magdoff

---

[5] However, for our argument, it is not essential that money wages should fall in proportion with the cost of the living index. The assumption of fall in money wages is a mere simplification.

[6] If the right hand side of Equation 5.2 remains constant, then a X per cent reduction in the primary commodity prices (p_a) leads to a X per cent reduction in the manufactured goods prices (p_i), leaving the terms of trade unaltered.

[7] Further, if the increase in productivity is not passed on to lower the primary commodity prices, then at given money wages, it would essentially lead to an increase in the profit margin of the primary commodity–producing sector. However, this also would leave the terms of trade unaffected.

(1969) criticised the latter argument on the grounds that even though the requirement of raw materials for industrial production had been going down over the years, it did not imply that the industrialised countries do not need raw materials at all. There still exists a huge demand for raw materials for the manufacturing sector and raw materials continue to be an essential component in the production of finished manufactured goods. The other criticism put forward by Patnaik (1997: 156) relies on Marx's distinction between 'use value' and 'exchange value'. Patnaik's argument is that the requirement of raw materials has not declined over the years; technological progress in the advanced countries has been successful in replacing one form of raw material with another. He argues that even if the value of raw material used per unit of manufactured output is lower, then also it does not entail that there have been any physical savings in the use of raw materials since a new substitute raw material is used in the production of the manufactured goods. This is due to the fact that one use value cannot be directly compared to another. The value of this new substitute raw material being less than the one used earlier is due to the fact that the amount of labour needed to produce this new raw material is less than that of the one used earlier. However, the wage rate in this new raw-material-producing sector has not gone up *pari passu* (at the same rate) with the increase in labour productivity in this sector. This means that the productivity of labour in terms of the value equivalent that its product replaces has gone up while its real wages have not gone up correspondingly and, thereby, explains the factors behind the decline in the share of the value of raw materials in the gross value of the manufactured output. Hence, the issue of reduction in the raw material use per unit of gross output does not have theoretical or empirical support, the latter being difficult to estimate and beyond the scope of this study.

Arguing on similar lines, there is another view in the literature that demand–supply imbalances in the global primary commodity sector lead to secular changes in the international terms of trade. Many arguments come from this demand–supply framework, namely an excess supply of the primary commodities (or a deficient demand) causing a secular fall in terms of trade. For instance, Borensztein and Reinhart (1994) considered supply and demand conditions playing a key role in explaining the weakness in international terms of trade, particularly since the 1980s.[8] According to this theory, an excess supply of the primary commodities in the international commodity market was responsible for the secular decline in the terms of trade. In the next section, we show that, when the capitalists in the manufacturing sector follow a prime cost plus pricing behaviour, demand and supply imbalances in the international commodity market cannot explain the secular trends in the terms of trade.

Demand–Supply Imbalances Cannot Cause a Secular Decline in the Terms of Trade

In a world of mark-up pricing as described by Equation 5.1, the prices of the manufactured goods also get affected by the rise or fall in the primary commodity prices, but it is from the cost side. If there is a decline in the prices of the primary commodities due to an excess supply in the market, then it also reduces the unit input cost of production and also the cost of the living index resulting in a fall in the unit labour costs. Given the same level of mark-up, this would reduce the price level in the manufacturing sector, leaving the terms of trade unaffected. Conversely, if the primary commodity prices rise due to excess demand, then also these leave the terms of trade unaffected given that they causes a *pari passu* rise in the prices of the manufactured goods (i.e., inflation in the industrialised countries; Kaldor, 1983: 545).

Arguments based on the changing prices of the primary commodity due to demand–supply imbalances can lead to movements in the terms of trade only if there is a lag in the adjustment of manufactured goods prices, that is, if the mark-up is applied with a lag. But even if there is such a lag, the theories that

---

[8] For a detailed analysis, see Aizenman and Borensztein (1988), Reinhart and Wickham (1994) and Gilbert (1989). Explaining the fall in the relative commodity prices of the 1980s, Bleaney and Greenaway (1993: 355) also supported this argument.

have been advanced, adducing demand–supply imbalances for an explanation of the decline in the terms of trade, can work only in the short run and not in the long run when adjustments in demand and supply themselves become possible.

In Prebisch–Singer hypothesis, there is no explicit theory of the demand–supply behaviour of primary commodities in explaining the secular decline in terms of trade. Although the authors mention the low income and price elasticity of demand for primary commodities, the impact of it on the terms of trade needs to be examined through the cost side as far as the manufactured goods sector is concerned (since its price is cost determined). In the Prebisch–Singer hypothesis, there is an implicit assumption regarding the supply and demand behaviour of the primary commodities. The presumption is that, in the long run, the supply of the primary commodity adjusts to the changes in the demand for it. Therefore, demand–supply equilibrium is always maintained in the primary commodity market in the long run.

Indeed the entire discussion along these lines is not quite distinguished between the short-run and long-run factors of price determination in these two sectors.[9] It is certainly true that, in the short run with some given configuration of money wages, the terms of trade clearly depends upon the sizes of the two sectors, which are the major determinants of the demand for and supply of primary commodities.[10] This is primarily because the supply of agricultural products is inelastic in the short run and responds to a change in demand after a time lag. In the short run, an increase in demand causes a reduction of stocks, and a rise in the price level, which might get enhanced by speculative behaviour in the commodity market. Assuming that the manufacturing sector prices are sticky in the short run, this will turn the terms of trade in favour of the primary commodities.[11] However, in the long run when supply adjustments can occur, so that the relative sizes of the two sectors become variable, this explanation of the secular decline in terms of trade does not hold any longer. Now, let us see how this takes place.

As mentioned earlier, the implicit presumption in Prebisch–Singer is that in the long run the supply of primary commodities adjusts to the demand for it, which after all is why they relate the movements in the terms of trade to more basic factors like the differential responses of the two sectors to productivity increases. This suggests that, in the long run, equilibrium can be maintained in the commodity market even for different values of terms of trade, that is, there is some mechanism in operation which ensures that there is an equilibrium rate of growth of supply and demand in the primary commodity sector at different levels of terms of trade in the long run. Here, we make an attempt to explain this mechanism through which the rate of growth of supply adjusts to the rate of growth of demand for the primary commodities in the long run.

Suppose there is an equilibrium rate of profit (r^*), at which there is an equilibrium achieved between the rates of growth of supply (s) and demand (d) in the primary-commodity-producing sector. We further assume that the rate of growth of demand for the primary commodities is exogenously given. Now, if the rate of profit (r) in the primary commodity sector exceeds that equilibrium rate of profit (r^*), then the rate of growth of supply (s) exceeds the rate of growth of demand (d). Likewise, the converse also holds true. From this it follows that if the rate of profit equals the equilibrium rate of profit, then the rate of growth of supply adjusts to the autonomous rate of growth of demand in the primary-commodity-producing sector. Therefore, demand–supply imbalances can get eliminated in the long run with the rate of growth of supply equalising the rate of growth of demand through a self-adjusting mechanism, that is, the adjustments of profit rate (Figure 5.1). By this mechanism, in the long run, the rate of profit will be equal to its equilibrium rate of profit, thereby eliminating any demand–supply imbalances in the primary commodity sector.

---

[9] Here, short run is defined in the sense that the primary sector output is given, whereas in the long run the primary sector output itself adjusts to changes in demand.

[10] These arguments are developed mainly on the basis of the arguments in Kalecki (1971).

[11] Chakraborty (2015) has argued that the recent increase in terms of trade since 2005 can be explained by this phenomenon.

Figure 5.1
Time Path of the Rate of Profit

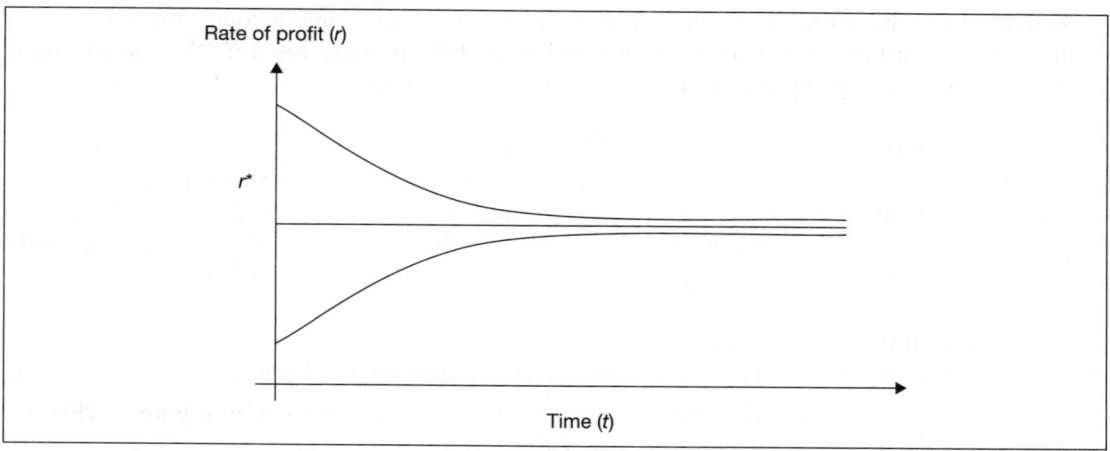

Mathematically, if in the primary [...] period t, then,

$$(s_t - d_t) = a \cdot (r_t - r^*), \quad (5.3)$$

where r_t is the rate of profit in the primary-commodity-producing sector, r^* denotes the equilibrium rate of profit and a denotes some arbitrary constant such that $a > 0$.

The change in the rate of profit over time can be written as:

$$dr/dt = b \cdot (d_t - s_t), \quad (5.4)$$

where dr/dt denotes the change in the rate of profit with time and b denotes some arbitrary constant such that $b > 0$.

Now, if $s_t = d_p$ then $r_t = r^*$, that is, at the equilibrium rate of growth of demand for and supply of primary commodities, the rate of profit in the primary commodity sector equals the equilibrium rate of profit.

Now, if $s_t \neq d_p$ then

$$dr/dt = -b \cdot (s_t - d_t)$$
or $\quad dr/dt = -ab(r - r^*) \quad$ (substituting from Equation 5.3)
or $\quad dr/dt = abr^* - abr$
or $\quad dr/dt = c - n \cdot r,$

where $c = abr^*$ and $n = ab$.

Therefore, if $s_t > d_p$ then $dr/dt < 0$, that is, the rate of profit in the primary-commodity-producing sector will tend to fall to the value of the equilibrium rate of profit over time, or if $s_t < d_p$ then $dr/dt > 0$, that is, the rate of profit in the primary-commodity-producing sector will tend to rise to the value of the equilibrium rate of profit in the long run.

In other words, it may be thought that the terms of trade determines the rate of profit in the primary commodity sector, so that at a given level of terms of trade, there will be some unique rate of profit which may differ from r^*. Putting it differently there will be only one particular terms of trade at which the equilibrium rate of profit can be obtained. But, this is not the case. The rate of profit not only depends upon the terms of trade but also on the share of wages in output in the commodity sector. If the share of wages can be adjusted so as to accommodate the movements in the terms of trade, then the equilibrium rate of profit can be maintained at different levels of terms of trade.

Suppose the capitalists in the primary commodity sector earn a certain amount of profit (P). We further assume that they have to import capital (K) in the form of machines from the manufacturing sector. Therefore, the rate of profit in such an economy can be defined as,

$$r = (P/K) \cdot (p_a / p_i) \tag{5.5}$$

$$\text{or} \quad r = (P/K) \cdot (\tau)$$

$$\text{or} \quad r = (P/O) \cdot (O/K) \cdot (\tau), \tag{5.6}$$

where O denotes the output, and therefore,

(P/O) (=π) denotes the share of profit, and
(K/O) denotes the capital–output ratio of the primary commodity sector.

We assume that the K/O ratio remains constant such that $\beta = O/K$ is given in the economy. Then, we can say that the rate of profit in the primary commodity sector is denoted by:

$$r = (\pi)(\beta)(\tau) \tag{5.7}$$

$$= f(\pi, \tau). \tag{5.8}$$

where f denotes a function of the share of profit and the terms of trade (τ).

From Equation 5.7, it can be seen that at any given terms of trade if the share of profit could be made to adjust appropriately, then the equilibrium rate of profit r^* could rule; if there is any decline in the terms of trade due to some exogenous factors, then an appropriate movement in the share of profit could still keep the primary commodity sector at the equilibrium rate of profit. Therefore, in such an economy, we can say that if the share of profit in the primary commodity sector can be adjusted so as to accommodate the movements in the terms of trade, then the capitalists can maintain the equilibrium rate of profit at different levels of terms of trade.

Here, the question which naturally arises is: "Is there any way that such changes in the share of profit occur in the primary commodity sector to maintain the equilibrium rate of profit in the long run at alternative levels of the terms of trade?" Such adjustments can be made (without affecting the equilibrium rate of profit) due to the fact that there is a class of primary commodity sector workers, whose wage shares can be adjusted to accommodate these changes in share of profit, that is, they act as price-takers.[12] Now suppose, there is a decline in the terms of trade. This decline in the terms of trade does not affect the rate of profit in the primary commodity sector because there lies a huge 'reserve army of labour' in this sector whose wages can be squeezed to maintain this equilibrium rate of profit. The adjustments in the share of wages in the primary commodity sector are possible because the large body of workers in this sector remain unorganised, or sufficiently weak in terms of their ability to bargain, and therefore cannot enforce in a sustained manner their *ex ante* claims on the output.

So far we have seen that changes in the share of profit *can* maintain the rate of profit at the equilibrium level even at different levels of the terms of trade. But does this *necessarily occur*? Or putting it differently, the fact that this can occur does not mean that it necessarily does occur. Is there any mechanism through which it necessarily occurs? In fact, there is. Let us imagine that there is a change in the terms of trade, which at the existing share of profits in the primary commodity sector lowers the rate of profit below r^*. This would

---

[12] Suppose we assume that output in the primary commodity sector gets distributed in the form of wages and profits only. Then, we can say that, $O = W + P$. Therefore, after re-arranging the terms, we can say that $(W/O) = 1 - (P/O)$.

cause a fall in the rate of growth of supply below the rate of growth of demand and, hence, an increase in the prices of the primary commodity in terms of the wage unit. This raises the share of profits in the primary commodity sector and the rate of profit, until r^* is reached, at which point there would be a lower level of the terms of trade for primary commodities, but a new market equilibrium with demand and supply growing in tandem. In this adjustment process, the entire brunt of maintaining the rate of profit of the capitalists at the equilibrium level is borne by the workers in the primary commodity sector. The wage share of these workers acts as a residue, that is, the burden of demand–supply equilibrium of primary commodities in the long run at any given terms of trade is borne by workers of the primary commodity sector.

Therefore, one can argue that though supply–demand imbalances can have an impact on the terms of trade in the short run, their impact gets eliminated in the long run with supply adjusting to demand. As a consequence, the changes in the terms of trade due to demand and supply imbalances are a transitory phenomenon since any such disparity, arising due to the differences in the rates of growth of the supply of and demand for primary commodities, disappears in the long run. However, in the long run, there are some autonomous factors which can cause a secular decline in the terms of trade at that equilibrium rate of profit. In the next section, we look into these long-run autonomous factors that have been responsible for the secular decline in the terms of trade and empirically test their validity in explaining this secular decline.

Factors Responsible for the Secular Decline in the Terms of Trade and Its Empirical Validity

We assume that there is an autonomous rise in the wage share of the manufactured goods sector (perhaps due to greater trade union strength in the manufacturing sector of the 'advanced' countries). This, in turn, leads to an increase in the price level of the manufactured goods, given that the profit mark-up in the manufacturing sector remains constant. Then, it follows that such a rise in the price level of the manufacturing sector will, *ceteris paribus*, lead to a decline in the terms of trade. From Equation 5.2, we can see that an increase in $\omega_i \lambda_i$ will, *ceteris paribus*, lead to a decline in the terms of trade. A similar case can be made out for an autonomous increase in the profit mark-up in the manufacturing sector. An increase in the profit mark-up will imply that the prices in the manufacturing sector go up, assuming that the wage share of the workers in the manufactured goods sector remains unchanged and, *ceteris paribus*, leads to a secular decline in the terms of trade. In Equation 5.2, this means that an increase in μ will lead to a secular decline in τ. Therefore, in our opinion, the two factors which can cause a secular decline in the terms of trade are: an increase in the wage share or an increase in the profit share in the gross output of manufacturing sector or an increase in both these shares.

In the following section, this proposition is empirically tested by studying the relationship between the terms of trade and the hypothesised variables discussed earlier, namely the wage share and the profit share in the gross value output of the manufacturing sector in advanced countries from 1970.[13] The underlying assumption of this empirical exercise is that the manufactured goods are exported by the developed economies, whereas the developing nations are the major exporters of primary commodities. Such an assumption has a strong empirical basis. Figure 5.2 shows the ratio of the developed economies' among the major exporters of manufactured goods in the world economy from 1970 to 2011. Although this ratio has declined in the recent past, it is evident that over the bulk of the period (i.e., from 1970 to 1993) the developed nations accounted for more than four-fifths in the exports of manufactured goods and continue to account for more than three-fifths of the manufacturing exports till date.

---

[13] An analysis of the pre-1970s period is not possible due to non-availability of data on profit, tax and wages of the manufacturing sector in the G7 countries. The definitions followed for these variables on an individual country basis are taken from United Nations (1994, 2005).

Figure 5.2
Share of Developed Countries among the Major Exporters of Manufactured Goods (1970–2011)

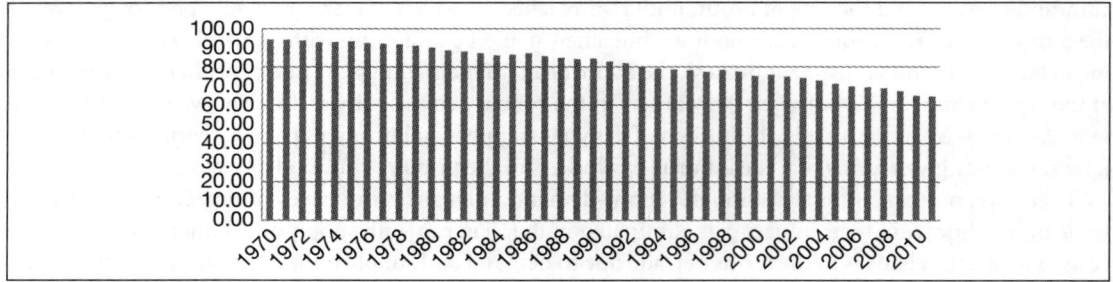

Source: *UNCTAD Handbook of Statistics*, various issues.

In the present world economic order, among the developed nations, the G7 is the nucleus of manufacture exports and has been a major player in the world trade of manufactured goods.[14] Figure 5.3 shows the ratio of these seven countries' exports to the exports of the major manufacturing exporters among the developed nations over the period 1980–2011. The domination of the world market in manufacturing exports by these seven countries clearly shows that the G7 is a major player in the manufacturing sector.

To find whether our hypothesis holds true, the behaviour of the wage share and profit share in the gross output of the manufacturing sector of the G7 countries is analysed. First, we consider the ratio of compensation to employees to the gross output in the manufacturing sector as an approximate alternative for wage share in the gross output. For the G7 countries on the whole, the ratio of wages to gross output of the manufacturing sector declined from 25.07 per cent in 1970 to 18.89 per cent in 2005 (Figure 5.4). The overall impression from the figure (as evident from the linear trend line) is that the ratio of wages to gross output of the manufacturing sector is declining over the study period. Second, we consider the ratio of the operating surplus to the gross output in the manufacturing sector as an approximate alternative for the profit share in the gross output. The overall impression is that of an increasing trend (observed from the linear trend line in Figure 5.5).

To estimate the extent of the effects of these variables, that is, the share of wages and the share of profits on the international terms of trade, we run a simple linear regression. The linear regression equation is of the following form:

$$\log(ToT)_t = \lambda + a \cdot \log(\text{wage})_t + b \cdot \log(\text{profit})_t + \varepsilon. \tag{5.9}$$

Our hypothesis is that an increase in the wage share or profit share leads to a secular decline in the terms of trade. However, from Figure 5.4, we can see from the linear trend line that the wage share has declined over the study period (1970–2005). Hence, the movements in wages could not have played a significant role in causing a secular decline in the terms of trade, whereas the rising ratio of profits to gross output in the manufacturing sector seems to be an important factor. To capture the impact of profits on the international terms of trade, Equation 5.9 is modified into:

$$\log(\text{ToT})_t = \alpha + \beta \cdot \log(\text{profit})_t + \varepsilon_t. \tag{5.9a}$$

---

[14] The G7, which is a group of seven highly advanced and industrialised nations, comprises the following nations: the United States of America, Canada, Italy, Germany, France, Japan and the United Kingdom.

Figure 5.3
Share of G7 Countries among the Major Manufacture Exporters: Developed Countries (1980–2011)

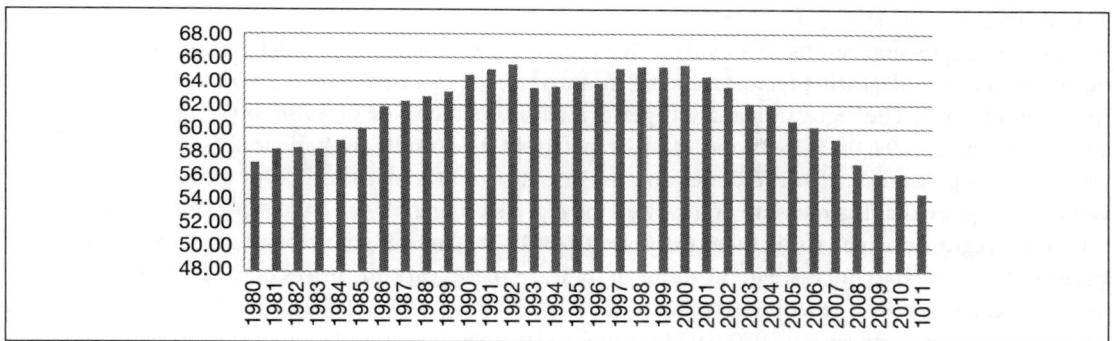

Source: UNCTAD *Handbook of Statistics*, various issues and International Trade Statistics, WTO, various issues.

Figure 5.4
Ratio of Wages to Gross Output in the Manufacturing Sector of the G7 Countries (1970–2005)

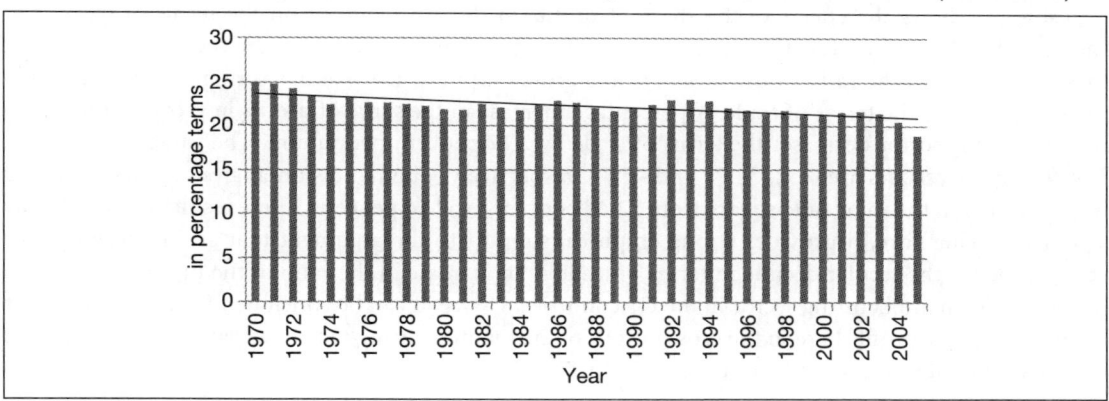

Source: Author's calculations based on National Accounts Main Aggregates Database, United Nations.

Figure 5.5
Ratio of Profits to Gross Output in the Manufacturing Sector of the G7 Countries (1970–2005)

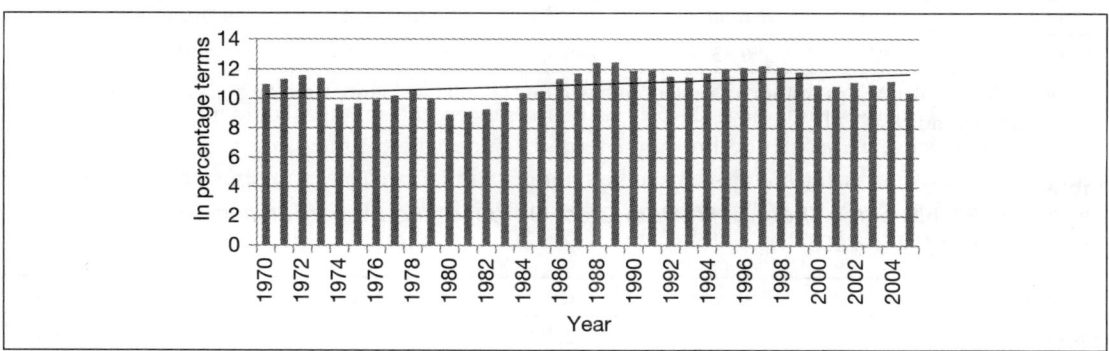

Source: Author's calculations based on National Accounts Main Aggregates Database, United Nations.

A linear regression is carried out by taking the share of profits in gross output as the independent variable and the international terms of trade as the dependent variable over a time period from 1970 to 2005. The observations are summarised in Table 5.1.

From the regression results, it is evident that a percentage increase in the share of profits in the gross output of the manufacturing sector of the G7 countries leads to a decline of 1.93 per cent per annum in the terms of trade. The regression analysis performed shows the value of *constant* (α), *R-square*, *F-value* and *t-value* to be −3.94, 0.33, 16.35 and −4.04, respectively. The results are statistically significant at 99 per cent level of significance. However, one can raise doubts from the statistical point of view about the low value of *R*-square that is a measure of how well the regression line fits the data. A possible reason for this is that our regression analysis includes the years 1970–1973. These are the years, that is, 1970–1973, that were marked by a sharp increase in the terms of trade. In these years, the prices of the primary commodities had nearly doubled, reaching stratospheric levels. The huge rise in the primary commodity prices spanning over this time period 1970–1973 is usually explained in terms of demand–supply imbalances in the primary commodity sector (Hone, 1973: 84–85). But here we are trying to empirically test the factors responsible for a decline in the terms of trade from the long-run perspective. Therefore, in our framework of analysis, we can consider the period from 1970 to 1973 as an 'aberration' and limit the time span of our analysis from 1974 to 2005.

Table 5.2 shows the effects of the share of profits in the gross output on the terms of trade over the period 1974–2005. Here, the results provide strong evidence in favour of the theoretical argument that an increase in the ratio of the profits to the gross output of the manufacturing sector results in a secular decline in the terms of trade. A percentage increase in the share of profits in gross output of the manufacturing sector decreases the terms of trade by 2.17 per cent per annum. The values of *R-square*, *F-value* and *t-statistics* are 0.52, 32.71 and −5.72, respectively. The regression analysis shows a marked improvement in the value of *R*-square from 32.47 per cent to 52.16 per cent. These results are statistically significant. Therefore, it provides strong empirical support to the argument that an important factor responsible for the secular decline in terms of trade is an increase in the ratio of the profits to the gross output of the manufacturing sector in the G7 countries. Hence, it can be concluded from this study that an increase in the profit share in the gross output of the manufacturing sector caused a secular decline in the international terms of trade over the period 1974–2005.

Table 5.1
Regression Results of the Share of Profits in Gross Output of the Manufacturing Sector on the Terms of Trade (1970—2005)

Variable	β	R-square	F-value	Root MSE	t-statistic	$P>|t|$
Profit	−1.93	0.33	16.35	0.26	−4.04	0.00

Source: Author's Calculations Author's calculations based on National Accounts Main Aggregates Database, United Nations and UNCTAD.

Table 5.2
Regression Results of the Share of Profits in Gross Output of the Manufacturing Sector on the Terms of Trade (1974–2005)

Variable	β	R-square	F-value	Root MSE	t-statistic	$P>|t|$
Profit	−2.17	0.52	32.71	0.21	−5.72	0.00

Source: Author's Calculations Author's calculations based on National Accounts Main Aggregates Database, United Nations and UNCTAD.

References

Aizenman, J., & Borensztein, E. (1988). Debt and conditionality under endogenous terms of trade adjustment. *IMF Staff Papers, 35*(4), 686–713.
Bernstein, E.M. (1960). *International effects of U.S. economic policy: Study of employment, growth and price levels* (Working Paper No. 16). Washington: United States Congress Joint Economic Committee.
Bleaney, M., & Greenaway, D. (1993). Long-run trends in the relative prices of primary commodities and in the terms of trade of developing countries. *Oxford Economic Papers, 45*(3), 349–363.
Borensztein, E., & Reinhart, C.M. (1994). The macroeconomic determinants of commodity prices. *IMF Staff Papers, 41*(2), 236–261.
Chakraborty, S. (2015). Explaining the rise in agricultural prices: Impact of neoliberal policies on the agrarian economy. *Agrarian South: Journal for Political Economy, 4*(2), 232–258.
Gilbert, C.L. (1989). The impact of exchange rates and developing country debt on commodity prices. *The Economic Journal, 99*(397), 773–784.
Hone, A. (1973). The primary commodities boom. *New Left Review, 1*(81), 82–92.
Kaldor, N. (1983). The role of commodity prices in economy recovery. *Lloyds Bank Review, 149*(July), 21–34.
Kalecki, M. (1971). *Selected essays on the dynamics of the capitalist economy.* Cambridge: Cambridge University Press.
Magdoff, H. (1969). *The age of imperialism.* New York: Monthly Review Press.
Patnaik, P. (1997). *Accumulation and stability under capitalism.* Oxford: Clarendon Press.
———. (2002). Globalization of capital and terms of trade movements. In V.K. Ramachandran & M. Swaminathan (Eds.), *Agrarian studies: essays on agrarian relations in less developed countries.* New Delhi: Tulika Books.
Prebisch, R. (1950). *The economic development of Latin America and its principal problems* (UN Document No. E/CN.12/89/Rev.1). Lake Success: United Nations Department of Economic Affairs.
———. (1959). Commercial policy in the underdeveloped countries. *The American Economic Review, 49*(2), 251–273.
———. (1962). The economic development of Latin America and its principal problems. *Economic Bulletin for Latin America, 7*(1), 1–22.
———. (1964). *Towards a new trade policy for development.* New York: United Nations, UNCTAD.
Reinhart, C.M., & Wickham, P. (1994). Commodity prices: Cyclical weakness or secular decline? *IMF Staff Papers, 41*(2), 175–213.
Ricardo, D. (1871/2004). *The works and correspondence of David Ricardo, Volume I: Principles of political economy and taxation* (Piero Sraffa & M.H. Dobb, Eds.). Indianapolis: Liberty Fund.
Sarkar, P. (1991). *Theories of worsening north-south terms of trade from Prebisch–Singer to Emmanuel: A survey and synthesis* (CSSS Occasional Paper No. 130). Kolkata: Centre for Studies in Social Sciences.
Singer, H.W. (1950). The distribution of gains between investing and borrowing countries. *The American Economic Review, 40*(2), 473–485.
———. (1975a). *The strategy of international development.* London: Macmillan.
———. (1975b). The distribution of gains from trade and investment-revisited. *Journal of Development Studies, 11*(4), 376–382.
———. (1982/1984, November). *Terms of trade controversy and the evolution of soft financing: Early years in the U.N.: 1947–1951* (IDS Discussion Paper No. 181). Republished in Meier, M. & Seers, D. (Eds.), *Pioneers in development.* New York: Oxford University Press.
———. (1987). Terms of trade and economic development. In J. Eatwell, H.M. Milgate, & P. Newman (Eds.), *The new palgrave: A dictionary of economics* (323–328). London: Macmillan.
Singer, H.W., & Meier, G.M. (1958). The terms of trade and economic development: Comment. *The Review of Economics and Statistics, 40*(1), 85–90.
Sundrum, R.M. (1983). *Development economics: Framework for analysis and policy.* New York: Wiley & Sons.
Torrens, R. (1852). *Tracts on finance and trade, No. II.* London: Chapman & Hall.
United Nations. (1949a). *Relative prices of exports and imports of underdeveloped countries.* Lake Success, New York: United Nations Department of Economic Affairs.
———. (1949b). *Post-war price relations in trade between under-developed and industrialized countries* (UN Document No. E/CN.1/Sub.3/W.5). Lake Success, New York: United Nations Department of Economic Affairs.
———. (1994). *System of national accounts 1993.* New York: United Nations, Department of Economic and Social Affairs.
———. (2005). *National accounts statistics: Main aggregates and detailed tables.* New York: United Nations Publications.

6
Global Rebalancing: Limitations of the East-Asia-centric Approach and the Role of Europe

Sabyasachi Kar*

Introduction

The group of 20 developed and emerging countries (G20), which has agreed to coordinate global macroeconomic policies, has identified rebalancing of global imbalances as one of their biggest priorities. These imbalances refer to the pattern of current account deficits and surpluses that had emerged in the global economy since the late 1990s (IMF, April 2009) and persisted until the beginning of the global economic crisis. In particular, it involved the large current account deficit of the US and corresponding surpluses of China, Japan and other East-Asian economies. An important aspect of this phenomenon is that large volumes of financial capital and savings were flowing from the surplus economies to the US economy. If these flows are not checked in time, this leads to an ever-increasing stock of net foreign liabilities for the latter, which is held by the rest of the world. This phenomenon is of great concern to the global economy, because it is felt that such trends in international movements in capital cannot be sustained forever, as there could be a ceiling to the demand for US assets made by international investors. Once these ceilings are reached (or even if we are close to it) there could be a sudden reversal in these trends in capital flows that would cause a collapse of the US dollar (Edwards, 2006; Feldstein, 2008). Since the US dollar is still the only global medium of exchange, its collapse could lead to a breakdown of the global financial architecture.

Apart from this major systemic cost that the global imbalances potentially pose to the global financial stability, they also have country-specific implications. These costs are different for deficit and surplus countries. As far as the deficit countries are concerned, the huge capital inflows due to the imbalance can overwhelm the capacity of even the most sophisticated financial systems to intermediate them, leading to a breakdown in this sector. A recent example is the period before the global crisis, when these capital

---

* This chapter was written as a part of the international research project AUGUR, which was funded by the European Commission's Seventh Framework Programme. I would like to thank Francis Cripps and Terry McKinley for useful comments on earlier drafts of the chapter. I also thank Jagadish Prasad Sahu for excellent research assistance.

inflows made the US markets highly liquid, resulting in low interest rates and under-pricing of risk. Another problem is the accumulation of external debts, which may be unsustainable in the future.

In the surplus economies on the other hand, particularly in the emerging markets, these imbalances imply that savings has not been channelled into emerging market investment, but rather into consumption and government expenditure in rich countries. For example in China, the domestic savings rate is higher than the investment rate, indicating lost opportunities in domestic investment. Surplus countries with undervalued exchange rates also generate under-investment in non-tradable (Bergsten, Freeman, Lardy & Mitchell, 2009). Such distortions can have major long-run consequences for them. The surplus countries also end up accumulating excess foreign exchange reserves. These generate low yield and have high opportunity costs for poor and emerging market economies (Mann, 2010). If the surplus country manages its exchange rate, it also faces the unpleasant choice between inflationary pressures and extensive sterilisation. As these costs—both systemic and country specific—have become clear, there has emerged a robust consensus among global policymakers as well as academicians that global imbalances are a major hindrance towards sustainable global growth, and hence in the future, global macroeconomic policies need to be coordinated in order to eradicate or minimise this phenomenon.

In order to adopt appropriate policies for the eradication of global imbalances, it is important to understand the factors that have given rise to this phenomenon in the first place. A large and growing literature—that has focused mostly on the large current account deficits of the US economy and the large and increasing surpluses of the East-Asian economies—has tried to identify some of these factors. Most contributions can be classified into three alternative approaches to the problem. These are (a) imbalances due to a decline in the US household savings (for instance, Feldstein, 2008) (b) imbalances due to a savings glut in Asia (for example, Bernanke, 2005) and (c) imbalances due to emerging Asia's export-led development approach with undervalued exchange rates and reserve accumulations (IMF, April 2009).

The first approach stresses that the US deficit had increased in the last decade as its private savings have remained low and its fiscal deficits had gone up. US households saved less and consumed more as the value of their wealth had increased, initially due to the late 1990s boom in stock markets and subsequently on account of the housing boom (Chinn, Eichengreen & Ito, 2011). Since saving was low, the US imported from the rest of the world in order to invest in domestic equipment. This led to higher US current account deficit (Backus, Henriksen, Lambert & Telmer, 2009).

Conversely, the high private savings rates in East Asia have been identified as the factor behind their large current account surpluses. The second approach has attempted to identify the factors that explain these high saving rates. Some explain this phenomenon by focussing on demographic characteristics like the fraction of the population in the prime working-age years and the rate of female labour force participation (Lim, 2010). Other studies claim that the high cost of residential property in many East-Asian countries also leads to high savings and low current consumption rates (Abeysinghe & Choy, 2004). Apart from the household sector, the corporate sector is a major contributor to high aggregate national savings in many of the Asian countries. This is the result of structural features of the corporate sector, mainly low shares of labour (wages) in national income. Both in China and Singapore, there are high and rising shares of state-owned enterprises or government-linked corporations in gross domestic product (GDP) that reinvest their profit rather than distributing their corporate incomes. In particular, in corporatist states like China, Singapore and Malaysia, there is little political pressure on state-owned enterprises and government-linked corporations to distribute their income to boost domestic consumption. This is a major reason for high government savings in these countries (Lim, 2010).

There have been a few studies focusing particularly on China and its high savings rate. Modigliani and Cao (2004) attribute China's high household saving to (a) the high growth following the economic reforms since the end of the 1970s and (b) the introduction of the one-child policy at around the same time, which led to a gradual increase in the ratio of employment to total population. The household saving rate (as a share of household disposable income) has been around 25 per cent since 2000. Government saving is also remarkably high in China compared with other countries, reaching 7.5 per cent of GDP in 2001. This is the result of a policy favouring government-financed investment over government consumption (Kuijs, 2005).

A few contributions have adopted the third approach and explained global imbalances as a result of undervalued exchange rate and reserve accumulation in certain Asian countries. According to Williamson and Cline (2010), the major disequilibria in the world remain the overvaluation of the dollar and the undervaluation of the renminbi. The absence of any action by China to correct its exchange rate will lead the disequilibria to persist. If China corrects its exchange rate, a number of other Asian currencies (India, Indonesia, Japan and Korea) will need to appreciate too. The appreciation of the renminbi against US dollar will make Chinese exports dearer in foreign market. This will lead to a decrease in the Chinese current account surplus.

It is clear from the wide range of the literature cited earlier that a number of factors could have accentuated the phenomenon of global imbalance. A consensus seems to be emerging that all of these factors have played some role in the overall imbalance in the global economy in the recent past. This has led to policy recommendations based on approaches that attempt to counter some of these factors. These have focused either on external sector policies (trade and investment) or on domestic demand management policies. Theoretically, imposing restrictions on cross-border trade and investment flows could reduce global imbalances. However, protectionist policies are not the best strategies to adopt as they imply a risky and highly uncertain trade-off. On the other hand, implicit or explicit subsidisation can lead to the accumulation of trade surpluses or deficits and removal of such subsidies would reduce trade imbalances (Deardorff, 2010). Trade imbalance could arise due to the asymmetry in the levels of trade protection. In other words, any asymmetries in the structure of trade barriers could result in the build-up of unsustainable imbalances. Trade imbalances may also occur if import barriers are persistently higher in services than in goods in both countries or if one of the countries has higher import barriers on both products. A removal of such subsidies could result in reduction of trade imbalances (Kowalski & Lesher, 2010).

The most influential contributions to this literature have focused on demand management in both the deficit and the surplus economies. This mainly involves encouraging US consumers to contribute less to the world's consumption and East-Asian consumers to contribute more. Theoretically, one option for policymakers is to adopt policies to reduce aggregate demand and hence external sector deficits of the US economy. However, such a policy will reduce global demand and push the US and the global economy into long-term recessions. Thus, the policy package for global rebalancing has to involve increasing aggregate demand sufficiently in the trade partners of the US, rather than focusing on reducing the demand in the US economy. In this context, the Chinese policymakers have been advised by the US that they cannot rely on their export-oriented strategy for their future economic growth. Accordingly, they should increasingly try to boost domestic demand in China. The recent evidence suggests that Chinese consumption is becoming a larger share of its GDP and current account surplus becoming much smaller. Demand-side adjustments have also been suggested to other developing Asian countries, in order to escape from the heavy reliance on exports. This involves expansion of domestic demand and broadening regional trade opportunities in the final demand for goods and services. Governments in these countries have been encouraged to target policies at increasing either domestic consumption or domestic investment or both.

The literature on global imbalances implicitly (or, in a few cases, explicitly) recognises the phenomenon as an outcome of the structure of the current global economy instead of an interaction between two or a few economies. However, when it comes to policy recommendation, a vast majority of the contributions focus exclusively on the role of the East-Asian economies in general and that of China in particular. For example, Kumar and Alex (2011) argue that policy measures to correct the global imbalances should focus on restructuring the current accounts of emerging Asian economies, especially that of China. As per their recommendation, rebalancing in Asia can be achieved by structural reforms that should be undertaken to raise domestic private consumption demand in East Asia, particularly in China. This will help the deficit countries, including the US to rebalance their economies by taking the advantage of external demand. It will also reduce the dependence of China on external demand to sustain its double-digit growth performance.

Similarly, the other contributions discussed earlier have identified various factors that lead to high savings/low consumption in East-Asian economies and prescribe policies to counter these factors. It may be noted that this literature does not include similar analysis for, say, Germany, although it was a significant contributor to the global imbalances. Thus, these studies suggest an East-Asia-centric approach to global rebalancing.

Is an East-Asia-centric approach sufficient to solve global imbalances? If the combined current account surplus of these economies is larger than the size of the US deficit, it may be tempting to conclude that a reduction in the East-Asian surpluses is sufficient to solve the problem. Unfortunately, such a conclusion may be fallacious since it does not recognise the interconnectedness of the global economy. Any reduction in the current account surplus of the East-Asian economies (as a result of, say, demand management policies in these economies) can lead to an equal reduction in US deficits only under the condition that there is no change in the external balances of other regional blocs. However, in a globalised world, the current account balance of other regional blocs is also affected by policies adopted by the East-Asian countries, and hence the result of reducing the surplus of these countries on the US deficit is uncertain. Under extreme circumstances, a reduction in East-Asian surpluses may lead to an equal increase in the external surplus of some other trade partners of the US, as a result of which there may be no reduction in the US deficits. Clearly, in order to attempt global rebalancing, it is important for global policymakers to know the precise impact of policy-induced reduction of East-Asian surpluses on the rest of the world economy, including the US. This requires a macro-modelling framework that adopts the important economic interlinkages between the major regional blocs of the world economy and can be used to simulate the impact of policies adopted in one or a few regional blocs on the rest of the world.

There is another reason why such a model-based analysis is useful for policymakers. Rebalancing involves adopting structural policies that change consumption and savings patterns of economies or blocs. It is well understood that such policies take time to work out. This implies that policymakers will not be in a position to identify and choose sets of regional blocs that must contribute to rebalancing sequentially, as this will give result after a very long time and may lead to a breakdown in global coordination. Thus, the regions have to be chosen simultaneously at the time such a policy is to be initiated. Bound by this constraint, the only reasonable approach involves comparing model-based scenarios with different sets of blocs and choosing that set of blocs that fulfil the policy objective in these scenarios.

In light of the above discussions, the objective of this chapter is to analyse the feasibility of the East-Asia-centric approach to global rebalancing using an existing global macro-econometric model that is regularly employed for global policy analysis. We choose the CAM global macro-econometric model that is also used by the United Nations Department of Economic and Social Affairs as a global policy model for their regular policy analysis.

The CAM Model[1]

The CAM model views the world economy as an integrated system comprising of regional blocs. The model assumes that the behaviours of the blocs have similarities as they are all part of a global economy but also differ because of their specific situations in terms of geography, level of development, financial position, etc. A common set of identities and behavioural equations is used for all blocs of countries to reflect the notion that they are part of the same world economy. Panel estimation methods are used to estimate the behavioural functions. Equations are thus estimated to yield common global parameter values for these behavioural functions while individual (country or bloc level) differences are captured in the intercept terms of the equation. Thus, all the estimated equations of the model have country or bloc fixed effects in the panel estimations.

The main sectors of the CAM are (a) private sector demand and income; (b) government demand and income; (c) international trade in manufactured goods, primary commodities, energy and services; (d) international factor payments and transfers, external positions, exchange rates and capital flows; (e) government and domestic banking sector flows and balances; (f) prices; (g) output and (h) capacity and inflation.

The whole model includes a large number of behavioural equations and identities, the details of which are given in Cripps, Izurieta and Vos (2010a, 2010b). Here, we shall discuss the principal macroeconomic identity and its components that lie at the heart of the model and determine the external imbalances across the countries/blocs in the model. From basic international macroeconomics, we know that for any economy,

$$Y = C + Ip + Ig + G + (X - M) \tag{6.1}$$

Here, Y is national income, C is domestic consumption, Ip is private investment, Ig is change in inventories, G is government expenditure, while X and M are total exports and imports of goods and services, including investment incomes and transfers. Next, defining private disposable income Yp as national income not absorbed by the government Yg, we have

$$Yp = Y - Yg \tag{6.2}$$

Again, private consumption can be rewritten in terms of the savings function Sp,

$$C = Yp - Sp \tag{6.3}$$

Thus, the above identity can be rewritten as

$$(Sp - Ip - Iv) + (Yg - G) = (X - M) \tag{6.4}$$

This identity shows that the sum of excess savings in the private and the government sector is identical to the current account balance of an economy. Thus, global imbalances are closely related to the domestic demand structure in major economies. In the CAM, all the variables that are components of the above identity are determined endogenously in the model. Detailed descriptions of how each of these components is modelled in the CAM are given in the Appendix.

---

[1] This section is based on Cripps, Izurieta and Vos (2010a, 2010b).

As discussed earlier, the current account balance of countries with large surpluses or deficits is the main focus of the literature on global imbalances. The discussion of the model, including the equations given above, describes how the CAM model determines the current account balance of the countries/blocs of the world. However, as noted previously, it is not only the flow variables in the external sector, but also the stock of net external assets or liabilities, particularly of the US economy, that is of central concern.

The net external assets or the net external position of an economy are determined by past levels of this stock variable and current addition through financial flows. In the CAM model, these financial flows are identical to the current account balance. In other words, the current account determines the capital account in this model and large current account balance ratios lead to large net external asset ratios. There is another factor, however, that determines the net external asset ratios. Like all assets or liabilities, the valuation of these assets also plays a role. In the model, the valuation of external assets, $rpax\$$ (Equation 6.5), is assumed to be a function of world inflation, phw, since the latter erodes the value of the former:

$$\log(rpax\$) = \Phi\left\{\overset{(-)}{\Delta \log(phw)}, \alpha_b, \varepsilon_b\right\} \qquad (6.5)$$

The model divides the world economy into 19 blocs. The developed world is represented by the 'US', 'North Europe', 'Central Europe', 'South Europe', 'East Europe', 'West Europe', 'Japan', 'Other Developed' and 'East Asia High Income'. The developing and emerging economies of 'China' and 'India' are taken individually. There are two main energy-exporting blocs—the former 'USSR' (CIS) and 'West Asia'. Other blocs include 'Central America', 'South America', 'Other East Asia', 'Other South Asia', 'North Africa' and 'Other Africa'. It is clear from the above discussions that variables like growth rates (from output in Equation 6.1), current account balance ratios (from Equation 6.4) and net external asset ratios (from Equations 6.4 and 6.5) for all 19 blocs are determined endogenously in the model. Thus, a baseline simulation (of the future) would generate the values of these variables of all the blocs solely on the basis of past behaviour (captured in the parameters of the estimated equations). We can, of course, run alternative scenarios with specific assumptions about one or more behavioural function in any of the countries or blocs contained in the model. In the next section, we shall use the baseline and alternative scenarios generated from the CAM in order to understand the issues related to global rebalancing that has motivated this study.

Some Results

In this section, we shall use the CAM model in order to investigate a number of issues related to global rebalancing. In particular, we shall try to throw light on the following questions:

1. Do global imbalances remain a major concern for the world economy?
2. Is an East-Asia-centric approach to global rebalancing sufficient to solve this problem or are their major limitations to such as approach?
3. What other regional blocs can play important roles in solving this problem?

In order to answer these questions, we generate a number of simulations of the world economy using the CAM model. Since our interest is in the future long-run trends related to global rebalancing, our simulations are forecasts for the period 2013–2014 to 2030–2031. The simulations include (a) the baseline scenario that projects the future of the world economy based on past economic structure and behaviour and (b) some alternative scenarios that are based on very specific assumptions about policy and/or the structure of the world economy.

In order to focus on global imbalances, the study looks at the current account balance (as a ratio to GDP) for the US and other major economic blocs (including East-Asian blocs) corresponding to the above scenarios. However, as we have noted earlier, it is not only the size of the current account balance but also the resultant accumulation of net foreign assets (or liabilities) that is critical. Given the relationship between the flow (current account balance) and the stock (net foreign assets) variables, even a stable current account balance to GDP ratio can give rise to an increasing net foreign asset (or liability) to GDP ratio under certain conditions. In the context of the US economy, such an increasing net foreign liability position carries the risk of a sudden and disorderly change in the value of the dollar. Hence, we also focus on the net foreign asset/liability ratios for the blocs corresponding to the various simulations.

Do Global Imbalances Remain a Major Concern for the World Economy?

Starting from the late 1990s, global imbalances became a resilient feature of the global economy, growing larger and larger over the course of the last decade. It was only with the outbreak of the global financial meltdown and the subsequent recession that there was some slowing down in the growth of these imbalances. As the global economy grapples to emerge from this recession, the concern is whether global imbalances can make a comeback in the future as and when we return to robust growth. Since our interest is in the future long-run behaviour of the world, we try to analyse this issue by looking at future trends of the world economy corresponding to the baseline scenario. Figure 6.1 shows the GDP growth rate of the world and major blocs corresponding to the baseline scenario. The simulation shows that global growth is expected to bounce back in the long run and stay at reasonably high levels thereafter. Among the blocs that have contributed to imbalances in the past, the US is expected to have a reasonably high and steady growth rate throughout, while China and EAH (bloc consisting of East-Asian high-income countries)—that initially have very high growth rates—shows a downward trend throughout the period. Are these patterns of growth going to increase or decrease global imbalances?

Figure 6.2 shows the current account balance ratios of all blocs corresponding to the baseline simulation. It clearly shows that in the long run, the global imbalances are set to return with the potential to cause disruption in the world economy. The current account balance ratio of the US is in deficit and falls continuously in the future despite a high growth in its GDP and reaches pre-meltdown levels (for example, levels reached before 2008–2010) in the long run. Among the major trade partners of the US, China, Japan, EAH and Central Europe all exhibit increasing current account surpluses during this period.

As noted earlier, it is not only the current account balance but also the net external asset position—particularly that of the US economy—that is critical from the view of global imbalances. Figure 6.3 depicts the net external assets to GDP ratio for all the blocs corresponding to the baseline scenario. Corresponding to the deterioration in the current account deficit, the net external liabilities of the US increase to nearly 100 per cent of GDP in the long run. As many contributions to the literature on global imbalances have shown, this is much higher than what is thought to be a sustainable level of net US assets demanded by the rest of the world. This further highlights the return of global imbalances in the future. It is clear from Figures 6.2 and 6.3 that global imbalances remain as pertinent as before the global meltdown and need to be tackled by the world economy. In order to look at this phenomenon a bit more closely, we separate the trade balance and the net invisibles next for some of the major contributors to the imbalance. Figure 6.4 depicts these variables, together with the current account balance, for the US, China, Japan and EAH.

Figure 6.1
GDP Growth: World Economy and Individual Blocs

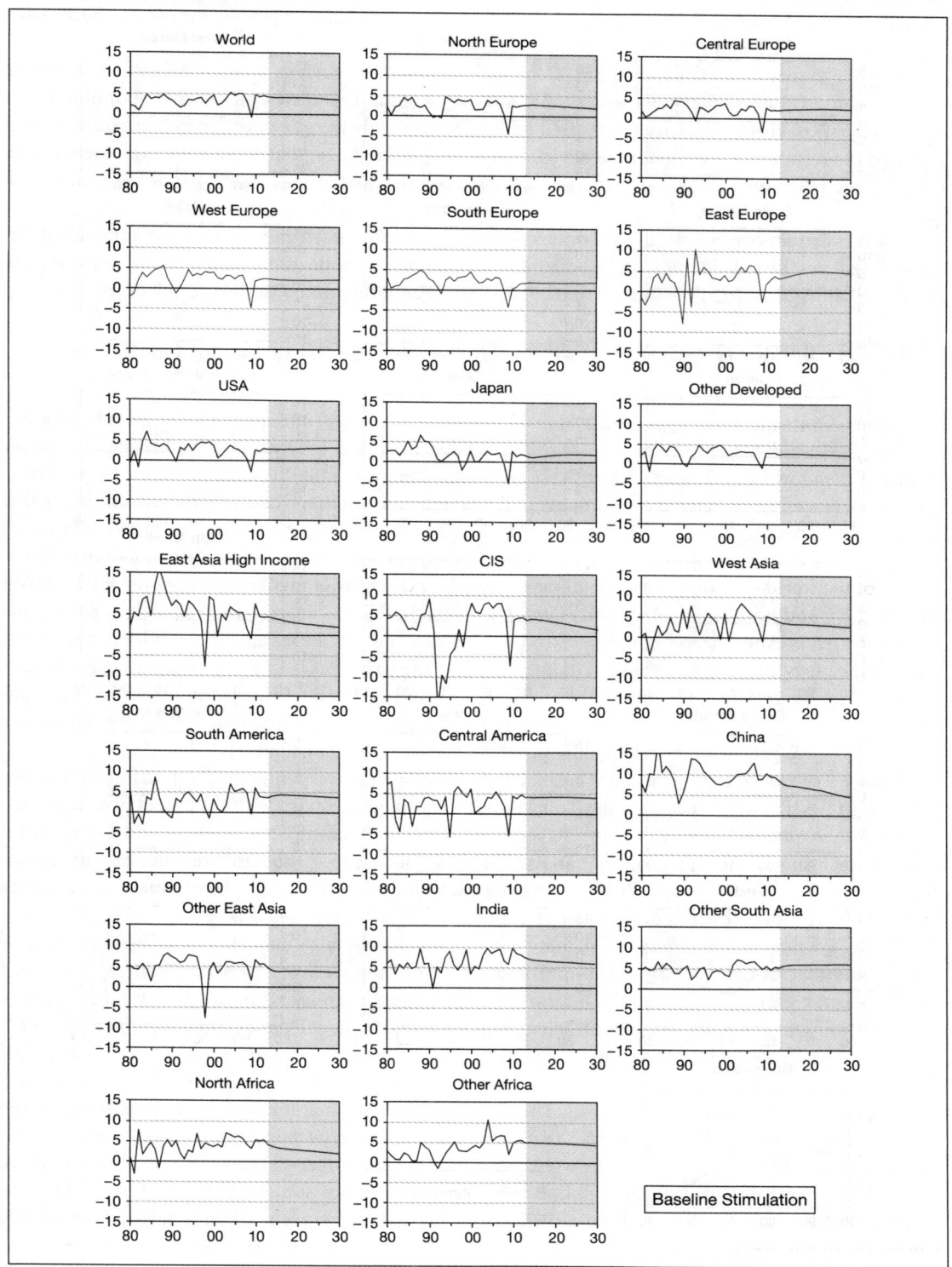

Baseline Stimulation

Figure 6.2
Current Account Balance as a Ratio to GDP

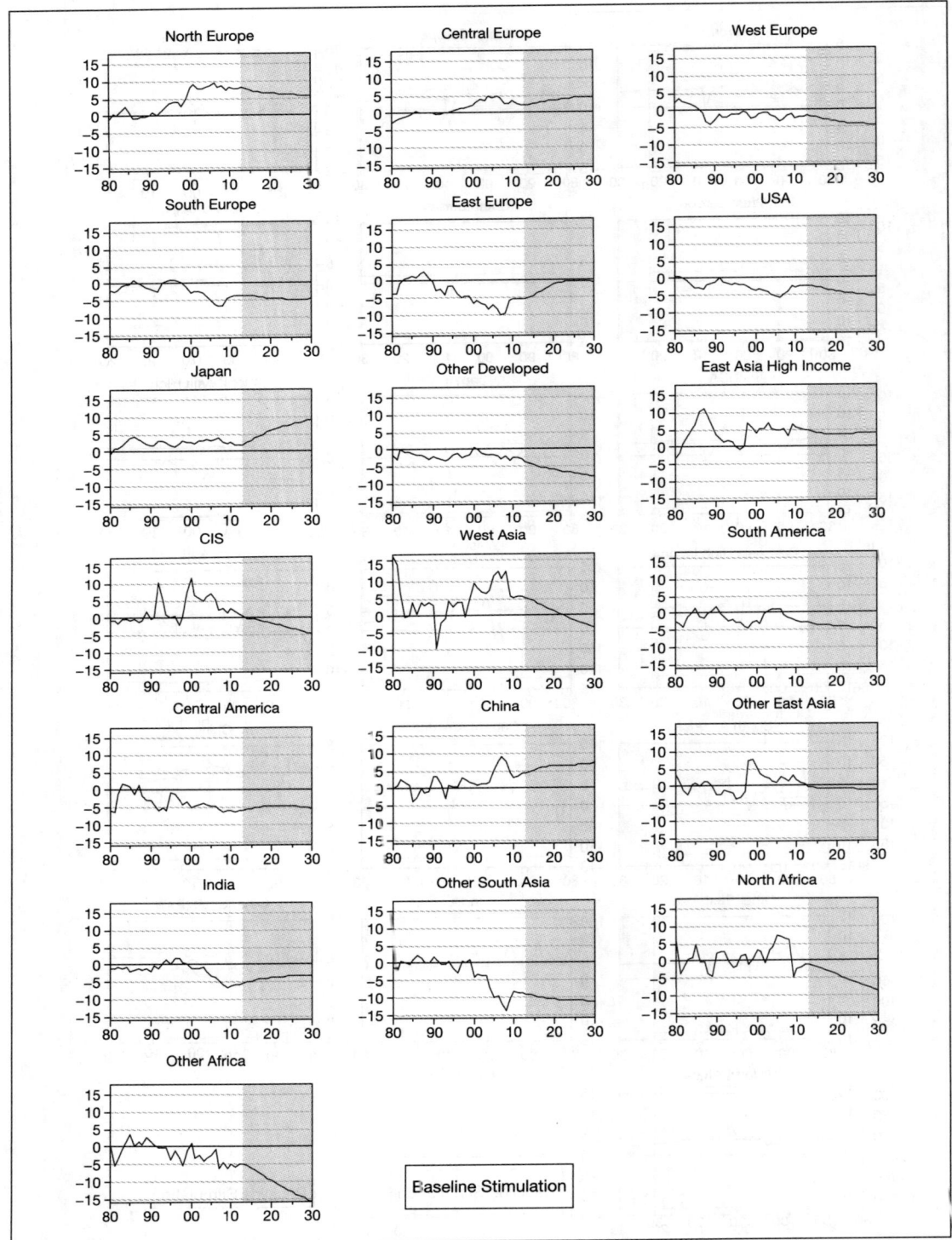

Figure 6.3
Net External Assets as a Ratio to GDP

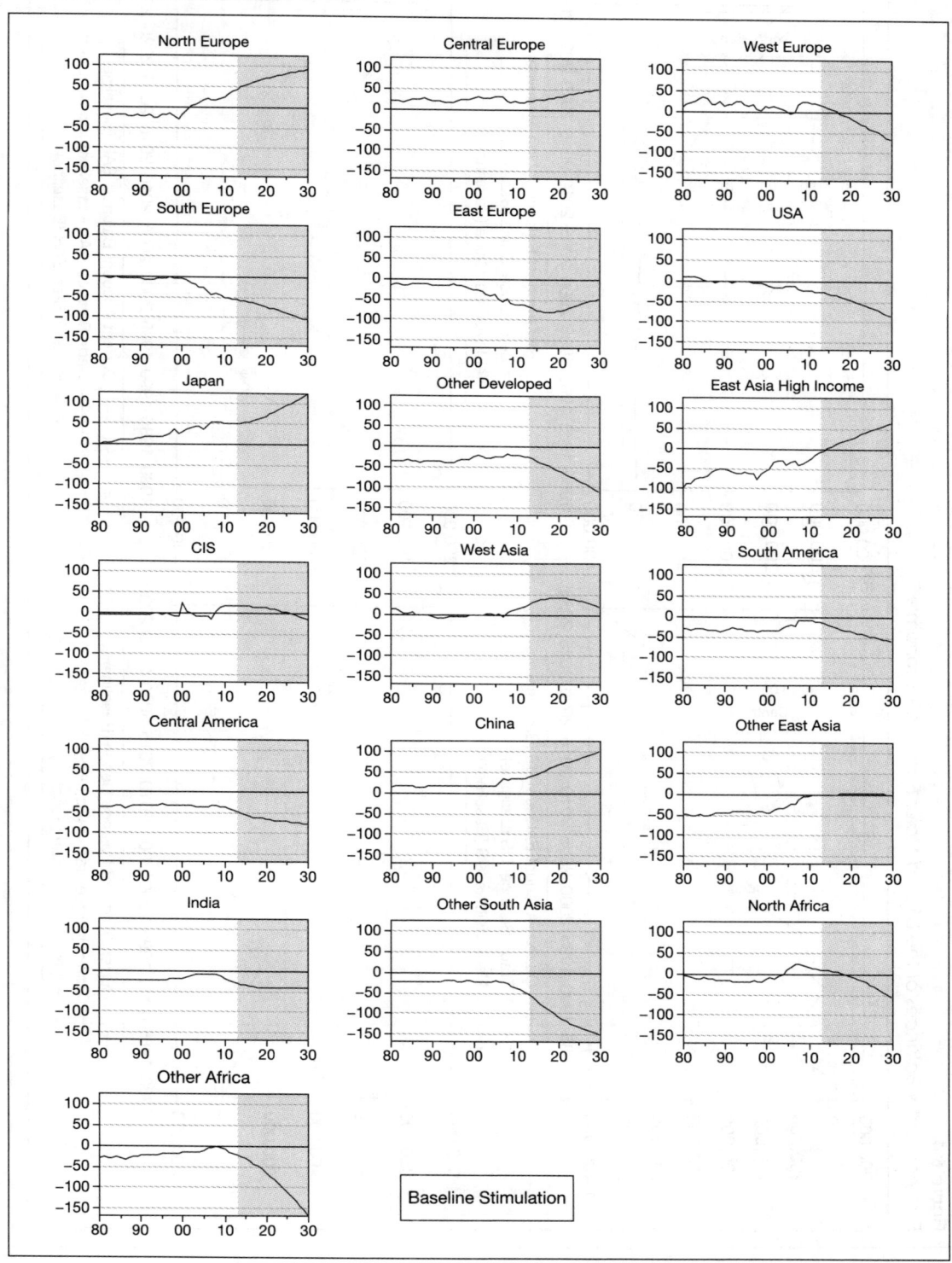

Figure 6.4
External Sector Balances of the US and Major East-Asian Economies

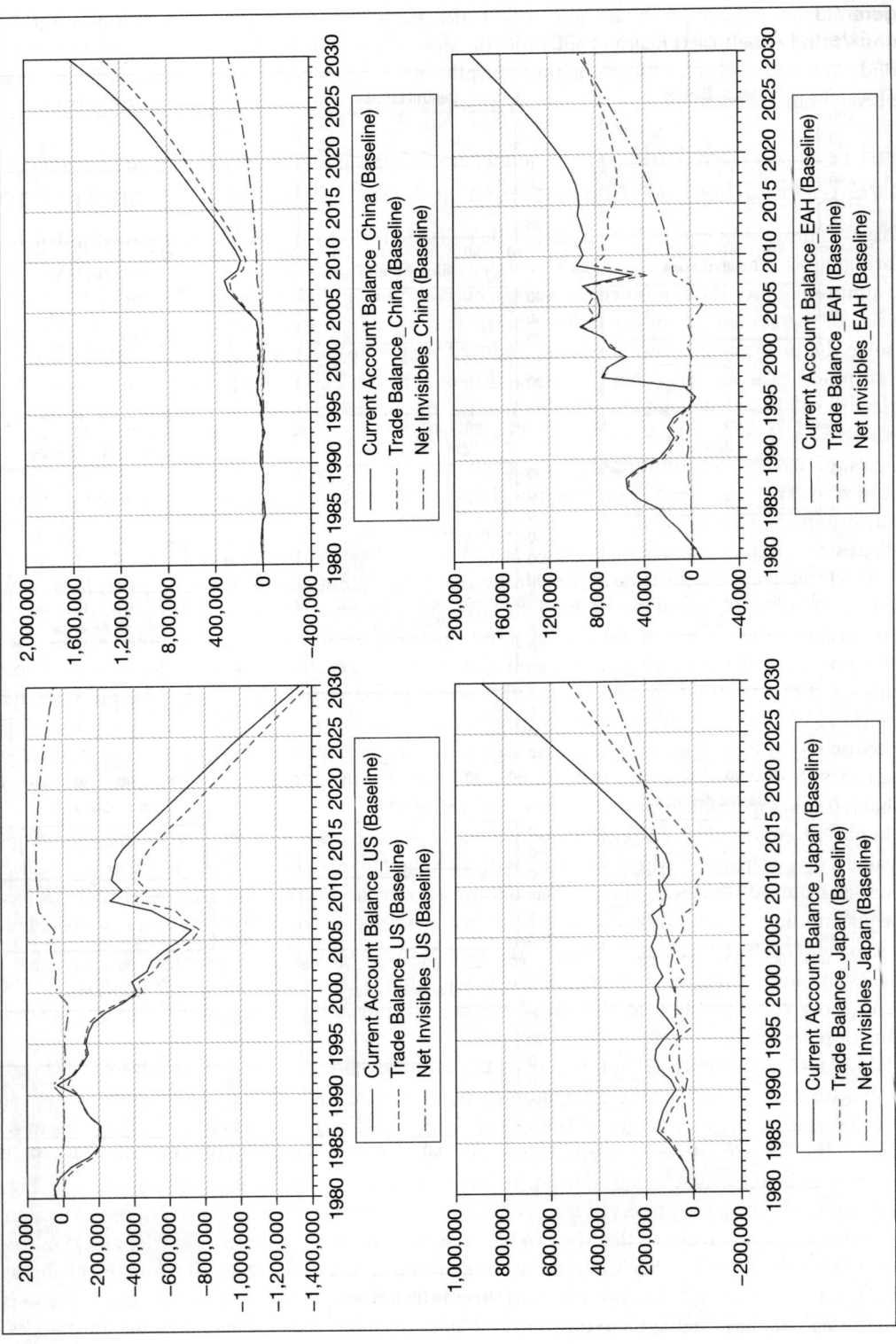

From Figure 6.4, we find that the constant increase in the size of the US current account deficit is almost entirely due to its trade deficit, while the net invisibles of the US are in surplus throughout the period. Among the surplus blocs, the trade surplus plays the biggest role in China, while for Japan and the EAH, both the trade surplus and the net invisibles play an important role.

Is an East-Asia-centric Approach to Global Rebalancing Sufficient to Solve This Problem or Are There Major Limitations to Such an Approach?

A large volume of literature has suggested that the solution to the problem of global imbalances lies in bringing about structural changes in East-Asian economies that lead to increases in their domestic consumption. Since the combined current account surplus in these East-Asian economies is larger than the size of the US deficit, these studies seem to assume that an East-Asia-centric approach is sufficient to solve the problem. However, a policy-induced reduction in East-Asian surpluses will also increase the surpluses of blocs other than the US and hence the net effect may not necessarily be sufficient to achieve the global rebalancing. In order to quantify this net effect, we have generated alternative scenario 1, where we assume that three major East-Asian blocs, namely China, Japan and EAH, adopt structural policies to increase consumption/decrease savings sufficiently to bring down their current account surplus to zero. The other variables in the model, including the current account balance of the other blocs, are determined endogenously.

Figure 6.5 shows the current account balance ratio for all the blocs corresponding to the baseline as well as alternative scenario 1. As expected, the current account balance ratio of China, Japan and EAH falls to zero for the period of the simulation. This leads to a definite improvement in the current account balance ratio of the US, which stabilises at about 3 per cent of GDP. However, as noted earlier, the extent of the global imbalance is also determined by the size of the net external liabilities of the US economy. Figure 6.6 shows the net external asset position of all blocs corresponding to the baseline and alternative scenario 1. We find that although the current account balance ratio for the US has stabilised following the reduction in East-Asian surpluses, the size of its net external liabilities increases continuously in the long run without showing signs of stabilisation. This clearly shows that the East-Asia-centric approach to global rebalancing is not sufficient to solve the problem.

In order to understand more clearly why the East-Asia-centric approach is not sufficient, we generate the alternative scenario 2, where we assume that China, Japan and EAH again bring down their current account surplus to zero, but only the US economy gains from this (for example, the US deficits reduce by an equal amount). Thus, in this scenario, the change in the current account balance, trade balance and net invisibles of the US is exactly equal to the sum of the changes in each of these variables for the three East-Asian blocs. Next, we compare the current account balance of the US corresponding to the baseline to those corresponding to alternative scenarios 1 and 2. Figure 6.7 shows these variables for the simulation period.

It is clear that if the reduction of the East-Asian surpluses had resulted in gains only for the US economy (alternative scenario 2), then the US economy would have ended up with a large current account surplus. However, due to the interaction of the global economy (alternative scenario 1), the current account deficit of the US remains very significantly large. This clearly implies that a reduction in the East-Asian surpluses leads to increase in surpluses or reduction in the deficits of the other blocs as well. Figure 6.8 shows some of the major gainers in terms of current account balances as a result of the reduction of the East-Asian surpluses. It shows that the two blocs comprising former Soviet countries and West Asia gain almost as much as the US while Central Europe gains much more as a result of structural changes in East Asia. As a result, although the combined surplus of the East-Asian blocs in the baseline scenario is larger than the US deficit, bringing them down to zero does not solve the problem of global imbalances.

Figure 6.5
Current Account Balance as a Ratio to GDP

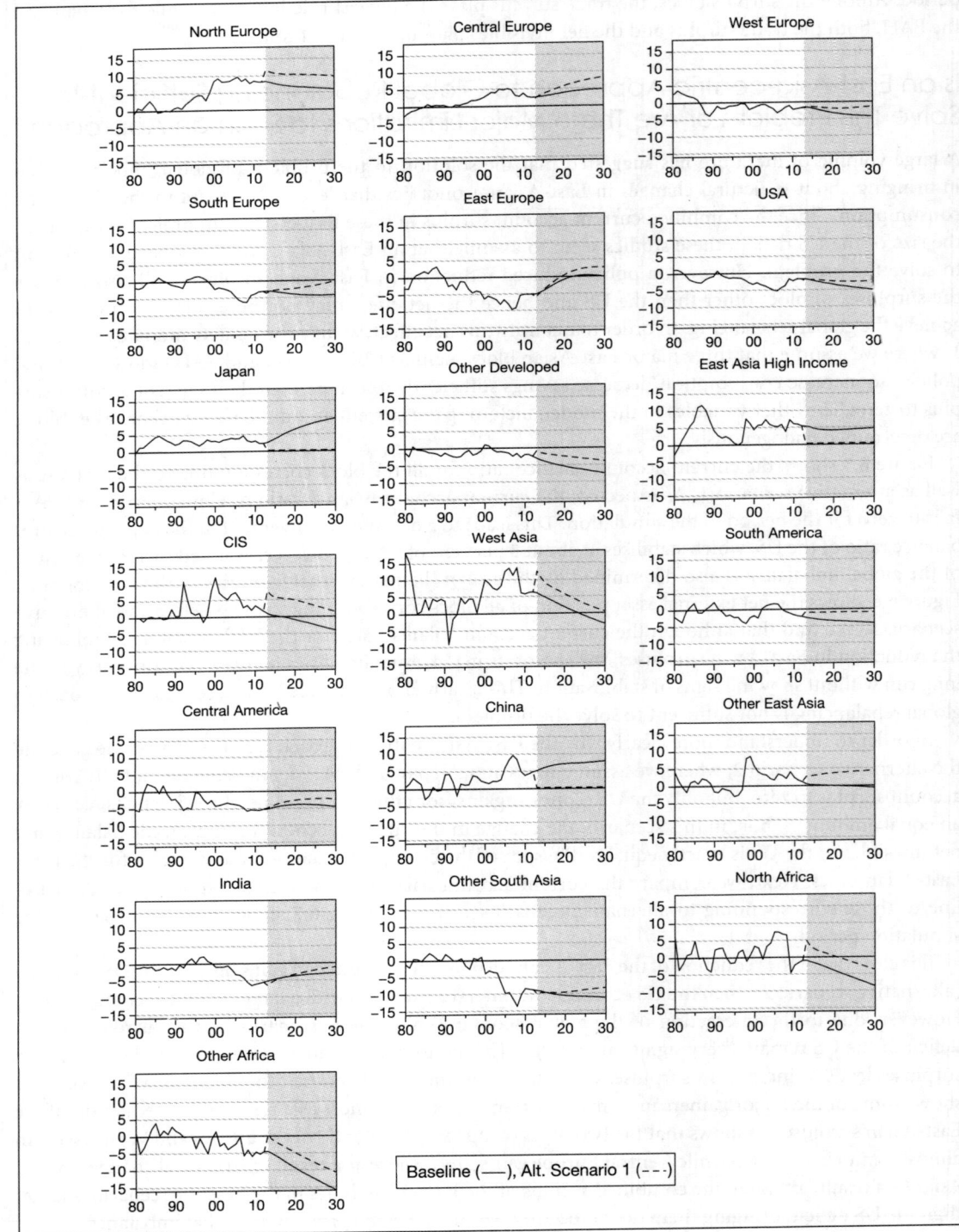

Figure 6.6
Net External Assets as a Ratio to GDP

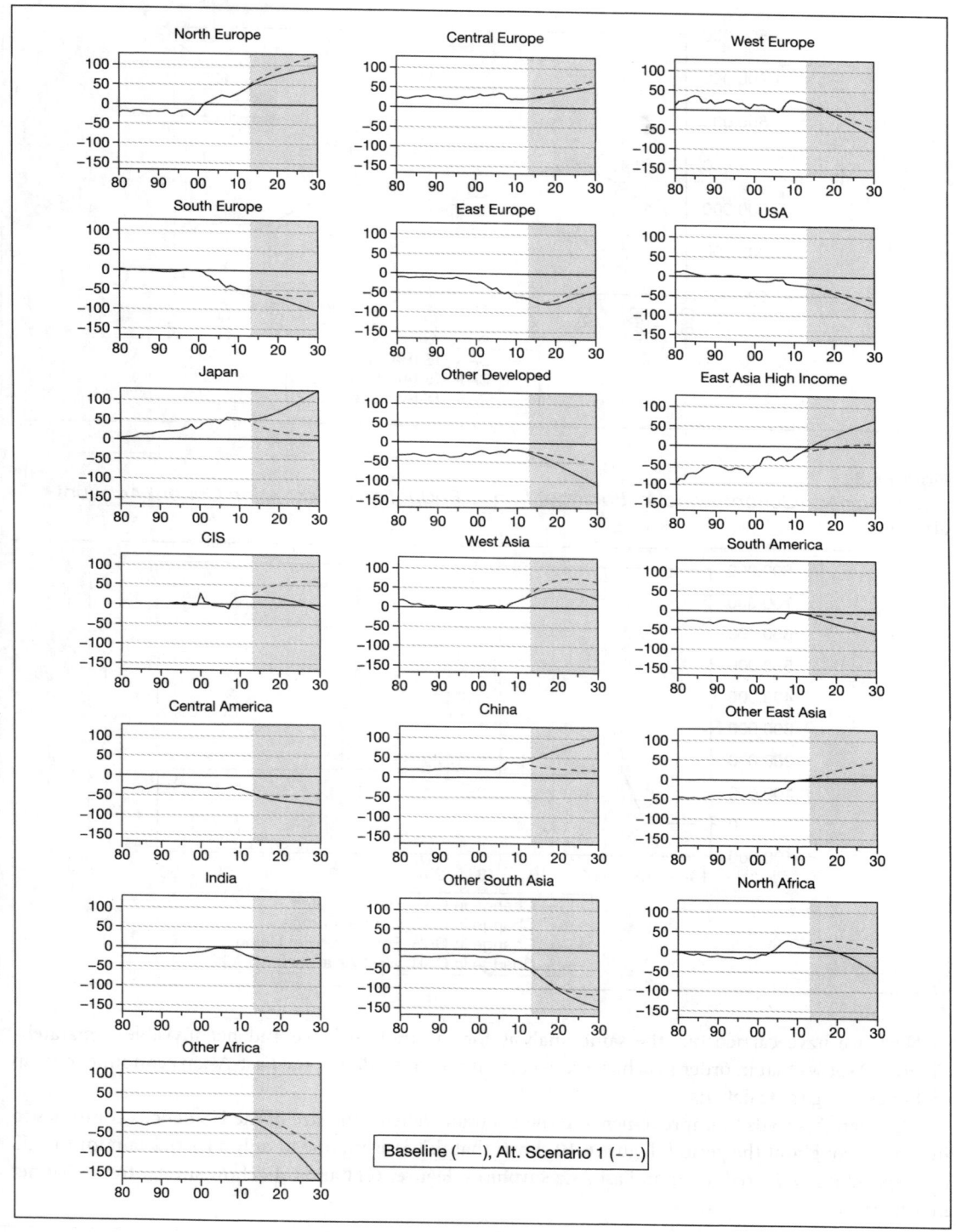

Figure 6.7
Current Account Balance of the US

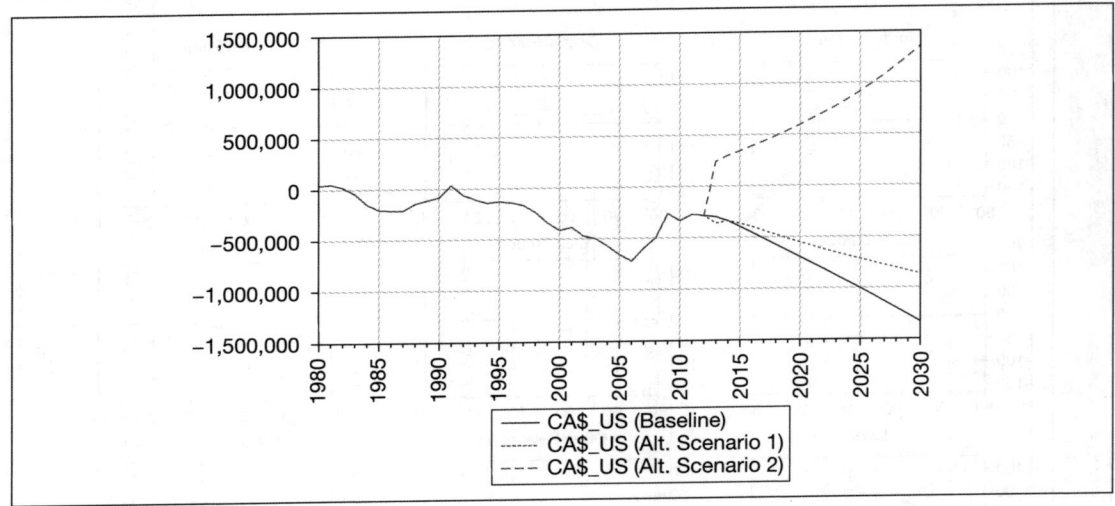

Figure 6.8
Major Gainers (Current Account Balance) from a Reduction of East-Asian Current Account Surplus

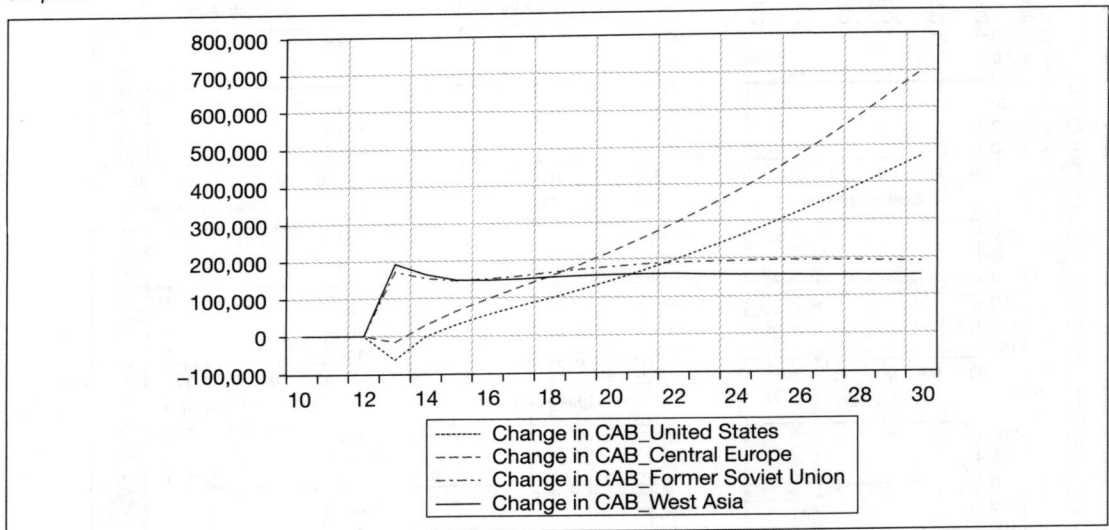

Next, we have carried out the same analysis for the trade balance and net invisibles separately. Figure 6.9 shows that in order to achieve zero current account balance, the East-Asian economies end up with increasing trade deficits.

Although this leads to improvements in the US trade deficits, the size of the US deficits continues to increase throughout the period. Figure 6.10 shows that this is again due to only a partial gain for the US corresponding to the reduction in East Asia surpluses. Figures 6.11 and 6.12 show similar trends for net invisibles.

Figure 6.9
Trade Balance of Some Major Deficit and Surplus Countries/Blocs

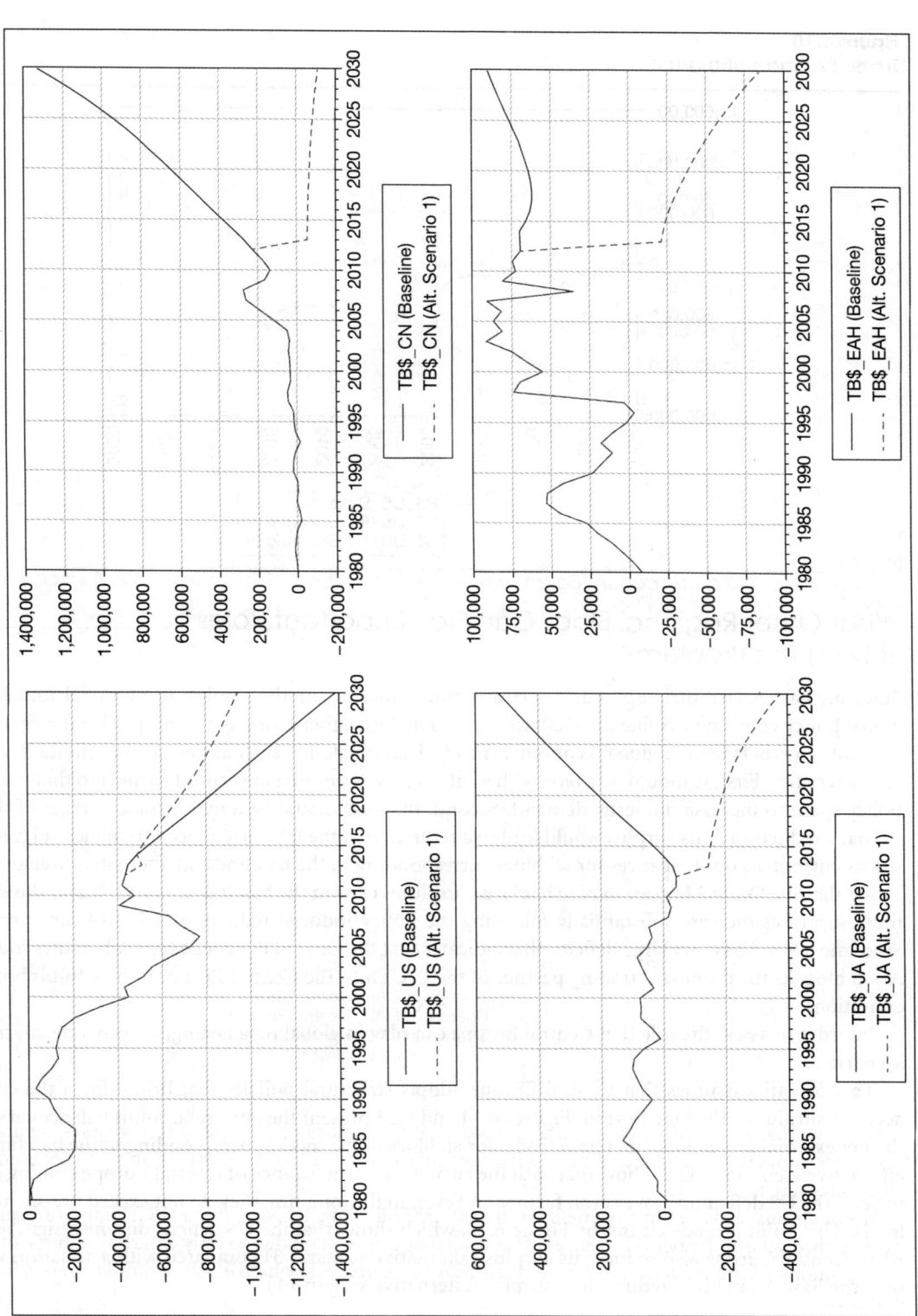

Figure 6.10
Trade Balance of the US

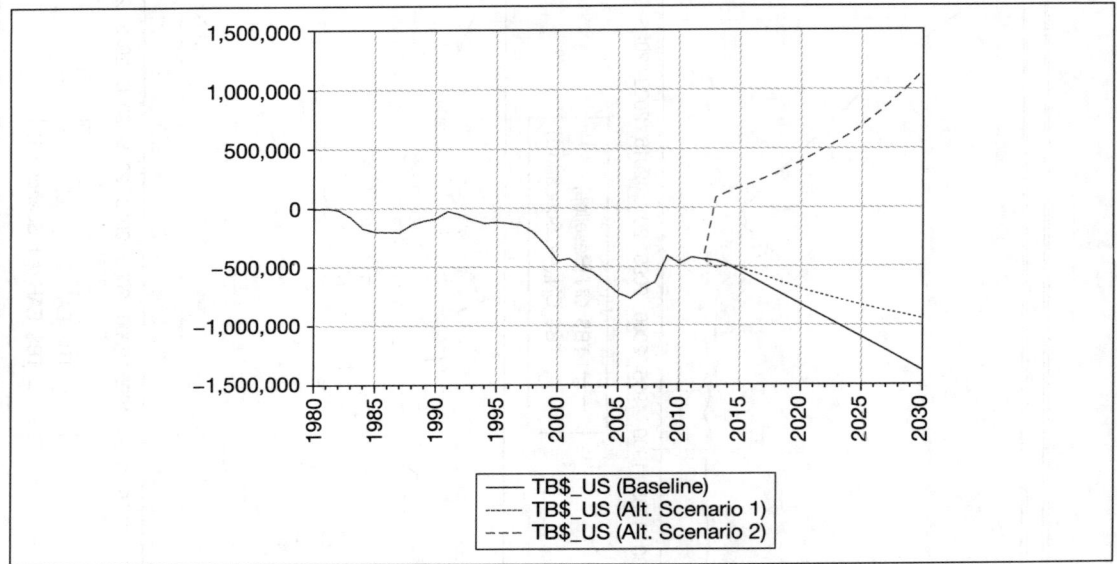

What Other Regional Blocs Can Play Important Roles in Solving This Problem?

Since an East-Asia-centric approach is clearly not sufficient for the resolution of global imbalances, global policy coordinators like the G20 will have to include other blocs to play a significant role in their attempts to rebalance the global economy. An ideal candidate for such as endeavour should have two characteristics. First, it should be a bloc with a sufficiently large current account surplus so that it has the policy space to increase domestic demand. Second, the bloc should be a major trade partner of the US so that a reduction in its surplus would lead to a reduction in the US current account deficit. Figure 6.13 shows current account balances for all blocs corresponding to the baseline and alternative scenario 1. It shows that the Central European bloc has large surpluses even in the baseline scenario. It also shows that these surpluses increase substantially following the policy-induced reduction of East-Asian surpluses. Since the US still has very large deficits, this indicates that the Central European bloc substitutes the East-Asian blocs as the dominant trading partner of the US. Thus, the Central European bloc fulfils both the conditions.

In order to assess the role that Central Europe can play in global rebalancing, we generate alternative scenario 3.

This scenario assumes that Central Europe adopts structural policies that bring down the current account surplus of the bloc to zero. Figures 6.14 and 6.15 present the current account balance ratio and the net external assets position, respectively, for all blocs of the model corresponding to the baseline and alternative scenario 3. They show that with the current account balance of Central Europe coming down to zero, the US deficit improves even further and even in the long run, they do not exceed pre-meltdown levels. This point is made clearer by Figure 6.16, which shows that the US deficits diminish significantly when Central Europe also reduces its surplus (alternative scenario 3) compared with a situation where only the East-Asian blocs reduce their surplus (alternative scenario 1).

Figure 6.11
Net Invisibles of Some Major Deficit and Surplus Countries/Blocs

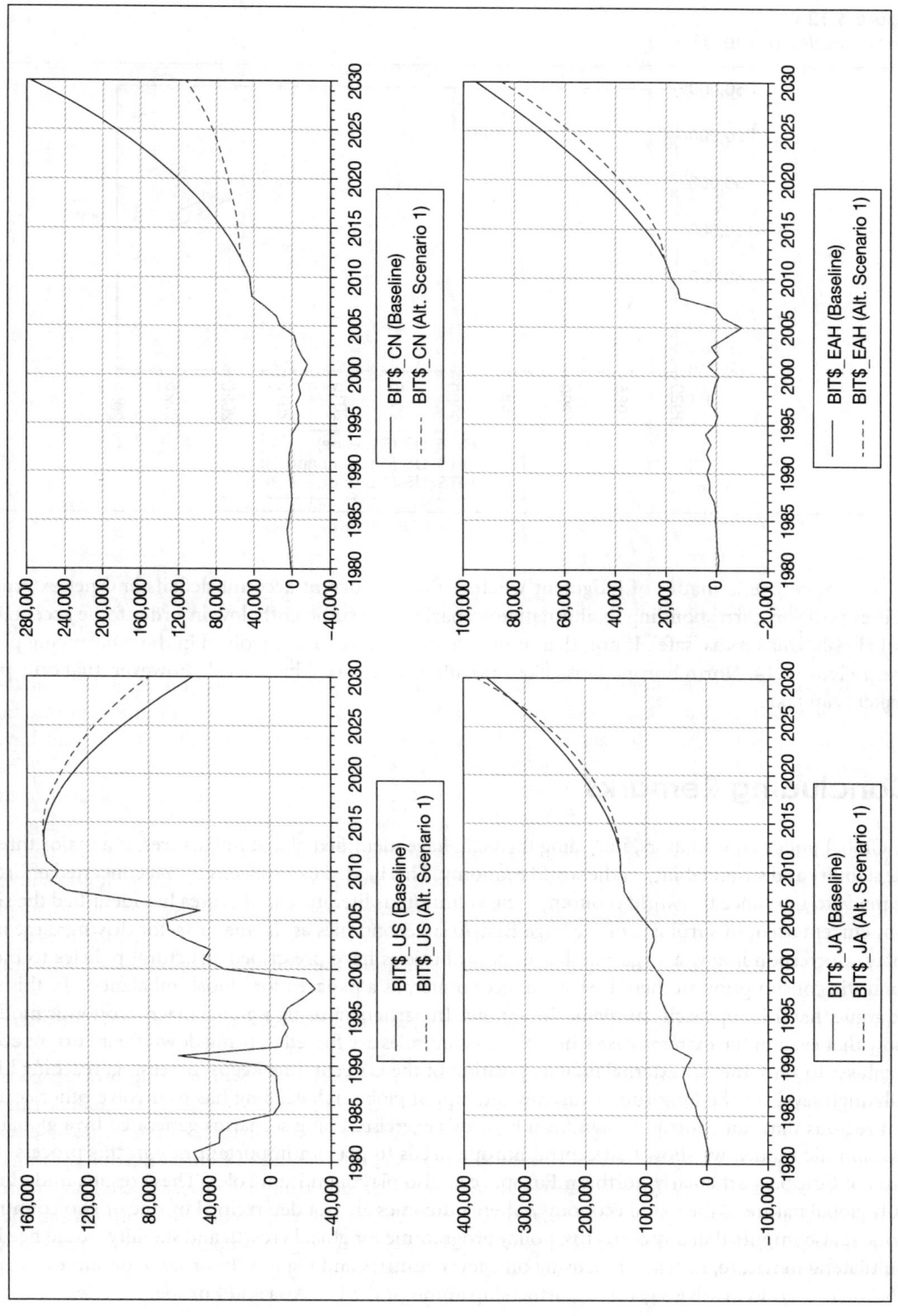

Figure 6.12
Net Invisibles of the US

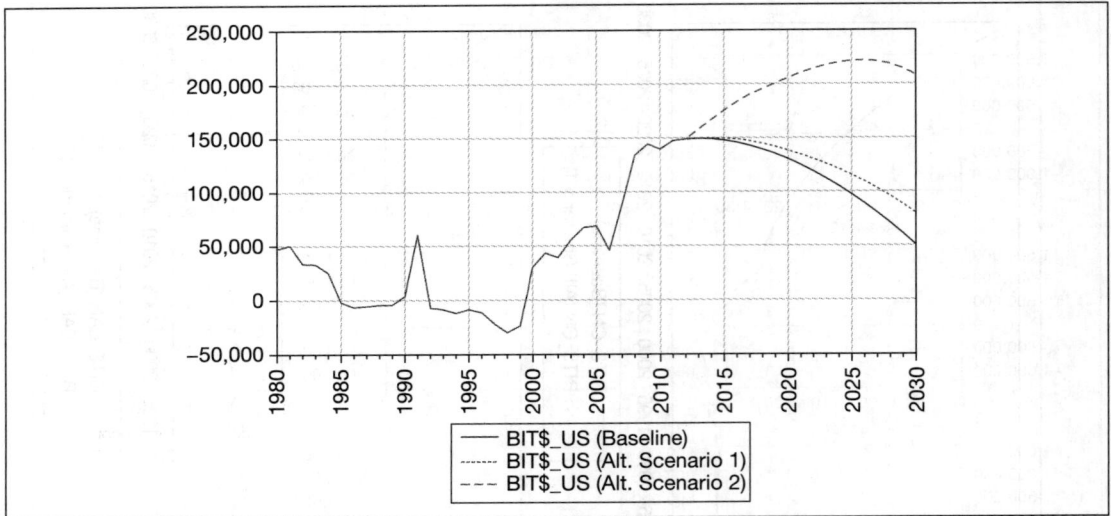

It is, of course, a matter of judgment whether the US current account deficits and net external liabilities position corresponding to alternative scenario 3 are sufficiently low in order to be acceptable by global policymakers as 'safe'. If not, then more blocs will have to be involved in the rebalancing process. From Figure 6.14, North Europe looks like a possible candidate. This is a call, however, that only policymakers can take.

Concluding Remarks

Global policy coordinators, including the G20, have identified global imbalances as a major threat for the stability and sustainability of the world economy. This has led to a consensus that concerted effort must be made to rebalance the world economy. The voluminous literature in this area has identified the significant current account surpluses of the large East-Asian economies as the major factor driving these imbalances. Correspondingly, a large number of contributions have prescribed structural policies to increase domestic consumption in these East-Asian economies, as a panacea for global imbalances. In this study, we argue that this approach has major limitations. In particular, using a global macroeconomic model, we show that even in the extreme case where these economies are forced to bring down their current account surpluses to zero, the net external liability position of the US economy keeps increasing, reaching historically high levels in the long run. Thus, any attempt at global rebalancing has to involve other countries and regions that can contribute significantly to this exercise. Using scenarios generated by a global macroeconomic model, we show that central Europe needs to play an important role in this process. Other parts of Europe, particularly northern Europe, can also play significant roles. These results underline the truly global nature of the world economy, where outcomes are not determined by one or two countries or blocs. It also implies that any corrective policy programme for global growth and stability would need to be multilateral in nature, instead of focusing on a few countries and regions. In order to be successful, global rebalancing has to involve a genuine partnership amongst the US, Asia and Europe.

Figure 6.13
Current Account Balance (in million dollars, 2005 Prices)

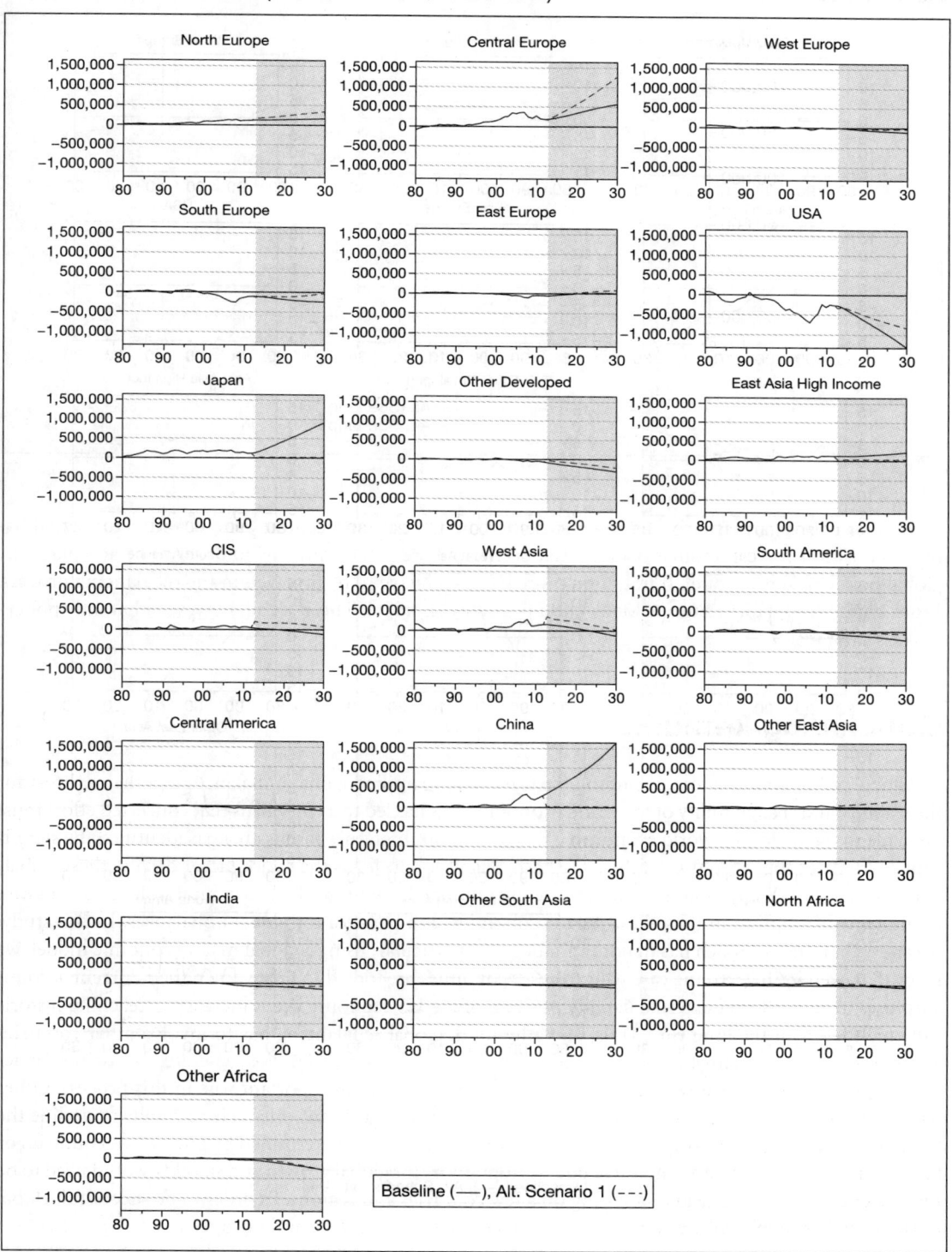

Figure 6.14
Current Account Balance as a Ratio to GDP

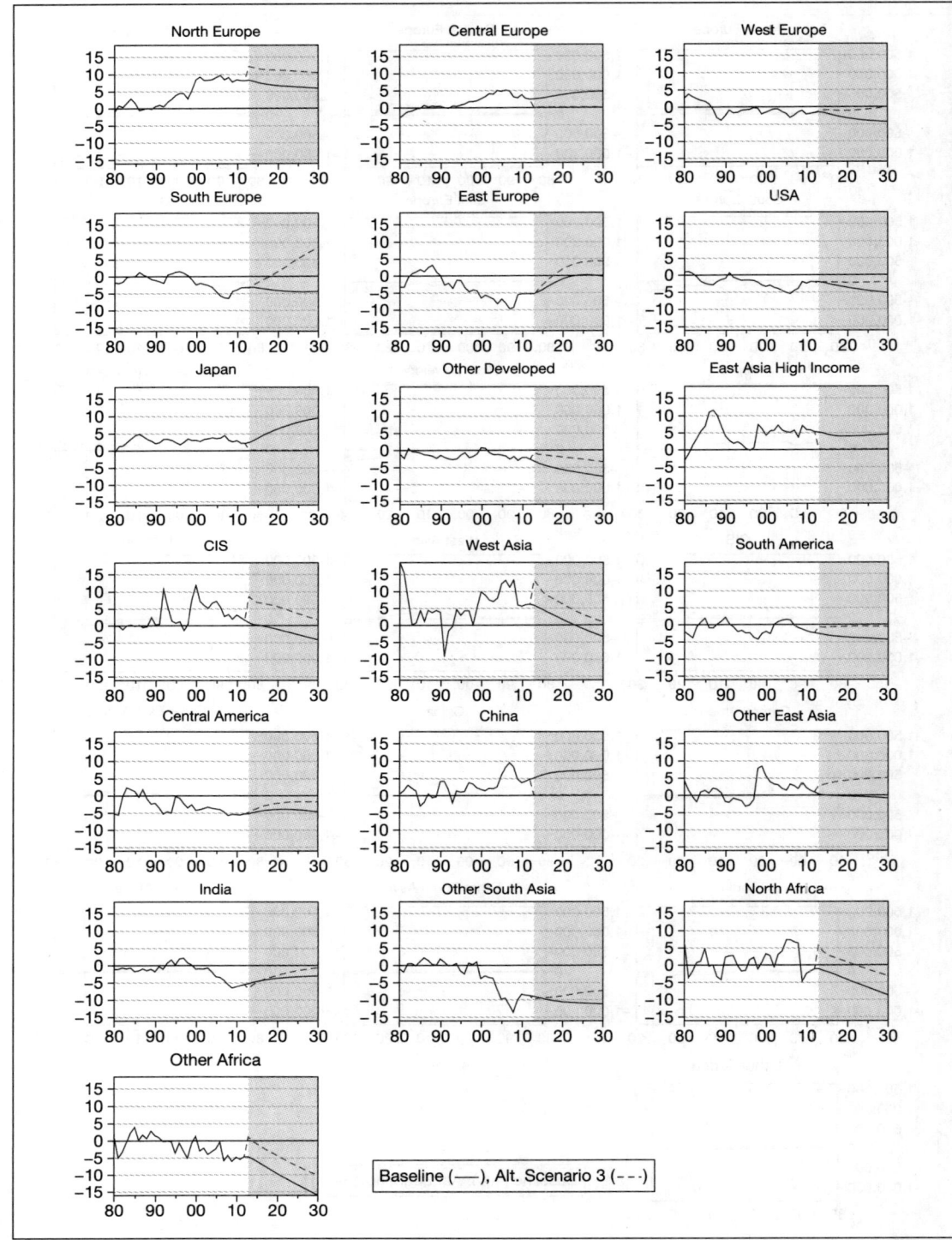

Figure 6.15
Net External Assets as a Ratio to GDP

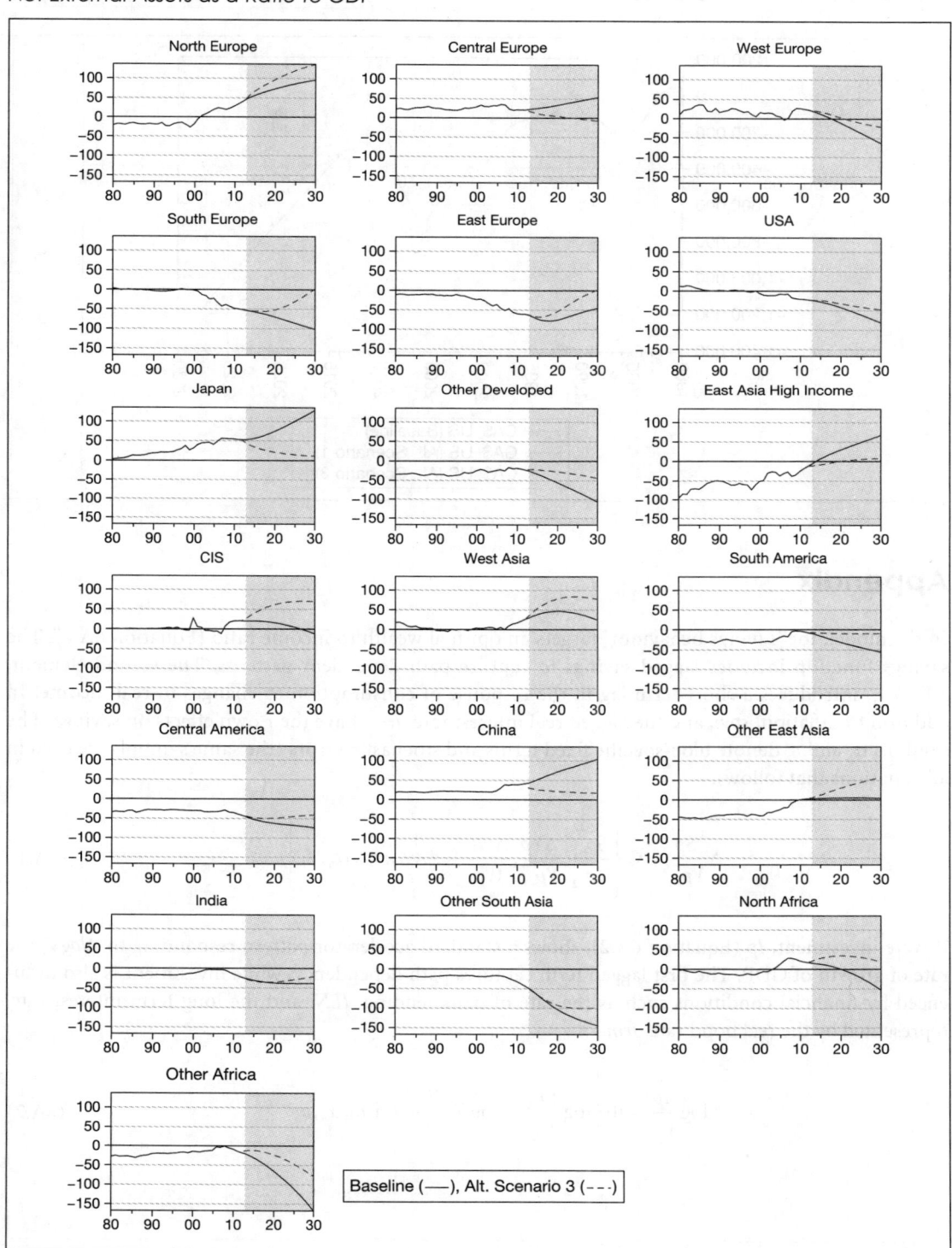

Figure 6.16
Current Account Balance of the US

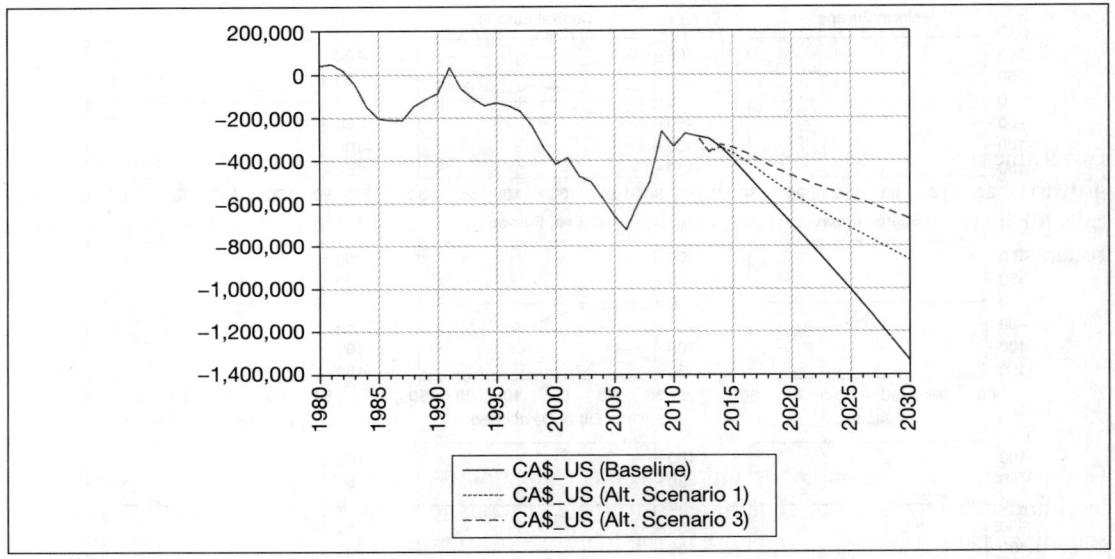

Appendix

In the model, the 'savings behaviour' targets an optimal wealth to income ratio (Equation 6A.1). The savings function includes lagged savings to capture path-dependent patterns. The second element, $\Delta Y_p/Y_{p-1}$, introduces a short-term lag in the response of consumption to changes in real income. In addition to inflation, *spvi*, and the lagged real interest rate, irs_{-1}, have their own effects on savings. The symbols α_b and ε_b denote bloc-specific fixed terms and stochastic errors (the same symbols are used in all equations that follow).

$$\Delta \frac{Sp}{Yp_{-1}} = \Phi \left\{ \overset{(-)}{\frac{Sp_{-1}}{Yp_{-2}}}, \overset{(+)}{\frac{\Delta Yp}{Yp_{-1}}}, \overset{(-)}{\frac{\Delta wp_{-1}}{Wp_{-2}}}, \overset{(+)}{spvi}, \overset{(+)}{irs_{-1}}, \alpha_b, \varepsilon_b \right\} \qquad (6A.1)$$

Private investment, *Ip* (Equation 6A.2), shows a standard accelerator pattern responding to $\Delta logV$, the rate of growth of GDP. The first lagged term captures path dependency, while investment is also influenced by financial conditions such as the rate of bank lending, *ILN*, and the long-term interest rate, represented by the real bond rate, *irm*.

$$\Delta \log \frac{Ip}{V_{-1}} = \Phi \left\{ \overset{(-)}{\log \frac{Ip_{-1}}{V_{-2}}}, \overset{(+)}{\Delta \log V}, \overset{(+)}{\frac{ILN_{-1}}{V_{-1}}}, \overset{(-)}{irm}, \alpha_b, \varepsilon_b \right\} \qquad (6A.2)$$

Inventory adjustment (Equation 6A.3) exhibits an accelerator response similar to the investment function with the short-term real interest rate, *irs*, replacing the bond rate.

$$\Delta \frac{IV}{V_{-1}} = \Phi \left\{ \overset{(-)}{\frac{IV_{-1}}{V_{-2}}}, \overset{(+)}{\Delta \log V}, \overset{(+)}{\frac{ILN_{-1}}{V_{-1}}}, \overset{(+)}{\Delta \frac{ILN}{V_{-1}}}, \overset{(-)}{irs}, \alpha_b, \varepsilon_b \right\} \quad (6A.3)$$

Government income, *Yg* (Equation 6A.4), is modelled to be path dependent, as well as a function of the growth of gross national income with some lag. The inherited stock of government debt, Lg_{-1}/Y_{-1}, usually calls for increased efforts to raise taxation, while interest on accumulated debt will erode government receipts.

$$\frac{\Delta Yg}{Y_{-1}} = \Phi \left\{ \overset{(-)}{\frac{Yg_{-1}}{Y_{-1}}}, \overset{(+)}{\frac{\Delta Y}{Y_{-1}}}, \overset{(+)}{\frac{\Delta Y_{-1}}{Y_{-1}}}, \overset{(-)}{\frac{Lg_{-1}}{Y_{-1}}}, \overset{(-)}{irm_{-1} \cdot \frac{Lg_{-1}}{Y_{-1}}}, \alpha_b, \varepsilon_b \right\} \quad (6A.4)$$

Government spending on goods and services, *G* (Equation 6A.5), is path dependent, responds to the level and rate of change of government income and tends to rise with population, *N*. Government spending is also adjusted in response to the inherited debt burden, Lg_{-1}/Y_{-1}, and the external balance as a ratio to GDP $\frac{CA\$_{-1}}{Y\$_{-1}}$ (external imbalances may require policy correction through contraction of domestic demand).

$$\Delta \log G = \Phi \left\{ \overset{(-)}{\log G_{-1}}, \overset{(+)}{\Delta \log Yg}, \overset{(+)}{\frac{Yg_{-1}}{Y_{-1}}}, \overset{(+)}{\log N_{-1}}, \overset{(-)}{\log \frac{Lg_{-1}}{Y_{-1}}}, \overset{(+)}{\frac{CA\$_{-1}}{Y\$_{-1}}}, \alpha_b, \varepsilon_b \right\} \quad (6A.5)$$

In the external sector, the model distinguishes between two parts of the current account balance, i.e., (a) the trade balance and (b) net incomes and transfers from abroad. International trade is modelled separately for the manufacturing, energy, primary and services sectors.

The international trade for manufactures is modelled on a bilateral basis between pairs of regional blocs. Imports of manufactures respond to activity, prices, the real exchange rate, etc., with the price being calculated as a weighted average of export prices of suppliers. Exports are driven by market shares (for example, share of imports of each bloc) responding to relative unit costs, calculated as a weighted average of domestic costs and costs of imports of primary commodities, energy and services as well as manufactures.

Energy production, demand and trade flows are determined in physical terms. A world pool for traded energy products is cleared by movements of the world price of oil. The oil price is treated as a benchmark and other kinds of energy (gas, coal and primary electricity) are measured in 'tons of oil equivalent'.

The international trade for primary commodities functions as a price-clearing pool with some friction resulting in partial quantity adjustment. Bloc equations, given world prices and domestic demand, determine net exports or imports. Exports of each bloc are scaled to ensure that world exports will equal world imports and the world price responds to growth of world imports.

The international trade for services is another pool. Net exports of each bloc are measured in international purchasing power and depend on the real exchange rate and service requirements of different branches of merchandise trade. Imports are determined as a function of net exports and the same variables, leaving exports (gross) to be calculated as the balancing item.

Finally, net income and transfers from abroad, $BIT_\$$ (Equation 6A.6), is estimated in a way that improves stability of the external balance. A lagged variable absorbs the error correction dynamic process, while $NX_\$$, the inherited net external position, when multiplied by the interest rate of reference of the reserve currency bonds, im_{US}, serves as a proxy for factor revenues.

$$\frac{\Delta BIT\$}{Y\$_{-1}} = \Phi\left\{\overset{(-)}{\frac{BIT\$_{-1}}{Y\$_{-1}}}, im_{US} \cdot \overset{(+)}{\frac{NX\$_{-1}}{Y\$_{-1}}}, \overset{(+)}{\frac{\Delta NX\$}{Y\$_{-1}}}, \alpha_b, \varepsilon_b\right\} \tag{6A.6}$$

References

Abeysinghe, T., & Choy, K.M. (2004). The aggregate consumption puzzle in Singapore. *Journal of Asian Economics*, 15(3), 563–578.

Backus, D., Henriksen, E., Lambert, F., & C. Telmer. (2009). *Current account fact and fiction*. NBER Working Paper No. 15525.

Bergsten, C.F., Freeman, C., Lardy, N.R., & Mitchell, D.J. (2009). *China's rise: Challenges and opportunities*. Washington, DC: Peterson Institute for International Economics and Center for Strategic and International Studies.

Bernanke, B.S. (10 March 2005). *The global saving glut and the U.S. current account deficit*. Remarks by Governor Ben S. Bernanke at the Homer Jones Lecture, St. Louis, Missouri. Retrieved from http://www.federalreserve.gov/boarddocs/speeches/2005/20050414/default.htm

Chinn, M.D., Eichengreen, B., & Ito, H. (2011). *A forensic analysis of global imbalances*. NBER Working Paper No. 17513.

Cripps, F., Izurieta, A., & Vos, R. (2010a). *The UN DESA global policy model: Underlying concepts and empirical illustrations*. United Nations: New York. Retrieved from http://www.un.org/en/development/desa/policy/publications/un_gpm.shtml

Cripps, F., Izurieta, A., & Vos, R. (2010b). *The UN DESA global policy model: Technical description of GPM version 3.0*. United Nations: New York. Retrieved from http://www.un.org/en/development/desa/policy/publications/un_gpm.shtml

Deardorff, A. (2010). A trade theorist's take on global imbalance. In S. Evenett (Ed.), *The US-Sino currency dispute: New insights from economics, politics and law*. London, UK: Centre for Economic Policy Research.

Edwards, S. (2006). *The US current account deficit: Gradual correction or abrupt adjustment*. NBER Working Paper No. 12154.

Feldstein, M. (2008). *Resolving the global imbalance: The dollar and the U.S. saving rate*. NBER Working Paper No. 13952.

IMF. (April 2009). *World economic outlook:* Washington, DC: International Monetary Fund.

Kowalski, P., & Lesher, M. (2010). A commercial policy package for rebalancing the global economy. In S. Claessens, S. Evenett, & B. Hoekman (Eds.), *Rebalancing the global economy: A primer for policymaking*. London, UK: Centre for Economic Policy Research.

Kuijs, L. (2005). *Investment and saving in China*. World Bank Policy Research Paper Series No. 3633: Washington, DC: World Bank.

Kumar, R., & Alex, D. (2011). Large Asian economies and the United States: Is rebalancing feasible? In K. Dervis, M. Kawai, & D. Lombardi (Eds.), *Asia and policymaking for the global economy*. Washington, DC/Tokyo: Brookings Institution Press/Asian Development Bank.

Lim, L.Y.C. (2010). Rebalancing in East Asia. In S. Claessens, S. Evenett & B. Hoekman (Eds.) *Rebalancing the global economy: A primer for policymaking*. London, UK: Centre for Economic Policy Research.

Mann, C.L. (2010). External imbalances: Costs and consequences of unsustainable trajectories. In S. Claessens, S. Evenett, B. Hoekman (Eds.), *Rebalancing the global economy: A primer for policymaking*. London, UK: Centre for Economic Policy Research.

Modigliani, F., & Cao, S.L. (March 2004). The Chinese saving puzzle and the life-cycle hypothesis. *Journal of Economic Literature, 42*(1), 145–170.

Williamson, J., & Cline, W.R. (2010). Exchange rates to support global rebalancing. In S. Claessens, S. Evenett, & B. Hoekman (Eds.), *Rebalancing the global economy: A primer for policymaking*. London, UK: Centre for Economic Policy Research.

7

Effect of Fiscal Policy on Level of Activity under Capital Flows

Surajit Das[*]

Models of Capital Mobility and Their Limitations

Incorporating the possibility of capital flows in an open economy set-up, an extension of the closed economy IS–LM analysis (Hicks, 1937) was introduced in the literature in the early 1960s by Marcus Fleming (1962) and Robert Mundell (1963). The Mundell–Fleming (M–F) model is one of the most influential macroeconomic models in the context of an open economy with capital flows whose presence is there right from high school textbooks to the highest level policymaking circles. This model is so celebrated because of its strengths lying in the following facts. First, it does not require the assumption of full employment or, in other words, it is perfectly compatible with the Keynesian assumption of downward rigidity of money wages. Second, it is one of the pioneering models recognising capital flows separately in the balance of payment (BoP) of any country. Third, it is a simple comparative static equilibrium framework that is easily comprehensible. And, most importantly, it deals with the basic macroeconomic aggregates of commodity market, money market and the BoPs, including capital flows, in order to determine the aggregate level of activity and employment (given technology/labour productivity).

The essential idea behind the M–F doctrine was to link the money and the monetary policy with the real economic activities in the context of an open economy with capital mobility. The primary focus on the money supply (and not even on the interest rate as an integral part of the monetary policy) made the foreign exchange market secondary in the M–F model. However, in reality, the monetary authority tries to influence the domestic interest rate as well as the exchange rate more directly rather than controlling the aggregate money supply per se.

The M–F model has two separate analyses—one is under fixed and another is under flexible exchange rate assumptions. The assumption of fixed or pegged exchange rate entails that there is little scope for monetary policy but that the expansionary fiscal policy may work in enhancing growth of level of activities and employment. On the other hand, under the assumption of flexible exchange rate, if there is perfect capital mobility, a monetary expansion leads to an increase in aggregate demand while a fiscal or export expansion has no effect at all on the level of output and employment even under a demand-constrained

---

[*] Views are personal. The author is deeply indebted to Professor Prabhat Patnaik and Professor Anjan Mukherji for their comments and inputs.

situation. Expansionary fiscal policies would not be effective because the entire additional demand would necessarily be leaked by an equivalent import surplus.[1]

The crux of the argument put forward by the M–F model (or popularly known as the IS-LM-BP model) in the context of floating exchange rate and 'perfect' capital mobility is quite clear. In the context of an open economy, the commodity market equilibrium equation or the IS curve is a negatively sloped schedule in the rate of interest–income (r–Y) plane. The aggregate supply of money (Ms) is assumed to be determined exogenously. Now, if the total demand for money be the sum of transaction demand for money (L_1) and the speculative demand for money (L_2), then the equation for money market equilibrium or equation for LM curve be $M_s = L_1(Y) + L_2(r)$, and it is a positively sloped curve in the r–Y plane. The BP schedule shows those combinations of real income and real interest rates that give equilibrium in the BoPs for a given exchange rate. The BP schedule is again a positively sloped schedule in the r–Y plane. The M–F assumption under 'perfect' capital mobility is that if the domestic rate of interest is higher than the world rate of interest, then unlimited capital inflow will take place and vice versa. And ultimately domestic interest rates of the concerned country cannot be different (exchange rate expectations and country risks are ignored for the time being for simplicity) from what prevails internationally. The model in its simplest terms can be described as

$$r = r^* \tag{7.1}$$

$$M_s = L(Y, r) \tag{7.2}$$

$$Y = C(Y - tY) + I(r, Y) + G + NX(Y, e) \tag{7.3}$$

where r is the domestic rate of interest, r^* is the prevailing world rate of interest, e is the exchange rate, NX is the net exports, t is the given tax rate (for simplicity without loss of generality) and the other symbols have their usual meanings. Note that $r = r^*$, because in equilibrium, it must necessarily hold, and we are concerned only with equilibria. These three equations determine the values of three unknowns, viz., r, Y and e (if G is given). In case of fixed exchange rate, e is given and therefore it is money supply that becomes an unknown or endogenously determined within the system.

There have been some extensions of the M–F model. Mussa (1976) and Dornbusch (1976) came out with two different papers, which were extensions of the M–F model incorporating expectations. As has been summarised by Parkin (1976), Mussa's paper talked about four basic propositions as follows. First, an exchange rate is a relative price of two national monies and is determined by the conditions for stock equilibrium in the markets for national monies and not in flow markets for goods. Second, one of the factors that influence the demand for money and, therefore, the exchange rate is the expected future exchange rate. That expectation is formed rationally and depends, therefore, on expected future monetary policy. Third, the exchange rate is not purely a monetary phenomenon. Real factors that affect the demand for money also affect the exchange rate. Fourth, the problem of policy conflict that exists under fixed rates is modified rather than eliminated by floating rates.

---

[1] "But this (increased government spending financed by borrowing) would increase the demand for money, raise interest rates, attract a capital inflow, and appreciate the exchange rate, which in turn would have a depressing effect on income. In fact, therefore the negative effect on income of exchange rate appreciation has to offset exactly the positive multiplier effect on income of the original increase in government spending. Income cannot change unless the money supply or interest rates change, the change in government spending is equal to the import surplus" (Mundell, 1963).

Parkin (1976) commented that the modern post-Keynesian view of the role of stock equilibrium in the money market reverses the two links in the 'Fisher causation'[2] story. The proximate determinants of the price level are now seen as the price expectations and assessments of excess demands by price setting firms (and households) in individual markets for goods and services (and factors of production). Given a price level thus determined, stock equilibrium in the money market arises from interest rate and real output adjustments. In other words, it is interest rates and real aggregate demand that are proximately determined by the equality of the supply of and demand for money. Now, if the exchange rates are, by definition, relative prices of national money, then it does not follow the central proposition of Mussa that the proximate determinants of exchange rates are the demand for and the supplies of various national monies.

On the other hand, Dornbusch's model is based on rational expectation and perfect foresight—more popular as the overshooting model. Later, Rogoff (2002) made another extension to it. Two relationships lie at the heart of the overshooting result. The first is the 'uncovered interest parity' condition. It says that the home interest rate on bonds, i, must equal the foreign interest rate, i^*, plus the expected rate of depreciation of the exchange rate, e_t (that is, $e_{t+1} - e_t$), where e is the logarithm of the exchange rate (home currency price of foreign currency). The second core equation of the Dorbusch model is the money demand equation: $M_t - P_t = -\eta i_{t+1} + \varphi Y_t$, where M is the money supply, P is the domestic price level and Y is the domestic output, all in logarithms, and η and φ are positive parameters. Higher interest rates raise the opportunity cost of holding money and thereby lower the demand for money. Conversely, an increase in output raises the transactions demand for money. Finally, the demand for money is proportional to the price level for given Y and i. Now if for a monetary shock, the money supply M rises relative to domestic price level P, the interest rate i must fall for any given level of Y. If i falls relative to i^*, then foreign currency outflow takes place, and the long-run impact of the money supply shock must be a proportionate depreciation in the exchange rate. The initial depreciation of the exchange rate must, on impact, be larger than the long-run depreciation. This initial excess depreciation leaves room for the ensuing appreciation needed to simultaneously clear the bond and money markets. The exchange rate must overshoot.[3] But Y is assumed to be given because of an underlying full employment assumption. However, the original formulation of the M–F model does not require this assumption at all.

On the other hand, Patnaik and Rawal (2005) argued:

> It is of course true that in a world with global mobility of finance the rates of interest (a proxy for the spectrum of returns) must be the same in all countries (net of risk-premia); but when the rates of interest are equal in all countries, it is not the case that capital would flow into each country exactly to match its current account deficit. It would have an autonomy in its global pattern of flows (which can of course be sought to be explained in terms of 'expected returns' but such an explanation would border on a tautology), the macroeconomic consequences of which were not investigated by Mundell and Fleming whose theory in effect precludes autonomous financial flows.

In today's world, nobody can deny the fact that finance capital is highly mobile across countries, and it is becoming more and more dynamic day by day with the strengthening of share markets, development of information technology and domestic policies of fuller capital account convertibility, various tax concessions given to foreign investors, etc. But, particularly in the context of developing countries, the

---

[2] "In the quantity theory tradition most convincingly presented by Irving Fisher (1911, ch. IV), the price level (and therefore the value of money) was regarded as being proximately determined by stock equilibrium in the money market. Any discrepancy between the rate of change of prices arising from this money market equilibrating process and the expected rate of price change would lead to adjustments in real output as producers responded to misread information about relative prices. Thus, the line of causation in the quantity theory of Fisher went from money to prices (i.e., money proximately determined the price level) and from prices relative to expected prices to real output and employment" (Parkin, 1976).

[3] See Obsfield and Rogoff (1996) for the elaboration about the mechanism.

assumption of perfectly elastic capital inflow is unrealistic. Rather, it would be more realistic to assume that a given amount of capital (say, k) becomes available to the country on the capital account during the single period under discussion. The destination and direction of international finance capital flows depend upon its profit opportunity net of perceived or expected risks. Now, this profit opportunity has very little (almost nothing) to do with the domestic interest rate of a particular economy in today's context. It is primarily the possibilities of capital gains based on various kinds of expectations (investors' confidence building spirals) and openness of the economy in terms of free in/out flows of finance capital which attract the foreign institutional investments (FIIs), which constitute a significantly large proportion of total net foreign capital flows. Apart from FIIs, other kinds of foreign investments or disinvestments are also dependent on profit opportunities, which are not really directly related to the rate of interest differential (vis-à-vis any given international interest rate like Federal Reserve System of United States [FED] rate or London Interbank Offered Rate [LIBOR] alone). In other words, the rate of interest is not at all a good proxy for the spectrum of returns expected by the international finance capital.

It is true that if the domestic interest rate is too high and the cost of credit is substantially lower elsewhere, then the domestic entrepreneurs may choose to borrow from abroad. It is also true that if the domestic interest is too low as compared with the internationally prevailing rate (FED rate or LIBOR), then there is a perceived risk of capital flight. However, the point is that the net foreign capital inflow in a particular economy and in a particular period of time should more realistically be assumed to be exogenously given rather than assuming it to be solely dependent on the domestic interest rate or interest rate differential or interest rate differential net of exchange rate fluctuation, etc. Interest differential may be one of the factors explaining a part of the aggregate capital flow given other things equal, but it is certainly not the dominant explanatory variable of the international financial flows in today's World. In the next section, we would elaborate this point with the help of available empirical evidences. In such a case, in addition to the three equations, there has to be a fourth one for the BoP equilibrium:

$$NX(Y,e) = -ke. \qquad (7.4)^4$$

now, since 'k' is given, the system is now overdetermined and the only way that equilibrium can exist if the money supply happens to be endogenous. Therefore, even in a world with flexible exchange rates, equilibrium in the foreign market can exist only if money supply ceases to be exogenous. Following the post-Keynesian concept of endogenous money supply, the endogeneity does not quite depend upon the degree of exchange rate flexibility[5] as is claimed by the M–F theorisation.

Capital Mobility: Some Empirical Evidence

The M–F doctrine makes the assumption that the interest rate differential net of risk of (expected) exchange rate fluctuation of a particular country solely causes net (in/out) flows of foreign capital. In Indian case, for example, we have witnessed that the net foreign capital inflows have dramatically increased particularly since 2003–2004 onwards, which have resulted in a phenomenal increase in the foreign exchange reserve of the order of US$320 billion (almost 30 per cent of India's gross domestic product, GDP) by 2007–2008 from less than US$60 billion during 1999–2000. However, interest rate has not increased at all during this period. Rather, the real interest differential of India with the US has

---

[4] Borrowed from Patnaik (2001).
[5] See Das (2010) for a literature survey of post-Keynesian endogenous money supply.

come down quite steadily, but the annual net foreign capital flow was surging up from virtually zero in 1999–2000 to over US$43 billion during 2007–2008. As a result of this huge net inflow, way above the current account deficit, the foreign exchange reserves have piled up and the exchange rate has appreciated to less than ₹40 per US dollar despite various government interventions in the foreign exchange market through sterilisation, market stabilisation schemes and other mechanisms. However, during the crisis of 2008–2009, the exchange rate depreciated to more than ₹50 per US dollar due to capital flight, and then again there was capital inflow and exchange rate appreciation in the recovery phase.

Clearly, the interest differential cannot really explain the sudden surge in inflow of foreign investment in the recent past in India. This capital flow has taken place mainly in the form of portfolio investment, although foreign direct investment (FDI; may be in the form of mergers and acquisitions or otherwise) has also increased since 2000–2001. During 2003 to 2007, the net portfolio investment (NPI) has been almost double of the net FDI in India. On the other hand, we find an extremely closed relation between the Bombay Stock Exchange (BSE) Sensex and aggregate net foreign investment. During 2008, we have witnessed capital flight before, during and after the financial crisis in the West followed by a recovery in the recent past. The BSE Sensex also moved accordingly.

The direction of flows of ever-increasing international pool of finance capital cannot be seen in isolation only from one country's point of view. How this pool gets distributed among countries and in which proportion they fly away from various economies need to be discussed. It is also important to distinguish between the flow of FDI and that of the NPI. If we look at the worldwide flow of FDI during 2003–2007,[6] that is, the period when India witnessed maximum net foreign capital inflow, we see that the top 20 countries have received, on an average, more than 70 per cent of entire FDI available for all 170 countries (for which data are available). China alone has received 34 per cent of net FDI of what was available for these top 20 countries. India has been in the eighth position, with 3.33 per cent of net FDI of top 20 countries. As far as the top 20 countries with net outflow of FDI during 2003 to 2007 are concerned, they account for almost 100 per cent of the entire net outflow. The US tops with 16.7 per cent, followed by Euro countries and Japan (see Table 7.1). China is getting 24 per cent of world's FDI, and the developed world is facing net outflow in the recent development with the shift of manufacturing production base which everybody is talking about.

Similarly, if we look at the worldwide flows of portfolio capital, we see that, on an average, the top 20 countries receive 98 per cent of the entire NPI availability for 150 countries (for which data are available) during 2003 to 2007. Again, the top 20 countries facing an outflow of NPI account for 96 per cent of all outflows. The US alone attracts 60 per cent of NPI, and India was in the 10th position with 1.25 per cent of NPI among top 20 countries during 2003–2007. Countries that were experiencing portfolio capital outflow are France, Saudi Arabia, Switzerland, Norway, Chinese province of Hong Kong, Canada, Belgium, etc. Apart from the US, countries that have experienced significant net portfolio capital inflow are Spain, Luxemburg, UK, Germany, Italy, Australia, Japan, Greece, etc. (see Table 7.2). Net FDI inflow in all countries receiving positive FDI is just one-fourth of NPI on an average during 2003–2007.

Now, the crucial question is whether these flows of FDI and NPI are significantly dependent on the average interest rates of the respective countries or not. We have calculated some cross-sectional correlation coefficients between proportion of capital in/outflows and the average interest rates or average interest rates net of exchange rate fluctuations and their t-values and the respective probabilities of t-statistics

---

[6] The data source is International Financial Statistics (IFS) 2009a provided by the International Monetary Fund (IMF). For Indian data on trade deficit, exchange rate (₹/US$), international price of oil and petroleum product of Indian basket and domestic GDP at current market price, the source is *Handbook of Statistics on Indian Economy*, 2010, provided by the Reserve Bank of India (RBI), Government of India.

Table 7.1
Top 20 Countries in Terms of FDI Inlow/Outflow during 2003–2007

Net FDI Inflow (US Million $)		Percentage of	Net FDI Outflow (US Million $)		Percentage of
Country	Annual Average	Top 20 Countries	Country	Annual Average	Top 20 Countries
China, P.R.: Mainland	69,307	34.06	US	−54,936	−16.68
Mexico	16,612	8.17	Spain	−39,422	−11.97
Poland	10,340	5.08	Japan	−39,232	−11.91
Turkey	10,276	5.05	Germany	−38,396	−11.66
Singapore	9,864	4.85	France	−34,982	−10.62
Brazil	9,847	4.84	Switzerland	−23,859	−7.24
Romania	7,076	3.48	The Netherlands	−18,397	−5.59
India	6,780	3.33	Italy	−14,304	−4.34
Thailand	6,652	3.27	Luxembourg	−14,266	−4.33
Belgium	6,610	3.25	Ireland	−13,724	−4.17
Australia	6,504	3.20	Sweden	−10,987	−3.34
The Czech Republic	5,873	2.89	Norway	−9,017	−2.74
Chile	5,644	2.77	Kuwait	−4,827	−1.47
Egypt	5,480	2.69	Iceland	−3,250	−0.99
Ukraine	5,122	2.52	Denmark	−3,158	−0.96
Bulgaria	4,997	2.46	Korea	−2,305	−0.70
Kazakhstan	4,675	2.30	Austria	−1,711	−0.52
Colombia	4,588	2.25	Saudi Arabia	−1,573	−0.48
Canada	3,799	1.87	China, P.R.: Hong Kong	−762	−0.23
Finland	3,411	1.68	Venezuela, Rep. Bol.	−247	−0.08

Source: Calculated from IFS, IMF (2009a).

(Table 7.3). We have listed the average interest rate, exchange rate fluctuation and the interest rate net of exchange rate fluctuation of 48 countries (in alphabetical order) comprising of the top 20 countries with respect to either FDI in/outflows or NPI in/outflows during 2003 to 2007 in the Appendix.

Clearly, the above empirical evidence suggests that there is an insignificant correlation between FDI or NPI flows and the interest rates or that net of exchange rate fluctuations. However, external commercial borrowings may be related to the interest rate differential. But, these flows of FDI and NPI dominate the capital account, which, in turn, dominates the current account or the trade balance in countries with huge capital flows. The above-mentioned empirical evidence substantiates the proposition that the direction, origin and destination of international flows of finance capital are not solely determined by the interest rate differential for sure. Other factors dominate. In that sense, it is exogenous from any single country's point of view. The so-called 'investment-friendly environment', government guarantees like full capital account convertibility and tax concession on capital gains for the foreign investors in

Table 7.2

Top 20 Countries vis-à-vis Net Inflow/Outflow of Portfolio Capital during 2003–2007

NPI Inflow (US Million $)		Percentage of	NPI Outflow (US Million $)		Percentage of
Country	Annual Average	Top 20 Countries	Country	Annual Average	Top 20 Countries
US	633,996	59.79	France	−66,868	18.84
Spain	91,974	8.67	Saudi Arabia	−54,621	15.39
Luxembourg	65,933	6.22	Switzerland	−36,419	10.26
UK	50,036	4.72	Norway	−27,827	7.84
Germany	44,486	4.20	China, P.R.: Hong Kong	−26,849	7.57
Italy	34,082	3.21	Canada	−25,935	7.31
Australia	27,648	2.61	Belgium	−25,520	7.19
Japan	23,044	2.17	Kuwait	−19,280	5.43
Greece	14,701	1.39	Denmark	−13,452	3.79
India	13,269	1.25	Finland	−9,206	2.59
Brazil	12,681	1.20	Singapore	−8,867	2.50
South Africa	8,627	0.81	Sweden	−8,604	2.42
Mexico	7,008	0.66	Chile	−6,925	1.95
Austria	6,602	0.62	Bahrain, Kingdom of	−5,584	1.57
Turkey	6,403	0.60	China, P.R.: Mainland	−4,540	1.28
Iceland	5,373	0.51	Netherlands	−3,758	1.06
Indonesia	4,130	0.39	Korea	−3,350	0.94
Hungary	3,645	0.34	Kazakhstan	−3,065	0.86
New Zealand	3,432	0.32	Ireland	−2,583	0.73
Poland	3,234	0.31	Malta	−1,638	0.46

Source: Calculated from IFS, IMF (2009a).

the share markets, easy mobility of finance capital due to development of information technology and internet banking, etc., are anyway out of the scope of the M–F framework. Even if the interest parity is maintained all over the world after adjustments for various country risks and exchange rate fluctuations in forward market, then the finance capital would also move in search of profit. This expected rate of profit has very little to do with domestic interest rates.

However, these flows of finance capital affect the exchange rate significantly, which, in turn, affects the trade deficit. For example, in the Indian case, the exchange rate fluctuation has very strong and significant effect on the trade deficit and, in turn, on the aggregate level of activity. If the exchange rate appreciates, then historically the trade deficit increases at least in the Indian case and dampens the level of activity and employment. If we regress the logarithm of trade deficit of India with respect to the logarithm of the Indian exchange rate vis-à-vis US dollar (Rs/US$), the logarithm of India's GDP at current market price and logarithm of the international price of the Indian basket of oil and petroleum products, we obtain a significant negative relationship with the exchange rate with partial elasticity of 2.4 during the period 1977–1978 to 2007–2008. As expected, trade deficit is a positive function of domestic GDP

Table 7.3
Correlation between Capital Flows and Interest Rates

Dependent Variable	Independent Variable	Correlation Coefficient	P(t)
Average net FDI outflow of a particular country as a percentage of average net FDI outflow of 20 countries during 2003–2007	Average interest rate of respective countries during 2003–2007	(–)0.27	0.24
Average net FDI outflow of a particular country as a percentage of average net FDI outflow of top 20 countries during 2003–2007	Average interest rate net of average exchange rate fluctuation of respective countries during 2003–2007	(–)0.24	0.31
Average net FDI inflow of a particular country as a percentage of average net FDI inflow of top 20 countries 2003–2007	Average interest rate of respective countries during 2003–2007	(–)0.07	0.75
Average net FDI inflow of a particular country as a percentage of average net FDI inflow of top 20 countries during 2003–2007	Average interest rate net of average exchange rate fluctuation of respective countries during 2003–2007	0.00	0.99
Average net FDI in/outflow of a particular country as a percentage of average net FDI in/outflow of top 40 countries during 2003–2007	Average interest rate of respective countries during 2003–2007	0.18	0.28
Average net FDI in/outflow of a particular country as a percentage of average net FDI in/outflow of top 40 countries during 2003–2007	Average interest rate net of average exchange rate fluctuation of respective countries during 2003–2007	0.20	0.20
Average NPI outflow of a particular country as a percentage of average NPI outflow of top 20 countries during 2003–2007	Average interest rate of respective countries during 2003–2007	(–)0.32	0.17
Average NPI outflow of a particular country as a percentage of average NPI outflow of top 20 countries during 2003–2007	Average interest rate net of average exchange rate fluctuation of respective countries during 2003–2007	(–)0.06	0.79
Average NPI inflow of a particular country as a percentage of average NPI inflow of top 20 countries during 2003–2007	Average interest rate of respective countries during 2003–2007	(–)0.18	0.45
Average NPI inflow of a particular country as a percentage of average NPI inflow of top 20 countries during 2003–2007	Average interest rate net of average exchange rate fluctuation of respective countries during 2003–2007	(–)0.09	0.72
Average NPI in/outflow of a particular country as a percentage of average NPI in/outflow of top 40 countries during 2003–2007	Average interest rate of respective countries during 2003–2007	0.04	0.81
Average NPI in/outflow of a particular country as a percentage of average NPI in/outflow of top 40 countries during 2003–2007	Average interest rate net of average exchange rate fluctuation of respective countries during 2003–2007	0.09	0.57

Source: Calculated from IFS, IMF (2009a).

(as import demand rises with GDP) and a positive function of international price of oil and petroleum products of the average Indian basket (as it inflates the import bill given relatively inelastic demand for oil). The model is a fairly good fit with R^2 being 96.66 per cent and Durbin–Watson statistics being exactly 2 (see Table 7.4), with a dummy for 1998–1999 capturing the possible post-South East Asian crisis effect. The residual is fairly stationary.

Table 7.4
Relation of Trade Deficit with Exchange Rate during 1977–1978 to 2007–2008 in India

Dependent Variable: Log of Trade Deficit
Method: Least Squares
Sample: 1977–1978 to 2007–2008
Included Observations: 31

Explanatory Variables (Var)	Coefficient	Standard Error	t-Statistic	Probability (Prob)
Constant	−18.26503	1.806253	−10.11211	0.0000
Log of exchange rate	−2.364841	0.484321	−4.882793	0.0000
Log of domestic GDP	2.322476	0.288435	8.051991	0.0000
Log of international price of oil	0.716357	0.191822	3.734497	0.0009
Dummy 1998–1999	0.888159	0.233459	3.804338	0.0008
R^2	0.966581	Mean-dependent var		9.542392
Adjusted R^2	0.961440	SD-dependent var		1.507704
Standard error of regression	0.296063	Akaike info criterion		0.550200
Sum squared residual	2.278984	Schwarz criterion		0.781488
Log likelihood	−3.528104	F-statistic		188.0026
Durbin–Watson statistics	2.005778	Prob (F-statistic)		0.000000

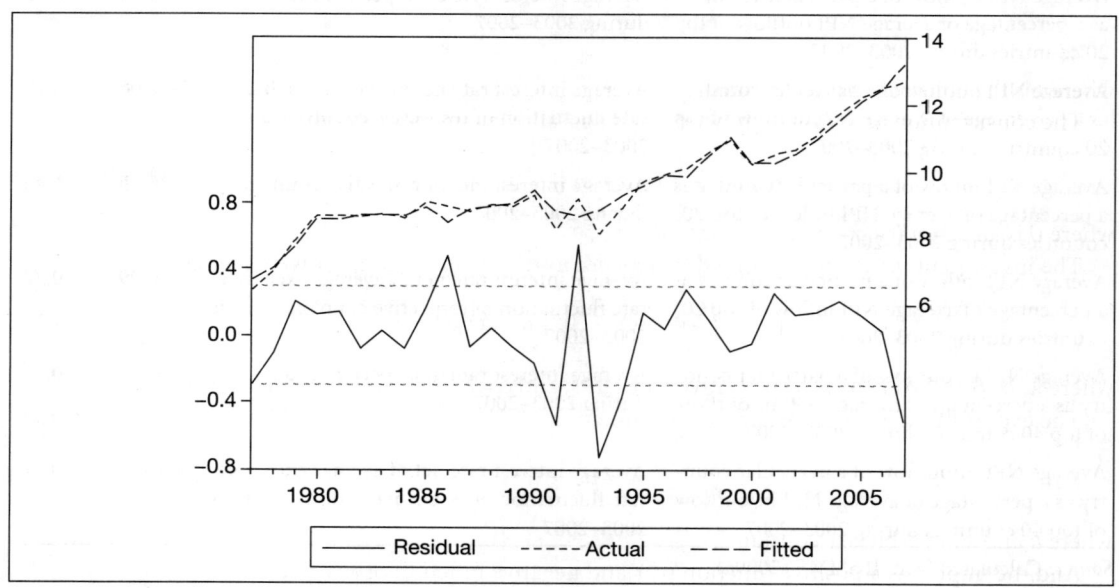

Source: Calculated from RBI (2010).

Note: Relationship between trade deficits with advanced country GDP is tested to be insignificant. The data for the advanced country GDP are taken from the World Economic Outlook 2009, IMF.

An Alternative Model

If the money supply happens to be endogenously determined and the net foreign capital inflow happens to be exogenous than in a simple comparative static framework, then some of the obvious corollaries of the M–F model are reversed. The M–F postulate is that the product and the money market equilibrium conditions would determine the overall level of activity and employment in the economy irrespective of the situation of the BoP, and the capital flow would always automatically necessarily adjust to it under a flexible exchange rate.

We believe that it would be more realistic to assume that the macroeconomic equilibrium is determined through the simultaneous equilibrium in the commodity market and BoP, and the money market automatically always adjusts to that equilibrium in the context of an open economy with free capital flows. Capital flow is not a passive residual variable as was postulated by the M–F doctrine, but, in today's context, it is one of the crucial exogenous variables that actively affect the level of activity and employment in an economy. For a formal derivation, let us assume some standard relationships in their simplest linear[7] form as follows.

Setting up the Model

The national income identity or the commodity market equilibrium condition is given by

$$Y = C(Y-T) + I(r,Y) + G + X(e) - M(Y,e), \tag{7.5}$$

where Y is the aggregate income, C is the consumption, T is the tax, I is the investment, r is the rate of interest, G is the government spending, X is the export, e is the exchange rate and M is the import.

Standard tax function, when the tax–GDP ratio is assumed to be given, takes the form

$$T = tY, \tag{7.6}$$

where t is the constant tax–GDP ratio.

The consumption as a positive function of disposable income is given by

$$C = \theta + c(Y-T) = \theta + cY(1-t), \tag{7.7} \text{ [since (7.6)]}$$

where θ is an arbitrary positive constant.

The investment function is assumed to depend positively on Y and negatively on r as

$$I = \lambda + \alpha Y - \beta r = \delta + \alpha Y, \tag{7.8}$$

where λ, α, β and δ are arbitrary positive constants, and $\delta = \lambda - \beta r^*$ when $r = r^*$ administered.

The export function is given as a positive function of the exchange rate and hence competitiveness is

$$X = \mu + ex, \tag{7.9}$$

where μ and x are arbitrary constants.

And the import as a positive function of Y and negative function of e is given as

$$M = \rho + mY - en. \tag{7.10}$$

---

[7] See Das (2008) for generalised derivation without the assumption of linearity and the stability condition.

Therefore, from Equation 7.5, we obtain the commodity market equilibrium condition as

$$Y = \theta + cY(1-t) + \delta + \alpha Y + G + \mu + ex - (\rho + mY - en)$$
$$\Rightarrow Y[1 - c(1-t)] - \alpha + m] = \varphi + e(x+n), \qquad (7.11)$$

where $\varphi = \theta + \delta + G + \mu - \rho$.

The equilibrium condition for the BoP in the foreign exchange market will be

$$\rho + mY - en - (\mu + ex) = ke = K, \qquad (7.12)$$

that is, the current account deficit is equal to net foreign capital inflow in terms of domestic currency.

Equation 7.11 shows the relationship between e and Y for the commodity market equilibrium, and Equation 7.12 gives the relationship between e and Y in BoP equilibrium. For fixed exchange rate $e = e^*$, we obtain a solution for Y from equation 7.12 itself as $Y = (ke^* + X - A)/m = Y^*$, where, $A = \rho - e^* n$.

For flexible exchange rate to get a unique solution for e and Y, we need equilibrium in the commodity and foreign exchange market simultaneously.

From Equation 7.11, we get the slope of the commodity market equilibrium condition as

$$\frac{de}{dY} = \frac{1 - c(1-t) - \alpha + m}{x + n}. \qquad (7.13)$$

From Equation 7.12, we get the slope of the foreign exchange market BoP equilibrium condition as

$$\frac{de}{dY} = \frac{m}{(x+n+k)}. \qquad (7.14)$$

Stability Condition

It would be fairly reasonable to assume in any economy that[8]

$$G > M - X$$
$$\Rightarrow G + \theta + \delta > M - X$$
$$\Rightarrow Y \equiv C + I + G + X - M > C - \theta + I - \delta \equiv \alpha Y + cY(1-t) \qquad \text{(from 7 and 8)}$$
$$\Rightarrow 1 > c(1-t) + \alpha, \quad \text{or} \quad [1 - c(1-t) - \alpha] > 0.$$

Since $[1 - c(1-t) - \alpha] > 0$, (the multiplier)

that is, $\dfrac{1 - c(1-t) - \alpha}{x + n} > 0.$ (since $x, n > 0$)

Again, $\dfrac{m}{(x+n)} > \dfrac{m}{(x+n+k)}.$ (since $m, k > 0$)

Therefore, $\dfrac{1 - c(1-t) - \alpha}{x + n} + \dfrac{m}{(x+n)} > \dfrac{m}{(x+n+k)},$

---

[8] We have looked at the data of the current account deficit to GDP ratio from the World Bank and data on government expenditure to GDP ratio from the World Economic Outlook database of the IMF for the years 2005, 2006 and 2007. Both the series were available for 169 countries. The government expenditure to GDP ratio is higher than the current account deficit to GDP ratio in the context of almost all the countries excepting only two (Grenada and Liberia).

that is, $\dfrac{1-c(1-t)-\alpha+m}{(x+n)} > \dfrac{m}{(x+n+k)}$

[where $m=|\delta M/\delta Y|$, $x=|\delta X/\delta e|$, $n=|\delta M/\delta e|$ and $k=|\delta K/\delta e|$],
that is, the slope of the commodity market equilibrium condition is greater than the slope of the BoP equilibrium condition. This is the stability condition of the existence of equilibrium.

Therefore, $\dfrac{(x+n)}{m} + \dfrac{k}{m} > \dfrac{(x+n)}{1-c(1-t)-\alpha+m}$.

The impact of a given change in exchange rate on the level of activity for BoP equilibrium is higher than that for equilibrium in the commodity market. A certain change in the exchange rate, for any given level of net capital inflow, would change the net availability of capital account surplus in terms of domestic currency. Given the stock of foreign exchange, for BoP equilibrium, the net import in terms of domestic currency has to be equal to that particular amount of capital account surplus. Net import, being a positive function of level of activity, would change with change in Y. Now, the commodity market would be affected due to change in import and export as a result of change in exchange rate. On the other hand, the BoP market equilibrium would be affected by change in export, import as well as value of net capital inflow due to exchange rate fluctuation. Moreover, in the commodity market, the effect of exchange rate fluctuation on the level of activity via change in import and export would be comparatively more moderate. In the above equation on the left-hand side, not only the positive factor (k/m) is extra but also $(x+n)/m > (x+n)/[1-c(1-t)-\alpha+m]$. Taking reciprocal in both sides, we get $m/(x+n) < \{1-c(1-t)-\alpha+m\}/(x+n)$

$$or, [m/(x+n)] < [m/(x+n) + \{1-c(1-t)-\alpha\}/(x+n)]$$

As $[1-c(1-t)-\alpha]/(x+n) > 0$ always, therefore, the effect would be moderate.

Equilibrium Condition

From Equations 7.11 and 7.12, we get a solution for e and Y in the following manner:

Equation 7.11 implies that $Y = \dfrac{\varphi + e(x+n)}{1-c(1-t)-\alpha+m}$.

From Equation 7.12, we get $Y = [ke + en + (\mu + ex)]/m$.

For simultaneous equilibrium in both the markets, equating these two, we get

$$\dfrac{\dfrac{e(k+n+x)}{m} - e(x+n)}{1-c(1-t)-\alpha+m} = \dfrac{\varphi}{1-c(1-t)-\alpha+m} - \dfrac{\mu}{m} \qquad (7.15)$$

$$\Rightarrow e^* = \dfrac{(\varphi m - \mu m - \mu \xi)}{[\xi(x+n+k)+mk]}$$

$$Y^* = \dfrac{(\theta m - \mu m - \mu \xi)(k+n+x)}{m\{\xi(x+n+k)+mk\}} + \dfrac{\mu}{m}, \qquad (7.16)$$

[from (7.12)]

where $\xi = [1-c(1-t)-\alpha]$.

Therefore, coordinate (Y^*, e^*) in the e–Y plane is a particular combination of exchange rate and income where both the commodity and the foreign exchange market would be in equilibrium simultaneously.

Comparative Static

Now, let us see the effect of a change in government expenditure G and the net capital inflow k on the exchange rate e and aggregate output Y in a comparative static framework. If, for example, G rises by ΔG, ceteris paribus, then Y changes by ΔY and e changes by Δe. Now, if G increases by ΔG, then φ also increases by ΔG. Therefore, from Equation 7.16, we get

$$\Delta Y^* = \frac{\Delta G m(k+n+x)}{[m\{\xi(x+n+k)+mk\}]}$$

$$\frac{\Delta Y^*}{\Delta G} = \frac{m(k+n+x)}{[m\{\xi(x+n+k)+mk\}]} \quad (7.17)$$

[since $\xi = \{1-c(1-t)-\alpha\}$]

$$\frac{\Delta Y^*}{\Delta G} = \frac{(k+n+x)}{[\{1-c(1-t)-\alpha\}(x+n+k)+mk]}.$$

And from Equation 7.15, we get

$$\Delta e^* = \frac{\Delta G m}{[\xi(x+n+k)+mk]}$$

$$\frac{\Delta e^*}{\Delta G} = \frac{m}{[\xi(x+n+k)+mk]} \quad (7.18)$$

[since $\xi = \{1-c(1-t)-\alpha\}$]

$$\frac{\Delta e^*}{\Delta G} = \frac{m}{[\{1-c(1-t)-\alpha\}(x+n+k)+mk]}.$$

Therefore, we get $(\Delta Y^*/\Delta G) > 0$ as well as $(\Delta e^*/\Delta G) > 0$. Hence, if G increases, ceteris paribus, both Y and e unambiguously rise and vice versa for any given level of net capital inflow k.

Similarly, if k rises by Δk, Y^* becomes Y_1^* and e^* becomes e_1^*. Therefore, from (7.12), we get

$$Y_1^* = \frac{[\Delta k(\varphi m - \mu m - \mu \xi) + (k+n+x)(\varphi m - \mu m - \mu \xi)]}{[\Delta km(\xi + m) + m\{\xi(k+n+x)+mk\}]} + \frac{\mu}{m} \quad (7.19)$$

Now, Y_1^* would be less than Y^* if the percentage rise in the numerator is less than the percentage increase in the denominator (hence the ratio comes down) and vice versa.

$$\frac{\Delta k(\varphi m - \mu m - \mu \xi)}{[(k+n+x)(\varphi m - \mu m - \mu \xi)]} < \frac{\{\Delta km(\xi + m)\}}{\{m\{\xi(k+n+x)+mk\}\}},$$

that is, $\dfrac{\Delta k}{k+n+x} < \dfrac{\Delta k(\xi + m)}{\{\xi(k+n+x)+mk\}}$,

that is, $\dfrac{1}{k+n+x} < \dfrac{\xi + m}{\xi(k+n+x)+mk}$, that is, $\xi(k+n+x)+mk<(k+n+x)(\xi+m)$,

that is, $mk<(k+n+x)m$,

that is, $k<k+n+x$,

that is, $n+x>0$, but this is always true because by assumption both n and x are positive.

Therefore, if the net capital inflow increases, then necessarily Y declines to keep both the product and the foreign exchange market in equilibrium.

Similarly, from (7.15), we get

$$e_1^* = \frac{(\varphi m - \mu m - \mu \xi)}{[\Delta k(\xi + m) + \xi(k+n+x) + mk]}. \tag{7.20}$$

Now, $e^* > e_1^*$ if $\Delta k(\xi+m)>0$, this is always true because Δk, ξ and m are positive.

Therefore, if net capital inflow increases, then necessarily the exchange rate appreciates to keep both the product and the foreign exchange market in equilibrium. Hence, the ultimate effect of an expansion of autonomous demand on the level of activity is positive, and net capital inflow eventually reduces the level of employment and output under the flexible exchange rate.

The above comparative static results suggest that the expansionary fiscal policy would have a net positive impact on the level of activity to keep the commodity market and the foreign exchange market in equilibrium simultaneously. For any given level of capital flows, the expansionary fiscal policy would widen the current account deficit (or reduce the current account surplus) and, as a consequence, the exchange rate would depreciate. The depreciated exchange rate would, in turn, improve the current account balance to some extent by reducing import and increasing export. Ultimately, the leakage of aggregate demand through import surplus would be less than the addition to the aggregate demand as a result of the larger government expenditure. If there is larger inflow of foreign capital, the exchange rate would appreciate. As a result, the current account balance would deteriorate, which would cause the aggregate demand and the level of activity (in demand-constrained situation) to decline in the absence of any increase in the autonomous demand (like the larger government spending). However, worsening of the current account would have some depreciating effect on the domestic currency, but it would not be large enough to more than offset the initial appreciation. The net effect of larger capital inflow, *ceteris paribus*, would result in an appreciation of the domestic currency and a net reduction in output and employment.

Summary and Conclusion

In the M–F model, under flexible exchange rate, the equilibrium is determined through intersection of the commodity market equilibrium condition and the money market equilibrium condition subject to an exogenous aggregate money supply, and the foreign exchange market always adjusts automatically to that common equilibrium point. The current study is significantly deviating from the M–F doctrine in a number of ways. First, we are saying that the equilibrium exchange rate and the equilibrium aggregate level of activities are determined by goods market and foreign exchange market equilibria. The money market would always be in equilibrium at any rate of interest or, in other words, the money supply would be endogenously determined according to the demand for it.[9] Second, we are claiming here that the net foreign capital

---

[9] See (among others) Kaldor (1958), Robinson (1970), Moore (1988) and Pollin (1991).

inflow is not really directly dependent on the interest rate differentials; rather, it would be more realistic to assume that the net capital flows into or out of a particular economy to be exogenously determined at any particular period of time. Particularly in today's context, when most of the foreign capital flows take place through share markets in terms FII, it will be an exaggeration to say that the profit or loss opportunity of foreign investment would depend solely on the interest rate differential even after the adjustment of expected exchange rate fluctuations. Rather, the direction and destination of international finance capital would be driven by profit motive based on expected capital gains (profit) net of various kinds of country risks.

Net export is a positive function of the exchange rate ($NX = ke$), because if the exchange rate increases (that is, depreciation), exporters would get more price as export earning, and their competitiveness increases and importables become comparatively more expensive and, as a result, imports reduce. On the other hand, if the exchange rate appreciates, then the importers would be encouraged to import more at a relatively cheaper rate and exporters would be discouraged as their competitiveness would fall. The domestic production would be substituted by relatively cheaper imported inputs given any fixed rate of import duties, and as an obvious consequence de-industrialisation takes place in an open economy exposed to foreign capital flows under a flexible exchange rate regime (necessarily if the Marshall–Lerner condition holds[10]). Therefore, we get a positive function of aggregate demand Y with the exchange rate for commodity market equilibrium. If autonomous components of consumption or investment or the government expenditure increase, then for each levels of exchange rate, we would get a larger level of aggregate demand and larger amount of Y and, as a result, the commodity market equilibrium function shifts parametrically.

In the absence of any increase in autonomous demand, due to larger net capital inflow, the exchange rate would appreciate and the employment and output would fall (however, the opposite is not true[11]) under a flexible exchange rate regime. If autonomous demand, for example government expenditure, increases, *ceteris paribus*, then the level of activity would increase. However, if the foreign capital inflow helps domestic demand to boost up by increasing, for example, investment, exports or government expenditure, then also the commodity market equilibrium condition or the IS schedule shifts rightward, increasing the level of activity. If both net capital inflow and autonomous demand increase simultaneously, then the net effect on the level of activity would depend on which effect more than offsets what. Therefore, under such a situation under flexible exchange rate and with larger net capital inflow, the expansionary fiscal policy would definitely work, but its effect would be dampened on expansion of employment and the level of activity.

For a fixed exchange rate, the overall aggregate level of activity is solely determined by the commodity market equilibrium condition. As opposed to the essential corollary of the M–F doctrine that the expansionary fiscal policy would be completely ineffective, we are concluding that under the assumption of Keynesian downward wage rigidity in the presence of persisting involuntary unemployment and money supply endogeneity, given any tax rate, the expansionary fiscal policy unambiguously increases employment and output when the exchange rate is flexible. Again, the increase in net foreign capital inflow, *ceteris paribus*, reduces the level of employment and output. Therefore, the demand expansion has to be large enough to more than offset this dampening effect, or the foreign capital flows have to be controlled or some combination of these two. Therefore, the expansionary fiscal policies coupled with some control over foreign capital flows are recommended, as opposed to conservative fiscal stance along with absolutely reckless capital flows that we are witnessing today.

---

[10] See Sodersten (1980).
[11] For an explanation, see Patnaik and Rawal (2005).

References

Das, S. (2008). *Macroeconomic policy under a regime of free capital flows* (PhD thesis). Centre for Economic Studies and Planning, Jawaharlal Nehru University, New Delhi.

Das, S. (2010). On financing the fiscal deficit and availability of loanable funds in India. *Economic and Political Weekly, XLV*(15), 67–75.

Dornbusch, R. (1976). Expectations and exchange rate dynamics. *Journal of Political Economy, 84*(6), 1161–1176.

Fleming, M. (1962). Domestic financial policies under fixed and flexible exchange rates. *IMF Staff Papers, 19*(3), 369–380.

Hicks, J.R. (1937). Mr. Keynes and the classics: A suggested interpretation. *Econometrica, 5*(2), 147–159.

International Monetary Fund. (2009a). *International financial statistics database*. Washington, DC: Author.

———. (2009b). *World economic outlook database*. Washington, DC: Author.

Kaldor, N. (1958). *Monetary policy, economic stability and growth*. A Memorandum Submitted to the Committee of the Working of the Monetary System (Radcliffe Committee), June 23. (Reprinted in Collected Economic Papers, Vol. 3. Essays on Economic Policy I. London: Duckworth, 1964)

Moore, B.J. (1988). *Horizontalists and verticalists – the macroeconomics of credit money*. Cambridge: Cambridge University Press.

Mundell, R.A. (1963). Capital mobility and stabilization policy under fixed and flexible exchange rates. *The Canadian Journal of Economics and Political Science, 29*(4), 475–485.

Mussa, M. (1976). The exchange rate, the balance of payments, and monetary and fiscal policy under a regime of controlled floating. *Scandinavian Journal of Economics, 78*(2), 229–248.

Obsfield, M., & Rogoff K. (1996). *Foundations of international macroeconomics*. Massachusetts: The MIT Press.

Parkin, M. (1976). Comment on Mussa. *Scandinavian Journal of Economics, 78*(2), 249–254.

Patnaik, P. (2001). Capital mobility and open-economy macroeconomics. In R.K. Sen & B. Chatterjee (Eds.), *Indian economy: Agenda for the 21st century: Essays in honour of P.R. Brahmananda*. New Delhi: Deep and Deep Publication Private Limited.

Patnaik, P., & Rawal, V. (2005). Level of activity in an economy with free capital mobility. *Economic and Political Weeky, XL*(14), 1449–1457.

Pollin, R. (1991). Two theories of money supply endogeneity: Some empirical evidence. *Journal of Post Keynesian Economics, 13*(3), 366–395.

Reserve Bank of India. (2010). *Handbook of statistics on Indian economy database*. Mumbai: Reserve Bank of India.

Robinson, J. (1970). Quantity theories old and new: Comment. *Journal of Money, Credit and Banking, 2*(4), 504–512.

Rogoff, K. (2002). Dornbusch's overshooting model after twenty-five years. International Monetary Fund's Second Annual Research Conference Mundell–Fleming Lecture. *IMF Staff Papers, 49*(Special issue), 1–34.

Sodersten, B. (1980). *International economics*. London: The McMillan Press Ltd.

Appendix

Table 7A.1
Interest Rate and Exchange Rate Fluctuation of 48 Countries during 2003–2007

Country	Annual Average, 2003 to 2007			Country	Annual Average, 2003 to 2007		
	Interest Rate (%)	Exchange Rate (%) Fluctuation	Net Interest Rate (%)		Interest Rate (%)	Exchange Rate (%) Fluctuation	Net Interest Rate (%)
Australia	9.15	−7.98	1.17	Japan	1.76	−1.12	0.65
Austria	7.64	−7.00	0.64	Kazakhstan	8.40	−4.34	4.06
Bahrain, Kingdom of	8.14	0.00	8.14	Korea	6.05	−5.73	0.32
Belgium	7.57	−7.00	0.56	Kuwait	7.14	−1.36	5.78
Brazil	54.38	−7.46	46.93	Luxembourg	3.94	−7.00	−3.07
Bulgaria	8.99	−7.02	1.97	Malta	5.71	−6.18	−0.46
Canada	5.00	−7.36	−2.36	Mexico	7.85	2.63	10.48
Chile	6.93	−5.28	1.65	The Netherlands	7.95	−7.00	0.95
China, P.R.: Mainland	6.01	−1.66	4.35	New Zealand	11.36	−8.36	3.00
China, P.R.: Hong Kong	6.45	0.00	6.45	Norway	4.87	−5.92	−1.05
Colombia	14.62	−3.14	11.48	Poland	10.11	−7.40	2.70
Czech Republic	5.83	−9.08	−3.25	Romania	9.60	−5.77	3.83
Denmark	5.90	−6.96	−1.06	Saudi Arabia	6.00	0.00	6.00
Egypt	13.03	7.09	20.12	Singapore	5.31	−3.34	1.97
Finland	8.61	−7.00	1.61	South Africa	12.24	−6.76	5.49
France	6.60	−7.00	−0.40	Spain	8.57	−7.00	1.56
Germany	9.18	−7.00	2.18	Sweden	4.44	−6.81	−2.38
Greece	13.03	−7.00	6.03	Switzerland	3.15	−4.96	−1.81
Hungary	9.63	−6.30	3.33	Thailand	6.33	−4.23	2.09
Iceland	15.19	−6.47	8.72	Turkey	28.31	−2.80	25.51
India	11.47	−3.11	8.35	Ukraine	16.11	−1.06	15.04
Indonesia	14.99	−0.18	14.81	United Kingdom	4.58	−5.60	−1.02
Ireland	8.96	−7.00	1.96	US	6.13	0.00	6.13
Italy	10.78	−7.00	3.78	Venezuela, Rep. Bol.	18.62	13.93	32.55

Source: Calculated from IFS, IMF (2009a).

8

Foreign Direct Investment, Intellectual Property Rights and Technology Transfer

Biswajit Dhar and Reji Joseph

Introduction

Technology flows from the advanced to the developing countries, and the factors influencing such flows have engaged the attention of development economists during most part of the past half a century. With developing countries aspiring to emulate the development experience of the advanced countries, acquisition of technologies from the latter assumed critical importance. Although most of the studies have described this process as transfer of technology, the reality of the technology acquisition was aptly described by Constantine Vaitsos as one of 'technology commercialisation' or technology trade, which brought into focus the nature of the market through which technology is 'transferred' to the developing countries (Vaitsos, 1974). Vaitsos argued that technology transfer is governed by a bargaining relationship between the suppliers and the recipients. In this relationship, purchasers are at an inherent disadvantage, owing to two factors: (a) the oligopolistic or even monopolistic nature of the international market for technology and (b) the nature of technology itself, which is highly complex and cannot be evaluated thoroughly by buyers before a particular transaction (Rath & Herbert-Copley, 1993).

The relevance of the above characterisation of the process of technology stems from the fact that technology generation is, in turn, influenced by two factors that have been extensively discussed in a large body of literature, namely intellectual property rights (IPRs) and foreign direct investment (FDI). While several generations of economists have recognised the role that IPRs can play in overcoming the problem of market failure in the process of generation and diffusion of new knowledge, studies have also commented critically about the control exercised by the owners of IPRs over the market for technology. The focus on FDI as a factor determining technology transfer owes to the domination of transnational corporations (TNCs) in the market for technologies. Viewed from the perspective of the developing countries, FDI has been seen as a provider of technologies and managerial skills essential for these countries to achieve rapid economic development.

This chapter examines the factors influencing technology transfer as has been elaborated in the available literature by dwelling on the nature of influence of IPRs and FDI on technology transfer. Although there are different mechanisms for the transfer of technology, FDI is the most important one. Technology transfer through FDI depends on many factors, in which IPRs play a very crucial role. Owners of technology seem to prefer the FDI route to service foreign markets where IPRs are weak and licensing options for IPRs are strong. It also appears that the quality of technology transferred varies depending on the strength of IPRs. In general, it has been the case that obsolete technologies are transferred, whether through the FDI route or licensing route, to those countries where IPRs are weak (Blyde & Acea, 2002; Maskus, 1997; Yang & Maskus, 2001). This does not mean that strengthening of IPRs would automatically result in transfer of better technologies. Strong IPRs would result in transfer of better technologies only when the technology holder (FDI firm) faces competition in the foreign market (FDI host country). This means that the host country will have to do the groundwork for building up science and technology (S&T) capabilities and human resources.

FDI and Technology Transfer

A technology may be defined as "the information necessary to achieve a certain production outcome from a particular means of combining or processing selected inputs" (Maskus, 2004: 9). Technology may be codified (formulas, blueprints, patent applications, etc.) or uncodified, as well as embodied (capital equipment) or disembodied (pure know-how). There is a wide variation in embodiment across products and services, and products like pharmaceuticals are relatively very easy to be copied as compared with complex machineries. Technology transfer is the process by which one party gains access to the knowledge of another party in such a way that the accessing party is able to successfully adapt the knowledge into the production processes. Technology transfer may take place through market-based and non-market-based mechanisms. Market-based channels include trade in goods and services, FDI, licensing, joint ventures and cross-border movement of personnel, whereas major channels in the non-market-based system are imitation, departure of employees (who join in another firm/institution or begin their own business) and data in patent applications and test data (Maskus, 1997, 2004).

Exports may result in transfer of technology to the extent that they are studied for design characteristics and reverse engineering. Import of capital goods and technological inputs like chemicals can directly improve productivity when they are employed in the production process. In FDI, the ownership of knowledge-based assets of multinational companies (MNCs) provides them with cost or quality advantages that can be adapted in multiple locations (Markusen, 1995). Licences involve purchase of production and distribution rights (protected by IPRs) and the know-how required to enable the exercise of production and distribution rights. Licences may involve subsidiaries or unrelated firms. In intra-firm licensing, the MNC retains the control over IPRs and know-how, whereas in licensing involving unrelated firms, access is provided to the licensee of the IPRs and know-how (Maskus, 2004). Joint ventures are arrangements between two or more firms where each one provides some advantages that result in a reduced cost of operations. In joint ventures, generally MNCs provide superior knowledge-based assets, whereas the local firms provide locational advantages like distribution networks, brand recognition, etc. Movement of technical people also plays an important role in the process of transfer of technology. Adaptation of certain technologies requires the transfer of complementary services of engineers and technicians to do onsite jobs. MNCs are better able to transfer such personnel to their subsidiaries. Transfer of skilled personnel to unrelated firms may be more restrictive and less flexible, which may raise the costs of transfer and adaptation (Maskus, 2004). It is reported that the bulk of the international technology transfer takes place through market-based mechanisms or within multinational firms (Maskus, 2004).

An Important Channel but Not a Panacea

Among the different channels of technology transfer, FDI is the most significant channel. FDI is defined as "act of establishing or acquiring a foreign subsidiary over which the investing firm has substantial management control" (Maskus, 1997: 7). By definition, firms engaging in FDI are MNCs. MNCs engage in FDI when they have advantages in terms of either capital or technology or both as compared to the firms in the host country to overcome the disadvantages it might face in terms of language and cultural barriers, jurisdiction-specific tax treatments, distance from headquarters and monitoring local operations. FDI is generally viewed less as a source of finance and more as a source of technology- or knowledge-based assets. This is because the capital required in the investment may be raised from host country or global financial markets or even from local capital markets of the home country (Maskus, 1997).

In order to understand the link between FDI and transfer of technology, it is important to know the factors influencing decisions on FDI vis-à-vis other options for serving a particular market. A firm has the options of exporting the goods to that country, producing locally by undertaking FDI and controlling the production process, licensing or franchising its technology to an unrelated firm in the particular country and undertaking a joint venture involving some joint production or technology-sharing agreement. These decisions would depend on characteristics of particular market, called location advantages. Location advantages include market size and growth, local demand patterns, distance and transport costs, wage costs, endowments of natural resources, trade protectionism that could encourage 'tariff-jumping' FDI investment, modern infrastructure and transparent and predictable government procedures (Maskus, 1997).

Exports may be the preferred mode of supply when transport costs and tariffs are low in comparison to the costs of FDI and licensing. The volume of exports, under this mode of supply, could depend on the strength of local IPRs. The study of Maskus and Penubarti (1995) based on Organisation for Economic Co-operation and Development (OECD) countries' exports in 28 manufacturing sectors to 25 developing countries in 1984 found that exporting firms discriminate in their sales decisions, taking account of local patent laws. Hence, exports were larger to countries with stronger patent laws. A later study by Smith (1999) based on more disaggregated industry-wise data[1] confirmed the view that export decisions of firms are influenced by the strength of patent rights in the importing countries. The study was based on US exports (of all manufacturing industries at two-digit level) to 92 countries in 1992. The study found that US exports have been significantly influenced by patent rights in the importing countries, but the direction of the relationship, that is, market expansion and market power effect,[2] depended on the threat of imitation. Strengthening of patent rights in the countries posing a strong threat of imitation would enhance the expansion of exports, whereas strong patent rights would enhance market power in countries where the threat of imitation is weak.[3]

When undertaking FDI involving knowledge-based assets, firms need to ensure that their advantages will not be undermined. MNCs have the advantage of using their knowledge produced in several plants

---

[1] The study was based on US exports (of all manufacturing industries at two-digit level) to 92 countries in 1992.
[2] The market power effect would reduce the elasticity of demand facing the foreign firm and would ordinarily induce the firm to export less of its patentable product, and market expansion effect would increase the elasticity of demand and firms would export more.
[3] The study had classified countries into four groups depending on their strength of patent rights and imitative capabilities: (1) countries with weak patent rights and weak imitative abilities, (2) countries with strong patent rights and weak imitative abilities, (3) countries with weak patent rights and strong imitative abilities and (4) countries with strong patent rights and strong imitative abilities.

in different countries (Markusen, 1984), whereas a local firm, in similar circumstances, would operate at a cost disadvantage. The knowledge is embodied in blueprints, software, chemical formulas and managerial or engineering manuals, and MNCs are able to use the knowledge numerous times at low marginal cost (Maskus, 1997). Thus, FDI is more likely to be important in industries in which intangible, knowledge-based assets (KBAs) specific to each firm are significant. IPRs play a crucial role where FDI involves KBAs; protection of IPRs provides assurance that the knowledge will not be copied. Firms in industries with high research and development (R&D) investments are likely to undertake FDI when IPRs are weak and are likely to license when IPRs are strong (Nicholson, 2007). Mansfield (1994) found that US-based MNCs were sensitive to IPRs in major developing countries while deciding on facilities abroad. The study also found that lagging technologies were transferred under licences, and R&D facilities were less likely to be established in those countries where enforcement of IPRs is weak. Similar conclusions were reached by Blyde and Acea (2002) and Yang and Maskus (2001). With improvement in the strength of IPRs, the risks associated with licensing get reduced, resulting in FDI paving way for licensing. In addition, the likelihood that the most advanced technologies are transferred rises with the improvement in the strength of IPRs (Maskus, 1997).

Although IPRs can have an impact on FDI, their relationship needs a careful analysis. This relationship is also influenced by the size of the market. Maskus has pointed out that if strong patents alone are sufficient to attract FDI inflows, recent FDI flows to developing countries would have gone mainly to sub-Saharan Africa and Eastern Europe (Maskus, 2000). FDI can also be dependent on the S&T base of the host country, depending on the motive of the TNC. Firms might invest in R&D abroad to gain access to local knowledge (Florida, 1997). In the FDI aimed at augmenting a firm's knowledge base, the S&T base of the target country becomes the deciding factor. For augmenting purposes, the FDI is directed to countries with relatively well-developed science base (Walter, 1998). A firm's decision on investing in R&D abroad for augmenting purposes would depend on the relative commitment to R&D by private and public sector in the host country as well the quality of the 'mental capital' and level of scientific achievement (Walter, 1999). Such FDI will create spillovers for the local environment because R&D sites provide employment and learning opportunities for the local researchers. The characteristics of national innovation system (which includes higher education, public funding for R&D, IPRs, venture capital, etc.) would determine the nature of spillovers (Walter, 1999). Maskus argues that developing countries' attempts to use FDI as a means for technology transfer must be accompanied by programmes to build local skills and ensure that the benefits of competition emerge (Maskus, 2000). Firms might also engage in FDI in R&D to adapt the technology to the local markets (Hakanson & Nobel, 1993). As the local demand becomes more sophisticated, local R&D facilities become useful in helping a firm to adapt its products better to the local needs (Bartlett & Ghoshal, 1990; Hakanson, 1990; Vernon, 1966). In the latter case also, the innovation system of the host country would play a crucial role in determining the quality and quantity of FDI as well as its spillover effects.

Although the impact of FDI and licensing on transfer of technology varies across developing countries, it holds promise for improving productivity and growth in developing countries. These flows provide access to the technological and managerial assets of MNCs, which provide a direct spur to both productivity and significant spillover benefits as they diffuse throughout the economy. The spillover takes place through numerous channels, such as the movement of newly trained labour among enterprises, the laying out of patents, product innovation through inventing around of patents and copyrights and the adoption of newer and more efficient specialised inputs that reduce production costs (Maskus, 1997). It might also result in increased competition. These beneficial impacts of inward FDI and technology transfer would come true only if the ground is ready for that. This calls for linkages with other relevant economic sectors, failure of which might result in enclave FDI. In enclave FDI, MNCs engage only in exports, and there are only limited spillovers into technologies adopted by local firms. The host country also needs to ensure that the MNCs do not engage in abusive practices of their protected market positions in exploiting stronger IPRs. The host country needs to put in place a policy system that promotes the maximum gains from FDI.

The Success Story of Korea

The experience of the Republic of Korea illustrates the importance of domestic policy in using FDI for the catching-up process. Korea chose the FDI and foreign collaboration route for technology development. Original equipment manufacturing (OEM) was a specific form of subcontracting that evolved out of the joint operations of TNC buyers and newly industrialised economy suppliers. Under OEM, finished products are manufactured under the specifications of the TNC, which then markets the products under its own brand name. In Korea, OEM accounted for a significant share of electronics exports in the 1970s, 1980s and 1990s. OEM has undergone changes over the years. Initially, OEM partners helped in the selection of capital equipment, the training of managers, engineers and technicians and advice on production and financing and management. Today, OEM overlaps with own design manufacture (ODM); local firms carry out most or all of the production design tasks usually according to the general design layout given by the partner TNC. Although ODM indicates some advancement in technology capability, it applies mainly to incremental or follower designs rather than leadership product innovations based on R&D (Michael, 2000). Samsung began making electronics in 1969 in joint collaboration with Sanyo of Japan. In 1981, Toshiba licensed microwave oven technology to Samsung. In 1982, Philips supplied colour TV technology, and videocassette recorder technology was licensed from JVC and Sony in 1983. One in five microwave ovens sold in the US in 1992 was made by Samsung mostly under OEM with government trading enterprise. Later, it emphasised on own brand sales, and its brand sales increased to 55 per cent in 1992, to 56 per cent in 1993 and to 57 per cent in 1994. In the 1980s, the Korean majors had become dominant producers and exporters. The Korean industrialisation process may be divided into three phases. Phase one (late 1950s to 1969) was dominated by FDI. In the 1960s, the US and Japanese firms invested in cheap labour assembly activities in Korea. US firms—Motorola, Signetics and Fairchild—began to assemble chips during the mid-1960s followed by Japanese–Korean joint ventures, such as Samsung–Sanyo, Crown Radio Corporation, Thoshiba and LG–Alps electronics. The second phase (1970 to 1979) was dominated by local firms and joint ventures. Exports included semi-finished, low-technology parts and components, shipped into Korea for final assembly by foreign firms. In the third phase (1980s), Chaebols became a dominant force for production and exports. Japanese firms, such as Matsushita, Sanyo and NCE, withdrew from joint ventures as tax advantages were cancelled and firms were encouraged by the government to leave (Michael, 2000).

IPRs and Technology Transfer

A literature review shows that the IPR regime plays a critical role in the transfer of technology. We shall argue below that a mere strengthening of the IPR laws will not result in the transfer of better technologies. Several studies have shown that IPRs will result in technology transfer only if domestic competencies are built up. In other words, increasing the strength of IPRs without strengthening the channels of technology transfer does not bring benefits to the countries seeking access to technologies.

IPRs: A Double-edged Sword

Knowledge has the characteristics of a public good that is non-rival and non-excludable. The knowledge/technology can be shared among multiple users without diminishing its productivity for any particular user and without affecting the availability of any one user. The non-excludability demands the developer not to prevent other users from using it without compensating. Competitors might use the technology to develop cost-effective production process, affecting the business interests of the innovator. As the generation of technology involves costs, the developer will be inclined not to share the technology or not to develop the technology at all if some kind of protection is not provided against unauthorised use of the technology. This is a market failure situation, and the governments need to subsidise innovators until the costs of subsidies equalled the benefits to society and then allow dissemination of technology at free of cost. Although this is the optimal solution to address the market failure, the issues in implementation call for a practical second-best solution—the IPRs.

An IPR is a "government protected right granted to an inventor or creator to exclude others from using the technology or product" in question (Maskus, 2004: 22). Granting temporary monopoly to innovators enables them to reap rents to recoup their investments in R&D. The scope of these rights refers generally to the ability of the inventor to exclude others from the use, production, sale and import of the product or technology for a specific period of time. The IPR system aims to serve three purposes: it provides legal means to ensure exclusivity rents to the inventor; it facilitates the disclosure of the knowledge, especially in IPRs like patents (Article 29 of TRIPS) and it provides a platform for the creation of markets in technology (Arora, Fosfuri & Gambardella, 2001). The third aspect is crucial in the discussion on IPR and technology transfer. IPRs provide the legal basis for the innovator to form a contract with its subsidiaries or licensees for the transfer of the proprietary technologies (Arora, 1996).

Among different kinds of IPRs, a patent is most crucial to the transfer of technology. The study of Mansfield (1994), which surveyed 100 major US firms, found that the influence of IPRs on transfer of technology varies across nature of industrial activities. All those firms engaged in R&D activities reported that their decisions on R&D investment would be influenced by strength of IPRs. An earlier study of Mansfield (1985) found that patents are very significant in promoting innovations in R&D-intensive industries. The study points out that 65 and 30 per cent of innovations in pharmaceuticals and chemicals, respectively, would not have been possible without patents. The study by Levin, Klevorick, Nelson and Winter (1987) showed that patents are most important to protect the process and product innovations in R&D-intensive industries like pharmaceuticals. It was found that the process patents were 40 per cent and product patent 51 per cent more effective as a means of protecting the returns from industrial innovations as compared to other industries.

Does a strong IPR regime mean more inbound transfer of technology? If it were true, the bulk of the technology transfer would have occurred in the African region. The country experience shows that IPRs alone are not sufficient to attract the inward movement of technology. Studies have shown that MNCs are not interested even in filing for patents in countries where the market is not attractive. A study conducted in 53 African countries for 15 antiretroviral drugs found that patenting prevalence was only 21.6 per cent (Attaram & Gillespie, 2001). The study by Blyde and Acea (2002), which looked into imports and FDI into Latin American countries, found that imports and FDI are sensitive to patent index only for the higher income countries and insensitive to patents in poorer countries.

A strong IPR regime will result in a better transfer of technology only if it meets certain conditions. In the absence of such conditions, a strong IPR regime may result in market power effect, which may raise the cost of transfer of technology. The framework for initial conditions for a national 'catching-up' strategy was first presented in a cogent manner by List (1841). This grew out of his concern about the relative technological backwardness of Germany in the first half of the nineteenth century and his perceived inability of his country to bridge the technology gap with Britain. Apart from advocating the policy of infant industry protection to promote industrialisation in the lesser developed Germany, for which he is better known, List proposed a broad set of policies aimed at developing a domestic technological base through the interaction between 'mental capital' and 'material capital', which in the present-day context may be called the software and the hardware. From the above, it has been inferred that List had clearly recognised the importance of both new investment embodying the latest technology and 'learning by doing' from the experiences of production with the equipment (Freeman, 1987: 99). Besides giving the framework of policy in this regard, List presented his views on the institutional mechanism, which should support the technology generation efforts. The crucial element was the link between the industry and the formal institution of science and education. List stated thus:

> There scarcely exists a manufacturing business, which has no relation to physics, mechanics, chemistry, mathematics or to the art of design etc. No progress, no new discoveries and invention can be made in these sciences by which a hundred industries and processes could not be improved or altered. In the manufacturing state, therefore, sciences and arts must necessarily become popular. (1841: 149)

It was not only in the absence of access to technology from the technologically advanced Britain that List saw the relevance of developing an indigenous system of innovation. He insisted that even if technologies were made available to the underdeveloped countries by the leading nations, the former would have to make attempts to assimilate them, depending essentially on the local capabilities that they were able to put in place. In addition, it was this complementarity between imported technologies and development of domestic skills that underlines the history of the growth of technology the world over during the past century and a half.

A number of advanced countries, such as US, Japan, Republic of Korea and Taiwan, have taken advantage, in their development process, of the foreign knowledge by tailor-making their respective IP regimes. During their development phase, these countries provided only the minimum IPR protection (Maskus, 2004). Japan's patent system was designed for facilitating innovation and diffusion (Ordover, 1991). It provided for utility patents, permitted only single claims in a patent application and required pre-grant disclosure. Japan's patent system also instilled an active opposition regime. All these features of Japanese patent system encouraged incremental and adaptive innovation. Japan also strongly encouraged innovative foreign firms to license their technologies to Japanese firms. The Ministry of Trade and Industry (MITI) was actively involved in the technology licensing process by examining the terms of the technology licensing contracts (Maskus, 2004). Japan revised its patent regime under pressure from the US during the period between 1988 and 1993.

The gains from IPR policies in terms of transfer of technology also depend on the industrial policy of the IPR granting country. The MNC may engage in FDI, joint venture or licensing depending on its motives. If the objective is to market its products, licensing may become the predominant strategy. However, for an MNC seeking to adapt its products to local conditions, FDI or joint ventures may likely become the dominant strategies. Similarly, if the MNC wants to gain from the advantages of the country, for example, the scientific talent at lower costs, FDI might become the strategy. All these modes would result in some diffusion of technology through the movement of personnel. However, more significant spillover will occur if forward and backward linkages are established for which the industrial policy plays an important role. A forward linkage exists where the firm produces inputs that reduce the costs of its customer firms or raises the quality of its products, and a backward linkage arises where the firm's operations increase demand for inputs from its local supplier companies and work to improve the technologies and standards used by those companies (Maskus, 2004).

With the strengthening of IPRs, licensing might become the dominant mode of transfer of technology. Yang and Maskus (2001) concluded, after analysing the pattern of licence fee payment to the US by 26 countries, that payment of licence fees was positively and significantly affected by the strength of patent laws. An increase of one percentage in the strength of patent index (Ginarte Park Patent Index) would increase the licensing volume by 2.3 per cent. The study also points to the probability of enhanced market power contributing to increased licensee fees. The licensing contracts were not available to the authors to examine the terms of the contract. Studies have shown that licensing deals may contain restrictive provisions, such as no-compete and grant back, which would impede the spillover effects of the transfer of technology. Hence, it is important to have an effective competition policy that checks anti-competitive effects of the licensing deals. Taylor (1994) observed that technology transfer expands with stronger patents when there is competition between a foreign innovator and a domestic innovator. Interestingly, Smith (2001) found that the positive relationship between patent enforcement and licence fee payments is true only in the case of countries with strong imitative capabilities.

Very high IPR standards at the same time might prevent global innovation and technology transfer. The global innovative firms would expect slower loss of their technology advantages and would earn higher profits per innovation, reducing the need to engage in R&D (Glass & Saggi, 1995; Helpman, 1993). Where the imitation is based on licensed technology, the licensor may provide low-quality technologies, and this, in turn, reduced the licensee's incentive to imitate (Rockett, 1990). In order to counter the abusive powers arising out of IPRs, the industrial policy should also have provisions for compulsory licensing when the innovator fails to transfer the latest technology or fails to transfer the same in the required manner. Without such provisions, patent laws may become a tool merely for preventing others from using the technology. Blocking patents and patent thickets can come in the way of both transfer and diffusion of technology. The blocking patents are in the nature of complementary patents that are essential for the development of new products or processes, implying thereby that these patents must be licensed out in order to successfully launch products or processes in the market.[4] Patent thickets pose a serious problem in technology transfer arrangements as they can affect the possibilities of arm's length transfers. This problem affects developing countries, in particular, as technology transfer opens up the possibilities of strengthening their domestic production capabilities. Compulsory licensing is a very effective policy instrument widely used in the advanced countries to check anti-competitive practices. Compulsory licensing provisions were introduced into the British patent law as early as 1623 and into the US patent law in 1790 (Penrose, 1951).

IPRs are important for the international transfer of technology. However, it calls for certain initial conditions in the IPR-granting country. Experience from advanced and emerging developed nations shows that these initial conditions include forward and backward linkages, competent domestic industry, skilled personnel and strong policies to check anti-competitive practices and to support indigenous innovation. In other words, IPRs should be seen as a part of the indigenous innovation system and have to be adequately linked to other components of the innovation system in order to maximise gains from the international transfer of technology. Studies have shown that in the absence of such conditions, market power effect emerges, resulting in no effective transfer of technology or transfer of lagging technologies.

---

[4] A more formal characterisation of a blocking patent was provided by Merges and Nelson thus: "Two patents are said to block each other when one patentee has a broad patent on an invention and another has a narrower patent on some improved feature of that invention. The broad patent is said to 'dominate' the narrower one. In such a situation, the holder of the narrower ('subservient') patent cannot practice her invention without a license from the holder of the dominant patent. At the same time, the holder of the dominant patent cannot practice the particular improved feature claimed in the narrower patent without a license" (Merges & Nelson, 1990: 860–861).

How Japan and China Managed IPRs

In Japan, the IPR system was a part of the broader innovation system. Japan rejected FDI as a means of technology transfer and encouraged local firms to assimilate imported technology. This led to improvements in the total system (Freeman, 1987). They had a systems approach to design, which recognises the integrative, coupling role of innovation management, relating the product design and process design to world technology. The 'quality circles' were a social innovation designed to maximise the contribution of the lower levels of the workforce and to assign to lower management levels a responsibility for technical change. The government adopted an 'integration strategy' that brought together the best available resources from universities, government research and private or public industry to solve the most important design and development problems (Peck & Goto, 1981). In order to cater to the innovation strategy, Japan reformed the education and training system. As a result, the rate of enrolment, especially in S&T education, increased steeply. In Science and Technology (S&T) education, industrial training is carried out at an enterprise level. The aim is to build up all-round capability at lower levels in workforce so that breakdown and maintenance are far more rapidly dealt with, and there is a smoother assimilation and readier acceptance of new process technology (Gregory, 1985). Further, the Japanese system of 'decentralised management' permitted greater horizontal integration or design, development and production (Aoki, 1986). Technology forecasting was carried out to decide on focus of technology. This orchestration of strategy was achieved by a combination of central government coordination (mainly by MITI) and Keiretsy (large conglomerate groupings in Japanese industries) initiatives.

In recent times, China provides a very good example to use of industrial policy to gain from IPR-technology transfer linkage. A study conducted by the United States International Trade Commission (USITC, 2011) showed that the indigenous innovation policy in China has crucial provisions to effect international transfer of technology, its local adaptation and dissemination. The study identified six policy areas as relevant to indigenous innovation in China: (a) Government procurement—this has been used both by the central and provincial governments as an early market to encourage the new technology products manufactured by Chinese companies. A catalogue of the products of indigenous innovation is prepared every year, and the products in the catalogue get preference in the government procurement; (b) Chinese standards—China has introduced its own technical standards different from international standards. Such standards encourage local adaptation of foreign technology as well as Chinese-made products; (c) China has introduced a strong anti-monopoly law; (d) tax incentives on R&D in China—Chinese firms are entitled to tax benefits if R&D is undertaken within China and IP is owned locally; (e) technology transfer policies and joint-venture requirements—in a number of high-technology industries, including aviation and automotive, foreign firms' access to Chinese market has often been contingent on the requirement of the transfer of specified technology to a Chinese firm, generally a joint-venture partner and (f) local content requirement for FDI firms. This would create backward linkages.

With the support extended to Chinese firms and indigenous innovation, the share of residents in total patents granted in the country is steadily growing, as shown in Figure 8.1.

Lessons Learnt

The literature surveyed in this section provides few clear messages regarding the North–South experience of technology transfer. The role of IPRs in determining technology transfer appears somewhat ambiguous. The strong case made in favour of a strong regime of intellectual property protection for enabling developing countries to get access to the technologies that they need to pursue their development

Figure 8.1
Share of Residents in Total Patents Granted in China (per cent)

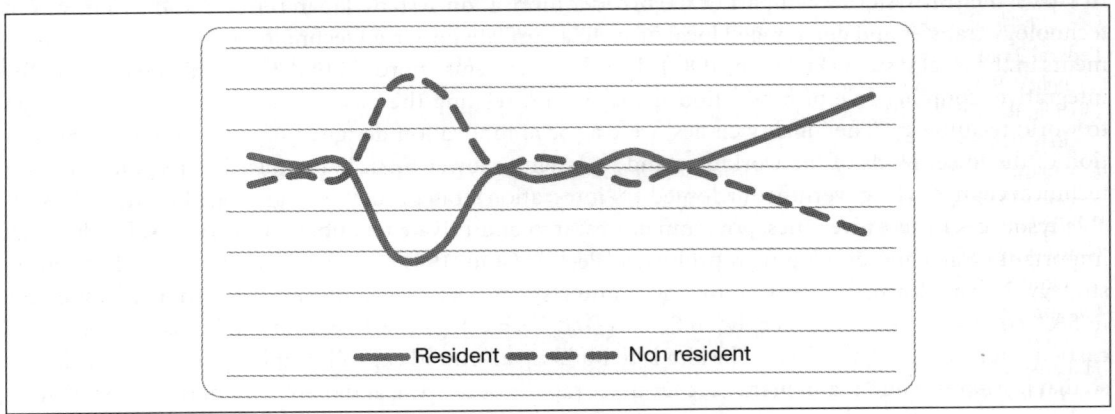

Source: WIPO database.

objectives does not find adequate empirical support. Studies reviewed in this chapter have pointed out that the owners of patented technologies were inclined to enter into licensing agreements only if the recipients have adequate domestic capabilities to assimilate the technologies. Most developing countries have weak local innovation systems and hence they do not stand to gain from the strengthening of the intellectual property regime. Again, while several studies have argued that a strong intellectual property regime will result in technology spillovers, which would, in turn, have a positive impact on the R&D systems of the recipient countries, the empirical support for this argument appears rather weak. In fact, there is now evidence emerging from the developed countries, such as the US, which have historically been supporting strong intellectual property regimes, that the impact of such a regime can be detrimental to its own innovation system (Federal Trade Commission, 2003).

Evidence linking the FDI regime and technology transfer is equally inconclusive. Like in the case of IPRs, studies reviewed in this chapter have indicated that the foreign firm usually exercises its superior bargaining power to refuse technology transfer to the host countries. Interestingly, technology transfer via foreign investors seems to be more successful only when the host country governments have imposed conditions on the investors. China, more recently, and India, in an earlier period, provide ample examples of what may be termed as 'policy-induced' technology transfer.

References

Aoki, M. (1986). Horizontal vs. vertical information structure of the firm. *American Economic Review, 76*(5), 971–983.
Arora, A. (1996). Contracting for tacit knowledge: The provision of technical services in technology licensing contracts. *Journal of Development Economics, 50*(2), 233–256.
Arora, A., Fosfuri, A., & Gambardella, A. (2001). *Markets for technology: The economics of innovation and corporate strategy.* Cambridge: MIT Press.
Attaram, A., & Gillespie-White, L. (2001). Do patents for antiretroviral drugs constrain access to AIDS treatment in Africa? *The Journal of American Medical Association, 268*(15), 1886–1892.
Bartlett, C.A., & Ghoshal, S. (1990). Managing innovation in the transnational corporation. In C.A. Bartlett, Y. Doz, & G. Hedlund (Eds.), *Managing the global firm.* London: Routledge.

Blyde, J.S., & Acea, C. (2002). *The effects of intellectual property rights on trade and FDI in Latin America*. Washington, DC: Inter-American Development Bank.

Economic Policy Research Centre. (2010). *Governing health service delivery in Uganda: A tracking study of drug delivery mechanisms*. Retrieved from http://www.eprc.or.ug/pdf_files/research_report1.pdf

Federal Trade Commission. (2003). *To promote innovation: The proper balance of competition and patent law and policy*. Retrieved from http://www.ftc.gov/os/2003/10/innovationrpt.pdf

Florida, R. (1997). The globalization of R&D: Results of a survey of foreign-affiliated R&D laboratories in the USA. *Research Policy, 26*(1), 85–103.

Freeman, C. (1987). *Technology policy and economic performance: Lessons from Japan*. London: Pinter Publishers.

———. (1997). The national system of innovation in historical perspective. In D. Archibugi & J. Michie (Eds.), *Technology globalisation and economic performance*. Cambridge: Cambridge University Press.

Glass, A., & Saggi, K. (1995). *Intellectual property rights, foreign direct investment, and innovation*. Columbus, OH: Ohio State University.

Gregory, S. (1985). Strategy and design: A micro level view. In R. Langdon & R. Rothwell (Eds.), *Design and innovation: Policy and management*. New York, NY: St. Martin's Press.

Hakanson, L. (1990). International decentralization of R&D—the organizational challenges. In C. A. Bartlett, Y. Doz, & G. Hedlund (Eds.), *Managing the global firm*. London: Routledge.

Hakanson, L., & Nobel, R. (1993). Foreign research and development by Swedish multinationals. *Research Policy, 22*(5–6), 373–396.

Helpman, E. (1993). Innovation, imitation, and intellectual property rights. *Econometrica, 61*(6), 1247–1280.

Kondo, E.K. (1995). The effect of patent protection on foreign direct investment. *Journal of World Trade, 29*(6), 97–122.

Levin, R.C., Klevorick, A.K., Nelson, R.R., & Winter, S.G. (1987). Appropriating the returns from industrial R&D. *Brooking papers in Economic Activity*, No. 3, 783–820.

List, F. (1841). *The national system of political economy*. Trans. Sampson S. Lloyd with an Introduction by J. Shield Nicholson. London: Longmans, Green & Co. Retrieved from http://lf-oll.s3.amazonaws.com/titles/315/List_0168_EBk_v6.0.pdf on 8 January 2016.

Mansfield, E. (1985). How rapidly does industrial technology leak out? *Journal of Industrial Economics, 34*(2), 217–223.

———. (1994). *Intellectual property protection, foreign direct investment, and technology transfer*. Discussion Paper 19, International Finance Corporation, USA.

Markusen, J.R. (1984). Multinationals, multi-plant economies, and the gains from trade. *Journal of International Economics, 16*(3–4), 205–226.

———. (1995). The boundaries of multinational enterprises and the theory of international trade. *Journal of Economic Perspectives, 9*(2), 169–190.

Maskus, K.E. (1997). The role of intellectual property rights in encouraging foreign direct investment and technology transfer. *Paper presented at the Conference on Public–Private Initiatives after TRIPS: Designing a Global Agenda*, Brussels, July 16–19.

———. (2000). *Intellectual property rights in the global economy*. Washington, DC: Institute for International Economics.

———. (2004). Encouraging international technology transfer. UNCTAD-ICTSD Project on IPRs and Sustainable Development, Issue Paper No 7.

Maskus, K.E., & Penubarti, M. (1995). How trade-related are intellectual property rights? *Journal of International Economics, 39*(3–4), 227–248.

Merges, R.P., & Nelson, R.R. (1990). On the complex economics of patent scope. *Columbia Law Review, 90*(4), 839–916.

Michael, H. (2000). East versus South East innovation systems comparing OEM and TNC led growth in electronics. In L. Kim & R. Nelson (Eds.), *Electronics in technology, learning and innovation*. New York: Cambridge University Press.

Nicholson, M. (2002). *Intellectual property rights and international technology transfer: The impact of industry characteristics*. Washington, DC: U.S. Federal Trade Commission.

Nicholson, M. (2007). The impact of industry characteristics and IPR policies on foreign direct investment. *Review of World Economics, 143*(1), 27–54.

Ordover, J. (1991). A patent system for both innovation and exclusion. *Journal of Economic Perspectives, 5*(1), 43–60.

Peck, M.J., & Goto, A. (1981). Technology and economic growth: The case of Japan. *Research Policy, 10*(3), 222–243.

Penrose, E.T. (1951). *The economics of international patent system*. Baltimore, MD: John Hopkins Press.

Price, G. (2005). *Diversity in donorship: The changing landscape of official humanitarian aid—India's official aid programme*. London: Humanitarian Policy Group, Overseas Development Institute.

Puttitanun, T. (2003). *Essays on intellectual property rights, innovation, and technology transfer* (unpublished dissertation). Boulder, CO: University of Colorado.

Rath, A., & Herbert-Copley, B. (1993). *Green technologies for development: Transfer, trade and cooperation*. Ottawa: International Development Research Centre.

Rockett, K. (1990). The quality of licensed technology. *International Journal of Industrial Economics, 8*(4), 559–574.

Sampath, P.G. (2011). Case study 8: Uganda. In *Local production of pharmaceuticals and related technology transfer in developing countries: A series of case studies by the UNCTAD Secretariat*. New York/Geneva: UNCTAD.

Smith, P.J. (1999). Are weak patent rights a barrier to US exports? *Journal of International Economics, 48*(1), 151–177.

———. (2001). How do foreign patent rights affect U.S. exports, affiliate sales, and licenses? *Journal of International Economics, 55*(2), 411–440.

Swarns, R.L. (2001, March 8). AIDS drug battle deepens in Africa. *New York Times*, p. A6.

Taylor, M.S. (1994). Trips, trade, and growth. *International Economic Review, 35*(2), 361–381.

United States International Trade Commission (USITC). (2011). *China: Effects of intellectual property infringement and indigenous innovation policies on the US economy* (Investigation No 332–519). Washington, DC: Author.

Vaitsos, C. (1974). *Intercountry income distribution and transnational enterprises*. Oxford, UK: Clarendon Press.

Vernon, R. (1966). International investment and international trade in the product cycle. *Quarterly Journal of Economics, 80*(2), 190–207.

Walter, K. (1998). Strategic interaction, knowledge sourcing and knowledge creation in foreign environments—An analysis of foreign direct investment in R&D by multinational companies. In M.A. Hitt, J.E. Ricart, & R.D. Nixon (Eds.), *Managing strategically in an interconnected world* (pp. 149–166). Chichester: John Wiley.

———. (1999). The drivers of foreign direct investment into research and development: Empirical investigation. *Journal of International Business Studies, 30*(1), 1–24.

Yang, G., & Maskus, K.E. (2001). Intellectual property rights and licensing: An econometric investigation. *Weltwirtschaftliches Archiv, 137*(1), 58–79.

SECTION 3
Mitigating Immiserisation:
Poverty, Inequality, Joblessness

9

Aspiration, Inequality and Growth

Mausumi Das

Introduction

> We asked Oucha Mbarbk, a man we met in a remote village in Morocco, what he would do if he had more money. He said he would buy more food. Then we asked him what he would do if he had even more money. He said he would buy better-tasting food. We were starting to feel very bad for him and his family, when we noticed a television, a parabolic antenna, and a DVD player in the room where we were sitting. We asked him why he had bought all these things if he felt the family did not have enough to eat. He laughed, and said, "Oh, but television is more important than food!"
>
> —A.V. Banerjee and E. Duflo (2011)

Poverty is believed to limit one's 'capacity to aspire'. In the recent development literature, aspiration, or rather lack of it, has been projected as one of the reasons why poor people stay poor (see, for example, Appadurai, 2004; Genicot & Ray, 2010; Ray, 2006). It has been argued that agents form their aspiration by looking around them, and since the poor and rich often occupy segregated socio-economic as well as geographical spaces, the standard of living that the former group aspires for also remains low, discouraging savings and investment in future income-generating activities. This line of thinking would therefore suggest that bringing the rich and the poor closer within the same neighbourhood would positively impact on the investment decisions of the poor, allowing them to move out of persistent poverty. In this chapter, we argue that 'aspiration'—a subjectively established goal for achievement (Heath, Larrick & Wu, 1998; Siegel, 1957; Starbuck, 1963)—could be a double-edged sword. Indeed, when aspirations are formed by looking at one's neighbours, its effect on investment could go in either direction. The outcome depends crucially on whether aspirations are formed in terms of current consumption or future consumption. While aspiring for a certain lifestyle 'in future' could indeed promote investment, the effect would be diametrically opposite if one is striving to attain the same standard of living in the current period itself. And this negative effect would get amplified in a society where there is no segregation between poor and rich. The 'aspiring' poor, trying to emulate the 'current' lifestyle of the richer group, could actually disinvest. In a growing economy where the benefits of growth are unevenly distributed to begin with, the resulting inequality may further encourage poorer people to overspend on current consumption, which, in turn, accentuates the initial inequality and hampers growth.

One of the primary mechanisms through which inequality persists across generations is the difference in the savings propensities of the poor vis-à-vis the rich. That marginal propensity to save is lower for poorer households is well established in the literature (for example, Dynan, Skinner & Zeldes, 2004; Menchik & David, 1983; Tomes, 1981). This suggests that household preferences are non-homothetic.[1] Moav (2002) constructed a model with non-homothetic preferences to show that credit market imperfection could lead to poverty traps such that poor people stay poor perpetually. In Moav, the source of non-homotheticity arises from a subsistence consumption requirement, which is the same for all households, but will spell out different savings propensities for different income groups. Das (2007) provides another micro-foundation for non-homothetic preferences by linking the discount factor of the agents to the level of current consumption. Poverty—and the concomitant threat of imminent starvation—makes the future look more distant, thereby distorting the relative marginal utility of a unit consumption today vis-à-vis in the future.

One limitation of the aforementioned theory is that there is no feedback from the society/neighbourhood to household behaviour. Thus, inequality has no direct bearing on the decisions undertaken by the poor. Moreover, these subsistence consumption-based explanations seem inadequate when one comes face to face with another empirically established fact, namely that the poorer people also spend a large proportion of their income on absolutely inessential non-food items like alcohol and tobacco and other forms of wasteful expenditures like festivals. Based on household surveys conducted in 13 less-developed countries (Cote d'Ivoire, Guatemala, India, Indonesia, Mexico, Nicaragua, Pakistan, Panama, Papua New Guinea, Peru, South Africa, Tanzania and East Timor), Banerjee and Duflo (2007) show that even though requirement for additional calories is high among the extremely poor (those who live on less than $1 per day), they "do not seem to put every available penny into buying more calories". Among the 13 countries, food typically represents from 56 to 78 per cent of consumption among rural households, and 56 to 74 per cent in urban areas. Yet, among the non-food items that the poor spend significant amounts of money on, alcohol and tobacco show up prominently. In some countries, spending on festivals also constitutes an important component of the households expenditure. For example, a typical extremely poor household in Udaipur (Rajasthan, India) could actually spend up to 30 per cent more on food than it actually does, just based on what it spends on alcohol, tobacco and festivals. Rao (2001) reports a similar pattern, noting that 15 per cent of households' total expenditures in rural India are spent on festivals. The magnitude of these expenditures seems puzzling especially because these households spend only 2 to 3 per cent of their income on the education of their children. Clearly what the poor or extremely poor consider 'necessary' goes beyond the conventional notion of 'subsistence' consumption. As the quote at the beginning shows, for some of them, "television is more important than food".

In this chapter, we argue that the minimum consumption level that an agent desires to attain is influenced by the society around him. In particular, we postulate that agents aspire to catch up with the living standards of their richer neighbours. We interpret neighbourhood in the narrow economic sense to mean the income class that is immediately above. The postulated association between aspiration level and economic neighbourhood signifies a crucial role of inequality in determining the savings behaviour of agents. In a perfectly egalitarian society where all agents belong to the same income class, there is no catching up to be done and savings are guided by agents' 'natural' tendencies towards intertemporal substitution between current and future. However, in an unequal society characterised by different income and wealth categories, agents belonging to different categories will aspire to different consumption levels, resulting in different savings propensities. Thus, we provide here an alternative explanation of the empirically observed convex savings, an explanation that is also consistent with the expenditure pattern of the poor, as noted by Banerjee and Duflo (2007) and Rao (2001).

---

[1] Recall that homothetic preferences would imply that marginal propensity to consume and save would be independent of households' income/wealth.

Like the existing poverty-trap models (for example, Galor & Zeira, 1993; Moav, 2002), poor households in our model also get entrapped in a low-income–low-savings long-run trap, which has implications for the aggregate macroeconomy. In particular, the initial inequality matters for the long-run growth. However, unlike Galor and Zeira, it is not just the initial distribution (proportion of poor vis-à-vis rich) that matters. In our model, the precise income gap between the rich and the poor at the initial point of time also influences the long-run macroeconomic outcome. In other words, both the distribution and the 'degree' of inequality play a crucial role in determining the long-run growth. This spells out different policy implications in our model than the existing poverty-trap literature.

General Framework

The economy is populated by a continuum of overlapping generations of dynasties, represented by the unit interval [0,1]. Each member of a dynastic household lives exactly for two periods and has a single offspring at the beginning of the second period. Thus, the total population in the economy remains constant over time.[2]

Agents differ in terms of their income. We start with a given initial distribution of income, which then evolves endogenously over time depending on the education decisions of the agents. For simplicity, we shall assume a simple two-point distribution where there are exactly two income groups in the society—'rich' and 'poor'. A constant fraction λ of the total population is rich and the rest are poor. Initial income levels of all agents within the groups are identical, denoted by y_0^R and y_0^P, respectively, such that $y_0^R > y_0^P$.

The lifecycle of an agent belonging to either group is as follows. Each agent is endowed with one unit of time in both periods of his life. In the first period (childhood), he consumes nothing and spends the entire time period in acquiring skill. However, skill acquisition is costly, and the amount of skill acquired by the agent depends on the amount of resources spent by his parent towards his schooling. In the second period of his life (adulthood), the agent works fulltime to earn a wage income that is positively related to his acquired skill level. He spends his adulthood income upon his own consumption and in educating his child. He dies at the end of this period.

Preferences

Agents care about their own consumption as well as their children's education. In other words, an agent i derives utility from his adulthood consumption (c^i) and the amount spent in educating his child (e^i). However, the crucial assumption in our model is that how much utility or satisfaction an agent derives from own consumption depends crucially on whether he is able to attain the consumption level that he aspires for (denoted by $\bar{C}^i$). In particular, the agent derives negligible (zero) or even negative utility when his consumption level lies below the corresponding aspiration level and begins to enjoy positive utility if and only if he has been able to attain the consumption level that he aspires for. Another important feature of this aspiration-driven preference pattern is that at the point where he attains his aspiration level, the marginal utility from own consumption is infinitely high. Marginal utility begins to diminish as he

---

[2] Constant population is a simplification. One can easily add an exogenous rate of growth of population without changing any of the results that follows. Since our focus here is on savings behaviour rather than on the population dynamics, we abstract away from unnecessary complexities.

goes on consuming beyond this point. In other words, the utility function has a convex stretch near the aspiration point and is concave thereafter.[3]

On the other hand, utility associated with educating one's child exhibits a standard concave pattern. Notice that the agent derives direct utility from the amount spent in child's education, which indicates the presence of 'warm glow' altruism (Andreoni, 1989).

The preference pattern described above is captured in this model by the following utility function for agent i:

$$U(c^i, e^i) = \frac{(c^i - \bar{C}^i)^{1-\sigma}}{1-\sigma} + \beta \frac{(e^i)^{1-\sigma}}{1-\sigma} \text{ for } c^i \geq \bar{C}^i; \quad (9.1)$$
$$= 0 \text{ otherwise,}$$

where the parameter σ measures the elasticity of marginal utility with respect to $(c^i - \bar{C}^i)$ as well as e^i. The parameter β, on the other hand, measures the degree of parental altruism. Both σ and β are positive fractions.

Determination of Aspiration Level

We postulate that aspirations are formed by looking around one's neighbourhood. In particular, agents aspire to attain at least a fraction θ of the living standards of their immediate neighbour, who is richer than him in the income ladder. For convenience, we consider only discrete distributions such that population is concentrated on a finite number of discrete points along the real line. If we arrange these points (each representing an income group) in ascending order, then for any agent belonging to income group y^i, his immediate richer neighbour is identified by the income group y^{i+1}. Thus, the aspiration level of an agent belonging to income group y_t^i is then defined by

$$\bar{C}^i = \theta c^{i+1}; 0 < \theta < 1. \quad (9.2)$$

Notice that by this definition, agents belonging to the richest income group (that is, the income group that is at the highest rung at the income ladder) have no richer neighbours whose lifestyle they aspire to attain. For this group, therefore, the aspiration level is by definition zero.

In this chapter, however, we have assumed a simple two-point distribution with only two income classes—rich and poor. Hence at any time t, the respective aspiration levels of the poor and the rich are given, respectively, by

$$\bar{C}_t^P = \theta c_t^R;$$
$$\bar{C}_t^R = 0. \quad (9.3)$$

Skill Formation and Income

We assume a simple linear skill formation technology that requires investment in terms of resources as well as a fixed time investment of one unit. Thus, if parental investment in skill formation at time t is

---

[3] This 'S'-shaped characterisation of the relationship between aspiration and preferences is consistent with the literature that looks at aspiration as a reference point (for example, Bogliacino & Ortoleva, 2009; Genicot & Ray, 2010).

given by e_t, then the corresponding skill level acquired by the child (to be used in the production process next period) is given by

$$h_{t+1} = 1 + \gamma e_t; \gamma > 0. \tag{9.4}$$

Notice that even when the parental investment in child's education is zero, the child still acquires some basic innate skill level, represented by unity. The parameter γ represents the effectiveness of schooling in skill formation.

Aggregate production technology is represented by an AK production function with human capital as the only input:

$$Y_t = AH_t; A > 0. \tag{9.5}$$

Thus, human capital is associated with a constant marginal (as well as average) product A, which also represents the per unit wage rate.

It then follows that an agent, whose parent spent e_t in educating him as a child, enters the labour market upon reaching adulthood (that is, in the second period of his life) with certain amount of skills, $h_{t+1} \equiv 1 + \gamma e_t$, which enables him to earn an adulthood income of

$$y_{t+1} \equiv A(1 + \gamma e_t). \tag{9.6}$$

Optimal Choices

Optimal Choices of the Poor

Recall that the a poor agent in our economy has an aspiration level represented by $\bar{C}_t^P = \theta c_t^R$, where c_t^R is the consumption level enjoyed by the rich, which the poor agent takes as given. Thus, the optimisation problem of a poor agent at period t, who earns an income y_t^P, is given by

$$\underset{\{c_t^P, e_t^P\}}{\text{Max.}} \frac{(c_t^P - \bar{C}_t^P)^{1-\sigma}}{1-\sigma} + \beta \frac{(e_t^P)^{1-\sigma}}{1-\sigma}$$

subject to

$$c_t^P + e_t^P = y_t^P; c_t^P \geq 0; e_t^P \geq 0.$$

From the first-order condition,

$$(c_t^P - \bar{C}_t^P)^{-\sigma} = \beta(e_t^P)^{-\sigma}$$
$$\Rightarrow e_t^P = (\beta)^{1/\sigma}(c_t^P - \bar{C}_t^P).$$

Substituting this value in the budget constraint, we obtain the optimal level of consumption by the poor as

$$c_t^P = \frac{1}{1+(\beta)^{1/\sigma}} y_t^P + \frac{(\beta)^{1/\sigma}}{1+(\beta)^{1/\sigma}} \bar{C}_t^P. \tag{9.7}$$

Noting that $e_t^P \geq 0$, the optimal level of investment by the poor agent in educating his child is given by

$$e_t^P = \frac{(\beta)^{1/\sigma}}{1+(\beta)^{1/\sigma}} (y_t^P - \bar{C}_t^P) \text{ for } y_t^P \geq \bar{C}_t^P;$$
$$= 0 \text{ for } y_t^P < \bar{C}_t^P. \tag{9.8}$$

Optimal Choices of the Rich

Recall that in our two-income-class economy, a rich agent does not have a richer neighbour whose lifestyle he would want to emulate. Thus, the aspiration level of the rich agent is zero. Accordingly, the optimisation problem of a rich agent at period t, who earns an income y_t^R, is given by

$$\underset{\{c_t^P, e_t^P\}}{Max.} \frac{(c_t^R)^{1-\sigma}}{1-\sigma} + \beta \frac{(e_t^R)^{1-\sigma}}{1-\sigma}$$

subject to

$$c_t^R + e_t^R = y_t^R; c_t^R \geq 0; e_t^R \geq 0.$$

From the first-order condition,

$$(c_t^R)^{-\sigma} = \beta(e_t^R)^{-\sigma}$$
$$\Rightarrow e_t^R = (\beta)^{1/\sigma} (c_t^R).$$

Substituting this value in the budget constraint, we obtain the optimal level of consumption by the rich as

$$c_t^R = \frac{1}{1+(\beta)^{1/\sigma}} y_t^R. \tag{9.9}$$

Similarly, the optimal level of investment by the rich agent in educating his child is given by

$$e_t^R = \frac{(\beta)^{1/\sigma}}{1+(\beta)^{1/\sigma}} y_t^R. \tag{9.10}$$

Intergenerational Dynamics

Since the educational investment by the parent determines the income earned by the child upon adulthood (via Equation 9.6), from Equations 9.8 and 9.10, we can derive the intergenerational income dynamics (and the concomitant education dynamics) for both the poor and the rich dynasties.

Income Dynamics of the Rich

Let us first analyse the intergenerational income dynamics of the rich. Combining (9.10) and (9.6), we obtain the following difference equation representing the income dynamics for the rich:[4]

$$y_{t+1}^R \equiv A(1+\gamma e_t^R)$$

$$\Rightarrow y_{t+1}^R = A + A\gamma \frac{(\beta)^{1/\sigma}}{1+(\beta)^{1/\sigma}} y_t^R. \tag{9.11}$$

This is a linear and autonomous difference equation that can be solved explicitly to derive the time path of y_t^R. In what follows, we analyse the dynamics using the phase diagram technique, which brings out more clearly the qualitatively nature of the solution.

From Equation 9.11, it is obvious that there are two mutually exclusive possibilities:

1.
$$A\gamma \frac{(\beta)^{1/\sigma}}{1+(\beta)^{1/\sigma}} \geq 1.$$

In this case, the phase line—the plotting of the y_{t+1}^R function with respect to y_t^R—will have a positive intercept and a slope greater than or equal to unity. Thus, the y_{t+1}^R line will never intersect the 45° line, as shown in Figure 9.1. Hence, the income of the rich dynasties will grow without bound.

2.
$$A\gamma \frac{(\beta)^{1/\sigma}}{1+(\beta)^{1/\sigma}} < 1.$$

In this case, the phase line—the plotting of the y_{t+1}^R function with respect to y_t^R—will have a positive intercept and a slope less than unity. Thus, the y_{t+1}^R line will intersect the 45° line only once, generating a unique steady-state point (y^{R^*}) that is globally stable. The precise value of the steady-state y^{R^*} is given by

$$y^{R^*} = \frac{A}{1-A\gamma \frac{(\beta)^{1/\sigma}}{1+(\beta)^{1/\sigma}}} > A. \tag{9.12}$$

Thus, the income level of the rich dynasties will converge to y^{R^*}, irrespective of the initial position. This case has been depicted in Figure 9.2.

---

[4] It is easy to verify that the corresponding education dynamics will be exactly symmetric. Noting that $y_{t+1} = 1 + \gamma e_t$ for all t, one can transform the dynamic equation representing the income dynamics to the dynamic equation representing the educational dynamics as follows:

$$e_t^R = \frac{1}{\gamma}(A-1) + A\frac{(\beta)^{1/\sigma}}{1+(\beta)^{1/\sigma}}(1+\gamma e_{t-1}^R).$$

The dynamic behaviour of the latter equation is qualitatively similar to that of the former.

Figure 9.1
Income Dynamics of the Rich: Perpetual Growth

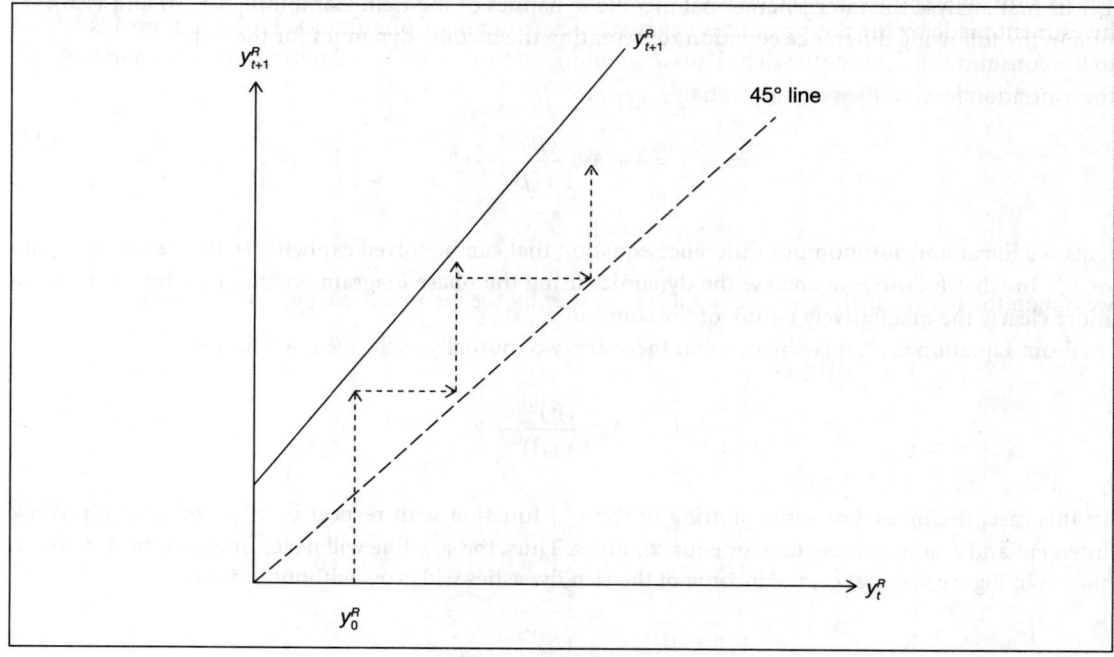

Figure 9.2
Income Dynamics of the Rich: Convergence to a Steady State

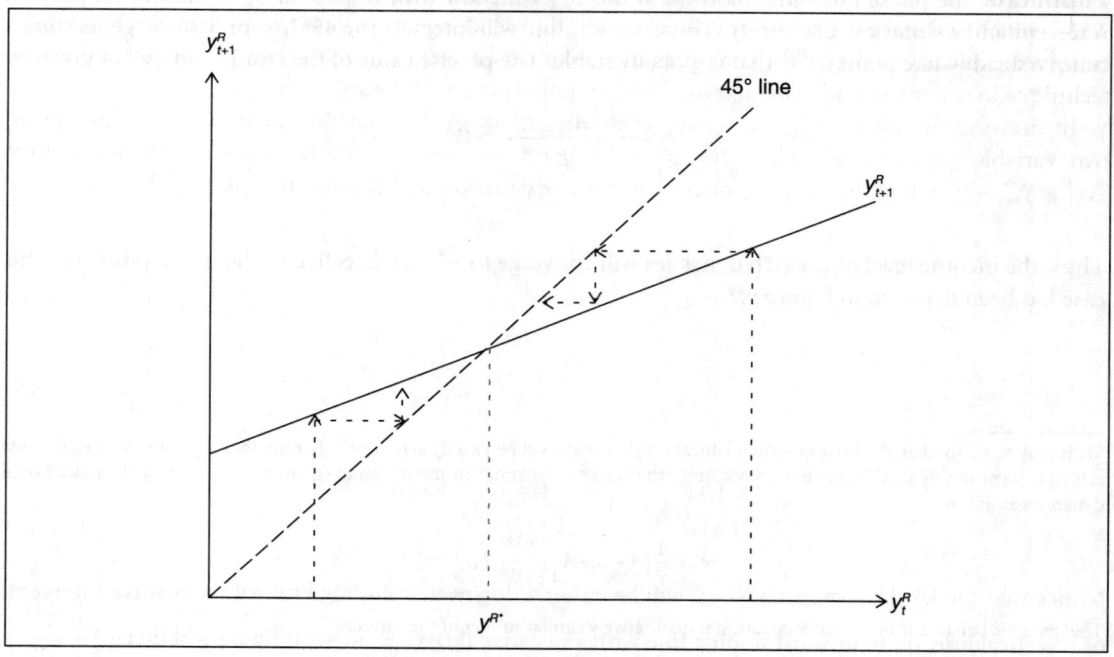

Income Dynamics of the Poor

Let us now analyse the intergenerational income dynamics of the poor. Recall that the educational investment made by the poor parent is negatively related to his aspiration level, which in turn is related to the consumption level of the rich. Thus, combining (9.8) and (9.6), and noting (from 9.3 and 9.9) that the aspiration level of the poor is given by

$$\bar{C}_t^P = \theta c_t^R$$
$$= \frac{\theta}{1+(\beta)^{1/\sigma}} y_t^R,$$

we obtain the following difference equation representing the income dynamics for the poor:

$$y_{t+1}^P \equiv A(1+\gamma e_t^P)$$

$$\Rightarrow y_{t+1}^P = \begin{cases} A + \gamma \dfrac{(\beta)^{1/\sigma}}{1+(\beta)^{1/\sigma}} (y_t^P - \bar{C}_t^P) \text{ for } y_t^P \geq \bar{C}_t^P \\ A \text{ for } y_t^P < \bar{C}_t^P \end{cases}$$

$$\Rightarrow y_{t+1}^P = \begin{cases} A + \gamma \dfrac{(\beta)^{1/\sigma}}{1+(\beta)^{1/\sigma}} \left(y_t^P - \dfrac{\theta}{1+(\beta)^{1/\sigma}} y_t^R \right) \text{ for } y_t^P \geq \dfrac{\theta}{1+(\beta)^{1/\sigma}} y_t^R \\ A \text{ for } y_t^P < \dfrac{\theta}{1+(\beta)^{1/\sigma}} y_t^R \end{cases} \qquad (9.13)$$

Notice that the income dynamics of the poor depends on the income level of the rich. Since the income dynamics of the rich can be solved independently, we can replace the explicit solution for y_t^R in Equation 9.13—which will make it a non-autonomous linear difference equation in y_t^P alone, and which can again be solved explicitly to derive the time path of y_t^P. However, we shall once again use the phase diagram technique in order to clearly characterise the qualitative nature of the solution.

In drawing the phase diagram to depict the dynamics of y_t^P, first note that y_{t+1}^P is a function of two variables: y_t^P and y_t^R. Thus, the phase diagram analysis will involve drawing the level curve $\Delta y^P \equiv y_{t+1}^P - y_t^P = 0$ in the (y_t^R, y_t^P) plane. The precise equation of this level curve is given by

$$y_t^P = A + \gamma \frac{(\beta)^{1/\sigma}}{1+(\beta)^{1/\sigma}} \left(y_t^P - \frac{\theta}{1+(\beta)^{1/\sigma}} y_t^R \right)$$

$$\Rightarrow y_t^P \left[1 - \gamma \frac{(\beta)^{1/\sigma}}{1+(\beta)^{1/\sigma}} \right] = A - \left(\gamma \frac{(\beta)^{1/\sigma}}{1+(\beta)^{1/\sigma}} \right) \left(\frac{\theta}{1+(\beta)^{1/\sigma}} \right) y_t^R.$$

$$\Rightarrow y_t^P = \frac{A}{1-\gamma \dfrac{(\beta)^{1/\sigma}}{1+(\beta)^{1/\sigma}}} - \frac{\gamma \dfrac{(\beta)^{1/\sigma}}{1+(\beta)^{1/\sigma}}}{1-\gamma \dfrac{(\beta)^{1/\sigma}}{1+(\beta)^{1/\sigma}}} \left(\frac{\theta}{1+(\beta)^{1/\sigma}} \right) y_t^R$$

(9.14)

Notice that the level curve for $\Delta y^P = 0$ will be either a downward sloping line with a positive intercept, or a vertical line, or an upward sloping line with a negative intercept, depending on whether $\gamma \dfrac{(\beta)^{1/\sigma}}{1+(\beta)^{1/\sigma}}$

is less than, equal to or greater than unity. Thus, in drawing the corresponding phase diagram, we have to consider three mutually exclusive possibilities:

$$\text{(a) } \gamma \frac{(\beta)^{1/\sigma}}{1+(\beta)^{1/\sigma}} < 1; \quad \text{(b) } \gamma \frac{(\beta)^{1/\sigma}}{1+(\beta)^{1/\sigma}} = 1; \quad \text{(c) } \gamma \frac{(\beta)^{1/\sigma}}{1+(\beta)^{1/\sigma}} > 1.$$

Second, recall that the nature of the relationship between y_{t+1}^P and y_t^P changes depending on whether $y_t^P \geq \frac{\theta}{1+(\beta)^{1/\sigma}} y_t^R$ or $y_t^P < \frac{\theta}{1+(\beta)^{1/\sigma}} y_t^R$. Thus, we also have to simultaneously draw the locus of y_t^R and y_t^P in the (y_t^R, y_t^P) plane, where this condition holds with equality. This line will demarcate the two areas where the relationships between y_{t+1}^P and y_t^P are different. This demarcation line is represented as follows:

$$y_t^P = \frac{\theta}{1+(\beta)^{1/\sigma}} y_t^R. \tag{9.15}$$

Finally, notice that we have to also plot the 45° line in the (y_t^R, y_t^P) plane and, in fact, must restrict our analyses to all combinations of y_t^P and y_t^R, which lie below this 45° line. Otherwise, it will violate the basic assumption that y^P represents the income of the relatively poorer group, which by definition has to be less than y_t^R—at least initially.

We capture all these pieces of information in a two-quadrant diagram, where the first quadrant plots the various relationships between y_t^P and y_t^R (namely Equation 9.14, Equation 9.15 and the 45° line signifying $y_t^P = y_t^R$), while the fourth quadrant reproduces the dynamic evolution of y_t^R (as captured by Equation 9.11 and as shown earlier in Figures 9.1 and 9.2), which is independent of y_t^P.

As we have seen earlier, the evolution of y_t^R differs, depending on whether $A\gamma \frac{(\beta)^{1/\sigma}}{1+(\beta)^{1/\sigma}} \geq 1$, or $A\gamma \frac{(\beta)^{1/\sigma}}{1+(\beta)^{1/\sigma}} < 1$. Thus, we have altogether six mutually exclusive parametric configurations. We discuss below the implications of these six mutually exclusive possibilities one by one.

Case A: $\qquad \gamma \frac{(\beta)^{1/\sigma}}{1+(\beta)^{1/\sigma}} < 1; \quad A\gamma \frac{(\beta)^{1/\sigma}}{1+(\beta)^{1/\sigma}} \geq 1.$

In this case, the $\Delta y^P = 0$ line (dotted line in Figure 9.3) is downward sloping with a positive intercept, while the demarcation line (solid line in Figure 9.3) is upward sloping, passing through the origin, with slope less than one (since θ is a fraction and $\frac{1}{1+(\beta)^{1/\sigma}} < 1$). Accordingly, the two lines intersect each other once in the first quadrant at the level where $y_t^P = A$. The corresponding direction of movements of y_t^P and y_t^R is shown in Figure 9.3.

It is easy to verify from Figure 9.3 that in this case the income of the rich is perpetually growing. The income of the poor, on the other hand, could be initially rising or falling (depending on the initial income gap between the rich and the poor), but eventually it moves below the demarcation line, whereupon it becomes constant at A (since, in their attempt to catch up with the lifestyle of the rich, the poor parents stop investing in children's education altogether).

Figure 9.3
Income Dynamics of the Poor: Poverty Trap Scenario

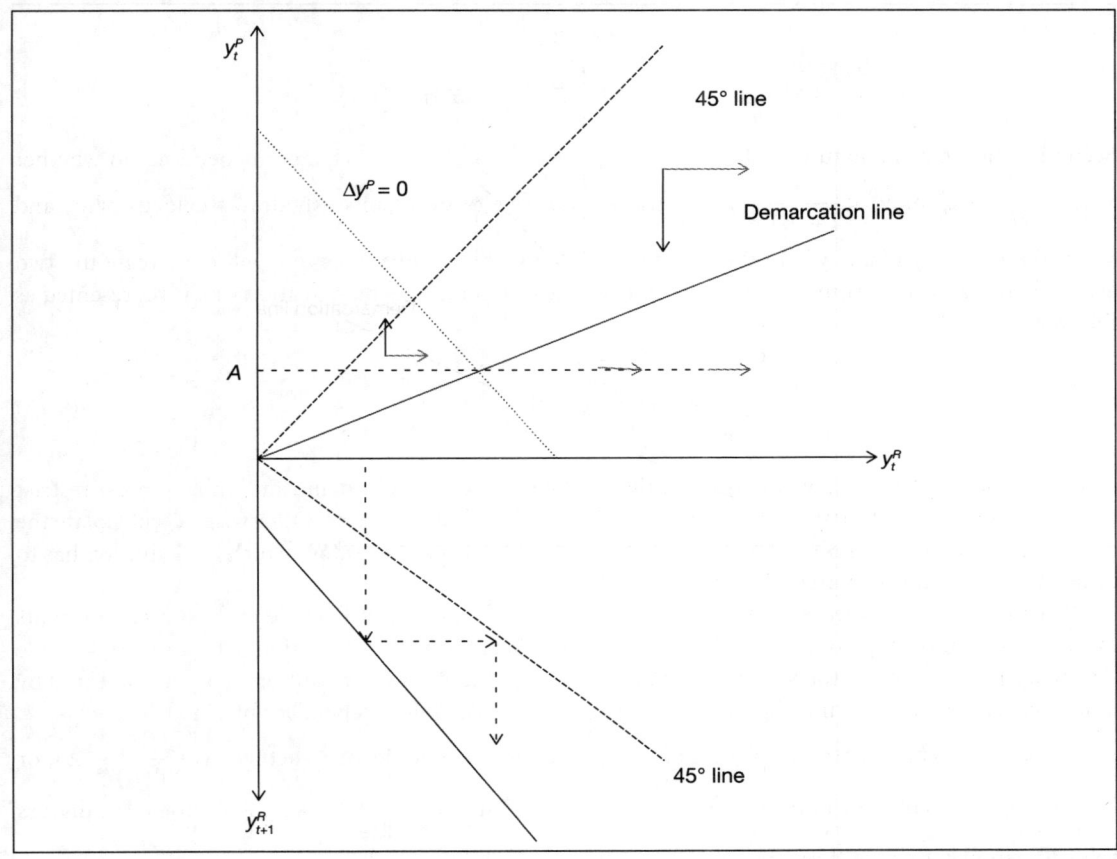

Case B:
$$\gamma \frac{(\beta)^{1/\sigma}}{1+(\beta)^{1/\sigma}} = 1; \quad A\gamma \frac{(\beta)^{1/\sigma}}{1+(\beta)^{1/\sigma}} \geq 1.$$

In this case, the $\Delta y^P = 0$ line (dotted line in Figure 9.4) becomes vertical at $y_t^R = A\frac{1+(\beta)^{1/\sigma}}{\theta}$, while the demarcation line (solid line in Figure 9.4) is the same as before. The two lines again intersect each other once in the first quadrant at the level where $y_t^P = A$. The corresponding direction of movements of y_t^P and y_t^R is shown in Figure 9.4.

Case C:
$$\gamma \frac{(\beta)^{1/\sigma}}{1+(\beta)^{1/\sigma}} > 1; \quad A\gamma \frac{(\beta)^{1/\sigma}}{1+(\beta)^{1/\sigma}} \geq 1.$$

In this case, both the $\Delta y^P = 0$ line and the demarcation line are upward sloping. Moreover, the $\Delta y^P = 0$ line has a negative intercept, and its slope is greater than that of the demarcation line. Once again, the two lines intersect each other once in the first quadrant at the level where $y_t^P = A$. The corresponding direction of movements of y_t^P and y_t^R is shown in Figure 9.5.

Figure 9.4
Income Dynamics of the Poor: Escape from Poverty Trap

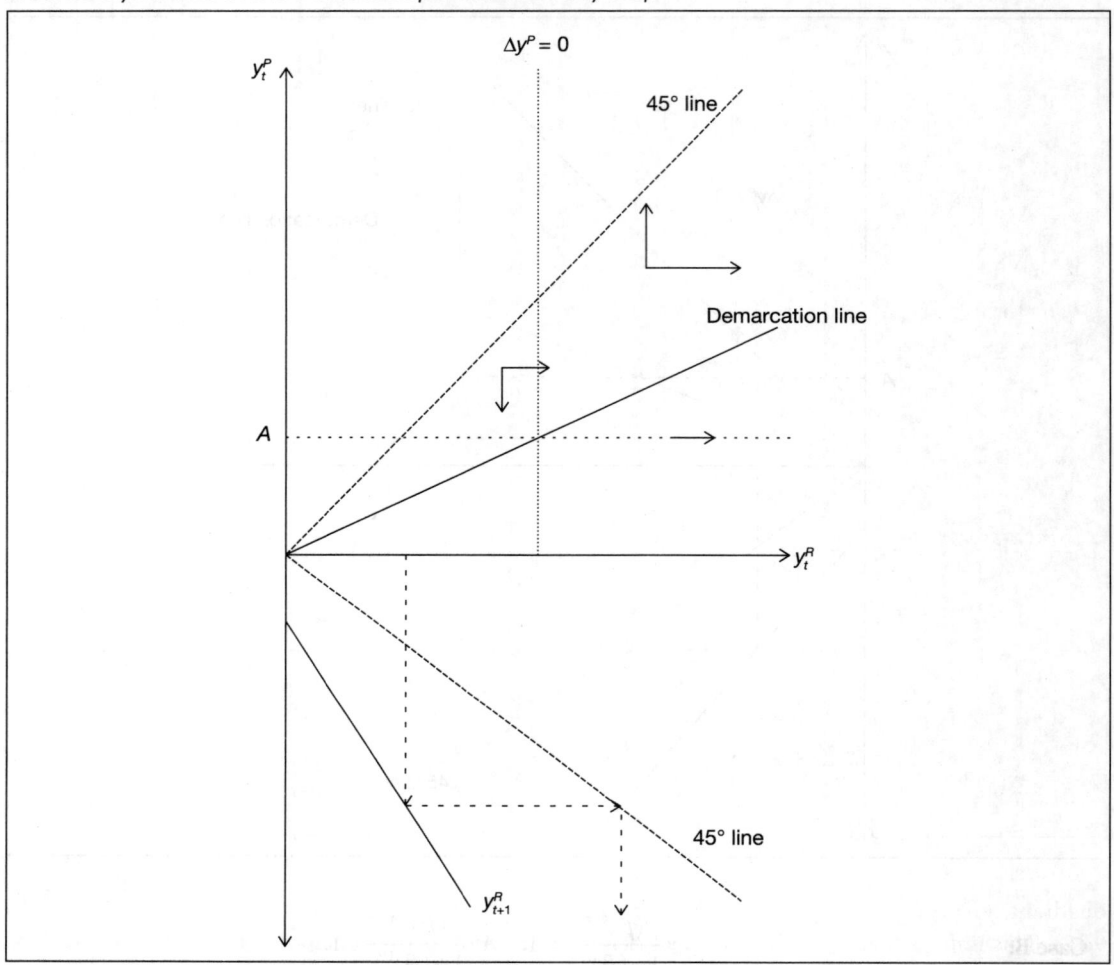

Figures 9.4 and 9.5 show that the dynamics of the rich and poor under cases B and C are similar. Once again, the income of the rich is perpetually growing. But now there is a possibility that income of the poor would also grow perpetually and never falls below the demarcation line. This happens when the initial income of both the rich and the poor is sufficiently high, so that even after trying to catch up with the lifestyle of the rich, the poor parents can invest enough in educating their children.

In our analyses so far, we have allowed y_t^R to grow without bounds (due to the assumption that $A\gamma \dfrac{(\beta)^{1/\sigma}}{1+(\beta)^{1/\sigma}} - 1$). What happens if y_t^R reaches a steady state? This possibility is discussed below.

Case D: $\qquad\qquad\qquad \gamma \dfrac{(\beta)^{1/\sigma}}{1+(\beta)^{1/\sigma}} < 1; \quad A\gamma \dfrac{(\beta)^{1/\sigma}}{1+(\beta)^{1/\sigma}} < 1.$

In this case, the $\Delta y^P = 0$ line and the demarcation line, drawn in the first quadrant, remain the same as in case A. As before, the two lines intersect each other at the level where $y_t^P = A$. However, in the fourth

Figure 9.5
Income Dynamics of the Poor: Low Aspiration

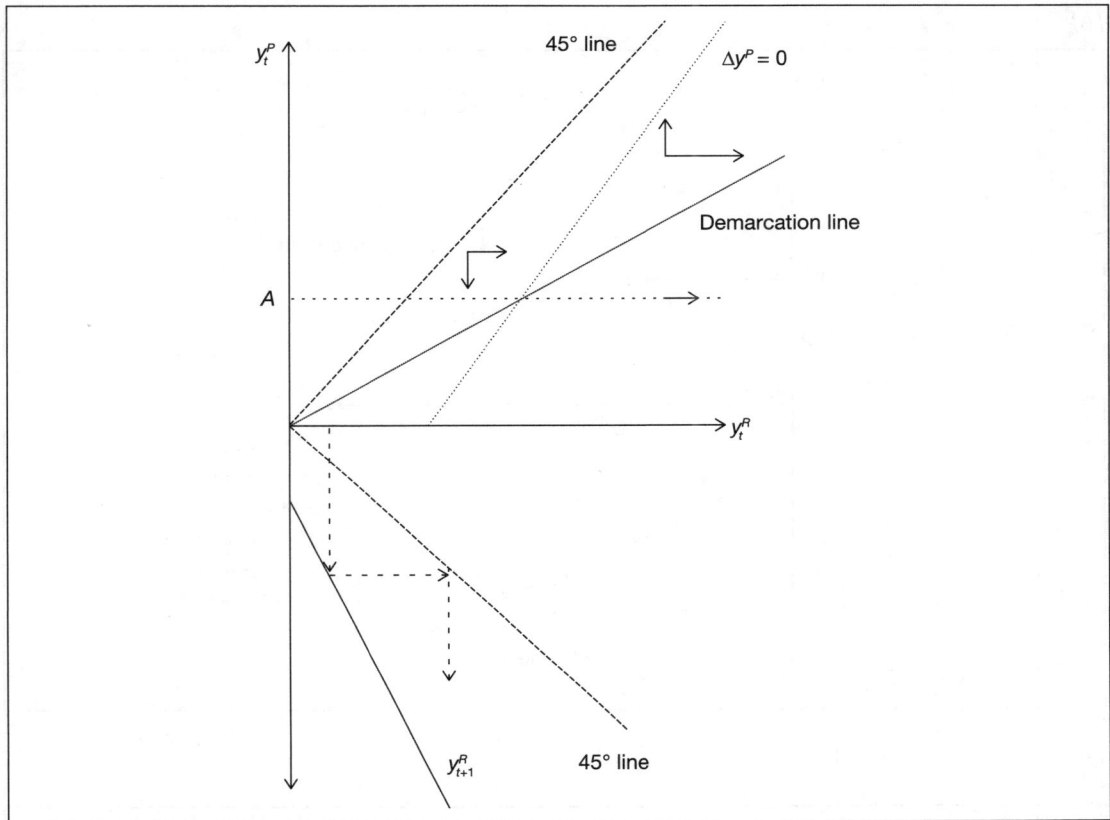

quadrant, y_t^R now approaches its steady-state value y^{R^*}, which is necessarily greater than A (see Equation 9.12). This implies that in the long run, all rich dynasties will spend some positive amount in educating their children. In the short run, now the direction of movements of y_t^R will be different depending on whether the initial value of y_t^R is to the left or to the right of y^{R^*}.

The position of the y^{R^*} line is crucial for the long-run value of y_t^P as well. In particular, the income level of the poor dynasties will approach a steady-state level $y^{P^*} > A$ (with positive investment in children's education) if and only if y^{R^*} lies to the left of the point of intersection between the $\Delta y^P = 0$ line and the demarcation line. Otherwise, the income of the poor dynasties eventually crosses over the demarcation line to fall to a constant level, A, with zero investment in educating their children.

Recall that $y^{R^*} = \dfrac{A}{1 - A\gamma \dfrac{(\beta)^{1/\sigma}}{1+(\beta)^{1/\sigma}}}$, whereas at the intersection point of the $\Delta y^P = 0$ and the demarcation line, the y^R value is given by $y^{\hat{R}} = \dfrac{A[1+(\beta)^{1/\sigma}]}{\theta}$. Thus, y^{R^*} would lie to the left of the point of intersection between the $\Delta y^P = 0$ line and the demarcation line if and only if

$$\dfrac{A}{1 - A\gamma \dfrac{(\beta)^{1/\sigma}}{1+(\beta)^{1/\sigma}}} < \dfrac{A[1+(\beta)^{1/\sigma}]}{\theta} \Rightarrow \theta < 1+(\beta)^{1/\sigma} - A\gamma(\beta)^{1/\sigma}$$

and it would lie to the right otherwise. These two alternative scenarios are depicted in Figures 9.6A and 9.6B, respectively.

Figure 9.6
Income Dynamics of the Poor: High Aspiration

(A)

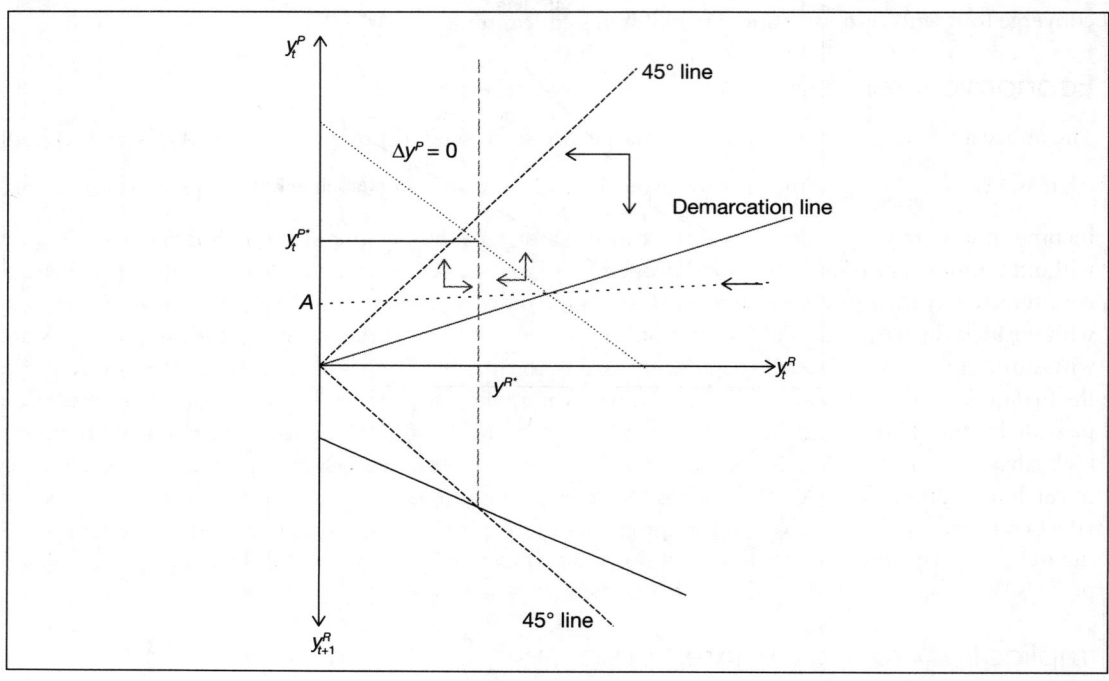

(B)

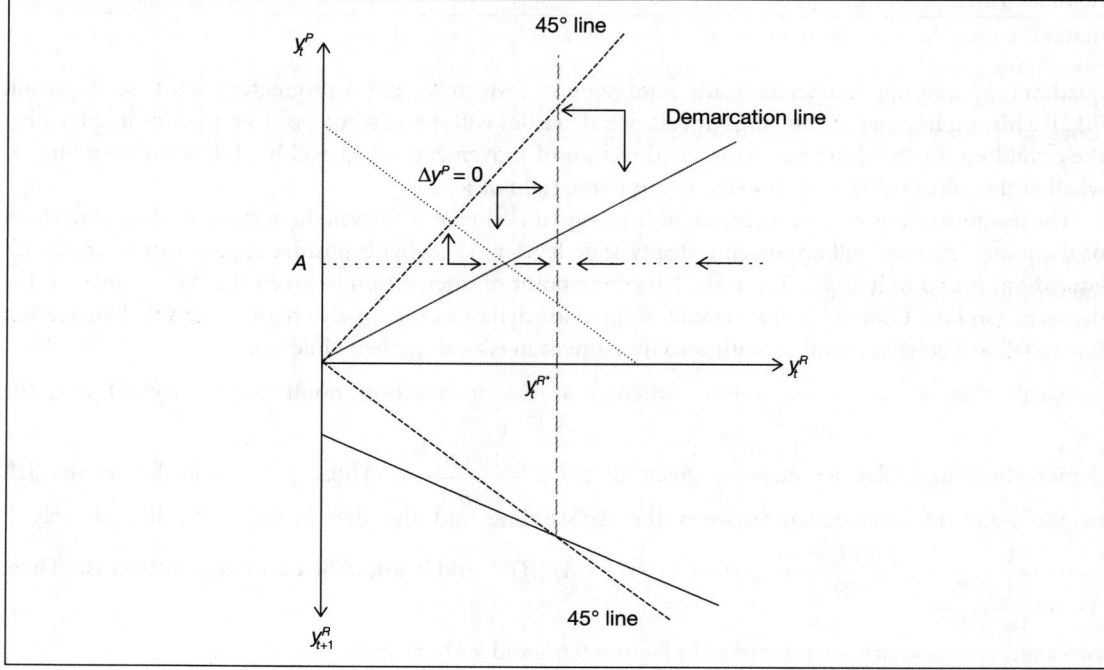

It is easy to verify that the same conclusion would hold in the other two cases as well, namely that the income of poorer people will converge to a level greater than A (with positive investment in educating their children) if and only if θ is low enough (that is, $\theta < 1 + (\beta)^{1/\sigma} - A\gamma(\beta)^{1/\sigma}$); otherwise, it would converge to A with zero investment in children's education.

Economic Interpretation

The above analysis shows that when the marginal return to education, captured by $A\gamma$, is high enough (that is, $A\gamma \dfrac{(\beta)^{1/\sigma}}{1+(\beta)^{1/\sigma}} \geq 1$), the rich dynasties keep on investing a sufficiently high proportion of their income in childrens' education, such that in the long run the income of the rich dynasties will grow without bounds. The poorer dynasties' propensity to invest in children's education, on the other hand, is counteracted by their predilection towards spending more on current consumption in order to catch up with the lifestyle of the rich. This 'aspiration' effect does not hamper the dynasty in the long run if it starts with sufficient level of income to begin with (that is, the initial point lies towards the north-east corner of the first quadrant), so that even after emulating the lifestyle of the rich, it still has enough resources left to provide for the child's education. However, if either (a) the income gap between the rich and the poor is high (that is, the initial point lies towards the south-east corner of the first quadrant) or (b) the tendency to catch up with the lifestyle of the rich is too strong (that is, θ is sufficiently high), then the 'aspiration' effect could be disastrous for the future progenies of the poor dynasties. In an attempt to catch up with the rich, their aspiring parents would cut down on educational expenditure of the child, which, in turn, propels the dynasty towards a zero-skill, low-income steady state in the long run.

Implications for Aggregate Economy

The negative 'aspiration' effect not only affects the long-run prospects of the poor dynasties but also has a negative impact on the growth rate of the overall macroeconomy. To see this, let us assume that we start with an initial point that lies below the demarcation line. Here, the negative aspiration effect that dominates the income of the poor dynasties is stagnant at A, and that of the rich dynasties grows perpetually at some rate, say g_t^R. Let λ_0 denote the proportion of people who are initially poor. Since under the present scenario, the rich become richer while the poor stay where they were to begin with, this proportion λ does not change over time. Thus, the average income in this economy at any point of time t is given by

$$\bar{y}_t = (1-\lambda_0)y_t^R + \lambda_0 y_t^P. \tag{9.16}$$

Noting that $y_{t+1}^R = (1+g_t^R)y_t^R$, while $y_{t+1}^P = y_t^P = A$, we can derive the growth rate of average (per capita) income in this economy as

$$\begin{aligned}
g_t &\equiv \dfrac{\bar{y}_{t+1}}{\bar{y}_t} - 1 \\
&= \dfrac{(1-\lambda_0)y_{t+1}^R + \lambda_0 y_{t+1}^P}{(1-\lambda_0)y_t^R + \lambda_0 y_t^P} - 1 \\
&= \dfrac{(1-\lambda_0)(y_{t+1}^R - y_t^R)}{(1-\lambda_0)y_t^R + \lambda_0 A} \\
&= \dfrac{(1-\lambda_0)y_t^R}{(1-\lambda_0)y_t^R + \lambda_0 A} g_t^R < g_t^R.
\end{aligned}$$

Moreover, $\frac{dg_t}{d\lambda_0} < 0$, that is, the higher the proportion of the poor in the economy, the lower is the growth rate. Thus, under the aspiration effect, the initial distribution of income impinges upon the overall macroeconomic performance through two distinct channels. First, a large initial income gap between the rich and the poor implies that the poorer people remain poor forever with a stagnant income. Second, a high proportion of the poor in the initial distribution implies a lower growth rate of per capita income.

Conclusion

In this chapter, we have analysed how in an unequal society, poorer households aspiring to catch up with the lifestyle of their richer counterparts may end up in a long-run poverty trap, which not only affects the future of their progeny but also has a negative impact on the overall macroeconomy. Such long-run poverty traps are not new in the development literature. Credit market imperfection along with indivisibilities in education investment would generate similar results (see, for example, Galor & Zeira, 1993). However, in this literature, inequality per se does not directly contribute to an emergence of the trap, and therefore, indirect measures like subsidising the education expenditure of the poor often work as an effective anti-poverty measure that pulls the poor people out of the trap. In our model, however, inequality directly feeds into the education decision of the poor. Hence, education subsidies may not be very effective in combating long-run poverty, unless the income difference between the rich and the poor goes down significantly. This calls for more direct and radical measures, like redistribution of income, which close the income gap sufficiently.

References

Andreoni, J. (1989). Giving with impure altruism: Applications to charity and ricardian equivalence. *Journal of Political Economy, 97*(6), 1447–1458.
Appadurai, A. (2004). The capacity to aspire: Culture and the terms of recognition. In V. Rao, & M. Walton (Eds.), *Culture and public action*. Palo Alto, CA: Stanford University Press.
Banerjee, A.V., & Duflo, E. (2007). The economic lives of the poor. *Journal of Economic Perspectives, 21*(1), Winter 2007, 141–167.
———. (2011). *Poor economics*. New Delhi: Random House.
Bogliacino, F., & Ortolevaz, P. (2009). *It's all about society: Growth when the consumption of others acts as a reference point*. Social Science Working Paper no. 1314, California Institute of Technology, USA.
Das, M. (2007). Persistent inequality: An explanation based on limited parental altruism. *Journal of Development Economics, 84*(1), 251–270.
Dynan, K.E., Skinner, J., & Zeldes, S.P. (2004). Do the rich save more? *Journal of Political Economy, 112*(2), 397–444.
Galor, O., & Zeira, J. (1993). Income distribution and macroeconomics. *Review of Economic Studies, 60*(1), 35–52.
Genicot, G., & Ray, D. (2010). *Aspirations and inequality*. Working Paper, New York University, USA.
Heath, C., Larrick, R.P., & Wu, G. (1998). Goals as reference points. *Cognitive Psychology, 38*(1), 79–109.
Menchik, P., & David, M. (1983). Income distribution, lifetime savings, and bequests. *American Economic Review, 73*(4), 672–690.
Moav, O. (2002). Income distribution and macroeconomics: The persistence of inequality in a convex technology framework. *Economics Letters, 75*(2), 187–192.

Rao, V. (2001). Poverty and public celebrations in rural India. *Annals of the American Academy of Political and Social Science, 573*(1), 85–104.

Ray, D. (2006). Aspirations, poverty and economics change. In A.V. Banerjee, R. Banebou, & D. Mookherjee (Eds.), *Understanding poverty*. Oxford, UK: Oxford University Press.

Siegel, S. (1957). Level of aspiration and decision making. *Psychological Review, 64*(4), 253–262.

Starbuck, W.H. (1963). Level of aspiration theory and economic behavior. *Behavioral Science, 8*(2), 128–136.

Tomes, N. (1981). The family, inheritance and the intergenerational transmission of inequality. *Journal of Political Economy, 89*(5), 928–958.

10
A Proposition on Convergence to Equality in a Growth Model with Bliss

Subrata Guha[*]

Introduction

Market economies have traditionally been based on the institutions of private property and private inheritance of wealth. The right to inherit wealth has, however, often been viewed as being unjust or unfair. A person receiving a larger bequest of wealth often does so due to her circumstances of birth and is not necessarily more 'deserving' than someone who receives a smaller amount. This, for example, violates the principle of 'justice as desert'. Similarly, two individuals born at the same time but endowed with different levels of inheritance, might be unequally placed while competing for a common goal in life. Thus, the institution of inheritance can be considered unfair because it does not provide a level playing field for members of society.

Measures like taxes and ceilings on bequests have long been advocated as being necessary to moderate these undesirable aspects of private inheritance. These measures, however, have also been criticised as violating principles of freedom and justice or dampening incentives for effort and enterprise. One can, for example, argue that if a person is free to consume her legitimately earned income, then she should also be free to transfer that income to whoever she pleases. Restrictions on the freedom to choose what to do with one's income might lead not only to lower consumption for potential inheritors of wealth but also to lower social income in a capitalist economy because 'animal spirits' are lower.

For most supporters as well as opponents of intervention, one's opinions about the necessity, urgency and extent of intervention must clearly depend on one's perception of what would happen, in the absence of intervention, to inequality in the distribution of bequests. Are there systemic tendencies within market economies that lead to the distribution of bequests becoming more unequal or less unequal in the long run? The answer must necessarily be based on a hypothesis about how the incomes of individuals in market

---

[*] The proposition is the result of a conjecture by Professor Prabhat Patnaik more than 15 years ago and forms an unpublished part of my doctoral thesis written under his supervision. It is published here in fond remembrance of my days as his research student in the Centre for Economic Studies and Planning.

economies are affected by their inheritances and how the distribution of incomes for one generation of individuals, in turn, determines the distribution of inherited wealth for the next generation of individuals. Different hypotheses would be encapsulated in different models of the economy and may well provide different answers to this common question. Our analysis in this chapter relates to one such model.

Perfectly competitive economies are known to satisfy the normative criterion of Pareto efficiency under certain conditions but, in the absence of some mechanism for reallocating initial endowments amongst members of society, might not achieve desired criteria relating to distribution. One possible objective of a society in which such reallocation is considered either not possible or not desirable is that there should be over time progressive achievement of equality in the distribution of inherited wealth. Does there exist systemic tendencies within perfectly competitive economies that promote this objective?

One way in which this question can be studied is by considering a hypothetical situation in which individuals in a perfectly competitive economy differ only with respect to the amount of wealth that they inherit and then study what happens to the distribution of bequests or inheritances over time. In the theory of economic growth, the Ramsey–Cass–Koopmans model provides a benchmark for studying the long-run dynamics of a perfectly competitive economy. Not only is the growth path in the Ramsey–Cass–Koopmans economy Pareto efficient, but the process of capital accumulation is driven by inter-generational transfers in the form of savings undertaken by infinitely lived dynasties or households. The model, therefore, provides a natural starting point for an analysis of the dynamics of inherited wealth in a perfectly competitive economy. The studies by Chatterjee (1994) and Caselli and Ventura (2000) provide the basis for most of the literature analysing the dynamics of wealth distribution within the model. By now, it is well understood that the model allows for a wide range of possibilities regarding the evolution of wealth distribution: convergence and divergence in distribution as well as monotonic and non-monotonic trends in wealth inequality.[1]

This chapter addresses a very simple question. Given an unequal initial distribution of inherited wealth, can the economy in the model ever converge to a situation of complete equality in wealth inheritances?

Stiglitz (1969) considered the dynamics of the distribution of inherited wealth in extended versions of the Solow growth model, assuming a variety of behavioural savings (bequest) functions. For some of these functions, he obtained strongly egalitarian results indicating that beginning from any unequal initial distribution of inherited wealth, the economy would asymptotically converge to a state of complete equality in wealth holdings (an equalitarian distribution of wealth).

In the case of the Ramsey–Cass–Koopmans model, however, although there exist various results outlining conditions under which there is decreasing inequality over time in the distribution of wealth, it is clear in most cases that the limiting distribution is unequal. This must, for example, be true for the basic model with technical progress in which instantaneous utility is an isoelastic function of the rate of consumption.[2] This must also be true for the model extended to include a minimum consumption requirement in which instantaneous utility is a time-varying isoelastic function of the excess of the rate of consumption over its minimum value, the latter being assumed to grow at the rate of technical progress.[3]

The intuition in both cases is similar. The basic model can be treated as a special case of the extended model in which the minimum consumption requirement is nil. We therefore confine ourselves to simply discussing the intuition in the latter case.

---

[1] Contributions to the literature include papers by Glachant and Vellutini (2002), Alvarez-Pelaez and Diaz (2005), Obiols-Homs and Urrutia (2005) and García-Peñalosa and Turnovsky (2009).
[2] See Guha (2004) for a formal proof.
[3] This model is considered, for example, by Chatterjee with a zero rate of technical progress and Alvarez-Pelaez and Diaz (2005) with a positive rate of technical progress.

Let us refer to the excess of a dynasty's consumption over the minimum requirement its 'surplus consumption'. The assumption that instantaneous utility is an isoelastic function of surplus consumption implies that the rate of growth of a dynasty's surplus consumption is equal to the rate of growth of surplus consumption in the economy as a whole. The economy asymptotically converges to a steady state in which surplus consumption per unit of effective labour is a constant. Therefore, for every dynasty, surplus consumption per unit of effective labour converges to some limiting value. Since, at any instant, the rate of growth of surplus consumption is the same for every dynasty, the larger the limiting value of surplus consumption per unit of effective labour the larger is the present discounted value at time 0 of the dynasty's stream of surplus consumption time 0 onwards.

The present discounted value of every dynasty's stream of current and future surplus consumption at any time is equal to the sum of its current wealth and the present discounted value of its stream of current and future wage income less the present discounted value of the dynasty's stream of current and future minimum consumption. Given our discussion in the previous paragraph, this equality has the following implications. Since, at any instant t, the present discounted values of the stream of wage income and the stream of minimum consumption t onwards per unit of effective labour at t are the same for every dynasty, it follows that dynasties with higher initial wealth have higher limiting values of surplus consumption per unit of effective labour. Further, because the present discounted values of the stream of wage income and the stream of minimum consumption divided by the present number of units of effective labour converge to limiting steady-state values, as does the present discounted value of the stream of surplus consumption per present unit of effective labour for any dynasty, it follows that current wealth per unit of effective labour for any dynasty also converges to a limiting value. Finally, because this value must then be greater for a dynasty with a greater limiting value of surplus consumption per unit of effective labour, it follows that the limiting value of wealth per unit of effective labour must be greater for dynasties with greater initial levels of wealth.

In this chapter, we prove that beginning from an initially unequal distribution of inherited wealth, it is possible for there to exist equilibrium growth paths in a Ramsey economy along which the economy converges to an equalitarian distribution of wealth. The major point of departure from the standard Ramsey–Cass–Koopmans model with technical progress is the assumption that instantaneous utility is a time-varying quadratic function of the rate of consumption.

The assumption of a quadratic function implies the existence of a finite rate of consumption at which the consumer is satiated (marginal utility becomes equal to zero), a state that Ramsey (1928) referred to as 'bliss'. The notion of bliss now appears fairly antiquated in growth theory but might be easier to appreciate if we remind ourselves that consumption requires time and there might be only so much that can be consumed by an individual within any finite time period without leading to a decline in total utility.

The time-varying nature of the utility function is required to allow for the possibility of a steady state with growing per capita income and follows from the assumption that the rate of consumption corresponding to bliss increases over time at the same rate as the rate of labour-augmenting technical progress. The last assumption may be rationalised on the ground that economy-wide increases in labour productivity are also accompanied by a continuous process of learning about ways to use and derive satisfaction from output produced in the economy. This leads to consumer satiation being attained at progressively higher rates of consumption.

The behaviour of wealth distribution in the presence of a quadratic instantaneous utility function[4] has been previously studied by Chatterjee (1994) in a neoclassical growth model with intergenerational altruism, where time is treated as a discrete variable and there is no technical progress. In his model, capital is

---

[4] For a more recent example of the use of the quadratic instantaneous utility function in a growth model, see Guerrini (2010).

taken to be the only factor of production, the number of firms in the economy is equal to the size of the constant population and the production function is the same as the intensive production function in the standard two-factor model. The time paths for aggregate consumption and capital stock are also those characterising equilibrium growth paths in the Ramsey–Cass–Koopmans model with the corresponding instantaneous utility function, and results relating to the distribution of wealth can be interpreted as relating to the distribution of human plus non-human wealth[5] in the standard model. The equilibrium growth paths considered in this chapter are, however, not analysed by Chatterjee.

The Model

We consider a closed economy without government intervention that produces a single good. The good can be consumed, or stocks of the good, constituting the capital stock of the economy, can be used in production along with labour. Capital stocks are not subject to depreciation,[6] and all capital is privately owned.

Individuals living at any point in time are identical except for the amount of (non-human[7]) wealth inherited by them. Wealth equals ownership of capital stock less net debts outstanding.[8] Individuals receive bequests, supply a fixed amount of labour (in physical units) during their lifetimes, earn wage income, rental income on capital and make or receive interest payments on debt. They decide upon the rates at which to consume and save during their lifetime. Accumulated assets and liabilities at death are distributed equally as bequests among descendants. Using a continuous time framework, it is assumed that each individual lives only for an instant and is replaced at death by a given number of descendants. The population of descendants of each individual grows at the same constant exponential rate n.

We know that, at any point in time, (a) individuals inheriting the same amount of wealth are identical, (b) each individual has the same number of descendants after any time interval of length $t(t>0)$ and (c) after an individual's death, her wealth is shared equally among descendants. Suppose, individuals comprising the social population at an initial point of time (denoted by, say, 0) are classified into groups according to the amount of wealth inherited by them. Then, at any time $t>0$, individuals descended from ancestors belonging to the same group (say, the ith) at time 0 have equal holdings of wealth and together constitute the same proportion (say, l_i) of the population as their ancestors at time 0. They are defined to constitute the ith group at $t>0$.

We assume that the number of groups is finite and equal to q, where q is a positive integer greater than unity. Therefore, at any instant $t \geq 0$, we have q groups of individuals, the ith group constituting a constant proportion l_i $(i=1,2,\ldots,q)$ of the total population ($\sum_{i=1}^{q} l_i = 1$). Within each group, individuals are homogeneous at any point of time.

Labour is homogeneous in quality across individuals at any point in time, and each individual supplies one natural unit of labour. The economy is assumed to undergo purely labour-augmenting technical progress. The number of efficiency units of labour (units of effective labour) corresponding to a natural unit of labour at time $t \geq 0$ is denoted by m_t and is assumed to grow at a constant exponential rate μ ($\mu \geq 0$).

---

[5] Human wealth can be defined as the present discounted value of the stream of current and future wage earnings.
[6] The analysis remains unaffected if we assume a constant exponential rate of depreciation of capital.
[7] For the purposes of our discussion, a dynasty at a point in time t refers to an individual living at point in time t and all her descendants. Human wealth of a dynasty at time t is defined as the present discounted value at time t of the current and future wage income of members of the dynasty.
[8] Net debts outstanding is defined as equal to the amount of loans taken (and awaiting repayment) less the amount of loans given (and awaiting repayment).

If k denotes the ratio of capital to effective labour, then the intensive production function f giving the average product of effective labour satisfies the following properties:

$$f(0) = 0;$$

$$\forall k > 0 : f'(k) > 0;$$

$$\forall k > 0 : f''(k) < 0;$$

$$\lim_{k \to 0} f'(k) = \infty \quad \text{and} \quad \lim_{k \to \infty} f'(k) = 0.$$

Factor markets are perfectly competitive. Let k_t denote the economy-wide ratio of capital to effective labour at time $t \geq 0 (k_t \geq 0)$. Let w_t denote the wage per unit of effective labour and r_t the rental price of capital in the economy at time $t \geq 0$. Then, for any $t \geq 0$, $w_t = f(k_t) - k_t f'(k_t); r_t = f'(k_t)$.

Let a_{it} denote the amount of wealth per efficiency unit of labour in the ith group at time t ($i = 1, 2, \ldots, q$; $t \geq 0$). The distribution of wealth in the economy at time $t \geq 0$ can therefore be represented by $(a_{1t}, a_{2t}, \ldots, a_{qt})$. Note that $\sum_{i=1}^{q} l_i a_{it} = k_t, \forall t \geq 0$.

Let c_{it} denote the rate of consumption per unit of effective labour in the ith group at time t ($i = 1, 2, \ldots, q$; $t \geq 0$). Let c_t be the average rate of consumption in the economy at time $t \geq 0$. That is, let $\forall t \geq 0 : c_t = \sum_{i=1}^{q} l_i c_{it}$.

The instantaneous utility function of an individual in the ith group at time t ($t \geq 0$) is the same for all $i \in \{1, 2, \ldots, q\}$ and is given by

$$u_t(c_{it} m_t) = (h m_t)(c_{it} m_t) - (1/2)(c_{it} m_t)^2,$$

where $h > 0$, and $\forall t \geq 0 : h \cdot m_t$ is the rate of consumption corresponding to bliss.

Individuals consider only those dynastic consumption plans for which c_{it} is a piecewise continuous function[9] of time. Moreover, the time path of a_{it} implied by any such dynastic consumption plan must be continuous, and the rate of change of a_{it} must be a piecewise continuous function of time.

Given a common positive rate of time preference θ, for every $i \in \{1, 2, \ldots, q\}$ and for every $\tau \in [0, \infty)$, an individual in group i at time τ chooses a programme $\{(c_{it}, a_{it})\}_{t=\tau}^{\infty}$ that solves the following optimisation problem:

$$\text{Problem } (i, \tau): \text{Max} \int_{\tau}^{\infty} u_t(c_{it} \cdot m_t) \exp(-\theta(t - \tau)) dt$$

subject to

$$\frac{d a_{it}}{dt} = w_t + (r_t - n - \mu) a_{it} - c_{it}, \quad \text{for all } t \geq \tau \quad (10.1)$$

$$\lim_{t \to \infty} a_{it} \cdot \exp\left(-\int_{\tau}^{t} (r_v - n - \mu) dv\right) \geq 0 \quad (10.2)$$

---

[9] This implies that the function has at most a finite number of points of discontinuity in any finite time interval; at any point of discontinuity, the discontinuity arises because both left-hand-side and right-hand-side limits exist but are unequal; and the value of the function at any point of discontinuity is assumed to be equal to the left-hand-side limit of the function at that point.

$$c_{it} \geq 0, \text{ for all } t \geq \tau \tag{10.3}$$

$$a_{i\tau} \text{ given} \tag{10.4}$$

There is, of course, no assurance that the utility functional in the above problem will converge. We assume that in comparing consumption programmes that do not converge, a feasible programme $\{(\hat{c}_{it}, \hat{a}_{it})\}_{t=\tau}^{\infty}$ will be considered optimal if for any other feasible programme $\{(c'_{it}, a'_{it})\}_{t=\tau}^{\infty}$ it is true that

$$\exists T' > \tau : \left[\forall T \geq T' : \int_{\tau}^{T} \{u_t(\hat{c}_{it} \cdot m_t) - u_t(c'_{it} \cdot m_t)\} \exp(-\theta(t-\tau)) dt \geq 0 \right].^{10}$$

We next define the concept of an equilibrium growth path in the context of the above definitions and assumptions.

Suppose, given k_0 and $(a_{10}, a_{20}, \ldots, a_{q0})$, a programme $\{(\bar{c}_{it}, \bar{a}_{it})\}_{t=0}^{\infty}$ exists for every $i \in \{1, 2, \ldots, q\}$ such that the following conditions are satisfied:

$$\forall i \in \{1, 2, \ldots, q\} : \bar{a}_{i0} = a_{i0} \text{ and } \forall i \in \{1, 2, \ldots, q\} \wedge \forall \tau \geq 0:$$

If $\left[\forall t \geq \tau : \bar{k}_t = \sum_{i=1}^{q} l_i \bar{a}_{it} \geq 0 \wedge \left[w_t = f(\bar{k}_t) - \bar{k}_t f'(\bar{k}_t) \wedge r_t = f'(\bar{k}_t) \right] \right]$ then $\{(\bar{c}_{it}, \bar{a}_{it})\}_{t=\tau}^{\infty}$ is a solution to Problem (i, τ).

Then, if $\bar{k}_0 = k_0$ and $\forall t \geq 0 : \bar{c}_t = \sum_{i=1}^{q} l_i \bar{c}_{it}$,

$\{(\bar{c}_t, \bar{k}_t); (\bar{c}_{1t}, \bar{a}_{1t}), (\bar{c}_{2t}, \bar{a}_{2t}), \ldots, (\bar{c}_{qt}, \bar{a}_{qt})\}_{t=0}^{\infty}$ is an equilibrium growth path for the economy.

Since, in this chapter, our objective is to merely demonstrate the possibility of existence of an equilibrium growth path along which the distribution of wealth converges to an egalitarian state, we make some additional assumptions. We assume that production technology is such that it is technologically possible to have a balanced growth path in which every individual has a rate of consumption corresponding to bliss. In particular, we assume that $h < f(k_g) - (n+\mu)k_g$, where $f'(k_g) = n+\mu$. This implies that the per capita rate of consumption in the economy along a balanced growth path satisfying the Golden Rule is always greater than the *bliss* rate of consumption. This implies that there exist two distinct positive values, k'_h and k''_h ($k'_h < k_g < k''_h$), of the ratio of capital to effective labour such that $f(k'_h) - (n+\mu)k'_h = f(k''_h) - (n+\mu)k''_h = h$. In addition, we assume that $f'(k'_h) > n + \theta - \mu$.

These assumptions imply that if there exists a steady-state growth path along which the rate of interest is equal to $n + \theta - \mu$, then for this growth path, the per capita rate of consumption is greater than the *bliss* rate of consumption, or the steady-state rate of interest is less than the rate of growth of effective labour.[11]

Finally, consider the dynamic system

$$\frac{dc_t}{dt} = (h - c_t)(f'(k_t) - (n + \theta - \mu)). \tag{10.5}$$

$$\frac{dk_t}{dt} = f(k_t) - (n + \mu)k_t - c_t. \tag{10.6}$$

---

[10] This is the 'overtaking' criterion for optimality. See von Weizsäcker (1965).
[11] These assumptions therefore rule out the growth paths considered by Chatterjee (1994) which asymptotically approach such steady states.

Figure 10.1
Phase Diagram for the System (10.5)–(10.6)

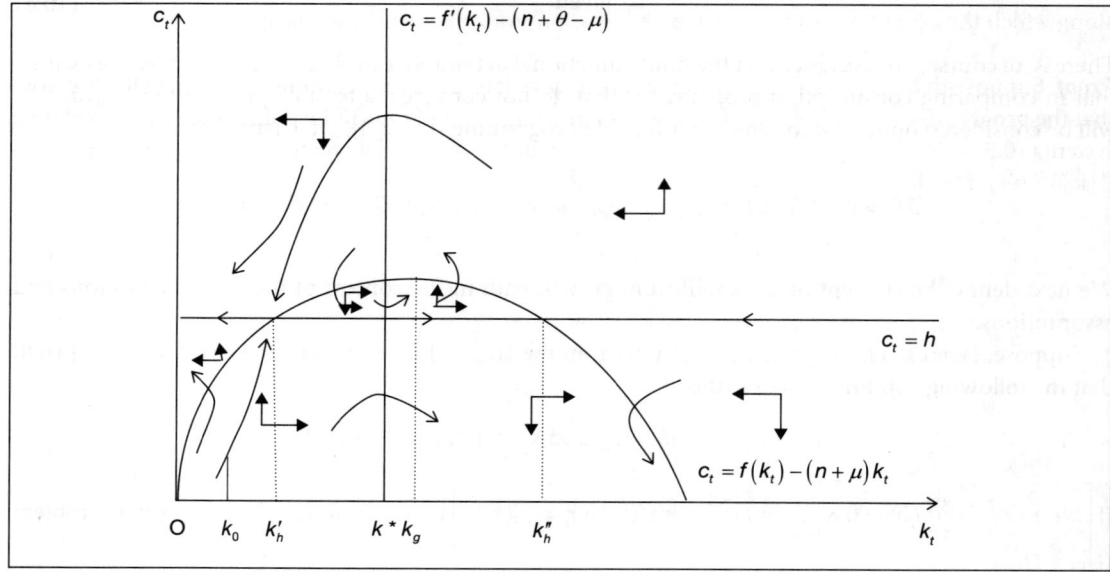

The Jacobian matrix for this system is given by

$$\begin{pmatrix} -f'(k_t)+n+\theta-\mu & (h-c_t)f''(k_t) \\ -1 & f'(k_t)-(n+\mu) \end{pmatrix}.$$

The Jacobian matrix evaluated at the equilibrium point (h, k'_h) is

$$J^* = \begin{pmatrix} -f'(k'_h)+n+\theta-\mu & 0 \\ -1 & f'(k'_h)-(n+\mu) \end{pmatrix}.$$

By assumption, $f'(k'_h) > n+\theta-\mu$ and $f'(k'_h) > (n+\mu)$. It follows that the determinant of J^* is negative and (h, k'_h) is a saddle point for this system. Further, it is simple to check using the phase diagram (see Figure 10.1) for the system that the saddle path is positively sloped.

Existence of Equilibrium Growth Paths with Convergence to an Equalitarian Wealth Distribution

In this section, we prove that there exist initial values of the ratio of capital to effective labour and a set of unequal initial distributions of wealth for which an equilibrium growth path exists in the economy with the property that the distribution of wealth converges to an equalitarian state in the long run.

We define restriction (R) on the initial value of the ratio of capital to effective labour in the economy as follows:

(R) $k_0 < k'_h$ and there exists $c > 0$ such that (c, k_0) is a point on a stable arm of the saddle point (h, k'_h) in (10.5) to (10.6).

A Proposition on Convergence to Equality in a Growth Model with Bliss

Proposition. Given an initial ratio of capital to effective labour satisfying (R), there exist unequal initial distributions of wealth $(a_{10}, a_{20}, \ldots, a_{q0})$ for which it is true that there exists an equilibrium growth path along which the distribution of wealth converges asymptotically to an equalitarian state.

Proof. Suppose that the initial ratio of capital to effective labour in the economy k_0 satisfies (R). Suppose that the programme $\{(\tilde{c}_t, \tilde{k}_t)\}_{t=0}^{\infty}$ with $\tilde{k}_0 = k_0$ lies on the stable arm of the saddle point (h, k_h') of the dynamic system (10.5)–(10.6) with monotonically increasing c_t and k_t. Given that $w_t = f(\tilde{k}_t) - \tilde{k}_t f'(\tilde{k}_t)$ and $r_t = f'(\tilde{k}_t) > f'(k_h') > n + \mu$ for all $t \geq 0$, the following conditions hold:

$$\forall t \geq 0 : \frac{d\tilde{c}_t}{dt} = (h - \tilde{c}_t)\{r_t - (n + \theta - \mu)\}. \tag{10.7}$$

$$\forall t \geq 0 : \frac{d\tilde{k}_t}{dt} = w_t + (r_t - n - \mu)\tilde{k}_t - \tilde{c}_t. \tag{10.8}$$

$$\lim_{t \to \infty} \tilde{k}_t \exp\left(-\int_0^t (r_v - n - \mu) dv\right) = 0. \tag{10.9}$$

$$\forall t \geq 0 : \tilde{c}_t > 0. \tag{10.10}$$

Further, since $k_h' < k_g$, it follows that

$$\lim_{t \to \infty} w_t = f(k_h') - k_h' f'(k_h') = w^* \text{ (say) and } \lim_{t \to \infty} r_t = f'(k_h') = r^* \text{ (say)} \tag{10.11}$$

$$\forall t > 0 : 0 < w_0 < w_t < w^* \wedge 0 < n + \mu < r^* < r_t < r_0. \tag{10.12}$$

From (10.11) and (10.12), we can show that $\int_0^z w_t \exp\left(-\int_0^t (r_v - n - \mu) dv\right) dt$ is a monotonically increasing function of z which is bounded above. Therefore,

$$\int_0^\infty w_t \exp\left(-\int_0^t (r_v - n - \mu) dv\right) dt = \lim_{z \to \infty} \int_0^z w_t \exp\left(-\int_0^t (r_v - n - \mu) dv\right) dt \text{ exists.} \tag{10.13}$$

From the definition of $\{(\tilde{c}_t, \tilde{k}_t)\}_{t=0}^{\infty}$, we know that

$$\lim_{t \to \infty} \tilde{c}_t = f(k_h') - (n + \mu) k_h' = h \text{ and } \forall t > 0 : 0 < \tilde{c}_0 < \tilde{c}_t < h. \tag{10.14}$$

From (10.11), (10.12) and (10.14), we can then show that

$$\int_0^\infty \tilde{c}_t \exp\left(-\int_0^t (r_v - n - \mu) dv\right) dt = \lim_{z \to \infty} \int_0^z \tilde{c}_t \exp\left(-\int_0^t (r_v - n - \mu) dv\right) dt \text{ exists.} \tag{10.15}$$

Moreover, from (10.12), it follows that

$$\int_0^\infty \exp\left(-\int_0^t (r_v - n - \mu) dv\right) dt = \lim_{z \to \infty} \int_0^z \exp\left(-\int_0^t (r_v - n - \mu) dv\right) dt \text{ exists.} \tag{10.16}$$

From (10.7), we get

$$\forall t \geq 0: \tilde{c}_t = h + (\tilde{c}_0 - h)\exp\left(-\int_0^t \{r_v - (n + \theta - \mu)\}dv\right). \tag{10.17}$$

Therefore, from (10.15) to (10.17), it follows that

$$\int_0^\infty \exp\left(-\int_0^t [\{r_v - (n + \theta - \mu)\} + (r_v - n - \mu)]dv\right)dt \text{ exists.} \tag{10.18}$$

Moreover,

$$\int_0^\infty \exp\left(-\int_0^t [\{r_v - (n + \theta - \mu)\} + (r_v - n - \mu)]dv\right)dt > 0. \tag{10.19}$$

Therefore, from (10.13), (10.16), (10.18) and (10.19), it follows that given any arbitrary initial distribution of inheritances $(a_{10}, a_{20}, \ldots, a_{q0})$, we can define $\forall i \in \{1, 2, \ldots, q\}$, a programme $\{(\tilde{c}_{it}, \tilde{a}_{it})\}_{t=0}^\infty$ such that

$$\forall t \geq 0: \tilde{c}_{it} = h + \left\{ \frac{a_{i0} + \int_0^\infty (w_z - h)\exp\left(-\int_0^z (r_v - n - \mu)dv\right)dz}{\int_0^\infty \exp\left(-\int_0^z [\{r_v - (n + \theta - \mu)\} + (r_v - n - \mu)]dv\right)dz} \right\}$$
$$\times \exp\left(-\int_0^t \{r_v - (n + \theta - \mu)\}dv\right) \tag{10.20}$$

$$\forall t \geq 0: \tilde{a}_{it} = \frac{a_{i0} + \int_0^t (w_z - \tilde{c}_{iz})\exp\left(-\int_0^z (r_v - n - \mu)dv\right)dz}{\exp\left(-\int_0^t (r_v - n - \mu)dv\right)}. \tag{10.21}$$

Since, by assumption, $f(\tilde{k}_t)$ and $f'(\tilde{k}_t)$ are differentiable functions of $\tilde{k}_t$ on $(0, \infty)$ and, by definition, $\forall t \geq 0: \tilde{k}_t > 0$; therefore, given (10.8), it can be shown that $\forall i \in \{1, 2, \ldots, q\}: \tilde{c}_{it}$ and $\tilde{a}_{it}$ are differentiable functions of t on $[0, \infty)$. In particular, we can show from (10.20) and (10.21) that

$$\forall i \in \{1, 2, \ldots, q\} \wedge \forall t \geq 0: \frac{d\tilde{c}_{it}}{dt} = (h - \tilde{c}_{it})\{r_t - (n + \theta - \mu)\}. \tag{10.22}$$

$$\forall i \in \{1, 2, \ldots, q\} \wedge \forall t \geq 0: \frac{d\tilde{a}_{it}}{dt} = w_t + (r_t - n - \mu)\tilde{a}_{it} - \tilde{c}_{it}. \tag{10.23}$$

Moreover, from (10.20) and (10.21), it can also be shown that

$$\forall i \in \{1,2,\ldots,q\}: \lim_{t \to \infty} \tilde{a}_{it} \exp\left(-\int_0^t (r_v - n - \mu)dv\right) = 0. \qquad (10.24)$$

Further, suppose, if possible, that $\forall i \in \{1,2,\ldots,q\}$:

$$-h\int_0^\infty \exp\left(-\int_0^z [\{r_v - (n + \theta - \mu)\} + (r_v - n - \mu)]dv\right)dz$$
$$+ \int_0^\infty (h - w_z) \exp\left(-\int_0^z (r_v - n - \mu)dv\right) dz < a_{i0} < \int_0^\infty (h - w_z) \exp\left(-\int_0^z (r_v - n - \mu)dv\right) dz. \qquad (10.25)$$

Since $\forall k > 0: \dfrac{d}{dk}\{f(k) - kf'(k)\} > 0$ and $k'_h < k_g$, therefore, by definition,

$\forall t \geq 0: h = f(k'_h) - (n + \mu)k'_h > f(k'_h) - k'_h f'(k'_h) > f(\tilde{k}_t) - \tilde{k}_t f'(\tilde{k}_t) = w_t$. Therefore, note that the right-hand-side expression in the second inequality in (10.25) is positive, and the first term on the left-hand side of the first inequality is negative.

From (10.12), (10.20) and (10.25), given $f'(k'_h) > n + \theta - \mu$, it follows that

$$\forall i \in \{1,2,\ldots,q\} \land \forall t \geq 0: 0 < \tilde{c}_{it} < h. \qquad (10.26)$$

From the definition of $\{(\tilde{c}_{it}, \tilde{a}_{it})\}_{t=0}^\infty (i = 1, 2, \ldots, q)$, and from (10.23), (10.24) and (10.26), it follows that if (10.25) holds, then

$\forall i \in \{1,2,\ldots,q\}: \{(\tilde{c}_{it}, \tilde{a}_{it})\}_{t=0}^\infty$ is an admissible programme for Problem $(i, 0)$ where

$$\forall t \geq 0: w_t = f(\tilde{k}_t) - \tilde{k}_t f'(\tilde{k}_t) \land r_t = f'(\tilde{k}_t). \qquad (10.27)$$

From (10.7)–(10.9), (10.13), (10.15), (10.18) and (10.19), it is possible to show that

$$\forall t \geq 0: \tilde{c}_t = h + \left\{ \frac{k_0 + \int_0^\infty (w_z - h)\exp\left(-\int_0^z (r_v - n - \mu)dv\right)dz}{\int_0^\infty \exp\left(-\int_0^z [\{r_v - (n + \theta - \mu)\} + (r_v - n - \mu)]dv\right)dz} \right\}$$
$$\times \exp\left(-\int_0^t \{r_v - (n + \theta - \mu)\}dv\right). \qquad (10.28)$$

$$\forall t \geq 0: \tilde{k}_t = \frac{k_0 + \int_0^t (w_z - \tilde{c}_z)\exp\left(-\int_0^z (r_v - n - \mu)dv\right)dz}{\exp\left(-\int_0^t (r_v - n - \mu)dv\right)}. \qquad (10.29)$$

Note that from (10.14) and (10.28), it follows that

$$-h\int_0^\infty \exp\left(-\int_0^z [\{r_v - (n+\theta-\mu)\} + (r_v - n - \mu)]dv\right)dz$$
$$+\int_0^\infty (h-w_z)\exp\left(-\int_0^z (r_v - n - \mu)dv\right)dz < k_0 < \int_0^\infty (h-w_z)\exp\left(-\int_0^z (r_v - n - \mu)dv\right)dz. \tag{10.30}$$

Therefore, it is possible to show that there exist unequal distributions $(a_{10}, a_{20}, \ldots, a_{q0})$ for which (10.25) and, therefore, (10.27) hold.

Further, from the definition of $\{(\tilde{c}_t, \tilde{k}_t)\}_{t=0}^\infty$ and from (10.20), (10.21), (10.28) and (10.29), it follows that

$$\forall i \in \{1,2,\ldots,q\} \wedge \forall t \geq 0 : \tilde{c}_t = \sum_{i=1}^q l_i \tilde{c}_{it} \wedge \tilde{k}_t = \sum_{i=1}^q l_i \tilde{a}_{it} > 0. \tag{10.31}$$

Consider any $i \in \{1,2,\ldots,q\}$. Consider any other distinct admissible programme $\{(\breve{c}_{it}, \breve{a}_{it})\}_{t=0}^\infty$ for the Problem $(i, 0)$, where $\forall t \geq 0 : w_t = f(\tilde{k}_t) - \tilde{k}_t f'(\tilde{k}_t) \wedge r_t = f'(\tilde{k}_t)$.

Let $\forall T > 0 : Z_T = \int_0^T u_t(\breve{c}_{it} m_t) \exp(-\theta t) dt - \int_0^T u_t(\tilde{c}_{it} m_t) \exp(-\theta t) dt.$

From (10.26), it follows that we can define $\forall t \geq 0$:

$$\tilde{\lambda}_{it} = \left[\frac{\partial u_t(c_{it} \cdot m_t)\exp(-\theta \cdot t)}{\partial c_{it}}\right]_{c_{it}=\tilde{c}_{it}} = (h - \tilde{c}_{it})m_0^2 \exp((2\mu - \theta)t) > 0.$$

Moreover, let $\forall t \geq 0$:

$$\tilde{H}_i(c_{it}, a_{it}, t) = u_t(c_{it} \cdot m_t)\exp(-\theta \cdot t) + \tilde{\lambda}_{it}\{w_t + (r_t - n - \mu)a_{it} - c_{it}\}.$$

Then, since both $\{(\tilde{c}_{it}, \tilde{a}_{it})\}_{t=0}^\infty$ and $\{(\breve{c}_{it}, \breve{a}_{it})\}_{t=0}^\infty$ satisfy (10.1), therefore

$$\forall T > 0 : Z_T = \int_0^T \left[\tilde{H}_i(\tilde{c}_{it}, \tilde{a}_{it}, t) - \tilde{\lambda}_{it}\frac{d\tilde{a}_{it}}{dt} - \tilde{H}_i(\breve{c}_{it}, \breve{a}_{it}, t) + \tilde{\lambda}_{it}\frac{d\breve{a}_{it}}{dt}\right]dt.$$

Integrating by parts, it follows that

$$\forall T > 0 : Z_T = \int_0^T \left[\tilde{H}_i(\tilde{c}_{it}, \tilde{a}_{it}, t) - \tilde{H}_i(\breve{c}_{it}, \breve{a}_{it}, t)\right]dt + \int_0^T \left(\frac{d\tilde{\lambda}_{it}}{dt}\tilde{a}_{it}\right)dt - \left[\tilde{\lambda}_{it}\tilde{a}_{it}\right]_0^T$$
$$- \int_0^T \left(\frac{d\tilde{\lambda}_{it}}{dt}\breve{a}_{it}\right)dt + \left[\tilde{\lambda}_{it}\breve{a}_{it}\right]_0^T.$$

Since $\tilde{a}_{i0} = a_{i0} = \breve{a}_{i0}$, it follows that

$$\forall T > 0: Z_T = \int_0^T \left[\tilde{H}_i(\tilde{c}_{it}, \tilde{a}_{it}, t) - \tilde{H}_i(\breve{c}_{it}, \breve{a}_{it}, t) + \frac{d\tilde{\lambda}_{it}}{dt}(\tilde{a}_{it} - \breve{a}_{it}) \right] dt + \tilde{\lambda}_{iT}(\tilde{a}_{iT} - \breve{a}_{iT}).$$

Let $\forall c : u(c) = hc - \frac{1}{2}c^2$. Then,

$$\forall T > 0: Z_T = \int_0^T [\{u(\tilde{c}_{it}) - u(\breve{c}_{it})\} m_0^2 \exp((2\mu - \theta)t) - \tilde{\lambda}_{it}(\tilde{c}_{it} - \breve{c}_{it})$$

$$+ \tilde{\lambda}_{it}(r_t - n - \mu)(\tilde{a}_{it} - \breve{a}_{it}) + \frac{d\tilde{\lambda}_{it}}{dt}(\tilde{a}_{it} - \breve{a}_{it})] dt + \tilde{\lambda}_{iT}(\tilde{a}_{iT} - \breve{a}_{iT}).$$

Given (10.22), from our definition of $\tilde{\lambda}_{it}$, it follows that

$$\forall t \geq 0: \frac{d\tilde{\lambda}_{it}}{dt} = -\tilde{\lambda}_{it}(r_t - n - \mu). \tag{10.32}$$

Further, it can be shown that

$$\forall t \geq 0: \left. \frac{\partial u(c_{it})}{\partial c_{it}} \right|_{c_{it} = \tilde{c}_{it}} m_0^2 \exp((2\mu - \theta)t) = \tilde{\lambda}_{it}.$$

Therefore, it follows that

$$\forall T > 0: Z_T = \int_0^T \left[\left\{ u(\tilde{c}_{it}) - u(\breve{c}_{it}) - \left. \frac{\partial u(c_{it})}{\partial c_{it}} \right|_{c_{it} = \tilde{c}_{it}} (\tilde{c}_{it} - \breve{c}_{it}) \right\} m_0^2 \exp((2\mu - \theta)t) \right] dt$$

$$+ \tilde{\lambda}_{iT}(\tilde{a}_{iT} - \breve{a}_{iT})$$

Since $\{(\tilde{c}_{it}, \tilde{a}_{it})\}_{t=0}^{\infty}$ and $\{(\breve{c}_{it}, \breve{a}_{it})\}_{t=0}^{\infty}$ are distinct programmes, both satisfying (10.1)–(10.4), let $t^* \in [0, \infty)$ such that $\tilde{c}_{it^*} \neq \breve{c}_{it^*}$. Since $\tilde{c}_{it}$ is continuous on $[0, \infty)$ and $\breve{c}_{it}$ is piecewise continuous on $[0, \infty)$, it therefore follows that

$$[\exists t' \in [0, t^*): [\forall t \in [t', t^*]: \tilde{c}_{it} \neq \breve{c}_{it}]] \vee [\exists t'' \in (t^*, \infty]: [\forall t \in [t^*, t'']: \tilde{c}_{it} \neq \breve{c}_{it}]].$$

From our definition of $u(\cdot)$, it can be shown using the Mean Value Theorem that

$$\forall t \geq 0: \left[\tilde{c}_{it} \neq \breve{c}_{it} \rightarrow u(\tilde{c}_{it}) - u(\breve{c}_{it}) - \left. \frac{\partial u(c_{it})}{\partial c_{it}} \right|_{c_{it} = \tilde{c}_{it}} (\tilde{c}_{it} - \breve{c}_{it}) > 0 \right].$$

Therefore, it follows that

$$\exists T^* > 0: [\forall T \geq T^*: Z_T - \tilde{\lambda}_{iT}(\tilde{a}_{iT} - \breve{a}_{iT}) > 0 \text{ and } Z_T - \tilde{\lambda}_{iT}(\tilde{a}_{iT} - \breve{a}_{iT}) \text{ is a non-decreasing function of } T].$$

From (10.32),

$$\forall T > 0 : \tilde{\lambda}_{iT} = \tilde{\lambda}_{i0} \exp\left(-\int_0^T (r_t - n - \mu) dt\right).$$

Therefore, it follows that

$$\exists T^* > 0 : \left[\forall T \geq T^* : Z_T - \tilde{\lambda}_{i0}(\bar{a}_{iT} - \tilde{a}_{iT}) \exp\left(-\int_0^T (r_t - n - \mu) dt\right) > 0 \text{ and}\right.$$
$$\left. Z_T - \tilde{\lambda}_{i0}(\bar{a}_{iT} - \tilde{a}_{iT}) \exp\left(-\int_0^T (r_t - n - \mu) dt\right) \text{ is a non-decreasing function of } T\right]. \quad (10.33)$$

Since, $\tilde{\lambda}_{i0} > 0$ and $\{(\tilde{c}_{it}, \tilde{a}_{it})\}_{t=0}^{\infty}$ satisfies (10.2), from (10.24) we get

$$\lim_{T \to \infty} (\bar{a}_{iT} - \tilde{a}_{iT}) \exp\left(-\int_0^T (r_t - n - \mu) dt\right) \geq 0. \quad (10.34)$$

Therefore, from (10.33) and (10.34), it follows that

$$\exists T' > 0 : [\forall T > 0 : T \geq T' \rightarrow Z_T > 0]. \quad (10.35)$$

Hence, from (10.27), (10.30) and (10.35), it follows that there exist initial distributions of inheritances $(a_{10}, a_{20}, \ldots, a_{q0})$ for which, under the assumed conditions,

$$\forall i \in \{1, 2, \ldots, q\} : \{(\tilde{c}_{it}, \tilde{a}_{it})\}_{t=0}^{\infty} \text{ is a unique solution to the Problem } (i, 0), \text{ where}$$

$$\forall t \geq 0 : w_t = f(\tilde{k}_t) - \tilde{k}_t f'(\tilde{k}_t) \wedge r_t = f'(\tilde{k}_t). \quad (10.36)$$

Moreover, it can be proved that $\forall \tau \geq 0 \wedge \forall i \in \{1, 2, \ldots, q\}$:

$$\forall t \geq \tau : \tilde{c}_{it} = h + \left\{\frac{a_{i\tau} + \int_\tau^\infty (w_z - h) \exp\left(-\int_\tau^z (r_v - n - \mu) dv\right) dz}{\int_\tau^\infty \exp\left(-\int_\tau^z [\{r_v - (n + \theta - \mu)\} + (r_v - n - \mu)] dv\right) dz}\right\}$$
$$\times \exp\left(-\int_\tau^t \{r_v - (n + \theta - \mu)\} dv\right) \quad (10.37)$$

and

$$\forall t \geq \tau : \tilde{a}_{it} = \frac{a_{i\tau} + \int_\tau^t (w_z - \tilde{c}_{iz}) \exp\left(-\int_\tau^z (r_v - n - \mu) dv\right) dz}{\exp\left(-\int_\tau^t (r_v - n - \mu) dv\right)}. \quad (10.38)$$

Using (10.37) and (10.38), it can then be proved in a manner analogous to that used for the case of $\tau=0$ that

$$\forall i \in \{1,2,\ldots,q\} \wedge \forall \tau > 0 : \begin{bmatrix} \{(\tilde{c}_{it},\tilde{a}_{it})\}_{t=\tau}^{\infty} \text{ is a unique solution to the Problem } (i,\tau) \\ \text{when } a_{i\tau} = \tilde{a}_{i\tau} \text{ and } \forall t \geq \tau : w_t = f(\tilde{k}_t) - \tilde{k}_t f'(\tilde{k}_t) \wedge r_t = f'(\tilde{k}_t) \end{bmatrix}. \quad (10.39)$$

From our definition of $\{(\tilde{c}_t,\tilde{k}_t)\}_{t=0}^{\infty}$ and from (10.30), (10.31), (10.36) and (10.39), it follows that, under the assumed conditions, there exist initial distributions of wealth $(a_{10}, a_{20}, \ldots, a_{q0})$ for which $\{(\tilde{c}_t,\tilde{k}_t);(\tilde{c}_{1t},\tilde{a}_{1t}),(\tilde{c}_{2t},\tilde{a}_{2t}),\ldots,(\tilde{c}_{qt},\tilde{a}_{qt})\}_{t=0}^{\infty}$ is an equilibrium growth path.

We next prove that over any such equilibrium growth path, the distribution of wealth converges to an equalitarian state.

Given that $f'(k_h') > n + \theta - \mu$, from (10.11), (10.12) and (10.20), it can be proved that

$$\forall i \in \{1,2,\ldots,q\} : \lim_{t\to\infty} \tilde{c}_{it} = h. \quad (10.40)$$

From (10.12), (10.21) and (10.24), it follows that

$$\forall i \in \{1,2,\ldots,q\} : \lim_{t\to\infty} \tilde{a}_{it} = \lim_{t\to\infty} \left\{ \frac{a_{i0} + \int_0^t (w_z - \tilde{c}_{iz})\exp\left(-\int_0^z (r_v - n - \mu)dv\right)dz}{\exp\left(-\int_0^t (r_v - n - \mu)dv\right)} \right\} \text{ is of the indeterminate form } \frac{0}{0}.$$

By assumption, $f(\tilde{k}_t)$ and $f'(\tilde{k}_t)$ are differentiable functions of $\tilde{k}_t$ on $(0,\infty)$ and, by definition, $\forall t \geq 0 : \tilde{k}_t > 0$. Further, from (10.8) and (10.22), we know that $\tilde{k}_t$ and $\forall i \in \{1,2,\ldots,q\}$, $\tilde{c}_{it}$, are differentiable functions of t on $[0,\infty)$. Moreover, $\forall t \geq 0 : \exp\left(-\int_0^t (r_v - n - \mu)dv\right) > 0$. Therefore, we can apply L'Hopital's Theorem to obtain

$$\forall i \in \{1,2,\ldots,q\} : \lim_{t\to\infty} \tilde{a}_{it} = \lim_{t\to\infty} \frac{\frac{d}{dt}\left\{a_{i0} + \int_0^t (w_z - \tilde{c}_{iz})\exp\left(-\int_0^z (r_v - n - \mu)dv\right)dz\right\}}{\frac{d}{dt}\left\{\exp\left(-\int_0^t (r_v - n - \mu)dv\right)\right\}}. \quad (10.41)$$

From (10.11), (10.40) and (10.41), it therefore follows that

$$\forall i \in \{1,2,\ldots,q\} : \lim_{t\to\infty} \tilde{a}_{it} = \frac{h - w^*}{r^* - n - \mu}.$$

The above result implies that for every wealth group $i \in \{1,2,\ldots,q\}$ in the economy, wealth per capita $(\tilde{a}_{it} m_{(t)})$ converges asymptotically to the same value.

Therefore, it follows that given initial values of the ratio of capital to effective labour satisfying (R) and initial distributions of wealth $(a_{10}, a_{20}, \ldots, a_{q0})$ satisfying (10.25), there exist equilibrium growth paths along which the distribution of wealth converges to an equalitarian state in the model economy.

Conclusion

The single proposition proved in this chapter adds another interesting possibility regarding the evolution of wealth inequality in the Ramsey–Cass–Koopmans model to an already wide array of possibilities that have been shown to exist in the literature. A result obtained by Stiglitz (1969) in extension of the Solow model using behavioural bequest functions is seen to be possible, albeit under more restrictive conditions, in a neoclassical growth model in which intergenerational altruism is explicitly introduced as a motive for bequests. The proposition might also be considered to be of some historical interest given that the optimal growth path under Ramsey's original assumptions is also one in which the economy asymptotically converges to a state of bliss.[12]

The result in the previous section demonstrates that if consumer preferences are such that there exists the possibility of satiation at a finite rate of consumption, then, unlike in the standard case of isoelastic instantaneous utility, it is possible to have an equilibrium growth path in the Ramsey–Cass–Koopmans model along which dynasties with lower current rates of consumption have faster rates of growth of consumption in transition to the steady state from below and the rates of consumption per unit of effective labour for all dynasties converge asymptotically to a common steady-state value. This implies that the present discounted value of any dynasty's stream of current and future consumption divided by its current number of units of effective labour also converges asymptotically to a common steady-state value. Since the present discounted value of the stream of wage earnings is always the same for every dynasty, this implies that dynastic wealth per unit of effective labour must also converge asymptotically to a common value.

The existence of an equilibrium growth path converging to a steady state in which all dynasties have same rates of consumption and the uniqueness of such a path depends critically on two assumptions. The first is that the production technology and the pace of technical progress are such that it is, in principle, possible with sufficient accumulation of capital to maintain per capita consumption at more than what is required for bliss. This ensures that there exists a steady state (an equilibrium for the dynamic system (10.5)–(10.6)) where per capita consumption is always at the level required for bliss. This also implies that for one and only one of these steady states does the present discounted value of capital stock per current unit of effective labour in the economy converge to zero over time, a necessary condition for any equilibrium growth path to converge to a steady state in the Ramsey–Cass–Koopmans model. The second important assumption is that the marginal product of capital at this steady state is greater than $n+\theta-\mu$. This ensures that the steady state with bliss is a saddle point equilibrium for the dynamic system (10.5)–(10.6) so that there is a unique and determinate growth path along which the economy converges to this steady state. This also rules out the possibility of an equilibrium growth path converging to a steady state in which per capita consumption is at a level less than what is required bliss.

References

Alvarez-Pelaez, M.J., & Diaz, A. (2005). Minimum consumption and transitional dynamics in wealth distribution. *Journal of Monetary Economics, 52*(3), 633–667.

Caselli, F., & Ventura, J. (2000). A representative consumer theory of distribution. *American Economic Review, 90*(4), 909–926.

Chatterjee, S. (1994). Transitional dynamics and the distribution of wealth in a neoclassical growth model. *Journal of Public Economics, 54*(1), 97–119.

---

[12] See Koopmans (1967).

García-Peñalosa, C., & Turnovsky, S.J. (2009). The dynamics of wealth inequality in a simple Ramsey model: A note on the role of production flexibility. *Macroeconomic Dynamics, 13*(2), 250–262.

Glachant, J., & Vellutini, C. (2002). Quantifying the relationship between wealth distribution and aggregate growth in the Ramsey model. *Economics Letters, 74*(2), 237–241.

Guerrini, L. (2010). The dynamic of the AK Ramsey growth model with quadratic utility and logistic population change. *International Journal of Pure and Applied Mathematics, 62*(2), 221–225.

Guha, S. (2004). Wealth distribution in Ramsey–Cass–Koopmans economies: Some further results. *Keio Economic Studies, 41*(1), 1–14.

Koopmans, T.C. (1967). Objectives, constraints and outcomes in optimal growth models. *Econometrica, 35*(1), 1–15.

Obiols-Homs, F., & Urrutia, C. (2005). Transitional dynamics and the distribution of assets. *Economic Theory, 25*(2), 381–400.

Ramsey, F.P. (1928). A mathematical theory of saving. *Economic Journal, 38*(152), 543–559.

Stiglitz, J. (1969). Distribution of income and wealth among individuals. *Econometrica, 37*(3), 382–397.

von Weizsäcker, C.C. (1965). Existence of optimal programs of accumulation for an infinite time horizon. *Review of Economic Studies, 90*(2), 85–104.

11

Education, Equity and Development

Sudhanshu Bhushan*

Education is crucial to the nation building and modernisation (Patnaik, 2009; Panikkar & Nair, 2012). In economic terms, higher level of education is associated with higher productivity and growth of a nation. The linkages between education and development that seem most straightforward need to be further explored in terms of equity dimensions. Growth can be inclusive, but it may also coexist with poverty. The links of education to development need to be fully understood, highlighting above asymmetries in the growth process. Education can simply reproduce class relations or cultural and social capital. It can, however, also be a source of producing equality of opportunities. The chapter explores the nature of educational process and outcomes that link it to development in which issues of distributive justice are central.

Colonial agenda of education was limited to the elites who could be exposed to western knowledge to support colonial administration. The root of nationalism was, however, founded during this period in finding out the logic against colonial rule and exploitation. Education created a new rationality in favour of independence and freedom from alien governance of the country. The idea of just society to be governed by the nationalist leaders was victorious in the granting of independence to the country. It was, however, a limited victory as the idea of just society was not fulfilled. The post-colonial phase of education and development witnesses various conflicts in realising the fuller opportunities to each and every individual and granting social justice. The idea of social justice might even suffer a severe jolt in the wake of recent education reform. The objective of the chapter is to examine how equality was denied in educational terrain on a substantive term. As a result, the development process suffered from exclusion. The nation-building task or the modernisation that education was supposed to bring in the development process was lopsided, sans social justice. The post-colonial phase may be divided into two periods—period since independence to the phase the process of liberalisation may be said to have begun and the phase of post-liberalisation.

---

* An earlier version of the chapter was presented in a seminar jointly with my MPhil student Shashi Ranjan Jha. In its little modified form, his contribution in extracting the results in section 'Education Level, Inequality in Education and Income Equality', preparing the appendix and discussion with me is acknowledged.

Theories and Hypotheses on Educational Linkages to Development

In the neoclassical literature, endogenous growth originates with Arrow (1962) and his analysis of learning by doing. Lucas, Mc Guire, Farley, & Ring (1968) introduced an average labour quality variable in the production function for producing aggregate output. Schultz (1961) estimates that between 36 and 70 per cent of the unexplained rise in the earnings of labour in the US is explained by the returns to the additional education of workers. The thrust of his argument is that education is an individually and socially productive investment. Labourers, like capitalists invest in education, enrich human resources and derive return. Thus, investment in education facilitates economic growth in two ways: (a) by fostering technological innovation and (b) by increasing the productivity of labour. Denison (1964) went on to argue that investment in education brings higher returns than investment in physical capital. An increase in educational expenditure is thus an effective means of increasing the gross national product. A direct policy implication of this, he noted, was that poverty could be reduced by an investment in human capital of low-income individuals. From this, it follows that education and development may go together with reduction in immiserisation through an appropriate strategy of investment in human resources.

It is further argued in the context of higher education that there are private benefits in terms of higher personal income and productivity. Further benefits are social in so far as personal income, when taxed, is translated through budgetary expenditures into public benefits. Besides, externality argument shows that whole society benefits when an individual becomes more educated. Estimates put the percentage of the income differentials between college graduates and non-college graduates due to innate ability somewhere between 12 and 40 per cent (Weisbrod & Karpoff, 1968). Recent evidence suggests that income differential due to a student's innate aptitude could be as high as 50 per cent (Hoxby & Terry-Long, 1999). From this, however, it does not follow that increased income of an individual will benefit society in a manner that there is increased equality of income. There may in fact be increased societal inequality and increased social stratification by increasing incomes among those who already are highest earners in the society.

It may, however, be argued that human capital argument suffers from many flaws. There may not be sufficient jobs for educated and trained manpower. Even if there is a job, it is not so easy to shift the job from a low-wage to high-wage job with increase in productive capacity through education and training. The more important criticism of the human capital approach is that it tends to ignore the institutional character of capitalist production where the process of immiserisation is endogenous to the accumulation and is independent of the level of education in an economy. Further, an important assumption in this whole argument is that acquisition of education is neutral to the social and economic groups, for example, educational facilities are equally available to everybody.

Assume that economic return on investment in human capital of the disadvantaged is less than that of the investment in human capital of the advantaged. If the government allocates resources towards the disadvantaged, then it leads to a move towards greater equality. However, income generation suffers. On the other hand, if the government allocates resources towards the advantaged, then it leads to a move towards income generation; however, equality suffers. It shows that there is a trade-off between income and equality. Investment decisions in human capital in most cases are indeterminate. Levin (1990) shows that in an egalitarian perspective, when society prefers greater equality, the high per capita educational expenditure of the disadvantaged in relation to that of the advantaged in the society becomes a rational investment policy only when economic return on investment in human capital of the disadvantaged is more than that of investment in the human capital of advantaged. In this case alone, there is no trade-off between income and equality. From this, it follows that there is a zone where a direct linkage between education and income is associated with an increase in inequality. This provides the justification for greater educational investment of those who are at high risk on account of various other factors. Greater investment for those sections of the student will mean reduced crime, better health and capability.

It is further argued that education itself could be the source of inequality. Education, like many other institutions, in a hierarchical social structure could be a source of inequality. It will allow entry to the few belonging to the high social status. Even if it presents equality of opportunities from an access point of view, educational practices and pedagogy may be such that success of socially deprived and marginalised groups may be low.

Bourdieu notes that "[t]he educational system reproduces all the more perfectly the structure of the distribution of cultural capital among classes (and sections of a class) in that the culture which it transmits is closer to the dominant culture..." (Bourdieu, 1973). He puts forward the argument that by converting social hierarchies into academic hierarchies, the education system fulfils a function of legitimation necessary to the perpetuation of the social order. Culture and education are thus central in the affirmation of differences between social classes and in the reproduction of those differences. In *La Reproduction,* Bourdieu (1970) argued that the French educational system reproduces the cultural division of society. He views economic and cultural capital as two distinct systems of social hierarchisation. Under the former, position and power are determined by money and property, the capital one commands. Under cultural capital, one's status is determined by how much cultural or 'symbolic capital' one possesses. Culture is also a source of domination, in which intellectuals play the key role as specialists of cultural production and creators of symbolic power.

In a Marxian perspective, economic inequality is the structural feature of a class-divided society based on property relations. Education is a part of the superstructure, and the inequality in the access to education goes hand in hand with class-based inequality. The state representing the interests of capitalist class provides the opportunities to education to the elites. However, in a democratic regime, the state has to cater to the needs of the poor, who are the instruments of managing the power through votes. The state is caught in this contradiction to yield to the pressure of politics to provide opportunities of education to the poor, yet manages to provide sufficient opportunities of high-quality education to the rich. Therefore, it is possible to find evidence that the educational growth process has led to the reduction in the inequality so far as access to education is concerned yet has not by itself reduced economic inequalities. There are fundamental contradictions of class-divided society based on property relations which education alone is not capable of sorting out. Education is, however, an important tool of class consciousness, and reduction of educational inequality on a substantive basis can, in the future, expose the roots of inequality by demanding a much more egalitarian structure.

Before turning to analyse the linkages of human capital and development with equity, it is worth examining the different dimensions of inequality in education.

Inequality in Higher Education

Inequality in access to education may be captured from the point of participation of social and religious groups and by the level of inequality at different stages of education. Participation is given by ratio, in percentage terms, of attendance in higher education to the eligible population (18–22 years). Gross attendance ratio (GAR), as per 64th National Sample Survey (NSS) round of survey, for the scheduled tribe (ST) and scheduled caste (SC) is 7.7 and 11.6 per cent, respectively, and is considerably below the GAR of others at 26.8 per cent. Even the GAR of the other backward classes (OBC) is way behind the GAR of others. In terms of religious category, the participation of Muslims in higher education lies

Education, Equity and Development 181

Figure 11.1
Gross Attendance Rates by Social and Religious Groups (2007–2008)

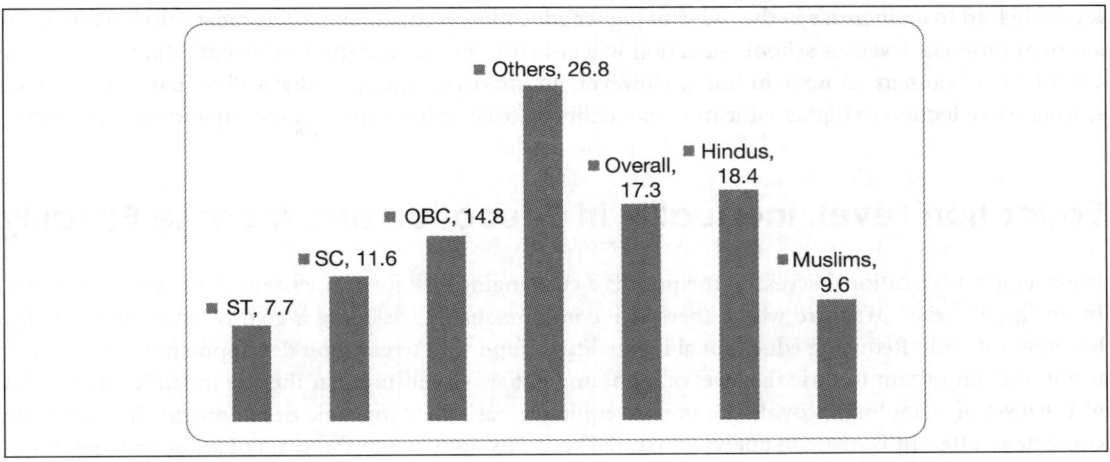

Source: Calculated from unit-level data of NSS 2007–2008 by Ravi Srivastava and reported to the subgroup on gross enrolment ratio constituted by the Planning Commission.

Figure 11.2
Inequality in Level Participation

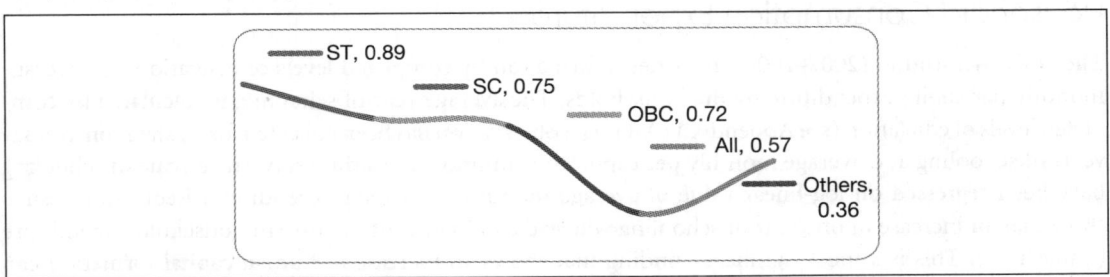

Source: Calculated from unit level data of National Sample Survey 2007–2008.

between ST and SC and is almost half of the GAR of Hindus. Thus, it may be noted that inequality in the participation along social and religious groups is quite high (Figure 11.1).

Further, inequality in access can be captured from the point of level inequality. Educational participation in terms of graduates at different levels of education can be shown in terms of index by taking the graduates at the elementary level as the base. With reference to the NSS round of survey in 2007–2008, the index of participation at different levels of education, such as at elementary (base = 100), secondary, senior secondary and higher education, may be calculated for different categories. Inequality in the level participation (INEP) may then be calculated by the coefficient of variation of index of graduates at the three levels. The higher the INEP, the higher is the level inequality. A higher INEP for the ST shows that the number of graduates at the secondary and senior secondary levels of education is considerably smaller in relation to that of elementary school graduates. Thus, access to higher education is constrained due to a smaller number of graduates in previous stages of education. The only way education inequality in terms of GAR in higher education can be reduced is by reducing the level inequality, thereby increasing the transition to higher levels of school education for the ST, SC, OBC and Muslims (Figure 11.2).

It has been further estimated, by treating INEP as an independent variable and index of participation for higher education as the dependent variable, that a 0.10 unit fall in the level of inequality at school level will lead to an increase in the index of higher education graduates by 6.4. It means that higher transition at different levels of school education will enhance the participation in higher education, raising the quality of human resource in India. However, an important question that still remains unanswered is whether reduction in higher education inequality by itself reduces the income/expenditure inequality.

Education Level, Inequality in Education and Income Equality

Improving an educational access to the poor is a challenging task for many of the developing countries. In an inegalitarian structure where there is income inequality, reaching a goal of education equality becomes difficult. Reducing educational inequality is important to carry on development with equity. It is not only important to raise the level of schooling but also to ensure that there is much less inequality in the level of schooling, providing a greater equitable basis for economic development. In the Indian context, an attempt is made to analyse, first, the relationship between the years of schooling and development. Second, the relationship between average years of schooling and educational inequality is examined. Third, the effect of average years of schooling and educational inequality on income inequality is analysed.

Empirical Result Showing Effect of Average Years of Schooling on Household Consumption Expenditure

The NSS, 64th round (2007–2008), provides information by completed levels of education and average monthly per capita expenditure by the households. The average year of schooling is calculated by completed levels of education (see Appendix 11A.1). The observation has been collected for 14 states on average years of schooling and average monthly per capita consumption expenditure. Average years of schooling have been regressed on log-linear value of average monthly per capita expenditure. Regression results show that an increase in one year of schooling will lead to 12 per cent increase in household expenditure (Table 11.1). This is a most significant finding that shows an increase in human capital formation can substantially enhance the consumption expenditure of the household, other factors remaining constant.

Declining Educational Inequality across States

As noted earlier, the effect of average years of schooling on increasing household consumption expenditure is not straightforward. There is no a priori effect of an increase in average years of schooling on reducing inequality in income/expenditure. Average years of schooling might result in an increase in

Table 11.1
Regression Statistics Dependent Variable in Average Monthly per Capita Expenditure

Observations	df	R^2	Adjusted R^2	F	Sig. F
14	13	0.31	0.26	5.59	0.035
	Coefficient	SE	t Stat	P value	
Constant	7.76	0.24	32.17	0.000	
Average years of schooling	0.12	0.05	2.36	0.035	

Figure 11.3
Education Gini Coefficient across States over the Years

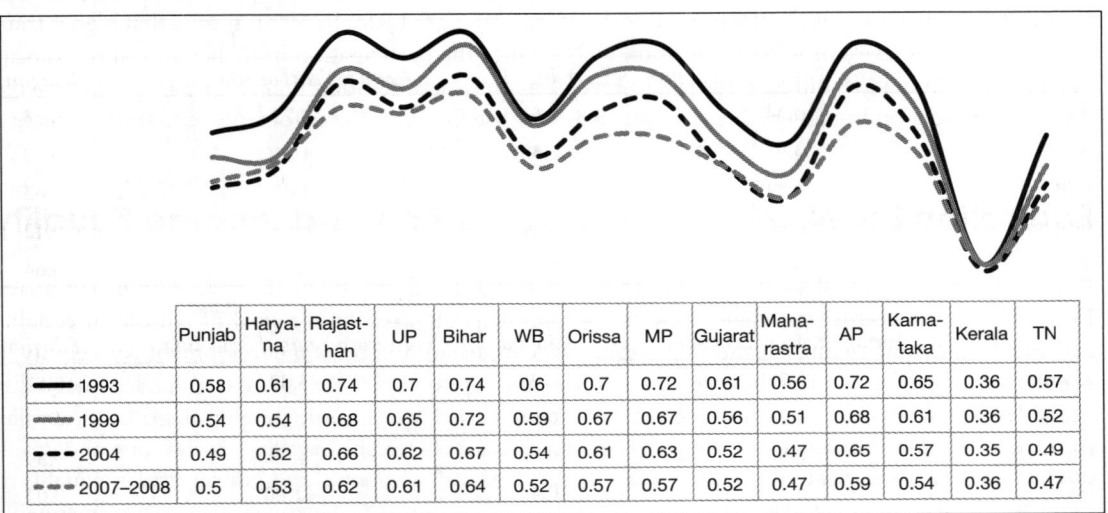

	Punjab	Haryana	Rajasthan	UP	Bihar	WB	Orissa	MP	Gujarat	Maharastra	AP	Karnataka	Kerala	TN
1993	0.58	0.61	0.74	0.7	0.74	0.6	0.7	0.72	0.61	0.56	0.72	0.65	0.36	0.57
1999	0.54	0.54	0.68	0.65	0.72	0.59	0.67	0.67	0.56	0.51	0.68	0.61	0.36	0.52
2004	0.49	0.52	0.66	0.62	0.67	0.54	0.61	0.63	0.52	0.47	0.65	0.57	0.35	0.49
2007–2008	0.5	0.53	0.62	0.61	0.64	0.52	0.57	0.57	0.52	0.47	0.59	0.54	0.36	0.47

educational inequality, and even if it reduces educational inequality, this might not result in reducing income/expenditure inequality.

Two empirical results are interesting to know. Education Gini as the measure of educational inequality can be calculated over the years for different unemployment rounds of survey by the NSS. (See Appendix 11A.2 for the calculation of the education Gini coefficient.) They are unemployment round of surveys in 1993–1994, 1999–2000, 2004–2005 and lastly the education survey conducted in 2007–2008. For each round of survey, Bihar witnesses the highest level of educational inequality measured by an education Gini coefficient. In the latest education survey, Bihar shows an education Gini coefficient of 0.64, which is highest in 2007–2008. It is interesting to note, however, that over the years, every state has shown a decline in the education Gini coefficient. It is also interesting to observe that in some states, where the education Gini coefficient was quite high, there has been a rapid decline in education inequality. The states such as Rajasthan, Odisha, Andhra Pradesh and Madhya Pradesh show a decline of 0.12, 0.13, 0.13 and 0.15, respectively, whereas Bihar shows a decline of 0.10 (see Figure 11.3).

Empirical Result Showing Effect of Average Years of Schooling on Educational Inequality

Another empirical result for all India with an exemplar of Bihar relates to the relationship between the average years of schooling and education Gini coefficient. With lower average years of schooling in Bihar across different social groups, education Gini is quite high as compared with that of all India. The same holds true across different religious groups. In the case of social groups, the 'others' category has the highest average years of schooling of 6.9 and the lowest education Gini coefficient of 0.39. In the case of religious groups, Christianity has the highest average years of schooling of 6.86 and the lowest education Gini coefficient of 0.36 at the all-India level. It is significant to note that Sikhs in Bihar have extremely high years of average schooling with an insignificant education Gini coefficient of 0.07, which demands a further explanation (Table 11.2).

Table 11.2
Average Years of Schooling and Education Gini by Caste and Religion: India and Bihar

	India		Bihar	
	Average Years of Schooling	Edugini	Average Years of Schooling	Edugini
ST	3.34	0.62	2.72	0.68
SC	3.91	0.58	1.81	0.80
OBC	4.84	0.51	3.47	0.63
Others	6.90	0.39	6.68	0.42
Total	5.17	0.50	3.68	0.64
	India		Bihar	
	Average Years of Schooling	Edugini	Average Years of Schooling	Edugini
Hindu	5.23	0.49	3.82	0.62
Islam	4.23	0.54	2.20	0.75
Christian	6.86	0.36	4.08	0.59
Sikh	5.80	0.45	11.00	0.07
Total	5.16	0.50	3.61	0.64

Source: NSS 64th round unit-level data.

Figure 11.4
Predicted Value of Overall Education Gini by Average Years of Schooling in Urban and Rural

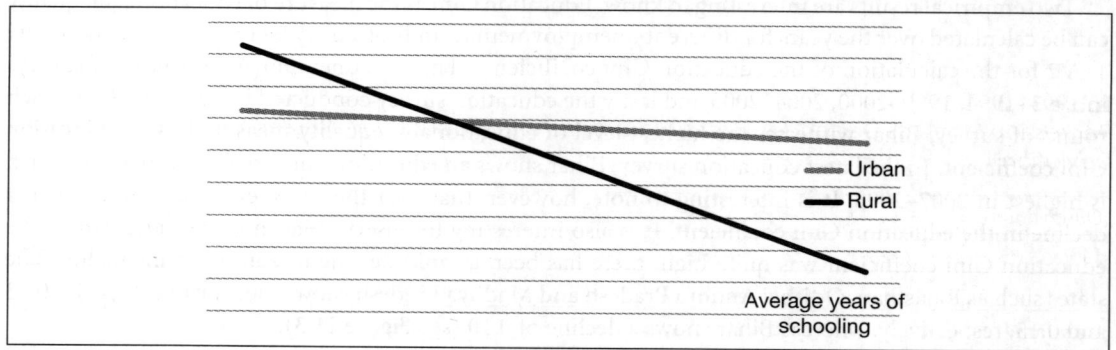

Overall, the education Gini coefficient was calculated for all India while taking average years of schooling for different states in rural and urban area separately. With the help of the regression result, the predicted value of the Gini coefficient at the all-India level has been plotted against the average years of schooling in rural and urban areas, respectively, in Figure 11.4. With a steep slope in rural line, an important message is that an increase in average years of schooling in rural areas will result in a sharp fall in educational inequality. With eight years of average year of schooling, educational inequality is expected to come down to less than 0.3. On the other hand, if average years of schooling in urban area are increased to 10 years, the educational inequality will still be more than 0.5. Hence, if we want to reduce educational inequality substantially, an investment in the rural sector in increasing average years of schooling will pay better dividends than an investment in the urban sector.

Empirical Result Showing the Effect of Educational Inequality on Income Inequality

Whereas Gini coefficient gives us a relative measure of educational inequality, a standard deviation of schooling simply gives us an absolute measure of educational inequality. Empirically, it was found that an absolute measure of educational inequality has a positive effect on expenditure inequality (Table 11.3). The same does not hold good in the case of relative measure of educational inequality. Regression results given below show that with a reduction in educational inequality (Gini), there is an increase in expenditure inequality (Table 11.4). The result indicates that one standard deviation decrease in educational inequality leads to 0.17 percentage point increase in expenditure inequality (Gini). The value of F statistics obtained suggests that the overall model is significant at one per cent. Educational inequality explains about 36 per cent variation in the expenditure inequality (Pose & Tselios, 2007).

In view of the above analysis, an important finding has been that with an increase in average years of schooling by one year, there is a 12 per cent increase in the consumption expenditure, other factors remaining constant. It has also been shown empirically that educational inequality over the last 15 years across the states has been declining. An important finding was that an increase in average years of schooling in rural area has a significant impact in reducing overall educational inequality. What is of interest to us is to know what impact a reduction in overall educational inequality will have on consumption expenditure inequality? Empirical results showed that a reduction in educational inequality measured in terms of a standard deviation results in lower expenditure inequality. Hence, an absolute measure of education inequality has a positive causal impact on expenditure inequality. However, the relative measure of educational inequality measured in terms of an education Gini coefficient has a negative causal impact on expenditure inequality. This calls for an explanation.

Table 11.3
Regression Statistics Dependent Variable Expenditure Inequality Measured in Terms of Standard Deviation

Observations	df	R^2	Adjusted R^2	F	Sig. F
14	13	0.29	0.23	4.99	0.04
	Coefficient	SE	t Stat	P Value	
Constant	9.39	10.29	0.91	0.37	
SD of Schooling	5.33	2.38	2.23	0.045	

Table 11.4
Regression Statistics Dependent Variable Expenditure Inequality Measured in Terms of Gini Coefficient

Observations	df	R^2	Adjusted R^2	F
14	13	0.41	0.36	8.49
	Standardised Coefficient	SE	t Stat	Sig. F
Constant	42.11	3.38	12.42	0.01
Education Gini	−0.17	0.060	−2.91	

Explaining the Negative Causal Impact of Education Inequality on Expenditure Inequality and a Way out of This Dilemma

The question that is of importance to us is whether increased human capital formation results in growth with equity. We found that even if average years of schooling are increased and educational inequality is reduced, there is no certainty that income inequality will also be reduced. Since education Gini coefficient measures inequality in terms of graduate at different levels of education in relation to the population, a reduction in education Gini coefficient means that at different levels of education, graduates in relation to population increases. A reduction in an education Gini coefficient means that in relation to population, both graduates at the lower level of education and graduates at higher levels of education may increase. It is due to the structure of the economy that favours labour market absorption for tertiary-level graduates, rewarding them with high wages and productivity. It also displaces labour with lower skill and education level. A reduction in education Gini coefficient does not mean that graduates at all levels of education get an equal opportunity to join labour market with proportionate wages and productivity. Persons with higher levels of education have much greater opportunity to earn proportionately higher wages than persons with lower levels of education. It is this fact that causes higher expenditure/income inequality in spite of a reduction in educational inequality measured in relation to the population.

Human capital formation does not, therefore, guarantee that it will also result in growth with equity. At this point, the role of the state acquires importance in increasing the public expenditure on education and other related human development parameters. The percentage share of social sector public expenditure to total expenditure was regressed on consumption expenditure inequality across states for different employment–unemployment rounds of an NSS survey. Interestingly, no significant causal effect between social public expenditure and income inequality could be found. Only for the year 2007–2008 education round of survey, a negative causal effect of the percentage share of social sector public expenditure to total expenditure on consumption expenditure inequality was observed at the five per cent level of significance (Table 11.5).

Social Expenditure and Income Inequality

We could find that with an increase in the ratio of social expenditure to total expenditure by the government, there is a decline in consumption expenditure inequality only for the 64th round data, and for other rounds, the results were not significant. This indicates that an increase in social expenditure

Table 11.5

Income Inequality to Social Expenditure as a Ratio to Total Expenditure (2007–2008)

	Standardised Coefficients Beta	T	Significance	R^2	F	Sig. F	df
(Constant)		10.78	0.000	0.311	5.405	0.038	13
Percentage share of social expenditure to total public expenditure	−0.557	−2.32	0.038				

by the government may not necessarily reduce income inequality. It probably indicates that the problem of inequality is much more rooted in the structure of the economy and society. Increasing public investment, unless the hierarchical structure is broken, cannot solve the problem of inequality. Education by increasing capital formation may lead to development. However, as long as the dominant structure of class, caste and other groups in society exists, it is very difficult to achieve development with equity with investment in education by the state. In fact, all counteracting measures to achieve equity by state investment in the social sector may also fail to yield the desired result if the developmental strategy of the state creates a pattern of labour market where persons with tertiary education have better chances of getting absorbed in the labour market with high wages. On the other hand, education may itself perpetuate inequality as mere access may not guarantee the high achievement of all irrespective of classes and social groups in the society.

Conclusion

There is no denying the fact that education helps in the formation of human capital. Higher level of human capital aids and supports the process of development. However, it was pointed out above that development with equity cannot be ensured with a higher level of education. Even if higher average years of schooling reduce educational inequality, it does not necessarily reduce income inequality. There are three important factors that account for income inequality in spite of the government effort to increase public expenditure on education and social sector. (a) Developmental strategy of the state may be such that it may favour the employment with high wages to those with higher levels of education. (b) As long as there is the dominant structure of class and social groups, the income inequality may be difficult to be reduced even with higher levels of education. (c) Education itself may perpetuate incoming inequality, as it may become the vehicle of social and cultural capital favouring the dominant social groups in society. Thus, what comes up from our understanding is that education has to be much more a political and social tool, not necessarily an economic tool for the developmental transformation of the state like Bihar. Political agenda should be oriented towards breaking the hierarchy, guiding the developmental process towards labour-intensive sectors and, above all, redefining education curriculum and pedagogy in favour of the oppressed.

Appendix 11.1

The Average Years of Schooling

The calculation of average years of schooling is required for finding educational Gini. The average years of schooling are used as a proxy of educational attainment. Further, this also indicates the level of educational progress in terms of human capital accumulation. The average years of schooling can be calculated by following formula, given by Thomas, Wang, & Fan (2000), as follows:

$$\mu = \sum_{i=1}^{n} p_i y_i,$$

where μ is the average years of schooling for the concerned population, n is the number of levels in attainment data ($n=7$), p_i is the proportion of population and y_i is the years of schooling of the ith educational level.

Standard Deviation of Schooling

Standard deviation of schooling reflects absolute dispersion in schooling among the concerned population. In other words, the higher the standard deviation, the higher is the dispersion in schooling. Quite a few studies have used standard deviation as measure of educational inequality (Birdsall & Londoño, 1997; Lam & Levinson, 1991; Londoño, 1990; Ram, 1990). The standard deviation of schooling can be measured through following formula:

$$\mathrm{SDS}(\sigma) = \sqrt{\sum_{i=1}^{n} p_i (y_i - \mu)^2},$$

where σ is the standard deviation, p_i is the proportion of population, y_i is years of schooling and μ is average years of schooling. Ram (1990) argues that standard deviation seems to be appropriate measure as it has the same dimension and unit as the mean (average years of schooling).

Appendix 11.2

Education Gini Coefficient

In the researches enrolment (flow variable), education finance and educational attainment have been used as an indicator of inequality in education. The educational attainment is considered to be a stock variable where 'the proper indicator of human development is the stock of education attainment defined as average years of schooling' (Psacharopoulos and Arriagada, 1986). Education Gini, which is similar to the Gini coefficient, is widely used to measure distributions of income, wealth and land, and ranges from zero, which represents perfect equality, to one, which represents perfect inequality.

In this chapter, the existing model of Thomas et al. (2000) is used to measure the education Gini. To measure the education Gini, the 64th round NSSO data on participation in education are used. The NSSO data provide very rich information on educational participation and educational attainment and cover all the 35 states and union territories.

$$E = \left(\frac{1}{\mu}\right) \sum_{i-2}^{n} \sum_{j=2}^{i=1} P_i |Y_i - Y_j| P_j,$$

where E is the education Gini based on education attainment distribution, large population; μ is the average years of schooling for the concerned population; P_i and P_j are the proportions of population with certain levels of schooling; Y_i and Y_j are the years of schooling at different education attainment levels; n is the number of levels/categories in attainment data.

Construction of Educational Level

Barro and Lee (1993) divided the population into seven categories: no schooling (or illiterate), partial primary, complete primary, partial secondary, complete secondary, partial tertiary and complete tertiary. The seven groups are both mutually exclusive and collectively inclusive. The NSS data provide educational attainment of individuals under seven levels. Based on the information available in NSS 64th round schedule 25.2, following educational levels were identified and accordingly years of education.

Table 11A.1
Construction of Educational Level from Educational Attainment of Individuals

Level of Education	Remark	Years of Schooling
Illiterate	Did not receive any education	0
Below primary	Literate without any schooling, literate without formal schooling, through NFEC/AIEP, literate though TLC/AEC, others; literate with formal schooling including EGS: below primary	2.5
Primary	Completed grade 1 to grade 5	5
Elementary	Completed grade 6 to grade 8	8
Secondary	Completed grades 9 to 10	10
Senior secondary	Completed secondary grades 11 to 12	12
Tertiary education	Completed graduate and above	15

Notes: NFEC, non-formal education centre; TLC, total literacy campaign; AEC, alternative education centre.

The formula for calculating the years of schooling at the seven levels of education as shown in Table 11A.1 can be calculated with following formula, where y_i is the years of schooling at educational attainment level i ($i = 7$ levels of schooling):

1. Illiterate: $y_1 = 0$
2. Below primary: $y_2 = y_1 + 0.5$ of completed primary (Cp) $= 0.5$Cp
3. Primary: $y_3 = y_1 + 5$ years of primary (Cp) = completed primary
4. Elementary: $y_4 = y_3 + 3$ of years upper primary (Cp+Cup) = completed elementary
5. Secondary: $y_5 = y_4 + 2$ years of secondary (Cup+Cs) = completed secondary
6. Senior secondary: $y_6 = y_5 + 2$ years of senior secondary (Cs+Css) = Completed senior secondary
7. Tertiary: $y_7 = y_6 +$ years (3+2/2) graduate and above = completed tertiary education.

Some adjustment in the educational level has been made in this chapter to that of Thomas et al. (2002) based on the nature of data provided in the NSS. People who have undergone some level of education but did not complete primary education are treated here as people with below primary level of education and are assumed to get half of the schooling cycle in their years of schooling. In order to find the proportion of population aged 15 and above, following method was used:

$$p_i = P_i/P,$$

where p_i is the proportion of population with educational attainment level i, P_i is the population with educational attainment level i and P is the total population.

Income Inequality

For studying the intrastate inequality, monthly per capita consumption expenditure (MPCE) data by household expenditure classes and the distribution of population in each MPCE class have been used (for calculation of Gini coefficients). Interstate inequality in household consumption has been studied using state-wise MPCE data at constant prices from the seven quinquennial rounds of the NSS.

$$G = \left(\frac{1}{2n^2\mu}\right)\sum_{j=1}^{m}\sum_{k=1}^{n} n_i n_j |Y_i - Y_i|.$$

Average income

$$\mu = \frac{1}{n}\sum_{i=1}^{n} n_i Y_i.$$

References

Arrow, K.J. (1962). Economic welfare and the allocation of resources for invention. In *The Rate and Direction of Inventive Activity: Economic and Social Factors* (pp. 609–626). Cambridge, MA: National Bureau of Economic Research, Inc.

Barro, R.J., & Lee, J.W. (1993). *International comparisons of educational attainment.* NBER Working Paper No. 4349, Massachusetts, Cambridge. Retrieved from http://www.nber.org/papers/w4349 on 10 January 2016.

Birdsall, N., & and Londoño, J.L. (1997). *Asset inequality does matter: Lessons from Latin America.* OCE Working Paper 1, Inter-American Development Bank March 1997 Washington, DC 20577. Retrieved from http://www.iadb.org/res/publications/pubfiles/pubwp-344.pdf on 10 January 2016.

Bourdieu, P. (1970). *La reproduction. Elèments pour une théorie du système d'enseignement,* 1977 (with Jean-Claude Passeron). *Reproduction in education, society, and culture* (translated by Richard Nice). London: SAGE Publications.

Bourdieu P. (1973). Cultural reproduction and social reproduction. In J. Karabel & A. H. Hasley (Eds.), *Power and ideology in education* (pp. 1–13). New York: Oxford University Press.

Denison, E.F. (1964). *Measuring the contribution of education (and the residual) to economic growth alternative.* Paris: OECD.

Hoxby, C., & Terry-Long, B. (1999). *Explaining rising income and wage inequality among the college educated.* National Bureau of Economic Research, Working Paper 687.

Lam, D., & Levinson, A. (1991). Declining inequality in schooling in Brazil and its effects on inequality in earnings. *Journal of Development Economics, 37*(1–2), 199–225.

Levin, H.M. (1990). The economics of justice in education. In D.A. Verstegen & J.G. Ward (Eds.), *Spheres of justice in education, the 1990 American education yearbook.* New York: Harper Collins.

Londoño, J.L. (1990). *Kuznetsian tales with attention to human capital.* Paper presented at the Third Inter-American Seminar in Economics, Rio de Janerio, Brazil.

Lucas, R.E., Jr., Mc Guire, T., Farley, J., & Ring, W. (1968). Estimation and inference for linear models in which subsets of the dependent variable are constrained. *Journal of the American Statistical Association, 63*(324), 1201–1213.

Panikkar, K.N., & Nair, M.B. (Eds). (2012). *Globalization and higher education in India.* New Delhi: Pearson.

Patnaik, P. (2009). Challenges before higher education in developing societies. *Social Scientist, 37*(7–8), July–August.

Psacharopoulos, G., & Arriagada, Ana-Maria. (1986). *The educational attainment of the labor force: An international comparison.* Report No. EDT38 World Bank. Retrieved from http://www-wds.worldbank.org/external/default/WDSContentServer/WDSP/IB/2005/09/01/000112742_20050901145133/Rendered/PDF/edt38.pdf on 10 January 2016.

Pose, A.R., & Tselios, V. (2007). *Education and income inequality in the regions of the European Union.* Working Papers, Department of Geography and Environment, London School of Economics, London, UK.

Ram, R. (1990). Educational expansion and schooling inequality: International evidence and some implications. *The Review of Economics and Statistics, 72*(2), 266–274. Retrieved from http://dx.doi.org/10.2307/2109716 on 10 January 2016.

Schultz, T.W. (1961). Investment in human capital. *American Economic Review, 51*(1), 1–17.

Thomas, V., Wang, Y., & Fan, X. (2000). *Measuring educational inequality: Gini coefficients of education.* World Bank Policy Research Working Paper No. 2525.

———. (2002). *A new dataset on inequality in education: Gini and Theil indices of schooling for 140 countries, 1960–2000.* Washington: The World Bank.

Weisbrod, B.A., & Karpoff, P. (1968). Monetary returns to college education, student ability, and college quality. *The Review of Economics and Statistics, 50*(4), 491–497.

12

Employment Growth and Informalisation of Workers in the Organised Manufacturing Sector

Shuji Uchikawa

Introduction

In India, the organised manufacturing sector[1] has maintained a stable and rapid output growth since 1981 onwards. But its employment did not increase much before 2004–2005. While the total number of workers in the organised manufacturing sector increased by only 0.9 per cent per annum between 1981–1982 and 2004–2005, gross value added (GVA) at 2004–2005 prices in the sector grew by 7.0 per cent per annum during the period [annual survey of industries (ASI) dataset].[2] In the East Asian countries such as Japan, South Korea, Taiwan and China, the manufacturing sector could absorb the surplus labour force in rural areas in the process of rapid industrialisation. But the organised manufacturing sector did not play an important role towards creation of employment opportunity in India; 'jobless growth' has been an important issue there.

Policy distortion has been argued to be one of the principal reasons behind jobless growth. In particular, before economic reforms, it was argued that multiple policy distortions have been instrumental in raising the capital intensity of the Indian industry (Ahluwalia, 1991). It implicitly suggested that the market mechanism may distribute more resources to labour-intensive industries, and the rise of capital intensity may slow down in an industry.

Although economic reforms were expected to address the problem, the capital–labour ratio increased continuously in all industries at the two-digit level after 1991 (Table 12.1).[3] Moreover, growth rates of the

---

[1] The organised sector is defined as those factories employing 10 or more workers using power and those employing 20 or more workers without using power. The unorganised sector includes smaller factories than the organised sector.
[2] Data on the organised manufacturing sector are available from ASI published by the Central Statistical Office. The section 'Conceptual and Empirical Issues' explains the way to construct the long-term ASI dataset in detail.
[3] Capital–labour ratio is calculated by dividing capital stock in 2004–2005 prices by number of workers. Capital stock is computed in the following way. Gross fixed capital at 2004–2005 prices in 1973–1974 taken from the ASI dataset was doubled to create the benchmark capital stock estimates for individual two-digit industries. To build the capital series from the benchmark capital stock estimate, the perpetual inventory method is used. Thus, gross fixed capital formation (GFCF) of individual two-digit industries is added to the benchmark capital estimate to obtain the capital stock estimate for the next year. The capital stock at current prices is deflated by implicit deflator of registered manufacturing sector in the National Account Statistics. In this manner, the entire capital series is built.

Table 12.1
Growth Rates of GVA and Capital–Labour Ratio in the Organised Manufacturing Sector

	National Industry Classification 1998	Growth Rates of GVA (%)		Capital–Labour Ratio in 1991 (Rs)	Growth Rates of Capital–Labour Ratio (%)	
		1973–1974 to 1990–1991	1991–1992 to 2012–2013		1973–1974 to 1990–1991	1991–1992 to 2012–2013
16	Tobacco products	5.5	4.1	2,630	−0.7	7.7*
18	Apparel; dressing and dyeing of fur	16.2	8.9*	9,838	2.6	4.6*
19	Tanning and dressing of leather	8.1	6.8	22,792	3.9	1.4
20	Wood and products of wood	2.5	5.1	23,324	6.1	5.8
36	Manufacture of furniture and other manufacturing	5.3	11.2*	24,483	4.9	3.1
15	Food products and beverages	6.8	6.4	30,516	4.3	5.7**
17	Textiles	4.0	6.5*	34,021	5.9	5.1
28	Fabricated metal products, except machinery and equipment	3.9	7.2*	36,258	3.1	3.2
22	Publishing, printing and reproduction of recorded media	2.5	2.3	40,754	6.2	7.9
35	Other transport equipment	5.1	7.8*	47,522	5.7	6.9
29	Machinery and equipment	6.8	9.9*	52,403	3.2	5.0*
26	Other non-metallic mineral products	7.3	8.7	55,730	4.8	4.2
33	Medical, precision, and optical instruments, watches and clocks	8.8	7.0	57,668	3.6	5.4**
31	Electrical machinery and apparatus	7.6	9.0	61,508	1.8	3.2**
32	Radio, television and communication equipment and apparatus	12.7	12.0	67,396	5.9	6.8
25	Rubber and plastics products	8.3	10.0	71,141	4.3	2.9
30	Office, accounting and computing machinery	13.7	10.6**	84,899	6.1	6.9
34	Motor vehicles, trailers and semi-trailers	6.7	12.0*	85,178	3.9	3.6
21	Paper and paper products	2.9	5.3*	94,597	4.4	4.0
24	Chemicals and chemical products	7.5	6.8	149,945	2.1	3.3**
27	Basic metals	4.9	7.6*	174,367	2.9	4.5*
23	Coke, refined petroleum products and nuclear fuel	9.4	10.1	352,101	4.4	8.3*
	Total	6.1	8.0*	61,465	4.3	4.7

Source: Author's calculation based on the ASI dataset.

Notes: *Acceleration is significant at the 99 per cent confidence level.
**Acceleration is significant at the 95 per cent confidence level.

capital–labour ratio accelerated significantly in nine industries after 1991. Employment in the organised manufacturing sector remained stagnant continuously. In sum, the liberalisation could not solve the problem. In fact, there were many arguments about the reasons for the jobless growth not just during the 1980s but also in the 1990s and beyond.

However, the total number of workers in the organised manufacturing sector increased by 5.5 per cent per annum between 2004–2005 and 2012–2013. This significant phenomenon signalled the end of jobless growth. This chapter examines the reasons behind the jobless growth for a prolonged period and the rapid increase of employment during the second half of the 2000s from a long-term viewpoint. Such an exploration will include examining the changes in the factors that had hampered employment creation before the mid-2000s for its contribution in employment creation after the mid-2000s.

Existing Views on Jobless Growth and Investment Boom

Jobless Growth

The existing literature offers five views on jobless growth up to the mid-2000s. The total number of workers in the organised manufacturing sector decreased continuously from 5.5 million in 1982–1983 to 5.0 million in 1986–1987 (ASI dataset). First, Fallon and Lucas (1993) observed that job security advanced by the Industrial Dispute Act affected growth of employment in the organised manufacturing sector after 1976.[4] Using the ASI dataset from 1959–1960 to 1981–1982, they found that the negative effects of job security regulation are statistically significant on a 90 per cent confidence level test in 14 out of 29 industries. In 1982, the coverage of the Act was extended to include factories employing not less than 100 workers. An International Labour Organization report (1996) also argued that job security regulation induced employers to keep their factory size artificially small, sacrificing economies of scale.

This argument was questioned by Uchikawa (2003) because the threshold effects at 100 workers could not be observed. It was shown that the share of factories employing 50 to 99 and 100 to 199 workers rose from 9.0 per cent to 13.1 per cent and 9.2 per cent to 12.9 per cent, respectively, between 1980–1981 and 1997–1998. Average gross profit ratio between 1979–1980 and 1997–1998 was highest in factories employing 50 to 99 workers and second highest in factories employing 100 to 199 workers. Medium-scale factories were sufficiently dynamic to gain employment and investment during the period.

Second, the World Bank (1989) attributes the decline of employment in the organised manufacturing sector to sharply rising labour costs. It was argued that the employers responded to it by virtually stopping new hiring and retrenching existing workers for short-run adjustments. Ghose (1994) ascribed the sharp decline of employment elasticity in the organised manufacturing sector to a strategy of capital deepening pursued by the firms. The rise of the relative price of wages deflated by the Wholesale Price Index (WPI) of products encouraged to adopt more capital-intensive technology to save on the wage costs. Underlying this argument is the perception that the growing power of trade unions exerted downward pressure on wages. Nagaraj (1994) contested the argument in three ways. First, the ASI data, which were used in these works, included contract workers in the total number of workers. He emphasised that share of contract workers increased in the 1980s. Second, the growth of working days increased the

---

[4] The Industrial Disputes Act was amended in 1976, which resulted in prohibition of lay-offs, retrenchment and closure by factories employing not less than 300 workers without prior permission of the government.

salaries paid to workers. He indicated that while the earnings per worker in the manufacturing sector grew by 3.2 per cent, those per man-day rose by only 1.6 per cent. Third, the power of the union declined. The proportion of workers unionised in the organised manufacturing sector fell from around 45 per cent in the late 1970s to around 30 per cent towards the end of the 1980s.

The third view on jobless growth is based on the extension of working hours in a day and increase in man-days. Bhalotra (1998) argued that employment depends on expected cyclical changes in demand, scale of production, hourly wages, productivity growth and hours of work. She had located a significant negative correlation between the number of workers and hours of work using state- and industry-wise ASI dataset between 1979–1980 and 1987–1988. Nagaraj (1994) suggested the possibility that casual workers accounted for most of the observed increase in man-days worked in the 1980s. Goldar (2000) regressed the growth rate of employment on growth rates in real wages, man-days per employee and output separately for the periods from 1980–1981 to 1990–1991 and 1990–1991 to 1997–1998. While the coefficient of real wages was found to be negative and significant, that of man-days was not significant. He concluded that the growth in man-days per employee was not a major cause of the stagnation of employment.

The fourth possibility explored was on the changes in composition of output in favour of less labour-intensive industries (Nagaraj, 1994). Kannan and Raveendram (2009) argued that effects of 'job-creating' and 'job-displacing' industries cancelled each other out between 1981–1982 and 2004–2005.[5]

The fifth reason advanced was on the question of over-employment. It could be that the organised manufacturing sector may have increased employment in a less competitive environment despite stagnation of growth during the 1970s: "when demand picked up in the 1980s firms would have first used their existing stock of labour (as well as capital) intensively before deciding to employ additional workers" (Nagaraj, 1994: 182).

Mazumdar and Sarkar (2008) analysed the determinants of employment elasticity. When the rate of growth of wage bill relative to value added in current prices was assumed to be constant over the period under consideration, the relationship of employment is specified by the following equation:[6]

$$\dot{L} = \alpha \dot{v} + \alpha \dot{P}_p - \dot{P}_c - \dot{w}.$$

Using an algebraic expression connecting the trade-off between employment growth and wage growth rate, they found a large shift to wage growth in the wage-employment trade-off between 1980 and 1996 and between 1996 and 2002. They argued that the employment elasticity has a cyclical pattern because employers regard labour force as a quasi-fixed factor. As a result, the employers are cautious to increase number of regular worker even when demand is expanding.

Investment Boom in the 2000s

In the second half of the 2000s, employment in the organised manufacturing sector grew rapidly as mentioned earlier. Nagaraj (2013) observed that output expansion was underpinned by a sharp increase in the investment rate, largely domestically financed and boosted by an unprecedented influx of foreign

---

[5] Food products, textile, wood products, publishing and printing, basic metals, electrical machinery and apparatus and other transport equipment were classified as job-displacing industries between 1981–1982 and 2004–2005.
[6] W is the real wage (average earning per worker). v is value (in constant producer prices). L is employment. P_p is the index of producer prices and P_c is index of consumer prices. α is the rate of growth of wage bill relative to value added in current prices. A variable written with a dot on top represents the proportionate rate of change of the variable concerned. This equation indicates the trade-off between employment growth and wage growth rates.

capital. He argued further that the incremental investment was skewed in favour of the capital-intensive organised manufacturing sector.

Goldar (2011a, 2011b) and Nagaraj (2011) expressed different views on the reasons for this growth. Goldar (2011a, 2011b) suggested that job creation in the organised manufacturing sector in different states may be related to the extent of labour reforms undertaken. On the other hand, Nagaraj (2011) argued that the unprecedented investment boom along with output growth has caused the employment boom.

Conceptual and Empirical Issues

The present study analyses growth trends in the organised manufacturing sector from a long-term viewpoint. The published results of the ASI from 1973–1974 to 2012–2013 at the three-digit level of industrial classification were used for this study. The industrial classification used for the ASI was the National Industrial Classification (NIC) 1970 up to 1988–1989, NIC-87 up to 1997–1998, NIC-98 up to 2007–2008 and thereafter NIC-08. All data were converted to the NIC-98 using the concordance at the three-digit level. The estimates at the two-digit level of industry classification from Division 15 to Division 36 were obtained by aggregating the relevant three-digit level industries. As coverage of ASI has changed, the organised manufacturing sector covers industries from Division 15 to Division 36 (NIC-98) and excludes other industries to maintain constancy.

In the ASI dataset, "workers are defined to include all persons employed directly or through any agency whether for wages or not and engaged in any manufacturing process or in cleaning any part of the machinery or premises used for manufacturing process or in any other kind of work incidental to or connected with the manufacturing process or the subject of the manufacturing process" (GoI, n.d.). Number of workers represents the average daily employment. Man-days are calculated by summing up the number of workers attending each shift across all the shifts worked on all days. The figures are furnished by each factory by dividing the total man-days worked during a year by the total number of working days during that year. Thus, they are based on actual attendance and not on the physical number of persons on the payroll. Wages are defined to include (a) basic wages and salaries, payment of overtime, various allowances, (b) remuneration for the period not worked and (c) bonuses and ex-gratia payment paid both at regular and less frequent intervals.

The GVA of each industry is deflated by the relevant WPI. The GVA of the organised manufacturing sector was obtained by aggregating the GVA deflated by the relevant WPI in each industry.

Economic Reform and Growth of the Manufacturing Sector

Economic reforms that started in 1991 included various changes in policies to eliminate bias against export-oriented, labour-intensive industries. First, exchange rates were shifted to a floating system. This change had caused the exchange rate of the rupee to depreciate, for example, against the US dollar from ₹24.5 per US dollar in 1991 to ₹47.7 in 1998–1999. Second, the industrial licensing regulation, which had regulated investment to the organised manufacturing sector for a long time, was abolished. Third, the private sector was permitted to enter the sector reserved for public sector undertakings (PSUs) that included particularly heavy ones such as steel, in which PSUs had dominated earlier. Fourth, the import quantity restrictions were phased out, and import duty rates were reduced after India became a founder member of the World Trade Organization in 1995. Fifth, the policy towards foreign direct investment

(FDI) was liberalised. New policy permitted existing companies with foreign equity to raise it to 51 per cent and provided automatic approval for foreign investment up to 51 per cent in 34 industries in 1991. Sixth, the number of items reserved for small-scale industries (SSIs) was reduced dramatically in the 2000s; the reservation policy prohibited large-scale factories to produce such items earlier.

Economic reforms caused an investment boom in the organised manufacturing sector in the mid-1990s. Abolition of industrial licensing might have encouraged investment on the basis of entrepreneurship. There are three reasons behind the investment boom. First, there was an expansion in demand in the first half of the 1990s. Certain industries manufacturing capital goods, intermediate goods, consumer durable goods and consumer non-durable goods showed rapid growth of GVA. Among consumer durable goods, GVA of the electrical appliance, automobile and motorcycle industries grew. Meanwhile, among consumer non-durable goods, GVA of food product and man-made textile industries rose. Growth of these industries increased the demand for intermediate goods through backward linkages; it was most prominent in plastic materials and synthetic rubbers, refined petroleum products and iron and steel. GVA at 2004–2005 prices in the manufacturing sector grew at a rate higher than 10 per cent between 1992–1993 and 1996–1997. To meet this expanding demand, lumpy investment was implemented in these three industry groups. Large-scale investment created demand for capital goods. Second, India had a stock market boom between 1992–1993 and 1994–1995, created by a small number of well-performing companies. They received alternative sources of funds in addition to loans from financial institutions and invested the funds towards capacity expansion. As a result of lumpy investment by a few big companies, the fixed capital formation in some industries jumped. Third, an increase in internal financing was advantageous to investment. Rapid growth of sales also raised profits.

These three factors had created an environment that led to the investment boom and caused entrepreneurs to overestimate the growth of demand in the organised sector. However, the investment boom was over by the mid-1990s. Growth of GVA in the manufacturing sector had stagnated since 1996–1997 and it continued till 2002–2003. Although lumpy investment raised output sharply, demand did not expand as much as increase of capacity. Under-utilisation of capacity became evident (Uchikawa, 2002).

Between 1997–1998 and 2002–2003, growth rate of the GVA at 2004–2005 prices in the organised manufacturing sector fluctuated. After the growth rate declined continuously for two years, it rebounded in 2002–2003. It was higher than nine per cent between 2002–2003 and 2010–2011, except in 2008–2009, during the 'Lehman shock'. GVA of consumer goods, intermediate goods and capital goods industries increased clearly in the second half of the 2000s. Stable and rapid expansion of domestic demand caused an investment boom again after 2004–2005. GFCF at 2004–2005 prices in the organised manufacturing sector rose from ₹718 billion in 2004–2005 to ₹2,350 billion in 2011–2012.[7]

The second investment boom was over by 2012–2013 because of the decline of economic growth. High inflation shrunk the domestic demand and pushed up the material and fuel costs. Growth rates of the WPI of all commodities were higher than nine per cent from February 2010 to November 2011. Recession in developed countries affected the exports as well. Finally, growth rates of the GVA of the organised manufacturing sector at 2004–2005 prices became negative in 2012–2013. GFCF at 2004–2005 prices declined between 2011–2012 and 2012–2013.

The differences between the first and second investment booms are in terms of investment scale and employment creation. The annual average GFCF at 2004–2005 prices in the organised manufacturing sector was ₹760 billion for three years from 1994–1995 to 1996–1997 and ₹1,634 billion for eight years from 2004–2005 to 2011–2012. The number of workers in the organised manufacturing sector increased

---

[7] Nominal GFCF, which is available from the ASI dataset, is deflated by implicit deflator of GFCF in the organised manufacturing sector in the National Account Statistics.

by only 0.8 million between 1993–1994 and 1995–1996 and by 3.7 million between 2004–2005 and 2011–2012. Between 2004–2005 and 2011–2012, five industries, namely food products, textiles, other non-metallic mineral products, basic metals and motor vehicles, created more than 300,000 employments.

Economic reforms did not lead to stable growth of the organised manufacturing sector, although it created an investment boom in the mid-1990s and the second half of the 2000s. For instance, a comparison of average growth rates of GVA at 2004–2005 prices between pre- and post-reform periods (Table 12.1) shows that the GVA of 10 industries out of 22 industries increased significantly at the 95 per cent confidence level and above after economic reforms. In 1991, the capital–labour ratio of refined petroleum products was highest, followed by those of basic metals, chemicals, papers and motor vehicles. Three industries among the top five capital-intensive industries accelerated their GVA growth rates following economic reforms. On the other hand, the capital–labour ratio of apparel was second lowest. Its GVA growth rate decelerated after economic reforms. In 9 out of 22 industries, growth rates of the capital–labour ratio rose significantly at the 95 per cent confidence level and above.

Long-term Changes in Industrial Structure of Four Industries

This section contrasts the long-term changes in the industrial structure of four industries: textile, basic metals, motor vehicles and apparel industries. The common points among textiles, basic metals and motor vehicles being acceleration of growth rates of GVA after economic reforms and creation of sizeable employment between 2004–2005 and 2011–2012 as noted above. In contrast, apparel has been the industry for which growth rates of GVA decelerated after economic reforms. But it created employment more than 220,000 between 2004–2005 and 2011–2012.

Textile Industry

Textile is a major traditional industry that has the largest share of employment in the organised manufacturing sector. Industrial sickness in the textile industry emerged soon after the Second World War and became a chronic phenomenon. The textile industry incurred losses continuously between 1982–1983 and 1988–1989 (ASI dataset). This suggests that many mills have suffered from industrial sickness since the 1980s onwards. There were three reasons for the chronic sickness in the textile industry. First, the power loom sector in the unorganised sector had deprived the mill sector in the organised sector of cloth market.[8] Up to 1985, the weaving capacity in the mill sector was regulated by the government. Even after the removal of restrictions, the weaving capacity in the mill sector consistently declined. As economies of scale are not effective in the weaving process, the power loom sector has an advantage over the mill sector because of the low wages of workers, the low fixed capital cost per unit of output and the flexibility of production. Further, labour regulations were imposed only on the mill sector. Second, the spinning sector, which supplies yarn to power looms, had greater capacity than the demand. Many mills were closed down or retrenched workers to reduce the labour costs. Before economic reforms, the appreciated exchange rates refrained exports of cotton yarn. Third, the lack of modernisation reduced competitiveness in the domestic and export markets. Because the textile industry was not profitable, owners hesitated to invest more funds in it. It is expected that the funds were diverted to other profitable industries under the control of the same owners (Uchikawa, 1998).

---

[8] The textile industry has three processes that include spinning, weaving and finishing.

After economic reforms, depreciation of rupee and export promotion policies gave incentive to set up export-oriented spinning mills. Average unit value realised on exports of cotton yarn rose from ₹ 57.3 per kg in 1990–1991 to ₹128.6 per kg in 1995–1996 (Textile Commissioner, 1997). Moreover, tax concessions became available under the scheme of 100 per cent export-oriented factories. The number of spinning mills, which included SSIs and non-SSIs, rose from 777 in 1990–1991 to 2,561 in 2000–2001 (Confederation of Indian Textile Industry, n.d.). Production and export of cotton yarn increased during the period. While old mills were closed down, new spinning mills were established. The number of closed mills, including spinning and composite mills, increased from 105 in 1990–1991 to 383 in 2000–2001 (Textile Commissioner, n.d.). Exports had stagnated after 1997–1998, faced with international competition (Figure 12.1). The textile industry suffered losses again continuously between 1997–1998 and 2002–2003. As a result, the number of workers in the organised textile industry declined from 1.3 million in 1979–1980 to 1 million in 2002–2003 (ASI dataset). Textiles became a job-displacing industry.

However, the situation changed dramatically afterwards. Production and exports of cotton yarn rose rapidly from 2004–2005. Under the export boom, the number of spinning mills increased from 2,727 in 2004–2005 to 3,097 in 2011–2012. As a result, installed spindles rose from 37.5 million to 48.3 million during the period (Confederation of Indian Textile Industry, n.d.). Establishment of new spinning mills expanded capacity and created employments.

The organised textile industry has concentrated on the spinning process, which is capital intensive. Export-oriented spinning mills, which were newly set up, introduced advanced machinery to compete in the export market. Before economic reforms, reduction of surplus labour might have contributed to the

Figure 12.1
Production and Exports of Cotton Yarn

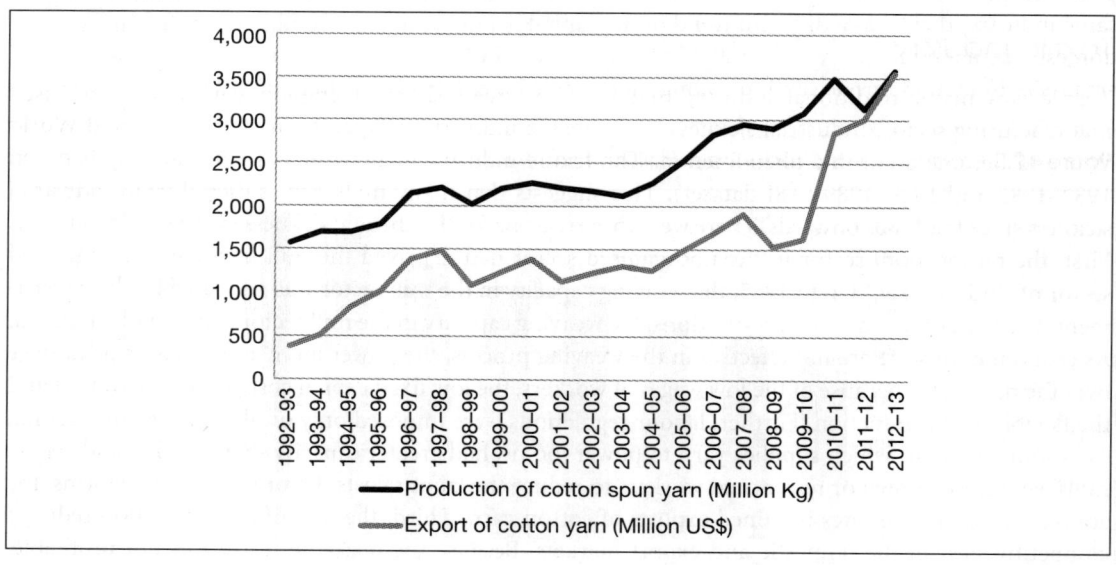

Sources: 1. Production
From 1992–1993 to 2006–2007: Confederation of Indian Textile Industry.
From 2007–2008 to 2012–2013: Ministry of Textiles.
2. Exports
From 1992–1993 to 1995–1996: Indian Cotton Mills' Federation (ICMF) (1998).
From 1996–1997 to 2012–2013: Department of Commerce, Ministry of Commerce and Industry.

hike of capital–labour ratio. On the other hand, introduction of advanced machinery during the export boom raised the capital–labour ratio in the 2000s. Newly set up spinning mills created employments. Increase in the number of workers did not conflict with the rise of the capital–labour ratio.

Basic Metal Industry

During the pre-reform period, the growth in steel production was mainly in the public sector factories because of reservation of large-scale capacity creation for these factories. Price and distribution were controlled for the integrated, large-scale producers in both private and public sectors, while the rest of the industry operated in a free market. Because of control on foreign technology agreements, the technology of the steel industry was considerably lower than the international standards.

Deregulation and decontrol of the iron and steel industry in 1991 and 1992 changed the situation. Large integrated steel plants were set up in the private sector by electric arc furnaces, such as Essar Steel, Ispat Industries and Jindal Group. In addition to these plants, small-scale induction furnace factories were developed. Using induction furnaces, they melted scrapped metal to produce crude steel. Small-scale re-rolling mills processed pencil ingots supplied by induction furnaces. Because the total investment cost to set up an induction furnace factory and a re-rolling factory is not large, entry was easy. Because their profits depended on market volatility, some plants were closed down soon after investment costs were recovered for them. The steel industry experienced a boom because of the rise of international prices after 2002. Production of steel by induction furnaces reached 10.5 million tonnes in 2003–2004 to 22.1 million tonnes in 2010–2011 (Figure 12.2).

The steel industry has a dualistic structure. A few large integrated steel plants and a large number of small-size induction furnace and re-rolling mills with low technology were established during the post-reform period. The former absorbed investment and the latter created employment; within the same industry, there was a different trend of the capital–labour ratio, as a result. While the shrinkage of domestic demand reduced employment in basic metal industry in the second half of the 1990s, entry of small-size induction furnace and re-rolling mills increased employment after 2004–2005.

Figure 12.2 *Production of Crude Steel (million tonnes)*

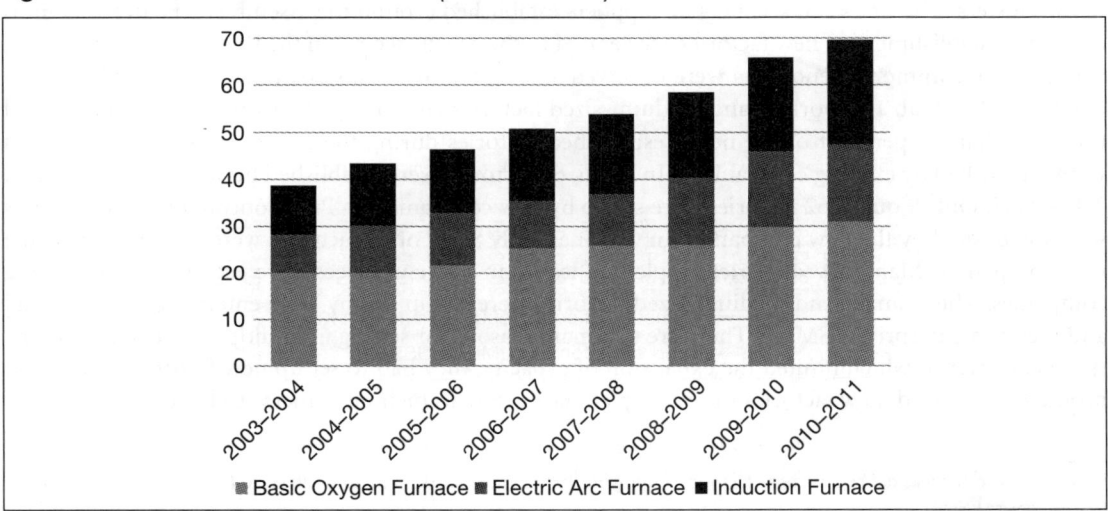

Source: Indian Bureau of Mines (2008, 2011).

Kundu and Bhatia (2002) conducted a survey in Gobindgarh in Punjab in 1999 and 2000. Some 220 of 300 re-rolling mills and 40 of 50 induction furnaces were found to be operational. It was found out that most workers, including the technical staff, acquired skills mostly by being on the job for a long period of time. Entrepreneurs, however, had registered only permanent and semi-permanent staff working in the administration departments and a few other technical personnel, in their official documents. Many of the unskilled and semi-skilled workers were recorded as contract workers with the designation of foreman or supervisor. Their positions were not secured.

Small-scale induction furnace and re-rolling factories maintain competitiveness because of flexibility advanced by small-lot production and easy access to the market. If modernisation of large integrated steel plants progress and transportation costs decrease because of improvement of road infrastructure, they may lose competitiveness. Further, if market conditions deteriorate, employers of induction furnace and re-rolling mills may retrench contract workers immediately.

Motor Vehicle Industry

In this sector, production increased rapidly after Maruti started operation in 1983. Prior to this, there was a tendency for assemblers of automobiles to produce parts and components in-house. As production of motor vehicles developed, many auto component manufacturers were set up and started to supply their products as first- and second-tier suppliers. Tierisation of subcontracting spread from the Maruti's operations. The monopolistic condition in passenger cars allowed Maruti to develop its suppliers. It was keen to develop subcontractors to improve its supply chain, giving technical and financial assistance (Okada, 2004). On the other hand, it adopted the strategy of procuring the same parts and components from two suppliers to avoid the risk of delayed delivery and encourage competition between them. Subcontractors were evaluated regularly from the viewpoints of cost reduction, product quality and delivery time. It changed the allotment of orders to its subcontractors, depending on the results. Suppliers had to try to improve their performance to get more orders (Uchikawa, 2011).

Because the industrial licensing regulation was abolished in 1991 and FDI was liberalised in 1993, more domestic and foreign enterprises entered the motor vehicle and component markets. Three motor vehicle industry clusters in Delhi, Pune and Chennai developed. Assemblers of motor vehicles located in the clusters. The first- and second-tier suppliers established around the assemblers. Figure 12.3 indicates that establishment of new factories accelerated in the census sector[9] in the three clusters during the 2000s. Some common phenomena were observed among the three clusters. First, small-sized factories employing less than 101 workers and medium-sized factories employing 101 to 300 workers accounted for more than 60 per cent of the newly established factories during the 2000s. Second, new factories were established by existing companies.[10] In Delhi, 62 factories were established between 2001–2002 and 2007–2008. Only 9 out of 62 factories were set up by new companies. In Pune, only 3 out of 38 factories were established by the new companies. In Chennai, only 8 out of 28 factories were put in place by the new companies. Many new factories employing less than 300 employees were established by existing companies. These small- and medium-sized factories were set up not by large enterprises but by small and medium enterprises (SMEs). There are two main reasons for setting up multiple factories. First, the space constraints, which limited the expansion of capacity; they had to set up new factories to increase production. Second, new factories were set up at places close to their customers (Uchikawa, 2011).

---

[9] The census sector was defined as those factories employing 100 or more workers in 2007–2008. ASI conducts survey on these factories every year.

[10] Unit-level data provide information on how many units a company has. If a company does not have any other units, it is a new company.

Figure 12.3
Distribution of Motor Vehicle Census Sector Factories Operating in 2007–2008

Delhi NCR

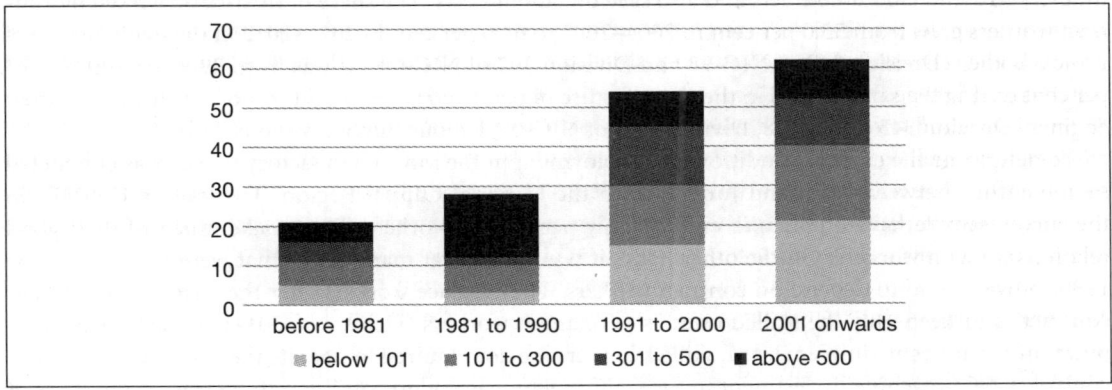

Pune

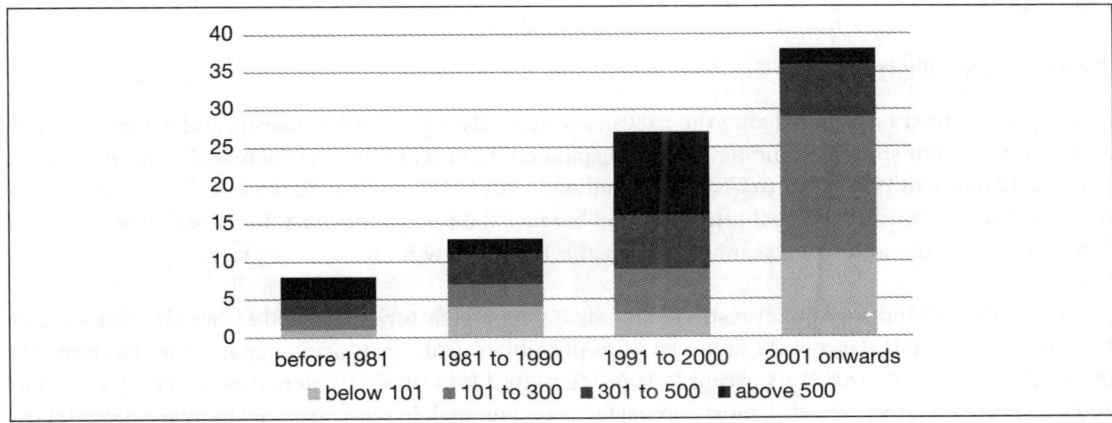

Chennai

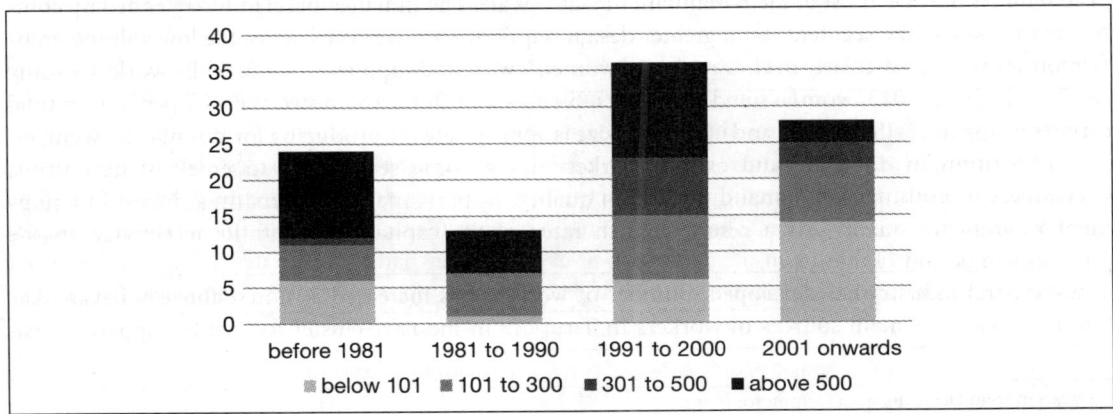

Source: Author's production based on unit-level data of ASI in 2007–2008.

The number of workers in the motor vehicle industry rose dramatically from 255,232 in 2004–2005 to 622,141 in 2011–2012 (ASI dataset). However, this does not mean that the workers in these industries had a stable job. The practice of introducing contract workers to the production line has spread in the industry to avoid labour conflicts and also save on labour costs. The share of man-days worked by contract workers grew from 55.0 per cent in 2004–2005 to 64.6 per cent in 2011–2012 in the manufacture of vehicle bodies (Division 342 of NIC-98 and Division 292 of NIC-08). It was from 29.9 per cent to 46.3 per cent during the same period in the manufacture of parts and accessories for motor vehicles and their engines (Division 343 of NIC-98, Division 293 of NIC-08; Labour Bureau, various years).

To determine the current conditions of employment in the industry, a factory survey was conducted by the author between April and June 2010 in the National Capital Region. Two out of 17 SMEs in the survey sample have a policy to employ only permanent workers. They make much of their good relationship with workers. On the other hand, it was found that many SMEs that were set up from the 1990s onward tend to depend on contract workers. They replace workers after the termination of their contracts and keep only the skilled ones as permanent workers (Uchikawa, 2011). In fact, once computer programmes are implemented, skilled workers are not required to operate the computer numerical control (CNC) machine. Investment in the CNC machine is the precondition to increasing the share of unskilled contract workers. Introduction of more advance machinery has pushed up the capital–labour ratio constantly.

Apparel Industry

The apparel industry developed after the 1980s onwards, catering to both domestic and export markets. As western fashion spread, domestic demand expanded. Exports of apparel increased constantly from US$3,753 million in 1996–1997 to US$15,001 million in 2013–2014.[11] Growth rates of GVA at 2004–2005 prices decelerated during the post-reform period because the base of the pre-reform period was too low (Table 12.1). As the industry was infant during the 1970s, growth rates of the pre-reform period were high.

The small-scale industry policy restricted the size of apparel factories as stated earlier. Because apparel was reserved for SSIs, large-scale factories were prohibited from producing apparel for the domestic market.[12] Ready-made garments except knit products and knit products were dereserved in 2001 and 2005, respectively. However, still, most apparel factories are small in size compared to international standards. Although some companies could adjust new environment and expand capacity to take advantage of economies of scale, most of them maintain the same scale. The Indian apparel industry ended up competing in low-volume segments with greater design requirements. It specialises in the low volume, mid-fashion segment, particularly in children's and women's wear and supplies to some of the world's leading retailers. In 2012–2013, women's and girls' suits, blouses and shirts accounted for 37.1 per cent of total exports of apparel (HS codes 61 and 62). Small size is appropriate for producing for this market segment.

Competition in domestic and export markets has become severe due to entry of new firms. Consumers in both market demand minimum quality. Apparel manufacturers must invest in equipment to improve quality. As a result, growth rates of the capital–labour ratio accelerated in the post-reform period (Table 12.1).

As apparel industry has developed, number of workers has increased as noted above. Vijayabaskar (2011) states three main sources of workers in Tirupur: an industry cluster for knitted apparel. First,

---

[11] Extracted from Department of Commerce (n.d.).
[12] Small-scale industries are defined by the investment in fixed assets in machinery, whether held on an ownership term or on a lease or hire purchase. The investment limit has been changed by the government from time to time.

agricultural labourers and workers engaged in other informal activities in the neighbouring villages. Workers commute by buses and trains from various villages within a radius of nearly 50 km of Tirupur. Second, migrants came from distant villages with their families and settled down in Tirupur. Third, migrants alternated between rural and urban workspaces.

The apparel industry has depended on seasonal cheap labour force in India. Workers learn skills in the workshop by learning through practice. Wages depend on experience. However, skill and extensive experience are not required much in the industry. Unskilled workers can adjust easily. Because design of apparel in the domestic and foreign markets changes every year, manufacturers must produce products intensively within a few months before the season starts. The fluctuation of demand enhances the need to rely on seasonal migrants from rural areas in the same and other states. They come in clusters to work in factories during production season and return to their villages after production season. Many migrants join the same factories again in the next season. The flexibility of labour supply and low wages are important for viability and maintaining the competitiveness of the apparel industry. Migrants who alternate between rural and urban workspaces are an important labour force.

Pais and Usami (2014) conducted survey on migrant workers in Ludhiana in Punjab, an industry cluster for knitted apparel in May–June 2012. A total of 199 out of 469 samples were engaged in hosiery, garment and textile industries. Other workers worked in auto components, bicycle manufacturing, etc. They collected data on workers' earning for a reference period of one month prior to the survey and estimated the earnings for an eight-hour workday, taking into account the overtime work done by workers. The average hours of work per day for production workers in hosiery garment and textile industries were 11 hours. Average monthly earnings for an eight-hour duty were ₹4,948 in these industries. The statutory minimum wages per month for an unskilled worker on an eight-hour shift in urban Punjab between March 2012 and September 2012 was ₹4,568. They pointed out that "while the average eight-hourly wage was a few hundred rupees above the statutory minimum wages, a large number of sample workers received wages that were below the minimum wages" (2014, p. 50).

To sum up, the capital–labour ratio in the four industries increased for different reasons. Various trends can be observed even within the same industry. Rise of wages did not affect the capital–labour ratio from a long-term viewpoint, albeit for different reasons. The common phenomenon among the four industries is active market entry in the second half of the 2000s. Establishment of new factories created employment. But the status of unskilled workers is unstable in the four industries. They work for long hours at low wage.

Explanation for Long-term Stagnation of Employment

This section investigates the reasons of long-term stagnation of employment. Five views on the jobless growth up to the mid-2000s have been examined earlier. Most of studies explained the stagnation of employment from the short-term viewpoint. Under the conditions of long-term period, three effects must be considered. First, entry and exit of factories that affect the capital stock. Second, existing factories can increase or reduce investment on capacity and number of workers easily. Third, extension of working hours and days and overlying of employment cannot continue.

Job security regulation by the Industrial Dispute Act may have given employers the incentive to maintain the number of regular workers at less than 100 as contract workers are not covered by this regulation. Increase of contract workers may not have been restricted total number of workers in the organised manufacturing sector. In fact, the rapid rise of contract workers increased the number of workers as reported in the ASI dataset in the 2000s. The share of man-days worked by contract workers increased clearly in all industries between 2001–2002 and 2011–2012 (Table 12.2). Growth rates of man-days worked by contract workers between 2001–2002 and 2011–2012 were higher than 10 per cent in 18 out of 22 industries. In the organised manufacturing sector, growth rates of man-days worked by directly employed workers and contract workers between 2001–2002 and 2011–2012 were 4.4 per cent and 11.0 per cent, respectively. Although Goldar (2011a, 2011b) regards labour reform as a main reason for the sharp rise of employment, flexible implementation of job security regulation affects only directly employed workers. Even under the job security regulation, number of workers could have increased.

The capital–labour ratio depends on changes in industrial structure, entry of new factories, exit of old factories and introduction of advance machinery (see section 'Long-term Changes in Industrial Structure of Four Industries' discussed earlier). It is noteworthy that the introduction of CNC machines even makes it possible to increase unskilled workers. Figure 12.4 indicates that wages deflated by the WPI of products rose sharply between 1981–1982 and 1984–1985, 1993–1994 and 1997–1998 and again between 2008–2009 and 2012–2013. During these three periods, the WPI of food articles increased by more than nine per cent per annum. Despite the rapid increase in wages between 2008–2009 and 2011–2012, the number of workers also increased. Although the sharp rise in wages may reduce employment for short-run adjustments, it does not affect the capital–labour ratio for the long term. The growth rate of wage bill relative to value added in current prices is not constant for long-term period; Mazumdar and Sarkar (2008) assumed it only for the short term. Thus, the rise in wages cannot be the reason for the long-term stagnation of employment.

There are four possible reasons for the long-term stagnation of employment before 2004–2005. First, the scale of investment was low, and the investment boom did not exist during the pre-reform period. Continuous growth of demand provided incentives for lumpy investment. During the pre-reform period, growth rates of GVA above 10 per cent in the organised manufacturing sector were not sustained for more than two years. Labour demand created by investment was adjusted by extending working hours and days. As a result, employment stagnation continued in the 1980s. The first investment boom increased the number of workers in the mid-1990s. However, the number decreased soon after the boom was over. Employment has been adjusted flexibly according to fluctuation of demand during the post-reform period.

Second, the negative effect by employment-displacing industries affected total number of workers in the organised manufacturing sector. Six industries, including textile and basic metal industries, reduced the number of workers between 1981–1982 and 2004–2005. However, the six industries increased employment after 2004–2005 onwards. Only two industries, tobacco product and precision instruments industries, reduced employment marginally between 2004–2005 and 2011–2012 (ASI dataset).[13] Employment increased in capital-intensive as well as in labour-intensive industries in the second half of the 2000s.

Third, a lack of skilled workers promoted introduction of capital-intensive technology to improve competitiveness. Skill is necessary to produce more sophisticated and accurate products and is accumulated through experience and training. It takes time and money to train workers. If a worker shifts to a competitor, the cost of training may become redundant. Computer-controlled machines can substitute skilled workers to some extent. When employers compare opportunity costs to raise skilled workers with investment in computer-controlled machines, most of them prefer the combination of computer-controlled machines and unskilled workers.

---

[13] While total lost employment in six industries between 1981–1982 and 2004–2005 was 320,395, which in two industries between 2004–2005 and 2011–2012 was only 31,407.

Table 12.2
Growth Rates of Man-days Worked by Directly Employed Workers and Contract Workers

		Growth Rates of Man-days Between 2001–2002 and 2011–2012 (%)		Share of Man-days Worked by Contract Workers (%)		
		Directly Employed Workers	Contract Workers	2001–2002	2006–2007	2011–2012
15	Food products and beverages	2.9	6.9	22.6	28.5	31.0
16	Tobacco products	−3.8	−0.2*	60.6	69.4	66.2
17	Textiles	3.4	8.6	8.6	12.6	14.2
18	Apparel; dressing and dyeing of fur	7.0	17.0	7.1	11.8	15.8
19	Tanning and dressing of leather	9.0	10.7	12.6	18.2	19.5
20	Wood and products of wood	4.3	13.2	12.9	26.7	25.1
21	Paper and paper products	3.9	5.8	24.5	30.9	28.5
22	Publishing, printing and reproduction of recorded media	2.9	12.0	7.7	12.5	18.3
23	Coke, refined petroleum products and nuclear fuel	4.1*	12.4	29.7	47.7	43.0
24	Chemicals and chemical products	2.7	10.7	22.4	31.5	40.2
25	Rubber and plastics products	6.5	16.3	14.9	24.5	30.5
26	Other non-metallic mineral products	2.6*	13.0	34.0	49.2	53.9
27	Basic metals	5.6	14.5	24.6	37.7	44.8
28	Fabricated metal products, except machinery and equipment	9.3	16.2	26.9	40.6	44.7
29	Machinery and equipment	5.0	16.6	14.3	26.6	34.3
30	Office, accounting and computing machinery	0.6*	11.0	38.5	45.9	52.2
31	Electrical machinery and apparatus	6.8	18.2	17.6	31.6	38.0
32	Radio, television and communication equipment and apparatus	4.3	19.5	11.3	26.3	32.8
33	Medical, precision, and optical instruments, watches and clocks	−4.0	10.6	5.7	11.1	20.8
34	Motor vehicles, trailers and semi-trailers	9.1	21.6	16.8	34.6	44.4
35	Other transport equipment	0.8*	18.0	12.7	41.5	48.3
36	Manufacture of furniture and other manufacturing	8.7	13.7	14.4	19.1	23.4
	Total	4.4	11.0	21.3	29.5	34.3

Source: Author's calculation based on Labour Bureau (various years).
Note: *Growth rate is not significant at the 95 per cent confidence level.

Figure 12.4
Trends in Number of Workers and per Capita Wages in the Organised Manufacturing Sector

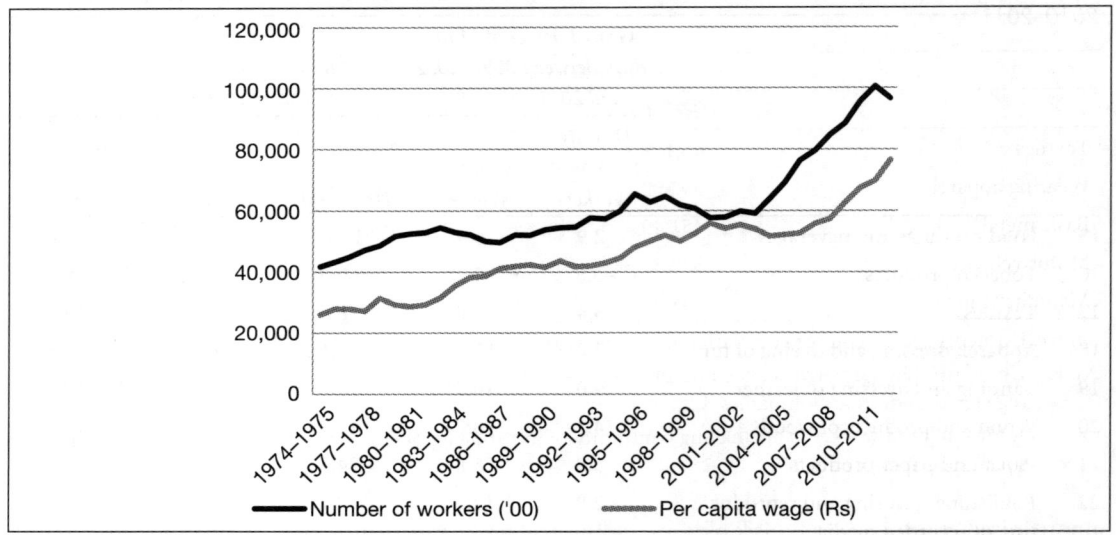

Source: Author's Production based on the ASI dataset.

Fourth, the unorganised sector did not want to turn into the organised sector to maintain its competitiveness. There are four reasons for the competitiveness of the unorganised sector: (a) low wages, (b) flexible labour force, (c) specialisation and (d) exemption from excise duty. Wages in the unorganised sector are much lower than those in the organised sector, for example, Table 12.3 shows that annual wages per worker in the organised sector are much higher than those in the unorganised sector.

Further, the organised sector must bear other expenditures for its workers, such as provident funds and other social security charges in addition to wages. The real gap in labour costs between the organised and unorganised sectors is much more. Because labour regulation is not imposed on the unorganised sector, it can fire and hire workers flexibly. Factories in the unorganised sector can specialise in a specific process and reduce initial investment amount. Low initial investment encourages entry. If they are built on inter-firm networking in an industrial cluster, they can compensate each other. This network functions as a de facto vertically integrated company. Exemption from excise duty is provided to the unorganised sector, depending on its turnover.

Informalisation of Employment

The second investment boom in the second half of the 2000s encouraged entry into the organised manufacturing sector. The number of factories increased dramatically from 128,056 in 2004–2005 to 202,524 in 2011–2012. The effects of large-scale investment compensated for the negative impact from the rise of the capital–labour ratio. As a result, the number of workers increased rapidly.

On the other hand, the share of contract workers rose in the 2000s as mentioned before. The main purpose to employ contract workers is not only to avoid job security but also to reduce labour costs as mentioned before. The National Commission for Enterprises in the Unorganised Sector (NCEUS) (2009) defines informal employment as follows: "unorganised workers consist of those working in the

Table 12.3
Annual Wages per Worker in the Organised and Annual Emoluments per Hired Worker in 2010–2011

	Unincorporated Enterprises		Organised Sector
	Formal Hired Worker	Informal Hired Worker	
Textiles	46,199	47,009	58,483
Wearing apparel	39,502	40,503	55,453
Basic metal	45,240	46,173	89,049
Motor vehicles	82,933	64,562	102,445
Manufacturing sector	45,229	43,293	67,442

Source: Unincorporated enterprises: National Sample Survey (NSS) Office (2013); Organised sector: ASI dataset.

Notes: Unincorporated enterprises include proprietary and partnership enterprises exclude enterprises which are registered under the Companies Act, 1956.

A formal hired worker is one having continuity of job and eligible for paid annual leave and also eligible for social security benefits.

unorganised enterprises or households, excluding regular workers with social security benefits, and the workers in the formal sector without any employment/social security benefits provided by the employers" (p. 12). The NCEUS estimated the formal and informal workers in the organised and unorganised sectors in the entire Indian economy, including agriculture and non-agriculture sectors. The study clarifies an important point in employment growth between 1999–2000 and 2004–2005. While formal employment grew slowly from 33.6 million to 35.0 million, employment in the organised sector increased rapidly from 54.9 million to 62.6 million.[14] This suggests that "the entire increase in the employment in the organised sector over this period has largely been of informal in nature" (NCEUS, 2009: 14). Informal employment spread not only in the manufacturing sector but also in the service sector.

Figure 12.4 indicates that per capita wages at 2004–2005 prices decreased from ₹54,220 in 2001–2002 to ₹51,603 in 2004–2005. The share of contract workers in total man-days in the organised manufacturing sector rose from 21.3 per cent in 2001–2002 to 25.8 per cent in 2004–2005. A portion of regular workers was replaced by contract workers. This might be the main reason for the decrease of per capita wages. It is confirmed from the ASI dataset that informalisation of employment took place even before the number of workers showed an increase.

Conclusion

Employment in the organised manufacturing sector had stagnated up to the mid-2000s despite its stable and rapid output growth. The reasons were argued from the short-term viewpoint. There are five views on jobless growth: (a) job security regulation by the Industrial Disputes Act, (b) adoption of capital-intensive technology to save on rising labour costs, (c) the extension of working hours in a day and increase in man-days, (d) changes in the composition of output in favour of less labour-intensive

---

[14] Total employment in the entire Indian economy, including both the organised and unorganised sectors, grew from 396.4 million to 455.7 million between 1999–2000 and 2004–2005. As a result, the share of formal employment in total employment declined from 8.5 per cent to 7.7 per cent during the period.

industries and (e) the question of over-employment. But jobless growth continued for more than two decades. The reasons should be argued from a long-term viewpoint. Extension of working hours and increase in man-days and overlying of employment cannot continue for long-term period. As contract workers are not covered by job security regulation, it may not have been restricted total number of workers in the organised manufacturing sector. Wages rose only for some years due to hike of food prices. The sharp rise in wages cannot be the reason for the long-term stagnation of employment. In fact, employment increased in the second half of the 2000s in spite of the rapid increase of wages.

The capital–labour ratio depends on changes in industrial structure, entry of new factories, exit of old factories and introduction of advance machinery. It has risen consciously in the organised manufacturing sector in both pre- and post-reform periods. As competition becomes severe in the post-reform period, some companies try to introduce advanced technology to improve productivity and quality of products.

Stable and rapid expansion of domestic demand caused an investment boom in the second half of the 2000s. New factories were set up, and well-performing companies expanded capacity. Indian economy has not seen such huge scale and long-term investment boom. Total number of workers in the organised manufacturing sector grew dramatically. The effects of large-scale investment compensated for the negative impact from the rise of the capital–labour ratio. The phenomenon signalled the end of jobless growth. However, this does not mean that the workers in these industries had a stable job. The share of contract workers in total man-days in the organised manufacturing sector rose constantly in the 2000s. A portion of regular workers was replaced by contract workers.

There are four possible reasons for the long-term stagnation of employment up to 2004–2005: (a) low scale of investment, (b) the negative effect by employment-displacing industries, (c) introduction of capital-intensive technology due to a lack of skilled workers and (d) hesitation of the unorganised factories to grow into the organised sector.

These arguments depend on demand side in labour market. There is a reason in supply side. Presently, labour shortage has emerged in some industrial areas. Employers in Delhi and Ludhiana had difficulty to employ unskilled workers.[15] Most of unskilled workers come from rural areas. Migrant workers flow into industrial areas to meet the labour demand in factories. However, the inflow of migrants cannot catch up with the rapid increase of labour demand. The supply-side conditions of workers should be investigated. Migrant workers compare expected income from factories and that from agricultural wage work and non-farm work in their villages before they come to industrial areas. Migration has many costs and risks associated with it. Contract workers cannot get stable positions and accumulate their skills to get better jobs in workshops. Contract work gives surplus workers in rural areas an alternative to agricultural work. If they find better income opportunities in their native villages, they may not risk coming to the cities. Thus, to solve the bottleneck of labour shortage, it is necessary to raise the wages of or give regular positions to migrant workers.

References

Ahluwalia, I.J. (1991). *Productivity and growth in Indian manufacturing*. New Delhi: Oxford University Press.
Bhalotra, S.R. (1998). The puzzle of jobless growth in Indian manufacturing. *Oxford Bulletin of Economics and Statistics*, *60*(1), 5–32.
Confederation of Indian Textile Industry. n.d. Retrieved from http://www.citiindia.com/images/database/table8.pdf on 12 January 2016.

---

[15] Survey conducted in Delhi in 2010 and in Ludhiana in 2011.

Department of Commerce, Ministry of Commerce and Industry. n.d. Import export data bank. Retrieved from http://commerce.nic.in/eidb/default.asp on 14 January 2016.

Fallon, P., & Lucas, R.E.B. (1993). Job security regulations and the dynamic demand for industrial labour in India and Zimbabwe. *Journal of Development Economics, 40*(2), 241–475.

Ghose, A.K. (1994). Employment in organised manufacturing in India. *Indian Journal of Labour Economics, 37*(2), 141–162.

GoI, n.d. Annual Survey of Industries (ASI), Ministry of Statistics and Programme Implementation, Government of India. Retrieved from http://mospi.nic.in/Mospi_New/upload/asi/ASI_main.htm?status=1&menu_id=88 on 12 January 2016.

Goldar, B. (2000). Employment growth in organised manufacturing in India. *Economic and Political Weekly, 35*(14), 1191–1195.

———. (2011a). Growth in organized manufacturing employment in recent years. *Economic and Political Weekly, 46*(7), 20–23.

———. (2011b). Organized manufacturing employment: Continuing the debate. *Economic and Political Weekly, 46*(14), 79–80.

Indian Bureau of Mines. (2008). *Indian Mineral Yearbook*. Nagpur: Indian Bureau of Mines, Ministry of Mines, Government of India.

———. (2011). *Indian Mineral Yearbook*. Nagpur: Indian Bureau of Mines, Ministry of Mines, Government of India.

Indian Cotton Mills' Federation (ICMF). (1998). *Handbook of statistics on cotton textile industry*. New Delhi: Author.

International Labour Organization (ILO). (1996). *India: Economic reforms and labour politics*. Delhi: Author.

Kannan, K.P., & Raveendar, G. (2009). Growth sans employment: A quarter century of jobless growth in India's organised manufacturing. *Economic and Political Weekly, 44*(10), 80–91.

Kundu, A., & Bhatia, S. (2002). *Industrial growth in small and medium towns and their vertical integration: The case of Gobindgarh, Punjab, India*. Management of Social Transformations Discussion Paper No. 57, United Nations Educational, Scientific and Cultural Organization, Paris.

Labour Bureau. *Annual survey of industries: Statistics on employment and labour cost*. Chandigarh/Shimla: Labour Bureau, Ministry of Labour and Employment, Government of India. Various years.

Mazumdar, D., & Sarkar, S. (2008). *Globalization, labour markets and inequality in India*. London & New York: Routledge.

Ministry of Textiles. Retrieved from http://www.txcindia.gov.in/html/data%20cotton%20and%20cotton%20yarn%20selected%20table.pdf on 12 January 2016.

Nagaraj, R. (1994). Wages and employment in manufacturing industries: Trends, hypothesis and evidence. *Economic and Political Weekly, 29*(4), 177–186.

———. (2011). Growth in organised manufacturing employment: A comment. *Economic and Political Weekly, 46*(12), 83–84.

———. (2013). India's dream run, 2003–08: Understanding the boom and its aftermath. *Economic and Political Weekly, 48*(20), 39–51.

National Commission for Enterprises in the Unorganized Sector (NCEUS). (2009). *The challenge of employment in India: An informal economy perspective* (Vol. I). New Delhi: Author.

National Sample Survey (NSS) Office. (2013). *Economic characteristics of unincorporated non-agricultural enterprises (excluding construction) in India* (Report No. 549). New Delhi: Author.

Okada, A. (2004). Skills development and interfirm learning linkages under globalisation: Lessons from the Indian automobile industry. *World Development, 32*(7), 1265–1288.

Pais, J., & Usami, Y. (2014). Migrant workers in Ludhiana. In S. Uchikawa (Ed.), *Industrial clusters, migrant workers, and labour markets in India*. London & New York: Palgrave Macmillan.

Textile Commissioner. (1997). *Compendium of textile statistics 1996*. Mumbai: Textile Commissioner, Ministry of Textiles, Government of India.

———. (n.d.). Closure of cotton/man-made fibre textile mills. Retrieved from http://txcindia.gov.in/html/closure%20report%20Mar06.htm on 20 January 2016.

Uchikawa, S. (1998). *Indian textile industry: State policy, liberalization and growth*. New Delhi: Manohar.

———. (2002). Investment boom and capital goods industry. In S. Uchikawa (Ed.), *Economic reforms and industrial structure in India*. New Delhi: Manohar.

Uchikawa, S. (2003). Employment in the manufacturing organized sector in India: The rise of medium scale units. In S. Uchikawa (Ed.), *Labour market and institution in India: 1990s and beyond*. New Delhi: Manohar.

Textile Commissioner. (2011). The rise of small and medium enterprises in Indian auto component industry. *Economic and Political Weekly, 46*(25), 51–59.

Vijayabaskar, M. (2011). Global crises, welfare provision and coping strategies of labour in Tiruppur. *Economic and Political Weekly, 46*(22), 38–45.

World Bank. (1989). *India: Poverty, employment and social services: A World Bank country study* (Vol. I). Washington, DC: Author.

SECTION 4
Envisioning the Institutional Changes

13

Monetary Equilibrium and Inertial Expectations

Jyotirmoy Bhattacharya[*]

Introduction

Contemporary economies use intrinsically valueless money. The material object corresponding to the unit of account is a token, such as a currency note, which is neither useful itself in consumption or production and nor does it directly give its holder any claim on any other object that can be so useful. Yet, this intrinsically valueless object is regularly accepted in exchange for objects that are in fact useful. It is one of the central problems in the foundations of monetary economics to understand why this is so.

While monetary economists, starting with Hume, have imagined economies where money is merely a token, for long, this remained merely a thought experiment since the value of money in the real world remained tied to the value of precious metals. It is only with the breakdown of the Bretton Woods system that the world of money has finally severed all its links with the world of commodities. Monetary theory now has no alternative but to take the intrinsically valueless nature of money as its starting point. How we choose to proceed from this starting point has real-world consequences to the extent that monetary theory guides monetary policy and monetary policy affects people's welfare.

Contemporary monetary theory also faces a challenge from another direction. Developments in financial systems and payments technology are making it more and more untenable to base monetary economics on the demand for a specific class of assets called 'money' whose supply is determined by monetary authorities. As a store of value, money was taken to be a distinguished from other assets by having a deterministic nominal return. But a modern financial system offers wealth holders a variety of short-term debt instruments with fixed nominal returns, most of which are not included in the usual monetary aggregates. Expanding the definition of money to cover all assets with a fixed nominal return does not help either since many of these assets are liabilities of the private sector and their supply cannot

---

[*] This chapter is based on Chapter 4 of my PhD thesis *Intrinsically Valueless Money and the Coordination of Intertemporal Exchange* (submitted 2007) written under the supervision of Professor Prabhat Patnaik at the Centre for Economic Studies and Planning, Jawaharlal Nehru University. It was from Professor Patnaik that I first learnt about the problem of valuedness of intrinsically valueless money and Grandmont's contribution to this area. I would like to express my deepest thanks to him not only for his very generous help and guidance during the writing of my thesis but also for initiating me into macroeconomics and monetary theory. Needless to say, the responsibility for any errors remains my own.

be taken to be exogenous or policy-determined. The alternative of defining money narrowly, such as cash plus demand deposits, and then deriving its demand from the transaction motive is also becoming harder to justify. The development of payment systems has reduced the costs of converting assets, which are not mediums of exchange (say, bonds or time deposits), into ones that are (say, demand deposits). Other developments, such as credit cards or mobile phone payments allow for payments to be made without making use of any assets whose supply is controlled by the central bank. The result of these developments has been to reduce the amount of narrowly defined money that must be held to support a given volume of transactions. There seems to be no lower bound below which the transactions demand for money cannot fall, and therefore an explanation for the value of money in a modern economy will be most satisfactory if it does not depend essentially on there being a transactions role for money.

Recognising these development and in line with other recent work such as Woodford (2003), in this chapter, we take money to be primarily a unit of account in terms of which prices are quoted and debt contracts are written. The economy in our model would have nominal assets, but there will be no special class of nominal assets distinguished as 'money' and there will be no transactions demand for money. In such a world, nominal assets will have a positive demand, and hence money will have a positive price in terms of goods, only if its current holders can expect to get something useful in exchange for it in the future. Thus, the positive price of money today depends on the expectation that it will have a positive price in the future, which in turn depends on the expectation that it will have a positive price at some point even further in the future. But this seems to leave us hanging uncomfortably by our bootstraps: why should money have a positive price at any date at all?

Fundamental contributions to this problem were made by Grandmont and his collaborators (Grandmont, 1977, 1983; Grandmont & Younes, 1972). Following the temporary equilibrium method, Grandmont takes expectations about the future to be determined by an exogenously given function of past and present economic variables. He shows that if we allow this expectation function to be chosen arbitrarily, then equilibrium may fail to exist in a monetary economy. However, if expectations are constrained to be 'inertial'—in a sense to be made precise below—then an equilibrium can be guaranteed to exist and money has a positive value in that equilibrium.

Grandmont's result can be seen as a response to the bootstraps problem. If we accept that expectations are formed not by arbitrary speculation about the future but are shaped by our past and present experiences, then the expectation function used in temporary equilibrium models can be interpreted as an embodiment of this learning from the past. Then, it follows from Grandmont's result that for an economy with a past that generates 'inertial' expectations, money would indeed have a positive value. The advantage of shifting the burden of the problem from the future to the past is that the past of actual economies is known to us, and if this past is one that makes our condition on expectations plausible, then we may claim relevance for our explanation of the value of money on empirical grounds even if one may be able to logically conceive of alternative pasts that would have been unable to support a positive value of money.

The present chapter extends Grandmont's work in two directions. First, we replace Grandmont's assumption of an exogenously given distribution of outside money with the alternative assumption that at the beginning of time some agents are entitled to receive and other agents are entitled to pay certain nominal amounts that are fixed from the past. This assumption makes clear that the fundamental role played by money in this class of models is that of a unit of account in terms of which some part of agents' wealth is predetermined. Thus, the requirement for expectations to be inertial would be equally applicable in a world where money is endogenous, but where at each point of time, there exist pre-existing nominal commitments, as is the case in actual economies. The extension of Grandmont's framework to allow for nominal liabilities, however, presents a complication in the form of a possibility that at low enough prices, some agents may turn out to have negative net wealth. In the next section, we set up a model that incorporates this case and establish an equilibrium existence result.

The second extension that we make is to allow for monetary policy in the form of a nominal interest rate that is determined by the central bank. This allows us to compare our results with the presently dominant new Keynesian framework for monetary theory. While in the model in the following section, the interest rate is determined exogenously, in section 'Endogenous Policy', we make the interest rate a function of the endogenous state of the economy through a policy rule. The sufficient condition for the existence of equilibrium now places a joint restriction on the expectations function and the interest rate rule. We compare this restriction to the conditions that need to be imposed on new Keynesian models under rational expectations in order to ensure determinacy of equilibrium.

The Basic Model

Assumptions

We consider a simple competitive pure-exchange economy. Time is discrete and there are two dates 0 and 1. There is no uncertainty. There is a single consumption good in the economy that cannot be stored across periods. There are H households that are the decision-making agents. Household h has endowments $\omega_0^h > 0$ and $\omega_1^h > 0$ in the two periods, respectively.

Spot markets in the consumption goods open on both days. Prices in these markets are quoted in terms of a unit of account which we refer to as 'money'. There are no future markets for commodities.

Households in the economy can make and receive commitments denoted in money terms. At the beginning of period 0, household h has a commitment, inherited from the past, to pay D^h units of money. D^h can be negative, in which case that particular household is entitled to receive money in the beginning of period 0.

In period 0, households can contract to borrow an amount b in money terms at the nominal interest rate i. Repayments of these loans are made in period 1.

The household's problem in period 0 is to decide on an optimum consumption plan (x_0, x_1) for the two periods. Each household's preference of ordering over consumption plans is given by a continuous, monotonic and strictly quasi-concave utility function $u^h(x_0, x_1)$. The budget constraint faced by each household is

$$px_0 \leq p\omega_0 + b - D$$
$$p_1^e x_1 + (1+i)b \leq p_1^e \omega_1$$
$$x_0 \geq 0, \; x_1 \geq 0,$$

where p is the price of the consumption good in the spot market on day 0, and p_1^e is the price expected to prevail in the spot market on day 1.

Since our household lives only on the two dates 0 and 1, they do not borrow in period 1. The model could be extended to infinitely lived households who could then borrow in each period. In that case, the budget constraint above would have to be augmented with a no-Ponzi-game condition.[1]

---

[1] A no-Ponzi-game condition requires that the present value of a household's debt position tends to a nonpositive limit as time tends to infinity. In the infinite horizon case, such a condition needs to be imposed to ensure that the present value of a household's expenditure stream does not exceed the present of value of its endowment stream.

We can eliminate b from the day 0 and day 1 constraints above to obtain the single constraint as follows:

$$px_0 + \frac{p_1^e}{1+i}x_1 \le p\omega_0 + \frac{p_1^e}{1+i}\omega_1 - D \quad x_0 \ge 0, x_1 \ge 0. \tag{13.1}$$

Expectations

The expectation p^e of the spot price on day 1 will in general depend on all the information available to agents on day 0. Also, different households will, in general, form different expectations even on the basis of the same information. While there is a considerable literature on the existence of monetary equilibrium under the assumption of rational expectations or perfect foresight, we do not feel the use of these assumptions justified in the absence of an argument showing the convergence over time of learning behaviour to rational expectations. In our model, where households form expectations only once, on date **0**, it is more natural to assume the expectation-formation mechanism to be given exogenously.

We, therefore, assume that p_1^e is some function $\xi(p)$ of current prices. While expectations may also depend on other information, including the past history of prices, these factors are fixed in our model, and therefore the dependence of expectations on them does not need to be explicitly modelled.

With these assumptions, the household's budget constraint now becomes

$$px_0 + \frac{\xi(p)}{1+i}x_1 \le p\omega_0 + \frac{\xi(p)}{1+i}\omega_1 - D \quad x_0 \ge 0, x_1 \ge 0.$$

For convenience, we define an auxiliary function $\eta(p)$ as

Definition 1

$$\eta^h(p) = \frac{\xi^h(p)}{1+i}.$$

This allows us to simplify the budget constraint to

$$px_0 + \eta(p)x_1 \le p\omega_0 + \eta(p)\omega_1 - D \quad x_0 \ge 0, x_1 \ge 0. \tag{13.2}$$

Bankruptcy

In (13.2), if the day 0 price is such that $p\omega_0 + \eta(p)\omega_1 - D < 0$, then there are no consumption plans satisfying the budget constraint. We refer to this outcome as 'bankruptcy'. In effect, prices are so low that the earnings of the household from selling its endowments is insufficient even to meet its prior nominal obligations. While we have not explicitly modelled the origin of D, one way to understand it would be to see it as $(1+i)b_{-1}$, where b_{-1} is the amount borrowed by the household in the period before period 0. In our model, households never wilfully plan to default on their borrowings. Therefore, bankruptcy occurs only when prices are lower than those expected by the households when formulating their plans in the previous period. Thus, the occurrence of bankruptcy is a direct result of our not assuming any form of perfect foresight.

We handle bankruptcy in our model with two assumptions. First, households that go bankrupt are assumed to consume nothing. Formally, we model this by setting their money income to zero. Second, the payments received by individuals with a negative D^h remain unchanged even if some other households go bankrupt. We may motivate this by assuming that there is a perfect debt guarantee and choosing to ignore in the current setup the informational problems associated with implementing such a guarantee.

With these assumptions about bankruptcy in hand, we define a household's expected money income as

Definition 2

The expected money income of household h is given by the function

$$M^h(p_0) = \max(p_0\omega_0^h + \eta^h(p_0)\omega_1^h - D^h, 0).$$

Now, a household's budget constraint can be written as

$$px_0 + \eta(p)x_1 \leq M(p) \qquad x_0 \geq 0,\ x_1 \geq 0. \tag{13.3}$$

Equilibrium

Let the household's demand for consumption goods on day 0 be given by the function $d_1^h(p)$ (we show in this appendix that this function is well-defined). Then that household's excess demand is given by $\zeta^h(p) = d_1^h(p) - \omega_0^h$. The aggregate excess demand is defined by

$$\zeta(p) = \sum_h \zeta^h(p).$$

A price $\hat{p} > 0$ is a temporary equilibrium for period 0 if it is the case that

$$\zeta(\hat{p}) = 0.$$

We investigate below the sufficient conditions for the existence of such a temporary equilibrium.

Continuity

We begin by assuming that expected future prices depend continuously on current prices.

Assumption 1. $\eta(p)$ is a continuous function of p.

Under this assumption, we can show that

Lemma 1. For all h, $\zeta^h(p)$ is a continuous function of p.

Proof. Deferred to the Proofs section.

Since the aggregate excess demand function is a sum of household excess demand functions, it follows that the aggregate excess demand too is continuous.

Proposition 1. $\zeta(p)$ is a continuous function of p.

Boundary Conditions

Since $\zeta(p)$ is a continuous function of p, we can obtain an equilibrium using the intermediate-value theorem provided we can find one price where excess demand is negative and another price where it is positive.

Naively, we would expect excess demand to go up as prices go to zero and excess demand to go down as prices go to infinity. However, the assumptions that we have made so far are not sufficient to establish this behaviour.

As is usual, we can divide the effect of a price change of demand into an income and a substitution effect. However, the existence of price expectations and nominal commitments requires some adjustments to this decomposition.

First, in addition to the usual income effect, we have an additional effect arising from changes in the real value of money commitments. This is the real balance effect. A rise in current prices raises the real income of creditors and reduces the real income of debtors.

Relative prices are given by

$$\frac{p_e}{p} = \frac{\xi(p)}{p}.$$

Hence, the substitution effect of a price change depends on the responsiveness of price expectations to current prices. Taking logarithms in the above equation and differentiating, we have

$$\frac{\dot{p}_e}{p} - \frac{\dot{p}}{p} = \frac{1}{p}\left(\frac{p\xi'(p)}{\xi(p)} - 1\right).$$

Thus, the direction of the substitution effect depends on the elasticity of expectations, namely

$$e = \frac{p\xi'(p)}{\xi(p)}.$$

When $e=1$, there is no substitution effect at all since expected prices move in the same proportion to current prices. When $e>1$, the substitution effect of a current price increase actually leads to an increase in current consumption since the price of future consumption rises by an even greater proportion. It is only when $e<1$ that the substitution effect works in the usual direction.

The presence of elastic expectations can cause our model to not to have a solution since the reverse substitution effect can result in demand not becoming positive when price goes to 0 or not becoming negative when price goes to infinity. Thus, a sufficient condition for existence of equilibrium in our model will require restrictions on admissible expectation functions. The assumption we choose is that expectations have both an upper bound and a strictly positive lower bound. More specifically,

Assumption 2. For each household h, there are numbers $L^h > 0$ and U^h such that $L^h(1+i) \leq \xi(p) \leq U^h(1+i)$ for all p, which implies that $L^h \leq \eta(p) \leq U^h$ for all p.

An expectation function that satisfies this assumption cannot be elastic for all prices. One economic interpretation of this assumption is that households have a notion of 'normal' prices and do not expect prices to go beyond these 'normal' limits. An extreme case of an expectation function that satisfies this assumption is zero-elastic expectations, that is, an expectation that does not change at all in response to current prices. It is this boundedness of expectations that essentially guarantees the existence of monetary equilibrium in our model.

While our assumption takes care of the substitution effect, the income effect for debtors can still cause problems. As prices fall, the real income of debtors falls, and in the limit, they become bankrupt and cannot consume anything. Therefore, an economy consisting only of debtors may once again fail to have a nonnegative demand at any prices as it may happen that before prices can fall enough to make demand positive, all households have become bankrupt. To rule out this pathological case, we assume that there is at least one creditor household.

Assumption 3. There is at least one household h with $D^h < 0$.

Taken together, the assumptions above are sufficient to establish our central result: the existence of a monetary equilibrium in this model.

Theorem 1. There exists a $\hat{p} > 0$ such that $\zeta p = 0$.

Proof. Deferred to the Proofs section.

Endogenous Policy

In the previous section, we have assumed that the nominal interest rate is exogenously given. In this section, we replace this assumption with a nominal interest rate rule

$$1 + i = \phi(p),$$

which makes the nominal interest rate a function of the present price level that is an endogenous variable.

The analysis of the existence problem under such a policy rule can be reduced to the analysis in section 'The Basic Model' provided that we redefine the function $\eta(p)$ used in that section to take into account the dependence of i on endogenous variables.

Definition 3.

$$\eta^h(p) = \frac{\xi^h(p)}{\phi(p)}.$$

With this change, the analysis proceeds as before, and the proofs for the propositions in section 'The Basic Model' continue to hold. The key sufficient condition for the existence of equilibrium now becomes

Assumption 4. For each household h, there are numbers $L^h > 0$ and U^h such that $L^h \leq \frac{\xi(p)}{\phi(p)} \leq U^h$ for all p.

If we make the plausible assumption that both $\xi(\cdot)$ and $\phi(\cdot)$ are increasing functions, then this condition can be interpreted as saying that the interest rate policy cannot forever be less responsive to the price level than the expectations of any household.

On the other hand, provided that the interest rate rule satisfies this condition, it is possible for an economy to have an equilibrium even if an otherwise identical economy with an exogenous interest rate would not have had an equilibrium because of the unboundedness of private sector expectations. All that is required is that the interest rate responds strongly enough to p to keep $\eta(\cdot)$ bounded. Thus, with an active monetary policy, we no longer have to appeal to private households' beliefs in a 'normal' range of prices in order to ensure the existence of equilibrium. A strong enough response by the monetary authority to changes in present prices is enough.

It is instructive to compare this result with constraints imposed on monetary policy in simple linearised new Keynesian models. In these models, it can be shown that the rational expectations equilibrium is locally determinate as long as nominal interest rate policy responds positively to the interest rate (see, for example, Proposition 2.3 in Woodford, 2003). While the property of local determinacy is not the same as that of existence of equilibrium which we have been using, it is still worthwhile to compare the two results since both of them ultimately rest on the effects of changes in current prices on the intertemporal terms of trade.

The new Keynesian criteria appear to be much simpler than ours since the set of acceptable policies—those where nominal interest rates respond positively to current prices—is independent of the values of the parameters characterising the behaviour of the private sector. However, this simplicity is a consequence of the overly restrictive assumption of rational expectations and the restrictive methodology of looking only at paths that are close to a given steady state. The complexity of our Assumption 4 is precisely a consequence of our modelling expectations of the future as arising from households' extrapolation from the past—with different households possibly drawing different lessons. The policy lessons that follow are that there cannot be a 'one-size-fits-all' monetary policy that can guarantee good outcomes in all possible economies. Rather successful monetary policy can be crafted only after taking into account the ever-changing beliefs and behaviour of the private sector.

Conclusion

We have shown that inertia in expectations and responsiveness of policy can ensure the existence of equilibria with a positive value of money even if money is intrinsically valueless. Moreover, we have done so without assuming a transactions role of money, thereby assuring us that our results would remain relevant even in a world where technological progress is ensuring that a large class of assets can easily be converted into a medium of exchange at a very low cost.

However, the demonstration of existence of equilibrium in a single period is only a first step in the analysis of monetary economies. Further work needs to be done to understand how economies of the kind we have analysed would behave over a sequence of periods and whether this behaviour would actually induce the kind of inertial expectations that we have assumed in this study. This extension, however, requires a theory of how households update their expectation functions in the light of experience. While there does exist a literature looking at such processes of learning in macroeconomic models (Evans & Honkapohja, 2001; Sargent, 1999), there is as yet no model of learning, which is either overwhelming supported by empirical evidence or broad enough to cover most reasonable forms of learning behaviour. Thus, it seems that the extension of our model to many periods must await further progress in our understanding of economic learning.

Proofs

The Budget Correspondence

Definition 4. For household h, the budget correspondence is a set-valued function of p, given, for $p \geq 0$ by

$$B^h(p) = \{(x_0, x_1) \in \mathbb{R}^2_+ \mid px_0 + \eta(p)x_1 \leq M^h(p)\}.$$

We now establish some properties of this correspondence. In what follows, we omit the subscript h for the household when this is not likely to cause any confusion.

Lemma 2. $B(p)$ is compact for all $p > 0$.

Proof. Since $x_1 \geq 0$,

$$x_0 \leq M(p)/p.$$

Similarly, since $x_0 \geq 0$,

$$x_1 \leq M(p)/\eta(p).$$

Thus, $B(p)$ is bounded.

We now show that $B(p)$ is also closed by showing that every convergent sequence in $B(p)$ converges to a point of $B(p)$. Let (x_0^n, x_1^n) be a sequence in $B(p)$ converging to (x_0, y_0). Since $(x_0^n, x_1^n) \in B(p)$,

$$p x_0^n + \eta(p) x_1^n \leq M(p).$$

Taking limits, we have

$$p x_0 + \eta(p) x_1 \leq M(p).$$

Hence, (x_0, y_0) also belongs to $B(p)$.

Being a closed and bounded subset of an Euclidean space, $B(p)$ is compact.

Lemma 3. If p^n is a sequence of prices that converge to p and $(x_0^n, x_1^n) \in B(p^n)$ is a sequence of consumption plans that converge to (x_0, x_1), then $(x_0, x_1) \in B(p)$.

Proof. From the definition of $B(p^n)$, we have

$$p^n x_0^n + \eta(p^n) x_1^n \leq M(p^n).$$

Taking limits and making use of the continuity of $M(\cdot)$ and $\eta(\cdot)$, we have

$$p x_0 + \eta(p) x_1 \leq M(p).$$

From which it follows that

$$(x_0, x_1) \in B(p).$$

Lemma 4. If p^n is a sequence of prices that converge to p and $(x_0, y_0) \in B(p)$, then there is a sequence (x_0^n, y_0^n) such that $\lim(x_0^n, x_1^n) = (x_0, x_1)$, and there is a number N such that for $n > N$, $(x_0^n, x_1^n) \in B(p_n)$.

Proof. We denote the expected cost of a particular consumption plan (x, y) at current price $q > 0$ by the function

$$f(q, x, y) = qx + \eta(q) y.$$

The function $f(\cdot)$ has the following properties:

1. $f(q, \lambda x, \lambda y) = \lambda f(q, x, y)$.
2. $f(q, x, y)$ is continuous: since $\eta(\cdot)$ is.
3. $f(q, x, y) \geq 0$.
4. $f(q, x, y) = 0$ if and only if $x = y = 0$.

Using $f(\cdot)$, we can write the consumer's budget set as

$$B(q) = \{(x,y) \in \mathbb{R}_+^2 \mid f(q,x,y) - M(q) \leq 0\}.$$

Now, we construct the sequence required by the lemma.

If $x_0 = y_0 = 0$, then we let $N=1$ and $(x_0^n, y_0^n) = (0,0)$ for all n. Since $(0,0) \in B(p^n)$ for all n and $\lim(0,0) = (0,0) = (x_0, y_0)$, so this sequence satisfies all the requirements.

Otherwise, let

$$\lambda_n = \frac{f(p, x_0, y_0) - M(p) + M(p^n)}{f(p^n, x_0, y_0)} \tag{13.4}$$

and

$$(x_0^n, x_1^n) = (\lambda_n x_0, \lambda_n y_0).$$

Since $M(\cdot)$ is continuous, $p^n \to p$ and $f(p,x,y) > 0$, we can find an N such that for $n > N$,

$$M(p) - M(p^n) < f(p,x,y).$$

From (13.4), this implies that for $n > N$, $\lambda > 0$.

We claim that N and (x_0^n, x_1^n) satisfy the requirements of the lemma.

For $n > N$,

$$\begin{aligned}
f(p^n, x_0^n, x_1^n) - M(p^n) &= f(p^n, \lambda_n x_0, \lambda_n x_1) - M(p^n) \\
&= \lambda_n f(p^n, x_0, x_1) - M(p^n) \\
&= f(p, x_0, x_1) - M(p) + M(p_n) - M(p^n) \\
&= f(p, x_0, x_1) - M(p) \\
&\leq 0 \text{ since } (x_0, x_1) \in B(p)
\end{aligned}$$

Thus, $(x_0^n, x_1^n) \in B(p^n)$ for $n > N$.

Also, $\lim(x_0^n, x_1^n) = (x_0, x_1)$ since $\lim \lambda_n = 1$ by the continuity of $f(\cdot)$ and $M(\cdot)$.

Individual Optimisation

Definition 5. If the solution to the household's maximisation problem

$$\max_{(x_0, x_1) \in B^h(p)} u^h(x_0, x_1)$$

is (x_0, x_1), then we define $d^h(p) = (x_0, x_1)$ and $d_0^h(p) = x_0$ and $d_1^h(p) = x_1$.

Since $B(p)$ is compact and $u_h(\cdot)$ is continuous, this maximisation problem has a solution. Since $u_h(\cdot, \cdot)$ is strictly quasi-concave, this solution is unique. Hence, the functions $d^h(\cdot)$, $d_0^h(\cdot)$ and $d_1^h(\cdot)$ are well defined.

Lemma 5. If p_n is a sequence such that $\lim p_n = p$ and the optimal consumption bundles $(x_0^n, x_1^n) = d(p_n)$ converge to (x_0, x_1), then $d(p) = (x_0, x_1)$.

Proof. By lemma 3, (x_0, x_1) belongs to $B(p)$.

Let (z_0, z_1) be an arbitrary bundle in $B(p)$. By lemma 4, there exists N and a sequence (z_0^n, z_1^n) such that $(z_0^n, z_1^n) \in B(p_n)$ for $n > N$ and $\lim(z_0^n, z_1^n) = (z_0, z_1)$.

Since $(x_0^n, x_1^n) = d(p_n)$ is the optimal bundle in $B(p_n)$ and it is the case that $(z_0^n, z_1^n) \in B(p_n)$ for $n > N$, it follows that for $n > N$,

$$u(x_0^n, x_1^n) \geq u(z_0^n, z_1^n).$$

Taking limits on both sides and using the continuity of $u(\cdot)$, we have

$$u(x_0, x_1) \geq u(z_0, z_1).$$

Since (z_0, z_1) was chosen to be an arbitrary point in $B(p)$, it follows that (x_0, x_1) is the optimal point in $B(p)$, that is, $d(p) = (x_0, x_1)$.

Lemma 6. The demand function $d(p)$ is continuous.

Proof. Let $p^n > 0$ be a sequence of prices converging to p. We shall prove that $\lim d(p)$ exists and is equal to $d(p)$.

We proceed by contradiction. Suppose $d(p^n)$ does not converge to $d(p)$. Then, there must be a $\varepsilon > 0$ and a subsequence p^{n_k} of p^n such that

$$|d(p^{n_k}) - d(p)| > \varepsilon. \tag{13.5}$$

We choose an arbitrary $0 < \delta < \min(p, \eta(p))$. Since $\lim p_n = p$ and $\eta(\cdot)$ and $M(\cdot)$ are continuous, there must exists an N such that for $n > N$,

$$p_n \geq p - \delta,$$
$$\eta(p_n) \geq \eta(p) - \delta,$$
$$M(p_n) \leq M(p) + \delta.$$

Since $x_1^n \geq 0$, $x_0^n \leq (M(p) + \delta)/(p - \delta)$ for $n > N$. Similarly, since $x_0^n \geq 0$, $x_1^n \leq (M(p) + \delta)/(\eta(p) - \delta)$ for $n > N$. This means that $d(p^n)$ and, hence, $d(p^{n_k})$, must be bounded. Being a bounded subset of an Euclidean space, it must have a convergent subsequence. Let us call this subsequence $d(p^{n_j})$. Since p^{n_j} is a subsequence of p^n and hence converges to p, $d(p^{n_j})$ satisfies the conditions of lemma 3 and hence must converge to $d(p)$. However, as $d(p^{n_j})$ is a subsequence of $d(p^{n_k})$, this contradicts (13.5).

Lemma 7. The excess demand function $d_0(p)$ is continuous.

Proof. Since $d_0(p)$ is just the first component of the continuous function $d(p)$, it must be continuous. The excess demand function is given by

$$\zeta^h(p) = d_0^h(p) - \omega_0^h$$

and, hence, it must be continuous too.

Aggregate Demand

Lemma 8. As $p \to 0$, $\zeta(p) \to \infty$.

Proof. We know that there is at least one household with $D^h < 0$. We begin by analysing the aggregate demand of such households.

Suppose p^n is a sequence with $\lim p^n = 0$. Since $0 < L \leq \eta(p^n) < U$ by assumption 2, $\eta(p^n)$ is a bounded sequence and must have a convergent subsequence. We assume that such a convergent subsequence has been chosen so that

$$\lim \eta(p_n) = p_1 \text{ (say)},$$

where

$$0 < L \leq p_1 \leq U.$$

Let $(x_0^n, x_1^n) = d(p_0^n)$ be the corresponding optimal bundles. We first show that the sequence (x_0^n, x_1^n) must be unbounded.

If $(x_0^n, x_1^n) = d(p^n)$ is bounded, then it must have a convergent subsequence $(x_0^{n_k}, x_1^{n_k})$. Let the limit of this convergent subsequence be (x_0, x_1). Since $D < 0$, this particular household can never go bankrupt, and therefore his budget constraint is always

$$p^{n_k} x_0 + \eta(p^{n_k}) x_1 \leq p^{n_k} \omega_0 + \eta(p^{n_k}) \omega_1 - D.$$

Taking limits, we have

$$p_1 x_1 \leq p_1 \omega_1 - D. \tag{13.6}$$

Choose some $\lambda \in (0,1)$ and let

$$x_0^\lambda = \lambda(x_0 + 1), \quad x_1^\lambda = \lambda x_1.$$

Note that since $D < 0$, the right-hand side of (13.6) is strictly positive. Therefore, if (13.6) holds with equality, then $p_1 x_1 > 0$ and hence

$$p_1 x_1^\lambda = \lambda p_1 x_1 < p_1 x_1 = p_1 \omega_1 - D.$$

On the other hand, if (13.6) holds with strict inequality, then

$$p_1 x_1^\lambda = \lambda p_1 x_1 \leq p_1 x_1 < p_1 \omega_1 - D.$$

In either case,

$$p_1 x_1^\lambda < p_1 \omega_1 - D$$

or
$$p_1(x_1^\lambda - \omega_1) < -D.$$

Since $p^n \to 0$ and $\eta(p^n) \to p_1$, we can use continuity to argue from the above that there is some K such that for $k > K$,
$$p^{n_k}(x_0^\lambda - \omega_0) + \eta(p^{n_k})(x_1^\lambda - \omega_1) < -D,$$

which means that $(x_0^\lambda, x_1^\lambda) \in B(p^{n_k})$. From the definition of $(x_0^{n_k}, x_1^{n_k}) = d(p^{n_k})$, it follows that
$$u(x_0^{n_k}, x_1^{n_k}) \geq u(x_0^\lambda, x_1^\lambda).$$

Taking limits and using the continuity of $u(\cdot)$, we have
$$u(x_0, x_1) \geq u(x_0^\lambda, x_1^\lambda)$$

or
$$u(x_0, x_1) \geq u(\lambda(x_0 + 1), \lambda x_1).$$

Since this is true for all $\lambda \in (0,1)$, we substitute $\lambda_i = (1 - 1/i)$ for $i = 2, 3, \ldots$, in the above inequality and take limits to get
$$u(x_0, x_1) \geq u(x_0 + 1, x_1).$$

This contradicts our assumption that $u(\cdot)$ is strictly monotonic. Hence, it must be the case that (x_0^n, x_1^n) is unbounded.

Now, we show that it is in fact x_0 that must become unbounded.
Recall the form of the budget constraint
$$px_0 + \eta(p)x_1 \leq p\omega_0 + \eta(p)\omega_1 - D.$$

Since $L \leq \eta(p) \leq U$, $x_1 \geq 0$ and $\omega_1 > 0$,
$$px_0 + Lx_1 \leq p\omega_0 + B\omega_1 - D.$$

Or, as $x_0 \geq 0$,
$$x_1 \leq \frac{p\omega_0 + B\omega_1 - D}{L}.$$

Hence, x_1 cannot become unbounded as p^n tends to 0, and it must be x_0 that becomes unbounded.

We have seen that the excess demand of households with $D_h < 0$ goes to infinity as p tends to 0. On the other hand, the excess demands of all households are bounded below since consumption cannot be non-negative. Hence, the aggregate excess demand $\zeta(\cdot)$ must go to infinity.

Lemma 9. As $p \to \infty$, $d_1(p) \to \infty$.

Proof. Suppose p^n is a sequence with $\lim p^n = \infty$. Let $(x_0^n, x_1^n) = d(p_0^n)$ be the corresponding optimal bundles. We first show that the sequence (x_0^n, x_1^n) must be unbounded.

If $(x_0^n, x_1^n) = d(p^n)$ is bounded, then it must have a convergent subsequence $(x_0^{n_k}, x_1^{n_k})$. Let the limit of this convergent subsequence be (x_0, x_1). For a sufficiently high price, no household goes bankrupt and therefore we can write the budget constraint as

$$p^{n_k} x_0 + \eta(p^{n_k}) x_1 \leq p^{n_k} \omega_0 + \eta(p^{n_k}) \omega_1 - D$$

or

$$x_0 + \frac{\eta(p^{n_k})}{p^{n_k}} x_1 \leq \omega_0 + \frac{\eta(p^{n_k})}{p^{n_k}} \omega_1 - \frac{D}{p^{n_k}}.$$

Taking limits and using the fact that $\eta(p) < B$,

$$x_0 \leq \omega_0. \tag{13.7}$$

Choose some $\lambda \in (0, 1)$ and let

$$x_0^\lambda = \lambda x_0, \quad x_1^\lambda = \lambda(x_1 + 1).$$

Note that since by assumption $\omega_0 > 0$, the right-hand side of (13.7) is strictly positive. Therefore, if (13.7) holds with equality, then $x_0 > 0$ and hence

$$x_0^\lambda = \lambda x_0 < x_0 = \omega_0.$$

On the other hand, if (13.7) holds with strict inequality, then

$$x_0^\lambda = \lambda x_0 \leq x_0 < \omega_0.$$

In either case,

$$x_0^\lambda < \omega_0$$

or

$$(x_0^\lambda - \omega_0) < 0.$$

Since $\eta(p^{n_k}) / p^{n_k} \to 0$, we can use continuity to argue from the above that there is some K such that for $k > K$,

$$(x_0^\lambda - \omega_0) + \frac{\eta(p^{n_k})}{p^{n_k}}(x_1^\lambda - \omega_1) < -\frac{D}{p^{n_k}},$$

which means that $(x_0^\lambda, x_1^\lambda) \in B(p^{n_k})$. From the definition of $(x_0^{n_k}, x_1^{n_k}) = d(p^{n_k})$, it follows that

$$u(x_0^{n_k}, x_1^{n_k}) \geq u(x_0^\lambda, x_1^\lambda).$$

Taking limits and using the continuity of $u(\cdot)$, we have

$$u(x_0, x_1) \geq u(x_0^\lambda, x_1^\lambda)$$

or

$$u(x_0, x_1) \geq u(\lambda x_0), \lambda(x_1 + 1).$$

Since this is true for all $\lambda \in (0, 1)$, we substitute $\lambda_i = (1 - 1/i)$ for $i = 2, 3, \ldots$, in the above inequality and take limits to get

$$u(x_0, x_1) \geq u(x_0, x_1 + 1).$$

This contradicts our assumption that $u(\cdot)$ is strictly monotonic. Hence, it must be the case that (x_0^n, x_1^n) is unbounded.

Now, we show that it is, in fact, x_1 that must become unbounded.

Recall the form of the budget constraint

$$px_0 + \eta(p)x_1 \leq p\omega_0 + \eta(p)p_1 - D.$$

Since $L \leq \eta(p) \leq U$, $x_1 \geq 0$ and $\omega_1 > 0$,

$$px_0 + Lx_1 \leq p\omega_0 + B\omega_1 - D.$$

Or, as $x_1 \geq 0$,

$$x_0 \leq \omega_0 + \frac{B\omega_1 - D}{pL}.$$

Hence, x_0 cannot become unbounded as $p^n \to \infty$, and it must be x_1 that becomes unbounded.

Hence, the result is proved.

Lemma 10. There is a $p > 0$ such that $\zeta(p) < 0$.

Proof. For sufficiently high prices, no household goes bankrupt, and we can write the budget constraint as

$$px_0 + \eta(p)x_1 \leq p\omega_0 + \eta(p)\omega_1 - D$$

or

$$p(x_0 - \omega_0) \leq \eta(p)(\omega_1 - x_1) - D.$$

We know from lemma 9 that the right-hand side becomes negative as $p \to \infty$. Hence, for a sufficiently large $\bar{p}$, it must be the case that

$$x_0 < \omega_0.$$

Repeating this analysis for all the H households and taking p greater than the largest of $\bar{p}$ for all households, the result is proved.

Proof of Theorem 1. Follows from using lemmas 8 and 9 to apply the intermediate-value theorem to the continuous function $\zeta(\cdot)$.

References

Evans, G.W., & Honkapohja, S. (2001). *Learning and expectations in macroeconomics.* Princeton, NJ: Princeton University Press.

Grandmont, J.M. (1977). Temporary general equilibrium theory. *Econometrica, 45,* 535–572.

———. (1983). *Money and value: A reconsideration of classical and neoclassical monetary theories.* Cambridge: Cambridge University Press.

Grandmont, J.M., & Younes, Y. (1972). On the role of money and the existence of monetary equilibria. *Review of Economic Studies, 39*(3), 355–372.

Sargent, T.J. (1999). *The conquest of American inflation.* Princeton, NJ: Princeton University Press.

Woodford, M. (2003). *Interest and prices: Foundations of a theory of monetary policy.* Princeton, NJ: Princeton University Press.

14

Stock Markets, Finance and Development: A View from History

Vineet Kohli

Stock Markets Versus Banks in Development: An Introductory Overview

In *A Theory of Economic History,* Hicks explored the relationship between stock market liquidity and economic development. According to Hicks (1969), much of the investment in the pre-industrial revolution period was in trade, where capital was circulating in nature. A bill of exchange would arise on the day of the sale and mature in a short period of time when the buyer received the shipment. With industry, however, things were different; industry required heavy doses of fixed capital that could only be recovered gradually in the form of profits earned over many years. Unlike merchants, industrial capitalists, therefore, had to remain illiquid for a much longer period of time. England, argued Hicks, was well suited to solve this problem because of the existence of developed stock markets on the eve of the industrial revolution. Markets provided liquidity to investors even as firms continued to hold fixed assets. Liquid stock markets, according to Hicks, were a precondition for the successful industrialisation of England.

Based on insights from Hicks (1969) on English industrialisation, Levine (1996) and Levine and Zervos (1998), among many other mainstream economists, have become vocal advocates of stock market development in less developed countries. Many such countries, including, as Singh (1999) pointed out, some of the poorest located in sub-Saharan Africa, have taken this policy advice very seriously.

Hicks (1969), it may be pointed out, never believed that the English experience with regard to stock market development needed to be replicated elsewhere. He only drew attention to the illiquidity barrier to development, which the banks were equally capable of surmounting but which, in the English case, was overcome through the creation of liquid stock markets:

> In order that people should be willing, in an uncertain world, to sink huge amounts of capital, they must either themselves be in possession of other resources, which they hold in a more liquid form, so that they can be quickly realized to meet emergencies, or they must be confident of being able to borrow–and that means borrowing from someone else (*it may be a bank*) who is able to borrow, or who has funds. In the end it is the availability of liquid funds that matters. (Hicks, 1969: 144–45, emphasis added)

What matters for economic development is liquidity, which the banks are as capable of providing as markets. Banks provide deposits that can be withdrawn freely (or at a short notice) while themselves making loans that are illiquid. They also provide credit lines to firms to meet their requirements of liquidity. Recent interpreters of Hicks, who insist on developing liquid stock markets, can be charged of a prejudice that Hicks never intended.

Seven years before Hicks' work appeared, Gerschenkron (1962) drew attention to the salutary role of large universal banks in the industrialisation of continental Europe. He argued that industrial development in a backward country differs from the past experience of already advanced countries, not only in terms of the speed and character of that development but also in the "application of institutional instruments for which there was little or no counterpart in an established industrial country" (Gerschenkron, 1962: 7). One such institutional arrangement, the use of which Gerschenkron emphasised, was long-term lending by German universal banks to industry in the nineteenth century. England, which industrialised before Germany, did not require the utilisation of banking for long-term investment because of the "more gradual character of the industrialisation process and more considerable accumulation of capital, first from earnings in trade and modern agriculture and later from industry itself" (Gerschenkron, 1962: 14). Direct interaction between lenders and borrowers in a financial market would have been difficult at this stage of German development due to distrust of industrial activities. The German experience of long-term industrial banking was also imitated in the European late developers of the nineteenth century like Austria, Italy, Switzerland, France and Belgium and, outside the European continent, in Japan.

This contrast between the British financial system, where most of the funds were either internally generated by the firms or obtained through the stock markets, and financial systems in late developers, where banks provided industrial finance, has been a starting point of some of the most celebrated studies on the interaction between financial systems and economic development.[1] Yet, in recent years, research has emerged that doubts this distinction. In particular, it has been argued that stock markets were much more important in the so-called bank-based systems like Germany and Japan than has so far been understood. This view emerged most forcefully in the historical account of finance produced by Rajan and Zingales (2003, 2004). Their account can be summarised in the following inter-related claims.

1. The distinction between bank-based and stock market-based financial systems is a relatively new one. Before the World War I, all economies, including those of continental Europe and Japan, possessed strong stock markets as, for example, indicated by high market capitalisation ratios and large number of stock market listings. Similar views have also been aired in the historical accounts of finance in Germany and Japan by Fohlin (2007) and Hoshi and Kashyap (2001), respectively.
2. Stock markets best flourish when economies are open to trade and capital flows. Strong stock market indicators before the World War I were an outcome of openness to trade and capital flows characteristic of the gold-standard era. As liberal policies towards trade and capital flows fell victim to the Bretton Woods regime, stock markets suffered, borrowing the phrase from Rajan and Zingales, a great reversal. Moreover, the reversal was more prominent in continental Europe than in the US and the UK.
3. Whereas bank-based systems concentrate credit in the hands of a few who possess collateral and enjoy close personal connections with financiers, market-based systems, based on property rights and public disclosure of information, tend to democratise access to finance.

---

[1] See, for example, Zysman (1983), who clearly distinguished between market-based system in the US and the UK and bank-based system in Germany, France and Japan.

The rest of this chapter would scrutinise the revisionist account of finance proposed by Rajan and Zingales and also make some general historical observations on the connection between stock markets and development.

Did Liberal Trade and Capital Flows Aid Stock Market Development?

Rajan and Zingales proposed an interest group theory of financial development to explain why liberal trade and capital flows should aid the stock market development. We first air our misgivings about their theoretical framework before producing some contrary evidence from history.

According to Rajan and Zingales, in the absence of strong property rights and public disclosure, lenders would not like to spread credit beyond the close circle of borrowers with whom they enjoy close ties. Close ties can be useful at the time of repayment and in generating valuable information about borrowers. Lack of property rights and information disclosure therefore becomes a source of market power, which the incumbents seek to protect by blocking efforts to develop a strong financial system based on respect for investors' rights and transparency. The opposition by the incumbents to stronger property rights and greater transparency, argued Rajan and Zingales, could be muted by an economy's openness to trade and capital flows. For example, 'discipline' imposed by capital flows may erode a government's ability to direct finance to incumbent firms through fiscal and monetary policy tools. In these circumstances, well-established industrial firms would like to attract finance from foreign investors who may require stronger protection under law as a condition for their investments. Rajan and Zingales further argued that over the course of the twentieth century, stock markets waxed and waned in accordance with the movement in trade and capital flows. High stock market indicators of 1913 were an outcome of openness to trade and capital flows that was characteristic of the gold-standard era. However, from the 1930s, financial markets entered a long period of decline as liberal policies towards trade and capital flows fell victim, first, to the Great Depression and, subsequently, to the Bretton Woods regime.

In Rajan and Zingales's theory, while incumbents can act together to block financial development, those refused access to finance, being large in numbers, cannot act as an interest group towards aiding stock market development. As Rajan and Zingales argued, this is a straightforward application of Olson's (1971) theory of collective action. However, the interest group theory of financial development proposed by Rajan and Zingales appears unconvincing. The government creates legal infrastructure of markets; it also decides on the degree of openness of the economy through its trade, industrial and financial policies. It is not clear why incumbents collectively act to block financial development directly but fail to do so when a government seeks to achieve the same goal indirectly, through liberalisation of trade and capital flows. Therefore, Rajan and Zingales's application of Olson's theory is selective.

The fact of the matter is that governments do possess a certain ability to act independently of the influence of powerful interest groups (Booth, 1978). The expression of such independence may not take the form preferred by Rajan and Zingales, namely in the creation of a liberal regime of trade and capital flows. Governments may exercise their independence from powerful interest groups to directly create stock market based on property rights and transparency or, what has been a preferred route, to improve access to finance of excluded groups through non-market means. An example would be the Indian government's decision to nationalise banks and administratively direct credit to small borrowers in 1969. This move was certainly to the detriment of big industrial houses that had until then controlled the Indian banking system and monopolised most of the credit that the latter had advanced.

Another example, from a more distant history, comes from Germany. There, besides large universal banks, savings and cooperative banks occupied an important place; by 1900, savings banks were the largest segment of the German banking system (Deeg, 2003; Edwards & Ogilvie, 1996). Both savings and cooperative banks lent to small craftsmen, workers and farmers. This, in turn, influenced the pattern of industrial growth through the creation of a large number of sole proprietorships, partnership firms and small private companies (Edwards & Ogilvie, 1996). What is of direct interest to us is that at various moments in German economic history, the government, sometimes through favourable legislation and, on other occasions, through outright incentives, supported both savings and cooperative banks (Deeg, 2003).[2] The moot question is as follows: why did the government act to benefit politically unorganised and scattered group of small-scale industrial and agricultural borrowers? Deeg (2003: 93) provided a simple answer in the form of the order-preserving role of the German state:

> The conjunctural pressures of industrialization, liberalism, and nascent socialism threatened to disrupt the existing social order and thus undermine political control by the state. In light of this the savings banks began to appear to the states—Prussia and Bavaria above all—as an ideal instrument to prevent the growth of a radical underclass by supporting production in agriculture and small firms [...]. (Deeg, 2003: 93)

Another major hurdle to Rajan and Zingales's interest group theory of financial development has been posed by the movements in openness and investor-friendly laws and institutions over the course of the twentieth century. The US, for example, had no federal laws for the protection of shareholders until 1933. Such protection as was available to shareholders at the state level was progressively weakened from about 1885 as states competed with each other to make their territories attractive to companies. As a result, "the statutory rights accorded to shareholders substantially diminished during the period 1885–1930" (O'Sullivan, 2007: 529). Coffee (2001) argued that the weakness of laws could be overcome through private initiatives of the New York Stock Exchange (NYSE) that stipulated disclosure requirements and provided listing to only large and well-established companies.[3] However, as O'Sullivan (2007) pointed out, a large number of stocks that were not admitted for listing in the NYSE could easily be traded outside the exchange on curb market. Competition from the curb market forced the NYSE to provide trading space to unlisted stocks, which continued until 1910.[4] Rajan and Zingales acknowledged the improvements in shareholder protection in the US brought about by the Securities Act of 1933 but insisted that the US was an outlier to the general trend of the deterioration of market-friendly institutions observed in the post-Great Depression period.[5]

---

[2] A good example of such support is the establishment of Preussenkasse, a central bank for all credit co-operatives in 1895. Preussenkasse gave subsidy to member cooperatives by borrowing deposits from them at higher than market interest rate and lending to them at below market rate (Deeg, 2003).

[3] Rajan and Zingales, however, argued that private initiatives cannot fully replace government in creating the legal infrastructure for market since only "government has the ability to coordinate standards and enforce non-monetary punishments such as jail terms" (2003: 14).

[4] Markham (2002: 4) described the unlisted department of the NYSE in the following manner: An unlisted department allowed trading in securities of corporations that refused to furnish any substantial information as to their business and which, therefore, could not be admitted to the regular list. The Amalgamated Copper Company and the American Sugar Refining Company were two such unlisted securities. Those companies were dealt in on the Exchange for many years without the public having any information regarding their affairs. They were in effect conducted and maintained as blind pools.

[5] Rajan and Zingales argued that the US could escape anti-market trends, unleashed after the Great Depression in other parts of the world, because of the political opposition to concentration of power within the American financial system. However, if this opposition (to concentration of power) was an enduring feature of the American financial system, it is not clear why the pro-market measures were adopted only after the Great Depression and not before it, as Rajan and Zingales's theory suggested.

However, the UK appears to have followed a more or less the similar path of greater market development in spite of opposing trends in trade and capital openness (Cheffins, 2003). Until about the 1940s, shareholders did not enjoy much legal protection in the UK. Directors' duties towards shareholders were not enunciated in law. Legal recourse to shareholders through derivative suits was also not easily available. Equally disquieting was the state of disclosure requirements. For example, until 1908, there was no formal requirement for companies to file a balance sheet and not before 1929 were companies required to provide information on current earnings to the Board. On the other hand, some gains in legal protection and especially in disclosure requirements were secured by the Company Act of 1948 that, for the first time in UK's business history, made it mandatory for companies to publicly file annual profit and loss statement. All in all, the shift towards greater investor protection and disclosure requirements became noticeable from the 1930s in the US and the 1940s in the UK, that is, much after the liberal capital and trade flow regimes of the gold standard were destroyed by the Great Depression. The claim that openness improves the institutional infrastructure for stock market development appears implausible on this reading of history.

Was Early Twentieth Century a Golden Age of Stock Markets?

Rajan and Zingales examined various indicators of stock market development, such as market capitalisation ratio, equity issues as a percentage of capital formation and number of listed companies and concluded that most economies possessed more developed stock markets in 1913 than they did in 1980. Their data revealed that market capitalisation ratio in France fell from 0.78 in 1913 to 0.09 by 1980; over the same period, it fell from 0.44 to 0.09 in Germany and 0.49 to 0.33 in Japan. The fall in market capitalisation ratio was much less pronounced in the UK, whereas the US witnessed an increase from 0.39 in 1913 to 0.46 by 1980. Only by the end of the 1980s did stock markets recover the position they had lost during the Bretton Woods period. Moreover, Rajan and Zingales's data revealed that both Germany and Japan had more developed stock market indicators than the US in 1913. They conclude that the distinction between continental Europe and Anglo-American countries is not confirmed by early data.

Rajan and Zingales's empirical claims have been questioned by Sylla (2006), who suggested that the size of US stock markets in 1913 was probably underestimated due to the non-inclusion of figures related to the curb and over-the-counter exchanges. This could have distorted Rajan and Zingales's analysis by making other countries appear more market based than the US in 1913. It may also have exaggerated the relative decline of stock markets outside the US after 1913. Sylla's suggestion was to use figures provided by Goldsmith (1985) that, he believed, were more dependable. In the following, we pursue Sylla's advice to examine the movement of stock markets in different countries using Goldsmith's estimates.

Table 14.1 gives market capitalisation to gross national product (GNP) ratio for 11 countries for which information is available in Goldsmith (1985) from 1875 onwards. Goldsmith's data also revealed a sharp decline in the average market capitalisation ratio in 1978 from its 1913 levels. However, in 1913, the US certainly appeared more market based than France or Germany. Moreover, Rajan and Zingales's claim that the decline was more pronounced in, what are today perceived as, bank-based economies failed to hold on a scrutiny of Goldsmith's data. Spearman's rank correlation coefficient between market capitalisation ratios in 1913 and 1978 is positive and statistically significant. The value of rank correlation coefficient is in fact very high at 0.782, and the P value is 0.0134. In other words, the ranking of different countries did not change much between these two time periods.

However, it may not be correct to rely on market capitalisation ratio for making an informed judgement about the size of stock markets. The reason is that market capitalisation ratio may fluctuate

Table 14.1
Ratio of Market Capitalisation to GNP

	1875	1895	1913	1929	1939	1950	1965	1973	1978
Belgium	0.64	0.58	0.87	0.69	0.34	0.32	0.24	0.18	0.18
Denmark	0.64	0.74	0.88	1.26	0.66	0.39	0.33	0.29	0.28
France	0.39		0.66	0.23		0.25	1.08	0.58	0.39
Germany	0.16	0.23	0.45	0.35	0.21	0.18	0.48	0.38	0.38
Great Britain	0.58	1.56	1.21	1.54	1.82	1.10	0.83	0.64	0.76
India	0.02	0.03	0.05	0.09	0.14	0.12	0.14	0.13	0.12
Italy	0.07	0.11	0.06	0.27	0.25	0.19	0.57	0.27	0.10
Japan	0.04	0.32	0.41	0.76	1.18	0.24	0.46	0.28	0.39
Norway	0.14	0.27	0.40	0.47	0.28	0.11	0.33	0.22	0.21
Switzerland	0.80	0.82	1.23	1.37	1.49	1.26	1.16	0.69	1.02
US	0.54	1.02	0.95	1.94	1.05	0.58	1.25	0.79	0.78
Mean	0.36	0.57	0.65	0.81	0.74	0.43	0.62	0.40	0.42
Median	0.39	0.45	0.66	0.69	0.50	0.25	0.48	0.29	0.38

Source: Author's calculations based on Table 15 (p. 37) and Table 57 (p. 153) of Goldsmith (1985).

with no change in stock market's ability to perform its fundamental function of funding long-lived assets.[6] A better indicator of stock market size would therefore be market capitalisation relative to the size of long-lived assets. Fortunately, since Goldsmith provided an estimate of the value of structures and equipment at different dates, such an exercise appears within our range. Table 14.2 provides information on the market value of corporate shares as a ratio of structures and equipment at different dates in the sample of countries for which information could be obtained since 1875.

Table 14.2 also fails to confirm Rajan and Zingales's hypothesis. Not only did the US have more developed stock markets in 1913 than, say, Germany or France, but the subsequent decline in the size of stock markets between 1913 and 1978 was more pronounced in Great Britain and the US than France and Germany. If we remove Great Britain and the US from our sample of countries in Table 14.2, mean value for the remaining countries is higher in 1965 than in 1913. Only in 1978 do we find a sharp decline in the size of stock markets in this sub-sample. The 'great reversal' hypothesis does not stand the scrutiny of different benchmark dates and other indicators, than the one used by Rajan and Zingales.

Finally, let us look at the size of the financial sector relative to the real sector of the economy. Table 14.3 lists the share of financial assets in national assets (defined as the sum of financial assets, tangible assets and monetary metals) using Goldsmith's data. The results are startling. The extent of financial deepening had in fact increased between 1913 and 1978. The mean value of the ratio of financial to national assets increased from 0.40 in 1913 to 0.45 in 1978; financial deepening increased until 1929 before levelling off in subsequent years. The claim that the shift to capital controls harmed financial sector is hard to maintain. Moreover, in the 50 years or so after 1929, there were some incredible examples of financial deepening. There was Italy, where the ratio of financial to national assets increased by 25 per cent between 1929 and 1978, and India, where the increase over the period was an incredible 80 per cent.

---

[6] With the same amount of fixed capital, an economy can produce more output due to improvements in capacity technical output capital ratio or, when capacity is underutilised, through improvements in capacity utilisation.

Table 14.2
Ratio of Market Capitalisation to Value of Structures and Equipment

	1875	1895	1913	1929	1939	1950	1965	1973	1978
Belgium	0.13	0.11	0.19	0.17	0.08	0.10	0.07	0.07	0.05
Denmark	0.59	0.45	0.47	0.62	0.28	0.14	0.14	0.14	0.09
France	0.21		0.40	0.13		0.22	1.18	0.63	0.36
Germany	0.07	0.13	0.14	0.09	0.08	0.08	0.35	0.15	0.15
Great Britain	0.33	1.23	0.90	1.23	1.57	0.86	0.58	0.36	0.26
India	0.01	0.02	0.04	0.05	0.08	0.09	0.06	0.06	0.04
Italy	0.06	0.08	0.04	0.16	0.13	0.11	0.39	0.23	0.07
Japan	0.03	0.26	0.33	0.56	0.83	0.37	0.47	0.29	0.28
Norway	0.08	0.15	0.18	0.23	0.14	0.05	0.04	0.03	0.02
Switzerland	0.20	0.30	0.36	0.44	0.35	0.29	0.35	0.45	0.27
US	0.49	0.54	0.74	1.36	0.73	0.51	0.81	0.48	0.41
Mean	0.20	0.33	0.35	0.46	0.43	0.26	0.40	0.26	0.18
Median	0.13	0.20	0.33	0.23	0.21	0.14	0.35	0.23	0.15

Source: Author's calculations based on country tables provided by Goldsmith (1985, Appendix A).

Notes: 1. Structure and equipment include residential structures, factories, stores, offices, roads, rail tracks and sewage installations (Goldsmith, 1985: 126–127).
2. Wherever possible, we have excluded residential structures since households do not issue securities to acquire dwellings. Due to non-availability of data, for Denmark, India and Switzerland, structures include both residential and non-residential structures.
3. For Belgium, market capitalisation has been divided by reproducible tangible assets due to lack of availability of data. Reproducible tangible assets include, besides structures and equipment, inventories, livestock and consumer durables.

Table 14.3
Ratio of Financial Assets to National Assets

	1875	1895	1913	1929	1939	1950	1965	1973	1978
Belgium	0.28	0.30	0.39	0.38	0.39	0.41	0.39	0.43	0.40
Denmark	0.49	0.56	0.58	0.59	0.54	0.51	0.49	0.53	0.50
France	0.34	0.00	0.47	0.44	0.00	0.35	0.55	0.44	0.41
Germany	0.24	0.37	0.40	0.27	0.36	0.29	0.44	0.43	0.43
Great Britain	0.38	0.51	0.47	0.60	0.63	0.64	0.60	0.56	0.53
India	0.12	0.11	0.13	0.16	0.19	0.22	0.29	0.31	0.29
Italy	0.28	0.30	0.31	0.40	0.42	0.29	0.45	0.52	0.50
Japan	0.23	0.25	0.38	0.54	0.58	0.35	0.45	0.48	0.50
Norway	0.26	0.35	0.41	0.50	0.42	0.44	0.44	0.46	0.46
Switzerland	0.43	0.48	0.48	0.55	0.54	0.48	0.50	0.46	0.48
US	0.37	0.40	0.43	0.54	0.51	0.50	0.54	0.50	0.47
Mean	0.31	0.33	0.40	0.45	0.42	0.41	0.47	0.47	0.45
Median	0.28	0.35	0.41	0.50	0.42	0.41	0.45	0.46	0.47

Source: Country tables provided by Goldsmith (1985, Appendix A).

All in all, Goldsmith's data fail to confirm Rajan and Zingales's main contention that continental Europe and Japan possessed stronger stock markets than Anglo-Saxon economies in 1913 and suffered more prominent reversals over the course of the twentieth century.

Did Stock Markets Provide Liquidity, Share Risk and Facilitate Competition?

Stock markets are expected to contribute to development through three principal mechanisms. First, as pointed out in the beginning, liquidity provided by stock markets may encourage fixed capital investment. Second, as Rajan and Zingales have pointed out, stock market finance is not based on collateral requirements and personal connections with financiers and therefore serves to spread finance beyond the close group of incumbents. Thus, stock markets may aid development by encouraging competition. Finally, unlike banks or owners of debt claims in general, equity owners share risk. Simply put, whereas interest payments are committed in nature, dividend payments are compressible and that makes equity an attractive source of finance for firms. How far did stock markets play these roles historically? We discuss the cases of Japan and the US to answer this question.

Let us take the case of Japan first. Hoshi and Kashyap (2001) pointed out that stock and bond markets occupied a pride of place in the pre-World War II Japanese financial system. Similar views were echoed by Miwa and Ramseyer (2000) and Hamao, Hoshi and Okazaki (2005). To take one example, averaged over 1902–1915, paid-in capital and reserves accounted for 82 per cent of total liabilities of joint stock companies (Hoshi & Kashyap, 2001). Also, market capitalisation ratio was high, at 40 per cent in 1920 and reaching 95 per cent in 1940 (also see Table 14.1). In spite of these impressive indicators, the role of stock markets in liquidity provision and risk sharing was rather limited. The reason is that whereas corporations relied on equity finance, purchase of equity depended on the ability of equity owners to obtain bank finance (Ishii, 1991, 2007; Patrick, 1967; Tamaki, 1995). Typically, loans obtained by equity owners were secured by the collateral of equity shares.[7] Banks accepted the collateral of shares because the Bank of Japan provided advances against the security of these shares.[8] In other words, liquidity for holders of shares was underwritten by the central bank.

On the other hand, stock markets were dominated by speculative fixed-term trading where investors (usually) squared up their positions through offsetting transactions within the settlement period.[9] The settlement period for transactions was three months. Such transactions, whatever other purpose they may have served, did not provide immediate liquidity to the owners of fixed capital.[10] On the other hand, spot transactions were rare, accounting for one-fourth of total trading on the Tokyo Stock Exchange and less than 5 per cent of total trading on Osaka Stock Exchange during the Meiji period (Teranishi, 2007).

Shareholders' indebtedness to banks had another implication; it circumscribed their ability to share risk in the enterprise. Companies, apparently, were not in a position to adjust dividends much since "shareholders were anxious to have dividend payouts at least sufficient to cover interest charges on

---

[7] Ishii (2007: 78) reported that in 1896, two-thirds of all industrial shares were pledged to banks as security.
[8] In providing finance against equity shares, the Bank of Japan was apparently in violation of its statutes. It nevertheless continued to use this policy and expanded the number of securities eligible for rediscounting so as to provide liquidity to banks' portfolio (Tamaki, 1995).
[9] That is, purchases (sales) are offset by sales (purchases) of an equivalent amount within the settlement period. At the end of the settlement period, the difference between sale and purchase values is received or paid.
[10] Since settlement took place on a future date.

loans" (Patrick, 1967: 283). Companies could well have survived without payment of dividends but not their shareholders who were in debt to the banking system.

Finally, what about Rajan and Zingales's idea that stock markets facilitate competition and entry? Could anyone become an entrepreneur, undeterred by collateral requirements, by raising funds on the stock markets? The answer is a clear no. New companies were not formed on the basis of public issues but private placements to few founding investors (Teranishi, 2007). Founders could leverage their investments through the mechanism of equity-secured loans from the banking system, which meant that investment size was a function of equity offered as collateral. Thus, both banks and their collateral requirements played an important role in the Japanese financial system, a role that would remain unknown to anyone focusing on indicators of stock market size alone.

Let us now take the case of the US. Economic historians have written about the ability of the US to develop strong stock markets early in its development trajectory (Sylla, 1998). The development of stock markets in the US was mainly triggered by the constitutional reform of 1788 that included the consolidation of existing federal debt with that of the states, which was then made available for trading on markets. Besides, the reforms prevented the states from printing fiat money, which was an important source of finance in the earlier period. The states could continue to charter new banks, which they did in ample measure, to earn revenues. Charters were granted against bonus payments, and the states also reserved the right to purchase shares at par value: this right was exercised when firms became profitable and started paying dividends or sold in the market when states did not wish to exercise it (Sylla, Legler & Wallis, 1987). The main outcome of these reforms was that banks emerged as equity-issuing entities, whereas industrial firms became reliant on bank finance (Kregel, 2001).

As Sylla (1998) has pointed out, liquidity provided by organised stock markets was probably an important factor in making corporate stocks attractive to both domestic and foreign investors. The US charted a different path, from Germany[11] and Japan, where markets were indeed important in liquidity provision. But it is interesting to note that the demand for bank charters arose not from people with independent interest in banking business but businesspersons engaged in manufacturing activities (Lamoreaux, 1986). Typically, a group of capitalists connected to each other through kinship, came together to float a bank. Over time, these capitalists reduced their share of ownership in banks but still remained firmly in control of its operations. Banks became engines to supply finance to insiders. Theoretically, those excluded by the existing banks could (and did) float their own banks. However, it was far more difficult for the new banks to accumulate capital compared to the existing institutions, whose directors were leading capitalists and prominent public figures (Lamoreaux, 1986). The US case tells us how both banks and markets were constructed by dominant capitalist groups to gain control over the society's savings.

Finally, the ability of stock market investors to share risk was circumscribed by the weakness of disclosure requirements and associated information problems in stock markets. To overcome this problem, firms tried to add those features to securities that could reduce the value of information. For example, debt securities with their fixed pre-announced returns typically require less information than equities where return is variable and sensitive to firm specific factors on which information may not be available. It is precisely for this reason, historically, bonds appeared on the scene before shares and preference shares before equity shares (Baskin, 1988). And when equity shares did become popular in the US in the late nineteenth century, the lack of information forced their issuers to market them as debt-like securities on which return in the form of dividends was more or less guaranteed. In the absence of sufficient information, firms desirous of tapping public investors regularly were forced to maintain a sustained record

---

[11] We have discussed the German case elsewhere (Kohli, 2012). The interested readers may also see De Cecco (2005) and Tilly (1991) for an illuminating account of the role of the Reichsbank in providing liquidity to German banks.

of dividends. The initial popularity of stock markets in the late nineteenth century in the US, therefore, came at the expense of the risk-sharing role of stock markets.

All in all, the early US history tells us that both banks and stock markets may play a crucial role in the process of development. As Kregel (2001) argued, everywhere banks are uniquely positioned to create credit that provides initial finance for implementing investment plans. When savings flow as a result of investment, either the borrowing firms or their banks can fund investment by issuing securities to savers.[12] Markets acquired importance in the early US history by providing liquidity to long-term securities, but in Japan, markets were (substantially) substituted by central banks who underwrote liquidity for long-term securities.

Conclusion

This chapter does not suggest what developing countries should do. Rather its aim is more limited. It only suggests that mainstream policy recommendations regarding stock market development in developing countries are based on a flawed reading of history. We reiterate some of the main points. First, the claim that stock markets were large at the dawn of the twentieth century and suffered more prominent reversals in bank-based economies is questionable. Second, the claim that financial openness has historically contributed to stock market development is unconvincing on theoretical as well as empirical grounds. Theoretically, it is based on a flawed application of Olson's collective action theory. Empirically, the claim is problematic because openness is supposed to contribute to stock market development through improvements in institutions of public disclosure and investor rights. Yet, improvements in these institutions happen much after openness became a victim of capital and trade controls instituted after the Great Depression. Finally, stock market size is not an indicator of its role in sharing risk, providing liquidity and aiding competition. Mainstream economists assume that stock markets played these roles reasonably efficiently in the past; our reading of history is that they probably did not.

References

Baskin, J. (1988). The development of corporate financial markets in Britain and the United States, 1600–1914: Overcoming asymmetric information. *Business History Review, 62*(2), 199–237.
Booth, D. (1978). Collective action, Marx's class theory and the union movement. *Journal of Economic Issues, 12*(1), 163–185.
Cheffins, B.R. (2003). Law as bedrock: the foundations of an economy dominated by widely held public companies. *Oxford Journal of Legal Studies, 23*(1), 1–23.
Coffee, J. (2001). *The rise of dispersed ownership: The role of law in the separation of ownership and control.* Working Paper No. 182, Columbia Center for Law and Economic Studies, New York.
De Cecco, M. (2005). Sraffa's lectures on continental banking: a preliminary appraisal. *Review of Political Economy, 17*(3), 349–358.
Deeg, R. (2003). On the development of universal banking in Germany. In D.J. Forsyth & D. Verdier (Eds.), *The origins of national financial systems: Alexander Gerschenkron reconsidered.* London: Routledge.
Edwards, J., & Ogilvie, S. (1996). Universal banks and German industrialization: A reappraisal. *Economic History Review, 49*(3), 427–446.
Fohlin, C. (2007). Does civil law tradition and universal banking crowd out securities markets? Pre-World War I Germany as counter-example. *Enterprise and Society, 8*(3), 602–641.

---

[12] Funding is the conversion of short-term liabilities into long-term liabilities.

Gerschenkron, A. (1962). *Economic backwardness in historical perspective: A book of essays*. Cambridge, MA: Harvard University Press.

Goldsmith, R.W. (1985). *Comparative national balance sheets: A study of twenty countries, 1688–1978*. Chicago & London: University of Chicago Press.

Hamao, Y., Hoshi, T., & Okazaki, T. (2005). The genesis and development of the capital market in pre-war Japan. Discussion Paper CIRJE-F-320. Retrieved from http://www.cirje.e.u-tokyo.ac.jp/research/dp/2005/2005cf320.pdf on 12 January 2016.

Hicks, J. (1969). *A theory of economic history*. Oxford: Oxford University Press.

Hoshi, T., & Kashap, A. (2001). *Corporate financing and corporate governance in Japan: The road to future*. Cambridge, MA: MIT Press.

Ishii, K. (1991). Japan. In R. Cameron & V.I. Bovykin (Eds.), *International banking 1870–1915*. New York: Oxford University Press.

———. (2007). Equity investments and equity investment funding in prewar Japan: comments on 'Were banks really at the center of the prewar Japanese financial system?' *Monetary and Economic Studies* (March). Retrieved from http://www.imes.boj.or.jp/english/publication/mes/2007/me25-1-3.pdf on 13 January 2016.

Kohli, V. (2012). Historical perspective on the role of stock markets in economic development. *Economic and Political Weekly, 47*(36), 58–64.

Kregel, J. (2001). Financial markets and economic development: myth and institutional reality. In G. Hodgson (Ed.), *The evolution of economic institutions: A critical reader*. Cheltenham: Edward Elgar.

Lamoreaux, N. (1986). Banks, kinship and economic development. *Journal of Economic History, 46*(3), 647–667.

Levine, R. (1996). Stock markets: A spur to economic growth. *Finance and Development 33*(1), 7–10.

Levine, R., & Zervos, S. (1998). Stock markets, banks and growth. *American Economic Review, 88*(3), 537–558.

Markham, J.W. (2002). *A Financial History of the United States* (Vol. II). New York: M.E. Sharpe.

Miwa, Y., & Ramseyer, J.M. (2000). *Banks and economic growth: Implications from Japanese history*. Centre for International Research on the Japanese Economy (CIRJE), Tokyo. Retrieved from http://www.cirje.e.u-tokyo.ac.jp/research/dp/2000/2000cf87.pdf on 11 January 2016.

Olson, M. (1971). *The logic of collective action: Public goods and the theory of groups*. New York: Shocken Books.

O'Sullivan, M. (2007). The expansion of the U.S. stock market, 1885–1930: Historical facts and theoretical fashions. *Enterprise and Society, 8*(3), 489–542.

Patrick, H. (1967). Japan. In R. Cameron (Ed.), *Banking in the early stages of industrialisation: A study in comparative economic history*. New York: Oxford University Press.

Rajan, R., & Zingales, L. (2003). The great reversals: the politics of financial development in the twentieth century. *Journal of Financial Economics, 69*(1), 5–50.

———. (2004). *Saving capitalism from capitalists: Unleashing the power of financial markets to create wealth and spread opportunity*. Princeton, NJ: Princeton University Press.

Singh, A. (1999). Should Africa promote stock market capitalism? *Journal of International Development, 11*(3), 343–365.

Sylla, R. (1998). US securities markets and the banking system, 1790–1840. *Federal Reserve Bank of St. Louis Review, 80*(May/June), 83–99.

———. (2006). Schumpeter redux: A review of Raghuram G. Rajan and Luigi Zingales' saving capitalism from the capitalist. *Journal of Economic Literature, 44*(2), 391–404.

Sylla, R., Legler, J.B., & Wallis J.J. (1987). Banks and state public finance in the new republic: the United States, 1790–1860. *Journal of Economic History, 47*(2), 391–403.

Tamaki, N. (1995). *Japanese banking: A history, 1859–1959*. New York: Cambridge University Press.

Teranishi, J. (2007). Were banks really at the center of the prewar Japanese financial system? *Monetary and Economic Studies, 25*(1), 49–76.

Tilly, R. (1991). Germany. In R. Sylla & G. Toniolo (Eds.), *Patterns of European industrialisation: The nineteenth century*. London: Routledge.

Zysman, J. (1983). *Governments, markets, and growth: Financial systems and the politics of industrial change*. Ithaca: Cornell University Press.

15
Corporate Retailing in the Advanced Countries: Some Salient Features

Pradip Kumar Biswas

Introduction

Rapid growth of organised retailing in the developed countries over the past few decades has led to the decline of small retailers in large numbers.[1] Monopsonistic power of a handful of mega retailers enables them to dictate terms of purchases from the suppliers and producers in their favour (Dobson, 2003). They often follow other anti-competitive practices like 'predatory pricing' and 'price flexing' to weaken the small retailers and exploit consumers, but they usually escape penalty by manipulating evidence (Competition Commission, 2000; European Commission, 2007; European Competition Network, 2012). Following the footstep of the developed countries or under compulsion, several developing countries have adopted policies to open up their retail sector to the corporate retailers and, in consequence, there has been a massive expansion of corporate retailing, in the last one decade or so, posing severe threat to the survival of millions of small traders, producers and wholesalers in those countries.[2]

History of the evolution of capitalism has witnessed growth and predominance of the various forms of capital, such as usury capital, merchant capital, industrial capital and financial capital. Each form of capital has played its role, however limited, in the development of capitalism.[3] Retail capital, akin to

---

[1] See Dunford (2002), Fine (1998) and Dobson Consulting (1999) for EU countries; Verdict Research (2008) for France; GLA (2006) for England; Stone (1994) and McGee (1996) for the US and Takaoka (1999) for Japan.
[2] For a discussion on the size and recent growth of the micro, small and medium enterprises (MSMEs) in India and some EU countries, see Biswas and Pohit (2015); Biswas and Baptista (2012).
[3] For example, usury capital is generally parasitic, but when it is used for production, it allows very limited unleashing of production forces in a controlled manner so as to enable the usurer by suitably fixing the interest rates to extract the entire surplus generated from the rise in productivity (Biswas, 2003). Merchant capital thrives on the price differentials that is buying at cheaper prices from a large number of small producers and selling at higher prices in the lucrative markets often located at far off places. It indirectly enters into the production process and helps growth of production capacity to the extent new markets are located (Biswas, 2003; Patnaik, 1975). There are evidences of this accumulated merchant capital being invested in manufacturing in a big way, thereby raising technology and productivity of labour (Hilton, 1976). Industrial capital in its classic case in England evolved through a process of accumulation and differentiation of the small producers. This industrial capital ultimately brought about industrial revolution in the country, leading to major innovations, rapid growth and overall transformation of the economy (Dobb, 1963).

merchant capital, is now becoming a predominant form of capital tending to subjugate even the industrial capital—the large manufacturers who used to choose distributors/wholesalers of their products now depend on these big retailers for selling their products.[4] Within the retail sector, e-retailing is recently gaining tremendous popularity across the globe.[5] In any case, unprecedented explosion of the retail capital occurs at the cost of the productive capacity of a country. Its gigantic size provides it double advantages—while buying goods, it weakens the producers by extracting their surplus (producers' surplus) (Competition Commission, 2000; European Competition Network, 2012), and while selling goods, it wipes out a large section of the traditional or smaller retailers leaving the wholesalers redundant (McGee, 1996; Stone, 1994). Then the suppliers charge higher prices to the smaller retailers in order to recuperate the losses incurred while selling their products to the big retailers at below costs. This phenomenon has been termed as 'waterbed effect', which further weakens the competitive strength of the small retailers. Once the smaller retailers are eliminated, the large retailers soon exploit the consumers by over pricing the products (and thereby extracting the consumers' surplus). This process thus follows the basic nature of capital, which is the capital's tendency to monopolise the markets leading to concentration of capital. Nonetheless, retail capital contributes to improvement in productivity primarily through cost cutting as a result of process innovations, which are induced through monopsonistic pressure of price reduction exerted by the big retailers on the producers (Dobson, 2003; European Competition Network, 2012).

It is often adduced that the 'economies of scale' is the primary reason for such a concentration of economic power and, if so, nothing can be done to restrain its aggression through any legal means like competition act.[6] In reality, it is not necessarily the 'scale economies', rather 'de-listing of a supplier', 'predatory pricing' and 'price flexing' are some of the potent tools that the corporate retailer uses to establish hegemony over the producers, distributors, small retailers and consumers alike (Dobson Consulting, 1999). The likely consequence of the massive growth of retail capital would be economic involution induced through a negative multiplier effect, that is, decline of small and medium retailers, small and medium producers and wholesalers and their employment and income, which in turn reduce the demand for goods and services usually produced and marketed by the small and medium enterprises.[7]

Finance capital has been a potent instrument to establish control over a larger and larger sphere of production, but it also plays a progressive role as it is used for the creation of physical capital (Hilferding, 1981).

[4] In its 'Economic Note on UK Grocery Retailing', the Food and Drink Economics branch of DEFRA (2006) lamented that "[t]hirty years ago, food manufacturers controlled retailers through strong brands and enjoyed high margins. Because of their dominant market share and buying power, multiple retailers are now the leading influence on the supply chain. Negotiating power favours supermarkets as it is easier for them to change suppliers than for suppliers to find new customers". In the Competition Commission Report of 2000, it was noted that the top five supermarkets accounted for an average of 65.5 per cent of UK sales for a group of large suppliers; among Tesco's 2,600 suppliers, the largest accounted for only 2.6 per cent of its purchases.

[5] For detailed discussions on the recent growth of e-retailing, including volume transactions and capital invested and major players across countries, see Deloitte (2015).

[6] It is argued that if the cost and price decline is the result of economies of scale and from such decline if the consumers benefit, there would be no economic justification to counter the business expansion and thereby raising market concentration by any enterprise.

[7] Dobson Consulting (1999) analysing the impact of the growth of modern corporate retailing noted that "while the short run benefits may be substantial due to reduced costs, in the longer term the number of competitors may diminish which ultimately may give rise to adverse effects on competition and potentially lead to reduced product/service choice for consumers and higher final prices" (p. 184). It is noted in Deloitte (2006) that over the past few decades in most of the developed countries, such as France, UK, Germany, Italy, US, Canada, Australia, Japan, etc., small retailers have declined and the large retailers have grown rapidly multiplying their sales turnover, profit and asset value (Deloitte, 2006, 2015). This is apparently similar to the growth of large industries leading to the decline of small industries and the resulting concentration of the industrial capital. But a careful analysis would reveal that the former concentration is more injurious having much more adverse repercussion on the economy than the latter as the industrial monopoly or oligopoly has some positive effects in terms of bringing about innovations/inventions and technological dynamism as discussed, among others, by Schumpeter. The large retailers' only positive effect is cost cutting through process/organisational innovations.

In a more stylised form, Dobson (2003) presented it as a virtuous circle for the very large retailers whereby size and market share create bargaining concessions from suppliers. This provides a cost advantage for large retailers over small retailers, which allows the former to invest in either improved customer facilities or reduced prices. This increases the attractiveness of large retailers compared to small retailers and therefore leads to even greater sales for the large retailers, which further reinforces their buyer power and so the cycle continues again. The same process, however, acts on the small or medium enterprises (SMEs) in the reverse direction, more than a vicious circle, and may be termed as involution, inducing a negative multiplier effect. Thus, the changed dynamics of the relations have adverse effects on producers, wholesalers, small retailers and consumers, which in turn have implications on unemployment and poverty.

This warrants redesigning appropriate state policies not only to make the trade practices by the big retailers fair and provide safeguard to the smaller producers and retailers but also to mitigate the problems of unemployment and poverty. It is often noted that even in the developed countries, the influences of these big retailers are powerful enough to design state policies in their favour and escape penalty by the regulatory bodies in the event of their unfair practices.[8] This may provide some lessons for the developing countries that are also presently experiencing rapid growth of large retailers or planning to allow corporate retailing.

With this objective in mind, the present chapter makes an analysis of the nature of functioning of the big retailers, sources of their immense power and rapid growth and the consequences on the producers, small and medium retailers, wholesalers and the consumers based on the experiences in the advanced countries.

Growth of Big Retailers and the Decline of Smaller Ones: Experience of the Advanced Countries

This section would provide brief accounts of the decline of the small retailers as a consequence of the high growth of corporate retailing in selected advanced countries of the EU as well as in the US. Although most of advanced countries have passed through a phase of rapid growth of corporate retailing, they are invariably accompanied by decline of small retailers, such as local grocery shops or mom-and-pop stores and roadside vendors. Further, all these countries therefore witnessed a decline in the small retailers' share in total retail sales and an overall decline in the retail sector employment. We would however first describe the US experience, which would be followed by the experiences of the EU countries.

The US Experience

In terms of the ownership of retail business of a country, there can be several categories of retailers like independently owned, chain owned, franchisee operated, owned by manufacturers or wholesalers and consumer owned. Statistics of the US indicate that during the high growth phase of corporate retailing, primarily the three decades of the 1970s, 1980s and 1990s, there was a rapid decline of the small retailers. The single-location retail firms, primarily 'mom-and-pop' stores, accounted for 60.2 per cent of retail

---

[8] See Byrom, McDonald and Parker (2006) for an analysis of how they avoid penalty for anti-competitive activities. Several states in the US subsidised Wal-Mart to construct big stores (Mattera & Purinton, 2004), while some other advanced countries enacted laws regulating size, location and opening time of the store and advertisement. See Allain, Marie-Laure, Chambolle and Verge (2009) for a discussion on the various regulations and restrictions on the functioning of big retailers in France.

sales in 1967, which declined to 39 per cent by 1997. On the other hand, large retail firms with more than 100 establishments accounted for 18.6 per cent of the retail sales in 1967, which grew to 36.9 per cent in 1997. In 1963, retail firms with multiple location chain shared 20.2 per cent of all retail establishments, but this figure grew to 35 per cent by 2000. In terms of employment, both the single-location retailers and chains had almost equal share until around 1980, and by 2000, the share of chains increased to two-thirds of total retail employment (Jarmin, Klimen & Miranda, 2007). As observed by Stone (1994), the setting up of stores like Wal-Mart offering one-stop shopping and sector-specific stores like Home Depot compelled a large section of local retailers to close down their shops simply because they failed to compete with these large nation-wide chains.

Using a statistical model, Jia (2005) estimated that Wal-Mart's expansion from the late 1980s to the late 1990s was found to account for 50 to 70 per cent of the decline in small retailers. In the first half of the 1990s, Fine (1998) observed that more than 100,000 retail companies have filed for bankruptcy, and this figure is 60 per cent more than the corresponding figure in the previous five years. Table 15.1 shows that for the single unit firms, the exit rate far exceeded the rate of entry in both the rural areas and small towns. For the chains, entry rates were much higher than the exit rates in all types of locations. The proportion of enterprises surviving till the next year was much lower for the single unit category.

In Mississippi, Wal-Mart stores captured on the average 17 per cent of the existing grocery market within the first two years in non-metropolitan counties, and about 4 per cent of the sales of the existing grocery stores one year after the entry in metropolitan counties (Artz & Stone, 2006). Similarly, in Dallas area, Ingraham, Singer and Thibodeau (2005) estimated that for every new dollar of retail sales within the 15-mile radius of Dallas' centre, 34 cents represented 'cannibalisation' or capture of existing retail sales, while 66 cents represented incremental sales to that market diverted from nearby cities outside the 15-mile radius.

Table 15.1
Firm Entry and Exit Rates for the US Retail Sector (Mean by Market Type, 1976–2000)

	Single Units	Local Chains	Regional Chains	National Chains
Entry rate (ER)				
Rural areas	0.143	0.085	0.077	0.077
Micropolitan areas	0.144	0.087	0.082	0.077
Metropolitan areas	0.151	0.094	0.097	0.089
Exit rate (XR)				
Rural areas	0.153	0.078	0.061	0.064
Micropolitan areas	0.150	0.077	0.065	0.063
Metropolitan areas	0.151	0.087	0.079	0.070
Continuer rate (CR)				
Rural areas	0.847	0.922	0.939	0.936
Micropolitan areas	0.850	0.923	0.935	0.937
Metropolitan areas	0.849	0.913	0.921	0.930

Source: Jarmin et al. (2007, Table 4).
Notes: 1. Micropolitan refers to small town.
2. ER = number of newly set up firms/number of firms existed last year.
3. XR = number of firms closed down/number of firms existed last year.
4. CR = proportion of firms operating last year are also continuing this year.

Table 15.2
Supermarket Convenience Store Acquisitions

Date	Active Business	Target Business	Number of Stores	Price (£m)	Profit (£m)	Turnover (£m)	Area (thousand sq ft)
January 2003	Tesco	T&S Stores	1,215	520	933		46
February 2004	Sainsbury's	Bells Stores	54	21.5	56	108	1
March 2004	Tesco	Adminstore	45	53.7	72.8		2.1
August 2004	Sainsbury's	Jacksons	114	100	143	214	
November 2004	Sainsbury's JB	Beaumont	6	13			
April 2005	Sainsbury's	SL Shaw	5	11			

Source: Europe Economics (2005).

The US experience, thus, shows that the high growth phase of the corporate retailing was associated with rapid decline of small retailers. The decline was not confined to the big cities or urban areas alone; it spread in the rural areas also.

European Experiences

The picture in the European countries is not very different from the one narrated above. In Great Britain, the number of small retailers (employing between 0 and 10 persons) declined by 4 per cent and the number of large retailers increased by 9.5 per cent between 1998 and 2004 (GLA, 2006).[9] The large retailers steadily raised their market share—for instance, in food retailing, large multiples' share increased from 50 to 79 per cent of the turnover between 1976 and 1991 (Burke & Shackleton, 1996). Competition Commission (2006) inquiry into the grocery industry notes that the supermarket sales increased by 26 per cent in real terms between 2000 and 2006, and the sales at specialist grocery stores increased meagrely by 1 per cent during the same period. More importantly, the number of specialist grocery stores declined by 7 per cent in that period. In addition to this, the sales of non-grocery products by grocery retailers increased by an estimated 89 per cent between 2000 and 2004. It noted that "Tesco Express stores have reportedly caused drops in business of 30 to 40 per cent for other local shops" (GLA, 2006: 10–11).

Concentration of the large retailers not only increased due to decline of the small single-location retailers but also through mergers and acquisitions. During the first half of the 2000s, there had been an unprecedented growth of mergers and acquisitions, leading to a profound restructuring of the distribution system. Tesco and Sainsbury's have established their respective positions relatively rapidly as may be seen in Table 15.2.

There had been increasing concern particularly within the independent convenience store segment that supermarket entry raised site prices. Rise in property prices and rents not only raised the asset value of the large retailers but also raised the cost of operation of small retailers in the neighbouring areas where the former acquired property or set up outlets (Christie & Co., 2005: 18).

European Commission (2007) noted that while grocery sales increased, the number of grocery outlets declined, with the number of supermarkets, convenience stores and specialist grocery stores falling by 2 per cent, 8 per cent and 7 per cent per year, respectively, since 2000. Despite this, the number of stores

---

[9] For a discussion on the growth pattern of micro enterprises (employing 10 or fewer persons) in the major EU countries, see Biswas and Baptista (2012).

Table 15.3
Sale of Clothing by Type of Outlet (in percentages)

	EU15			France		Italy	
	1988	1996	2000	1986	1994	1986	1998
Independent retailers	48	41	37	39	27	67	54
Specialised chains	18	24	26	13	23		15
Department and variety stores	12	13	13				
Hypermarkets and supermarkets	5	6	7	17	19		15
Mail order	7	8	9	10	12		
Street vendors						14	9
Other	10	8	8				7
Total	100	100	100	78	82		100

Source: Dunford (2002).

operated by the four largest grocery retailers (namely Asda, Morrisons, Sainsbury's and Tesco) more than doubled since 2000. This observation reflects the effect of rising concentration through both the opening of new stores and the acquisition of competitors.

For long only small retailers enjoyed the privilege of opening long hours including on Sunday. Recently, this privilege was extended to the big outlets also. GLA (2006) cited a survey result of the London Chamber of Commerce, which found that just over 80 per cent of the independent retailers experienced a fall in their sales due to relaxation of Sunday Trading Laws. Therefore, large retailers moving into high streets as well as the general rise in property prices raising the cost of operations for the small retail outlets along with decline in sales led more small retailers to sell their premises.

In the case of the EU textiles and clothing industry, it is found that overall the specialised chains and hyper markets and super markets were becoming more and more powerful (Dunford, 2002). Although, traditional and independent retailers were still predominant but declining (as may be seen in Table 15.3). In Italy in 1986, independent retailers had 67 per cent of the clothing market, which declined to 53 per cent by 1996. There were 120,000 outlets in 1984, which declined to 70,000 outlets in 1997. The UK had the most concentrated structure—in 1996, the combined share of specialised chain stores, department and variety stores, supermarkets and mail order stood at 76 per cent compared with just 15 per cent for independent retailers (Dunford, 2002).

This survey of the literature is indicative of the phase of rapid growth of organised retailers operating through chains and franchises, which led to a steady decline of the small retailers, primarily the mom-and-pop stores on which detailed discussion will be made in the section that follows.

Nature of Functioning of the Large Retailers—Establishing Dominance over Producers and Out-competing Small Retailers

The process of building supremacy by the large retailers involves several innovations in organisation, management, marketing in tune with consumer behaviour, sourcing products and even inducing state policies. A large retail organisation may be treated as a summation of a number of vertically structured or quasi-tree organisations involving networks of producers at the top and small retailers at the bottom and layers of intermediaries like wholesalers or distributors in between, where each agent transacts vertically in the hierarchy along the tree.[10] The large retail organisation replaces segments of several such trees by supply chain and thereby economises many of the transaction costs like search costs, contracting costs, monitoring and enforcement costs, etc. Another advantage is the economies of scale, particularly in bulk transactions (not manufacturing) with pecuniary gain, and scope with the latter enabling larger and appropriate assortment of merchandise. This would effectively make the customer's visit to a grocery store a 'one-stop shopping'.

Along with the change in lifestyle, people prefer comfortable and one-stop buying. Thus, the act of shopping has been transformed from economic-purpose or utilitarian shopping into recreational/pleasure or hedonistic shopping.[11] Several recent studies have examined shopping as a source of entertainment, and hedonic consumption as critical to retail success globally[12]. In an examination of shopping motives, Roy (1994) found a negative correlation (−0.41) between functional-economic shopping orientations and the frequency of mall shopping, but a positive correlation (0.34) between recreational shopping orientations and the frequency of mall shopping. Varble (1976) found Sunday shoppers to have recreational orientations. Thus, shopping malls have emerged with all these provisions under one roof, and they are generally set up in the peaceful downtown areas with good road connections, parking facilities and many other recreational and entertainment facilities. The other innovation is the display and arrangement of specialised merchandise in locations with maximum footfalls within a store in order to induce the customers to make many unplanned impulse buying that often cover a large percentage of the consumers' budget (Gutierrez, 2004).

The real source of power of a large retailer rests in its ascendancy as monopsonist in the product market, thereby extracting the entire producers' surplus. This surplus provides it enough leverage and solvency to out-compete smaller retailers either through price cutting or through providing attractive incentives or non-price benefits to the consumers. Increasingly, grocery suppliers, like farmers, food processors and other producers, are becoming dependent on large supermarket chains to sell their produce. In contrast, the supermarkets are rarely dependent on any one supplier. For instance, the very largest grocery supplier in the UK accounted for less than 3 per cent of Tesco's total purchases, and the average supplier provided less than 100th of 1 per cent of their purchases.[13] The threat of de-listing therefore gives the supermarkets an overwhelming advantage in negotiating power over their suppliers. Having no other alternative, the suppliers give in to supermarkets' pressure fearing the loss of their main buyers.[14] As a matter of practice, supermarkets regularly take unilateral action to the detriment of suppliers, for example, by requiring suppliers to make payments or concessions to gain access to supermarket shelf space. There are numerous examples described in detail in paragraphs 2.460–2.550 of the Competition Commission (2000). These practices are grouped into eight categories shown in Table 15.4.

---

[10] See Biswas (2007, 2011).

[11] Bellenger and Korgaonkar (1980) distinguished between functional-economic shopping and recreational shopping, the former being more purposive and the latter being more entertaining. Holbrook and Hirschman (1982) revealed that consumption experiences can have hedonic qualities.

[12] For a review of the literature, see Gutierrez (2004).

[13] See European Commission's observations and decision in Rewe/Meinl 1999, http://europa.eu.int/abc/doc/off/bull/en/9901/p103089.htm.

[14] See Competition Commission (2000), particularly observation about Asda, Safeway, Sainsbury, Somerfield and Tesco (paragraph 2.458).

Table 15.4
Supermarket Practices Concerning Relations with Suppliers

Category of Practices	Number of Practices	Number of Retailers Engaging in Practice (Min–Max)	Percentage of Practices Against Public Interest
Payments for access to shelf space	8	5–13	50
Imposing conditions on suppliers' trade with other retailers	2	1–4	0
Applying different standards to different suppliers	1	3	100
Imposing an unfair imbalance of risk	12	1–12	83
Imposing retrospective changes to contractual terms	8	1–7	75
Restricting suppliers' access to the market	1	10	100
Imposing charges and transferring costs to suppliers	8	2–13	63
Requiring suppliers to use third-party suppliers nominated by the retailer	2	2–11	50

Source: Competition Commission (2000).

Governance Issues

Regulatory Measures against Acting Public Interest

In relation to suppliers, the Competition Commission (2000) identified 30 separate practices by five grocery retailers that were affecting the competitiveness of some of their suppliers and distorting competition among grocery suppliers—and in some cases among grocery retailers—and that 27 of these practices operated against the public interest. The Competition Commission recommended that a Code of Practice be adopted to address the concerns it identified (European Commission, 2007).

Concerns about buyer power have been raised in a number of EU and other countries. The fact that the European Commission commissioned a major study on buyer power indicates the level of concern at the EU level. The report, "Buyer power and its impact on competition in the food retail distribution sector of the European Union", was submitted on May 1999. An even broader study on buyer power in the retailing sector was carried out by the Organisation for Economic Co-operation and Development in its Round Table on Buyer Power held in October 1998 (OECD, 1998). Several countries have had laws regulating anti-competitive behaviour of the large retailers including (a) below cost selling or predatory pricing; (b) transparency of purchase prices (so that consumers can see the disparity between what farmers or other suppliers receive for their produce and what the supermarket charges); (c) unilateral changes in contract terms at short notice (which can devastate small suppliers); (d) demanding discounts that are not justified (a widespread practice, at least in the UK); (e) de-listing without adequate cause (widespread in every country) and (f) limiting acquisitions of smaller stores by large supermarket groups. European Competition Network (2012) report on competition law enforcement and market-monitoring activities by European competition authorities in the food sector reveals that anti-competitive practices by big retailers are still rampant.

Predatory Pricing and Price Flexing

Supermarket chains followed numerous other anti-competitive practices to out-compete small retailers, such as predatory pricing, that is selling at prices below the costs, and price flexing, that is, selling the same products at different prices in different markets in order to extract the maximum possible consumers' surplus and at the same time maintaining competitive advantage locally. These practices are severely damaging to smaller retailers and have adverse knock-on effects for consumers.

European Commission (2007) in its review noted that

> "below-cost selling practices of grocery retailers over the past 12 to 18 months shows that ten grocery retailers (Aldi, Asda, the Co-op, Lidl, Morrisons, Netto, Sainsbury's, Somerfield, Tesco and Waitrose) engage in below-cost selling to varying extents…predatory strategies towards smaller grocery retailers and specialist stores appear to be feasible in certain circumstances…[and] contribute to the exit of smaller grocery retailers and specialist stores."

In an earlier investigation also, the Competition Commission (2000) noted similar anti-competitive practices against the public interest by Asda, Morrison, Safeway, Sainsbury and Tesco (paragraph 1.6(a)).

No Penalty against Large Retailers for Predatory Pricing and Price Flexing

Large retailers often avoided penalty for their anti-competitive actions due to lack of sufficient evidence. Because of their substantial power, they could easily garner evidence favouring them, but the resource-poor small retailers often fail to act together and collect adequate evidence against the large retailers. Concerning pricing practices, the Competition Commission found that varying prices in different locations in response to local competitive conditions contributed to a situation in which the majority of grocery products were not fully exposed to competitive pressure and that these practices distorted competition in the supply of groceries and operated against the public interest. The Competition Commission also found that a number of multiple grocery retailers adopted pricing structures and regimes that, by focusing on a relatively small proportion of their product line, restricted active competition on the majority of the product lines. Though the Competition Commission found that there was a distortion of competition in the supply of groceries, it did not make recommendation for remedial action (European Commission, 2007).

Byrom, McDonald and Parker (2006) in responding to the various enquiries by the Office of Fair Trading (OFT) and the Competition Commission stated that the evidence base did not reflect the grocery sector in its entirety and was heavily slanted towards issues concerning the 'Big Four' only: "Undoubtedly the 'Big Four' will be investing heavily in preparing for any possible inquiry into the grocery sector as they have for the previous inquiries. The small retail sector however, is in the unfortunate position of having little representation in comparison. Small shops do not have the resources, skills or time to effectively influence competition and consumer policy". Thus, in spite of the existence of rules, code of conducts and OFT and Competition Commission, large retailers can pursue anti-competitive trade practices.

Large Retailers Influencing Public Policy and Using Public Money for Their Benefit

Mattera and Purinton (2004) used newspaper archives to identify Wal-Mart received incentives from the public sector—for the construction of 91 retail stores, a total of $245 million, about $2.8 million per store, was received. They estimated that total subsidies given to 81 distribution centres were $624 million. In Barnstable, Massachusetts, the estimated net cost to the community of a new big-box retailer was $468 per $10,000 square feet (cited in Irwin & Clark, 2006). Further, Artz and Stallmann (2006) noted that communities compete for big-box retailers by offering incentives so as to raise their sales tax revenues on which the local communities were becoming increasingly dependent.

Adverse Effects of Corporate Retailing

Decline in Retail Wages and Employment and Increase in Poverty

A recent study reveals that opening a Wal-Mart store would reduce average wage rate between 0.5 and 0.9 per cent, which implies a combined 1.3 per cent reduction in total earnings (wage bill) of workers in these sectors, and the retail workers in the country as a whole would lose an estimated $4.7 billion wage income (Dube, Lester & Eidlin, 2007). As regards loss of employment, Neumark, Zhang and Ciccarella (2005) estimated that Wal-Mart entry at county level reduced retail employment by about 180 to 270 workers, implying that each Wal-Mart worker displaced about 1.5 to 1.75 other retail workers. They further noted that on the average, retail wages declined by about 7.5 per cent at a county level. However, this observation has been contradicted by Basker (2005b), who noted that the immediate effect of Wal-Mart's entry was an increase of 100 retail jobs, and after five years, this number was reduced to an average of 50 jobs. But, the most noteworthy aspect of Basker's study is the negative impact on local wholesalers—on the average, 20 jobs would be lost in the local wholesale activities after five years of opening of a Wal-Mart store.

Wal-Mart has now got another bad reputation—that of raising poverty even in the most prosperous country like the US. Goetz and Swaminathan (2006) found that counties with more Wal-Mart stores in 1987 had higher rates of poverty in 1999 than counties with fewer or no Wal-Mart stores. They also found those counties in which new Wal-Mart stores were built between 1987 and 1998 experienced higher poverty rates in 1999. Specifically, the opening of a new Wal-Mart store was found to increase the average poverty rate in a county by 0.2 per cent, and this figure was arrived at after controlling the effects of other factors. In aggregate, an additional 20,000 families were in poverty as a result of the Wal-Mart's presence in local communities.[15] Shils and Taylor (1997) observed that "in exchange for 1 new part-time job in a mega-discount store, about 1½ full time jobs are eliminated in smaller stores". It is therefore not surprising that the prosperity of Wal-Mart would engender poverty in the local communities.

Price Reduction Benefits Consumers in the Short Run—Price Would Rise again in the Long Run

There is no doubt that the consumers benefit from the substantial decline in the prices led by the large retailers. For instance, Wal-Mart not only offered lower prices, but its entry also had the indirect effect of lowering prices at competing stores. Irwin and Clark (2006) found that the prices for various food items in Wal-Mart and other 'nontraditional' large discount food retailers are typically 5 to 48 per cent less than prices for the same product in conventional supermarkets. Similarly, Basker (2005a) estimated price declines of 7 to13 per cent in the long run as the result of a Wal-Mart store opening. Further, Hausman and Leibtag (2006) found that the direct effect of having access to lower priced goods generates a savings of 20.2 per cent in food expenditures for the average household. The competition effect generates additional savings of 4.8 per cent. Not surprisingly, lower income households benefit even more from lower food prices; the estimated saving in expenditures is close to 30 per cent for households with an annual income below $10,000.

Notwithstanding this decline in consumers' price in the US, in the EU, the large retailers are found to raise the prices of consumers' goods, particularly agro-based products, as well as reduce the farm-gate prices.

---

[15] It is argued that the higher paid 'mom and pop' retail jobs were lost to lower paid Wal-Mart jobs, resulting in lower average household income, which added to the poverty in the county.

Rising Price Spread for Agricultural Commodities

The combined effect of monopsony and monopoly power of the large retailers has been the rise in price spread for agricultural commodities as noted in the EU countries during the 1990s. Farm output prices fell sharply, whereas consumer retail food prices increased substantially during the 1990s. For all agricultural products, the producer price index (in real terms) declined by 27 per cent in the EU-15 area during 1990–2002. Real farm output prices declined as much as by 50 per cent in Finland, 42 per cent in Austria, 41 per cent in Portugal, 37 per cent in Denmark, 36 per cent in Luxembourg and 34 per cent in both Belgium and Sweden (DEFRA, 2004). Farm output prices in nominal terms remained more or less unchanged in the EU over the period, whereas aggregate consumer prices and consumer retail food prices increased substantially. This disparate trend in farm prices and consumer food prices has become an issue of discussion. Table 15.5 displays the changes in real farm-gate prices for crop products as well as animal and animal products for the 15 countries in the EU during 1990–2002, and Table 15.6 shows the changes in consumer prices.

Excepting for the wheat/bread, potato and flour, price spread ranges between 1 and 5 times the farm-gate price. In the case of wheat/bread, the price spread varies between 6.9 and 35 times the farm-gate price across countries. In case of potato, the largest spread is noted for Germany (19 times the farm-gate price). For flour, it is 3.9 times in the UK and 5.9 times in Austria (Table 15.7). Further, it may be seen in Table 15.8 that the ratio of price spread to farm-gate price increased rapidly in the 1990s for the products like apples, potato, onion, tomato, bread, flour and egg across the EU countries. For

Table 15.5
Change in Real Farm-gate Prices (1990–2002)

Country	Changes in Real Farm-gate Price Index—Crop Products	Changes in Real Farm-gate Price Index—Animal and Animal Products
Austria	−40.2	−42.6
Belgium	−29.0	−36.3
Denmark	−36.4	−35.0
Finland	−58.4	−45.4
France	−29.9	−26.1
Germany	−28.3	−31.2
Greece	−11.5	−23.6
Ireland	−22.6	−31.2
Italy	−10.4	−25.4
Luxembourg	−17.9	−40.1
Netherlands	−5.1	−35.5
Portugal	−37.8	−44.5
Spain	−22.9	−27.5
Sweden	−28.6	−36.0
UK	−36.9	−31.2
EU-15	**−23.4**	**−31.2**

Source: DEFRA (2004, Table 1.1).

Table 15.6
Change in Agriculture Output and Consumer Prices in EU-15 in Percentage (1990–2002)

Total output	5.3
Production of crops	14.3
Animal and animal products	8.0
Overall consumer price level	36.0
Consumer prices: food and non-alcoholic beverages	29.8

Source: DEFRA (2004, Table 1.2).

Table 15.7
Farm-gate and Retail Price Spreads Ratio in EU Member States (2001)

Country	AP	CA	PO	ON	CB	TO	BE	LA	PI	BR	FL	EG	CH
UK	1.74	1.24	7.08	3.52	1.31	0.92	1.29	1.43	1.28	6.86	3.9	4.66	
Austria	3.99	3.46	9.28	4.7	2.93					34.52	5.6	1.57	0.89
France						2.05	0.72	1.23		21.42		3.19	
Germany	3.44	2.32	19.08	3.04	3.24	0.74	1.35	0.46	1.74	30.61		0.46	1.46
Ireland		1.46		3.6		1.3	1.83	0.59		10.64		2.69	
Netherlands			6.23			3.22			3.2	12.58		1.56	2.94
Spain		1.6								10.23		0.42	

Source: DEFRA (2004, Table 2.1).
Notes: AP, apples; CA, carrots; PO, potatoes; ON, onions; CB, cabbage; TO, tomatoes; BE, beef; LA, lamb; PI, pork; BR, bread; FL, flour; EG, egg; CH, chicken.

Table 15.8
Percentage Change in Farm-gate and Retail Price Spreads Ratio in EU Member States (1990–1991 to 2000–2001)

Country	AP	CA	PO	ON	CB	TO	BE	LA	PI	FL	EG	BR
UK	54.80	−35.64	193.88	36.31	−10.86	22.84	68.56	49.43	30.38	76.05		59.67
Denmark			28.38					16.90	59.85		86.95	
France						103.87	−25.07	42.90		44.55	87.59	
Germany	60.46					145.16	−49.76	27.15				
Ireland				53.45			32.83	62.72	−1.39	−25.20	64.60	73.03
Netherlands			299.12			148.65						
Spain			55.16							4.28	108.32	

Source: DEFRA (2004, Table 2.2).
Notes: AP, apples; CA, carrots; PO, potatoes; ON, onions; CB, cabbage; TO, tomatoes; BE, beef; LA, lamb; PI, pork; BR, bread; FL, flour; EG, egg.

potato, the ratio increased by 300 per cent in the Netherlands and 194 per cent in the UK. In France, the ratio of price spread to farm-gate price increased by 104 per cent for tomato, 43 per cent for lamb, 46 per cent for flour and 88 per cent for egg. Does the large and rising price spread in relation to farm-gate price indicate the large and increasing share of non-farm costs in the final product? Is it caused by concentration in the retail sector? A detailed study conducted by DEFRA (2004) identified "a number of factors affected the size of the spreads during the nineties. The key factors … are the exchange rate, overall domestic demand and supply and costs in the supply chain in the case of meat products, and, in the case of fruits and vegetables, the concentration of the food retail industry" (p. 94).

Suggestive Policies for the Developing Countries

Given these negative effects of large retailing in the advanced countries where the powerful states can protect the interests of their people and the SMEs, can the governments of the developing countries protect millions of SMEs against these powerful retailers? For instance, in India, as per National Sample Survey Office estimates of 2010–2011, there were 34 million persons engaged in trading and around 35 million in manufacturing in the informal sector who are likely to be affected. Thus, the long-term consequence of the growth of the large retailers in the developing countries is likely to be much more adverse than that of the developed countries.

In these countries, the regulatory machinery needs to be strengthened so as to keep a close vigil over the day-to-day functioning of the big retailers. It would ensure that the latter do not act against public interest. Anti-competitive practices by the big retailers, whether applying monopsonistic power over the small producers and suppliers, or below cost selling/price flexing to weaken the small retailers, or monopoly price discrimination to exploit consumers, must be prevented at the initial stage. In line with French regulations, store location, store opening hours, and modalities of advertisement in various media must be appropriately defined and effectively regulated. A fixed proportion of the total procurement must be obtained from the local MSMEs. Unlike in the advanced EU countries where SME unions are strong and in a position to demand protection against unfair practices by the big retailers or ask for mandatory procurement by the state and big retailers from the SMEs, in the developing countries such unions are not very effective. In these circumstances, the Government has to play proactive role in protecting the interest of the SMEs as well as the consumers.

References

Allain, M.L., Chambolle, C., & Verge, T. (2009). *The galland law and its reforms, La loi Gallandsur le commerce: jusquou la reformer?* Opuscule du Cepremap, Editions Rue d'Ulm. Retrieved from http://innovation-regulation2.telecom-paristech.fr/wp-content/uploads/Documents/thematiques/Digital_Distribution/chambolle.pdf on 23 October 2013.

Artz, G., & Stallmann, J.I. (2006). Recruiting big-box retailers as an economic development strategy. *Paper presented at the National Public Policy Conference*, Fayetteville. Arkansas, September 17–19.

Artz, G., & Stone, K. (2006). Analyzing the impact of Wal-Mart supercenters on local food store sales. *American Journal of Agricultural Economics*, 88(5), 1296–1303.

Basker, E. (2005a). Selling a cheaper mousetrap: Wal-Mart's effect on retail prices. *Journal of Urban Economics*, 58(2), 203–229.

———. (2005b). Job creation or destruction? Labor-market effects of Wal-Mart expansion. *Review of Economics and Statistics*, 87(1), 174–183.

Bellenger, D.N., & Korgaonkar, P.K. (1980). Profiling the recreational shopper. *Journal of Retailing, 56*(3), 77–92.

Biswas, P.K. (2003). *Rural industrialisation in West Bengal: Institutions, innovations and growth*. New Delhi: Manak Publishers.

———. (2007). Indigenous systems of organizations and the development of MSMEs in India. *The Innovation Journal: The Public Sector Innovation Journal, 12*(2), 1–30.

———. (2011). Networks of small enterprises, architecture of governance and incentive alignment: Some cases from India. *AI & Society, 26*(4), 383–391.

Biswas, P.K., & Baptista, A. (2012). Institutions and micro-enterprises demography: A study of selected EU countries, 1997–2006. *Journal of Small Business and Entrepreneurship, 25*(3), 283–306.

Biswas, P.K., & Pohit, S. (2015). Present structure of Indian enterprises, in CSIR-NISTADS. *India: Science and Technology* (Vol. 3). New Delhi: CUP.

Burke, T., & Shackleton, J. (1996). *Trouble in store? UK retailing in the 1990s*. London: Institute of Economic Affairs.

Byrom, J., McDonald, O., & Parker, C. (2006). *Response to the office of fair trading's proposed decision to make a market investigation for the grocery sector*. Retail Enterprise Network Papers for Practitioners Series. England: Manchester Metropolitan University Business School.

Christie and Co. (2005). *Business outlook*. Retrieved from http:www.christie.com/christie/index.asp on 21 January 2016.

Competition Commission. (2000). *Supermarkets: A report on the supply of groceries from multiple stores in the United Kingdom*. London: Author.

———. (2006). *Groceries market investigation: Statement of issues*. London: Author.

Deloitte. (2006). *2007 global powers of retailing*. Deloitte & Touche LLP. Retrieved from http://public.deloitte.com/media/0460/2009GlobalPowersofRetail_FINAL2.pdf on 22 October 2013.

———. (2015). *2015 Top 250 global powers of retailing*. Retrieved from https://nrf.com/news/2015-top-250-global-powers-of-retailing on 15 February 2015.

DEFRA. (2004). *Investigation of the determinants of farmretail price spreads*. UK: London Economics.

DEFRA, Government of UK. (2006). *Economic Note on UK Grocery Retailing*. UK: Author.

Dobb, M.H. (1963). *Studies in the development of capitalism*. New York, NY: International Publishers.

Dobson Consulting. (1999). *Buyer power and its impact on competition in the food retail distribution sector of the European Union*. Brussels: European Commission DGIV.

Dobson, P.W. (2003). Competition and collaboration in European grocery retailing. *European Retail Digest, 39*(Autumn), 13–21.

Dube, A., Lester, T.W., & Eidlin, B. (2007). *Firm entry and wages: Impact of Wal-Mart growth on earnings throughout the retail sector*. Working Paper Series, Paper iirwps 126-05, Institute for Research on Labour and Employment, Berkeley, CA. Retrieved from http://irle.berkeley.edu/workingpapers/126-05.pdf on 20 February 2013.

Dunford, M. (2002). *The changing profile and map of the EU textile and clothing industry*. Falmer, Brighton: School of European Studies, University of Sussex.

European Commission. (2007). *Emerging thinking: Groceries market Investigation*. Retrieved from http://webarchive.nationalarchives.gov.uk/20140402142426/http://www.competition-commission.org.uk/inquiries/ref2006/grocery/pdf/emerging_thinking.pdf on 26 February 2013.

European Competition Network (ECN). (2012). *Report on competition law enforcement and market monitoring activities by European competition authorities in the food sector*. European Commission. Retrieved from ec.europa.eu/competition/ecn/food_report_en.pdf on 25 February 2013.

Europe Economics. (2005). *Impact of supermarket expansion in the convenience retailing sector: A report for the association of convenience stores*. London, UK: Author.

Fine, M. (23 February 1998). The European market beckons. *Discount Store News, 37*(4), 15.

GLA. (2006). Retail in London. Working Paper G, March, GLA, London.

Goetz, S., & Swaminathan, H. (2006). Wal-Mart and county-wide poverty. *Social Science Quarterly, 87*(2), 211–225.

Gutierrez, B.P.B. (2004). Determinants of planned and impulse buying: The case of the Philippines. *Asia Pacific Management Review, 9*(6), 1061–1078.

Hausman, J., & Leibtag, E. (2006). Consumer benefits from increased competition in shopping outlets: Measuring the effect of Wal-Mart. *Journal of Applied Econometrics, 22*(7), 1157–1177.

Hilferding, R. (1981). *Finance capital: A study in the latest phase of capitalist development.* London: Routledge & Kegan Paul.

Hilton, R. (1776). *The transition from feudalism to capitalism.* London: New Left Book.

Holbrook, M.B., & Hirschman, E.C. (1982). The experimental aspects of consumption: consumer fantasies, feelings, and fun. *The Journal of Consumer Research, 9*(2) 132–140.

Ingraham, A., Singer, H.J., & Thibodeau, T.G. (2005). Inter-city competition for retail trade: Can tax increment financing generate incremental tax receipts? *Social Science Research Network Electronic Journal.* Retrieved from http://ssrn.com/abstract=766925 and http://dx.doi.org/10.2139/ssrn.766925 on 10 January 2013.

Irwin, E.G., & Clark, J. (2006). *Wall Street vs. main street: What are the benefits and costs of Wal-Mart to local communities?* Columbus: The Ohio State University.

Jarmin, R.S., Klimek, S.D., & Miranda, J. (2007). *The role of retail chains: National, regional, and industry results.* Washington, DC: Center for Economic Studies, U.S. Census Bureau.

Jia, P. (2005). What happens when Wal-Mart comes to town: An empirical analysis of the discount retail industry. Working paper, Yale University, USA.

Mattera, P., & Purinton, A. (2004). *Shopping for subsidies: How Wal-Mart uses taxpayer money to finance its never-ending growth.* Washington, DC: Good Jobs First.

McGee, J.E. (1996). When Wal-Mart comes to town: A look at how local merchants respond to the retailing giant's arrival. *Journal of Business and Entrepreneurship, 8*(1), 43–52.

Neumark, D., Zhang. J., & Ciccarella, S. (2005). The effect of Wal-Mart on local labor markets. Paper presented at the Allied Social Sciences Association Meeting, Boston, MA, January 6–8.

OECD. (1998). *Buying power of multiproduct retailers.* Retrieved from http://www.oecd.org/officialdocuments/publicdisplaydocumentpdf/?cote=DAFFE/CLP(99)21&docLanguage=En on 23 October 2013.

Patnaik, U. (1975). *The process of commercialisation in agriculture in colonial condition: A hypothesis.* Occasional Paper no.14, CESP, JNU.

Roy, A. (1994). Correlates of mall visit frequencies. *Journal of Retailing, 70*(2), 139–161.

Shils, E.B., & Taylor, G.W. (1997). *Measuring the economic and sociological impact of the mega-retail discount chains on small enterprise in urban, suburban and rural communities.* Philadelphia: University of Pennsylvania, Wharton School, Wharton Entrepreneurial Center.

Stone, K.E. (1994). *Competing with retail giants: how to survive in the new retail landscape.* New York: John Wiley and Sons.

Takaoka, M. (1999). *Globalization of the distribution system and the 1985 shock in Japan.* Institute of Social Science, University of Tokyo, Discussion Paper No. 7. Retrieved from http://project.iss.u-tokyo.ac.jp/Findings/Contents.htm and http://project.iss.u-tokyo.ac.jp/kikkawa/iss-7.pdf on 21 March 2013.

Verdict Research. (2008). *Retailing in France 2008.* Datamonitor Research Store. Retrieved from http://www.datamonitor.com/Products/Free/Report/DMVT0463/020DMVT0463.htm on 15 March 2013.

Varble, D.L. (1976). Sunday shopping and promotion possibilities. *Journal of the Academy of Marketing Science, 4*(4), 778–791.

SECTION 5
Reimagining the Political Hegemony

16
Empire or Imperialism?
Prasenjit Bose

Introduction

An intense debate over imperialism took place in the backdrop of the First World War, which broke out just about a 100 years ago. Months after the war started, German theorist Karl Kautsky published an article arguing that imperialism was digging its own grave by indulging in war and becoming a hindrance to the peaceful development of capitalism. He also contended that it is possible to conceive of 'a phase of ultra-imperialism', where the notion of cartelisation between giant firms and banks would be carried into the sphere of foreign policy. The result of the world war between the imperialist powers, Kautsky surmised, would then be the emergence of "a federation of the strongest, who renounce their arms race" (Kautsky, 1914).

Launching a scathing attack against this position, Russian revolutionary leader V.I. Lenin argued that one may 'theoretically' conclude that over time business magnates can unite into a 'world trust' replacing the rivalries between imperialist nations, but to advocate such a position 'in practice' amounts to shifting the focus away from 'the sharp tasks' confronting the anti-imperialist revolutionaries in the context of war. This, according to him, amounted to harbouring a petty-bourgeois dream of 'peaceful capitalism'. While not denying the possibility of the development towards an 'internationally united finance capital', Lenin reasoned that such development was ridden with 'such contradictions, conflicts and convulsions' that before a world union of national finance capitals—'ultra-imperialism'—can come into being, "imperialism will inevitably explode, capitalism will turn into its opposite" (Lenin, 1915).

How do we appraise such prognoses made about a 100 years ago? Lenin's assessments were certainly more valid till the Second World War, when the 'contradictions, conflicts and convulsions' characterising the imperialist world order were not only manifest but also drove the dynamics of economics and politics at the global level. In the post-war period, the rivalries between the advanced capitalist nations—inter-imperialist rivalry—gave way to the 'cold war' between the US-led capitalist world and the socialist bloc led by the erstwhile Union of Soviet Socialist Republics (USSR). Decolonisation also led to the emergence of the Third World and the Non-aligned Movement. As far as the advanced capitalist world is concerned, it had started moving in a Kautskite direction.

The world we are in today, since the fall of the USSR and the disappearance of the socialist bloc, is marked by the globalisation of capitalism. It is noteworthy that the end of the cold war has also not witnessed a revival of the 'contradictions, conflicts and convulsions' between the old imperialist powers, in contrast to the scene prevalent in the early decades of the last century. On the face of it, Kautsky's prognosis of 'ultra-imperialism' seems to have turned out to be more prescient than Lenin's.

However, the unity of the traditional imperialist powers has neither led to a slowing down of the 'arms race' nor a world without wars, as can be seen from the recent military invasions by the US and its North Atlantic Treaty Organization allies, in Afghanistan and Iraq, and the interventions in Kosovo and Libya, besides the lingering conflicts in other parts of the world under the rubric of an 'endless' war on terrorism. Thus, the contemporary world not only defies Lenin's notion of an imperialism marked by intense inter-imperialist rivalries but also the Kautskite notion of a peaceful world order under 'ultra-imperialism'.

Attempts to interpret these complex realities from a radical (anti-capitalist) standpoint have led to renewed debates. Hardt and Negri in their opus, *Empire*, questioned the very utility of the concept of imperialism to analyse contemporary capitalism and the world order (Hardt & Negri, 2000). Their work posits a 'passage' from 'modern' imperialism in the last century to a 'post-modern' global empire of the contemporary times and seeks to unravel its historical and philosophical evolution, as well as its political, economic, sociological and cultural dynamics. Marxist scholars of political economy, while critiquing Hardt and Negri's arguments, have also felt the need to conceptualise a 'new economics' or 'new phase' of imperialism as against the old.[1] This paper, while exploring some aspects of this imperialism/empire/new imperialism debate, makes a critique of 'empire' and looks at how imperialism remains to be a valid theoretical category in analysing contemporary economics and politics.

'Empire': The Concept

The political economic logic of Hardt and Negri regarding a 'passage' from imperialism to empire needs to be distilled from a complicated set of arguments. According to them, the post-war era, often considered as the golden age of capitalism, ushered in a new world order where the capitalist world was shaped by the New Deal, inaugurated in the US. The process of decolonisation gathered pace during this period, and after the Vietnam War, hegemony and the international hierarchisation of power and authority were established primarily through economic rather than military means.

This new hierarchisation was also accompanied by the decentralisation of capitalist production across the world, facilitated by the rise of transnational corporations (TNCs). Capitalist interests across the world got aligned with the TNCs, leading to the emergence of new regional economies. Alongside, there was a process of homogenisation of production processes and labour regimes across the world, first with the universalisation of modern factory production and later with the 'postmodernisation' of production—implying the growth of employment in services, particularly those based on knowledge, information and communication technologies.

Hardt and Negri argue that with decolonisation and the collapse of the USSR, capitalism has finally realised a unified world market, marked by the free mobility of capital, labour, commodities and technologies across national borders. As a result of this globalisation, the earlier division between the First, Second and the Third World has got much scrambled, so that "we find the First World in the Third, the Third in the First, and the Second almost nowhere at all" (Hardt & Negri, 2000: xiii). They further argue that the sovereignty of the erstwhile nation-states has declined under globalisation, and a 'new imperial form of sovereignty' has emerged through a 'network' of national and supra-national organisations, like the International Monetary Fund (IMF), World Bank, TNCs and non-governmental organisations.

---

[1] See Albo (2004), Harvey (2003), Patnaik (2010, 2011).

While the US is considered to have a 'privileged' position in this network, which is identified as a global extension of the imperial constitutional project of the US, this 'new imperial form of sovereignty' is deemed to be incomparable with the European imperialisms of the earlier centuries: "*The United States does not, and indeed no nation-state can today, form the centre of an imperialist project.* Imperialism is over. No nation will be world leader in the way modern European nations were" (Hardt & Negri, 2000: xiii–xiv; emphasis as in original).

Hardt and Negri characterise this 'new global form of sovereignty', a power network of national and supra-national organisations that rules without any territorial boundaries or socio-economic limits, as the 'empire'. This empire is confronted with a 'multitude', implying a proletariat that comprises not only of the industrial working class—which in their opinion has lost its hegemonic position in the anti-capitalist struggle—but also of all those who labour and cooperate to reproduce life, from migrant 'illegal labour' to the knowledge workers. The political programme of this insurgent multitude against the imperial power is outlined as a set of universal demands: the right to global citizenship, the right to a social wage (guaranteed income for all) and the right to reappropriate the means of production, which includes free access to and control over knowledge, information, communications, etc.

Hardt and Negri's work has been widely critiqued for attempting to rewrite the *Communist Manifesto* for the twenty first century.[2] What the authors have sought to rewrite or rather discard, however, is not so much the basic thesis of the *Manifesto* but the 'classical' theories of imperialism developed by Marxists like Rosa Luxemburg and Lenin, through the early twentieth century debates over the political economy of monopoly capitalism as well as international politics, war and peace.[3] *Empire* can be read more as a call to return to the *Manifesto* rather, in a world where there are only two classes left, face to face with each other: the empire of capital and the multitude of the proletariat.

Globalisation of capitalism, in Hardt and Negri's view, has obliterated all other divisions, based on nation-states or the spatial distinction between the First and the Third World. Hence their assertion 'imperialism is over' and their explicit reference to the 'missing volumes of *Capital*' on the state and the world market, which they think was not possible to write during Marx's time because the conditions, were only nascent (Hardt & Negri, 2000: 236). It is only in the globalised world of today that they find the centrality of class struggle between capital and labour becoming globally relevant and the only resolution possible through the global appropriation of the means of production, including the means of knowledge creation, information and communications, by the proletarian multitude. In other words, for those who want to change the world or make revolution, there is no material basis left for anti-imperialism at the national/local levels; transformative praxis is possible only through a global anti-capitalism.

Empire or New Imperialism?

The State under Capitalism

There are three basic problems with Hardt and Negri's thesis in *Empire*. The first concerns the understanding of how a capitalist economy functions and the role in it played by the state. Capitalism functions through the process of expanded reproduction, where capital extracts surplus from labour, realises it as profit and reinvests it as additional capital. In *Capital*, Marx had dissected how this process of capital accumulation often breaks down into crises because of the failure of capital to realise the surplus

---

[2] See for instance Zizek (2001).
[3] See Lenin (1917/1963) and Luxemburg (1917/1951).

as profit owing to the limitations of the market. Marx had also analysed how capital accumulation leads to concentration of capital and the emergence of giant blocs of monopoly capital.

The classical theories of imperialism developed by Luxemburg and Lenin were based on these Marxian concepts. For Luxemburg, capital's quest to realise its surplus inevitably led to intrusions into pre-capitalist markets, which formed the basis of imperialism. Lenin saw imperialism more as a multifaceted manifestation of the concentration of capital, the growth of gigantic monopolies and the emergence of finance capital through the coalescence of giant banks and monopoly firms, which led to a quest for markets, raw materials, avenues for capital exports and extending 'spheres of influence' outside national boundaries. Imperialism was thus theorised as a natural outcome of the process of capital accumulation and an elaboration of how capitalism actually expanded on a global scale. In other words, the theories of imperialism were as much attempts to fill the gap left by the 'missing volumes of *Capital*' on the state and the world market, as they were analytical tools to interpret the world events from a radical standpoint.

One can, however, argue that the role of the state remained under-theorised in the classical theories of imperialism, since both Luxemburg and Lenin saw the state more as an instrument for imperialist ventures, waging wars and capturing colonial markets and resources on behalf of capital. The fact that the state under capitalism can and has historically played a vital role in the accumulation process by expanding the domestic market through incurring debt/deficit-financed expenditures was not given much theoretical attention. The New Deal kind of solution to the problem of capitalist crisis was therefore never properly anticipated. The other vital role played by the state under capitalism in ensuring price and monetary stability, without which the process of capital accumulation in a money-using economy can also get jeopardised, has largely remained outside the scope of the classical theories of imperialism.

This is not to suggest that the role played by the state under capitalism makes imperialism redundant, but to underscore the point that neither capital accumulation nor imperialism can be fully comprehended without understanding the 'economic' role played by the state under capitalism in 'stabilising' the accumulation process. The market-enhancing role of the state has increased manifolds over the past century to reduce capitalism's reliance on pre-capitalist markets, which was at the heart of Luxemburg's analysis. Lenin's prognosis of competition between the rival national blocs of finance capital inevitably leading to inter-imperialist military conflicts also seems to have been overrun by later-day developments. But neither has the realisation problem vanished from the capital accumulation process nor has the expansionary and predatory nature of finance capital under monopoly capitalism been reversed. If anything, these trends have become more acute and the importance of the economic functions of the state has increased accordingly.

Hardt and Negri's analysis of the nation-state has been carried out from a narrow prism of declining 'sovereignty'. There is much truth in the argument that the sovereignty of nation-states has declined under globalisation. Such erosion of national sovereignty has had major implications for the economic functions played by the state under capitalism. However, *Empire* assumes away those functions altogether in the name of a power network of national and supranational organisations replacing the nation-state. In *Empire's* globalised world therefore, there are only capital, labour, commodities and technologies freely flowing across national boundaries, but no fiscal or monetary policies, no financial, trade or immigration policies and no intellectual property rights. This robs the concept of its analytical depth and explanatory capacity.

For instance, even after several decades of economic globalisation, the degree or extent of cross border mobility of capital or commodities is not matched by that of technologies or labour. What explains the differentiated speed at which these factors of production move across the national boundaries? Moreover, when Hardt and Negri argue that after the Vietnam War, hegemony has been pursued more through the dollar than through military hardware, it begs the question how it was possible to establish or maintain this hegemony in the first place? Or why has military expenditure not come down in the US or for the world as a whole despite the end of the cold war?[4] Since they deny the status of the US as a 'world leader' or argue that the US nation-state does not lie at the centre of any imperialist project, how can they possibly explain the ongoing global recession following a financial crisis in the US? There was no global recession following the earlier instances of financial crisis in South East Asian or Latin American countries.

These questions cannot be addressed within the framework of *Empire* precisely because of its inadequate analysis of the political economy of globalisation and the functions played by the state. Imperialism, as a concept, helps us to (a) explain the hegemonic nature and unequal structure of the present world order in terms of its underlying class processes and (b) analyse the inter-relationships between economic globalisation and persisting international conflicts and wars.

Post-war Capitalism: Finance and US Hegemony

Empire's narrative of the 'passage' from imperialism to empire brings out the conceptual problems more vividly. Hardt and Negri argue that the New Deal and decolonisation during the post-war period brought about the shift in the way world capitalism functioned, with old-style imperialism gradually giving way to the new form of 'empire'. For them, globalisation has followed as a natural corollary or a continuum of the post-war restructuring of capitalism. This is both ahistorical and analytically problematic.

The post-war restructuring of capitalism and decolonisation were forced upon the capitalist classes and states of the advanced countries, partly by the massive working class and anti-colonial struggles of that period, partly by the exigencies of the generalised crisis of the 1930s, which led to the Second World War and partly by the existence of the USSR-led socialist camp, which posed a credible threat. Thus, it was in many ways a triumph of the 'multitude', which succeeded in pushing imperialism on the back foot and forcing it to amend its ways. The institutional architecture put in place during the post-war 'golden age of capitalism' reflected this balance of class forces at the international level.

Far from being a continuum, the beginning of economic globalisation signified a reversal of this class balance and a dismantling of that post-war institutional architecture. This was accomplished through the neoliberal counter-revolution of the 1970s witnessed in the US and other advanced capitalist countries. This involved dumping the Bretton Woods arrangement of the gold-dollar standard, doing away with the capital controls, allowing all currencies to adjust in the market vis-à-vis the dollar and abandoning Keynesian demand management policies domestically in favour of privatisation and deregulation. The class force driving these changes was a resurgent finance capital, originating in the US and other advanced countries but international in its scope and ambition. The emergence of international finance—much more autonomous of national or industrial linkages than the finance capital of early twentieth century—and its quest to break down all the barriers that hinder its global mobility lies at the heart of the globalisation process.

The incursions of international finance have been so intense and pervasive under globalised capitalism, from shaping the trajectories of capital accumulation, to influencing the prices of commodities and assets and to determining the policies of the state, that this process in its totality has been identified as

---

[4] Data from the SIPRI Military Expenditure Database show that world military expenditure (in constant dollars) first declined from around $1.5 trillion in 1990 to around $1 trillion in 1998, but has risen progressively since then to reach $1.75 trillion in 2012 (2.5 per cent of world GDP), well past the cold war peak. Thirty-nine per cent of total world military expenditure in 2012 was incurred by the US, 9.5 per cent by China, 5.2 per cent by Russia, 3.5 per cent by the UK, 3.4 per cent each by Japan and France, 3.2v by Saudi Arabia and 2.6% each by India and Germany.

'financialisation' of contemporary capitalism.⁵ *Empire* misses this point completely when it characterises globalisation as an 'irresistible and irreversible' process of 'economic and cultural exchanges', failing to identify the class forces driving the process.

The 'post-modern' features of the globalised economy identified in the *Empire*, the decentralisation of capitalist production through the growth and spread of TNCs, the growth of the services sector or the innovations in information and communications technologies have all been shaped by international finance capital, which seeks to permeate economic activities and appropriate surplus from all corners of the world. Far from a diffusion of economic and political power within a mystical global network of national and supra-national organisations, as the *Empire* will have us believe, globalisation has led to an unprecedented concentration of power and resources in the hands of a global financial oligarchy.

While international finance is globally mobile and not tied to any specific nation-state, the US state has played a central role in stabilising capital accumulation and maintaining the institutional architecture within which global finance operates.⁶ This entails the hegemony of the dollar, in which bulk of the world's assets and resources are held or traded, including the foreign exchange reserves held by nation-states around the world.⁷ Dollar hegemony facilitates the flow of financial resources into the US from across the world and allows its state to stimulate the accumulation process, not only within the domestic economy but in all other economies that export goods and services to the US. This makes the rest of the capitalist world dependent on the US market, which is a major reason for the muted inter-imperialist rivalries under globalisation. Rather than fiercely competing with the other capitalist economies for markets in goods and services, the US provides its own market to other countries in exchange for their acceptance of its financial supremacy.

This regime, under which globalisation functions, has two major problems. First, the sustenance of this regime is crucially dependent on the continued expansion of the US economy, which is the largest economy of the world accounting for over a fifth of world GDP. The accumulation process within the US has, however, become highly unstable because of its reliance on asset price bubbles and debt-financed consumption spending owing to financialisation. Second, the leadership role played by the US in the world economy by running external deficits and providing market access to other countries implies growing external indebtedness. This cannot go on endlessly, without either eroding global confidence in the dollar or the big foreign creditors, like China and Japan, eventually making claims over physical assets within the US. Efforts to bring down its external debt or deficit, on the other hand, will undermine US' leadership role in the world economy.⁸ The 2007 financial crisis and the subsequent global recession have brought both these problems to the fore, making US hegemony less secure.

The enormous military apparatus under US command continues to be maintained and expanded to pre-empt any threat to its hegemonic position, especially the position of the dollar as the reserve currency. For dollar hegemony to be stable, the value of the dollar vis-à-vis the primary factors of production needs to be stable. This underlies US' military-strategic thrust towards control of natural resources across the world, especially oil, which is the principal energy resource. The most devastating and expensive war

---

⁵ Epstein (2005: 3) defines 'financialisation' as "the increasing role of financial motives, financial markets, financial actors and financial institutions in the operation of the domestic and international economies".
⁶ See Panitch and Gindin (2008).
⁷ Out of the $6 trillion foreign exchange reserves held by countries reporting to IMF's Currency Composition of Official Foreign Exchange Reserves (COFER) in 2013-Q1, 62 per cent were held in US dollars. The UN World Economic Situation and Prospects, 2013, shows net transfer of financial resources from the developing to the developed countries to be more than $600 billion in 2012. Bulk of this is on account of holding high foreign exchange reserves.
⁸ For an elaborate discussion, see Chapter 20 on "Capitalism and imperialism" in Patnaik (2008).

in recent times fought against Iraq by the US and its allies, which has killed over hundreds of thousands of Iraqi civilians since 2003 and costed over $3 trillion to the US exchequer, was fought over oil.[9]

Defending *Empire*'s thesis in the backdrop of the Iraq war, Hardt argued that the 'Bush administration's unilateralist policies and imperialist adventures' like the Iraq war ended up in 'fiascos', and these 'failures' marked the 'end of imperialism'. He contrasted this with the Bush administration's 'collaboration' with Europe, Russia and China on Iran, which showed how 'Washington feels the pressure to develop wider collaborations to achieve a stable global order', similar to the 'collaboration between a monarch and a group of aristocrats' within an *Empire* (Hardt, 2006).

The foreign oil companies operating in Iraq today following the auctioning of the nationalised oilfields would hardly consider the Iraq war as a 'failure'. Whoever else lost or failed in the war so far, they have clearly won for the time being. And if the logic is that the US becomes imperialist only when it goes to war and acts as empire when it collaborates with others, question arises why the *Empire* needs to turn imperialist at all after the 'passage' from imperialism to empire?

The Third World Persists

Is the World Flattening?

A glance through the annual Forbes lists of Global 2000 leading companies or the world's dollar billionaires of the past decade will show how corporations and business magnates from the 'emerging' economies like China, Russia, India, Brazil, Turkey, Mexico and others have gradually secured their place in it alongside those from the US (which continues to dominate all such lists), Japan and the west European countries.[10] Does this signify an end to the geographical distinction between the First World and the Third, as has been argued in *Empire*?

Rather than flattening the world and modernising the developing countries on the image of advanced capitalism, what has happened under globalisation is the creation of a limited number of globally integrated enclaves within a select group of developing countries. Within these enclaves, rapid industrialisation/modernisation is taking place through the diffusion of global capitalism. This enclavised accumulation process, given the global pattern of its demand, technologies, labour processes, skill requirements and financial networks, is failing to absorb surplus labour of the Third World and transform the landscape of backwardness.

Thus, economic dualism continues to persist, besides widening socio-economic inequalities on an unprecedented scale. The paradoxical nature of this development process can be seen in the 'convergence' of wealth and assets of the big capitalists in the Third World with those of the First, even while the gap between the wages, income levels or standards of living for the labouring classes in the First and the Third World refuses to close. For the vast majority of the Third World people, the world does not appear as scrambled as *Empire* suggests. The Third World remains where it was, as 'economically' distant from the First World, and as exploited as ever.

The question of underdevelopment therefore remains central in the Third World context as it was during the phase of anti-colonial struggles or the early days of decolonisation. What has changed,

---

[9] See Stiglitz & Bilmes (2008) and Wikipedia (n.d.).
[10] Most of the Chinese, Russian and Brazilian companies that figure in the Forbes Global 2000 lists are state controlled but publicly listed banks and oil companies. Russia and China ranked second and third, respectively, after the US in the number of dollar billionaires in 2012.

however, is the nature and role of the big capitalist class in the Third World, which has moved from their earlier position of relative autonomy with regard to imperialism in the post-war period to one of strategic alignment with international finance capital under globalisation.[11] The co-option of the 'national bourgeoisie' of the Third World by global finance does not imply their relegation to a 'comprador' status, but their emergence as junior or sub-imperialist powers themselves. This has made it difficult to pursue anti-imperialism as a national project within the Third World, but it has neither done away with the unequal structure of the world economy nor the perpetuation of underdevelopment for the vast majority of the Third World masses. What this calls for is a renovation of the theory of imperialism and reworking anti-imperialist strategies, not its conceptual negation à la *Empire*.

Three Forms of Exploitation

In *Capital*, Marx had explicated how the people are subjected to three distinct forms of exploitation or oppression by capital. The first is of course the extraction of surplus value from the workers by capital in the production process. The second is by the creation or preservation of the reserve army of the unemployed by introducing labour-displacing techniques in production; the existence of the reserve army keeps workers subjugated to capital and tethers the wage rate to a subsistence level. The third is through the 'primitive accumulation' of capital whereby there is an expropriation of the resources and means of production of the pre-capitalist producers, turning them into proletariats or even paupers, slaves, beggars, robbers and vagabonds. In contrast to the world of the *Empire*, where only the first form of exploitation exists (perhaps a bit of the second too), the Third World continues to witness all the three forms of exploitation and oppression.[12]

The processes unleashed by globalisation—financial speculation, the privatisation of public sector assets, transfer of natural and common resources like land, water and minerals to big corporations, rents extracted through intellectual property rights and the squeeze on the petty producers brought about through deflationary policies and trade liberalisation, alongside the displacement of peasants and rural workers from their lands, forests and habitats—are together being viewed as a variant of 'primitive accumulation'. It has been argued that this form of expropriation or grab of resources—as distinct from the appropriation of profit through expanded reproduction—has become an increasingly important form of capital accumulation under the neoliberal regime, particularly in the Third World. Harvey (2003) termed this as 'accumulation by dispossession' and considered it as the 'primary contradiction' of the post-1973 era, which lies 'at the heart' of imperialist practices. Patnaik (2005) sees this as 'accumulation through encroachment' whose 'relative importance' in the overall accumulation process has witnessed a 'vast increase' during the 'new phase of imperialism' (Harvey, 2003; Patnaik, 2011).

There are conceptual problems involved in clubbing together a whole range of neoliberal processes in the Third World together as a variant of primitive accumulation and characterising it as imperialist appropriation. In so far as all this ultimately translates into transfer of resources from petty producers or the state to big capital, both domestic and foreign, a differentiation needs to be made between the transfers made through market mechanisms and what comprises actual primitive accumulation: (a) expropriation of petty private property or common resources by big capital, involving direct displacement and colonial-style coercion of the people or (b) ex gratia transfer of public or common resources by the state to big capital through cronyist processes. Some proportion of such transfers also contributes

---

[11] While the degrees of autonomy varied greatly across countries, the relative autonomy of the Third World bourgeoisie as a whole was reflected in the Non-aligned Movement (NAM) until the 1980s. The relevance and influence of the NAM have greatly declined under globalisation.

[12] For a detailed discussion, see Bose (2011).

to domestic capital accumulation within the Third World. A significant proportion of such transfers through primitive accumulation, however, are sucked out of the Third World into the circuits of global finance, which amounts to imperialist appropriation.

The exclusion of a vast section of the working population from the system of capitalist production is the other major aspect of exploitation in the Third World. This leads to the persistence of a huge pool of reserve labour, not only the openly unemployed but also those who are under-employed in a wide range of informal economic activities or even unpaid labour, both in agriculture and non-agriculture. A significant proportion of this workforce is also self-employed and engaged in petty economic activities. Sanyal (2007) characterises this Third World condition as a 'capital–non-capital complex', where non-capitalist production involves self-employment and household-based work.[13] He sees the forces of globalisation both destroying non-capitalist production in some instances and creating conditions for it to exist and thrive in others. Sanyal also insists that 'non-capital' coexists with capital not because of any specific functional need of capitalism—unlike what the dependency theories of imperialism argued—but because of the peculiarities of 'post-colonial capitalism', where capitalist transition gets blocked owing to the weakness of the bourgeoisie.

There are two important ways, however, in which the 'non-capitalist' sector is functionally related to capitalist production. To the extent that the self-employed workers, at least a sizeable proportion of them, exchange commodities with the capitalist sector, there is an unequal exchange. Second, this 'non-capitalist' sector together with the informal sector workers (who are not self-employed) comprises a huge pool of reserve labour, which keeps wages low in the Third World, and facilitates the super-exploitation of labour even within the enclaves of capitalist production through contractualisation of labour. Bulk of the manufacturing production under globalisation is organised today around this 'cheap' Third World labour, which creates super-profits for the big corporates and helps to keep inflation low, even within the advanced capitalist countries.[14]

Anti-imperialist Resistance

The structure of exploitation under globalised capitalism is more complex than what Hardt and Negri suggest. Just as the concept of *Empire* seeks to oversimplify that structure, the political programme outlined for the multitude tends to generalise the terrain of resistance, without identifying the target. Today's radical or progressive struggles, however, are being fought at different levels.

There is the struggle within the First World between the proletarian multitude against their ruling classes, to defend whatever is left of the welfare state and reigning in finance capital. Then there are the struggles in the Third World against all the three forms of exploitation and oppression by big capital and the neoliberal state: struggles against primitive accumulation, struggles against exclusion/underdevelopment for livelihood rights and democracy and the struggle against 'cheapness' of labour. Finally, there is a common global struggle against international finance capital and US imperialism. All this taken together comprise the global anti-imperialist resistance. Not only has imperialism not been defeated yet, but it also cannot possibly be defeated straightaway at the global level. The success of the struggles in the Third World as well as the first, to reclaim the nation-state from the respective ruling classes, can pave the way for larger anti-imperialist victories.

---

[13] See Sanyal (2007).
[14] For a similar argument, see Chapter 18 on "Capitalism as a Mode of Production" in Patnaik (2008).

References

Albo, G. (2004). The old and the new economics of imperialism. In C. Leys & L. Panitch (Eds.), *Socialist register 2004: The new imperial challenge*. London: Merlin Press.

Bose, P. (2011). The three stories of capital and their relevance today. In *Marx's capital: An introductory reader* (77–103). New Delhi: Leftword Books.

Epstein, G.A. (2005). Introduction: Financialization and the world economy. In G.A. Epstein (Ed.), *Financialization and the world economy* (pp. 3–16). Northampton, MA: Edward Elgar.

Hardt, M. (31 July 2006). From imperialism to empire. *The Nation*, 35–40.

Hardt, M., & Negri, A. (2000). *Empire*. London: Harvard University Press.

Harvey, D. (2003). *The new imperialism*. Oxford: Oxford University Press.

Kautsky, K. (1914). Ultra-imperialism. *Die Neue Zeit (Journal of the Social Democratic Party of Germany)*. Retrieved from https://www.marxists.org/archive/kautsky/1914/09/ultra-imp.htm on 12 January 2016.

Lenin, V.I. (1915). Introduction. In *Imperialism and world economy* (pp. 9–14). London: Martin Lawrence Limited.

———. (1917/1963). *Imperialism, the highest stage of capitalism* in *selected works* (Vol. I). Moscow: Progress Publishers.

Luxemburg, R. (1917/1951). *The accumulation of capital*. London: Routledge & Kegun Paul.

Panitch, L., & Gindin, S. (2008). Finance and American empire. In L. Panitch & M. Konings (Eds.), *American empire and the political economy of global finance* (pp. 17–47). Basingstoke: Palgrave Macmillan.

Patnaik, P. (2008). *The value of money*. New Delhi: Tulika Books.

———. (2010). Notes on contemporary imperialism. *The Marxist*, *XXVI*(October–December), 4.

———. (Ed.). (2011). The economics of the new phase of imperialism. In *Re-envisioning Socialism*. New Delhi: Tulika Books.

Sanyal, K. (2007). *Rethinking capitalist development: Primitive accumulation, governmentality and post-colonial capitalism*. New Delhi: Routledge.

Stiglitz, J.E., & Bilmes, L.J. (2008). *The three trillion dollar war: The true cost of the Iraq conflict*. New York, NY: W.W. Norton.

Wikipedia (n.d.). Casualties of the Iraq War. Retrieved from http://en.wikipedia.org/wiki/Casualties_of_the_Iraq_War on 22 January 2016.

Zizek, S. (2001). Have Michael Hardt and Antonio Negri rewritten the communist manifesto for the twenty-first century? *Rethinking Marxism*, *13*(3/4), 190–198.

17

Output and Price (In)Stability under Neoliberalism: A Kaleckian Approach

Rohit

Introduction

Since the withdrawal of Keynesianism in the 1970s as a result of 'stagflation', there has been an increasing thrust both in mainstream macroeconomic theory and policy derived from it towards a laissez-faire economy as far as possible.

Patnaik (1997, 2009) has worked extensively to expose the limitations of mainstream macroeconomics by showing that an isolated mature capitalist economy faces twin problems of output and price instability. It is only when the non-capitalist periphery is included as an *intrinsic* part of the system that one could logically argue that these instabilities are kept muted over longer periods of time, as has historically been the case.

This chapter proposes to interpret his argument in the case of a purely laissez-faire economy in the era of neoliberalism. I argue that while neoliberalism has aggravated the problem of output instability, it has muted price instability.

With respect to output instability, I argue that because of the limitations vis-á-vis demand generation capacity of the state under neoliberalism, the economy increasingly gets dependent on asset price booms, which could result in spectacular booms but equally spectacular busts, as witnessed in the Great Recession today. In other words, there is a tendency towards stagnation with violent business cycles.

On the other hand, because of the exposure to competitive labour markets located in the periphery, the working class in the capitalist core itself gets weakened, thereby undermining the very source of price instability.

Instabilities under Capitalism

While growth under capitalism has been the subject matter of enquiry since Adam Smith, modern growth theory came into existence arguably through Harrod (1939). It was an attempt to dynamise Keynes' static analysis of a capitalist economy.

Harrod (1939) had argued that under capitalism, where expectations about the market drive accumulation, there will be instability in this process, because the market gives the capitalists contrary signals. Also, while the decision to invest by capitalists is individual, their decisions have a collective effect *ex post* on the extent of market available. Investment generates output in a proportion determined by the Keynesian multiplier, say a. If the capitalists desire the output–capital ratio to be, say b^1, there is a specific level of investment-capital ratio given by b/a, the famous Harrodian warranted rate of growth, which will realise their expectations. Let us see how the market gives contrary signals.

If they happen to invest (investment–capital ratio) more than b/a, say $1.1b/a$, then the *actual* output–capital ratio will turn out to be $1.1b$, that is, even higher than they expected, giving them the impression that they were unnecessarily pessimistic. In the next period, instead of cutting down the investment–capital ratio to b/a, they will end up increasing it beyond $1.1b/a$, thereby pushing the economy away from b/a, that is, the one consistent with expectations. If, on the other hand, to begin with they happen to invest less, say $0.9b/a$, then the actual output–capital ratio will be even lower than their expectation, giving them the impression that they were a little too optimistic. On either side of the warranted rate of growth, the actual rate of growth diverges, which gives it the 'knife-edge' nomenclature. We can call this the *first* knife-edge of Harrod because there was another knife-edge, namely the balance between the warranted and natural rates of growth. Out of the 20 odd pages, Harrod spent just the last four on the second knife-edge, which should give a sense of the importance he gave to the first knife-edge.

Unfortunately, the first knife-edge, which is central in understanding problems of accumulation under capitalism, has been erased from the discourse in the mainstream growth theory beginning with Solow (1956). Without providing a solution to the first knife-edge, Solow (1956) proceeds to provide a solution to the second knife-edge. Much as it draws attention to the rigidity of the output–capital ratio in Harrod (1939), it misses almost the entire point made. Solow (1956: 65) says this about Harrodian instability: "[w]hen the results of a theory seem to flow specifically from a special crucial assumption, then if the assumption is dubious, the results are suspect". It is ironical that Solow does exactly that in his own paper by assuming all savings are necessarily invested, thereby erasing the first knife-edge by *assumption*. Sen (1970a) shows that if this crucial assumption is removed from Solow (1956) by introducing an independent investment function, Harrodian instability reappears *despite* assuming a neoclassical production function with perfect substitutability between labour and capital. He goes on to show that such a flexibility makes the process of accumulation even more unstable.

This criticism will hold for the entire modern mainstream growth theory, ranging from the Cass–Koopmans' to the endogenous growth theories, as they all assume the first, and the more crucial, knife-edge away. So, while the Cass–Koopmans' model endogenises the savings rate (in effect the multiplier above), the endogenous growth theories make the rate of growth of labour productivity (one of the components of the natural rate of growth) endogenous to the growth process itself.

As opposed to this, there is a tradition of demand-driven growth models, which takes the first knife-edge as a point of departure and develops it. Kalecki (1962) presented a critique of Harrod (1939) from a different perspective. He argued that it is true that the warranted rate of growth is unstable (Kalecki called it 'ephemeral') in that the economy slides down or explodes in either direction. But what is more, if the economy slides down, it actually *stabilises* at a zero rate of growth in the absence of an exogenous

---

[1] A careful reading of section 'Instabilities under Capitalism' tells us that this (in his terminology, 1/C) is *not* necessarily the technological given output–capital ratio as has been made out to be the case by almost the entire growth literature, including the authoritative essay by Sen (1970b). To be precise, he writes (p. 18), "... C, the amount of capital per unit required by technological and *other* conditions (including the *state of confidence*, the rate of interest, etc.)..." (emphasis added). This distinction is important as it makes expectation intrinsic to the very definition of warranted rate of growth itself and is not determined purely by the savings ratio and technologically given capital–output ratio. It makes the Harrodian knife-edge problem come out even more clearly.

stimulus. In other words, the problems of accumulation under capitalism are such that the normal state of affairs would be no accumulation, that is, Marx's simple reproduction. So, for there to be a positive level of accumulation, some form of exogenous stimuli (exogenous to the process of accumulation) is required. Kalecki believed that innovations play that role from within the capitalist system, whereas the state could also play the role from outside the pure system.

Patnaik (1997) takes the Kaleckian argument even further. He presents an investment function on the lines suggested by Kalecki (1962) which generates two rates of growth (more on this later) but goes on to argue that what Kalecki considered as exogenous, that is, innovations, cannot strictly be taken as exogenous to the system. This is so because the expenditure required for innovations itself will be dependent on the level of investment. In such a situation, we are back to the original problem that Kalecki had proposed that a *pure* capitalist system will stabilise at zero rate of growth. Aside from the cyclical ups and downs, the fact that the system has not behaved like this historically (except during the Great Depression) need not have anything to do with a fundamental stability assumed in Solow (1956) but to the fact that capitalism has never existed without the crutch of semi-capitalist periphery, which has acted as a market on tap as well as a provider of raw materials at cost-effective rates.

This chapter, as is Patnaik (1997), is in the tradition of demand-driven growth models. Before we proceed further, let us place certain definitional issues in order. In this tradition of growth models, an independent investment function is central. So, while a short period is defined as one where investment is given exogenously, in the long period, the investment function comes into play. In other words, investment creates its own savings and not the other way round, as assumed in the mainstream growth models.

Let us look at the short period more formally. Kalecki assumed that workers consume all their wages, whereas capitalists consume only a portion of their profits. In the short run, the capacity utilisation is determined by the level of demand in the following manner. Since we are discussing a pure capitalist sector, i.e., without the outside help of the state or external markets, there are three sources of demand: consumption demand of the workers and the capitalists and investment demand of the capitalists. Gross domestic product (GDP) from the income side is on the left-hand side (LHS) and demand side on the right-hand side (RHS) in the following:

$$W + P = W + (1-s)P + \bar{I}$$

$$s\frac{P}{O}\cdot\frac{O}{K} = \frac{\bar{I}}{K}$$

$$shu = \bar{g} + d$$

where W = Wages

P = Profits

s = Savings propensity out of profits

I = Gross investment (17.1)

O = Output

K = Capital stock

h = Share of profits in output

u = Output – capital ratio

g = Net investment as a proportion of capital

d = Radioactive rate of depreciation of capital

Bounds of a Laissez-faire System

Patnaik (1997) blends the Harrod–Kalecki problem of accumulation (he calls it output instability) with the question of price instability, which advanced capitalist countries have to grapple with because of a significant bargaining position of the working class. In a system where the division of output is determined through negotiations between classes whose interests are antagonistic, there is an attempt by these classes to tilt the distribution in their favour. The weapon of negotiation is their collective strength, which for capitalists could be represented by the 'degree of monopoly', whereas for workers it could be the rate of employment. This will generate a lower limit to unemployment below which the price system will come under threat as the prices would increase without bound. Moreover, while prices in the aggregate are upwardly flexible, they are seen to be downwardly rigid. So, it generates a long-run L-shaped Phillips curve in the unemployment–inflation plane with the kink at the lower limit (more on this later in this section). Assuming an inverse relation between unemployment and capacity utilisation of machinery, this process sets an upper bound to the latter.

Patnaik (2009) brings another issue to the table. Not only is there an upper bound to the system, there is also a lower bound to a credit-based economy. Investment plans are also financed through credit, payment commitments on which are in nominal terms. On an average,[2] for the economy as a whole, at any given point in time, the rate of profit has to be at least at a level high enough to be able to service the accumulated debt. For a given profit margin and technology, this sets a lower limit to the level of capacity utilisation.

Lower Bound: Nominal Debt Commitments

At any given point in time, firms have past debt with interest commitments mutually agreed upon in the past which cannot be altered in the present. So, independent of the current rate of profit, to save themselves from bankruptcy, firms are supposed to service the accumulated debt. This requires the net rate of profit to be *at least* equal to the interest payments required on these commitments, which sets a lower bound for the system to be viable (also see Figure 17.1).

$$r = \frac{P - dK}{K} \geq i\frac{D}{K}$$

$$\frac{g + d}{sh} - d \geq i\delta \text{ (using Equation 17.1)}$$

$$\rightarrow r \geq i\delta \ \forall g \geq g_{min}, \text{ where } g_{min} = shi\delta - (1 - sh)d \quad (17.2)$$

where r = Net rate of profit

i = Nominal rate of interest

D = Past debt commitments

δ = Debt – capital ratio

Upper Bound: Non-accelerating Inflation Rate of Unemployment (NAIRU)

Assuming that the working class bargains for a wage share, which is positively related to the level of activity (inversely related to unemployment) and disinflation is a rarity ($\hat{x}$ represents the rate of growth of variable x),

---

[2] While it might be true that a fraction of firms might have revenues lower than that, financial stability requires this fraction to be low. Indeed, a higher fraction signifies a financial system in a precarious condition, an example of which is the global economic crisis of today.

Figure 17.1
(Im)Possibility of a Viable Range

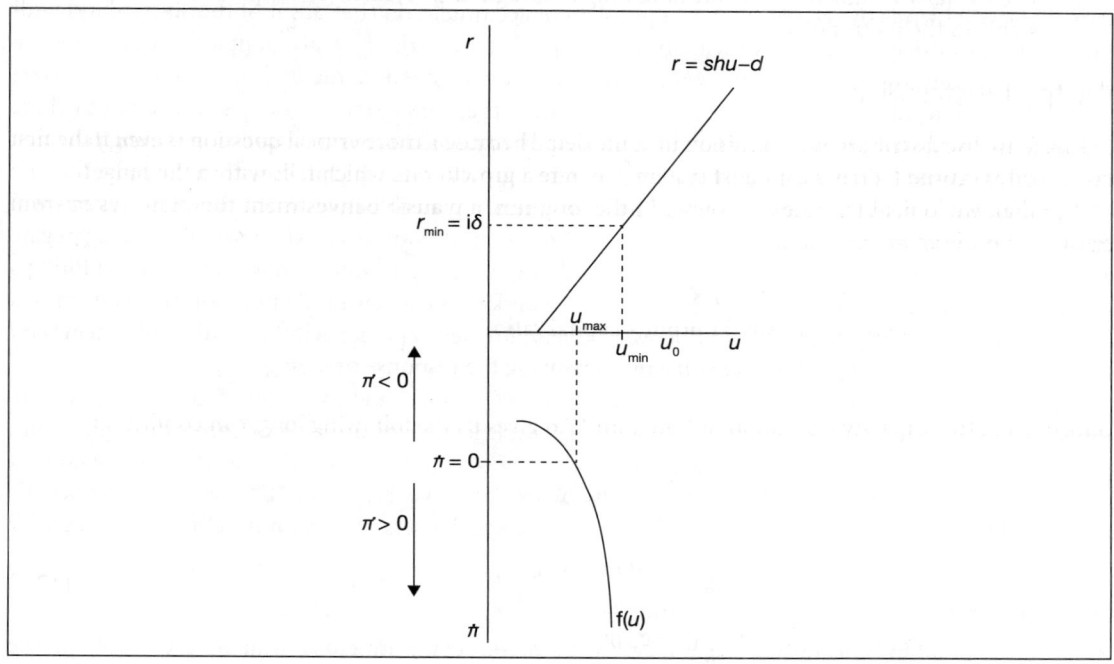

$$\hat{w} = \hat{p}^e + f(u) \; f > 0$$
$$\hat{p} = \max[0, \hat{w}]$$

where w = Nominal wages inclusive of labour productivity (17.3)
p = Price level
p^e = Price expected by the working class

This can be further explored under a plausible formulation of expectation formation, that is, adaptive expectations, which would give us (also see Figure 17.1)

$$\therefore \hat{p}^e = \hat{p}_{t-1} \; [\text{adaptive expectations}]$$
$$\dot{\pi} = \max[-\pi, f(u)]$$
$$\dot{\pi} = 0 \; \forall u = [0, u_{max}], \text{ where } f(u_{max}) = 0 \quad (17.4)$$
$$\rightarrow \dot{\pi} = 0 \; \forall g \leq g_{max} = shu_{max}$$
where π = Rate of inflation

Three Conditions

In light of the above discussion, three conditions need to be satisfied for this system to be self-correcting (also see Figure 17.1).

1. The range given by the lower and upper bounds is not an empty set. In other words,

$$[g_{min}, g_{max}] \neq \phi \quad (17.5)$$

2. The system, through its internal logic, creates a stable growth rate which falls within this range.
3. Even if falls within range, it produces high enough employment to keep the system politically stable in the metropolis.

Output Instability

We need to discuss the second condition in some detail because a more critical question is *even if* the first condition is satisfied, does a capitalist system generate a growth rate which falls within the range?

For that, we look at the rate of growth. In the long run, a plausible investment function (taken from Patnaik, 1997) can be formulated as

$$\dot{g} = \gamma_u (u - u_0) g$$

where u_0 = Desired output – capital ratio (17.6)
γ_u = Positive constant measuring the response of u on g

Substituting this capacity utilisation in Equation 17.6 gives us the following long-run condition:

$$\dot{g} = \gamma_u \left(\frac{g+d}{sh} - u_0 \right) g$$

$$= \frac{\gamma_u}{sh}[g - (shu_0 - d)]g \qquad (17.7)$$

$$= \frac{\gamma_u}{sh}[g - g_w]g$$

where g_w = Harrodian warranted rate of growth

This system has two steady states:

$$g_s = 0 \text{ or, } \frac{I}{K} = d$$

$$g_w = shu_0 - d \text{ or, } \left(\frac{I}{K}\right)_w = shu_0$$

The first rate of growth is the case of Marx's simple reproduction where the system is in stagnation (g_s), that is, just replicating itself by replacing the depreciated capital. The second growth rate is the Harrodian warranted rate of growth (g_w), where the economy would stay *if* it happens to be on it but would diverge in either direction if per chance it deviates. In other words, it is an unstable steady state. This can be easily established by taking the first derivative of the differential Equation 17.7.

$$\frac{d\dot{g}}{dg} = \gamma_u \left(\frac{2g+d}{sh} - u_0 \right)$$

Stable steady state: $g_s \therefore \left. \frac{d\dot{g}}{dg} \right|_{g_s} = -\frac{\gamma_u g_w}{sh} < 0$ (17.8)

Unstable steady state: $g_w \therefore \left. \frac{d\dot{g}}{dg} \right|_{g_w} = \frac{\gamma_u g_w}{sh} > 0$

Figure 17.2
Questioning the Viability of the Capitalist Core

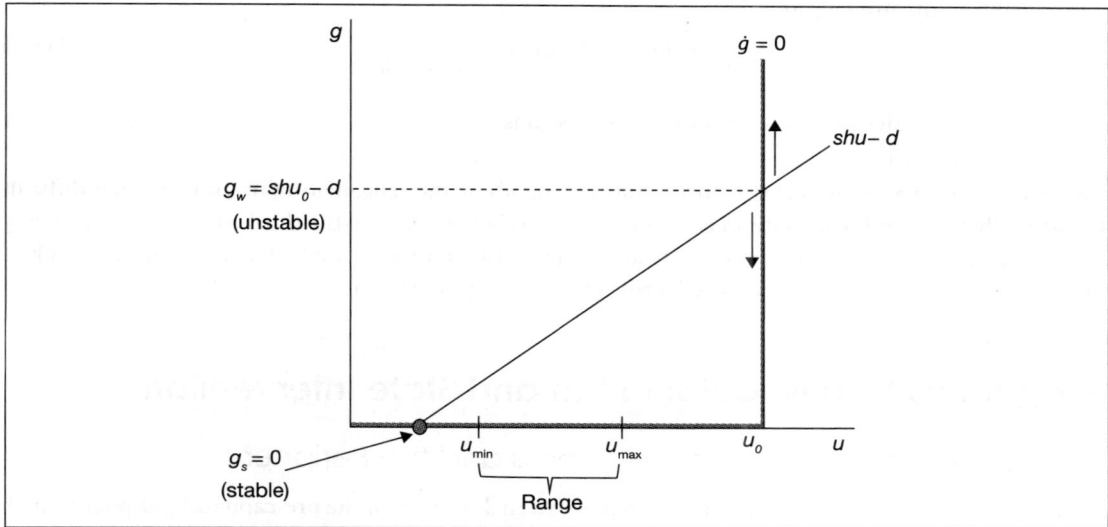

A laissez-faire capitalist system stabilises at simple reproduction. This is what Kalecki (1962) had argued, that is if one takes the Harrodian argument to its logical conclusion, then not only is the warranted rate unstable but the only stable rate is zero rate of growth, unless there exists an exogenous stimulus to investment. Bringing in the second condition in this discussion, for $g^* = 0$, the system can be above the threshold level of activity only if $g_{min} \leq 0$ (see Equation 17.2). Now there is no reason why the rate of depreciation would be such as to make it possible. So, there is no inherent mechanism under an isolated capitalist system to be working beyond this threshold. This violates the second condition mentioned earlier (in Figure 17.2, this stable steady state falls outside the range of viable options).

Despite such a logical impossibility, the system has worked historically. This begs the question: either this theoretical structure is incorrect or there are ways in which these conditions have been fulfilled with the help of external mechanism. We will focus on the second question here as a lot has been written on the debate between the heterodox and mainstream theoretical structures. About the merits of different theoretical structures on this important question and the need to focus on the second question, we quote Patnaik (1997: 53–54):

> When we observe a dog standing on its hind legs, we can theorise either that the dog is a biped animal, or that it needs a support to be able to stand up. ... we can attempt to find out from its muscular development and muscular effort, as observed in the standing position itself, whether it is these alone which contribute to its standing position. But there is no reason why, observing the dog standing, we should necessarily conclude that it is inherently stable on two legs, nor rule out any questions regarding its need for external support. Yet this is what economic theory has done systematically for decades.

Kalecki (1962), however, argued that there is an 'internal' component, innovations, which could ensure that the economy fulfils the second condition even as the third condition might not be satisfied.

$$\dot{g} = \gamma_0 + \gamma_u(u - u_0)g$$

which gives us

$$g^I = \frac{shu_0 - \sqrt{(shu_0)^2 - 4\gamma_0 sh/\gamma_u}}{2} > 0 \text{ [stable]} \qquad (17.9)$$

where e = Autonomous innovations

But precisely for the reason that this growth rate g^I depends on the exogeneity of innovations, it is difficult to ensure that the level of activity so generated is relatively high to fulfil the third condition. And, at any rate, innovations by themselves need not satisfy the first condition as well. Hence, we need to look at other external factors which have played a role in sustaining capitalism.

Exogenous Stimuli: Colonialism and State Intervention

Unequal Interdependence: Metropolis and the Periphery

Patnaik (1997, 2009) argues that it is the crutch of external support of the pre-capitalist periphery which has helped capitalism in the metropolis function smoothly with just some blips intermittently. How has that happened?

The periphery has, through its role as the raw material provider, historically ensured that the first condition is fulfilled. And through its role as the market on tap ensured that the other two conditions are fulfilled too. Let us take a look at these two roles of the pre-capitalist periphery.

It opens up the higher bound by becoming the shock absorber (to be more precise inflation absorber) of the capitalist core. Let us see how.

$$p = \mu(w + \sigma p_a)$$
$$= \frac{\mu w}{\phi}$$

where σ = Production coefficient of raw material from the periphery

p_a = price of raw material in the same currency as p

$$\phi = \frac{w}{w + \sigma p_a} \text{ Share of wage cost in the total cost}$$

An increase in the share of wages in total cost is a decline in the share of the raw material in total metropolitan output. Using Equation 17.4 and assuming the markup to be given as earlier, we can write

$$\dot{\pi} = \max[-\pi, f(u) - \hat{\phi}] \qquad (17.10)$$

If the share of the periphery acts as the residual of this system as far as the distribution of shares of metropolitan output is concerned, the share of workers or capitalists or both can rise in the metropolis without threatening the system with inflationary instabilities of the kind discussed above. In other words, a high level of capacity utilisation (despite putting an upward pressure on the wage share) can materialise. Actually, if they absorb these shocks all the time, there is, *logically* speaking, no upper bound to this system, at least on this count, which means that the first condition is automatically satisfied (see Figure 17.3).

Figure 17.3
Periphery Ensures the Viability of the Capitalist Core

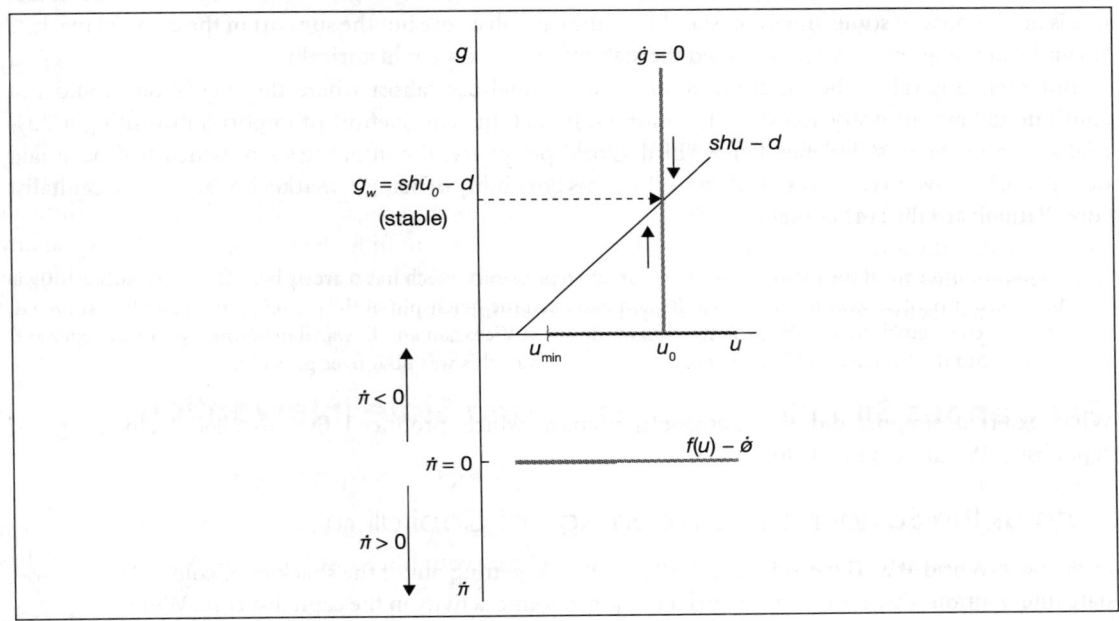

$$[g_{min}, \infty] \neq \phi \tag{17.11}$$

But this is just a *potential* set of feasible growth rates. What ensures that the system stabilises at a high rate of growth within the range which ensures political stability in the capitalist core?

It is the role of the periphery as a market on tap which ensures that the system works at the desired rate of capacity utilisation ($u = u_0$), because it gives the confidence to the capitalists in the core not to worry *ex ante* about the profitability of their investment decision. In the event that the domestic demand is such that output produced at u_0 is not exhausted, the core could push the extra production to its colonies and vice versa and ensure that in the long run the economy functions at the desired rate of capacity utilisation (see Figure 17.3). This can be seen in the following:

$$\therefore \frac{X - \frac{p_a}{p}M}{K} = g_w - g$$

$$shu = g + d + \frac{X - \frac{p_a}{p}M}{K} \quad [\text{short-run equilibrium}] \tag{17.12}$$

$$\dot{g} = \frac{\gamma_u}{sh}[g_w - (shu_0 - d)]g = 0 [\text{long-run equilibrium}]$$

where X = Exports
M = Imports

So, the warranted rate of growth becomes a stable steady state (see the change in the direction of arrows at the warranted rate of growth in Figure 17.3 in relation to Figure 17.2). But, as is to be noted, this is not because of some 'inherent' stability in the capitalist core but the support of the colonial markets (as and when required) which provided the stability to this system historically.

But then this raises the question about post-colonial capitalism where the metropolis could not continue to have arbitrary access to the colonies. In fact, the entire effort of import-substituting industrialisation in the post-independence Third World periphery, the initial seeds of which had been laid during the inter-war years, was in effect to close this possibility of being a 'market on tap' for the capitalist core. Patnaik (1997: 214) argues:

> [O]ne component of the picture [the 1930s Great Depression] which has scarcely been discussed sufficiently is the loss of British hegemony over Asia. Britain had been the lynch-pin of the earlier system, and had survived, and thereby contributed to the prolongation of the Great Victorian and Edwardian boom, by going deeper and deeper into the Indian and Chinese markets. After the war, this was no longer possible.

What external support did the metropolis manage which produced the so-called Golden Age of capitalism? We discuss that below.

State as the Saviour: The Golden Age of Capitalism

In the post-World War II period, with the Third World getting out of the shackles of colonial rule, it was state intervention which was active in driving the economic activity in the capitalist core. While geographically, this support was located within the metropolis, it was still an 'external' sector to the capitalist system as Luxemburg (1913/2003) had argued. However, it is important to note here that the state could still only ensure that the second and the third conditions are fulfilled, the first one still required the periphery as discussed earlier. So, it will be incorrect to argue that Keynesian demand management *alone* stabilised the system during the so-called Golden Age of capitalism. In fact, as we will see later, Keynesianism came under attack precisely when the first condition was threatened as the shock-absorbing capacity of the raw material producers in the Third World was under a severe strain due to the oil crisis of the 1970s.

State intervention in the economy ensured that there was an external source of demand which would keep the animal spirits high for the capitalists. It can be seen in the following manner. The short-run equilibrium changes to

$$W + P = W + (1-s)P + I + G - T$$
$$(sh - \xi)u = \bar{g}$$

where G = Fiscal expenditure (17.13)
T = Taxes (assumed to be indirect for simplicity)
ξ = Fiscal deficit as a proportion of output

By substituting the short-run equilibrium level of u arrived above in the investment function, the long-run stable rate of growth of the Golden Age can be derived as

$$g^{GA} = \frac{(sh-\xi)u_0 - \sqrt{((sh-\xi)u_0)^2 - 4e(sh-\xi)/b}}{2} > g^I \qquad (17.14)$$

And this rate would be higher, the higher is the share of fiscal expenditure in total output. An increase in ξ is the same as a decline in the savings ratio or an increase in the profit share. In such demand-driven growth models, these have a *positive* effect on the growth rate.

While state intervention might have solved the second and the third conditions, the metropolis still needed the periphery for the first condition. And herein laid the contradiction of Keynesianism, which saw government intervention as the route to smooth functioning of an otherwise unstable capitalist system. The crisis of Keynesianism hit the mainstream economic theory and policy circles precisely when the question of price instability came back on the agenda of the capitalist core. And what was the source behind that instability in the 1970s, the decade of end of Keynesianism in the West? The oil-exporting countries in the periphery had formed a cartel, that is the Organization of the Petroleum Exporting Countries, which hiked the prices of oil as a response to US aid to Israel. Prior to this period, despite very low rates of unemployment and high rates of growth in the metropolis during the two decades of the Golden Age, it did not face an inflationary crisis. Only when the terms of trade p_a/p became a shock-giver, by demanding a higher share in the metropolitan output, instead of being the shock absorber of the system as described above, that the metropolis faced an unprecedented inflationary crisis. The events of the 1970s clearly exposed the limitations of seeing state intervention as the panacea for a crisis-prone system and point to the critical role that the periphery played even during the Golden Age.

Neoliberalism: Suppression of the Working Class

As a response to the inflationary crisis of the 1970s, there was a resurrection of the old classical ideas of Say's law, with Milton Friedman leading the charge against Keynesian economics and its policy prescriptions. It resulted in what is called the neoliberal phase of capitalism. Some striking components of this paradigm were withdrawal of the welfare state (both within the core and the periphery); disciplining the working class; within the surplus owners, increased strength of the rentier class (a process came to be known as financialisation); aggressive free trade policies with respect to the periphery. Let us see how it affected the three conditions.

Globalisation and the Upper Bound

Rohit (2013) has argued that the bargaining function $f(u)$ of the working class in the metropolis turns redundant as their wages get tethered to their brethren in the periphery. This gives us another role that the periphery can play in ensuring that the first condition is fulfilled. This assumes greater importance than the terms of trade route because over a period, the latter could lose its shock-absorbing capacity as its magnitude itself would keep falling if there is increased pressure from the metropolis.

$$\hat{w} = \min[\theta\hat{w}_a, \hat{P}_{t-1} + f(u)] \theta > 1$$
$$\dot{\pi} = \max[-\pi, \min\{\theta\hat{w}_a - \pi f(u)\}] \tag{17.15}$$
where w_a = Wage share of the peripheral workers

The steady state of inflation would be given as follows:

$$\pi^* = \begin{cases} \theta\hat{w}_a & \text{if } \hat{w}_a > 0 \\ 0 & \text{if } \hat{w}_a \leq 0 \end{cases} \tag{17.16}$$

Unlike the case where the burden of adjustment fell on the share of the periphery, here the working class within the geographical boundaries of the capitalist system itself becomes the shock absorber. This has the potential of aggravating the political instability, both because the bargaining power of the working class gets severely limited and because the tendency towards stagnation reappears, as we see below.

Aggravated Output Instability

While globalisation eases the first condition, it has the potential of violating the second and the third conditions. This is for two reasons.

First, as a matter of policy, there was withdrawal of the state from active fiscal intervention, thereby limiting the role that it had hitherto played during the so-called Golden Age. This was evident in the 1990s when the US under Bill Clinton not only curtailed the fiscal deficit but actually ran a budget surplus for the first time since the 1950s.

Second, catching up on technological innovations by advanced capitalist countries other than the leader as well as outsourcing of certain activities to destinations with cheaper labour closes the opportunity of using the Third World as a market on tap. The US has been running trade deficit with the rest of the world for more than four decades now.

How, if at all, has the system coped with this problem? On the one hand, there has been a tendency towards more militarism, which was visible during Bush's presidency. On the other hand, there has been an increased dependence on asset-price bubble-based growth stories. We dwell upon the latter possibility in what follows. It needs to be mentioned that while such bubbles can alter the fluctuations in the level of activity, they cannot change the underlying trend rate of growth. Far from it, they make recovery more difficult, as is visible in the current global crisis.

Real Versus Speculative Investment

Investment is normally divided between non-residential and residential investment. While the investment plans in the former category are more likely to be made based on the level of demand in the economy, for the latter, it is more for speculative purposes since returns for this category of assets is essentially in terms of asset-price appreciation. However, these are not straightjacketed compartments. Yet for purposes of clarity, we argue that the first category of investment is dependent on the level of capacity utilisation, whereas the second is dependent on whether the market value of the asset (sales price of a residential property) is greater than its book value (say, the price of construction).

Let us explain the relation between the market value and book value through Tobin's q. The book value of assets can be defined as pK, where p is the production price of capital goods K (which, in one good model, is the general price level). The capitalists hold their entitlements to this capital stock in the form of equities E. Let p_E be the price of these equities. The relation between the market value and its book value is given by a proportion q.

$$q = \frac{\overbrace{p_E E}^{\text{Market value}}}{\underbrace{pK}_{\text{Book value}}} \tag{17.17}$$

It can be easily seen that the market value can deviate from its book value (the denominator) because of a relative increase (decrease) in the price of equities, that is the q-ratio can be different from one. In the presence of highly speculative markets, this ratio would be greater than 1 because higher demand for equities would push the prices of the existing equities up.

Joining the two components of investment, we get the following relation:

$$\dot{g} = \gamma_0 + \gamma_u(u-u_0)g + \gamma_q(q-1)$$

$$u = \frac{g+\varepsilon}{sh-\xi} \text{ [short-run equilibrium]}$$

where q = Tobin's q

γ_q = Constant measuring the response of q on investment

$$\varepsilon = \frac{X - \frac{p_a}{p}M}{K} \text{ [trade surplus]}$$

Determinants of Tobin's q

In this case, it is the rate of growth which has a primary influence over Tobin's q. We propose that the positive effect of the rate of growth on the desired values of q depend on the rate of growth itself. To be specific, at lower rates of growth, the effect is weaker compared to when it is higher. Also, the desired value varies positively with q, which captures the element of speculation that is, *independent* of the 'fundamentals' (captured by the rate of growth), speculation itself begets speculation. Also even if hypothetically the rate of growth and q-ratio are zero, the desired rate is positive owing to some exogenous factors like the animal spirits working in the asset markets. Let us formulate this relation in the following manner:

$$q^d = \lambda_0 + \lambda_g g^2 + \lambda_q q, \text{ where } \lambda_q < 1; \lambda_0 > 0 \tag{17.18}$$

A dynamic version of adjustment towards the desired value can be assumed in the following form:

$$\begin{aligned}\dot{q} &= \Theta_q(q^d - q) \\ &= \Theta_q[\lambda_0 + \lambda_g g^2 + \lambda_q q - q] \\ &= \Theta_q[\lambda_g g^2 + (\lambda_q - 1)q + \lambda_0] \\ \text{for } \dot{q} = 0; \ g^2 &= \frac{1-\lambda_q}{\lambda_g}\left(q - \frac{\lambda_0}{1-\lambda_q}\right)\end{aligned} \tag{17.19}$$

where Θ_q = Speed of adjustment

Steady States and Stability Analysis

$$\dot{q} = \Theta_q[\lambda_g g^2 + (\lambda_q - 1)q + \lambda_0] \tag{17.20}$$

$$\dot{g} = \gamma_0 + \gamma_u(u-u_0)g + \gamma_q(q-1) \tag{17.21}$$

Here, we will just focus on the phase diagram, while the mathematical proof of their stability can be found in the appendix.

To plot these two functions, we need to know their slopes from which we can derive the shape of these demarcation curves.

Figure 17.4
Transitional Dynamics from the Golden Age to Neoliberalism

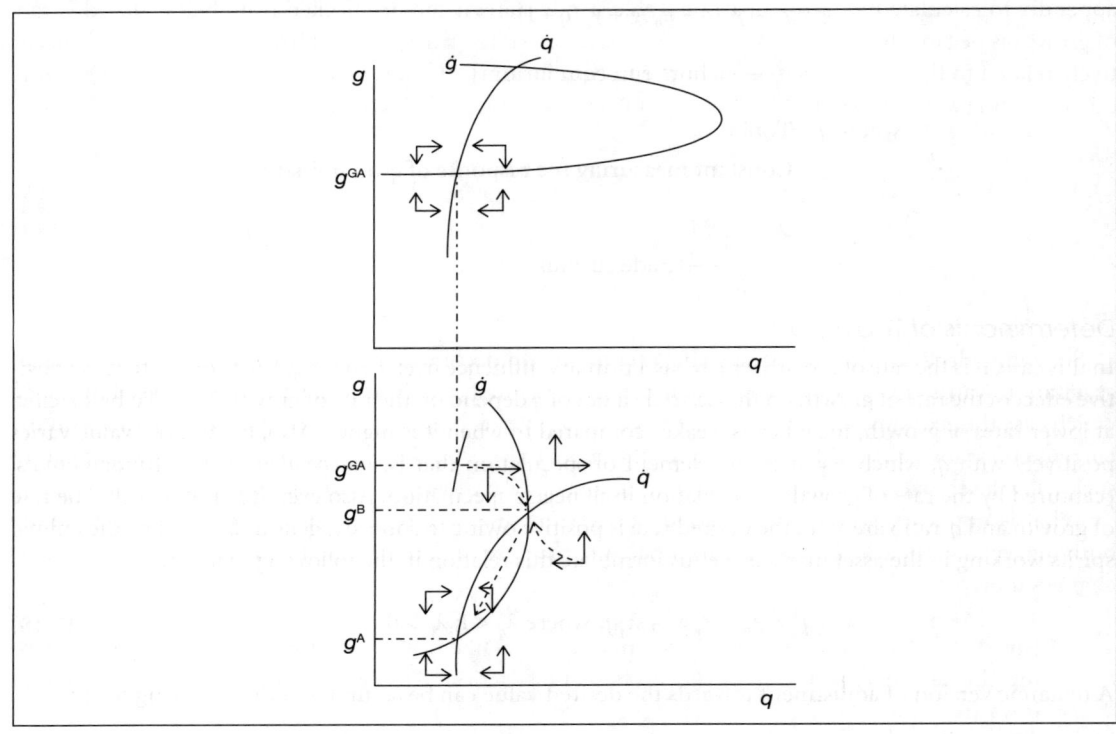

$$\left.\frac{dg}{dq}\right|_{\dot{q}=0} = -\frac{\lambda_q - 1}{2\lambda_g g} > 0 \,\forall g > 0$$

$$\left.\frac{d^2 g}{dg dq}\right|_{\dot{q}=0} = \frac{\lambda_q - 1}{2\lambda_g g^2} < 0$$

$$\left.\frac{dg}{dq}\right|_{\dot{g}=0} = -\frac{\gamma_q(sh - \xi)}{\gamma_u[2g + \varepsilon - (sh - \xi)u_0]} \lessgtr 0 \quad (17.22)$$

$$\left.\frac{d^2 g}{dg dq}\right|_{\dot{g}=0} = \frac{2\gamma_u \gamma_q (sh - \xi)}{\{2\gamma_u g + \varepsilon - (sh - \xi)u_0\}^2} > 0$$

From the derivatives of the growth function, one could tell that it is a parabola in the qg-space and concave with respect to g (as shown in Figure 17.4). On the other hand, the q-function is also a parabola but convex with respect to g.

To draw the streamlines, we need to know the sign of the arrows for the two demarcation curves, which can be derived from the following:

$$\frac{d\dot{q}}{dq} = \Theta_q(\lambda_q - 1) < 0$$

$$\frac{d\dot{g}}{dg} = \frac{2\gamma_u g + \varepsilon - (sh - \xi)u_0}{sh - \xi} \quad (17.23)$$

These arrows tell us that out of two steady states g^A and g^B, the former is a stable node, while the latter is a saddle point. g^A is the counterpart of Kalecki's stable rate of growth g^t. Using the mathematical appendix to calculate the Jacobian at the stable steady state, it can be checked from below that this rate of growth is negatively related to fiscal contraction as resulted from the neoliberal order. Also, it is negatively related to the trade deficit faced by the leading country, the US, as a result of countries like China outcompeting them in critical areas like manufacturing during the neoliberal phase.

$$\frac{\partial g^A}{\partial \xi} = \frac{1}{J_A} \cdot \frac{\Theta_q \gamma_u (g^2 + \varepsilon)(1-\lambda_q)}{(sh-\xi)^2} > 0$$
$$\frac{\partial g^A}{\partial \varepsilon} = \frac{1}{J_A} \cdot \frac{\Theta_q \gamma_u (1-\lambda_q)}{sh-\xi} > 0$$
(17.24)

So, with a decline in ξ and ε, the stable rate of growth declines. The economy in the long run would gravitate towards this growth rate, which could incidentally be even lesser than the lower bound, in which case the economy would not be able to even service its past debt. One could compare this with the current condition of the US economy with the subprime crisis where the rate of growth plummeted to such a low level that it threatened the system to go below the lower-bound condition.

What is noteworthy here is the second rate of growth, g^B. Here, the rate of growth and q-ratio are both higher in comparison to g^A (Figure 17.4). We propose that in the era of neoliberalism, two notable changes took place:

1. Investment tilted in favour of speculative activities like residential investments, thereby increasing the response factor γ_q in the investment function. This makes the growth function shift inwards.
2. With increased financialisation, q^d increased both with respect to the rate of growth and, in particular, to the q-ratio. Speculation dominated the asset-price markets because of the mantra of downsize and distribute in the era of neoliberalism (Lazonick & O'Sullivan, 2000). This means, in terms of our simplified model, an increase in both λ_g and λ_q. In terms of the diagram, this meant an outward shift in the q function with higher convexity than earlier. An economic interpretation of this would be that the asset-price markets became loosely linked to the rate of growth and closely related to the q-ratio.

Transition from the Golden Age to the Neoliberal Era

A brief look at the economic aggregates for the US in the post-war period will help the discussion that follows.

A few important conclusions can be drawn from Table 17.1. First, the rate of growth was higher during the Golden Age than in the neoliberal era. Even within the cycles across these two periods, it is the 1960s that perform the best. For all the hype about the fabulous decade of the 1990s, if one takes the average across the whole cycle, even that decade seems to be just as good or as bad as the others during the neoliberal era. It is easy to see why high growth of the 1990s is not showing in the present data because we have presented the data as cyclical average. It is only if we break the data for the 1990s into two halves that we get the more 'expected' result. Blinder & Yellen (2001) show that if we take only the second half of the 1990s into consideration, then the GDP grew at 4 per cent per annum, inflation at 2.4 per cent, while unemployment remained at 5 per cent, which seems quite impressive compared to the rest of the period during the neoliberal era. However, as correctly argued by Pollin (2005), if one compares the 1990s with the 1960s, then the fabulous 1990s pale in every indicator of economic performance.

Table 17.1
Comparative Analysis of Growth in the US: 1955.4–2006.4

Period	G	uκ	C/O	G/O	(X−M)/O	I/O	(Net I)/O
Golden Age (1955.4–1973.1)	4.1	83.5	62.1	21.9	0.5	15.5	8.0
Neoliberal Era (1978.4–2006.4)	3.1	79.6	65.9	19.7	−2.0	16.4	6.7
Business Cycles							
Golden Age							
1955.4–1959.2	1.7	82.2	62.5	21.7	0.4	15.4	7.6
1959.2–1966.1	4.8	83.0	62.3	21.7	0.8	15.3	8.0
1966.1–1973.1	3.1	84.5	61.7	22.3	0.2	15.8	8.4
Transition Age							
1973.1–1978.4	3.0	81.3	62.6	20.8	−0.2	16.7	7.9
Neoliberal Era							
1978.4–1989.2	3.2	79.0	64.0	20.5	−1.7	17.2	7.3
1989.2–1997.4	2.8	81.3	66.8	19.3	−1.1	15.0	5.4
1997.4–2006.4	2.6	77.9	69.3	18.3	−4.1	16.5	6.3

Source: Rohit 2013.
Note: κ = Technologically given capital–output ratio.

Second, the average rate of capacity utilisation has gone down from 83.46 per cent during the Golden Age to 79.6 per cent during the neoliberal era. Even though it goes up in the 1990s as compared to the other business cycles within the neoliberal era, but it is still lagging behind the average rate of the 1960s.

Third, the share of government expenditure has declined during the neoliberal era. This has especially happened during the 1990s when Clinton's Budget Agreement of 1993 proposed to balance the government budget. One can see that during the Golden Age, the average government expenditure as a proportion of GDP had increased through each passing business cycle, whereas exactly the opposite happened during the neoliberal era where there was a special attempt to make the government small.

What does this hold for our analysis? There was a transition from a high to a low growth trajectory between these two periods. However, in the latter period, there have been spectacular rates of growth, almost comparable to high rates of the Golden Age, before the economy fell back to the lower trajectory. We can see this possibility in Figure 17.4. A higher trajectory is represented by g^{GA} while the intermittent high rate of growth is shown by g^B before falling down to a lower trajectory at g^A.

Starting from a high rate of growth g^{GA} and the downward movement of the $\dot{g}$ function, along with the increased convexity of the $\dot{q}$ function, the intermittent rate of growth could fall on the stable arm especially if the speed of adjustment also increases with financialisation Θ_q. In such a case, the rate of growth will decrease marginally with a significant surge in the asset price markets, a process reminiscent of the bubble-based high growth phases in the US in the 1980s, 1990s and 2000s before the respective recessions set in. However, given that such a growth rate is a saddle point, the tendency of the economy to diverge away from it if per chance the economy falls off it is equally high. So, the economy will always have an inherent tendency to move towards g^A, a stagnationist regime. The tendency of such a growth regime, which depends on debt-financed growth riding on the booming asset-price markets, to end up in a range lower than g_{min} is also high particularly because the lower bound ($shi\ \delta$) itself keeps increasing with a rising debt–capital ratio (δ).

Conclusion

This chapter is an attempt to extend the work of Patnaik (1997, 2009) for the neoliberal era. Patnaik (1997) argues that a mature capitalist economy is faced with twin instabilities. On the one hand, there is a tendency of the system to stagnate. On the other hand, it faces the problems of unstable inflation except at the NAIRU. Unlike the mainstream argument that the system is self-correcting or the Keynesian argument that the capitalist state stabilises the system, he has argued that it is the non-capitalist periphery which acts as the shock absorber of the system, as has historically been the case.

Patnaik (2009) further buttresses this point from the money side. This later work also came with a slightly revised position against the uniqueness of NAIRU (in the absence of the periphery) while adding that past debt commitments place an additional constraint on the system, that is, there is lower bound to the system. So, for the viability of the system (a) there needs to be a non-null set between the upper and lower bounds; (b) the system settles within this range. According to him, the presence of the pre-capitalist periphery ensured both.

We have extended this work for the so-called Golden Age and the era of neoliberalism. We believe that while the periphery has played a critical role in ensuring a non-null viable set exists, the capitalist state during the Golden Age has played a role in making the system settle within this range. This argument can be appreciated especially if one looks at the events that posed a challenge to the so-called Golden Age. The crisis of Keynesianism erupted only when the periphery refused to act as the shock absorber during the oil crisis of the 1970s. By destabilising the Golden Age, this crisis ended up resurrecting a free market ideology, which has been known as the neoliberal era.

However, the neoliberal era, in particular the world economic crisis that started in 2008, has brought the questions raised by Patnaik (1997, 2009) back on the agenda. We argue that while aggravating the problem of output instability, neoliberalism has muted the problem of price instability.

We show that under neoliberalism, the periphery plays an additional role. Due to globalisation, a credible threat of moving the work base to a peripheral country has kept the working class in the capitalist core on a tight leash, thereby taking care of the price instability. On the other hand, with the withdrawal of the state and absence of the colonies as markets on tap, the output instability has got aggravated. The tendency towards stagnation looms large, and the only way the system has avoided it intermittently is by depending on asset-price bubble-based growth trajectories. The system hops on from one kind of a bubble to another without stabilising at a high enough rate of growth comparable to either the colonial era or the Golden Age.

This has come at its own peril. The very process of muting the price instability and aggravated output instability has the potential of generating a political instability of the kind that the world has witnessed in recent times. In the US itself, the Occupy Wall Street movement is a reflection of the kind of political instability Patnaik (1997) hinted at. Now whether the crisis or the resistance to it signals something larger on the political front is a moot question. What is important, however, is to see this system fundamentally as a crisis-prone system.

Appendix

Mathematical Appendix

Verifying the Stability of the Steady States

To establish stability of the two this steady states, we check the trace of the Jacobian and its determinant at each of these points. Here $\Gamma = sh - \xi$.

$$J = \begin{pmatrix} 2\Theta_q \lambda_g g & \Theta_q(\lambda_q - 1) \\ \dfrac{2\gamma_u}{\Gamma}\left[g - \left(\dfrac{u_0\Gamma - \varepsilon}{2}\right)\right] & \gamma_q \end{pmatrix}$$

To check for stability of this steady state, we need to find out the signs of trJ and $|J|$ at the two points:

$$\begin{aligned} trJ &= \Theta_q(\lambda_q - 1) + \frac{2\gamma_u}{\Gamma}\left[g - \left(\frac{u_0\Gamma - \varepsilon}{2}\right)\right] \\ |J| &= 2\Theta_q \lambda_g g \cdot \gamma_q - \Theta_q(\lambda_q - 1) \cdot \frac{2\gamma_u}{\Gamma}\left[g - \left(\frac{u_0\Gamma - \varepsilon}{2}\right)\right] \end{aligned} \tag{17A.1}$$

To find out the nature of the two steady states g^A, g^B, we need to calculate the value of the jacobian along with its trace at the two points.

Stability at g^A

To find out the sign of the trace, we need to know the sign of the second term as we know that the second term is already negative ($\lambda_q < 1$). It can be derived from the shape of the $\dot{g}$ function. Rearranging the $\dot{g}$ function gives us the following:

$$\left[g - \left(\frac{u_0\Gamma - \varepsilon}{2}\right)\right]^2 + \frac{\gamma_q \Gamma}{\gamma_u}(q - 1) + \frac{\gamma_0 \Gamma}{\gamma_u} - \left(\frac{u_0\Gamma - \varepsilon}{2}\right)^2$$

The axis of the parabola occurs at $\dfrac{u_0\Gamma - \varepsilon}{2}$, which means that if the $\dot{q}$ curve cuts it below this point, which is definitely the case with g^A (or even for g^B according to our figure), $g^A < \dfrac{u_0\Gamma - \varepsilon}{2}$.

$$\because \lambda_q < 1, g^A < \frac{u_0\Gamma - \varepsilon}{2}; trJ < 0 \tag{17A.2}$$

The determinant depends on the relative slopes of the two curves.

$$\because \left.\frac{dg}{dq}\right|^B_{\dot{g}=0} < \left.\frac{dg}{dq}\right|^B_{\dot{q}=0}$$

$$-\frac{\gamma_q \Gamma}{\gamma_u[2g + \varepsilon - \Gamma u_0]} < -\frac{\lambda_q - 1}{2\lambda_g g} \tag{17A.3}$$

$$\text{then } |J_B| > 0$$

These two points establish the fact that g^A is a stable node as argued in the text.

Stability at g^B

For g^B, the determinant gets the opposite sign because the (modulus of the) slope of the $\dot{g}$ curve is more than that of $\dot{q}$.

$$\because \left.\frac{dg}{dq}\right|^B_{\dot{g}=0} < \left.\frac{dg}{dq}\right|^B_{\dot{q}=0}$$

$$-\frac{\gamma_q \Gamma}{\gamma_u [2g + \varepsilon - \Gamma u_0]} < -\frac{\lambda_q - 1}{2\lambda_g g} \quad (17A.4)$$

$$\text{then } |J_B| > 0$$

Irrespective of the sign of the trace, this steady state is a saddle point as argued in the text.

References

Blinder, A.S., & Yellen, J. (2001). *The fabulous decade: Macroeconomic lessons from the 1990s*. New York: The Century Foundation Press.

Harrod, R.F. (1939). An essay in dynamic theory. *The Economic Journal*, 49(193), 14–33.

Kalecki, M. (1962). Observations on the theory of growth. *The Economic Journal*, 72(285), 134–153.

Lazonick, W., & O'Sullivan, M. (2000). Maximising shareholder value: A new ideology for corporate governance. *Economy and Society*, 29(1), 13–35.

Luxemburg, R. (1913/2003). *The accumulation of capital*. New York: Routledge.

Patnaik, P. (1997). *Accumulation and stability under capitalism*. Oxford: Clarendon Press.

———. (2009). *The value of money*. New York: Columbia University Press.

Pollin, R. (2005). *Contours of descent: US economic fractures and the landscape of global austerity*. New York: Verso.

Rohit. (2013). *It's not over: Structural drivers of the global economic crisis*. New York: Oxford University Press.

Sen, A. (1970a). Interest, investment and growth. In A. Sen (Ed.), *Growth economics* (219–232). England: Penguin Books.

———. (1970b). Introduction. In A. Sen (Ed.), *Growth economics* (9–40). England: Penguin Books.

Solow, R. (1956). A contribution to the theory of economic growth. *Quarterly Journal of Economics*, 70(1), 65–94.

18

Agricultural Investment in India in Recent Decades: A Political Economic Note of Its Causes and Consequences

Debarshi Das[*]

Introduction

The mode of production debate (the Debate henceforth) has been one of the most thought-provoking discussions on the political economy of India. The Debate sought to characterise the relations of production in agrarian India. This was not a purely eclectic exercise: it had obvious and immediate political ramifications. This is the reason why analytical issues churned out by the Debate remain relevant to this day. Risking simplification, we propose an upshot of the Debate as follows. A set of conditions needs to be fulfilled for a mode of production to be called capitalist: (a) production is based on wage labour; (b) production is carried out mainly for the market and (c) there is reinvestment of surplus value in production.[1] Condition (c) would mean that fruits of scientific research embodied in the new investment are constantly applied, provided there is technological progress. As a result, accumulation of capital would roll on in the right earnest, and forces of production would be relentlessly strengthened.[2]

---

[*] A brilliant mind and a wealth of patience are essential for a successful researcher and teacher. However, these two qualities do not completely explain Professor Prabhat Patnaik's stature. The residual is his unflinching commitment for the exploited. More importantly, a coherent political understanding informs this commitment and gives it meaning. Knowingly or unknowingly, many of us pay respect to this commitment through modest academic efforts.

The present chapter has been in the making for quite some time. A preliminary version had appeared on Sanhati website (http://sanhati.com/excerpted/2905/). It has undergone several revisions since. I thank all those who have provided helpful suggestions. The errors are entirely mine.

[1] This set as a whole is both necessary and sufficient. Individually, the conditions are necessary but not sufficient.

[2] Accumulation of capital is an essential feature of capitalism. The maniac and somewhat helpless state of the capitalist in the accumulation process has been famously described in *Capital I* (Marx, 1867/1976: 739):

> [T]he development of capitalist production makes it necessary constantly to increase the amount of the capital laid out in a given industrial undertaking, and competition subordinates every individual capitalist to the immanent laws of capitalist production, as external coercive laws. It compels him to keep extending his capital, so as to preserve it, and he can only extend it by means of progressive accumulation.

Importance of investment in the above characterisation is noteworthy. The increase in investment in agriculture that took place after the late 1950s made many researchers hopeful for the development of capitalist production.[3] With the beginning of economic planning in 1951, the state had been actively promoting research and dissemination of new technology. Although the Green Revolution, which started in the mid-1960s, had its detractors from the early days,[4] the role of the state in crowding-in private investment is well known (Vaidyanathan, 1997). The demand side was also favourable. In the mid-1950s, there were signs that large public spending and population growth were tilting the terms of trade in favour of the agricultural sector (Hazell, Misra & Hojjati, 1995). After the mid-1960s, rising terms of trade became a secular trend (Hazell et al., 1995). With the first of the three conditions listed earlier getting increasingly satisfied from colonial times[5] while the other two receiving ample assistance from the Nehruvian State, some observers had reasons to believe that a virtuous cycle of high agricultural investment would soon be created. The pre-capitalist agrarian scene of stagnant productivity would be soon swept away by the dynamism of accumulating capitalist farms, it was perceived.

Has the hope been validated as the subsequent decades unfolded? This chapter would seek to answer this question and examine associated political implications. But before that, two points need to be clarified. First, not many researchers claimed that production conditions in Indian agriculture 'had already been' transformed into a capitalist mode. The claim has been that the capitalist mode was in the ascendancy.[6] Second, it was never in doubt that rising investment would be incapable of absorbing the surplus labour of rural economy.[7]

In spatial and temporal terms, considerable variation can be observed in the putative motion of capitalist development. To simplify the task, we shall concentrate only on the condition (c).[8] This condition demands reinvestment of surplus. We thus focus on agricultural accumulation.[9]

---

[3] See Omvedt (1981). A long passage by Patnaik (1971: A-126) is worth quoting,

> [T]he mid-1950s onwards, marks a definite break with earlier trends. The creation of an expanding domestic market owing to the large investment outlays by the state under the plans combined with a lagging behind of agricultural production, has sharply raised the profitability of agriculture vis-a-vis other avenues of surplus utilisation. For the first time in decades investible funds generated in agriculture are flowing back to the land, and even urban funds are tending to flow in this newly profitable direction. Post-independence land reforms have played a positive role in penalising absenteeism. The dominant landholder is intensifying operations by investing in irrigation, double and triple cropping, and thus stepping up cash outlays considerably. Landlords in many areas find it profitable to turn tenants off the land ... and operate with wage-labour instead. The rich peasant who can generate an investible surplus and has access to credit similarly intensifies operations, employs more wage-labour and moves up the economic scale.

[4] Rudra, Majid and Talib (1969a, 1969b, 1970), for instance, questioned the existence of capitalist farmers in the cradle of the Green Revolution.
[5] Patnaik (1972a) cites evidence of rising percentage of agricultural labourers in South, Central and West India in the early twentieth century.
[6] The Communist Party of India (Marxist) holds a similar view on the development of agrarian capitalism of present times: "the development of capitalism in agriculture has assumed certain specific forms and led to changes in the relations of production. Increasingly capitalism is the mode of production in agriculture" (Karat, 2000).
[7] "The short-run increase [in labour employment] can at best reduce marginally the existing overt unemployment among labourers, before being subordinated to the labour-displacing tendency which will accentuate the already acute problems of underemployment" (Patnaik, 1972b: 18).
[8] The main protagonists of the debate were more or less in agreement that the first two conditions were satisfied. Thus, the third condition alone becomes the necessary and sufficient condition.
[9] Note that the requirement of reinvestment of surplus makes sense if one has an entire economy as the point of reference. That economy needs to be autarkic as well: an open economy can experience capital inflow-led accumulation, without any reinvestment. Here, the agricultural sector, a part of the economy, is being considered. In essence, the feature one is looking for is the development of productive forces in a process of expanded reproduction. If productive forces in agriculture are strengthened through the investment of economic surplus produced outside agriculture, the third condition will still be satisfied. However, this is only

A brief outline of the contention of the chapter is in order. Capital formation in Indian agriculture has declined in the last three decades. A reason for this is fall in public investment. Public investment could have boosted private investment, thus raising aggregate investment. In the absence of robust capital accumulation, petty peasant agrarian relations (rather than capitalist or semi-feudal production relations) dominate Indian agriculture.[10] Thus, capitalist transition is not as imminent as it was supposed to be in the early 1970s, nor can capitalism be considered the mode of production.

If the above assessment is correct, it has important political implications. The demand of land distribution loses appeal in a petty peasantry-dominated agrarian economy where the amount of ceiling surplus land is negligible. Second, the contradiction between 'feudalism and broad masses' would not constitute the principal contradiction, as is claimed by some communist parties.

There exists a rich literature on production relations in Indian agriculture (Jodhka, 2012; Lerche, 1999; Rodgers & Rodgers, 2001; Upadhya, 1988a, 1988b). Many of these studies are based on meticulous village surveys. While they present fascinating accounts of rural transformation, most of them do not emphasise enough the role of capital accumulation in the development of capitalism. Prevalence of wage labour, decline of attached labour, investment by farmers outside agriculture, increasing monetisation and production for market are often taken as signs of capitalist development. These observations are unmistakable indicators that semi-feudal relations are waning. However, the Debate's principal insight was to underline the importance of investment. Drawing on this, we contribute to the literature by putting investment at the centre of the analysis. Given the poor state of accumulation, we argue, while semi-feudalism is on the way out, it is premature to characterise the mode of production in Indian agriculture as capitalist.

Agricultural Investment after Independence

The trajectory of agrarian accumulation in the post-Independence period can be divided broadly into two phases: 1947 to the 1970s and the 1980s and thereafter. The final phase of colonial rule was characterised by near stagnation in agriculture, especially of foodgrains production. Blyn's estimation shows that from 1891 to 1947 foodgrains production rose at an average annual rate of merely 0.11 per cent. Production of rice fell in absolute terms during this period (Blyn, 1966). A structural break in production came about with Independence. The first 15 years of planning saw growth of primary sector output at 2.6 per cent per annum, which is in fact higher than the average annual growth rate it achieved during the first five decades after Independence (Balakrishnan, 2010). A reason behind this turnaround can be attributed to increase in agricultural investment. The difference in agricultural investments between pre-independence and post-independence periods is stark. Data on net private investment (as a percentage of agricultural income) of years before and after Independence are presented in Table 18.1.

A reason for the rise in private investment after independence was the stimulus provided by public investment. During the first 15 years of economic planning, public investment claimed a greater share of aggregate investment than private investment, and it also rose at a faster rate than private investment (Table 18.2).

---

an academic point. For it is difficult to conceive that surplus from agriculture would emigrate to other sectors, when funds from outside flow inward in agriculture. In Upadhya's (1988a, 1988b) study, for example, it moves in one direction, from agriculture to trade and industries.

[10] This is akin to 'small-scale peasant ownership' agrarian economy discussed in *Capital III* (Marx, 1893/1981). See Basu and Das (2013) for elaboration.

Table 18.1
Net Private Investment as a Percentage of Agricultural Income

Period	Net Private Investment to Agricultural Income
1935–1936 to 1940–1941	2.54
1940–1941 to 1945–1946	0.84
1945–1946 to 1950–1951	0.7
1950–1951 to 1955–1956	4.25
1955–1956 to 1960–1961	4.03

Source: Shukla (1968).

Table 18.2
Public and Private Investment in First Three Five-year Plans (Crores of Rupees at 1960–1961 Prices)

	Public Investment	Private Investment	Public Investment as a Percentage of Total Investment
First Plan (1951–1956)	532	530	50.09
Second Plan (1956–1961)	718	712	50.21
Third Plan (1961–1966)	1,310	800	62.09

Source: Shukla (1968).

Table 18.3
Percentage Growth of Inputs Use, Irrigated Area in Different Periods

	1962 to 1982	1982 to 1992	1992 to 2003
Tractors (Nos/0000Hc)	1,133	132	94
Pump sets (Nos/000Hc)	880	61	41
Fertiliser consumption (Kg/Hc)	1,000	109	49
	1962–1965 to 1980–1983	1980–1983 to 1990–1993	1990–1993 to 2003–2006
Percentage of irrigated area	53	24	14

Source: Calculated from Bhalla and Singh (2009).

Dhawan and Yadav (1995) establish the positive link between public investment in irrigation and private investment in agriculture empirically. Vaidyanathan (1997) has pointed out four areas where the state has a salient role to play towards raising productivity: (a) irrigation; (b) soil and moisture conservation of rain-fed agriculture; (c) the development and spread of biochemical inputs, in particular, fertilisers and (d) state policy that affects agrarian institutions and prices. Notice, these factors are affected by public investment. From the early 1960s to the early 1980s, investment and input use in agriculture rose at a high rate (second column of Table 18.3).

High growth of public investment in agriculture during the initial years of planning rejects the myth that the Mahalanobis Strategy, which was followed during those years, ignored the wage goods constraint—that is, it paid scant attention to the agricultural sector. First, such an accusation does not match with the data cited above that the growth of primary sector was higher in the first 15 years of planning

Table 18.4
Annual Percentage Change in Capital Formation in Indian Agriculture, at 1980–1981 Prices

Time Period	Public Sector	Private Sector	Total
1962–1963 to 1975–1976	4.19	7.65	6.39
1975–1976 to 1982–1983	12.2	3.91	6.45
1982–1983 to 1984–1985	−0.78	−2.05	−1.56
1984–1985 to 1987–1988	−4.73	3.39	0.16
1987–1988 to 1993–1994	−3.58	6.45	3.05

Source: Purohit and Reddy (1999).

than in the first 50 years of Independence. Second, even by its face value, the myth unfairly discredits the rich vision the Mahalanobis Strategy entailed. Interdependence between agricultural and industrial sectors was indeed factored in. To quote Mahalanobis,

> [A]dvance of one step in agriculture would supply food and raw materials for advance of one step in manufacturing industries which again, in its turn, would speed up irrigation and increase the supply of fertilizers and pesticides and help in the promotion of scientific research, which would lead to further advance in agriculture. (cited in Balakrishnan, 2010: 51)

As Patnaik (1994) persuasively argued, what blunted the Mahalanobis Strategy stemmed from the realm of political economy, not its neglect of agriculture.

Public investment started to decline from the 1980s. From high positive growth per annum in 1975–1976 to 1982–1983, public investment dipped to negative growth after the early 1980s. It remained negative till the period 1987–1988 to 1993–1994 (Table 18.4). As could be predicted from the positive association between public and private investment, the latter followed suit as the former slowed down. Growth of private investment dropped to negative values in the early 1980s. There was recovery of private investment afterward, but it could not compensate for the negative growth of public investment. Overall investment growth from the early 1980s to the mid-1990s has been substantially lower than the preceding period.

Reflecting decelerating investment, between the early 1980s and the early 1990s, growth of inputs slowed down (Table 18.3).

The trend of low public investment continued even after the mid-1990s (Table 18.3). In recent years, agricultural investment as a percentage of total investment has remained unchanged: 6.7 per cent in 2009–2010 to 6.5 per cent in 2012–2013 (Government of India, Ministry of Finance, 2014). Public investment as a proportion of private investment has continued to fall: we find that private gross capital formation as a percentage of agricultural gross domestic product rose 16.7 per cent to 18.1 per cent from 2009–2010 to 2012–2013 (Government of India, Ministry of Finance, 2014).

Two points can be inferred from the fragmented evidences cited above. First, public investment has decelerated in the agricultural sector. Second, agricultural investment as a whole has decelerated as a consequence.

In order to have a cogent picture of the last 30 years, we have estimated two parameters from the Central Statistical Organisation (CSO) data of 'Gross domestic product (GDP) from Agriculture and Allied Sector and its percentage share to total GDP'. The first is public investment as a ratio of aggregate investment in agriculture, and the second is agricultural investment as a ratio of aggregate investment. The values of these two parameters are plotted in Figure 18.1 (data range: 1980–1981 to 2012–2013, at constant 1999–2000 prices). The first parameter is represented by the dark line on the top. From close to 46 per cent

Figure 18.1
Public Investment in Agricultural Sector, Agricultural Investment and Total Investment

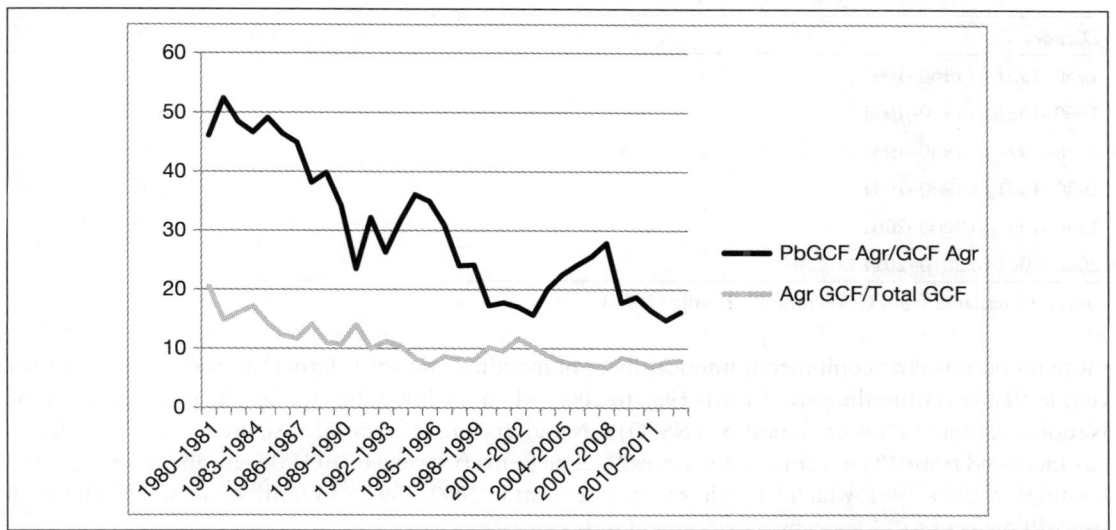

Source: Calculated from the CSO data.

the share of public investment in agricultural investment has come down to around 16 per cent. The line at the bottom represents a percentage of gross capital formation (GCF) in the agriculture and allied sector to the total GCF of the economy. This also has seen a long-run decline from 20 per cent to 7 per cent.

Other Evidences of Low Investment

High rate of accumulation often causes rising size of landholding. Accumulating farms reinvest surplus to acquire land and thus grow in size. Owing to economies to scale, large farms earn more and invest more. From small to large scale, change in quantity translates into qualitative changes: a chain of cumulative causation begins to operate. Centralisation of land is thus a sign that capitalist development is in progress.[11]

On the other hand, low accumulation and fragmentation of landholding reinforce each other. As there is low creation of jobs in the agrarian economy due to low investment, petty farmers become reluctant to let go of their parcels, making it difficult for the investors to buy them out. Small farms have little scope to scale up.[12] Thus, there could be multiple equilibria in a coordination failure-like set-up: one with high investment and large farms, and the other with low investment and petty holdings (Das, 2007).

Centralisation of land has not been a prominent feature in India agriculture. The data from 1961–1962 to 2002–2003 show that average operational size of landholdings has declined from 2.63 to 1.06 Ha (Basole & Basu, 2011a). Marginal farms (less than 1 Ha of land) and small farms (1 to 2 Ha) are becoming

---

[11] "[I]n industry, capital grows as a result of *accumulation*, as a result of the conversion of surplus-value into capital; *centralisation*, i.e., the amalgamation of several small units of capital into a large unit, plays a lesser role. In agriculture, the situation is different. The whole of the land is occupied (in civilised countries) and it is possible to enlarge the area of a farm only by *centralising* several lots; this must be done in such a way as to form *one continuous area*". (Emphasis in the original; Lenin, 1899).
[12] "Small-scale production permits of the employment of machinery within narrower limits; the small proprietor finds credit more difficult to obtain and more expensive" (Lenin, 1899).

Table 18.5
Annual Growth Rate of Yield of Food Grains

Decades	Annual Growth Rate of Yield
1950–1951 to 1960–1961	3.6
1960–1961 to 1970–1971	2.28
1970–1971 to 1980–1981	1.73
1980–1981 to 1990–1991	3.49
1990–1991 to 2000–2001	1.78
2000–2001 to 2010–2011	1.86

Source: Calculated from Government of India (2015).

more numerous. The combined numerical share of marginal and small farms has gone up from 75 per cent to 91 per cent in the period 1961–1962 to 2003, when the last published landholding survey of the National Sample Survey Organisation (NSSO) was undertaken. In terms of area, the share of these farms has increased from 20 per cent to 43 per cent.[13] Large farms (more than 10 Ha) were about 5 per cent of holdings in 1960–1961, which fell to less than 1 per cent in 2002–2003.[14] In terms of area, their share fell from 29 per cent to 12 per cent (Government of India, 2006.)[15]

Rising size of landholdings can be one manifestation of higher investment. However, it is not necessary that higher investment would always lead to rising size of holdings. Investment can lead to more capital being applied on the same piece of land. In such a case, the plot becomes more productive even as its size remains the same. Has investment in India led to capital deepening, rather than land centralisation? A sign of capital deepening is the rate at which crops yield grows.[16] Bhalla and Singh (2009) have estimated that the growth rate of yield has been going down. From the annual growth rate of 1.73 per cent (1962–1965 to 1980–1983), yield of crops rose to 3.17 per cent (1980–1983 to 1990–1993) and then fell to 1.52 per cent (1990–1993 to 2003–2006) (Bhalla & Singh, 2009). Our own estimation of decadal growth of foodgrains yield is presented in Table 18.5. The evidence does not suggest that capital deepening is taking place at a quick pace. If we leave aside the 1970s, yield growth rate has been lower in the post-liberalisation period.[17]

Thus, centralisation of land is absent, and capital deepening seems to be slowing down. Instead of centralisation, there is a tendency in the opposite direction of subdivision of holdings.

---

[13] Agriculture Census data over 10-year period 2000–2001 to 2010–2011 indicate a similar trend. Share of small, marginal holdings rose from 81.8 per cent to 84 per cent in terms of number of holdings. In terms of land, their share rose from 38.9 per cent to 44.6 per cent (Government of India, 2015).

[14] Upadhya (1988a, 1988b) claimed that land ceiling was a barrier against land consolidation. If ceiling indeed acted as a barrier, there would be high frequency of holdings just below the ceiling limit (this can range from 2.5 Ha to 13 Ha depending on land quality). This is not the case, and frequency seems to be much higher below 1 Ha.

[15] Declining big farms may not necessarily imply that capitalist farms are losing land. A small farm can be run with capitalist production relations. Besides land size, other parameters need to be examined. I thank Professor Utsa Patnaik and Roshan Kishore for pointing this out. My research on this indicates that growth of capitalist farms, although not altogether absent, cannot be considered robust (Das, 2014).

[16] Agricultural output can be taken as a function of land, labour and capital. Increment of land area is near zero, so is marginal product of labour due to the existing high application of labour. Thus, as long as technological progress growth is constant, yield growth is directly proportional to capital investment.

[17] Desai, D'Souza, Mellor, Sharma and Tamboli (2011) point out that curtailing of State's involvement in many areas has adversely affected the potential of farming. These include irrigation, flood control, watershed development, infrastructure, soil and water conservation, regulated market, agricultural research, education and extension. All this may have had a bearing on yield growth.

Table 18.6
Annual Growth Rate of Employment in the Organised Sector

	1983–1994	1994–2008
Public sector	1.53	–0.65
Private sector	0.44	1.75
Total organised	1.2	0.05

Source: Government of India, Ministry of Finance (2011).

Two more factors contributed to land subdivision. The first is the high population pressure on land. From 1950–1951 to 2010–2011, gross cropped area (which accounts for change in land under cultivation, as well as changing intensity of cultivation) rose at the annual compound rate of 0.69 per cent. In contrast, the population of cultivators grew at a much faster rate of 0.89 per cent during 1951 to 2011.[18] The second factor is the scarce employment opportunities outside agriculture. We turn to this in the next section.

Opportunities outside Agriculture

In development economics literature, migration of surplus labour from agricultural to industrial sector raises agricultural sector's marginal productivity of labour, which eventually rises to the real wage level of industrial sector (the 'commercialisation point' in Ranis & Fei, 1961). Outflow of labour reduces peasants' dependence on land, making it easy for capitalist development to proceed. Thus, the ability of the non-agricultural sector to absorb unskilled labour from agricultural sector is critical.

From the data available, it is found that the organised sector employment has expanded sluggishly since 1994 (Table 18.6). In the absence of employment in the organised sector, surplus labour of agriculture, which is mostly unskilled,[19] is forced to seek employment in the unorganised/informal sector.[20] All these informal jobs are not necessarily non-agricultural: many farm labourers and marginal farmers from eastern India travel to Punjab and Haryana farms (Rodgers & Rodgers, 2001). Such jobs provide the peasants an alternative, seasonal livelihood. However, informal sector labour is less productive than formal sector labour. For example, in 2001 the gross value added of a worker in an informal manufacturing sector was less than 6 per cent of the formal sector gross value added (Kar & Marjit, 2009). Despite low productivity and meagre income, the unorganised sector is absorbing labour at a much faster rate than the organised sector (see Table 7 and Figure 8 in Kotwal, Ramaswami & Wadhwa, 2011). Demand for labour in informal jobs is helped by subcontracting of formal sector work, which is a route to escape regulations of the formal sector (Basole & Basu, 2011b; Kotwal et al., 2011). Lack of regulation or enforcement of labour laws in informal sector contributes to keeping wage at a bare minimum. The consequence is a booming

---

[18] Calculated from the data of Reserve Bank of India and Agricultural Statistics at a Glance 2004, both available at Indiastat.com (http://www.indiastat.com/table/agriculture/2/landuse19502013/448932/293157/data.aspx and http://www.indiastat.com/table/agriculture/2/agriculturalworkforce/41/17528/data.aspx).
[19] The study by Government of India, Ministry of Finance (2015) tacitly acknowledges that the surplus labour is 'unutilisable' in sectors that can transform the economy "…the choice confronting India is really about how to make it a Lewisian economy that has unlimited supplies of labor. India can either create the conditions to ensure that its existing unlimited supplies of unskilled labor are utilisable…" (Government of India, Ministry of Finance, 2015: 115).
[20] Although unorganised and informal sectors are not exactly synonymous, they overlap to a large extent (Mehrotra, Gandhi, Sahoo & Saha, 2012). Here, we use the terms interchangeably. An enterprise in the unorganised sector is one that employs less than 10 workers (and uses power) or less than 20 workers (and does not use power).

informal sector. During 1994–1995 to 2000–2001, share of employment in unorganised manufacturing of total manufacturing went up from 71 per cent to 86 per cent (Kar & Marjit, 2009).

To be sure, migration from villages is not a new phenomenon. Migration of farmers and agricultural labourers from South Gujarat villages to Surat, Bombay and East Africa rose as transport network developed in the late-nineteenth and early-twentieth centuries (Breman, 2007). Byres (1981) commented on the loss of land of small farmers as the Green Revolution gained momentum in North-Western India during the 1970s. However, small farmers were not giving up land completely, even while they became more dependent on wage income. This prompted him to term the process as 'partial-proletarianisation'. Lerche (1999) documented the rising tide of emigration since the 1960s in the villages of Uttar Pradesh. Some analytical differences aside, the flow of footloose labourer observed at present is the continuation of the same long procession through history. Rapid expansion of the unorganised sector and declining growth of the agricultural sector in recent decades suggest that the flow has risen of late.[21] In spite of rising migration, it is observed that land acquisition drives often encounter resistance (Bhaduri & Patkar, 2009), which is not surprising in view of the observation made by Byres about peasants' unwillingness to give up their land entirely. Uncertain nature of employment of the migrated labourers makes them reluctant to give up the only secure source of livelihood, namely their land.[22] Even as the peasants go to seek work elsewhere, they remain tethered to land. This has important political implications which we shall comment on later.

Let us summarise before we move to the next section. Slowing down of public investment is a probable cause for low accumulation: low public investment leads to low profitability of cultivation resulting in low accumulation. Low accumulation and subdivision of land holdings reinforce each other. Dearth of gainful employment outside agriculture adds to the stagnation.

Semi-feudalism?

An alternative explanation of low investment in agriculture is the presence of feudal production relations. The literature of semi-feudalism is old and rich: Bhaduri (1973), Prasad (1973) and Chandra (1974) among others have been its notable contributors. Is semi-feudalism responsible for slowing down of investment?

From the above discussion, it does not appear that the bonds of semi-feudalism have remained strong. Migration renders the labourer less dependent on the landlord for his livelihood (Djurfeldt et al., 2008; Jodhka, 2012; Lerche, 1999; Rodgers & Rodgers, 2001). The fact that agricultural labourers and petty peasants are undertaking seasonal migration indicates loosening of the bonds that had tied labourer to land so that he remains available to render his service to the landlord. Sharecropping is regarded as another marker of semi-feudalism. However, official data show declining incidence of sharecropping and other forms of land tenancy. Official data could be questioned for deliberate misreporting of tenancy land.[23] However, declining tenancy has been confirmed by field surveys as well (Wilson 1999, for example). Concentration of land in the control of big landlords is a feature of semi-feudalism. According to official estimates, the amount of ceiling surplus land has been going down rapidly (Rao, 1992). This is supported by the NSSO data on the falling percentage of large farmers cited earlier.

---

[21] Rodgers and Rodgers (2001), who have surveyed a set of Bihar villages over a period of 30 years, have confirmed this rise of migration.
[22] Marginal farmers, *bargadars* (tenants) and farm labourers were at the forefront of Singur resistance (Banerjee, 2006).
[23] See Bardhan (1970) for an early discussion on underestimation of tenancy.

Usury is another channel through which semi-feudal exploitation takes place. In Bhaduri's model of semi-feudalism, land lease market and credit market interlock with each other to produce a state of stagnation (Bhaduri, 1973). On the prevalence of usury, data show a non-linear trajectory. Before liberalisation, there was a secular declining tendency of non-formal credit, which can be taken as a proxy of usurious loans. This has been attributed to bank nationalisation, priority sector lending, etc. (Shah, Rao & Sankar, 2007). After liberalisation, there has been a reversal: share of non-formal credit has been rising (Basu & Das, 2013). However, it would be a leap of faith to conclude from the rising incidence of usury that semi-feudalism has strengthened. Usury alone does not imply semi-feudalism—it is only a component of a system. Other parts of the system are disintegrating, as mentioned earlier.[24]

Field Study

Aggregative data do not reveal many micro-level details of cultivation. For example, how much income does the farmer earn per acre, after all imputed costs are accounted for? Or, which are the possible areas where public investment can raise farmer's earning? Field studies by researchers have tried to answer some of these questions. In our study, respondents come from five villages of Bihar: three in the East Champaran district and two from the Buxar district. The first three villages depend on rabi crop, because frequent monsoon floods render kharif uncertain. The last two villages are more prosperous as both crops are secure. The respondents were not chosen on the basis of a random sample. Stray visits were made to villages, the respondents talked in groups and their conversations were examined to draw conclusions. The study has no claim to formal generalisability. However, most our observations are in line with those of Rodgers and Rodgers (2001) inter alia, hinting that the observations may be valid for a large swathe of rural India.

The questions that we were interested in are earning/acre from farming, reasons for low earning if it exists, possibility of public investment in boosting profitability, extent of usury and tenancy, incidence and reasons for migration and possibility of land redistribution. We interviewed farm labourers, marginal, small peasants, and large farmers, who were few in number. We recorded the caste of the respondent, size of the land he owns, land he leases in/out, frequency of cultivation, crops he grows, harvest per acre, price of the crop, sale to the Food Corporation of India, costs of farming—labour cost: both own and hired, other inputs costs, frequency of his and his family members' migration, wages he receives, if he thinks public investment can improve the harvest, his investment plans and so forth. The responses have been collated, analysed and are summarised as follows.

First, majority of peasants own small land parcels. Their low earning per acre is inadequate to meet subsistence requirements. Male, able-bodied, peasants resort to seasonal migration to make ends meet. Decision to migrate is a function of many variables, such as economic condition and caste status of the person, distance from local urban centres and value of the harvest. Second, for those who earn economic surplus, or have access to organised credit, profitability of farming is too low to undertake investment. Third, power, flood control, irrigation and regular harvest procurement (and payment of procured grain on time) are some of the areas where more public spending can make difference. However, as majority of peasants have small parcels of land, the gain from higher public investment is likely to be limited.[25]

---

[24] Rodgers and Rodgers (2001) report a decline in usury because of fall in the prevalence of attached labour.
[25] How to break the deadlock then? Migration of labourers from agriculture can release land and help the accumulation process. Or, collectivisation through cooperative farming can be a way out. Economies of scale enjoyed by large capitalist farms could benefit cooperative farms as well. An alternative could be coordinated, large-sized, public investment. Piecemeal investments are likely to

Fourth, rising input price without commensurate rise in crop price is a main reason for low profitability. Fifth, tenancy and interlinked markets are not widespread. Sixth, there is a demand for land among the landless and marginal farmers. But potential of land redistribution does not seem to be immense as there exist few above-ceiling holdings.[26]

Conclusion and Comments

After the inauguration of economic planning, capital formation in agricultural sector started to improve. This was propelled by the stimulus of public investment. Public investment decelerated from the 1980s, which adversely affected aggregate agricultural investment. Rising population pressure on land combined with low investment resulted in a subdivision of landholdings. Outside the agricultural sector, organised industries and services do not absorb unskilled surplus labourers. The informal sector benefits from the flow of migrating labourer. But poor working conditions in the informal sector do not encourage permanent migration.

Before we conclude, a few political economic comments are in order. In the documents of Marxist Leninist (ML) stream of communist parties, feudalism is considered as a major impediment on the path of social revolution.[27] Contradiction between feudalism and the broad mass of people is the principal contradiction according to them. However, the agrarian economy in our discussion is found to be increasingly less held back by semi-feudal production. Matters of concern for the marginal farmers and the landless are more macroeconomic in character: public spending in irrigation, flood control, extension service, price of diesel, fertiliser, pesticides, seeds and procurement price of crop for instance. As these variables are a function of state policy and operation of large corporations, it is the big capital and the state—acting at big capital's behest—which the interests of 'revolutionary classes' are increasingly at odds with.[28] Although national and global influences get mediated through the local power structure, local power does not appear to be a part of the principal contradiction.[29] Coming from the other end, given the moribund state of accumulation, it is too early to conclude that Indian agriculture is characterised by capitalist mode of production.

The high degree of subdivision of holdings poses a dilemma for the communist movement as a whole. In the populous regions, ceiling surplus land is undergoing severe erosion, which robs the demand

---

be futile. This is because desperation for land creates a coordination failure-like condition. A big-push, planned investment strategy, by raising job opportunities boosts profitability and breaks the deadlock (Das, 2007).

[26] Kumar (2003) has made similar observations for Jehanabad and Arwal districts.

[27] The Party Programme of the Communist Party of India (Maoist): "[c]ontradiction between feudalism and broad masses is the principal contradiction at present. During the process of resolving this contradiction through the armed agrarian revolution, which is the axis of the new democratic revolution, that is, protracted people's war, the resolution of other contradictions will be facilitated". (Communist Party of India [Maoist], 2004). The existing Party Programme of the CPI (ML)-Liberation identifies a similar principal contradiction (Communist Party of India [ML], 2007): "[t]his alliance [between imperialism, big capital and feudal remnants] can only be overthrown by grasping and resolving the principal contradiction between feudal remnants and the broad Indian masses". Interestingly, the Draft General Programme for the 9th Party Congress has modified the principal contradiction: "[t]he antagonism between this nexus [of big capital, imperialism and feudalism] and the broad Indian masses thus constitutes the principal contradiction of present Indian society" (Liberation, 2013).

[28] By revolutionary classes, we are referring to the united front of four classes: the proletariat, the peasants, the petty bourgeoisie and the national bourgeoisie (Mao, 1940).

[29] We concur with Chatterjee (2008: 56): "there is a distinct ascendancy in the relative power of the corporate capitalist class as compared to the landed elites. The political means by which this recent dominance has been achieved needs to be investigated more carefully, because it was not achieved through the mechanism of electoral mobilisation". Patnaik (2006) also observed a change in the nature of primary contradiction.

for land redistribution of its traditional appeal. This is not to claim that slogans of land redistribution have lost their meaning, because there is no surplus land left to be redistributed. There could be underreporting of land under big holdings, which would give a low, inaccurate estimation of ceiling surplus land. There are regional variations of the degree of subdivision, which means there are states that have substantial amount of ceiling surplus land. Nonetheless, the NSSO data that large farms occupy zero or negligible percentage of land in many states indicate that the old slogan of 'land to the tiller' can become increasingly ineffective.[30]

It is evident that in relation to the big bourgeoisie, the hold of the landlords on the state power is slipping. For, when land holdings have been divided to such a high degree, economic foundation of feudalism has not stayed unscathed. This is not to say that landlords or their progenies have been emasculated. Many have diversified to trade, transport and other services.[31] But the fact that they are taking up other occupations suggests their growing powerlessness as a class. Peasant struggles under various communist parties have contributed to this erosion. Simultaneously, social domination of landlords has been challenged by caste movements.[32]

The present state of affairs produces its own contradictions. Having established a firm grip on the state, capital seeks to appropriate new resources with the help of state instruments to reproduce itself. This appropriation is unlike the appropriation of surplus value that takes place by 'the silent compulsion of economic relations' (Marx, 1867/1976: 899) in the course-expanded reproduction. It is achieved through extra-economic coercion, and, expectedly, it encounters resistance.[33] Land acquisition drives are being opposed by peasants. Their meagre land parcels may not support the peasant families throughout the year, but those parcels act as a valuable fallback option. In short, agriculture may have been rendered unprofitable, but that is not sufficient for the capitalists to take over peasants' land uncontested. It is more important to understand these resistances than to get imprisoned in questionable formulations.

References

Balakrishnan, P. (2010). *Economic growth in India*. New Delhi: Oxford University Press.
Banerjee, P. (2006). Land acquisition and peasant resistance at Singur. *Economic and Political Weekly*, 41(46), 4718–4720.
Bardhan, P. (1970). Trends in land relations: A note. *Economic and Political Weekly*, 5(3–5), 261–265.
Basole, A., & Basu, D. (2011a). Relations of production and modes of surplus extraction in India: Part I—Agriculture. *Economic and Political Weekly*, 46(14), 41–58.
———. (2011b). Relations of production and modes of surplus extraction in India: Part II—'Informal' industry. *Economic and Political Weekly*, 46(15), 63–79.
Basu, D., & Das, D. (2013). The Maoist movement in India: Some political economic considerations. *Journal of Agrarian Change*, 13(3), 365–381.
Bhaduri, A. (1973). A study in agriculture backwardness under semi-feudalism. *Economic Journal*, 83(329), 120–37.

---

[30] If we take 10 Ha as the uniform ceiling across states, 4.78 million Ha of land was ceiling surplus in 2003. This is too little for the 14.8 million landless households, not to speak of the 117.6 million marginal farmer households with the average 0.21 hectare holding (Government of India, 2006).

[31] In Bihar, 83 per cent of the bureaucracy was upper caste in 1970s (Kumar, 2003). In UP in 1984, 94 per cent of principal secretaries and secretaries, 79 per cent of district magistrates were from upper castes. They constituted 95 per cent of managing directors of public sector units (Jaffrelot, 2003).

[32] See Harriss, Jeyaranjan and Nagaraj (2010), for example.

[33] See Levien (2011) on the element of extra-economic coercion of the process, which he refers to as accumulation by dispossession rather than primary accumulation.

Bhaduri, A., & Patkar, M. (2009). Industrialisation for the people, by the people, of the people. *Economic and Political Weekly*, *44*(1), 10–14.

Bhalla, G.S., & Singh, G. (2009). Economic liberalisation and Indian agriculture: A statewise analysis. *Economic and Political Weekly*, *44*(52), 34–44.

Blyn, G. (1966). *Agricultural trends in India, 1891–1947: Output, availability and productivity*. Philadelphia, PA: University of Pennsylvania Press.

Breman, J. (2007). *Labour bondage in West India: From past to present*. New Delhi: Oxford University Press.

Byres, T.J. (1981). The new technology, class formation and class action in the Indian countryside. *The Journal of Peasant Studies*, *8*(4), 405–454.

Chandra, N.K. (1974). Farm efficiency under semi-feudalism: A critique of marginalist theories and some Marxist formulations. *Economic and Political Weekly*, *9*(32–34), 1309–1331.

Chatterjee, P. (2008). Democracy and economic transformation in India. *Economic and Political Weekly*, *43*(16), 53–62.

Communist Party of India (Maoist). (2004). Party programme. The Central Committee (Provisional) of the CPI (Maoist). Retrieved from http://www.bannedthought.net/India/CPI-Maoist-Docs/Founding/Programme-pamphlet.pdf on 27 January 2016.

Communist Party of India (ML). (2007). General programme. 8th Congress Documents. Retrieved from http://cpiml.org/8th_congress/partyprogramme.html on 1 February 2016.

Das, D. (2007). Persistence of small-scale, family farms in India: A note. *The Journal of International Trade and Economic Development*, *16*(3), 401–10.

———. (2014). Changing distribution of land and assets in Indian agriculture. *Review of Radical Political Economics*, *47*(3), 1–12.

Desai, B., D'Souza, E., Mellor, J.W., Sharma, V.P., & Tamboli, P. (2011). Agricultural policy strategy, instruments and implementation: A review and the road ahead. *Economic and Political Weekly*, *46*(53), 42–50.

Dhawan, B.D., & Yadav, S.S. (1995). Private fixed capital formation in agriculture: Some aspects of Indian farmers' investment behaviour. *Economic and Political Weekly*, *30*(39), A103–A109.

Djurfeldt, G., Athreya, V., Jayakumar, N., Lindberg, S., Rajagopal, A., & Vidyasagar, R. (2008). Agrarian change and social mobility in Tamil Nadu. *Economic and Political Weekly*, *43*(45), 50–61.

Government of India. (2006). *Some Aspects of Operational Land Holdings in India, 2002–03*, Report 492, NSSO 59th round.

———. (2015). *Agricultural statistics at a glance 2014*. Ministry of Agriculture, Department of Agriculture and Cooperation, Directorate of Economics and Statistics, New Delhi: Oxford University Press.

Government of India, Ministry of Finance. (2011). *Economic Survey 2010–11*. New Delhi: Author.

———. (2014). *Economic Survey 2013–14*. New Delhi: Author.

———. (2015). *Economic Survey 2014–15*. New Delhi: Author.

Harriss, J., Jeyaranjan, J., & Nagaraj, K. (2010). Land, labour and caste politics in rural Tamil Nadu in the 20th century: Iruvelpattu (1916–2008). *Economic and Political Weekly*, *45*(31), 47–61.

Hazell, P.B.R., Misra, V.N., & Hojjati, B. (1995). Role of terms of trade in Indian agricultural growth: A national and state level analysis. EPTD Discussion Paper No. 15, International Food Policy Research Institute, USA.

Jaffrelot, C. (2003). *India's silent revolution*. New Delhi: Permanent Black.

Jodhka, S.S. (2012). Agrarian changes in the times of (Neo-liberal) "Crises". *Economic and Political Weekly*, *47*(26–27), 5–13.

Kar, S., & Marjit, S. (2009). Contemporary perspective on the informal labour market: theory, policy and the Indian experience. *Economic and Political Weekly*, *44*(14), 60–71.

Karat, P. (2000). *Marxist analysis of Indian society*. Lecture delivered at the 20th anniversary Meeting of *Marxbadi Path*. Retrieved from http://cpim.org/node/1349 on 3 February 2016.

Kotwal, A., Ramaswami, B., & Wadhwa, W. (2011). Economic liberalization and Indian economic growth. *Journal of Economic Literature*, *49*(4), 1152–1199.

Kumar, A. (2003). Violence and political culture: Politics of the ultra-left in Bihar. *Economic and Political Weekly*, *38*(47), 4977–4983.

Lenin, V.I. (1899). *Capitalism in agriculture*. Retrieved from https://www.marxists.org/archive/lenin/works/1899/agriculture/ on 12 January 2015.

Lerche, J. (1999). Politics of the poor: Agricultural labourers and political transformations in Uttar Pradesh. *The Journal of Peasant Studies, 26*(2–3), 182–241.

Levien, M. (2011). Special economic zones and accumulation by dispossession in India. *Journal of Agrarian Change, 11*(4), 454–483.

Liberation. (2013). Draft General Programme. Retrieved from http://cpiml.org/library/print-liberation-full?cat=137&id=4643 on 11 January 2016.

Mao, T. (1940). *On new democracy*. Retrieved from https://www.marxists.org/reference/archive/mao/selected-works/volume-2/mswv2_26.htm on 12 January 2016.

Marx, K. (1867/1976). *Capital: A critique of political economy* (Vol. I). London: Penguin Classics.

———. (1893/1981). *Capital: A critique of political economy* (Vol. III). London: Penguin Classics.

Mehrotra, S., Gandhi, A., Sahoo, B.K., & Saha, P. (2012). Creating employment in the twelfth five-year plan. *Economic and Political Weekly, 47*(19), 63–73.

Omvedt, G. (1981). Capitalist agriculture and rural classes in India. *Economic and Political Weekly, 16*(52), A-140–A-143, A-145–A-159.

Patnaik, P. (1994). P.C. Mahalanobis and the theory of development planning. *Economie Appliquée, 47*, 153–165. (Reprinted in *Whatever Happened to Imperialism*, pp. 107–119, 1995, New Delhi: Tulika).

Patnaik, U. (1971). Capitalist development in agriculture: A note. *Economic and Political Weekly, 6*(39), 123–30.

———. (1972a). Development of capitalism in agriculture: I. *Social Scientist, 1*(2), 15–31.

———. (1972b). Development of capitalism in agriculture: II. *Social Scientist, 1*(3), 3–19.

———. (29 January 2006). The agrarian crisis and importance of peasant resistance. *People's Democracy*. Retrieved from http://pd.cpim.org/2006/0129/01292006_utsa.htm on 1 February 2016.

Prasad, P. (1973). Production relations: Achilles heel of Indian planning. *Economic and Political Weekly, 8*(19), 869–872.

Purohit, B., & Reddy, V.R. (1999). *Capital formation in Indian agriculture: Issues and concerns*. Occasional Paper 8, NABARD, Mumbai.

Ranis, G., & Fei, J.C.H. (1961). A theory of economic development. *The American Economic Review, 51*(4), 533–565.

Rao, V.M. (1992). Land reform experiences: Perspective for strategy and programmes. *Economic and Political Weekly, 27*(26), A50–57, A59–64.

Rodgers, G., & Rodgers, J. (2001). A leap across time: When semi-feudalism met the market in rural Purnia. *Economic and Political Weekly, 36*(22), 1976–1983.

Rudra, A., Majid, A., & Talib, B.D. (1990). Big farmers of Punjab. In U. Patnaik (Ed.), *Agrarian relations and accumulation: The 'mode of production' debate in India* (pp. 13–32). Bombay: Sameeksha Trust and Oxford University Press (originally published in Economic and Political Weekly [1969a, 1969b, 1970]).

Shah, M., Rao, R., & Sankar, P.S.V. (2007). Rural credit in 20th century India: Overview of history and perspectives. *Economic and Political Weekly, 42*(15), 1351–1364.

Shukla, T. (1968). Investment in agriculture. *Economic and Political Weekly, 3*(45), 1729, 1731–1732.

Upadhya, C.B. (1988a). The farmer-capitalists of coastal Andhra Pradesh. *Economic and Political Weekly, 23*(27), 1376–1382.

———. (1988b). The farmer-capitalists of coastal Andhra Pradesh. *Economic and Political Weekly, 23*(28), 1433–1442.

Vaidyanathan, A. (1997). Performance of Indian agriculture since independence. In K. Basu (Ed.), *Agrarian questions* (pp. 18–74). New Delhi: Oxford University Press.

Wilson, K. (1999). Patterns of accumulation and struggles of rural labour: Some aspects of agrarian change in Central Bihar. In T.J. Byres, K. Kapadia, & J. Lerche (Eds.), *Rural labour relations in India* (pp. 316–354). London: Frank Cass.

19
Political Economy of Contemporary Indian Agricultural and Rural Dynamics

Praveen Jha[*]

Introduction

One of the major threads in Prabhat Patnaik's work has been the political economy of the trajectories of economic transformation, in particular, ramifications of shifts in macroeconomic policy regimes. In this context, theoretical insights emerging from his analysis of the 'crisis in the countryside' in the era of neo-liberalism have been extremely illuminating. This chapter attempts to connect with some of his writings in this regard to investigate the nature and causes of India's 'agrarian crises' in the recent years.

India's countryside has come under tremendous pressure with respect to all the relevant major economic indicators in the recent years. It is well documented (Ghosh & Chandrasekhar, 2002; Patnaik & Chandrasekhar, 1995) that gradual changes in the country's macroeconomic regime commenced in the late 1980s with trade liberalisation alongside slow but steady deregulation of investment and output controls; by the early 1990s, there was already a sea change in the overall macroeconomic policy regime. The shift from *dirigiste* regime to largely a market-driven regime has had profound implications for the wellbeing of the masses in rural India. It is well acknowledged that agriculture continues to be the lifeline for millions in the countryside, and the state's action through appropriate public policies (for example, in terms of providing appropriate rural infrastructure: physical, social, etc.) has been central to a healthy performance of this

---

[*] It is deeply gratifying to contribute to a volume in honour of Professor Prabhat Patnaik, who is not only an outstanding economist but also a social scientist of great distinction with wide-ranging interests. Apart from his formidable scholarship that has had enduring appeal across disciplinary boundaries, Professor Patnaik's stellar role in shaping one of the finest and highly respected economics departments in India, namely the Centre for Economic Studies and Planning at Jawaharlal Nehru University, New Delhi, is well known. To his students, Professor Patnaik has been an adorable teacher and mentor, in the best senses, and a remarkable example of engaged and organic intellectual. His most exacting intellectual standards combined with an extremely sensitive approach towards his students have been a much appreciated attribute. For me, to be his student has been a matter of immense privilege and pleasure, both intellectually and personally. I can only say: Thank You Professor!

Towards preparation of this chapter, the author is happy to acknowledge valuable research assistance provided by his research student, Nilachala Acharya. This chapter also draws substantially on our arguments from earlier two papers (Jha, 2006; Jha & Acharya, 2011).

Figure 19.1
Share of Agriculture in Total GDP (at Constant 2004–2005 Prices, in percentage)

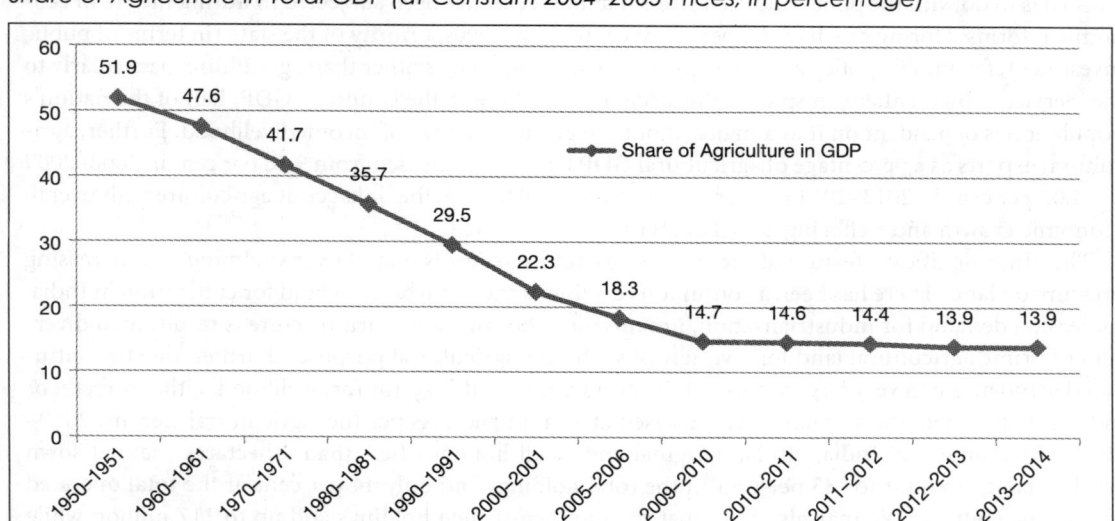

Source: Computed from the base data given in the Planning Commission, Government of India.

sector over the decades since Independence (Jha & Acharya, 2011). Before I come to the key elements of the contemporary agricultural and rural crisis, its causes and manifold consequences, a word or two may be useful to flag the moments of significant shifts in public policies towards the countryside since Independence.

Depending on a particular analytical lens one wishes to use, the entire post-Independence period can be classified into different phases based on alternative typologies.[1] My own preference, as discussed later briefly, is for a three-phase classification, at a high level of generality, from the point of view of public policies for agricultural and rural development. In this chapter, I do not get into a detailed discussion of all these phases, as also those of structural issues underlying the current state of the Indian agriculture (such as inadequate attention to the land question soon after Independence), or the interplay between the structural and conjunctural.[2] Here, my focus is on the conjunctural, in particular, the change in the macroeconomic policy regime since the early 1990s, and its correlations with the agrarian crises. It goes along with the view 'that the crisis of the countryside is intimately linked to the neo-liberal policies themselves and that it cannot be overcome within a neo-liberal regime' (Patnaik, 2005: 4).

A Profile of Indian Agriculture at the Current Juncture: Some Key Features

As is well known, the share of agriculture in the country's gross domestic product (GDP) has come down very substantially over the years, and currently it accounts for 14 per cent (Figure 19.1). However, from this, one must not deduce that agriculture has lost its importance in the overall scheme of things; part of

---

[1] For further details of such an analysis, please refer to Jha and Acharya (2011).
[2] Such as the factors that have facilitated a transition from a dirigiste nationalist policy framework to a neo-liberal regime or the factors which may account for the gaps between the rhetoric and reality of the erstwhile dirigiste regime.

this decline is expected as a common feature in any trajectory of economic transformation. Nevertheless, it also has to do with the policy-induced stress that the sector has been subjected to during the era of economic reforms. During much of the period since the early 1990s, priority of the state (in terms of public investment, favourable policy environment, etc.) shifted to sectors other than agriculture, particularly to the 'Services'. Incidentally, in spite of this decline in its share in the country's GDP, half of the nation's population is dependent on it as a major, if not the primary, source of income/livelihood. Further, agricultural exports as a percentage of agricultural GDP have also increased from 9.10 per cent in 2008–2009 to 14.05 per cent in 2013–2014 (Government of India, 2015: 89), the linkages of agriculture with overall economic growth and wellbeing is well established.

The other significant feature of the Indian agriculture sector is that of overwhelming and increasing pressure on land. There has been a continuous decline of the availability of land for cultivation in India. Increasing demand for industrialisation, urbanisation, housing and infrastructure is resulting in diversion of prime agricultural land for a variety of such non-agricultural purposes. Further, due to continued dependence of a very large section of the population on this sector for livelihood, either directly or indirectly, fragmentation of land has increased at a rapid pace. As per the Agricultural Census, 2010–2011 (Government of India, 2014), marginal and small holdings (less than 2 hectares [ha; net sown area] of land) account for 85 per cent in the total holdings and only 44 per cent of the total operated area in the country. We may also note that the number of such holdings add up to 117 million while accounting for a total of 70 million ha of cultivable land. Taking all the categories of farm sizes together, the average size of operated holding is at 1.16 ha (Table 19.1). Needless to add, the average size of operated area per holding has been declining at a significant rate. The point worth highlighting here is that economic viability of the small-sized holdings is a huge challenge without appropriate institutional and technological support. As regards the (total) area under crops, it has shown an increase during the period 1990–1991 to 2009–2010 (from 185.74 to 192.2 million ha), and this increase is on account of increase in cropping intensity. However, as regards the area under food crops, there is a marginal dip

Table 19.1

Distribution of Number of Holdings and Area Operated in India as per Agricultural Census 2010–2011

Serial Number	Size Group	Number of Holdings (in Million)	Area Operated (in Million ha)	Average Operated Area Per Holding (ha)	Percentage of Holdings to Total Holdings	Percentage of Area Operated to Total Area
1	Marginal (below 1 ha)	92.4	35.4	0.38	67.04	22.25
2	Small (1–2 ha)	24.7	35.1	1.42	17.93	22.07
3	Semi-medium (2–4 ha)	13.8	37.5	2.71	10.05	23.59
4	Medium (4–10 ha)	5.9	33.7	5.76	4.25	21.18
5	Large (above 10 ha)	1.0	17.4	17.38	0.73	10.92
All holdings		137.8	159.2	1.16	100.0	100

Source: Government of India (2013).

Table 19.2
Cropping Pattern in India (Area in million ha)

Years	1990–1991	2003–2004	2009–2010 (P)
Total area under crops	185.74	189.67	192.20
Net area sown	143.00	140.71	140.02
Cropping intensity (per cent)	129.89	134.80	137.26
Area under food crops	141.03	142.12	141.06
Area under non-food crops	44.71	47.55	51.14
Net irrigated area	48.02	57.05	63.26
Total/gross irrigated area	63.20	78.04	86.42

Source: Government of India (2013).
Note: P, provisional.

from 142.12 to 141.06 million ha during 2003–2004 and 2009–2010. Further, total net area sown has also tended to decline, that is, from 143 in 1990–1991 to 140 million ha in 2009–2010 (Table 19.2).

The third feature worth highlighting here relates to the shift in cropping pattern. As already hinted earlier, the area under foodgrain crops has shown a decline since the 1990s. This retrenchment in area under cultivation, during the period of analysis, is more acute with regard to millets cultivation followed by paddy. However, a small increase in area under cultivation of wheat has been observed over the period. On the whole, there has been a reduction in an area under cultivation for total food crops during the same period (for the overall as well as a disaggregated picture, across crops, see Table 19.3).

The fourth feature I would like to highlight here is that the Indian agriculture's performance has been well below its potential almost all through since Independence, and the problems have become more serious in the neo-liberal era largely because of the change in policy regime. The most obvious indicators of the health of the agricultural sector, such as the production and yield growth rates, clearly corroborate this argument. In the 1950s, the annual average rate of growth of total foodgrain was 5.08 per cent; which tended to decline during the next couple of decades before picking up in the decade of the 1980s (4.96 per cent) with spread and deepening of the Green Revolution. However, this was halved to 2.18 per cent in the decade of 1990s, and in the subsequent period, it nose-dived to about 1 per cent. The disaggregated picture with respect to major crops shows almost a similar picture. For instance, there has been a considerable decline in rate of growth of production of rice, since Independence; it was 5.52 per cent in the decade of the 1950s, which declined to 2.09 per cent in the 1990s and 0.68 per cent in the decade of the 2000s. Trends with regard to wheat, coarse cereals and pulses tell us similar stories (Table 19.4). On the whole, the 1980s was the best decade in terms of yield growth rates since Independence, and last decade (2000–2001 to 2009–2010) clearly stands out for its worst performance (both with respect to yield and output).

Features and Correlates of Agrarian Crisis

Given the World Trade Organisation (WTO) commitments, a progressive opening up of the domestic agriculture to the world market since the second half of the 1990s has been a source of considerable distress for farmers in general, and in the recent years, a very acute one for those growing cotton, spices, plantation crops, among others. By now, it is well acknowledged that as a result of import liberalisation,

Table 19.3
Trends in Cropping Pattern in India (Percentage Share—Crop Wise)

Years	1990–1991	2003–2004	2008–2009 (P)	2009–2010 (P)
Total area under crops (in million ha)	185.74	189.67	195.36	192.20
Rice	23.0	22.3	23.1	22.0
Jowar	7.6	5.0	3.9	4.1
Bajra	5.8	5.8	4.5	4.7
Maize	3.2	3.8	4.2	4.3
Ragi	1.2	0.9	0.8	0.7
Wheat	12.9	14.2	14.3	14.9
Barley	0.5	0.4	0.4	0.3
Other cereals and small millets	1.3	0.6	0.5	0.4
Total cereals and millets	55.5	53.0	51.6	51.4
Gram	4.0	3.7	4.1	4.2
Arhar	1.9	1.8	1.7	1.8
Other pulses	7.4	7.3	6.4	6.5
Total pulses	13.4	12.9	12.2	12.5
Total foodgrains	68.9	65.9	63.8	63.9
Sugarcane	2.1	2.4	2.5	2.4
Total condiments and spices	1.3	1.7	1.6	1.7
Total fruits and vegetables	3.6	4.9	5.2	5.4
Other food crops	0.1	0.1	0.1	0.1
Total food crops	75.9	74.9	73.2	73.4
Groundnut	4.5	3.3	3.2	2.9
Castor seed	0.5	0.4	0.4	0.4
Sesamum	1.3	1.0	1.0	1.2
Rapeseed and mustard	2.8	2.7	3.1	2.8
Linseed	0.5	0.2	0.2	0.2
Coconut	0.8	1.0	1.0	1.0
Other oilseeds	3.2	5.2	6.4	6.4
Total oilseeds	13.5	13.8	15.2	14.9
Cotton	4.1	4.2	4.8	5.2
Jute	0.4	0.5	0.4	0.4
Other fibres	0.2	0.1	0.1	0.1
Total fibres	4.7	4.8	5.3	5.7
Tobacco	0.2	0.2	0.2	0.3
Tea	0.2	0.3	0.3	0.3
Coffee	0.2	0.2	0.2	0.2
Fodder crops	4.5	4.6	4.4	3.9
Other non-food crops	0.8	1.1	1.2	1.4
Total non-food crops	24.1	25.1	26.8	26.6

Source: Government of India (2013).
Note: P, provisional.

Table 19.4
Growth Rates of Production of Cereals, Pulses and Total Food Grains since the 1950s

	Annual Average Growth Rates					
Year	Rice	Wheat	Coarse Cereals	Total Cereals	Pulses	Total Food grains
Annual average (1951–1952 to 1959–1960)	5.52	6.02	5.00	5.19	4.83	5.08
Annual average (1960–1961 to 1969–1970)	3.13	8.15	2.32	3.62	1.62	3.25
Annual average (1970–1971 to 1979–1980)	1.53	5.30	0.71	1.99	−1.99	1.58
Annual average (1980–1981 to 1989–1990)	6.56	4.91	3.26	4.98	4.90	4.96
Annual average (1990–1991 to 1999–2000)	2.09	4.52	−0.08	2.29	0.94	2.18
Annual average (2000–2001 to 2009–2010)	0.68	0.77	2.47	0.87	1.99	0.93

Source: Computed by the author based on the data available on RBI (2012).

several crops have been hit by unfavourable price trends, and may be more importantly, by violent fluctuations. For instance, between 1995 until about 2004, the agricultural commodity prices in the world market have witnessed a secular downtrend, although within this, there were significant fluctuations. Similarly, between 1997 and 2002, most prices had taken a nosedive, but subsequently they started climbing (Jha, 2006). Obviously, one requires careful and disaggregated accounts as regards the impact of long-term price trends on India's farmers. However, it may be appropriate to argue that the increased openness, through price fluctuations, has increased the vulnerability of a very large section of the peasantry, given severe limitations of their coping mechanism. Along with this, state intervention and support in domestic market for agricultural produce tended to weaken considerably, (for example, government procurement has been abandoned or scaled down; for crops covered by minimum support prices, such as paddy or wheat, minimum support price has not kept pace with rising costs of cultivation, to note a couple of policy measures in this regard), and private players, including multinational corporations, have been allowed to have a significant say on the course of events. In fact, the Indian government appears to have been more loyal to the emperor than the emperor himself, as it removed quantitative restrictions on agricultural imports in 2001 itself, that is, two years before the WTO stipulated date. Combination of these factors has increased the vulnerability of the Indian peasantry to the fluctuations in global markets, while also inflicting substantial losses on them. Coupled with increasing the openness, the neo-liberal regime has also pushed up the input prices, for instance through a curtailment of subsidies (for example, fertiliser subsidies, cost of power for irrigation, etc).

As is well acknowledged, the crisis in agriculture in the recent days is an outcome of a long negligence of public policies relating to investment towards this sector (as discussed later in some details). For instance, it has been observed that the share of gross capital formation (GCF) in agriculture and allied sector in total country's GCF shows a declining trend (Figure 19.2). This reflects the neglected priorities of public investment in this sector since long. Further, as regards the share of capital formation by the public sector, there has been a continuous decline as compared to the share of capital formation in this sector by the private players (Government of India, 2012).

It is, in fact, on account of poor performance of public investment in particular, and neglect with respect to public policies in general, that the yield growth rates have tended to decline for various foodgrains during the last couple of decades. This decline in yield is quite sharp for major crops, such as rice and wheat (for disaggregated information, across crops, see Table 19.5). The declining trends in area, yield and production are witnessed in the case of almost all crops, except for the marginal improvement in

Figure 19.2
Share of Public Sector GCF in Agriculture and Allied Sector in the Total GCF (in Percentage and Figures are Based on 2004–2005 Prices)

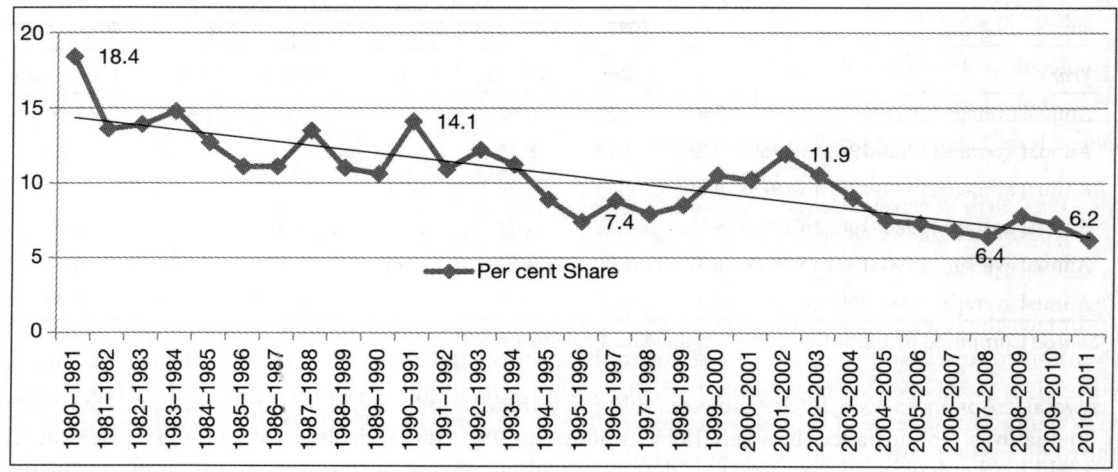

Source: Government of India (2013).

Table 19.5
Growth Rates of Yield of Cereals and Pulses and Total Food Grains in India since the 1950s

	Annual Average Growth Rates					
Year	Rice	Wheat	Coarse Cereals	Total Cereals	Pulses	Total Food grains
Annual average (1951–1952 to 1959–1960)	4.3	2.1	3.0	3.3	1.4	2.9
Annual average (1960–1961 to 1969–1970)	1.9	5.3	1.3	2.3	2.6	2.4
Annual average (1970–1971 to 1979–1980)	0.7	2.0	1.7	1.6	−2.6	1.2
Annual average (1980–1981 to 1989–1990)	5.5	4.2	4.0	4.7	4.0	4.6
Annual average (1990–1991 to 1999–2000)	1.4	2.9	2.0	2.4	1.8	2.4
Annual average (2000–2001 to 2009–2010)	1.1	0.2	2.5	1.0	−5.8	0.8

Source: Computed by the author based on the data available on RBI (2012).

the growth rate of yield of coarse cereals and the growth rate of area cultivated under wheat. The decline in yields for most crops is quite dramatic, and careful explanations are required to explain this; however, it may not be inappropriate to put one's finger on the dwindling of government research effort, in particular on seed varieties, along with the shrinking of public support in many other ways, as one of the more important elements in this story.

Another notable feature of recent decades, obviously connected with the above noted policies, has been growing landlessness among the peasantry. As per a recent study, based on the National sample Survey (NSS) data,

> about 49 per cent of households did not have any operational holding of land (in 2011–12). Data from successive rounds of NSS surveys show a sharp rise in landlessness over the last two decades. Data on land cultivated show that proportion of households that did not cultivate any land increased from 35 per cent in

Table 19.6
Agriculture Labour Households with/without Access to Cultivable Land (Percentage of Total Agricultural Labour Households)

Year	1983	1987–1988	1993–1994	1999–2000	2004–2005	2009–2010
Households without cultivable land	55.9	52.2	57.0	57.3	61.72	63.63
Households with some land	44.1	47.8	43.0	42.7	38.28	36.37

Source: Rural Labour Enquiry (RLE), Government of India.

1987–88 to 49 percent in 2011–12. Data on ownership holding of land, which include homesteads and all other types of land, show that proportion of households that did not have land (or had less than 0.01 hectares of land) increased by 9 percentage points over this period. (Rawal, 2013)

In fact, the lower rungs of the peasantry, many of whom are in the agricultural labour market, have been forced to sell or give up their land due to the growing difficulties of cultivation. Thus, it is hardly surprising, as may be seen from Table 19.6, that within agricultural labour households, there has been a very significant increase in landlessness between 1987–1988 and 2009–2010; also, it is worth noting that the trend in the 1980s was in the opposite direction.

It is hardly surprising, given the above-noted context, that there was a sharp decline in the availability of foodgrains (per capita net availability) over the period of neo-liberal reform. It is commonly acknowledged that during the period immediately after Independence, there has been a serious crisis experienced in terms of production and availability of foodgrains; however, the per capita net availability of foodgrains has increased significantly up to the period of the late 1980s, and much of this increase is due to the introduction of the Green Revolution and its outcome. However, since the 1990s, there has been a marked reduction in the per capita net availability of foodgrains; it reached to 438.6 grams per capita per day in 2010 compared to 510 grams per capita per day in 1991 (Government of India, 2012).

In popular discussions and in the pink press, one often comes across arguments that subsidies for agriculture are guzzling huge amount of scares resources. In this context, it is worth noting here that the share of total subsidies to the GDP does not substantiate such a view. For instance, the total Union government subsidy for the most recent period (2004–2005 to 2013–2014) has fluctuated between 1.42 and 2.03 per cent of the GDP and 9.22 and 13.88 per cent of the total Union government expenditure.[3] Similarly, another important factor contributing to the stress of agriculture has been the overall input use profile. As is well known, electricity for irrigation is quite critical to modern agriculture. During the 1980s, the share of electricity use in agriculture out of total electricity use was around 20 per cent, which increased to 30 per cent by the mid-1990s and has come down significantly in the subsequent period of 2009–2010 to 21 per cent.

Drying up of institutional credit for agriculture has been among the most serious concerns leading to an increased dependence on moneylenders and traders, that is, private sources of usurious credit. The percentage share of agricultural credit in the total credit of all the Scheduled Commercial Banks since the early 1990s has taken a severe beating compared to the levels reached in the 1980s. For instance, the annual growth rate of agricultural credit was 6.8 per cent between 1981 and 1990, which fell down to 2.6 per cent between 1991 and 2000, with a large-scale closure of commercial bank branches in rural areas. In fact, between 1995 and 2005, the number of rural branches of commercial banks fell by 922. Also, there has been a clear sidelining of small and marginal farmers in the supply of agricultural credit

---

[3] For further details, see Centre for Budget and Governance Accountability (2013).

and is evident from the share of agricultural credit to these groups of farmers out of total credit disbursement. In total credit disbursement to agriculture sector, the share of small and marginal farmers has declined to 50 per cent in 2004 compared to 55 per cent in 1990. It is true that in the last couple of years, particularly since 2003, there has been a substantial increase in absolute amount of credit for agriculture, and it may have eased the pressure on the relatively better off farmers (Jha, 2006).

At the same time, it is quite possible that for a very large section of the peasantry, there has been no turn around in this respect. It is worth emphasising that the share of 'indirect credit'[4] in the total agricultural credit showed a declining trend during the 1970s and 1980s; however, from the mid-1990s onwards, the share of indirect credit in the total agricultural credit is increasing.[5] As is well known that a great deal of the indirect credit is outside the reach of farmers, and thus a shift in composition of credit for agriculture in favour of the indirect component may be considered a cause of concern from the point of view of the immediate wellbeing of farmers, particularly so when almost every other aspect of the macroeconomic policy has put them in a tighter spot. It is important to note here that about 33 per cent of the total agricultural credit in India was disbursed through either urban or metropolitan branches of banks, and even in direct finance, almost 26 per cent was disbursed through either urban or metropolitan branches of banks (Jha, 2006).

Inadequate Budgets and Budgetary Priorities towards 'Rural Economy'

As is well known, public spending through budgets has been one of the most direct and effective instrument that governments can use to promote desirable trajectories of development. Furthermore, there is enough evidence to suggest that public policies favouring appropriate budgetary investments towards agriculture and rural development play a crucial role in shaping the overall growth of the economy while ensuring agricultural development and reducing the incidence of absolute poverty (for elaborate discussions on these issues, see Bates, 1997; Chand, 2010; Fan, Hazell & Haque, 2000; Hayami & Ruttan, 1985; Paroda & Kumar, 2000; Patnaik, 2003; Pinstrup-Andersen, Ruiz de Londono & Hoover, 1976; Ramachandran & Swaminathan, 2002; Vyas, 2003, 2005).

The relevant literature lends strong support to the view that there exists a high degree of positive association between public investment towards agriculture and rural infrastructure on the one hand, and agricultural development, increased rural household income and consumption, reduction of poverty in rural areas, etc., on the other (for further elaboration of these arguments, see Bhalla, 2007; Fan et al., 2000; Fan & Rao, 2003; Ghosh, 2010; Patnaik, 2005; Vaidyanathan, 2006). A growing body of research has also attempted to explore the linkages between agricultural development and different components of physical infrastructure,[6] namely roads, irrigation, electricity supply, banking,[7] communications, etc. Studies have also focused on the impact of social infrastructure (like education and health facilities, agricultural extension services and information dissemination systems, participatory mechanisms, etc., supported by appropriate public investments in agricultural research and technology) on the pace and distribution of agricultural growth (Bhalla & Singh, 2001; Fan, Mogues & Beni, 2009; Fan & Rao, 2003;

---

[4] For further details, see Ramakumar (2013).
[5] For details, see Jha (2006).
[6] It is worth emphasising that rural infrastructure plays a significant role in the successful adoption and utilisation of research and technology for agricultural development. For instance, using data for 44 developing countries from Africa, Asia and Latin America, it has been observed that the economic returns of agricultural research and technology are usually high in countries and regions with good rural infrastructure.
[7] Among the major deficiencies in rural infrastructure, inadequate provision of financial institutions for mobilising savings and disbursing credit to farmers, particularly to the small and marginal landholders, has often been highlighted as a pervasive problem in most developing countries.

Fan, Yu & Saurkar, 2008; Thirtle, Piesse, & Lin, 2003). Key message emerging from such research is that good rural infrastructure is critical for enhancing the growth of agricultural output and productivity, and the former is largely dependent on public investment particularly in early to middle stages of economic transformation (that is, the context appropriate for developing countries).

As is generally well acknowledged, agriculture in much of the developing world has been experiencing serious difficulties in the recent years, in large measure on account of policies rooted in neo-liberal macroeconomic frameworks. One major element of such policy regimes has been relative neglect of agriculture in particular and the rural areas in general. Given that almost three-quarters of the world's poor live in rural areas and are largely dependent on the agriculture sector for their livelihood, inadequate public provisioning and states' inaction can have serious adverse consequences for agricultural development and wellbeing of the masses, as witnessed across developing world, in varying measure, and India is no exception to this general trend.

As hinted earlier, the recent stress experienced by the Indian agriculture and decline in its rate of growth is, in large measure, due to low public investment priorities accorded in the respective budgets by both the Union and state governments.[8] In particular, since the early 1990s, the inadequacy of capital formation has been a major factor in contributing to the slackened pace and pattern of technological changes and the infrastructural development with adverse consequence on agricultural productivity and output. As discussed in the foregoing, since the early 1990s, the share of capital formation in agriculture out of GCF of the country has declined sharply, and public sector capital expenditure for agricultural development in many states of India has witnessed varying degrees of decline.

Without getting into a detailed discussion of the structural issues plaguing the Indian agriculture or the political economy of the development trajectories that the country has witnessed, attempt here is to look at the trends and patterns of public investment and priorities accorded in different budgets over the years towards 'rural economy' (henceforth, RE). An attempt has been made here to map the status of public investment towards rural economy in India (both Union and state governments combined) since the 1950s and also to look at priorities within this broad head.

In the analysis here, the sector defined as rural economy, goes beyond the conventional meaning of 'Agricultural and Allied Activities' and 'Rural Development' sectors taken together, as per the accounting classifications maintained in the budgets of the Union and state governments. While conceptualising rural economy, an attempt has been made to take into account the combined budgetary allocations made towards rural economy by the Union, states and Union territory governments (for details of expenditure under major heads that constitute rural economy as per the definition used in this chapter, the relevant data sources and methodological issues, readers may refer to Jha & Acharya, 2011).

The relevant data show that the share of budgetary expenditure towards rural economy out of total combined budgetary expenditure constituted 11.4 and 12 per cent, respectively, during 1950–1951 and 1960–1961. Subsequently, there was a noticeable dip during 1970–1971 (that is, 9.5 per cent), before it rose during 1980–1981. For instance, during 1980–1981, these shares moved upward and reached 10.1 per cent compared to 9.5 per cent during 1970–1971. Thereafter, its share reached 12 per cent in 1990–1991 but declined throughout the decade of the 1990s and reached 8.8 per cent in 2000–2001. However, an increasing trend is observed in the past decade (Figure 19.3).

Similarly, the trend line of shares of rural economy out of the country's GDP shows an increasing trend during the 1950–1951 to 1960–1961; however, its shares stagnated during the decade of the mid-1960s and 1970s. Subsequently, during the late 1970s and the decade of the 1980s, its share shows an increasing trend. As can be seen, the share of rural economy out of the GDP reached its all-time high

---

[8] For a discussion of trends relating to public expenditure since the early 1990s, see contributions in Jha (2011).

Figure 19.3
Share of Combined Budgetary Expenditure towards Rural Economy (RE) out of Total Combined Budgetary Expenditure and GDP since 1950–1951 (in percentage)

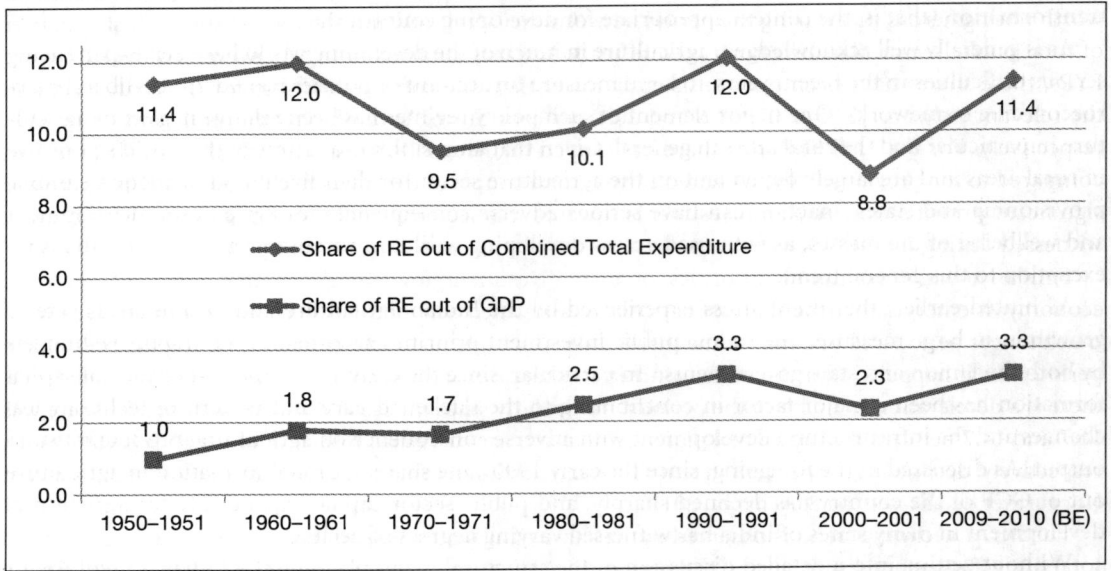

Source: Reproduced from Jha and Acharya (2011).

(3.3 per cent) during the 1990–1991 before exhibiting a declining trend since then. In fact, its share reached 2.3 per cent in 2000–2001 before making an upward move (Figure 19.3).

Further, while examining the priorities of public investment towards various major components within rural economy since 1950–1951, it clearly emerges that the three components, namely agriculture and allied activities, rural development and irrigation, received most of the allocations during the entire period under examination. For instance, the share of agriculture and allied activities out of total expenditures towards rural economy was 4.1 per cent during 1950–1951, which increased to 25.9 per cent during the decade of the 1990s. However, during the subsequent decade, that is, during the period 2000–2001 to 2009–2010, this share has come down further and reached 17.1 per cent. As regards the share of budgetary expenditures towards rural development programmes out of total budgetary spending on rural economy since the 1950s, it has been observed that the trend shows an increasing one. The share of expenditure on rural development during 1950–1951 was 23.6 per cent, which increased to 48 per cent during the decade of 2000s (annual average, 2000–2001 to 2009–2010).

With regard to share of irrigation and flood control, substantial attention was paid and major chunk of resources had been utilised during the early decades of Independence. For instance, its share out of total budgetary spending towards rural economy during 1950–1951 was 68.5 per cent. However, in the subsequent decades, particularly since the mid-1970s, its share witnessed a sharp decline. As may be seen in the relevant data that during the most recent decade (that is, annual average, 2000–2001 to 2009–2010), its share was pegged at as low as 5.5 per cent.[9]

While examining trends relating to the share of public sector plan expenditure towards rural economy out of the total public sector plan expenditure, very important insights were revealed. As is the case with

---

[9] For a detailed discussion on this, please refer to Jha and Acharya (2011).

the trends of combined budgetary expenditure, similar pattern for the plan expenditures towards rural economy over the years has been observed. For instance, this share was 23.3 per cent during the third five-year plan (FYP, henceforth), and the same had increased to 25.7 per cent in the sixth FYP. The point worth noting here is that during the period between the late-1960s and the mid-1980s, almost a quarter of total public sector plan investments were made towards rural economy. However, in the successive FYPs, these shares have been put consistently lower than the comparable ratio for the sixth FYP, and the relevant ratios are 23.5, 23.7, 21.6 and 20.1 per cent during seventh, eighth, ninth and tenth FYP, respectively. For the 11th FYP, this share has dipped further to 18.5 per cent, which is an all time low, compared to the previous FYPs. As noted earlier, for a couple of decades since the early 1970s, there was significant prioritisation of plan investments towards this sector to pull it out of a near-crisis situation witnessed during the late 1960s.

Similarly, while examining priorities of plan investment towards different components of rural economy, it emerges that the share of agriculture and allied activities has been an area of concern for a much longer period and one may argue that it did receive adequate attention even during the pre-reform period.[10] As it happens, after the initial spurt in its share during first couple of decades of Independence, there is a deceleration in much of the periods, particularly since the late 1970s. For instance, its share was 16.7 and 14.7 per cent during annual plans (annual average of 1966–1969) and fourth FYP (1969–1974), respectively, declined to 3.9 per cent in tenth FYP and for the eleventh FYP, its share is as low as 3.7 per cent (for further details, see Jha & Acharya, 2011).

Further, a declining trend is observed in the share of all states expenditure towards rural economy in total budgetary expenditure during the period since the early 1990s. During 1990–1991, share of rural economy was 21.9 per cent, which increased to 24.2 per cent in 1993–1994 and thereafter it showed a marked decline reaching 11.8 per cent in 2003–2004; the subsequent period shows reversal of the above-noted trend. The observed decline is largely due to a drastic compression of expenditure towards rural economy by quite a few states, which include Gujarat, Haryana, Himachal Pradesh, Karnataka, Kerala, Madhya Pradesh, Odisha, Punjab, Rajasthan, Tamil Nadu and West Bengal. As already noted, the declining trend in combined rural economy expenditure by all states is reversed since 2003–2004, and the relevant figure for 2009–2010 was 17.14 per cent.[11]

The other point worth highlighting is that of wide fluctuations in expenditure on rural economy across states during most of this period. Apart from this, share of expenditure towards rural economy in total budgetary spending in a few states is extremely inadequate and requires urgent attention (Table 19.7).

As regards distribution of expenditure during the last two decades, taking all states together, within agriculture and allied activities, almost half the share is on account of crop husbandry, the head which primarily takes care of the development of agricultural activities. Further, on an average, around 10 per cent is spent under soil and water conservation and about 18 per cent towards the development of animal husbandry during last two decades. Expenditure towards other sub heads, such as dairy development, fisheries, marketing, quality control and food storage and ware housing, have been disappointing.

As regards spending under the head of agriculture research and education, although there is an increase in nominal amount during the last decade compared to the 1990s, the problem is that the absolute allocation itself is extremely inadequate with reference to any appropriate benchmark. In terms of expenditure

---

[10] In absolute term, and in current prices, 10-fold growth of plan expenditure towards agriculture and allied activities has been seen during the period between the seventh and eleventh FYPs.
[11] We may note here that in terms of nominal value of absolute expenditure towards rural economy (taking all states together), there was an increase of almost 9 times during the period 1990–1991 to 2009–2010. However, for obvious reasons, it is more appropriate to look at the 'proportions' instead of absolute expenditure.

Table 19.7
Share of Expenditure on Rural Economy in Total Budgetary Expenditure since the 1990s (in percentage)

State/Year	1990–1991	2000–2001	2001–2002	2002–2003	2003–2004	2004–2005	2005–2006	2006–2007	2007–2008	2008–2009 RE	2009–2010 BE
Andhra Pradesh	23.41	16.63	16.55	15.78	15.78	18.77	24.77	27.05	28.08	28.23	27.19
Arunachal Pradesh	19.10	15.65	16.37	17.09	17.01	14.95	15.09	15.14	21.94	16.33	13.02
Assam	18.66	12.25	12.45	10.34	11.55	10.74	12.69	14.94	14.79	17.44	15.80
Bihar	19.82	15.32	15.87	16.79	15.65	12.58	13.40	15.91	17.00	20.93	19.26
Chhattisgarh	NA	18.93	17.10	19.32	19.23	20.52	21.28	20.51	23.55	21.19	19.67
Goa	15.19	6.01	5.19	4.89	5.85	6.88	10.92	9.95	9.40	9.18	7.92
Gujarat	23.62	17.52	14.30	15.04	9.90	11.61	13.26	16.49	15.80	20.49	15.17
Haryana	19.78	19.28	18.19	9.45	4.52	7.63	11.71	10.18	14.96	14.36	10.81
Himachal Pradesh	17.74	9.43	8.03	7.56	6.68	6.61	7.57	8.43	10.15	10.07	10.18
J&K	14.56	10.75	13.42	13.35	12.57	12.14	9.55	12.54	8.88	9.30	11.30
Jharkhand	NA	NA	19.72	22.05	21.00	20.77	18.96	19.43	17.99	16.44	13.79
Karnataka	21.89	18.92	16.14	17.23	13.27	17.62	21.31	20.47	20.98	15.44	16.88
Kerala	15.89	14.74	12.34	12.81	8.95	12.44	13.05	8.01	7.18	8.60	7.66
MP	25.56	15.70	14.48	15.32	12.28	13.02	13.35	16.09	18.04	17.77	17.06
Maharashtra	27.14	14.83	16.42	18.80	19.05	19.26	21.45	19.95	17.39	22.93	32.55
Manipur	20.68	10.86	11.09	7.94	10.68	13.06	17.24	16.04	15.36	19.38	16.99
Meghalaya	19.30	13.44	15.07	12.43	12.12	11.77	15.31	16.69	15.57	18.71	18.25
Mizoram	15.91	11.56	12.08	13.05	12.26	14.61	14.55	16.03	17.81	17.79	13.80
Nagaland	18.28	12.29	11.72	9.76	11.77	11.76	14.02	14.75	14.06	15.61	15.10
Odisha	25.00	14.14	12.61	12.37	10.82	10.64	11.22	11.47	15.34	16.74	17.52
Punjab	14.66	13.66	13.65	4.45	5.04	6.05	7.12	6.36	6.76	8.79	7.34
Rajasthan	19.71	11.61	11.83	10.40	11.22	12.08	14.52	12.09	12.23	13.49	13.51
Sikkim	12.99	9.62	4.95	5.57	8.51	5.36	7.91	9.27	8.47	10.53	8.58
Tamil Nadu	18.31	12.66	10.82	9.23	9.42	9.49	10.59	15.21	13.28	12.43	12.21
Tripura	19.34	14.20	14.19	12.53	10.57	10.00	11.07	12.15	11.85	12.98	12.76
Uttar Pradesh	25.98	17.02	16.79	15.31	9.56	12.51	13.77	12.44	14.40	15.44	14.04
Uttarakhand	NA	40.14	14.57	12.33	13.44	13.61	12.90	14.46	15.33	16.96	12.74
West Bengal	19.39	12.18	11.12	8.48	6.22	7.95	8.21	8.59	9.72	8.54	9.69
All States	21.93	15.00	14.40	13.66	11.80	13.40	15.08	15.50	15.97	16.91	17.14

Source: Compiled by the author from the base data given in RBI (2010).

Notes: NA, not applicable.

RE, revised estimate.

BE, budget estimate.

on rural development programmes, taking all states together, the average spending increased in nominal terms from ₹9,873 crore during the 1990s to ₹29,463 crore during 2000–2001 and 2009–2010. Likewise, the relevant figure towards irrigation and flood control in the decade of the 1990s was ₹13,487 crore, which went up to ₹39,516 crore (annual average) during the period 2000–2001 and 2009–2010.

Concluding Remarks

It should be evident from the foregoing discussion that there is a strong basis to argue that India's contemporary crisis is organically connected with the neo-liberal regime that has been ascendant since the early 1990s. The performance of India's RE, in particular agriculture, has been a subject of serious concern in the recent years. One of the important reasons for the disappointing outcomes is that this sector seems to have been facing inadequacy of the public policies by the successive governments, at different levels.

In this context, it is clearly important to understand the underlying shifts in the balance of class relations in the Indian economy that has led to a significant transition in policy choices. In other words, one needs to come to grips with the political economy of India's transition from the *dirigiste* to a neo-liberal regime in which the countryside has been affected relatively more adversely. In particular, the question is how do we relate the drastic shift in economic policy regime vis-à-vis rural India to the nature of the Indian State? Whatever happened to the politico-ideological programme that was supposed to be the bedrock of 'passive revolution' in the post-independent India which had sought to avoid the unnecessary rigours of an industrial transition?

A proper treatment of answers to these questions cannot be captured within the scope of this chapter as there are several issues and dimensions that need to be addressed. The best one can do here is to flag a couple of ideas that may serve as pointers to any attempt towards arriving at reasonable answers. One may recall here that soon after the spread and presumed 'success' of the Green Revolution during the 1970s and 1980s, commentators often talked about the rising power and voice of the Indian countryside. Often there were allusions not only to the rise of the 'kulak' power but also that of 'bullock-capitalists', middle-peasantry, etc.; it was as if the 'rural' had found much greater voice in the policy setting within the country. Journalistic accounts talked of the likes of Mahendra Singh Tikait's ability to hold Delhi to ransom at will. Of course, the backdrop to all this was well-demonstrated ability of the 'farmers' to mobilise themselves in different parts of India during the 1970s and 1980s. Hence, one may find it surprising how the presumed power of the 'rural' has taken a drubbing in the era of neo-liberal reforms.

However, we would suggest that there is not much of a surprise, if one attempts a careful class analysis of the economic transformation in rural India during the 1970s and 1980s. The leadership of the so-called farmers typically was with the landlords and the rich peasants who happened to be the major beneficiaries of the Green Revolution. They were the ones who had benefitted disproportionately from the public policy support regime, had got into a variety of 'mobility channels' (social-political and economic) and were restive for more. The surplus generated by the better off among the rural elite was already being channelised into a number of non-agricultural options. As a well-known commentator puts it,

> [...] a typical family of this class has a landholding in its native village, cultivated by hired labour, *bataidar*, tenant or farm servants and supervised by the father or one son; business of various descriptions in town managed by other sons; and perhaps a young and bright child who is a doctor or engineer or a professor. It is this class is most vocal about the injustice done to the village. (Balagopal, 1987)

In other words, the success of the Green Revolution also reflected an acceleration in differentiation, and much of the so-called rise of the 'rural' was basically vested in, and manipulated by, the rural oligarchy and the elite. As it happens, this section had already started 'voting with their feet' vis-à-vis the RE and society and begun to align with the interests of the urban elite, and did not quite feel threatened by the policy changes since the early 1990s. Further, one may even suggest that with respect to their stake in the countryside itself, they felt that the policy transition may be in their interest in important ways (for instance, through their access to export markets for their surplus).

In other words, in any case, the overwhelming majority of the peasantry did not have any significant say as regards the policy regime of the 1970s and 1980s. Hence, the transition since the early 1990s, which has affected them extremely adversely, may not be viewed as a surprise. The real question then is as follows: what is the range of legitimation strategies unleashed by the state in the face with huge adversities confronting the peasantry.

It is important to recognise that the Indian agriculture is in dire need of a 'big push' public investment (which in turn can also attract private investments). Given the crisis of declining/stagnant productivity in agriculture and the increasing demand for foodgrains to feed an ever-growing population (as well as other demands on agricultural output), it is crucial to prioritise public investment towards this sector. Further, to bridge the gap between demand–supply mismatches, there is a need for increasing productivity through various technological advancements that largely depend on greater public investment. Also, the role of the public sector in this regard is very critical with reference to distributional considerations. Provision for rural infrastructures like rural roads and other means of connectivity, creation of food storages and godowns, re-energising rural market hubs for better marketing facilities, restructuring the farm extension services with the deployment of adequate manpower and capital investments, encouragement to the farming community through various incentives like declaration of minimum support price of different products on time, extended farm insurance, etc., can ensure sustained growth of this sector.

Given India's fiscal/financial architecture as per the Constitution, agriculture is primarily the domain of the state governments; however, support from the Union government has been an extremely important component in facilitating development of this sector. In this context, it is worth emphasising that central assistance to states should be provided with as little conditionalities with respect to the use of funds while ensuring their non-diversion. Besides, states should also prioritise their public investment basket in favour of agriculture and rural development. It hardly needs emphasis that apart from increasing the crop yields, adequate provisions should also be made to develop allied sectors, such as animal husbandry, fisheries, etc. Areas such as agricultural research and education have clearly not received due attention and must be on the front burner, so as to help developing appropriate and advanced technologies suited to different agro-climatic zones. Apart from making primary investments, funds should also be allocated for the proper management, continuation and upgradation of the existing infrastructure, such as medium and minor irrigation projects.

In a country like India, agriculture in particular and petty production in general can hardly do without the substantial state support, and it is precisely this support that has been hit hard by neo-liberalism.

References

Balagopal, K. (1987). An ideology of the provincial propertied class. *Economic and Political Weekly*, 21(36–37), 2177–2178.

Bates, R. (1997). Institutions as investments. *Journal of African Economies*, 6(3), 272–287.

Bhalla, G.S. (2007). *Indian agriculture since independence.* New Delhi: National Book Trust.
Bhalla, G.S., & Singh, G. (2001). *Indian agriculture: Four decades of development.* New Delhi: Sage Publications.
Centre for Budget and Governance Accountability. (2013). *How has the dice rolled? Response to union budget 2013–14.* New Delhi: Author.
Chand, R. (2010). SAARC agricultural vision 2020. *Agricultural Economics Research Review, 23*(2), 197–208.
Fan, S., Hazell, P., & Haque, F. (2000). Public investments by agro-economical zones to achieve growth and poverty alleviation goals in rural India. *Food Policy, 25*(2000), 411–428.
Fan, S., Mogues, T., & Beni, S. (2009). *Setting priorities for public spending for agricultural and rural development in Africa.* Washington, DC: International Food Policy Research Institute (IFPRI).
Fan, S., & Rao, N. (2003). *Public spending in developing countries: Trends, determination and impact.* Discussion Paper No. 99, International Food Policy Research Institute (IFPRI), Washington, DC.
Fan, S., Yu, B., & Saurkar, A. (2008). Public spending in developing countries: Trends, determination and impact. In S. Fan (Ed.), *Public expenditures, growth, and poverty: Lessons from developing countries* (pp. 20–55). Baltimore, MD: Johns Hopkins University Press.
Ghosh, J. (2010). The political economy of hunger in 21st century India. *Economic and Political Weekly, 45*(44), 33–38.
Ghosh, J., & Chandrasekhar, C.P. (2002). *The market that failed: neoliberal economic reforms in India.* New Delhi: Left Word Books.
Government of India. (2012). *Economic survey of India 2011–12.* New Delhi, India: Ministry of Finance.
———. (2013). *State of Indian agriculture 2012–13.* New Delhi: Author.
———. (2014). *Agricultural census of India 2010–11.* New Delhi: Agriculture Census Division, Department of Agriculture and Cooperation, Ministry of Agriculture.
Government of India. (2015). *Economic survey of India 2014–15.* New Delhi, India: Ministry of Finance.
———. (1994–1995 to 2009–2010). *Indian public finance statistics.* New Delhi, India: Author.
———. (1961–1962 to 1987–1988). *Indian economic statistics—public finance.* New Delhi, India: Author.
Hayami, Y., & Ruttan, V. (1985). *Agricultural development: An international perspective.* Baltimore, MD: Johns Hopkins University Press.
Jha, P. (2006). Some aspects of the well-being of India's agricultural labour in the context of contemporary Agrarian Crisis. *Indian Journal of Labour Economics, 49*(4), 741–764.
———. (2011). *Towards progressive fiscal policy in India.* New Delhi: SAGE Publications.
Jha, P., & Acharya, N. (2011). Expenditure on the rural economy in India's budgets since the 1950s: An assessment. *Review of Agrarian Studies, 1*(2), 134–156.
Paroda, R.S., & Kumar, P. (2000). Food production and demand in South Asia. *Agricultural Economics Research Review, 13*(1), 1–24.
Patnaik, P. (2005, November). *The crisis in India's countryside.* Paper presented at the Seminar on India: Implementing Pluralism and Democracy, Chicago, United States.
Patnaik, P., & Chandresekhar, C.P. (1995). Indian economy under structural adjustment. *Economic and Political Weekly, XXX*(47), 3001–3013.
Patnaik, U. (2003). Deflation and Déjà vu: Indian agriculture in the world economy. In V. K. Ramachandran & M. Swaminathan (Eds.), *Agrarian studies: Essays on agrarian relations in less developed countries* (pp. 111–143). New Delhi: Tulika Books.
Pinstrup-Andersen, P., Ruiz de Londono, N., & Hoover, E. (1976). The impact of increasing food supply on human nutrition: Implications for commodity priorities in agricultural research and policy *American Journal of Agricultural Economics, 58*(2), 131–142.
Ramachandran, V.K., & Swaminathan, M. (2002). Rural banking and landless labour households: Institutional reform and rural credit markets in India. *Journal of Agrarian Change, 2*(4), 502–544.
Ramakumar, R. (2013). Bank credit to agriculture in India: Trends in the 1990s and 2000s. *The Marxist, XXIX*(3), 1–11.
Rawal, V. (2013). Changes in the distribution of operational landholdings in rural India. *Review of Agrarian Studies, 3*(2), 73–104.
Reserve Bank of India (RBI). (2010). *Handbook of statistics on state government finances.* Mumbai, India: Author.
———. (2012). *Handbook of statistics on Indian economy,* 2011–2012. Mumbai, India: Author.

Rural Labour Enquiry (RLE). *Reports on general characteristics of rural labour households—1999–2000, 2004–2005 and 2009–2010* (based on the data for 55th round, 61st round and 66th round of the National Sample Survey Organisation, Government of India). Shimla/Chandigarh: Ministry of Labour Bureau, Government of India.

Thirtle, C., Piesse, J., & Lin, L. (2003). The impact of research led productivity growth on poverty in Africa, Asia and Latin America. *World Development, 31*(12), 1959–1975.

Vaidyanathan, A. (2006). Farmers' suicides and the agrarian crisis. *Economic and Political Weekly, XLI*(38), 4009–4013.

Vyas, V.S. (2003). *India's agrarian structure, economic policies and sustainable development: Variations on a theme.* New Delhi: Academic Foundation.

———. (2005). Agrarian distress: Strategies to protect vulnerable sections. *The Indian Journal of Labour Economics, 48*(1), 19–28.

About the Editors and Contributors

Editors

Mausumi Das is Associate Professor, Department of Economics, at the Delhi School of Economics, University of Delhi. Her areas of expertise include macroeconomics, economic growth and development. She has published research articles in various reputed international journals, such as *Journal of Economic Growth* and *Journal of Development Economics*. Her current research work includes impact of inequality on health investment and its implications for growth; the trade-off between teacher quality, teacher quantity and their growth effects; and choice of public versus private provision of merits goods and its welfare implications. Her doctoral thesis is titled as 'Savings Behaviour and Macro-dynamics of Neoclassical Growth Models: Stability and Other Issues' (June 1999).

Sabyasachi Kar is Associate Professor at the Institute of Economic Growth, University of Delhi. He has published a number of books and academic articles on macroeconomics, growth and development economics, with particular focus on the Indian economy. He is currently collaborating with the Effective States and Inclusive Development (ESID), University of Manchester, and the Kennedy School of Government, Harvard University, on an extensive cross-country study of political and economic institutions and their relationship with growth. His doctoral thesis is titled as 'Factors Underlying Growth in Low Income Economics: A Theoretical and Empirical Analysis Based on a Cross-section of Countries' (July 2000).

Nandan Nawn is Associate Professor, Department of Policy Studies, at TERI University, New Delhi. His publications have been in journals like *Economic and Political Weekly* and *Journal of Agrarian Change*. His research interests include areas of ecological economics, agrarian studies and law and economics as distinct sub/trans-disciplines, apart from the cross-disciplinary areas like agricultural energetics and law and ecology, and frameworks like classical political economy. His doctoral thesis is titled as 'A Comparative Study of Modern Chemical Based Agriculture and Organic Farming in Terms of Sustainability' (January 2012).

Contributors

Jyotirmoy Bhattacharya is Assistant Professor at the School of Liberal Studies, Bharat Ratna Dr B.R. Ambedkar University, New Delhi. His primary area of research interest is the dynamics of beliefs and learning in economic models. He is particularly interested in understanding the ways in which self-fulfilling beliefs can contribute to the stability or instability of macroeconomic systems. His doctoral thesis is titled as 'Intrinsically Valueless Money and the Coordination of Intertemporal Exchange' (July 2007).

Sudhanshu Bhushan is Professor, Department of Higher and Professional Education, at the National University of Educational Planning and Administration (NUEPA), New Delhi. He specialises in internationalisation of higher education, policy issues in higher education and educational planning. His recent contributions in books include *Quality Assurance of Transnational Higher Education: The Experiences of Australia and India*, *Public Financing and Deregulated Fees in Indian Higher Education* and *Restructuring Higher Education in India*. His present responsibility includes providing policy support to the government, University Grants Commission (UGC) and the Planning Commission of India. His doctoral thesis is titled as 'Resurgence of the Classical Approach in the Light of Theoretical Controversies' (1993).

Pradip Kumar Biswas is Associate Professor at the College of Vocational Studies, University of Delhi. His research areas include institutional economics, micro, small and medium enterprises (MSMEs), industry, bio-energy, innovations, science and technology and agricultural economics. He is presently working on industrial policies and development of entrepreneurship in India. His doctoral thesis is titled as 'Rural Industrialization with Special Reference to West Bengal after Independence' (September 1997).

Prasenjit Bose is associated with the Indian Council of Social Science Research sponsored project on 'Financial Globalisation and India'. His research interests include macroeconomics and political economy. His doctoral thesis is titled as 'Capital Accumulation and Crisis: A Theoretical Study' (July 2003).

Shouvik Chakraborty is Research Fellow at the Political Economy Research Institute, University of Massachusetts Boston, Amherst, Massachusetts. He has published on a variety of progressive economic policy issues, especially in the areas of development banking and international trade, in *Economic and Political Weekly*, *Journal of South Asian Development* and others. His current work focuses on the recent increase in commodity prices and the generation of jobs through investment in clean renewable energy. His doctoral thesis is titled as 'Movements in the Terms of Trade of Primary Commodities vis-à-vis Manufactured Goods: A Theoretical and Empirical Study' (July 2010).

C.P. Chandrasekhar is Professor at the Centre for Economic Studies and Planning, and presently Dean, School of Social Sciences, JNU, New Delhi. His areas of interest include the role of finance and industry in development and the experience with fiscal, financial and industrial policy reform in developing countries. Besides having published widely in academic journals, he is the co-author of *Crisis as Conquest: Learning from East Asia* and *The Market That Failed: A Decade of Neoliberal Economic Reforms in India*. He is a regular columnist for *Frontline* (titled 'Economic Perspectives') and *Business Line* (titled 'Macroscan'). His doctoral thesis is titled as 'Growth and Technical Change in the Indian Cotton Mill Industry: 1947–77' (November 1981).

Debarshi Das is Associate Professor, Humanities and Social Sciences Department, at the Indian Institute of Technology, Guwahati. His research interests include development economics, macroeconomics and political economy. He is currently working on profitability analysis of Indian industries, growth of services sector in India and employment elasticity in different sectors in India. His doctoral thesis is titled as 'Role of International Trade in Transforming an Agrarian Economy: A Theoretical Study' (November 2003).

About the Editors and Contributors

Surajit Das is Assistant Professor at the Centre for Economic Studies and Planning, JNU, New Delhi. His primary area of research is macroeconomic policy. He is currently working on macroeconomic effects of fiscal deficit and public debt. His doctoral thesis is titled as 'Macroeconomic Policy under Regime of Free Capital Flows' (July 2008).

Biswajit Dhar is Professor at the Centre for Economic Studies and Planning, Jawaharlal Nehru University (JNU), New Delhi. Before joining the university, he was the Director General of Research and Information System for Developing Countries, a think-tank specialising in international economic issues. He has also served as the Head of the Centre for World Trade Organization (WTO) Studies in the Indian Institute of Foreign Trade, New Delhi. His doctoral thesis is titled as 'Problems of Technology and Development in the Indian Fertilizer Industry' (1989).

Subrata Guha is Associate Professor at the Centre for Economic Studies and Planning, JNU, New Delhi, where he currently teaches courses on growth theory and monetary economics. His research has been primarily in the area of neoclassical growth and distribution. His doctoral thesis is titled as 'Some Issues Relating to the Distribution of Wealth in the Context of Models of Economic Growth' (August 1999).

Praveen Jha is Professor at the Centre for Economic Studies and Planning and the Centre for Informal Sector and Labour Studies, JNU, New Delhi. He is one of the Editors of *Agrarian South: Journal of Political Economy*. Major areas of his research and teaching include political economy of development, with particular reference to labour, agriculture, natural resources, public finance, education and history of economic thought. His doctoral thesis is titled as 'Changing Conditions of Agricultural Labourers in Post-independence India: A Case Study from Bihar' (December 1995).

Reji K. Joseph is Associate Professor at the Institute for Studies in Industrial Development, New Delhi. His areas of research interests include trade and public health, intellectual property rights, and access to medicines and Indian pharmaceutical industry. He teaches courses on international political economy.

Vineet Kohli is Assistant Professor at the Tata Institute of Social Sciences, Mumbai. His research uses heterodox economic theory and draws on historical evidence to evaluate financial sector policies in least developed countries. He is currently engaged in developing an applied macroeconomic model for India. His doctoral thesis is titled as 'Stock Market, Corporate Financing, and Corporate Investment: Studying for Interlinkages with Special Reference to India' (July 2008).

Pranab Mukhopadhyay is Professor at the Department of Economics, Goa University, India. His primary area of research includes environment and macroeconomics. He has published research articles in *Ecology and Society*, *Economic and Political Weekly* and *Environment and Development Economics*. He is the co-editor of *Promise, Trust and Evolution: Managing the Commons of South Asia* and *Nature, Economy and Society* and co-author of *Common Property Water Resources: Dependence and Institutions in India's Villages*. His doctoral thesis is titled as 'Public Debt and Economic Growth: A Theoretical Essay in the Context of a Developing Labour Surplus Economy' (April 2005).

Rohit is Assistant Professor at the Centre for Economic Studies and Planning, JNU, New Delhi. He has recently authored a book titled *It's Not Over: Structural Drivers of the Global Economic Crisis*. His primary areas of research include growth and distribution, monetary theory and policy with special focus on developing countries. His doctoral thesis is titled as 'Concentration of Capital and Its Macroeconomic Impact: A Case Study of the United States in the 1980s and 1990s' (March 2009).

Shuji Uchikawa is Professor at the School of Economics, Senshu University, Tokyo. His primary areas of research include industry policies and labour policies. He has published a number of articles on the manufacturing sector in India. He is currently working on industrial clusters in India, exploring how entrepreneurs come out and small industries are developing, especially focusing on examples in Ludhiana and Tirupur. His doctoral thesis is titled as 'India's Foreign Trade Policies and the Development of the Textile Industry' (March 1993).

Index

agents, 147
aggravated output instability,
   transition from golden age to neoliberal era, 281, 283
   realvs speculative investment, 278
   steady states and stability analysis, 279, 281
   determinants of Tobin's q, 279
aggregate economy,
   implications, 160
agrarian crisis,
   features and correlates of, 303, 305, 307
   rural economy, budgets, 308–311, 313
agricultural investment, 288–290
agriculture,
   in total GDP, 1, 316
Anglo-Saxon, 23
apparel industry, 202–203
ASI dataset, 195
aspiration level,
   determination of, 148
average income, 190

balance of payment (BoP), 114
   market equilibrium, 125
banks in development, 229–230
basic metal industry, 199
basic model, 215
   assumptions, 215–216
   expectations, 216
      bankruptcy, 216
      equilibrium, 217–218
big retailers, growth, 242
   European experience, 244–245

   large retailers, 245–246
   US experience, 242–243
      firm entry and exit rates, 254
      Wal-Mart stores, 243
BRICS, 34–35, 37–38, 46
   initiative with China's Balancing Act, 39
   growth in India, 39–40
British financial system, 230

calorie intake, 54
CAM model, 92–93
   Asia-centric approach,
      global imbalances, 99
   net external assets, 93
   regional blocs, 104
   results, 93–94
      global imbalances, 94
   sectors, 92
   trade deficits, 102
CAM-AUGUR model, 35
capital flows, 114, 118, 123
capital flows aid stock market development, 231–233
capital mobility,
   empirical evidence, 117–119
capital stocks, 165
capital-intensive technology, 204
capital-labour ratio, 203–204
capitalism,
   instabilities, 267–268
      criticism, 268
      ephemeral, 269
      growth theory, 268
      Kaleckian argument, 269

   post-war capitalism, 261–262
      foreign oil companies, 263
   state, 259
      HN's analysis, 260
      Marxian concept, 260
capitalist growth and exogenous stimuli, 23–24
   identifying of, 25–27
   temporary, 27–28
capitalist production, 53
centralisation of land, 291–292
charters, 237
Chinese policymakers, 90
closed economy, 165
colonialism and state intervention, metropolis and periphery, 274–276
Company Act of 1948, 233
comparative static, 126–227
Competition Commission (CC), 240
competitive economies, 163
compulsory licensing, 138
conceptual and empirical issues, 195
construction of educational level, 188–189
contemporary economies, 213
contemporary Indian agricultural rural dynamics,
   political economy of, 300–301, 303, 305, 307–311, 313
contemporary monetary theory, 213
coordinated policy, 46
corporate retailing (CRs), 240
   adverse effects, 249

price reduction, 249–250, 252
retail wages and employment, 249
current account balance, 94
as ratio to GDP, 96
current account deficit, 124
and surpluses,
pattern of, 88

debate, 286
decolonisation, 257
depreciated exchange rate, 127
developing countries,
policies, 252
development, 145, 160
Dornbusch's model, 116

East Asia,
private savings rates, 89
East-Asian economies,
surpluses of, 89
ecological Marxism, 14
ecological unsustainabilities, 54
economic interpretation, 159
economic reform and growth of manufacturing sector, 195–197
economies of scale, 241
economy, 147
agent, 147
life cycle of, 147
education, 178–180
and culture, 180
colonial phase, 178
level, 182–183
post-colonial phase, 178
theories and hypotheses, 179
elements of human physiology, 62
emerging markets, 89
empire, 258
capitalism, globalization, 259
capitalist interest, 258
empirical issues, 195
employment elasticity, 194
employment rates, 41, 44, 46, 51
in Europe, 51
employment-displacing industries, 204
endogenous policy, 219
energy (balance) analysis (EBA), 54, 56
energy return on investment (EROI), 58

energy surplus, 55–57
envisioning, institutional changes,
finance, 16
market, 16
money, 16
equilibrium,
boundary conditions, 218
condition, 125
continuity, 217
growth path, 167
European blocs, 46
European crisis, 33–34, 38–39, 43, 50
backdrop of, 34
country concerns, developing, 34
European reflation, 41, 43–44
export function, 123

factor markets, 166
field studies, 295
finance,
adverse effects on growth 30–31
as exogenous stimulus, 28, 30
debt, 29
demand and growth, 28
domestic demand, 28
financial assets, 234
financial development, 231
flexible exchange rate, 124
food-calorie,
adoption of, 54
foodgrain crops, 303
foreign direct investment (FDI), 131–134, 196
and transfer of technology, 133
impact, 134
defined, 133
foreign institutional investments (FIIs), 117

German banking system, 232
German economic history, 232
gigantic size, 241
Gini coefficient, 184–186, 188
global imbalances, 88, 91–92, 94
global innovative firms, 138
global policy coordinators, 106
global recession, 33
globalization,
capital, 14
technology, 14
trade, 14

golden age of capitalism, 276
state intervention, 277
golden age of stock markets, 233–234
Goldsmith's data, 236
good, 165
governance issues,
large retailers, 248
predatory pricing, 247–248
price flexing, 247–248
public interest, 247
government debt, 51
government income, 111
government spending on goods and services, 111
Grandmont's work, 214
gross attendance ratio (GAR), 180
gross fixed capital formation (GFCF), 196
growth in per capita income, 51
in Europe, 51

high inflation, 196
HN characterizes, 259
household saving rate, 90
human capital, 149
human capital formation, 186
human capital,
economic return on investment, 179
human labour,
accounting for, 57–58
industrialised agricultural systems, 57
empirical illustration, 63, 68
energy-value, 64
higher energy efficiency of small farms, 66
metabolic framework, 65
scale P farming, 66
metabolic framework, 62–63
human muscular labour, 59

imports, 112
income equality, 182–183
income inequality, 186, 189
Indian agriculture, 288
profile of, 301–303
Indian Council of Agricultural Research (ICAR), 57

Index

industrial licensing regulation, 200
industrial structure of four industries,
  apparel industry, 202–203
  long-term changes, 197
  basic metal industry, 199
  motor vehicle industry, 200, 202
  textile industry, 197–198
inequality, 145–147, 160, 180
  GAR, 180
  in education, 182
    declining, 182–183
    participation, 181
  INEP, 181–182
  religious category, 180
inequality in the level participation (INEP), 181
informal jobs, 293
informalisation of employment, 206–207
inheritance of wealth, 162
intellectual property rights (IPRs), 131, 135–136
  influence of, 131
  Japan and China, 139
    quality circles, 139
    studies, 140
    technology forecasting, 139
intergenerational income dynamics,
  of poor, 153–155, 159
  of rich, 151
International Federation of Institutes of Advanced Study (IFIAS), 57
International finance capital (IFC), 8
International Labour Organization, 193
international trade,
  for manufactures, 111
  for primary commodities, 111
  for services trade, 112
inventory adjustment, 111
investment,
  boom, 194, 196
  capital ratio, 268
  friendly environment, 119
  function, 123

Jacobian matrix, 168
Japanese financial system, 236

Japanese patent system, 137
job security regulation, 203
jobless growth, 193, 194
joint ventures, 132

Korea,
  success story,
    OEM, 135
Korean industrialization, 135

labour, 165
labour-power, 56, 62
  quantitative assessment of, 56
laissez faire economy, 267
laissez faire system,
  bounds,
    NAIRU, 270
    nominal debt commitments, 270
    output instability, 272–274
    three conditions, 271
less developed countries (LDCs), 229
less labour-intensive industries, 194
liberal trade, 231–233
liquid stock markets, 229
long-term stagnation of employment, 203–204, 206

macro-modelling framework, 91
Mansfield,
  study of, 136
manufacturing sector, 191, 193
  economic reforms, 191, 193
  and growth, 195–197
  policy distortion, 191
marginal farms, 291
marginal propensity, 145
market capitalisation ratio, 236
market economies, 162
market failure, 136
markets, 229
Marxian perspective economic inequality, 180
material capital, 137
mean value theorem, 173
medium-scale factories, 193
mental capital, 137
The Ministry of Trade and Industry (MITI), 137
mitigating immiserisation,
  inequality, 15

joblessness, 15
poverty, 15
monetary economists, 213
monopsonistic power, 240
motor vehicle industry, 200
  numbers of workers, 202
Mundell-Fleming (M-F) model, 114–117, 123

National Industrial Classification (NIC), 195
neoclassical growth model, 164
neoliberalism,
  working class, suppression,
    aggravated output instability, 278, 280–281
    globalisation and upper bound, 277–278
net foreign capital inflow, 117
net foreign direct investment (FDI), 118
net income, 112
net portfolio investment (NPI), 118

original equipment manufacturing (OEM), 135
outflow of labour, 293
over-employment, 194
own design manufacture (ODM), 135

Pareto-efficiency, 163
peaceful capitalism, 257
Physiocrats, 55
Podolinsky, 58–59, 61
  myth, 59
  numerical illustration, 61
  societal level, 59, 61
policy distortion, 191
political hegemony, 16, 17
poor agent,
  optimal choice, 149
portfolio capital,
  worldwide flows of, 118
positing sustainability of farming, 13
post-liberalisation, 295
poverty, 145
poverty trap models, 147
Prabhat Patnaik, 1, 2
  academic and professional life, 2
  birth, 2

Festschrift project, 2
scholarships, 2
works, 3
   capitalism, 5–8
   growth in the Indian economy, 3–5
   social projects, 8–11
private inheritance, 162
private investment, 110
production technology, 167
produit net, 55
proofs, 220
   aggregate demand, 224–225, 227–228
   budget correspondence, 220, 222
   individual optimisation, 222–223
public investment, 288, 290, 294–295
public sector undertakings (PSUs), 195
purchasing power parity (PPP) measures, 35

quadratic function,
   assumption of, 164

Rajan and Zingales (RZs), 231–232
   hypothesis, 234
   idea, 237
   interest group theory, 232
Ramsey-Cass-Koopmans model, 163–165
rate of savings targets, 110
rational investment policy, 179
real exchange rate, 35
real wages,
   coefficient of, 194

recommended dietary allowance (RDA), 58
regression results, 182
restriction (R),
   define, 168
restrictions on the freedom, 162
retail capital, 240
rich agent,
   optimal choice, 150
rural dynamics,
   political economy of, 300–301, 303, 305, 307–311, 313

scale P, farming, 66
schooling,
   standard deviation of, 188
Securities Act of 1933, 232
semi-feudalism, 294
shareholders' indebtedness, 236
skill formation technology, 148
small-scale industry policy, 202
social expenditure, 186
spillover, 134
stability condition, 124–125
standard tax function, 123
stock markets, 229–230, 236–237
   investors, 237
surplus consumption, 164
surplus countries, 89
sustain,
   define, 52
sustainability of agricultural practices, 53
sustaining, growth process, 13

t-statistics, 118
t-values, 118

technology flows, 131
technology transfer, 132, 135, 138
   IPRs, 136
textile industry, 197–198
Theory of Economic History, 229
third world persists,
   exploitation,
      creation or preservation of reserve army, 264
      extraction of surplus value, 264
      primitive accumulation, 264–265
   world flattening, 263
      economic dualism, 263
time-varying nature, 164
trade imbalance, 90
trade practices, 242
transfers from abroad, 112
transnational corporations (TNCs), 258
   domination of, 131

US deficit, 89
US public debt and net export of assets, 51
USA reflation, 40
   employment, 41
   public debt, 41
USA slowdown, 39

wage-employment trade-off, 194
wealth, 165
wholesale price index (WPI), 193